S0-AXM-393

Housing

DECISIONS

by

Evelyn L. Lewis
Professor Emeritus, Home Economics
Northern Arizona University
Flagstaff, Arizona

Contributing Authors:
Clair S. Hill
Associate Professor
College of Engineering and Technology
Northern Arizona University
Flagstaff, Arizona

Susan Sherman Differding
Susan Sherman Differding and Associates
Hoffman Estates, Illinois

L. Annah Abbott
Windsor, Vermont

The Goodheart-Willcox Company, Inc.
South Holland, Illinois

Copyright 1994

by

THE GOODHEART-WILLCOX COMPANY, INC.

Previous editions copyright 1990, 1987, 1984, 1980, 1978

All rights reserved. No part of this book may be reproduced, stored in a retrieval system, or transmitted in any form or by any means, electronic, mechanical, photocopying, recording, or otherwise, without the prior written permission of The Goodheart-Willcox Company, Inc. Manufactured in the United States of America.
Library of Congress Catalog Card Number 93-23858
International Standard Book Number 0-87006-071-6

1 2 3 4 5 6 7 8 9 94 99 98 97 96 95 94 93

Library of Congress Cataloging-in-Publication Data

Lewis, Evelyn L.
Housing Decisions / Evelyn L. Lewis
p. cm. -- (The Goodheart-Willcox home economics series)
Includes index.
Summary: Discusses selecting and furnishing a home and career opportunities related to housing.
ISBN 0-87006-071-6
1. Housing. 2. Dwellings. 3. Interior decoration. 4. House furnishings. [1. Housing. 2. Dwellings. 3. Interior decoration.] I. Title. II. Series.
TX301.L46 1994
643--dc20 93-23858
CIP
AC

Cover photos courtesy of Marvin Windows & Doors, California Redwood Association, James F. Parnell, The Kohler Co., and Lowden, Lowden & Co.

Introduction

Housing Decisions prepares you to make wise choices concerning your housing. It helps you understand your housing needs, and it shows you how to meet those needs. Many housing alternatives are presented throughout the book. You will learn to evaluate them and select the best ones for you.

Housing Decisions gives you a broad understanding and appreciation of the housing field. A logical progression of topics leads you through the decisions you face when selecting and furnishing your home. A chapter describing career opportunities related to housing is also included.

Housing Decisions is easy to read and understand. It includes hundreds of illustrations that give you ideas you can adapt to fit your own home. References to the illustrations are made in the copy. They help you link the visual images to the written material.

Each chapter begins with objectives that help you set goals for your learning. Following the objectives are a list of key words. At the end of the chapter, questions are provided to help you review the chapter's important points as well as suggestions for some learning activities.

Appendices, a glossary, and an index are found at the end of the book. They will provide you with additional help as you use *Housing Decisions.*

Contents

Part One
Housing for You

Chapter 1
Housing and Human Needs 9
People and Their Housing 10 Meeting Needs through Housing 10
Values and Housing Choices 15 Housing Needs Vary 17
Life-styles Influence Housing Decisions 20 Housing and the Quality of Life 24

Chapter 2
Influences on Housing 26
Historical Influences on Housing 27 Cultural Influences on Housing 32
Societal Influences on Housing 33 Environmental Influences on Housing 36
Economic Influences on Housing 38 Technological Influences on Housing 39
Governmental Influences on Housing 41

Part Two
Making Housing Choices

Chapter 3
Using Decision-Making Skills 47
Types of Decisions 48 Resources for Housing Decisions 50
The Decision-Making Process 52

Chapter 4
Choosing a Place to Live 56
Location 57 Housing 69 Choosing Housing to Meet Special Needs 72
Moving to a New Location 76

Chapter 5
Acquiring Housing 81
Acquisition 82 A Place to Rent 83 A Place to Buy 91
Condominium Ownership 101 Cooperative Ownership 102

Part Three
From the Ground Up

Chapter 6
The Evolution of Exteriors **105**
Traditional Houses 106 Modern Houses 111
Contemporary Houses 114 Future Trends 116

Chapter 7
Understanding House Plans **119**
Architectural Drawings for a House 120 The Space Within 124

Chapter 8
House Construction **135**
Housing Begins with the Foundation and Frame 136
Materials Used for Exterior Construction 138 Windows and Doors 140

Chapter 9
The Systems Within **145**
Electrical Systems 146 Gas As an Energy Source 148 Plumbing Systems 149
Heating Systems 150 Cooling Systems 154 Conserving Energy 155

Part Four
The Inside Story

Chapter 10
The Elements of Design **161**
Design Characteristics 162 Elements of Design 163

Chapter 11
Using Color Effectively **172**
Understanding Color 173 The Color Wheel 174
Color Harmonies 176 Using Color Harmonies 179

Chapter 12
Using the Principles of Design **185**
The Principles of Design 186 Goals of Design 192 Sensory Design 193

Chapter 13
Textiles in Today's Home **196**
Understanding Fibers, Yarns, and Fabrics 197 Selecting Textiles for Home Use 203
Textiles for Kitchen, Bath, and Bed 207 Textiles for Floor Treatments 204
Textiles for Upholstered Furniture 205 Textiles Used in Window Treatments 206
Textile Laws 209

Chapter 14
Creating Interior Backgrounds **212**
Floor Treatments 213 Walls 216 Ceiling Treatments 219
Planning Your Background Treatments 220

Chapter 15
Furniture Styles and Construction **223**
Choosing Furniture Styles 224 Evaluating Furniture Construction 230
Consumer Protection 237

Chapter 16
Arranging and Selecting Furniture **240**
Arranging Furniture 241 Selecting Furniture 244
Stretching Your Furniture Dollars 247

Chapter 17
The Finishing Touches **252**
Window Treatments 253 Artificial Light 256 Let Light Work for You 259
Structural and Nonstructural Lighting 262 Choosing Accessories 265

Chapter 18
Selecting Household Equipment **268**
Appliance Considerations 269 Consumer Satisfaction 271
Choosing Kitchen Appliances 272 Choosing Laundry Appliances 279
Choosing Climate Control Appliances 280 Choosing Other Appliances 281

Part Five
A Safe and Attractive Environment

Chapter 19
The Outdoor Living Space **287**
Planning the Landscape 89 Landscape Elements 89
Designing the Outdoor Living Spaces 293 Landscaping for Conservation 300
Complete Scaled Plans 303

Chapter 20
Keeping Your Home Safe and Secure **307**
A Safe Home 308 A Secure Home 314
Equipping a Home for People with Disabilities 319

Chapter 21
Maintaining Your Home **325**
Keeping the Home Clean 326 Outdoor and Lawn Care 330
Making Home Repairs 331 Meeting Storage Needs 337 Redecorating 340
Remodeling 341 Resources for Home Care, Maintenance, and Improvements 343

Part Six
Progress in Housing

Chapter 22
Housing for Tomorrow **347**
Recent Developments in Housing 348 Housing Concerns 350
New Solutions in Housing 359

Chapter 23
Careers in Housing **365**
Who Provides Housing? 366 Career Clusters 366 Job Descriptions 369
Career Levels 378 Qualities for Success 381 Careers and Life-style 383
Balancing Work and Family 384

Appendix A
Housing Legislation **387**

Appendix B
Energy-saving Tips **392**
Protect Your Home from Outside Heat and Cold 392
Heating and Cooling 393 Hot Water Energy Savers 394
Energy Savers in the Kitchen, Laundry Room, and Bathroom 394
Appliance Energy Savers 395 Lighting Energy Savers 396
Yard and Workshop Energy Savers 396

Glossary **397**

Index **406**

Drexel Heritage

Chapter 1 Housing and Human Needs
Chapter 2 Influences on Housing

PART 1

Housing for You

C H A P T E R 1

Housing and Human Needs

Georgia-Pacific

To Know

adobe
beauty
blended family
creativity
esteem
extended family
housing
human ecology
life cycle
life situations
life-style
living unit
microenvironment
needs
nuclear family
one-person living unit
physical needs
psychological needs
quality of life
self-actualization
self-esteem
self-expression
single-parent family
values

Objectives

After studying this chapter, you will be able to:

- Explain how you interact with your housing.
- Show how you move toward self-actualization through housing.
- Explain how your housing helps you satisfy your needs and values.
- Describe how housing needs change with the life cycles.
- Compare housing needs with various life-styles.
- Describe how housing affects the quality of life.
- Define human ecology.

Housing, good or poor, has a deep and lasting effect on all people. Winston Churchill once said, "We shape our buildings, and then they shape us." This is especially true of the buildings in which people live. First, people find shelter to satisfy their needs, and then this shelter affects the way they feel and behave.

Housing, as used in this text, is any dwelling that provides shelter. This includes the furnishings, neighborhood, and community. The relationship between people and their housing will be considered throughout this text.

People and Their Housing

Housing is your ***microenvironment,*** or a small and distinct part of the total environment in which you live. Although housing is just one part of your total environment, it is a very important part. It has a great effect on your life-style and personal development.

Whether you live alone or with others, you interact with your housing. Housing affects your actions, and in turn, your actions affect your housing. For example, if you live in a small apartment, you will not be able to host large parties. You will not have enough room, and your neighbors might complain about the noise. However, if you want to host large parties, you might choose to live in a large house that is set apart from other houses.

This type of interaction can also be seen on a smaller scale. Suppose a room in your house is decorated with many fragile and expensive accessories. This would give you a feeling of formality and elegance. You would not want to exercise in this room. However, if exercise is important to your life-style, you could furnish the room differently. You could adapt your housing to match your way of life.

Meeting Needs through Housing

Your well-being is affected by everything around you. Your microenvironment, in the form of housing, helps you meet your needs. ***Needs*** are the basic items that people must have in order to live. All people share physical, psychological, and other needs.

A director of a rescue mission once said that he saw human needs arranged in the following order: soup, soap, salvation. When people came to him for help, their basic needs had not yet been satisfied. They were hungry and could think only of food. Once they had eaten, their next concern was to be comfortable. Only when their most basic needs were met, could they think of their psychological needs.

Psychologist Abraham Maslow prioritized human needs as shown in 1-1. According to Maslow, as each type of need is met, you progress up the pyramid to the next level. Your basic physical needs must be met first. When they are satisfied, you can think about other needs, such as security, love, esteem, and self-actualization.

Physical Needs

Physical needs are the most basic human needs. They have priority over other needs, because they are essential for survival. Physical needs include shelter, food, water, and rest. They are sometimes called basic needs or primary needs.

Shelter as a physical need. The need for shelter and protection from the weather has always been met by a dwelling of some type. The earliest dwellings were in natural settings, such

Human Needs

1. Physical needs. Your physical needs, such as shelter, food, water, and rest, must be at least partially satisfied before you can think about anything else.
2. Security. Next, you need to feel safe in your surroundings and to know what to expect. You need protection from physical harm and economic disaster.
3. Love and acceptance. At this point, you will do many things to gain affection. You need to be praised and accepted by others. A small failure can make you feel rejected as a person. You need much support, assurance, and personal warmth.
4. Esteem. Not only do you want to be liked, you also want to be respected. In this way, you gain confidence and feel necessary in the world.
5. Self-actualization. To reach this level, all other needs must be fulfilled to some degree. Your need is to develop your full potential. You learn because you want to be a "fuller" person. You have pride and self-respect. You can show individuality despite social pressures. You have your own opinions and are able to express them.

1-1
Maslow shows the priority of human needs by arranging them in the shape of a pyramid.

as caves, 1-2, and overhanging cliffs, 1-3. Later, crude dwellings were built from materials that were readily available. The Pueblo used ***adobe,*** which is building material made of sun-dried earth and straw, and rafters made from native materials. The thick walls and flat roofs, as shown in 1-4, provided shelter from the hot climate. The

1-2
The Qumran Caves shown here are located near the Dead Sea. You can see the entrances to caves that were used for shelter by shepherds over 2,000 years ago.

W.H. Troxell

1-3
This large cliff dwelling called Montezuma Castle is located in central Arizona. It gave shelter to Native American farmers who probably lived there over 1,000 years ago.

Apache built houses from branches. See 1-5. They offer protection from the scorching sun, while breezes circulate through the branches.

1-4
Adobe is still used in housing today to help keep houses cool in warm climates.

Western Ways Features

1-5
The housing of the Apache is a clue to their way of life. Here you see a summer house that is under construction. Sturdier houses, like the one in the background, offer more protection from the elements in the winter.

Today, some Bedouins, nomadic Arabs, still use tents, such as the one pictured in 1-6. These simple dwellings can be taken apart and carried from place to place. This is important since the Bedouins travel continually, searching for food.

Food and water as physical needs. In the past, people located their housing near sources of food and water. They stored food and a small supply of water in their dwellings, while they prepared and ate their food outside.

Today, areas within dwellings are set aside for storing, preparing, and eating food. See 1-7. However, people still like to prepare food and eat outside. Some houses are designed with this in mind. Food preparation areas are sometimes located in enclosed patios to make outside eating easier.

Psychological Needs

Once the basic physical needs are met, people strive to meet the psychological needs, which are higher on Maslow's pyramid of human needs. ***Psychological needs*** are needs related to the

1-6
The Bedouin tent is made from a frame of poles and ropes. These are covered with cloth of goat hair. The tent is divided into separate quarters for men and women. They sit and sleep on cotton quilts.

Carol G. Brown, ASID–Certified in the State of California

1-7
Today's modern kitchen has developed from simply a place to store food and water to a place to store, prepare, and eat food.

mind and feelings that must be met in order to live a satisfying life.

Security as a psychological need. Housing provides security from the outside world. It offers protection from physical danger and the unknown. It helps you feel safe and protected. Living in a dwelling that is well-built and located in an area free from crime can help you feel secure.

Love and acceptance as psychological needs. Housing affects your feelings of being loved and accepted. If you have your own bedroom or a private place of your own, you know that others care about you. They have accepted you as a person who has needs. When you are assigned chores to do around the house, it is because you have been accepted as part of a group.

Esteem as a psychological need. You need to be ***esteemed,*** or respected, admired, and held in high regard, by others. Your housing tells other people something about you and can help you gain esteem. A house that is clean, neat, and attractive will gain the approval and respect of others.

You also need self-esteem. ***Self-esteem*** is awareness and appreciation of your own worth. When you have self-esteem, you think well of yourself and are satisfied with your own role and skills. See 1-8. Living in a pleasant, satisfying house can help you gain self-esteem.

Self-actualization. When you meet the need for ***self-actualization,*** you have developed to your full potential as a person. You have become the best that you can be, and you are doing what you do best. If your talent is baseball, you will be playing baseball as well as you can play. If your talent is building houses, the houses will be well-built.

For self-actualizing people, housing is more than a place to live. It is the place where each person can progress toward becoming what he or she is capable of being. Striving toward self-actualization is often a lifelong process.

Other Needs Met through Housing

Recognizing the levels of human needs as described by Maslow can help you understand how important needs are in relation to housing. Beauty, self-expression, and creativity are also important needs. They can be achieved through your housing decisions.

Beauty. ***Beauty*** is the quality or qualities that give pleasure to the senses. Your concept of

John Running

1-8
As this son gives his mother a table that he made, both of them gain self-esteem.

beauty is unique. What is beautiful to you may not be beautiful to someone else. In fact, the same objects may not appear beautiful to you as you mature. An appreciation of beauty develops over time as you are exposed to beauty around you. Beautiful surroundings, such as the one in 1-9, can make you feel good about yourself and release you from tensions.

Self-expression. Showing your true personality and taste is called ***self-expression.*** Self-expression is evident when you choose colors to decorate your house. Those colors are often a clue to your personality. For instance, if you have an outgoing, vibrant personality, you might show it by using bright, bold colors inside your house. If you have a quiet, subdued personality, you might show it by using pale, soft colors, 1-10. Furnishings can also help you express yourself.

Creativity. ***Creativity*** is the ability to create. You show creativity when you express your ideas to others. Your housing provides opportunities for you to express your creativity. Primitive people exhibited creativity when they painted pictures on the walls of their cave dwellings. Today, people may show their creativity by painting, 1-11, or gardening. If you enjoy working with flowers, you can arrange a special design in your flower garden. You may also create flower arrangements to display around your house.

Andersen Windows, Inc.

1-10
Quiet, subdued people may show their personalities by decorating with soft, pale colors.

California Redwood Association

1-9
Beauty in a room can help you feel happy, content, and peaceful.

Grosfillex

1-11
Providing a room in the house for a person to paint can help them meet their need for creativity.

Values and Housing Choices

Values are strong beliefs or ideas about what is important. They can be views, events, people, places, or objects that you prize highly. When you choose something freely and act upon that choice, you are acting on a value. This gives meaning to your life and enhances your growth.

All of the values you hold, such as family, friendship, money, status, religion, and independence, form your value system. Your value system is different from that of anyone else's. You have formed your value system as a result of the experiences you have had. The people you've known and the activities in which you have participated have all influenced your value system.

You use your value system whenever you choose between two or more items. The choice you make depends on which items you desire most. Suppose you had a choice between spending a day by yourself, with your family, or with your friends. Your decision would depend on whether you value privacy, family, or friends most highly.

If you share a house with others, you will find that some of your values are not the same as the other people's. Therefore, the values you have in common will control the thinking and actions of the group; the shared values will influence your housing decisions.

How Needs and Values Relate

Your needs and values are closely related. For example, you need a place to sleep. A cot can satisfy this need. However, the cot may not meet your value of comfort. If you have a choice, your value of comfort may cause you to choose a better bed than the cot.

You may also need space in the room you sleep in for activities other than sleeping. Therefore, your values will determine whether you choose a large or a small bed for the room. While the large bed may provide more comfort, the small bed will give you more space. See 1-12.

Ethan Allen, Inc.

1-12
This bunk bed may offer less than your ideal for comfort, but it does not take up as much space in the bedroom as a larger bed. The extra space can be used for activities other than sleeping.

Values That Influence Housing Choices

Housing can help you express your values. Consider some of the values discussed below that influence housing choices. See if any of these values are a part of your value system.

Space. People have spatial needs. While too much space can make people feel lonely, they need a certain amount of space around them to keep from feeling crowded. They create invisible boundaries around themselves, and others can sense those boundaries. These other people know whether or not they have permission to enter the boundaries.

Hobbies and activities can influence the need for space. For example, people who like to garden need space for a garden. People who enjoy spending time with friends need space for entertaining.

The way space is used also influences the amount that is needed. In places where space cannot be added or removed, the right furnishings can make the space seem larger or smaller. For example, by changing the furnishings, a crowded room can become more spacious and airy. Likewise, a large room can become warm and cozy.

Privacy. People need privacy to maintain good mental health. Sometimes they need to be completely alone. They need to be where others cannot see or hear what they are doing, nor can they see and hear what others are doing. They may want to be able to think, daydream, read, or study without being disturbed.

Since the need for privacy varies among people, it can be satisfied in a number of ways. One of the most extreme ways is to live alone in a dwelling that is set apart from other dwellings, 1-13. Another way is to have a private room or some other private place where people can enter only when they are invited.

Some people may not have the opportunity to live alone or have their own, private place. However, they can still meet their need for privacy. Doing a task that must be done alone, such as mowing the lawn, provides some privacy as does driving alone in a car. A chair that is set apart from other furnishings in a room can be a private place. Activities that require people to concentrate, such as woodworking or playing the piano, can free them from others. Even the sound of a vacuum cleaner gives some degree of privacy. It isolates people from other sounds.

Family unity. If people consider the well-being of their family as a whole to be important, they value family unity. Decisions in families that value family unity are made to benefit all family members, rather than just one.

When family unity is an important value, several areas of the house are designed for group living. A great room may be used for family activities. A large eat-in kitchen may be desired, so several family members can cook and eat together. Other families may have an outside area for recreation, as in 1-14. Even a chair can provide a place for family unity.

Economy. People who place a special emphasis on cost have a value of economy. Economy can apply to effort as well as money.

Housing costs money whether people rent or buy housing. Additional costs include the furnishings and equipment people put inside a house; utilities, such as electricity, gas, and water; caring for the house; and repair and maintenance bills.

If people highly value economy, they choose dwellings that have only the amount of space they need and buy only the furnishings and equipment they need. They use conservation methods to control their utility bills, such as turning off the lights in empty rooms and setting thermostats at moderate temperatures. They keep their houses in good shape. Maintenance bills nearly always cost less than repair and replacement costs. They may also make their own house repairs.

Effort costs in housing are high, since everything people do takes some amount of effort. Washing dishes, making beds, cleaning floors, painting walls, and mowing the lawn are only some of the many tasks that require human effort.

La Marr Hubbs

1-13
This house, which is located in a remote, wooded area, provides privacy for its occupants.

Weber-Stephen Products Company

1-14
Having a family barbecue provides a chance for family unity.

Although tasks cannot be eliminated, effort can be economized. Dwellings can be designed for efficient use of effort. For example, effort can be saved by storing dishes near the dishwasher or sink, locating the linen closet near bedrooms and bathrooms, or storing cleaning supplies near the rooms to be cleaned. Efficiency and orderliness can save effort.

Housing Needs Vary

On almost a daily basis, you can be sure of change. ***Life situations,*** sometimes called circumstances, cause change and affect the way you live. They are related to every aspect of your life. They set the stage for the way you interact with other people and with your housing. Changes occur, not only in your personal life but also in your living unit.

Living Units

People who share the same living quarters are called a ***living unit.*** The size of a living unit can vary from a single person to hundreds of people.

A ***one-person living unit*** may be someone who has never married or whose marriage has ended because of the loss of a spouse through death, desertion, or divorce. Although some single people live alone, others are part of larger living units. A college residence hall, 1-15, houses a large living unit of single people. Retirement centers and nursing homes house large living units of older, single people.

Many singles are the heads of ***single-parent families.*** In some of these families, one parent has died or left the home. Other single-parent families consist of an adult who has never married and one or more children. A single-parent family may be a separate living unit, or the unit may share housing with other people and be a part of a larger living unit.

Another living unit is the ***nuclear family.*** It includes parents and their children, 1-16. A married couple, even if childless, is considered a nuclear family.

A living unit is sometimes an ***extended family.*** This happens when relatives share a dwelling with one another. There are different types of extended families. One type consists of several generations of a family. For instance, children, their parents, and their grandparents make an extended family. Another type of extended family consists of people related to one another, but in a horizontal direction. Perhaps you know of living units consisting of aunts, uncles, and their nieces and nephews. Some families extend in both directions. They may include grandparents, parents, children, in-laws, aunts, uncles, or cousins, 1-17. Still another extended family is the ***blended family.*** That is usually parents and children from previous marriages.

1-15
Students who live in a residence hall, such as this one, form one type of living unit.

Kent Hayward

1-16
A nuclear family can consist of a mother, father, and two daughters.

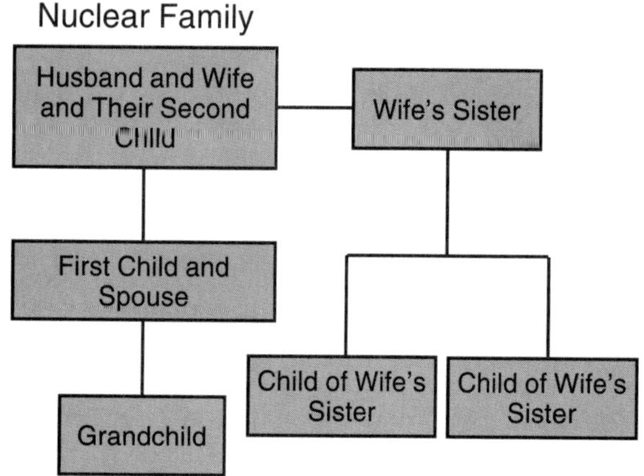

1-17
Some families are extended in more than one direction.

Your living unit affects your housing. In turn, your housing affects your living unit. In fact, certain types of housing are made for special types of living units. For example, residence halls are for students, retirement communities are for retirees, and efficiency apartments are for people who live alone.

Life Cycles

Life cycles are another way to view your housing needs. A ***life cycle*** is a series of stages through which an individual or family passes during its lifetime. In each stage, you have new opportunities and face new challenges. You develop new needs and values. These changes are related to your housing.

Individual life cycle. Each person follows a pattern of development called an *individual life cycle.* It is divided into four stages according to age groups:

1. Infancy.
2. Childhood.
3. Youth.
4. Adulthood.

Each stage can be divided into substages, as in 1-18. What stage do you belong to? Do you have brothers or sisters in other stages?

Family life cycle. Just as you have a place in an individual life cycle, your family has its place in the *family life cycle.* A family life cycle has five stages, 1-19. There is also a substage or substages in each stage.

The beginning stage is the time the married couple is without children. The husband and wife make adjustments to married life and to each other.

The expanding stage is the time when the family is growing. It includes the childbearing periods and the years of caring for young children.

The developing stage is the time when the children are in school. This stage includes the years of caring for school-age children and teenagers.

The launching stage is the time when the children become adults and leave their parents'

Infancy Stage	Childhood Stage	Youth Stage	Adulthood Stage
• Newborn, birth to 1 month old. • Infant, 1 month to 1 year old.	• Early childhood, 1 to 6 years of age. • Middle childhood, 6 to 8 years of age. • Late childhood, 9 to 12 years of age.	• Preteens. • Early Teens. • Middle Teens. • Late Teens.	• Young Adults. • Mature Adults. • Aging Adults.

1-18
This chart shows one way to divide the individual life cycle into substages.

Beginning Stage	Expanding Stage	Developing Stage	Launching Stage	Aging Stage
• Married couple without children.	• Couple with child(ren) up to 30 months old. • Couple with child(ren) 2 1/2 to 6 years old.	**Substages** • Couple with child(ren) 6 to 13 years old. • Couple with child(ren) 13 to 20 years old.	• Couple with child(ren) leaving home. • Couple with child(ren) away from home until couple retires.	• Couple from time of retirement until death of both spouses.

1-19
The family life cycle includes both stages and substages.

house. They may leave to go to college, to take a job, or to get married, 1-20. When all the children have left home, the couple is again on its own.

The aging stage is the time after retirement. At some point in this stage, either the husband or the wife lives alone after the death of his or her spouse. As people live longer, this stage increases in the length of time.

Artlynn Photography

1-20
These two people have just been launched and are starting a new family life cycle.

Family groups usually include more than one stage, or substage. In some cases, the stages overlap. For example, when a family has both a preschool child and a school-age child, the family is in overlapping stages.

Other families may have gaps between the stages or substages. An example would be a family with a teenager, in which the mother is pregnant.

Life Cycles and Housing Needs

As you move from one stage or substage of a life cycle to another, your housing needs change. Therefore, you should consider what stage or substage of the life cycles you are in as you plan your housing. If you think about both your present and future needs, your housing can help you live the kind of life you desire.

One example of a need that changes as you move through the life cycles is the need for space. When you were a baby, you probably slept in a crib that took up very little space. As you grew, you needed more sleeping space. You may have slept in a twin bed, 1-21, or a bunk bed. Finally, you may have moved to a double bed.

The need for space also changes throughout a family's life cycle. A young married couple in the beginning stage may not need very much space. However, once they enter the expanding stage, their need for space will increase. During this stage, the number, ages, sexes, and activities of their children will affect their space needs.

As families add new members, additional space is required, 1-22. As each member grows, he or she requires even more space. Teenagers need space for studying and entertaining friends. They also need space to store sports equipment, stereo equipment, clothes, and personal belongings.

Photo courtesy of Georgia-Pacific Corporation

1-21
When a child outgrows a crib, he or she may sleep in a twin bed, which has more room.

Sally Riggs

1-22
An expanding family must realize that each new member needs space.

As a family moves into the launching stage, it usually requires less and less space. When family members are launched, they take many of their belongings with them. This leaves more space for the rest of the family. An older married couple may have more space than they need when all of the children have been launched.

At this time some couples desire a change of scenery. They want to "buy down" to a smaller house with fewer demands. However, other couples choose to stay in their present house. They may not want to leave behind the memories their family house holds. They may also want to have plenty of room when their children and grandchildren come to visit.

Life-styles Influence Housing Decisions

You have seen how your needs and values affect your housing. You know how the make up of your living unit affects housing choices. Now you will see how life-styles and housing are related.

A ***life-style*** is a living pattern or way of life. Each person and living unit has a life-style. To a degree, all life-styles are alike. That is, they must satisfy the basic human needs. Beyond that, life-styles can take many different directions.

Your life-style is an extension of you. It is influenced by your needs, values, and life cycles. It reflects your experiences, personality, and goals.

The people who live in the house pictured in 1-23 like having a beautiful house with expensive furnishings. Their life-style may include hosting formal dinner parties. Look at 1-24. Can you guess the type of life-style the living unit of that house has? Would you enjoy the same life-style?

Specific life-styles are described below. You may find one that seems to fit your life situation. You may see your life-style as a combination of two or more types. You may desire a life-style that is not described in this section. Whatever life-style you have, living in the right kind of place can help you make the most of it.

Thomasville Furniture Industries, Inc.

1-23
This formal dining room reflects the life-style of the people who live in this house.

Individualistic Life-style

If your prefer to "do your own thing," you have an individualistic life-style. You do what you want to do. You are not concerned about what others think. If you want to live in a house with purple trim, you will paint the trim of your house purple. If you want to travel, you will, even if it means quitting your job and selling your house.

The first owner of the Winchester Mystery House, 1-25, had a very individualistic life-style. Sarah Winchester was a widow who lived alone in the huge dwelling. She believed that no harm could come to her as long as work continued on the house. Therefore, 16 people worked around the clock every day of the year. The house grew until it had 160 rooms, 10,000 windows, and 44 stairways.

People with individualistic life-styles are not necessarily eccentric. They simply follow their inner desires and feelings. They are not concerned about the praise or scorn they may receive from others.

Spiegel, Inc.

1-24
The values of the people who live in this house can be seen in the furnishings used in this room.

Winchester Mystery House, San Jose, Ca.

1-25
Most windows in the Winchester Mystery House have 13 panes; stairways have 13 steps.

Supportive Life-style

You have a supportive life-style if you like to help others. You may help family members, or you may work away from home helping others. You might combine the roles of a helper at home and a wage earner outside the home. The right housing will permit you to support others. The support may be psychological, physical, or financial.

Basic Life-style

If you can live simply without many modern conveniences, you have a basic life-style. Many people who are concerned about the effects of pollution and the depletion of natural resources have chosen to try this way of life. Depletion of the ozone layer may influence other people in this direction.

Sometimes a basic life-style is forced upon a living unit. In 1-26, you can see how one couple met its basic housing needs after its house was destroyed by fire. At first, the two used the "temporary" dwelling, because they had no money for other housing. Later, they chose to remain there and spent the money they could have used for better housing to satisfy other desires.

Danny Clevenger

1-26
This converted goat shed is the home of one couple who has a basic life-style. The hammock to the right provides a place to sleep.

Community Life-style

If you enjoy group activities, you may like group living and a community life-style. Communities vary widely. In some, members differ in age, sex, and background. In others, the members are very much alike. Some communities are small, and they may consist of only one living unit. Others, meanwhile, are as large as a village or town.

In every community, the members have at least one aspect of their lives in common. They may share the same religious beliefs or the same outlook on life. They may have the same career goals or be in the same stage or substage of the life cycle.

Community living arrangements are often found near college campuses. The members of each community are students who share housing responsibilities while attending school. The members have a lot in common, such as saving money and getting an education.

People who desire a community life-style may choose to live in a planned community. Some planned communities have a lot of apartments. People living there are renters rather than homeowners. Other types of planned communities are retirement communities. Older people, who have similar interests and hobbies, live there. Most of them have a great deal of leisure time. Many leisure activities are provided in this type of community. A typical layout of a retirement community is shown in 1-27. It has housing, a shopping center, and recreational facilities close together.

Influential Life-style

If you like to influence, or have some control over, people and events, you have an influential life-style. You are highly motivated and have a strong desire to reach goals that include leadership. You use your talents, energy, and money to create and support projects. These projects may be to promote religious, civic, or political activities.

Your housing should let you and your associates perform your activities with ease. You may need a private work place, 1-28, or a room where committees can meet. If you host large groups for

Thomasville Furniture Industries, Inc.

1-28
A home office is needed by many people who work at home.

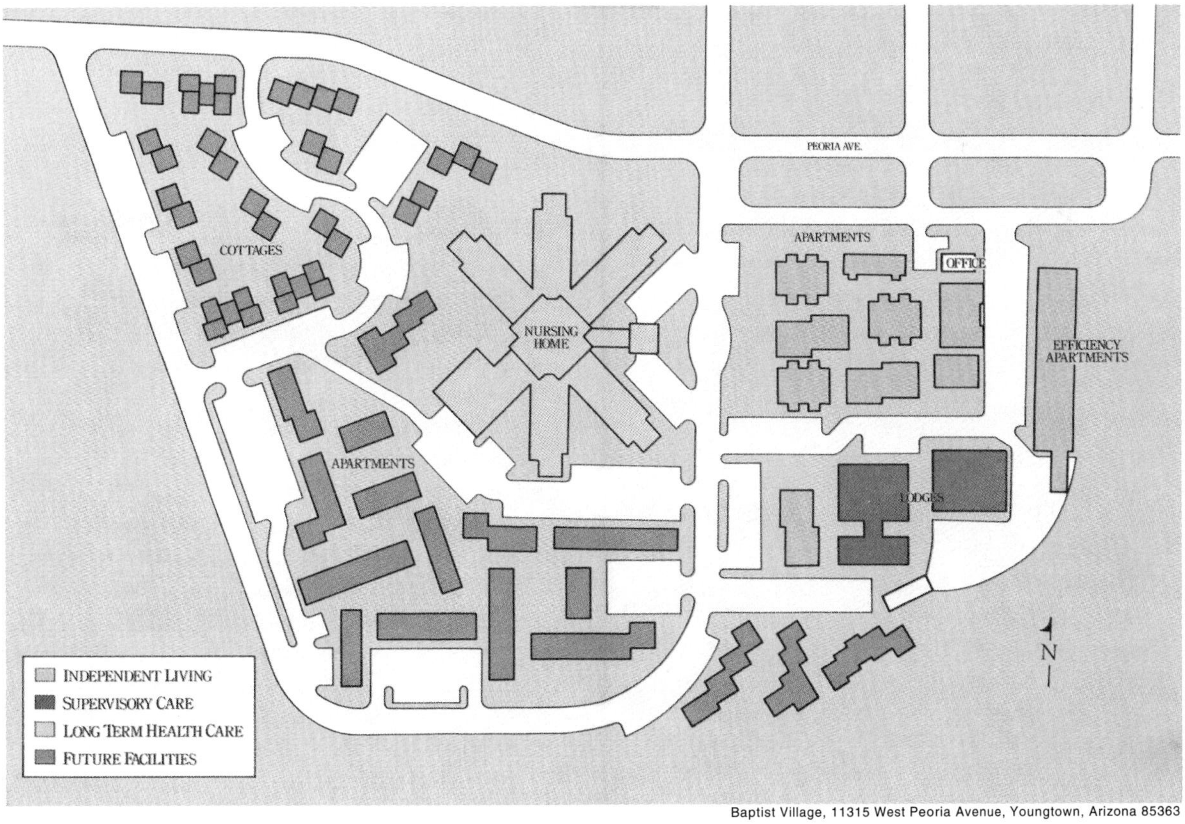

Baptist Village, 11315 West Peoria Avenue, Youngtown, Arizona 85363

1-27
This retirement community has various types of housing for the living units. In addition to housing, there is a recreation center, dining room, beauty and barber shop, and gift shop. A hospital and shopping mall are located close by.

your organizations, a large outdoor or indoor area may be an asset. You may need housing that will let you be active and efficient, so you can devote more of your time and energy to the activities that are important to you.

Housing and the Quality of Life

Quality of life is the degree of satisfaction obtained from life. Good housing provides people with satisfying surroundings that can improve their quality of life.

Personal Quality of Life

Quality of life is important to you as an individual. Just as you are unique, your concept of the quality of life is unique. What you think improves the quality of life may not appeal to someone else. Your housing environment helps you meet your needs and values. It also adds satisfaction to your life and, therefore, improves the quality of your life.

Quality of life is also important to the other members of your living unit. Your living unit, whether it is your family or some other group, is one part of your life situation. The members play a part in shaping your attitudes and values. In turn, the combined needs and values of the members determine the type of housing environment in which you live. If all of the members are concerned about the well-being of the group as a whole, the quality of life for everyone will be satisfactory.

Quality of Life for Society

The future of a society depends on individuals and groups who work to make life better for everyone. Some of the work is social in nature. That means groups of people must cooperate to reach a common goal. The goal is to improve the quality of life for society. All people cannot make equal contributions toward any given goal. Some degree of "give and take" is required. An example is the plight of people who are homeless. They do not have the resources to secure housing for themselves. Therefore, groups of people work together to see that housing is available for the homeless.

People must also work together and use their resources of time, money, and energy to maintain and support beautiful surroundings, such as well-kept buildings and natural landscapes. These surroundings satisfy the needs and values of many people in society.

Human Ecology

Human ecology is the study of people and their environment. Much research is being done in this field. People are becoming aware of the problems caused by pollution. For instance, untreated wastewater from houses and factories dumps pollutants into streams, lakes, and underground water supplies. Fuel burned for heat and power adds harmful elements to the air.

Instead of wishing for the "good old days," people must move ahead to find ways to solve problems, such as noise and air pollution, traffic congestion, and the waste of natural resources. Solving these problems will improve the microenvironment of housing and the quality of life for society.

Summary

People interact with their housing. Their housing affects them, and they affect their housing. Housing helps satisfy people's physical and psychological needs and can help them move toward self-actualization. Beauty, self-expression, and creativity in housing are other needs that can be met through housing.

Needs and values are closely related. However, the needs and values of people and living units vary as they move through the life cycles.

Each person chooses a life-style, and it is reflected in his or her housing. People can choose from a variety of life-styles, including individual, supportive, basic, community, and influential.

Housing affects the quality of life for both individuals and society. The study of human ecology can help people improve housing.

To Review

Write your responses on a separate sheet of paper.

1. The word housing refers to the dwelling and what is _____ it and _____ it.
2. Housing is your:
   a. Microenvironment.
   b. Macroenvironment.
   c. Total environment
3. List three physical needs people have.
4. Four psychological needs people have are _____, _____, _____, and _____.
5. Describe a person who has met his or her need for self-actualization through housing.
6. Define the term values.
7. Explain how space and privacy are related.
8. Describe five ways to achieve privacy.
9. People who place a special emphasis on cost, value:
   a. Esteem.
   b. Self-expression.
   c. Family unity.
   d. Economy.
10. Give an example of how housing can help you meet each of the following needs:
    a. Security.
    b. Creativity.
    c. Self-expression.
11. Given the chance, how would you change your housing to better meet your need for self-actualization?
12. Define the term life situations.
13. List three circumstances that influence your life situations.
14. People who share the same living quarters are called a(n) _____ _____.
15. List the four stages of the individual life cycle.
16. Give an example of the way housing needs change as a family moves from one stage of the life cycle to another.
17. Explain how a couple in the beginning stage of the family life cycle differs from a couple in the aging stage.
18. Define the term life-style.

To Do

1. Work with your classmates to create a bulletin board display. Draw a large pyramid similar to the one in 1-1. Then find or draw pictures that show how housing can meet the different kinds of needs.
2. List in order of importance needs and values that are met by your housing.
3. Collect pictures of rooms and tell how you would use creativity to change them.
4. Write a description of the area you consider to be your own private space.
5. If you have permission, rearrange furniture in some part of your house, so that someone has more privacy. Report to the class about your actions and results.
6. List the circumstances that determine the life situations of your living unit. Then list some of the housing needs your living unit has because of life situations.
7. Survey your classmates to find out how many types of living units they represent.
8. List housing needs for each of the four stages of the individual life cycle. Be sure to consider privacy, recreation, and clothing storage. Compare your list with a classmate's.
9. Consider a specific housing need, such as space, and explain how it changes during each stage of the family life cycle.
10. Look at a friend's house. Then write a short essay describing how his or her house reflects his or her family's life-style.
11. Ask an older person to tell you how his or her housing has changed during his or her lifetime. Ask how his or her life-style and housing affect each other. If possible, tape-record the interview and share it with the class.

CHAPTER 2

Influences on Housing

James F. Parnell

to Know
agrarian
building codes
census
climate
computer-aided drafting and design (CADD)
culture
density
disabilities
dual-income family
dysfunctional
environment
Gross Domestic Product (GDP)
hogans
housing market
new town
resources
row houses
subdivision
substandard
Sunbelt
tax exemption
technology
topography
tract houses
zoning regulations

Objectives

After studying this chapter, you will be able to:

- Relate historical events to housing.
- Discuss culture and housing characteristics.
- Determine the relationship between societal changes and housing.
- Analyze concerns about environmental aspects of housing.
- Relate the effects of economy and housing on each other.
- Understand the impact of technology on housing.
- Identify the role of government in housing decisions.

Housing changes according to the needs and desires of the members of the living unit. It also changes because of outside influences such as historical, cultural, societal, environmental, economic, technological, and governmental influences.

Historical Influences on Housing

The story of housing in the United States begins before the colonies were established by the first European settlers. There is a sharp contrast between the houses of today and those of early North America.

Early Shelter

Early humans lived in caves that provided a degree of safety and protection from the weather and wild animals. These caves helped people meet the basic need of shelter–a place to sleep and rest.

Another form of early shelter was a dugout, which is a large hole dug in a bank. Dugouts were warm in cold weather and cool in warm weather. Sometimes a dome-shaped covering was added to the dugout to make it roomier. The covering was often made of animal skins, mud and bark, or mud and branches.

Housing of Native Americans. A crude rock overhang or cliff was often used for housing by early Native Americans, who were known as cliff dwellers. The overhangs were improved by enclosing them. The enclosure gave warmth, privacy, and security to the cliff dwellers. Living in cliffs gave cliff dwellers the advantage of being able to see great distances, which added to their security.

Native Americans occupied much of North America before European settlers began to arrive. The materials used for their housing depended on what was available in the section of the country in which they lived. Some lived in huts that were constructed with a framework of poles and coverings of thatch, hides, or mud placed over the poles. Others lived in tepees and wigwams. Some Native Americans lived in permanent dwellings constructed of adobe. Study 2-1 and notice the different types of Native American dwellings and where they were located.

Housing of the colonists. The first shelters used by the European settlers were copied after Native American dwellings. Other houses were built of sod. Dirt floors were common.

The early colonists built their own houses. Sometimes house raisings were held where neighbors would come over to help build a house. Since many people helped with the work, a house could be built in a short amount of time. The quality of these early dwellings was limited due to the lack of skills, tools, and materials.

After the colonists became settled, they attempted to copy the houses in their homeland. However, the styles had to be adapted to the materials available. Some housing styles of the old country were not well-suited to the climate of the new land and were discarded. For instance, the thatched roof, commonly used in England, was not suited to the cold New England climate, 2-2.

The abundance of trees in the eastern forests made the *log cabin* convenient to build. It is believed that the first log cabins were built about 1640 by Swedish and Finnish colonists. They began as one-room structures with fireplaces for heating and cooking. See 2-3. The chimneys were located on the outside of the cabins.

Later, the log cabin was built in a variety of styles. Rooms were often added as families grew

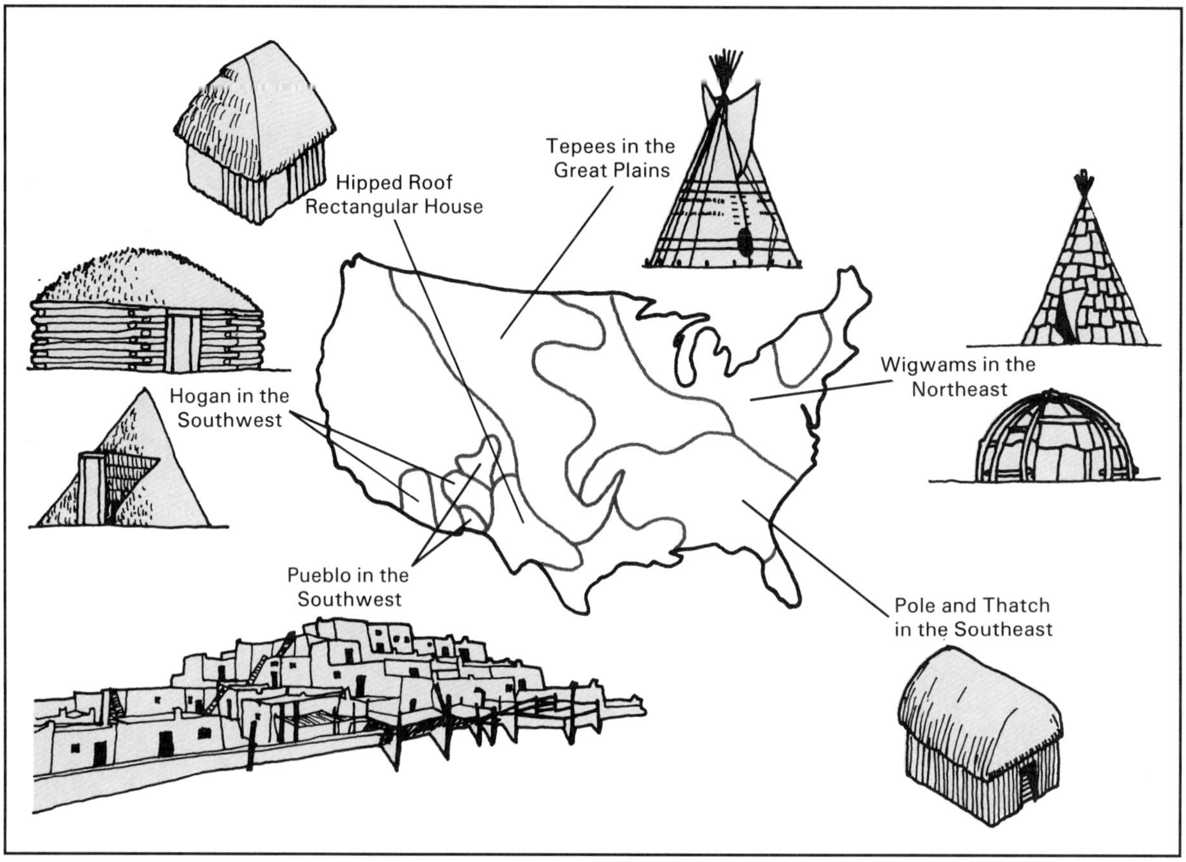

2-1
Early Native Americans lived in an assortment of housing. Housing designs varied, according to the region of North America in which they were located.

2-2
The thatched roof, which is not appropriate for cold climates, is frequently found in warmer climates.

Fern Mountain Historic Homestead

2-3
The typical log cabin looked similar to this one.

larger. Some log cabins were built with three rooms–an entryway, kitchen, and sleeping room. Others were even two stories tall. The kitchens in these log cabins were large, so food could be both processed and prepared in the house. Sleeping rooms were small and sometimes located in a loft. If a small log cabin was replaced by a larger dwelling, the small log cabin was sometimes used for storage.

The log cabin spread from the Northeast into the South and onto the western frontier. It became a symbol of the early United States.

Most housing in early settlements could be found in group settings. The houses were placed close together for security reasons. The houses were generally square or rectangular. Many had one or two rooms and a fireplace. When other rooms were added around the main room, it became the "great room."

As the country became settled, more people with building skills arrived. They helped build houses and taught others their skills. When logs were made into lumber, many houses were built of lumber. Other houses also appeared that were built of stone or brick.

Housing during the 1700s and 1800s

Throughout the 1700s and 1800s, many people moved west and settled on large plots of land. They lived on their land in a variety of dwellings. *Farmhouses* ranged in design and construction from sod houses to log cabins to ranch houses. At the same time, large *plantation houses* were being built in the South, 2-4.

Madewood Plantation, Louisiana Office of Tourism

2-4
Plantation houses were common dwellings for large landowners of the South.

In the late 1700s, a majority of the settlers who had come to North America were ***agrarian,*** or people who earned their living from the land. By 1890, the rural population had decreased as a result of the Industrial Revolution. People began to move to the cities along with immigrants looking for jobs. The birth rate also increased, and the cities grew. This increased the demand for housing in the urban areas.

Urban housing. The high ***density,*** or number of people in a given area, in the cities resulted in housing being built close together and houses being crowded with people. Most houses were frame houses that varied in design. The first *tenement houses,* which were built mainly for the immigrants, appeared in New York City about 1840. They were constructed without any regulations. Most were built on a city lot 25 by 100 feet. A typical tenement house was a five-story building measuring 25 by 25 feet. Next to each dwelling was another 25 by 25 feet building.

The typical tenement house consisted of as many as 116 two-room apartments. The outdoor toilets were located on the land between the buildings. Conditions were very poor and the landlords earned the title of "slumlords."

By 1890, government regulations required that each room in a new tenement house have a window. Each apartment was to have running water and a kitchen sink. Community toilets were to be located in the stairway area going from one floor to another.

The first row houses were built in the 1820s. ***Row houses*** are a continuous group of dwellings connected by common sidewalls. Many of them were built to house factory workers. See 2-5. Two-story row houses sometimes housed as many as six families at a time.

Eventually, row houses without as many common walls evolved. They grew from a dwelling planned for one family to multifamily housing. Two family dwellings called duplexes were built. Others were built for four families or six families.

The tenement houses and row houses were forerunners of modern apartments. Some apartments first appeared during the housing shortage caused by the Industrial Revolution. At the same time, mansions were being built for the well-to-do. See 2-6.

Changes in housing. Many changes were taking place in housing and the housing industry in the 1700s and 1800s. There were new inventions, machinery, and technology.

Wood and coal burning stoves appeared in houses. Steam heating systems were installed. Oil and gas lamps replaced candles. Ice boxes were available. Water supplies, plumbing, and sanitation were improved. Some houses had indoor toilets and bathtubs. However, only people with high incomes could afford to take advantage of the new developments. Rural areas were slow to adopt the improvements.

Machinery, craftsworkers, and architects were all important in the housing industry. Machinery helped the buildings go up rapidly. Craftsworkers were responsible for a high quality of work. Architects got ideas from designs used in buildings in other countries. No one housing style dominated the scene.

Historic Pullman Foundation

2-5
Many employees of The Pullman Palace Car Company lived in these rowhouses in the late 1800s.

W. Metzen/H. Armstrong Roberts

2-6
Mansions, such as the Vanderbilt Mansion shown here, were often built for wealthy industrial families in the late 1800s.

Housing in the 1900s

During the early 1900s, the number of immigrants coming to the United States was increasing. More and more people were moving to the cities. A housing boom in the early 1900s began to meet this need for housing.

Then, during World War I, almost no housing was built except by the federal government. This caused a housing shortage. House ownership declined. Housing was overcrowded. There was also a shortage of materials and, as a result, structures fell into disrepair. After World War I, about one-third of the population was living in substandard housing. ***Substandard*** means the houses are not up to the standards that are best for people. Only a halfhearted housing reform was taking place.

By the time the Great Depression began in 1929, more than half the population lived in cities. However, the building of houses had slowed down. People of all income levels had to struggle to meet their own housing needs. However, private enterprise, as well as the government, soon saw the need for housing reform and began to lay the foundation.

The first census of housing in the United States was taken in 1940. (A ***census*** is an official count of the population taken by the government.) The census supported what the people knew–the housing needs of people at all income levels had not been met. The impact of the increased population, World War I, and the Great Depression had left housing conditions in a sad state.

New solutions to housing shortages. In response to the housing shortage, new forms of housing were developed. Mobile homes became popular. They first appeared as travel trailers in the 1920s and 1930s. Then they evolved into house trailers in the late 1930s and 1940s. They served as year-round housing for many people, including defense workers, factory employees, and military personnel. Mobile homes were a solution to the desire for house ownership, since the cost of a mobile home was considerably less than for a house.

Manufactured housing, or factory-produced housing, has evolved from the mobile home to include many different types. In general, manufactured housing comes in three types–modular, panelized, and precut. Models may be purchased at various levels of completion depending upon the type. Some are completely finished at the factory. Some come in finished sections that need to be put together. Others are not finished until they are erected. All involve a certain amount of labor when being placed on the site.

Following World War II, building resumed. ***Tract houses,*** which are groups of similarlydesigned houses built on a tract of land, appeared. They were moderate in size and built to meet the needs of the moderate income family. The living units who live in the tract houses today, have adapted them to fit their life cycles and life-styles, 2-7.

Steps to improve housing. Several new housing ideas were developed to improve housing. Two of these were new towns and subdivisions. A ***new town*** is an urban development consisting of a small to medium-sized city with a broad range of housing and planned industrial, commercial, and recreational facilities. See 2-8. It covers up to 6,000 acres. The number of residents ranges from 10,000 to 60,000. The industrial facilities provide opportunities for employment. People of all ages, economic levels, races, educational backgrounds, and religions live there.

2-7
Tract houses look alike when built, but many owners decide to alter them. In this picture, the garage has been converted to a room, and a two-car garage with rooms above has been added at the rear of the house.

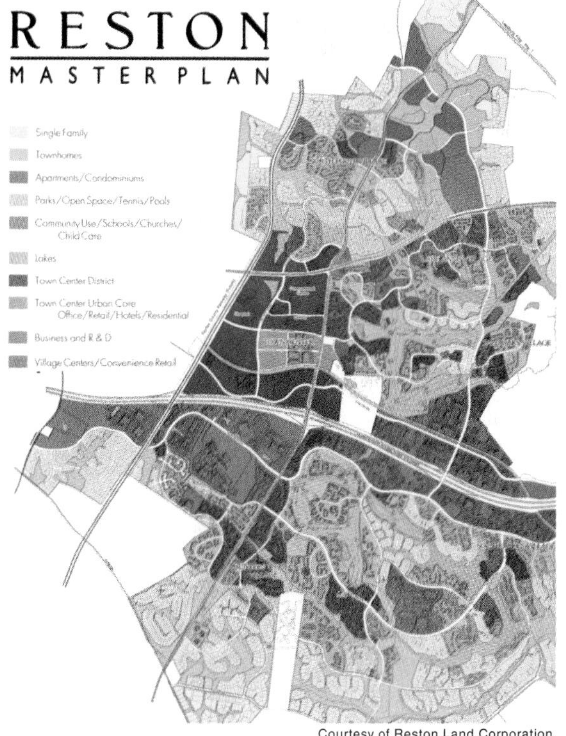

Courtesy of Reston Land Corporation

2-8
A master plan is used when developing the planned community of Reston, Virginia.

The idea for new towns dates back to the 1910s. However, it was 1960 and later before the idea caught on. By the early 1970s, about fifteen new towns were started. The idea continued and by 1990, 60 new towns were in progress in the United States.

A subdivision is a smaller version of the new town concept. In a ***subdivision,*** the density and types of buildings are controlled. Schools, but not industry, are included in the plan.

By 1930, the federal government had stepped up efforts to improve the housing conditions. Many policies and programs were put into action. Efforts were made to rebuild the slum areas. Housing programs for low-income families and older people increased. Even more tract houses were built. Numerous apartments and town houses appeared on the scene. Efforts to house the homeless became important. The demand for more housing was being met. However, adequate housing for everyone has never been achieved in the United States.

Ideally, the supply of housing will continue to strive to meet the needs of the United State's diverse population, which includes older people, people with disabilities, singles, first-time homeowners, and people of all income levels.

Cultural Influences on Housing

The beliefs, social customs, and traits of a group of people form their ***culture.*** The culture of a group of people influences its housing. Its housing also becomes part of the culture. The following examples illustrate how housing influences culture.

The Navajo, a Native American tribe of the early North American Southwest, lived in ***hogans,*** which were buildings made of logs and mud. The windows faced west, and a single door faced east. The placement of the door had religious significance. The Navajo believed that the door must face east, so the spirit guardians can enter. The tradition exists today, even though the type of housing for many has changed. The Crow, a Native American tribe of the Northwest, also have doors that face east.

The Native American tribes who were scattered throughout North America had cultures related to their region and the local environment. They typically viewed the land and water as common property that belonged to everyone. Then, European settlers who had contrasting views arrived. In North America, they saw the opportunity for private ownership of the land and water.

Before regions in the South and Southwest became states, they were settled by the Spanish. The Spanish built missions with white-washed walls and red-tiled roofs. The style of the Spanish missions greatly influenced the local architecture. In the early 1900s, there was a revival of Hispanic heritage, including architecture. The old missions were preserved and early Spanish architecture was copied in houses and other buildings. Today, the Hispanic influence can be found in architecture throughout the South and Southwest, 2-9. It has also spread north.

When the Pilgrims arrived on Plymouth Rock in the winter of 1620, they needed shelter immediately. They duplicated the housing of the Native Americans. After the winter was over, they began to duplicate the English cottages of their homeland. They used wood, which could be found in abundance and was the traditional building material of their homeland. The first cottages

San Xavier Del Bac Mission, Arizona Office of Tourism

2-9
Spanish missions, such as this one, influence architecture even today.

were often crude and made of timber. They had few windows, dirt floors, and chimneys built of sticks and heavy clay. As better materials and skills became available, the cottages were built to better resemble the cottages in England.

As other cultures came to North America from Europe, they also contributed their styles of housing to the American culture. As mentioned before, the Swedish log cabin became a popular form of housing. The Dutch Colonial, Pennsylvania Dutch (German) Colonial, French Normandy, and Italianate housing styles are other examples of European influences on American housing.

Throughout history, houses have been strong indicators of culture. Heritage as well as traditional resources and skills are reflected in housing. As cultures change, the changes are evident in the housing.

Societal Influences on Housing

Signs of societal change are everywhere. They can be seen in the growth of the cities and the movement of people to new jobs and locations. They can be seen in relationships and lifestyles. Many of these changes affect housing.

Household Size

One important social change that has influenced housing is the number of members of a living unit. This number has been gradually decreasing since the first U.S. census was taken in 1790. This census showed that a majority of the households had between three and seven members. In 1900, the majority had between two and five members. The 1990 U.S. census showed that the majority had between one and two people.

Household Composition

The decrease in the number of household members is not the only change that can be seen in living units. During the twentieth century, for example, the composition of living units has changed. In 1940, 75 percent of all households were headed by married couples, and 7 percent were single-person households. By 1990, the single-person household had increased to almost 25 percent of the total. Households headed by married couples had decreased to 56 percent.

In the past, married couples were more likely than single people to own their own houses. However, this has changed in part, due to an increase in the number of singles. The 1990 U.S census showed that there were 65 million single people, as compared to 38 million single people in 1980. This increase has occurred for many reasons, such as many singles are putting off marriage until their careers are established. The divorce rate has also been steadily increasing.

Some singles prefer to live alone, while others live with roommates and share housing costs. Many singles are renters and live in apartments. Others own houses, condominiums, cooperatives, or town houses.

Some singles continue to live in their parent's houses. Never-married singles or single-again adults may return to their parent's houses after living in their own housing for awhile. They may return for a short or extended period of time. Their children may or may not accompany them.

An Older Population

The continual aging of the population is another change in society that affects housing. The age group with the largest population growth increase is the elderly, people over 65 years of age. According to the 1990 U.S. census, there were 29 million people classified as elderly. The numbers continue to grow. Any population that shows such rapid growth demands attention. Thus, housing for older people has become a national concern.

Housing needs for many older people differ from those of the general population. Many older people lose some of their physical abilities as they age. They may have a partial loss of hearing or sight. They may also become more sensitive to heat and cold. Their housing needs to be adapted to meet these changes. Many older people live in older housing, which has not been designed to accommodate these changes. Housing that is adapted or designed to fit the needs of older people helps them remain independent.

People with Disabilities

Many people have either physical or mental ***disabilities*** that limit their activities. This affects their housing needs, since they need housing that allows them to carry out day-to-day activities with as little restriction as possible.

When their housing limits their activities, they need to consider how housing can be built or adapted to meet their needs. This will be discussed further in Chapter 4, "Choosing a Place to Live" and Chapter 20, "Keeping Your House Safe and Secure."

Finding Affordable Housing

Many people live in inadequate housing. They may live on fixed incomes, such as Social Security or welfare benefits, where their incomes remain the same regardless of other economic changes, such as inflation. Other people become homeless as a result of unemployment and loss of income.

Inadequate housing has many effects on society. Substandard dwellings become overcrowded, which results in a lack of privacy, the spread of disease, and increase of family conflicts.

The middle-income group is the largest in the United States. Most jobs fit in the middle-income level, and most houses and furniture are designed for middle-income families. However, today's middle-income families sometimes have difficulty buying houses. This is because family incomes are not increasing at the same rate as the cost of housing. It used to be that families should spend no more than two and one-half times their annual income to purchase a house. Today, the average house in the United States is priced higher than this figure. The average family spends at least one-third of its income on housing. Some of those who purchase houses may pay up to four times their annual income for an average house.

Since the prices of houses have risen faster than incomes, the middle-income people have faced, and will continue to face, some major changes in their housing and life-styles. Instead of buying houses, they may choose to live in apartments, condominiums, cooperatives, or town houses. See 2-10.

2-10
Due to the high cost of housing, many families today have chosen to live in multifamily housing, such as this four-plex.

Changing Roles

Today, many women are working outside the home. Some are working to support themselves. Others are working to support their families, which might include children or older parents. Many women own their own houses.

When both the husband and wife are employed outside the home, they have a ***dual-income family.*** This situation has become common and necessary for many families, because income has not kept up with the cost of living. While dual-income families may have more income, they may have less time for household chores. They may desire more convenient housing and time-saving devices.

Planning for Leisure Time

People today do not have much time for recreation and relaxation. They may have to juggle their jobs and home responsibilities. This can include making time for commuting to work and caring for children, if there are any. These activities and others all require time and cut down on leisure activities. However, many people plan how they use their leisure time and, therefore, use it more wisely.

How you choose to use your leisure time affects your housing decisions. You may choose housing with low maintenance requirements, so you can spend more time on leisure activities. On the other hand, you may spend your leisure time decorating or fixing up your house.

You may choose housing that provides opportunities for leisure activities. Your house might have a special room or space to work out in or do hobbies. Your housing may include a swimming pool, 2-11, golf course, or tennis court. A large backyard may be the place you want to spend your leisure time with your friends.

Marilyn Brandon, photo by Philip Bartholomew

2-11
A swimming pool helps you enjoy leisure time.

A Mobile Society

In a mobile society, people often travel from one location to another. The average vehicle owner travels 15,000 miles a year. Many people frequently travel long distances by air. Add other methods of transportation, such as trains and boats, and the picture is clear that today's society is very mobile.

In a mobile society, people often move to housing in new locations. The average living unit moves every six years, which can add up to 13 moves in a lifetime. The main reason is employment. Other reasons include adventure, retirement, and better climate.

Some people may have more than one house and move between the two. Others move with their portable dwellings, 2-12. Some people move across the country. Others move shorter distances. They may move across town or between urban, suburban, and rural areas. They may move because of employment, the desire for larger or smaller housing, or to change neighborhoods. They may be changing from renters to homeowners or vice versa.

Population increases in some areas of the United States are evidence of our mobile society. Before 1970, there was a slow, continuing westward movement. People were also moving

Winnebago Industries, Inc.

2-12
Many people use motorized mobile homes to travel around the country and visit relatives.

toward large bodies of water such as the Atlantic Ocean, Pacific Ocean, Great Lakes, and Gulf of Mexico. Then, after 1970, people began moving to the Sunbelt. The ***Sunbelt*** is the southern and southwestern states of the United States.

Environmental Influences on Housing

Your ***environment*** is the conditions, objects, places, and people that are all around you. People adapt to their environments in the housing they design and build. They are also able to manipulate their environments through their housing decisions.

The Natural Environment

The *natural environment* is provided by nature. Land, water, trees, and solar energy are elements of the natural environment. ***Climate*** is part of the natural environment. It is the combination of weather conditions in a region over a period of years as shown by temperature, wind velocity, and precipitation. The altitude and distribution of the land and water help produce the climate.

Shelter varies according to the climate in which it is located. For instance, in areas where it snows or rains often, roofs are sloped to shed snow and rain. In warm areas where it does not rain or snow often, roofs may be flat and accessible, so people can sleep on the cooler rooftops at night. In cold regions, houses may have smaller doors and fewer windows.

Many early people expected to live in harmony with nature. Living in caves and tents enhanced that concept. Today, people want protection from nature, while having the opportunity to enjoy it. Large windows can frame views of the outdoors, while providing protection from the elements. On mild days, decks, patios, and swimming pools provide great opportunities for outdoor living, 2-13.

The climate and ***topography,*** or lay of the land, of a region both influence the location and design of dwellings. Houses that are designed and located to harmonize with the natural setting and climate are more likely to be efficient.

During the 1950s, integrating houses with the natural environment was explored. Architects designed houses to fit various natural environments. One of the most influential architects concerned with the environment was Frank Lloyd Wright. He broke away from traditional housing designs, saying people should have the courage to follow nature. He used natural settings and many native building materials, 2-14. Wright positioned houses to take advantage of natural

Photo courtesy of Georgia-Pacific Corporation

2-13
This patio gives people a chance to spend time outdoors in beautiful surroundings.

Courtesy of The Frank Lloyd Wright Foundation

2-14
Frank Lloyd Wright designed this building, so it seems to be a part of the hill.

sunlight and prevailing breezes. He also located them so they had a great deal of privacy. Much of today's housing is designed to take advantage of the natural environment.

The Constructed Environment

The *constructed environment* includes the natural environment after it has been changed by human effort. A constructed environment is created whenever a dwelling is built; trees and bushes are planted around the dwelling; and heat pumps, heaters, or air conditioners are used to change the dwelling's indoor climate.

Together, natural and constructed environments can provide pleasing surroundings. Highways through the mountains make the beautiful scenery accessible to people. Dwellings located along beaches allow people to enjoy a view of the ocean, 2-15.

The Behavioral Environment

Housing creates an environment for people to interact with one another. This interaction is called the *behavioral environment.* Human resources, such as intelligence, talent, energy, and attitude, are part of this environment. Feelings, such as happiness, loneliness, love, and anger, are another part of it.

The behavioral environment overlaps with the natural and constructed environments. It is found wherever people interact with one another–in child care centers, schools, shopping centers, neighborhoods, and houses. See 2-16.

Housing fosters social behavior. It may restrict certain types of behavior and permit others. Housing is more than a response to the physical environment. It is a setting for the development of the members of the living unit.

A positive behavioral environment is desired. However, sometimes a living unit or family is ***dysfunctional.*** This means the behavioral environment produces a negative effect on members of the living unit. For instance, drug addiction, alcoholism, and violence cause families to become dysfunctional. Substandard housing can be the cause of negative behavior and result in a dysfunctional family, while satisfactory housing contributes to positive behavior.

Interaction of the Environments

Each type of environment affects the other two, causing a chain reaction, 2-17. One example is a community that has a limited amount of land. Houses in this community are built close together, covering most of the land. No land is set aside to preserve part of the natural environment.

2-15
The people who live in this building have easy access to the ocean in addition to a beautiful view.

H.L. Rolf

2-16
The cooperation of people who are making the most of their human resources is an example of a good behavioral environment.

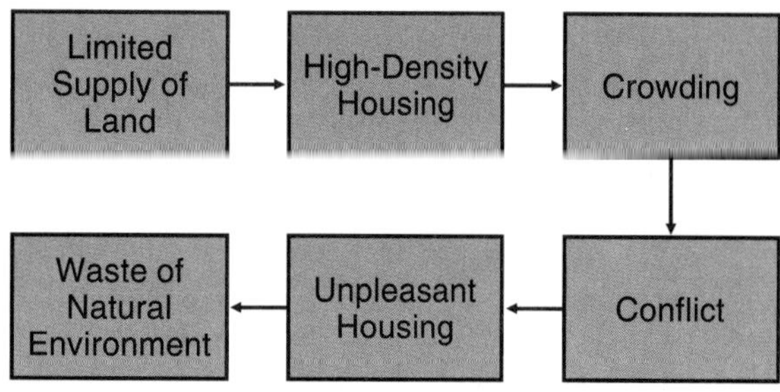

2-17
One type of environment affects another type. The result is a chain reaction.

The behavioral environment in this community is full of conflict, because the constructed and natural environments are not satisfying to the people. The people are crowded too close together. They do not have the space they need or the natural beauty they want. Because their environments are not controlled, all of their needs and wants cannot be met. They cannot move toward self-actualization.

Economic Influences on Housing

The economic influences on housing are those that involve the production and consumption of goods and services related to housing. These influences include the interaction among consumers, businesses, and government in meeting housing needs.

People make economic decisions every day. Their decisions concern how they use their resources to meet their goals. ***Resources*** are items that can be used to reach a goal. One resource people have is money, or purchasing power. A goal they may also have is buying housing.

Houses are expensive and the cost keeps rising. For example, in 1923, a three-bedroom house could be bought for $4,325. In late 1992, the average cost cost of a three-bedroom house for resale was $104,400, according to Dr. J. Butler of Arizona State University. This is an increase of over 240 times in almost 70 years. In addition to the purchase price of a house, the cost of utilities and maintenance needs to be considered. Their costs also continue to rise.

How Housing Affects the Economy

One way the economy is measured is to determine the number of families that can afford to buy a new, medium-priced house. High mortgage rates and high unemployment affect the ability of living units to purchase housing. In 1970, 45 percent of families were able to afford new, medium-priced housing. By 1986, the number had risen to 53 percent. In 1990, according to the U.S. Census Bureau, there was a decrease to 30 percent.

Another measure of the economy is the number of housing starts, or houses being built, in a given year. In an average year, the housing starts should number two million, which would meet the demand for new housing. When the economy is up, that number may be reached. When the economy is down, the number of housing starts is less than expected.

How the Economy Affects Housing

The economy affects and is affected by the production of houses. A large amount of nationally-produced goods and services is related to the housing industry. Employment goes up and down in relation to the condition of the housing industry. See 2-18. (The housing industry employs planners, developers, builders, material suppliers, buyers and sellers, and financial

Lowden, Lowden & Co.

2-18
Construction workers have plenty of employment opportunities when the housing industry is up.

experts.) There are millions of enterprises involved in the housing industry.

The housing industry is dependent on the housing market. The ***housing market*** is the transfer of dwellings from the producers to the consumers. The condition of the housing market depends on supply and demand. It changes considerably from year to year, since it follows a general pattern of economic prosperity and decline. You have already read that war, recession, depression, and inflation have all impacted the housing market.

Housing is traditionally the first major sector of the economy to rebound after a slump. Growth in the housing industry has a positive impact on the ***Gross Domestic Product (GDP),*** which is the value of all goods and services produced within a country during a given time period, regardless of who owns the production facilities. The GDP is the most accurate indicator of the national economy.

Mortgage interest rates and tax advantages affect growth in the housing industry. Interest rates on home mortgages and inflation seem to increase at the same time. When mortgage rates are down, there may not be enough housing to meet the demand. When the rates are high, fewer living units invest in new housing.

Tax advantages include the ongoing personal income tax exemption on mortgage interest. A ***tax exemption*** means that you do not have to pay taxes on the designated portion of income. Homeowners age 55 and older receive a special tax exemption when they sell their houses. Other house sellers may have a capital gains tax advantage, which means there may be an exemption on the profit made by a sale. Those who move because of a job change may have another tax advantage.

Technological Influences on Housing

Technology is a scientific method of achieving a practical purpose. A knowledge of tools, materials, and processes allows people to adapt to their environment. Technology changes over time as new and better ways of meeting human needs are discovered.

Early Technology

Technology began with the early cave dwellers. Caves met the cave dwellers housing needs, because they were dry and secure, and the temperature was moderate. However, caves were in short supply, and they were often located far from food and water.

When people evolved from being hunters and gatherers to being farmers, living in caves became less desirable. People then used technology to build dwellings. They used naturally occurring materials, such as logs, sticks, bark, rocks, leaves, grass, mud, and snow, to construct houses. These houses were temporary and would last only two or three years. They were easily abandoned if the living unit wanted to move on, or if better housing became available. The main shortcoming of these houses was the quality of materials used, rather than the design. When the early dwellings are examined, some of the same technology used in basket weaving and pottery making is found. See 2-19.

Over time, technology continued and natural materials were improved. Old techniques were modified and new techniques were generated. Logs were made into wood planks and stones were chipped into blocks. Animal hides became coverings for windows and doors. Later bricks, tiles, pipes, and cement were developed.

2-19
Can you see the resemblance between pottery and the adobe bricks used in this modern structure?

Industrialization

The Industrial Revolution had a large technological impact on housing. Goods were being mass-produced. The expansion of the railroad system was in progress. Factories and farmers could ship their products, which included housing materials, by rail. Prefabricated houses became popular, because they could be shipped in sections. Sears, Roebuck & Company shipped 110,000 mail-order houses in a 40-year period.

Industrialization has changed housing in many ways. Many parts of houses, such as doors and windows already in frames, come from the factory ready to install. Climate control units, such as heat pumps, are factory produced and have replaced fireplaces and simple fans. Today, machines are performing tasks once done by humans. The pace of life has become faster than ever before.

In his book *Future Shock,* Alvin Toffler says that in the past change was so slow that it was hardly noticed. One could live an entire lifetime and not feel the impact of the changes taking place. He says that of the last 800 lifetimes, humans spent 650 of them as cave dwellers. Only in the last three lifetimes has anyone used an electric motor. In just the last two lifetimes, most of the objects people take for granted in everyday life, such as microwave ovens and TV sets, have been developed. Future shock is the term Toffler uses to describe these fast-moving changes.

The rate of change today is so rapid that sometimes people have difficulty knowing where they are or what they want. Seeing the changes occur is like watching a movie with the projector running on fast forward. You cannot tell very much about what is taking place at any one time.

High Tech

Technology has an ever-growing influence on housing decisions. Today is a *high tech,* or high technology, era. It has already become a part of traditional housing, 2-20. For example, high tech lets you program outlets and light fixtures to save energy and give the house a lived-in

Photo courtesy of GE Plastics

2-20
By touching a button, interior windows can change from clear to translucent through the use of a crystal polyester film material.

look when you are away from home. It has also made available telephones with built-in speakers and microphones that let them become intercoms for easy communication throughout the house.

Computer technology can also be found throughout housing. You probably do not even think about all of the computer systems you use in your house. Do you have a touch-tone telephone or push-button microwave oven? These both use computers to operate. Other, more complex computer operated systems are also in use in the house.

Computer-aided drafting and design (CADD) is software and hardware that lets designs be created using a computer. Many architects and interior designers use CADD to create their designs. CADD lets them quickly adjust plans to improve the structure, conserve materials, or improve the energy efficiency of a house. Adjustments based on clients' needs and desires can also be easily made.

While technology is used to solve some problems, it sometimes causes others. One example is a freeway system in a large city that helps people drive quickly and easily from their houses to work and back. However, due to the large amount of traffic, there is an increase in pollution and decrease in air quality.

Governmental Influences on Housing

Government at all levels–federal, state, and local–influences housing decisions. This influence began early in this country's history.

Legislation

Laws regulating housing were made during colonial times. Some laws prohibited the building of houses on the village green, which was often set aside for government and church buildings. Other laws helped control the spread of fire between houses located near one another. Fireplaces used to cook food and heat the house were often inferior. They caught fire easily and soon the whole house would catch on fire. The fire would often spread to other dwellings, and sometimes a whole settlement would be wiped out by a single fire. In 1649, the British ordered that houses be built of brick or stone and the roofs be made of slate or tile to help prevent the spread of fire.

Over the years, the government has played an increasingly stronger role in safeguarding people and their housing. In the past, housing often was unsafe and unhealthy. People lived in poorly-built, crowded conditions, and landlords often took advantage of them. In the late 1800s, Congress began enacting laws and allocating money for housing. Laws were also introduced at the turn of the twentieth century to control the use of land, prevent overcrowding, and encourage beautification.

Even today, some land developers are more interested in making money than serving people and protecting natural resources. They build poorly-constructed buildings. Congress continues to pass housing legislation and to allocate money for housing programs.

States also pass laws related to housing. State laws are required to conform to federal legislation. More and more responsibility for regulating housing is being delegated to states.

Local ordinances may be established by city or county governments. These laws must conform to both federal and state laws. Most local housing legislation falls into one of the following categories:

- Standards for quality construction.
- Control of land and density.
- Funding for housing.
- Housing for people in need.
- Environmental protection.

Housing standards. Much of the housing legislation sets minimum standards of quality in various areas. Standards are set for land use and dwelling construction. They are also set to control density and separate residences from industry. Other standards are set to protect the people's health.

Standards include building codes. ***Building codes*** establish minimum standards for materials and construction methods. There are codes for electrical, plumbing, heating, and ventilation systems. Placement of stairways and exits are also included in the codes. The codes are used to assure healthy, safe, and sanitary conditions. Some standards also have to do with appearance. They indicate roof styles or maximum height. Codes are formulated and enforced by local and state governments. The *Uniform Building Code* is a popular national guide that sets minimum standards for building construction.

Some housing codes are set to determine the use, occupancy, and maintenance of buildings. One reason is to prevent overcrowding. Another is to guarantee that major alterations made to a dwelling meet required standards. These codes may not be found in all communities and are sometimes difficult to enforce when they are. This is because inspection officials are often unavailable, and some people resist inspections that will result in exposure of code-breaking.

Zoning regulations control land use in certain areas. They state that only specific activities can take place in a certain area. An area may be zoned for residential, commercial, or industrial use. In a residential zone, only houses can be built. In a commercial zone, only stores and office buildings can be built. See 2-21. In an industrial zone, only industrial businesses can be built. Sometimes within a residential area, only one type of dwelling may be built. The location of manufactured housing and multifamily dwellings are usually restricted to specific areas. Sometimes, the minimum size of dwellings to be built is specified.

Jack Klasey

2-21
The land this sign sits on is zoned to only be used for commercial purposes.

Density is also controlled through zoning. Density control reduces the risk of fire and controls traffic and pollution. It also restricts excessive noise and lighting. Lot size and the placement of a building on a lot are also indicated.

Government controls at all levels seem to make the cost of housing increase. However, building and zoning controls are intended to serve the best interests of the public.

Funding for Housing

Funding is another example of government involvement in housing. Several government agencies are involved in the buying and selling of home mortgages. The government assures some loans, which means it stands behind the lender if homeowners do not meet their obligations. It helps special groups, such as older people, people with disabilities, veterans, and low-income living units, secure funding. First-time homeowners are also given assistance.

Most of the financial organizations are a part of the Department of Housing and Urban Development (HUD). HUD is a policy-making body in the federal government. It works to ensure that affordable housing is available to everyone.

Housing for people in need. Government assistance is provided for people who cannot afford housing. It provides rent supplements for low-income living units. It builds public housing and rents it to those who are unable to fully pay for satisfactory housing.

The government also gives support to private programs created to help the homeless. In recent years the number of homeless people has increased dramatically. It is estimated that there are between 250,000 and three million homeless people in the United States. Over one-third are members of families with children. About one-fourth are veterans. Many are newly homeless–those who have suddenly lost a job or the ability to work. Others are chronically homeless–those who seem to have accepted their homeless condition as a way of life.

Many people have benefited from government housing assistance. However, there never seems to be enough to go around to everyone.

Environmental Protection

In recent years, the awareness of environmental problems related to housing has increased. This concern has led to a number of environmental protection laws.

In addition to laws, several government agencies, such as the U.S. Environmental Protection Agency (EPA) and the U.S. Consumer Product Safety Commission (CPSC), have been formed to support a positive natural environment, 2-22. They are engaged in research and provide information to consumers, so the housing environment, as well as the total environment, will be safe and protected. Some agencies have hot line numbers to assist consumers with their problems concerning the environment.

2-22
A clean environment exists where there are no pollution problems.

The concern of the EPA and CPSC is not limited to the natural environment. They are also concerned about the constructed environment. For example, they are concerned about the use of pesticides that make water unsafe. They are concerned about the use of asbestos, a form of housing insulation, and lead paint in dwellings, because they have both had health problems linked to them.

Environmental programs are monitored and research continues. Legislation continues to be enacted at all levels. You can find out more about housing legislation by studying Appendix A.

Summary

Many forces work together to influence housing. Some, such as history, culture, and society, involve people. Others, such as the environment, economy, technology, and government, involve conditions. They are all interrelated.

The cultural development of housing in North America occurred when settlers arrived from all over the world to join the Native Americans. They brought their unique cultures with them, which influenced their housing.

Historical events, such as the Industrial Revolution, Great Depression, and World Wars I and II, impacted how people were housed. Societal events, such as changes in needs, wants, and lifestyles of living units, affected housing designs.

The Industrial Revolution, population increases, and economic crises all caused housing shortages. To ease the shortages, technology and government were used to help develop new solutions for affordable housing.

Housing is a part of the constructed, natural, and behavioral environments. Each type of environment impacts the other two. The government passes legislation that establishes building standards, zoning regulations, and environmental protection. It works to make sure all three environments work together well and to ensure affordable housing for all people by providing funding.

To Review

Write your responses on a separate piece of paper.

1. List three types of early Native American dwellings.
2. How does housing of the colonists differ from housing today?
3. Why is the log cabin the symbol of the early United States?
4. What was the main cause of the population shift from rural to urban areas in the late 1700s?
5. What were two housing problems created by the population shift?
6. Describe the differences between tenement houses and row houses.
7. Name three historical events that resulted in substandard housing.
8. Describe new towns and explain why they were developed.
9. Give an example of how culture influences housing.
10. Briefly explain how the changes in living unit composition have influenced housing.
11. Why may older people have special housing needs?
12. Why are many middle-income families choosing to live in apartments, condominiums, cooperatives, or town houses instead of buying houses?
13. How can leisure time affect housing decisions?
14. The average living unit moves every _____ years.
15. After the natural environment has been changed by human effort, it is called the _____.
16. List three ways housing and the economy affect each other.
17. How is the housing industry dependent on the housing market?
18. Two ways CADD is used to improve housing are _____ and _____.
19. Give one example of what HUD does to improve housing.

To Do

1. Interview older members of your family about what housing was like when they were young. Ask them how housing has changed and improved over time. Ask them what historical events have had an impact on their housing.
2. Research the housing of a country of your choice. Then write a short essay describing how it has influenced housing in the American culture.
3. Look through newspapers and magazines for articles that discuss how social problems and housing are related. Then mount them on a bulletin board to share with the class.
4. Choose one of the following topics and write a two-page report telling how it has influenced housing:
   a. Changing roles.
   b. Divorce rates.
   c. Life expectancy.
   d. Culture.
   e. Government.
5. Survey the students in your class to see how many have changed houses in the past year.
6. Take a walk around your neighborhood and look for ways people have altered the natural environment for housing purposes. Report your findings to the class.
7. Obtain brochures from different housing developers and house builders. List the advantages they give for the type of house they promote and explain how the advantages are related to the natural, constructed, and behavioral environments.
8. Read the classified ads to learn current purchasing and rental costs of housing. Share your findings with the class.
9. Work in small groups to predict what new technology will be used in houses in the year 2020.
10. Identify a problem in the environment. Research how this problem could be solved and which government agencies could help you.

Acorn Structures, Inc.

When you look at a new home today, think of the cultural, economic, and societal influences that have played a role in its design.

Acorn Structures, Inc.

Chapter 3 Using Decision-Making Skills
Chapter 4 Choosing a Place to Live
Chapter 5 Acquiring Housing

PART 2

Making Housing Choices

CHAPTER 3

Using Decision-Making Skills

To Know

central-satellite decision
chain decision
habitual behavior
human resources
nonhuman resources
rational decision
spur-of-the-moment decision

Objectives

After studying this chapter, you will be able to:

- Define the different types of decisions.
- List some of your human and nonhuman resources.
- Discuss the steps of the decision-making process and make wise decisions.

In the first two chapters of this book, you read that many decisions affect housing. These decisions are related to your needs, values, life situations and leisure time or to environmental and governmental influences. Since these factors are constantly changing, you continually face making new decisions. By making these decisions wisely, you and your living unit will have the chance to grow and develop into better people.

Types of Decisions

All decisions are not alike. Learning to recognize the different types of decisions will help you develop decision-making skills.

Decisions can be classified into two groups. See 3-1. One group consists of those decisions that vary according to the thought and care used in making them. The other group classifies decisions by their relationships to other decisions.

Decisions Made According to Thought and Care

The three types of decisions that are made according to the amount of thought and care used to make them are rational, spur-of-the-moment, and habitual.

Suppose you have your own bedroom and you want to place an upholstered chair in it. If you shop until you find a chair that looks good with what you already have in your room, you would be making a ***rational decision,*** or one based on reasoning. However, if you buy the first chair that appeals to you without thinking about how it would look in your room, your decision would be a spur-of-the-moment one. A ***spur-of-the-moment decision*** is one that is made quickly, with little thought of the possible consequences.

Habitual behavior, on the other hand, is an action that is done as a matter of routine without thought. It does not call for you to make a decision unless there is a new factor in the situation. For instance, turning on the faucet in your bathroom is a habit. You do not have to make a decision unless water fails to come out of the faucet.

Interrelated Decisions

Central-satellite decisions and chain decisions are examples of decisions that can be described according to their relationships to other decisions.

Central-satellite decisions. A ***central-satellite decision*** is a group of decisions consisting of a major decision that is surrounded by related,

Types of Decisions	
Grouped According to Amount of Thought Taken to Make the Decision	
Rational decisions	Choices are made only after looking at problems carefully. The consequences are considered.
Spur-of-the-moment decisions	Choices are made hurriedly. Little thought is given to possible outcomes.
Habitual behavior	Action is done as a matter of habit. Decisions are made only when new situations arise.
Grouped According to Relationships Between Decisions	
Central-satellite decisions	A major decision is surrounded by related, but independent, decisions.
Chain decisions	One decision creates other choices that must be made to complete the action.

3-1
Decisions are classified by the amount of thought devoted to them or by their relationships to other decisions.

but independent, decisions. The concept of central-satellite decisions is illustrated in 3-2.

Chain decisions. A ***chain decision*** is a sequence of decisions in which one decision triggers others. All decisions in the chain must be made to complete an action. See 3-3 for a diagram of a chain decision related to housing.

One example of making interrelated decisions would be that some of the grass in your yard is dying. When you planted the grass, you chose it because it was attractive. Now the backyard is used by children and pets as a playground, 3-4. It is also used as a path from one part of the yard to another. This heavy traffic is preventing the grass from growing.

Suppose that you have decided not to replace the grass. Instead, you want to protect the grass from heavy use. In this case, the decision to keep the same grass becomes a central decision. Satellite decisions are needed. You may move some of the play activities to a patio, since they are better suited to hard-surfaced areas. Other activities could be moved to another part of the yard. You could also set up traffic barriers. Careful placement of lawn furniture or flower beds can force people to walk around the grassy area instead of through it.

Find Long-Term Financing

Change Vacation Plans

Cut Food Costs

Build a House for the Desired Life-Style

Cut Clothing Costs

Find a Job for Spouse

3-2
The central decision is to build a house; the others are satellite decisions. They are related to the central decision, but they are not dependent on it.

John Oehler

3-4
Children and pets can result in a lot of wear and tear on the lawn.

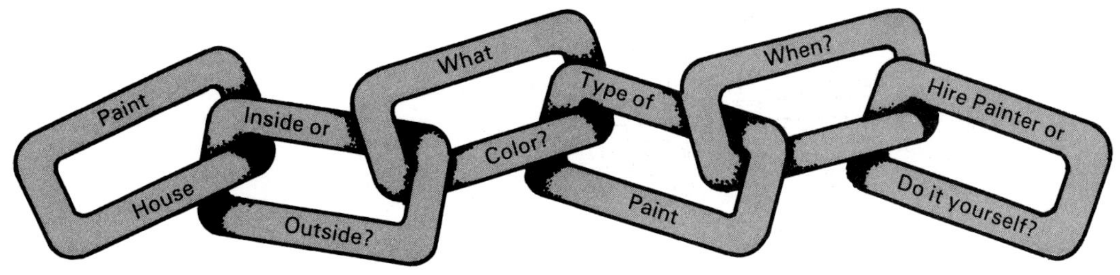

3-3
In chain decisions, additional decisions are needed to complete the action of the first decision.

One the other hand, you may choose to remove the grass and replace it with a hardier variety. The new variety will withstand the traffic and still look attractive. It will also require less care.

The decision to replace part of the grass is the first decision in a chain. The second "link" is the decision to replace only the grass in the backyard. The next decision is to decide which variety of grass to plant. Other "links" include deciding where you will buy the grass, whether you will plant it yourself or have someone else do it, when you will plant it, and how you will pay for it. Each of these decisions must be made before the grass can be replaced.

Resources for Housing Decisions

As you learned in Chapter 2, "Influences on Housing," resources are items that can be used to reach a goal. You need resources to carry out any type of decision you make. They are available to you in many forms.

Human Resources

Human resources are resources that are available from people. They include ability, knowledge, attitude, energy, and health. See 3-5.

You may have many resources that help you make housing decisions. For instance, if you have the ability to make house repairs, you have skill as a human resource. If you are willing to learn how to make house repairs, you have attitude as a human resource. When these resources are developed and used, decisions can be made, and results can be achieved.

If you are a person with a high energy level, you may spend time after school and on weekends doing extra projects to improve your housing. If you have a low energy level, you may choose to hire someone to do what is needed to keep your house in shape. You can rest while they work.

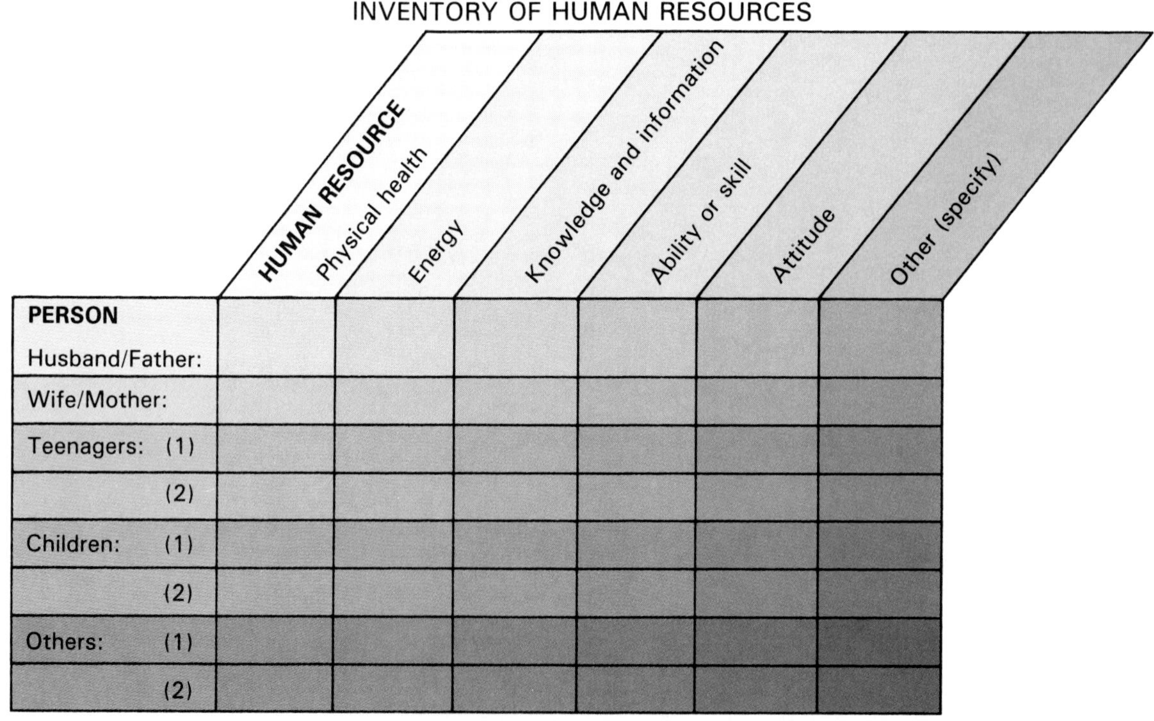

INVENTORY OF HUMAN RESOURCES

PERSON / HUMAN RESOURCE	Physical health	Energy	Knowledge and information	Ability or skill	Attitude	Other (specify)
Husband/Father:						
Wife/Mother:						
Teenagers: (1)						
(2)						
Children: (1)						
(2)						
Others: (1)						
(2)						

3-5
Human resources are resources that are available from people. To make an inventory of the human resources in your living unit, make a similar chart on a separate sheet of paper. Rate members on a scale of 0 to 5 with 0 being the lowest and 5 being the highest.

If you have good health, that resource will enable you to use other human resources to an advantage. For example, when you are healthy, you are likely to be motivated to use your knowledge and skills. You might decide to remodel your kitchen. If you have poor health, you are likely to postpone the project or hire someone to do it for you.

You will seldom use only one resource at a time. They are all closely related. To develop a new skill, you will need a good attitude, knowledge, energy, health, and time.

Time is also a human resource. How you use time is what counts. You have 24 hours a day, 365 days a year, just as everyone else has. Time is the only resource all people have in equal amounts. Other resources come in different quantities for different people. You will have different quantities of resources at different times in your life. For instance, today, you may have more energy than you will 30 years from now. On the other hand, in the future, you may have more money to spend than you have now.

Some people are short of both money and energy. To make their resources meet their needs, they must know how to use their knowledge and abilities to save money and energy.

You can choose which resources you wish to spend and which ones you wish to save. Suppose that you own a house that needs painting. You could paint it yourself. This would take a lot of time that you may prefer spending in some other way. In that case, you might decide to buy someone else's time to have them paint the house. You could hire a painter or a friend.

Some of your human resources are depleted as you use them. Others increase with use. You may use up all of your energy and time, but you can increase your abilities and knowledge as you use them.

Nonhuman Resources

Nonhuman resources are resources that are not directly supplied by people. They include money, property, and community resources. These are shown in 3-6.

Money. Consider how the nonhuman resource of money is used in housing. Everyone has some housing expenses. Money is needed to buy or rent a place to live. Additional money is needed for furnishings, equipment, utilities, and repairs. You must decide what you can afford to

3-6
Books, land, buildings, money, and tools are a few examples of nonhuman resources.

spend for these items. That amount will be determined by a number of factors, such as:

- The income you are making.
- The amount of money you have saved for housing.
- Your life-style.
- Your other property.

Property. The property you acquire and the way you use it are related to your housing decisions. Property resources include such items as land, buildings, and furnishings. The housing you can afford is partly determined by choices you have made about other property. Perhaps you are willing to live in a less expensive apartment building, so you can have new furniture. If you choose a more expensive apartment, the furniture or some other feature of your housing may have to wait. You may decide to reupholster or repair older furniture rather than replace it.

Community resources. Community resources are often taken for granted, but they can play an important part in your housing decisions. You may base the decision of where you will live on the quality of the community resources available. For example, you may want to have a good public library in your community. This will allow you to study books to prepare for a job or do your homework. You can also read books for recreation.

A city park with a playground and a picnic area is another community resource. If you know that a park is nearby, you may decide to choose housing with a small yard.

Some communities offer special classes for self-improvement. By taking advantage of these classes, you can learn such skills as furniture refinishing, upholstery, remodeling, and house maintenance.

Other community resources include hospitals, fire stations, police departments, schools, shopping centers, and recreational facilities, 3-7. What community resources are available where you live?

The Decision-Making Process

To make a wise decision, you must know the goal or problem to be solved. Then you can determine the best way to reach the goal or solve the problem, following the steps in the decision-making process. See 3-8.

Sun Lakes Development Company

3-7
Some communities offer outdoor recreation centers such as the one shown here.

Steps in the Decision-Making Process
Problem Identification • State the problem. • Find the causes. • Consider the effects on people.
Seeking Alternate Solutions • Look for ways to solve the problem. • Study each solution. • Answer questions concerning the solution.
Choosing One of the Alternatives and Taking Action • Select one of the solutions. • Carry out the decision. • Evaluate the decision.

3-8
Following the steps in the decision-making process will help you make good decisions.

Steps in Decision Making

The first step in the decision-making process is called *problem identification.* It includes:

- Defining the problem.
- Finding the cause.
- Considering the effects of the problem on the people involved.

The second step is *seeking alternate solutions.* You look for ways to solve the problem. Each possible solution is studied. At this time, the following questions must be answered:

- What resources are needed?
- What will happen as a result of each solution?
- Will the outcome give lasting satisfaction?
- Will everyone involved be satisfied?
- What other decisions need to be made?

The third step is *choosing one of the alternatives and taking action.* You need to select one of the solutions and carry it out. Then you need to evaluate it. Hopefully, you have chosen the best alternative. However, if your decision does not work, you will need to go back to the second step and look at the alternate solutions again. In some cases, you will also have to go back to the first step and reidentify the problem.

Sometimes your decisions have to be changed because you could not foresee the outcome. Suppose you decide to use the money you earn mowing lawns to buy a pet rabbit. However, if the outcome is that your family does not want you to have a rabbit, you might have to change your decision.

Other decisions must be changed because the necessary resources are not available. Suppose you decide to barbecue steaks for dinner. If you forget to buy charcoal and lighter fluid, you will have to change your decision. You will have to cook indoors instead.

Going through the Steps

One way to learn about the decision-making process is to consider one housing problem and think through all the steps needed to make a decision about it.

For example, your grandmother is coming to spend a winter with you and your family. As a result, the housing needs and desires of your family will change. How will your new needs and values be met? How will your grandmother's needs and values be met?

Step one: Problem identification. The problem is to find a way to satisfy the needs and values of all members of the new, larger living unit.

Find the causes of the problem:

- Grandmother needs to spend the winter in a milder climate.
- Grandmother cannot afford to pay a separate rental price.
- Your family enjoys Grandmother and wants her to come for the winter.

Consider the effects of the problem:

- Some or all members of the living unit will be more crowded.
- The life-style of the living unit will change.
- Extra money may be needed to provide housing for Grandmother.

Step two: Seeking alternative solutions. One solution that you may choose is to have

Grandmother occupy the room that the family uses as both a home office and a guest room.

Determine the additional resources needed:

- Another office area.
- A place for guests.
- Money to make the needed changes.
- Time to reorganize the room.

Consider the consequences:

- There will be less chance for use of the home office unless it is moved.
- Members of the living unit will need to double up when there are guests.
- There will be more use of the shared facilities, such as laundry equipment and the bathroom.
- Less money will be spent on some items–perhaps recreation.
- Items may be stored in places where they are hard to find and use.
- Leisure time will be given up by one or more members of the living unit to get the room ready.
- The arrangement is temporary (for the winter) and may not provide lasting satisfaction for Grandmother.
- Members of the family may not be satisfied with their changed life-styles.

Other decisions must also be made:

- Where will belongings be stored?
- Will there continue to be a home office?
- Where will guests sleep?
- How will the extra money be obtained?
- Who will get the room ready?
- What will Grandmother do next summer?

Another solution is to add a room with a bathroom to the house. What resources will be needed to carry out this alternative? What are the possible consequences? What other decisions will need to be made? Can you think of other solutions to the problem?

Step three: Choosing one of the alternatives and taking action. Your family has decided that Grandmother will occupy the dual-purpose room. (You may choose to make a different decision.) It is time to take the necessary action.

- Make the other decisions listed and carry them out in the order that seems best.
- Check to see if the outcome is satisfactory for all involved.
- Change some of the minor decisions for more satisfaction, if necessary.

Going through the decision-making process takes time and thought. It helps you make rational and wise decisions. The decisions based on Grandmother's move, such as when she will move, how she will move, and what items she will bring with her are both rational decisions and chain decisions.

The decisions made by your family can also be classified as central-satellite decisions. The central decision is that Grandmother is coming to stay with the family for the winter. The other decisions are satellite decisions.

In addition to the example given above, there are many different types of decisions to make as you choose housing. For example, you will need to decide about location, financing, style, and interior and exterior decoration. The skills learned in this chapter will help you make these decisions.

Summary

There are three types of decisions that are grouped according to the amount of thought or care used. They are rational, spur-of-the moment, and habitual. Other types of decisions, such as central-satellite and chain decisions, are grouped according to the relationships between decisions.

You use resources in your decision-making. Human resources, such as ability, knowledge, attitude, energy, health, and time, are factors in making decisions. Nonhuman resources, such as money, property, and community resources, affect decisions.

If you follow the logical steps of the decision-making process, you are more likely to make wise decisions. There are three steps in the decision-making process. They are problem identification, seeking alternate solutions, and choosing one of the alternatives and taking action.

To Review

Write your responses on a separate sheet of paper.

1. A(n) _____ decision is one that is made after thinking carefully about a problem or goal.
2. When you make a decision with little thought of the possible consequences, it is called a(n) _____ decision.
3. True or False. Closing the door as you leave your house is called an habitual behavior.
4. When one decision requires other decisions to carry it out, it is called a:
   a. Central-satellite decision.
   b. Chain decision.
5. List five community resources.
6. Describe the three major steps in the decision-making process.

To Do

1. Divide a separate sheet of paper into three columns. Label the first column "Degree of satisfaction," the second column "Decision," and the third column "Type of decision." In the second column, list some housing decisions that have been made by members of your living unit. In the third column, list the type of decision (rational, spur-of-the-moment, or habitual behavior). In the first column, write a (+ +) if there was a great deal of satisfaction from the outcome, a (+) if there was some satisfaction, and a (-) if there was no satisfaction.
2. Have a class debate about this statement: Rational decisions give more satisfaction than spur-of-the-moment decisions.
3. In a small group, write and present a skit to the class, showing how resources can be decreased and increased at the same time.
4. Read the following case study and complete the suggested activities.

   Andy and Noelle are both students at a community college. They plan to be married in June. Both have part-time jobs and will continue in school after their wedding.

   They will both graduate after another year. Andy plans to work in an auto repair and welding shop. Noelle wants to continue her job in the college library. In four or five years, they plan to start a family. They want two children.

   Noelle likes music and wants a piano. Andy likes to fish and garden.

   a. Identify a major housing decision this couple will face.
   b. What resources will be available to them? What are the alternatives they may consider? What are the possible outcomes of each alternative? What other related decisions will they have to make?
   c. Which alternative would you choose as a solution? Give reasons for your choice.

C H A P T E R 4

Choosing a Place to Live

U-Haul International

To Know
architect
attached houses
bill of lading
community
condominium
con-ops
contractor
cooperative
freestanding houses
graduated-care facilities
home
house
kit house
landscaping
manufactured housing
minimum property standards (MPS)
mobile home
motor home
multifamily house
neighborhood
owner-built houses
physical neighborhood
planned neighborhood
private zone

public zone
region
reverse mortgage
service zone
single-family house
site

Objectives

After studying this chapter, you will be able to:

- Describe different regions in which people live.
- List factors people consider when choosing a community or neighborhood.
- Discuss decisions involved in choosing a site and house.
- List special needs to consider when choosing housing.
- Compare the different ways to move.

Once you decide you need a new place to live, you will have many other decisions to make. Some of those decisions will concern location. Others will involve the type of dwelling, adapting to the special needs, and how you will move to the new location.

Location

When you choose a place to live, you will need to make five major decisions about the location. They are:

1. The region or area of the world, country, or state.
2. The community–country, suburbs, or city.
3. The neighborhood or section of the community.
4. The site or lot within the neighborhood.
5. The specific house.

Region

Region is the specific part of the world, country, or state in which you live. The reasons for choosing to live in a certain region vary. You may like the scenery. Perhaps the climate is important to you. See 4-1. You may want to be close to family members or friends. Employment

A

B

C

4-1
Many different types of climates can be found in the United States. They include (A) desert regions, which are noted for mild winters and very hot summers; (B) mountain regions, which offer cool summers and very cold winters; and (C) coastal regions, such as this New England coast, where the weather is affected by the ocean.

may also lead you to a certain region. Jobs are usually easier to find in regions with large cities.

Several items to consider when you are choosing a region are listed in 4-2. Which ones would you like to find in your ideal region?

Community

A region is divided into communities. A ***community*** may be a large city, small village, or rural area.

Cities are high-density areas. Many people live close together. If you enjoy being in contact with people most of the time, you are a *contact person.* You may enjoy city life.

Rural areas and the outskirts of towns and cities are low-density areas. If you enjoy limited contact with other people, you are a *noncontact person.* You may choose to live in a community of this type.

Some communities are designed for specific groups of people. For instance, retirement communities are built especially for retired people. University communities are planned for large groups of students and professors. Some communities are developed by businesses for their employees and their families.

Before choosing a community, you should consider more than just its size and social aspects. The number and type of services offered in a community should also be studied. For instance, what kinds of stores are in the community? Is the school system good? Does your religious group have a meeting place? Are there good medical facilities? Will you have good fire and police protection? Are resources available for self-improvement? What recreational facilities are offered? Are jobs easy to find? If some of these services are not available in the community, how far away are they? What kinds of public transportation are offered?

The chart in 4-3 can serve as a guide for evaluating a community. Which factors apply to your present community? Which ones would you like in your ideal community?

The Region			
Decisions	Range of Available Choices		
General Climate	Hot Dry Constant temperature	to to to	Cold Wet Varying temperature
Topography (Prairie, lakes, mountains, etc.)	Flat Desert Low altitude	to to to	Mountainous Forest High altitude
Employment Opportunities	Limited in type Limited in number Low-paying Seasonal	to to to to	Varied Plentiful High-paying Steady
Cost of Living	High	to	Low
People	Family and friends	to	No acquaintances
Value System (A set of values that seems to dominate the thinking and actions of people)	All people equal Conservative	to to	Class conscious Liberal

4-2
These are some of the choices that will influence your selection of a region in which to live.

The Community				
Decisions		Range of Available Choices		
Type		Rural Industrial Commercial Suburban		
Size		Farm Village Town City Metropolis Megalopolis		
Density of Population		Sparse	to	Dense
Cost of Living		Low	to	High
Population Composition Age Income Occupation	 Religion Ethnic group Interests	Homogenous (similar)	to	Heterogenous (varied)
Community Facilities Educational Recreational Medical Shopping Job opportunities	 Environmental protection Transportation Fire and police protection Banking Religious organizations	Few	to	Many
Value System (A set of values that seems to dominate the thinking and actions of the people)		Prejudiced	to	Free from prejudices

4-3
When you look for a community to live in, these factors may be considered.

Neighborhood

While regions are divided into communities, communities are divided into neighborhoods. A ***neighborhood*** consists of a group of houses and people. The buildings in any one neighborhood are usually similar in age, design, and cost. The people in a neighborhood usually have some similarities, too.

Physical neighborhood. The ***physical neighborhood*** is determined by the way the land and buildings are used. Some neighborhoods are all residential. They include dwellings that are occupied by living units. Commercial neighborhoods include stores and businesses. A shopping center is a kind of commercial neighborhood. Industrial neighborhoods include businesses, factories, warehouses, and industrial plants.

Some neighborhoods combine residential, commercial, and industrial buildings. For instance, when a local grocery is surrounded by houses, the neighborhood is a combination of residential and commercial buildings.

Zoning regulations and other restrictions. As you read in Chapter 2, "Influences on Housing," zoning regulations control land use in certain areas. A neighborhood may be zoned for either residential, commercial, or industrial use or for a combination of uses.

Housing developers can set additional limits that are called restrictions. (Developers improve and subdivide land and build houses, apartment complexes, shopping centers, etc.) These restrictions may control the design of the buildings that can be constructed. They may also limit the kind and number of animals that can be kept in a neighborhood. In 4-4, you can see a set of restrictions drawn up for a subdivision.

Declaration of Restrictions for Swiss Manor Subdivision

1. All of said lots in Swiss Manor Subdivision shall be known and designated as residential lots and shall not be used for any business purpose whatsoever.
2. No structure whatsoever other than one private dwelling, together with a private garage or carport, for not more than three cars, shall be erected, placed, or allowed to remain on any of the lots.
3. No dwelling house shall be erected which contains less than 1200 square feet of livable space, exclusive of attached garage, porches, patios, and breezeways. No residence shall be built which exceeds the height of 2 1/2 stories or 30 feet from the curb level. All structures on said lots shall be of new construction and no building shall be moved from any other location on to any of said lots.
4. There shall be no trailer houses, or homes built around or incorporating trailer homes. All camper trailers, campers, or boats shall be stored behind the dwelling house, or be stored within the garage.
5. There shall be no unused automobiles, machinery, or equipment allowed on these premises outside of enclosed garages. All driveways or parking areas used for parking vehicles shall be constructed of concrete.
6. All clotheslines, equipment, service yards, woodpiles, or storage piles shall be kept screened by adequate planting or fencing to conceal them from view of neighboring lots or street. All rubbish, trash, or garbage shall be removed from the lots and shall not be allowed to accumulate thereon. All yards shall be kept mowed and all weeds shall be cut. Garbage and refuse containers may be brought to the street not more than 12 hours before collection time and must be removed within 12 hours after collection time.
7. No animals, livestock, or poultry of any kind shall be raised, bred, or kept on any lot, except for dogs, cats, and other household pets may be kept, provided that they are not kept, bred, or maintained for commercial purposes, and so long as applicable laws in respect to restraining or controlling animals are observed.
8. No lot may be subdivided, or a portion sold unless it becomes a part of the adjacent property.
9. No solid wall, hedge, or fence over 2 1/2 feet high shall be constructed or maintained past the front wall line of the house. No side or rear fence shall be constructed more than 6 feet in height.
10. All utility lines must be brought underground to the dwelling house.
11. No structure shall be built nearer than 25 feet to the front property line. No living areas shall be located nearer than 10 percent of the lot widths to any side property line and no carport or garage closer than 5 feet.
12. No billboards, signs, or advertising devices, except suitable "For Sale" or "For Rent" signs shall be maintained.
13. Before construction of the initial structure of any building, plans, specifications, and materials must be approved by the Developer or its successor.
14. Construction of homes must be started within one year after purchase of lot and must be completed within one year after commencement of construction.
15. No property owner shall in any way divert the drainage water in such a way that it will encroach upon a neighbor's property.
16. These declarations shall constitute covenants to run with the land, as provided by law, and shall be binding on all parties and all persons claiming under them, and are for the benefit of and shall be limitations upon all future owners in said Swiss Manor Subdivision.

4-4
This list of restrictions was made by the developers of a subdivision. Its purpose is to assure that all owners will maintain a certain style of living.

A planned neighborhood is usually in a zoned area with restrictions. In a ***planned neighborhood,*** before dwellings are built, the size and layout of individual lots are determined. This creates the shape of the neighborhood. Three ways to arrange lots are shown in 4-5.

All houses built in a planned neighborhood must fit into the overall plan. Some planned

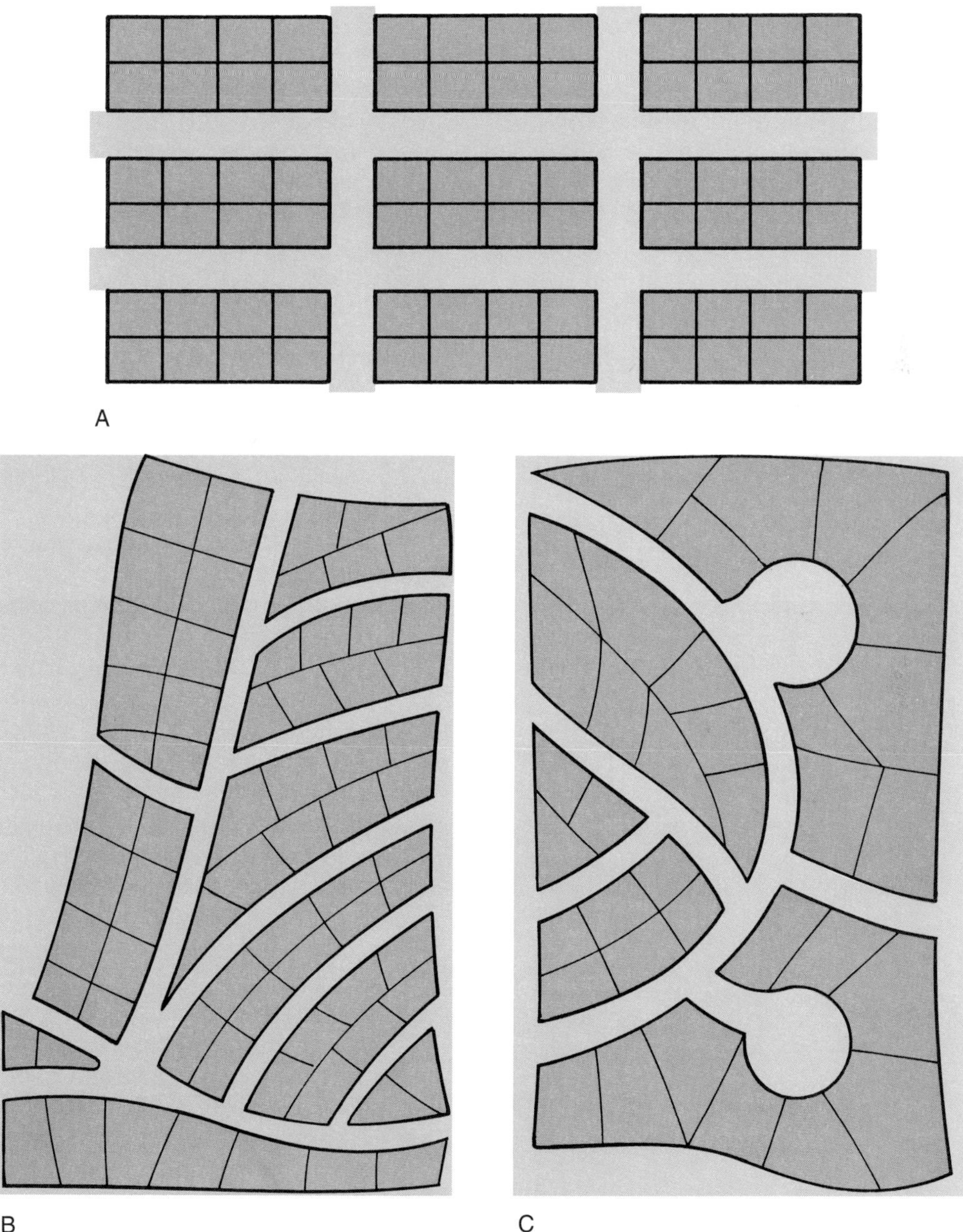

4-5
There are many ways to arrange lots. They include (A) the traditional "gridiron" arrangement, where all of the lots are the same size and shape; (B) the contour arrangement, where the shape of streets and lots adds variety and interest to the neighborhoods; and (C) the cluster layout, where fewer houses are placed together in groups with less traffic on the streets.

neighborhoods have only single-family houses. Some have only apartment buildings. Other planned neighborhoods are for only manufactured housing. Still others are designed to include more than one type of housing with each type of housing grouped together.

The quality of construction and the type of design are sometimes controlled in a planned neighborhood. This assures the residents that the neighborhood will not become run-down.

Many planned neighborhoods include recreational facilities. Parks and playgrounds, 4-6, are built in locations that are convenient to the people living in the neighborhood. Clubhouses are often built as places for meetings and social activities.

Social neighborhood. The type of people in any neighborhood may be quite varied. When this happens, the neighborhood is *heterogeneous.* If the people are very similar to one another, the neighborhood is *homogeneous.* Sometimes neighborhoods or whole communities are made up of people who are similar in age, ethnic background, income level, or occupation. These patterns occur in both rural and urban settings.

Another factor associated with social neighborhood is population density. A low-density neighborhood has more space for each individual than a high-density neighborhood. Smaller houses, smaller lots, and more people in less space create high-density neighborhoods. Apartment buildings and parks for manufactured housing also fit in this category.

Which kind of neighborhood would you choose? What are your reasons for making that choice? The factors listed in 4-7 can help you make a decision.

Presley Development Company

4-6
Playgrounds are a part of many planned neighborhoods.

Site

A location within a neighborhood is called a site, or lot. A ***site*** is the piece of land on which the dwelling is built. It extends as far as the property lines.

Each site has its own characteristics–size, shape, contour (hills and curves), and soil type. What kind of site would be your ideal? Would you like to have your house on a hill or on flat land? What kind of view would you like? Would you like to be close to your neighbors, or would you prefer to have more privacy? These characteristics should be considered before you choose a site for your house, 4-8.

If you are buying a house that someone else built, or if you are renting an apartment, you should look carefully at the placement of the house on the site. It will have a great effect on your microenvironment. It will determine the views, the amount of sunlight, and the amount of protection from wind you will have.

If you are building a house, you can choose the site and the type of house you want. You can place the house where you want it on the site. This gives you the chance to make the house and site work together to form a satisfying microenvironment for you.

When you plan your site, you will encounter restraints, or obstacles. Some will be natural restraints. Others will be legal restraints.

Natural restraints. Natural restraints are those that come from nature. One kind of natural

The Neighborhood			
Decisions	**Range of Available Choices**		
Physical	Residential Commercial Industrial Combination		
	Zoned	to	Unzoned
Organization of Lots	Attractive	to	Unattractive
	Much street traffic	to	Little street traffic
	Park and play areas	to	No park or play areas
Type of Structures	Single-family Multifamily Mixed		
Location in Community	Edge	to	Center
Density of Population	Sparse	to	Crowded
Population Composition Age, Occupation Income, Religion Interests, Ethnic group	Homogenous (similar)	to	Heterogenous (varied)
Value System (A set of values that seem to dominate the thinking and actions of the people)	Agrees with own values	to	Does not agree with own values

4-7
Which of these factors would you include in your ideal neighborhood?

The Site			
Decisions	**Range of Available Choices**		
Location in Neighborhood	Edge	to	Center
Orientation to Environment Sun, Prevailing wind Water, Erosion View, Pollution	Takes advantage of features	to	Ignores features
Physical Characteristics Size Shape Contour of the land Soil characteristics	Large	to	Small
	Regular	to	Irregular
	Level, Gentle slope, Steep slope, Sand, Gravel, Rock, Clay		

4-8
Before you choose a site, you should consider all your choices.

restraint is the topography of a site. Flat sites make the job of mowing grass easy. See 4-9. Flat lawns are also good places for children's games and lawn furniture.

Hilly sites are more difficult to maintain, but they are often very attractive. Some houses, such as split-level houses, look best on hilly sites.

Sites with extremely steep slopes have some disadvantages. A house built at the top of a slope may be difficult to reach, especially in icy weather. Also, soil may wash away and cause land erosion.

Landscaping can be used to change the appearance of a site by altering the topography and adding decorative plantings. See 4-10. For instance, small hills can be built to make the site more attractive. You will learn more about landscaping in Chapter 19, "The Outdoor Living Space."

Soil and water can be natural restraints. Soil conditions affect both the site and the house. Poorly-drained soil freezes and expands. This can cause sidewalks and driveways to crack and bulge. Plants have difficulty growing in shallow or nonporous topsoil. High water levels can cause swampy yards, wet basements, and poor plant growth.

Orientation to the sun can be a restraint or an advantage. Houses with southern and western exposures receive more sunlight than houses with northern and eastern exposures. In colder regions, houses are often built with large amounts of glass on the south and west sides of the dwelling. The glass allows sunlight to bring light and warmth into the dwellings.

Because of the earth's changing position in relation to the sun, more sunlight reaches the earth during the summer, 4-11. Therefore, houses may need protection from the intense summer sun. Some houses are shaded by trees. Shade can also be provided by built-in features, such as roof overhangs. The width of the

4-9
The topography of this site is very flat. It makes maintaining the yard easy.

Velux-America, Inc.

4-10
Landscaping adds to the beauty of this site.

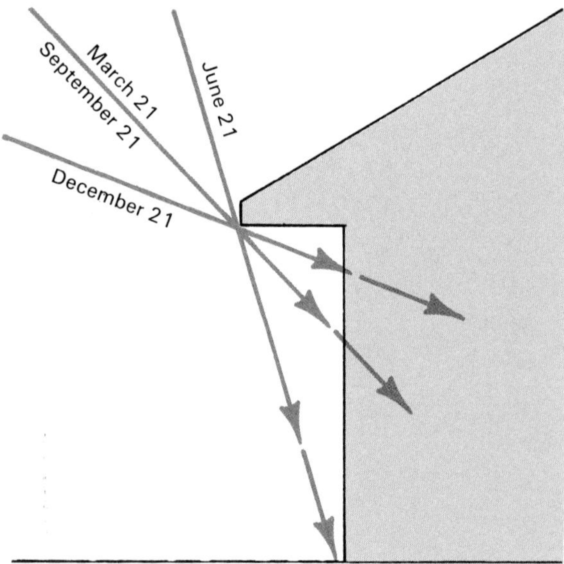

4-11
The sun shines at different angles on the south side of a house at different times of the year. By knowing this angle, architects can plan proper roof overhangs.

overhang on a roof affects the amount of sunlight that enters a building. Wider overhangs block out more sunlight.

Orientation to the wind is another natural restraint. Houses can be located so that they are protected from strong winds. Windbreaks are used to provide some of this protection. Trees and shrubs are natural windbreaks. Walls and stone or wood fences are also windbreaks. A garage placed on the north side of a house will usually eliminate drafts from cold winter winds and reduce heating costs in the house.

In most regions, the prevailing, or most frequent, wind changes direction with the season. This should be taken into consideration when planning for protection from the wind. The illustration in 4-12 shows a house that is well-oriented to both the sun and wind.

Orientation to scenery is also a consideration. A pleasant view is desirable, but it is not always provided by nature. If necessary, you can create a nice view through landscaping. Landscapers use gardens, shrubs, and decorative fences to change the scenery.

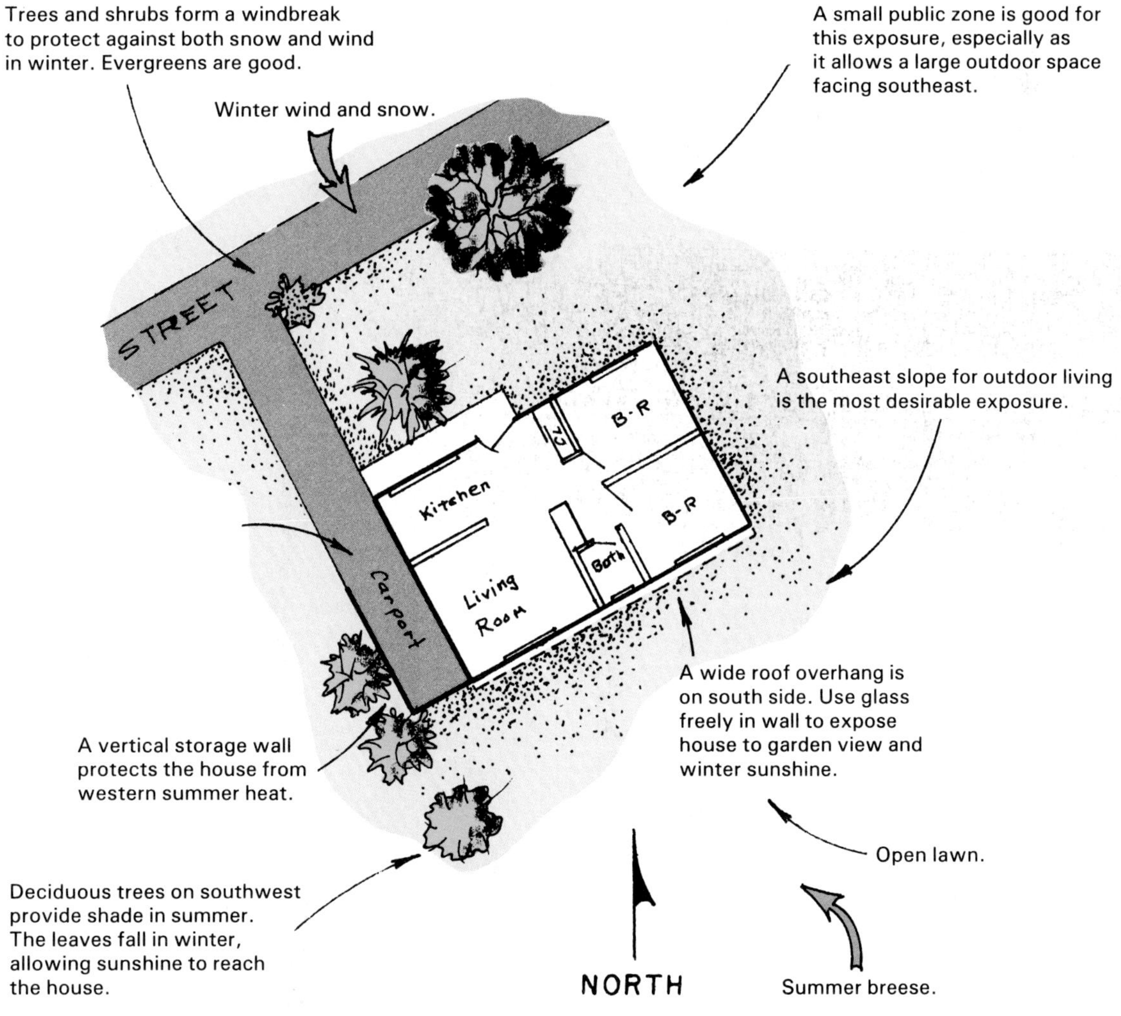

4-12
Orientation to sun and wind are important factors to consider when deciding about the location of a dwelling on a site.

Legal restraints. Legal restraints affecting sites may be federal, state, or local laws. They are established for your protection.

Minimum property standards (MPS) are standards set by the Federal Housing Administration (FHA) that regulate the size of lots. MPS vary according to the shape and location of a site. In some cases, the minimum size of a lot is 65 feet wide and 130 feet long. Look at 4-13 to see a plan for a lot that meets these MPS.

The local government or the developer may set higher standards than the MPS. State and local authorities also establish limits and standards for the quality of construction, water supplies, and disposal of wastes. Do you have a housing authority office in your community? If so, what legal restraints do they enforce?

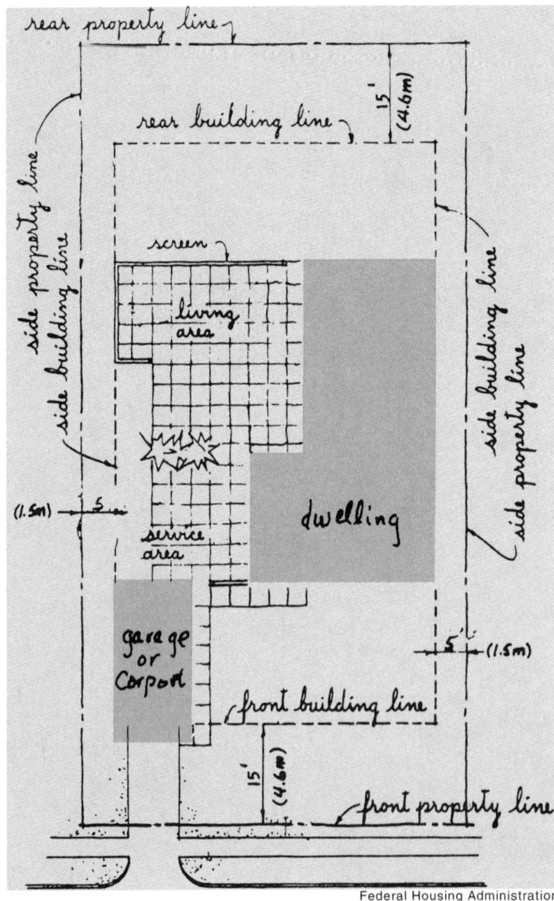

4-13
This plan meets the MPS (minimum property standards) for a rectangular lot in the middle of a block.

Zones within the Site

The part of the site that is not the actual dwelling is divided into three zones–public zone, service zone, and private zone.

The ***public zone*** is the part of the site that can be seen from the street or road. It is usually in front of the house. If the house is on a corner lot, the public zone is L-shaped. It includes the front and the side of the lot closest to the street. Since the public zone is seen more often than any other part of the site, people want to make it attractive, 4-14. It is seldom used for activities.

If the house is as far forward on the lot as the law permits, the public zone is small. Many people want small public zones, because they are easier to maintain.

The ***service zone*** is the part of the site that is used for necessary activities. It includes sidewalks, driveways, and storage areas for such items as trash, tools, lawn equipment, and cars. A service zone may include a clothesline for drying laundry. It may have a storage area for firewood.

At least part of the service zone can usually be seen by others, 4-15. However, many people choose to have as much of it screened from view as possible.

Versa-Lok Retaining Wall Systems

4-14
Many different materials were used to make this public zone attractive.

4-15
Sidewalks and driveways are parts of the service zone that can be seen by others. The garage door hides the inside of the garage, which is also part of the service zone.

In this zone, convenience is most important. The service area should be directly connected to the indoor service area, which includes the kitchen and laundry area. It is important that the service zone be accessible from the street, since deliveries are usually made in the service zone.

The ***private zone*** is the part of the site hidden from public view. It provides space for recreation and relaxation, 4-16, and a place where children and pets can play. Private zones can be separated from public zones by using shrubs, hedges, screens, fences, or walls.

Some living units want a large private zone. They may want a place for yard accessories, such as outdoor furniture and barbecue equipment, a swimming pool, or yard games. Other living units prefer a small private zone, so they can care for it easily. Some want all the available space inside the house and do not want an outdoor private zone.

In 4-17, you can see how a house is placed on the site to provide all three zones–public, service, and private.

Photo courtesy of Georgia-Pacific Corporation

4-16
This private zone provides a secluded area for people to relax.

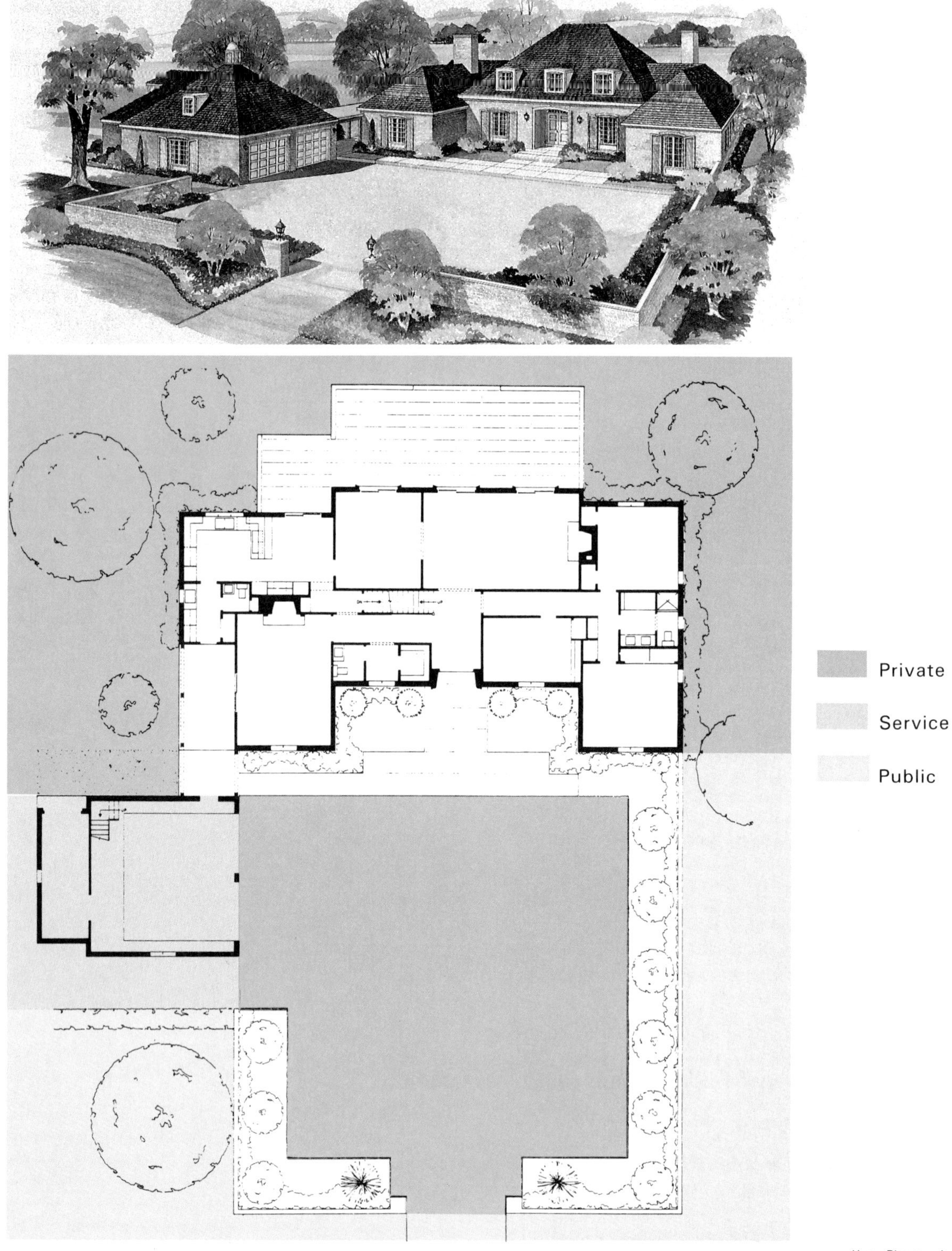

Home Planners, Inc.

4-17
The house shown above has a huge private zone. In the plan shown below it, you can see that the public and service zones are much smaller.

Housing

After choosing a region, community, neighborhood, and site, your next decision is to choose a form of housing. A ***house*** is any building that serves as living quarters for one or more families. A ***home,*** on the other hand, is any place a person lives. The two major groups of houses are multifamily and single-family. Within each group are several variations.

Multifamily Houses

A ***multifamily house*** is a structure that provides housing for more than one living unit. Each living unit within the dwelling has its own distinct living quarters.

Today, life-styles are changing, and the demand for multifamily housing is increasing. In the past, single people, young married couples, and retired people were the living units most interested in this type of housing. Now, more nuclear families, single-parent families, and other living units are turning to multifamily housing, too. This type of housing is usually less costly and easier to maintain than single-family houses.

Cityfront Place/Photographer, David Clifton

4-18
Cityfront Place is a series of high-rise buildings in Chicago where several hundred families live.

Some multifamily housing is in high-rise buildings, 4-18. Others are in low-spread buildings as shown in 4-19. Those in low-spread buildings may be large, or they may be just duplexes (with two living units) or quadraplexes (with four living units).

Rentals. Rental apartments range from tenement houses to penthouses, which are suites located at the top of apartment buildings. Rentals also vary in the number and type of facilities offered. Many apartment buildings have washing machines and dryers, tennis courts, and swimming pools available for the residents. Some large, high-rise buildings are like small cities. They include business offices, schools, stores, and recreational facilities.

Cooperative units. The word ***cooperative*** refers to a type of ownership where people buy shares of stock in a nonprofit housing corporation. These shares entitle them to occupy a unit in the cooperative building. Therefore, when people move into a cooperative unit, or co-op, they "buy" their apartment by purchasing shares in the corporation. If a resident wants a larger unit, he or she purchases more stock. Residents have an absolute right to occupy the unit for as long as the stock is owned.

4-19
Low-spread apartment buildings require larger lots per living unit than high-rise buildings.

Although residents do not own their units, they own an undivided interest in the entire property. They have a voice in how the corporation is run and even get the chance to select their neighbors. If a living unit wants to buy shares in the corporation and move into the building, the members of the corporation vote on admitting them.

An advantage of living in a co-op is that neighbors meet one another and work together to create a pleasant housing environment. A disadvantage is that if they disagree with the others on an issue, they will be forced to go along with the decision of the majority.

Condominium units. A ***condominium*** is a type of ownership where the buyer owns individual living space and also has an undivided interest in the common areas and facilities of the multiunit project. In comparison to co-ops, buyers purchase the units as if they were separate dwellings. At the same time, the buyers receive a portion of the common areas. They share the ownership of the site, parking areas, recreational facilities, and hallways and lobbies with the other condominium owners.

Although condominium owners own their units, they must answer to the desires of the entire group of owners for certain items. For instance, the appearance of the outside of their units and their yards may be under the control of the group's management.

There is some experimenting with ***con-ops,*** which are a blend of condominium and cooperative units. In con-ops, the buyers own their individual living spaces as in a condominium ownership. However, ownership of the common areas and facilities are cooperative ownership.

The terms cooperative and condominium refer to a type of ownership, not a building design. When you look at a multifamily dwelling, you cannot tell if it is a rental, cooperative, or condominium, 4-20.

Single-family Houses

In spite of the rising trend for multifamily dwellings, the ***single-family house*** is still popular. It is designed to house one family or living unit. Single-family houses can be rented or owned.

Attached houses. Some single-family houses are ***attached houses.*** That is, they are designed for one living unit but share a common wall with the houses on each side. Town houses and row houses are names for these houses. Usually, entire sidewalls of houses are shared, but there are variations, as shown in 4-21. The designs of the attached dwellings are often alike.

George Gale

4-20
These town houses could be rentals, co-ops, or condos. You can't tell by looking at them.

Danny Clevenger

4-21
These town houses share only part of their sidewalls.

The owners of an attached, single-family house own the dwelling itself and the land on which it is located. They have their own entrance and yard area.

Freestanding houses. When single-family houses stand alone and are not connected to another unit, they are called ***freestanding houses.*** They vary in size, design, color, features, and cost.

The most individualistic type of house is one that is custom-designed and custom-built by an architect and a contractor. This kind of house is "a dream house." It is often expensive and takes a long time to plan and build.

An ***architect*** is a person who designs buildings and supervises their construction. When custom-designing a house, an architect considers the needs, values, and life situations of a living unit. He or she then designs a house to "fit" the living unit.

A ***contractor*** is a person who contracts or agrees to supply certain materials or to do certain work for a stipulated fee, especially one who contracts to build buildings. With a custom-built house, a contractor builds the house according to the architect's plans and living unit's wishes.

Some houses are custom-built from stock plans. In these cases, people go to a contractor and look at house plans. They choose the plan that they want, and the contractor builds a house for them on their site.

Owner-built houses are for people with lots of time, energy, and building skills. These types of houses can be less expensive than other types of housing. This is because there is less investment in money and more investment in other resources, such as time and energy. Sometimes a contractor is hired to put up the house shell, and the living unit does the interior work. In other cases, the living unit builds the entire house. Building a house can be a great experience for a living unit if it has the necessary human resources.

On the other hand, *tract houses* are built by a developer who builds an entire neighborhood at once. The houses are built before they are sold to living units. One or two sets of plans are used over and over to save money. Because few variations are made, the houses lack individuality, but they are less expensive to buy than custom-built houses.

Manufactured housing is built in factories and then moved to a site and assembled. One type is modular houses, which are built in factories and moved in modules to the sites. Today's manufactured housing has improved in appearance and quality. You often cannot tell a manufactured house from a house that was built on the site piece-by-piece. See 4-22.

Schult Homes

4-22
When in place and landscaped, a manufactured house is difficult to distinguish from a site-built house.

Kit houses are a type of manufactured housing. ***Kit houses*** may be shipped to the site in unassembled parts or as a finished shell from the factory. The interior is then completed according to the buyer's wishes.

Kit houses are less costly than most other types of manufactured housing. The total cost is influenced by several factors. They include the size and style of the house, the distance from the factory to the site, and whether all the materials and labor for the house are purchased with the kit or separately.

Mobile homes are still another kind of manufactured single-family house. Most houses are "fixed." That is, they are attached to a foundation that is anchored to the ground. Mobile homes are an exception. They can be moved by attaching wheels to them. They should not be confused with ***motor homes,*** which are automotive vehicles equipped as houses.

When moving a mobile home, there are several laws you need to keep in mind. Each state has laws that must be followed when moving a mobile home. Some local governments have passed additional rules, such as zoning regulations that prohibit the placement of mobile homes in certain areas.

Small mobile homes can be moved by the owners as long as all laws are followed. Larger mobile homes have to be moved in parts, 4-23. A company specializing in moving mobile homes could handle the job. However, large units are usually fixed on a site.

More Decisions

Other items to consider when choosing a dwelling include the condition (if it is not new), price, size, design, and way it looks on the site. The chart in 4-24 can guide you as you make decisions about a house.

Choosing Housing to Meet Special Needs

By the 1980s, housing was a hot issue. Government officials, house builders and developers, as well as the general public found a need for safe, decent, affordable housing for everyone. Groups of people with special needs were targeted. They included older people, people with disabilities, and living units with children. Today, housing is being designed for those with special needs.

Housing Considerations for Older People

Many people look forward to retirement. They may plan to catch up on activities they have not had time for in the past, such as golf and

Schult Homes

4-23
Double-width mobile homes must be split into two sections to be moved.

The Dwelling			
Decisions	Range of Available Choices		
Ownership	Rental Cooperative Condominium Private		
Form Multifamily	High-rise Few units Few extra facilities	to to to	Low-spread Many units Many extra facilities
Form Single-family	Custom-designed and custom-built Custom-built from stock plans Owner-built Tract house Modular dwelling Kit house Mobile home		
Landscaping	Dwelling "fits" site Many trees and shrubs	to to	Dwelling looks out of place No trees or shrubs
Outside Zones Public Service Private	Large	to	Small
Structural Quality	High Standard Deteriorating Deteriorated		
Price	High Affordable Low		
Size	Huge Adequate Too small		

4-24
Many options are possible when you choose a house.

fishing. They may plan to travel and take advantage of events they have previously been unable to attend. These retirement plans may affect their housing decisions. They may want housing that requires less time for maintenance or that will be secure while they are away. The situations vary with each retiree and the housing choices vary.

As people age, their energy levels often decrease and their health may be on the decline. As a result, they find their houses difficult to maintain. Even simple, everyday activities are sometimes difficult. This makes it hard for older people who prefer to "age in place," or stay in their present houses. They need housing that requires little maintenance and where household routines can be done easily.

Some older people find that living in their old neighborhoods is inconvenient. They may be far from shopping centers and community centers where they can be with other older people. If they have difficulty driving, they may not want to leave home very often. This can lead to loneliness, especially if they live alone.

When older people can no longer live alone due to loneliness or health problems, they usually change housing. They may become a part of another living unit. It may be with a child or someone who is not a family member. They may live with a person who can help care for them. They may choose to become a part of a larger living unit, such as a retirement community, retirement home, or nursing home, 4-25.

Another option for older people is to move to a life care community. Many are ***graduated-care facilities,*** which means the residents move from their own apartments to a nursing home unit as needed. Facilities that are well designed and carefully administered offer comfortable living.

For older people who choose to live on their own, house ownership is high. However, they may find that they are "house rich and cash poor," because their savings have been tied up in their houses. While their houses are paid for, they may become run down. If older people's incomes are limited, they may not be able to cover the increasing cost of housing. They may not have money for maintenance, repairs, utilities, or taxes. They may not have the money to adapt their houses to meet their special needs.

Measures have been taken to assist older people. Some states allow reverse mortgages. A ***reverse mortgage*** enables older people to convert the money tied up in their houses into income. They receive a monthly payment as long as they live in the dwelling. When they no longer live in the house, the mortgage company assumes ownership of the dwelling. Reverse mortgages can help older homeowners stay in their houses.

George Gale

4-25
Retirement homes satisfy the housing needs of many older people.

Housing Considerations for People with Disabilities

There are many people with disabilities in the United States. They include adults who work and live on their own or with their families, children, and older people. The types of disabilities vary. Some people are visually impaired. Many have difficulty moving and must use wheelchairs, crutches, or walkers. Others are people with mental retardation.

These people need housing to meet their needs. They often are unable to live independently in the same dwelling as nondisabled people. Appropriate housing can assist people with disabilities in their daily living. For example, the bathroom in 4-26 has been adapted to meet the needs of a person in a wheelchair.

Several national organizations have taken steps to improve housing for people with disabilities. As a result of their research, the 1988 Fair Housing Act was passed. (See Appendix A for details.) It provided standards to make buildings usable by people with physical disabilities. Guidelines have also been developed for selecting and adapting housing for people with disabilities. If you or a member of your living unit has a disability, the following factors should be considered:

- Choose a one-story dwelling or ground-level unit in a multilevel building.
- Look for a level entryway or landing that will make opening doors easy.
- Look for wide doorways and hallways.

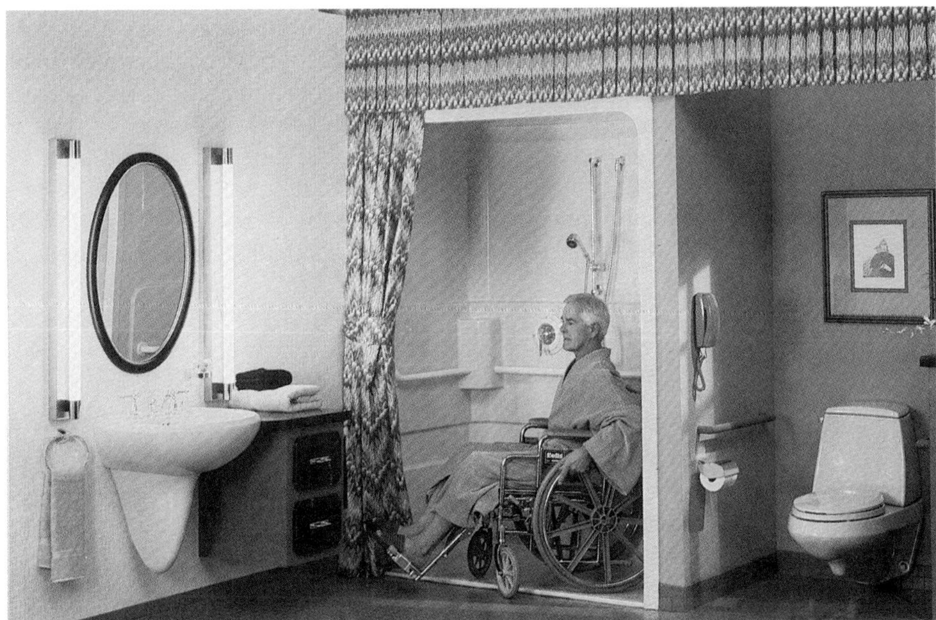

Photo courtesy of Kohler Company

4-26
The smooth floor, space around and under the sink and toilet, and the wide, level shower opening make this bathroom accessible to everyone in the living unit.

- Provide good lighting for people with low vision.
- Install audio and visual smoke detectors.
- Choose housing on or near public transportation lines.
- Choose housing near shopping areas.

When people with disabilities have housing that meets their needs, they can live more independently.

Housing Considerations for Living Units with Children

Another group with special housing needs is living units with children. Children develop physically, mentally, emotionally, and socially. No matter how old they are, they need to live in a safe and healthy housing environment that promotes positive development.

A housing choice that fits the needs and desires of a couple without children may not be satisfactory when a child arrives. Children need room to grow–to learn to crawl and walk. As they grow older, they need additional space for activities. See 4-27. An outdoor play area that is protected from street traffic is desirable. This gives them a place to play and move about.

Kate Shenberger Interiors, Flossmoor, Illinois

4-27
This playhouse gives this little girl her own special place to grow and develop.

The community in which children grow can influence their development. When choosing a place to live, look for communities and neighborhoods that will foster healthy growth and development.

Look for good schools, safe neighborhoods, park programs, and recreational facilities.

Pets also have special needs. Therefore, you may want to include your pets needs in your housing choices. If you are renting a house, you may find that neither children nor pets are wanted. However, discrimination laws prevent landlords from refusing to rent to living units with children. The same is not true for pets.

Moving to a New Location

Once you have chosen a house that meets your needs and those of your living unit, you are ready to move. How many times have you and members of your living unit moved from one place to another? How do you compare to the average American living unit who moves once every six years?

Many moves made by living units are from one house to another within the same neighborhood or community. Short moves may be expected as a living unit ends one stage of its life cycle and enters another. Changes in life-style, occupation, socioeconomic status, or other life situations also cause people to move.

A long distance move is a bigger job and has a greater emotional impact than a move across town. Relocating family and possessions is likely to cause stress. The amount of stress can be reduced if you take the right steps before your moving day.

No matter how far you are moving, it is a good idea to get rid of the household items you no longer need and do not want to move. People have often found out they paid to move items or boxes of trash they intended to discard. You may consider selling and then later replacing the heavy items, such as old refrigerators, that add to moving costs. If you decide to sell and replace goods, consider renting them at your new house. This gives you a chance to settle in, then look around for the best deals.

Another way to eliminate the amount of belongings you move is to have a garage sale. You can also give unwanted items to charity or recycle them. Items given to charity are good for an income tax deduction if you get a receipt.

Moving expenses may also qualify as an income tax deduction. If you move because of a job change or transfer and live at least 50 miles farther from work, you may qualify. You must be working full time and make the move within one year of the time you began the new job.

Use the moving expense checklist, 4-28, to be sure you have all the records you need to claim a tax deduction. Be sure you have the correct forms from the Internal Revenue Service (IRS) to claim your deductions.

Moving Expense Checklist

Records pertaining to your move should be kept in one place. They include:

Premove House Hunting Trip Receipts

- ☐ Transportation Costs (Air, bus, or train fares, or automobile expenses)
- ☐ Meals
- ☐ Lodgings

Residence Replacement Records

- ☐ Advertising Expense
- ☐ Real Estate Commissions
- ☐ Attorney Fees
- ☐ Title Fees and Costs
- ☐ Escrow Fees
- ☐ "Points"
- ☐ State Transfer Taxes
- ☐ Appraisal Fees
- ☐ Lease Settlement Costs

Mover's Documents

- ☐ Bill of Lading
- ☐ Inventory
- ☐ Packing and Unpacking Certificate
- ☐ Weight Certificate

Travel Expenses Receipts

- ☐ Transportation Costs (Air, bus, or train fares, or automobile expenses)
- ☐ Meals
- ☐ Lodgings

Temporary Quarters Receipts

- ☐ Meals
- ☐ Lodgings

United Van Lines

4-28
A moving expense checklist helps you when you move. Some items may be tax deductible.

Once you have decided to move, you need to decide how you will do it. You have two alternatives:

1. You may move yourself.
2. You may hire a moving company.

Moving Yourself

About two-thirds of all moves are do-it-yourself efforts. If you do not own a truck or trailer, you can rent one and move yourself. There are many good reasons for tackling the job yourself. First of all, the cost is about one-third that of a professional mover. Second, you can move on your own schedule. Third, you and your goods arrive at the same time.

On the other hand, you have to realize that what you save in money will cost you in time and energy. You will do all of the packing, loading, unloading, and unpacking yourself. Family and friends can help if the move is only a short distance. They can also help with packing and loading for a long move.

Before you begin the process of moving, you need to plan ahead. You need to make arrangements with a rental firm early to assure that the equipment you need is available when you need it. Also, before you reserve a truck or trailer, you will need to estimate the amount of items to be moved. This will help you choose the correct-sized truck or trailer. The rental firm can help you with this.

Trailers and trucks come in a variety of sizes and models. You can also rent equipment, such as furniture pads and dollies, or purchase moving cartons and other materials.

As you rent equipment, check on liability and damage insurance for the equipment. Find out the cost of insuring your belongings. Sometimes your homeowners or renters policy covers your goods. If not, you may buy supplemental insurance to cover them. Get a written estimate from the insurance company you are dealing with and ask if there will be additional charges.

You can begin packing early. As you pack, take an inventory of your household items. An inventory will help you check to see if all your belongings arrive at your new house. It will also provide information you may need to collect insurance if any of your goods are damaged or lost. See 4-29.

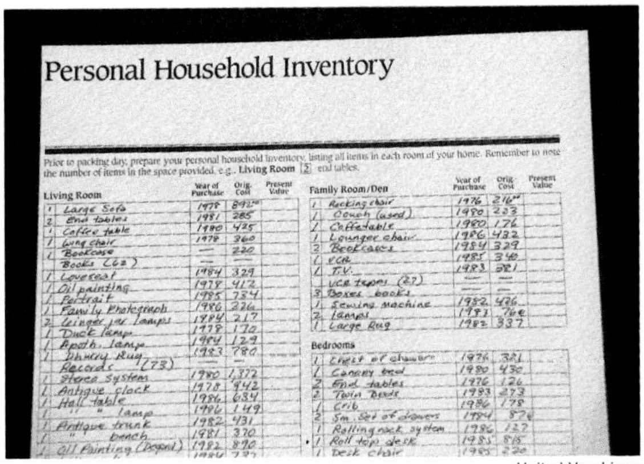

United Van Lines

4-29
An inventory of household items, similar to this one, is good to have when you unpack.

If all of this seems like a lot to do, think about the money you will save by being a do-ityourselfer!

Hiring a Moving Company

If you choose to hire a moving company, you will also need to plan ahead of time for the move. The checklist in 4-30 is a good one to use regardless of the moving method you have chosen.

There are over 2,000 moving companies in the United States. About 15 major van lines do most of the business, especially for interstate moves. To decide which one to hire, you can ask your friends, neighbors, or business associates who have moved recently about a dependable carrier. The relocation manager of your company or a reliable real estate agent can also be valuable resources. Choose only licensed movers and obtain at least three written estimates. Be sure to compare the estimates.

After you have chosen a moving company, you need to ask about insurance. Be sure to read the fine print and ask about additional costs. Also ask about discounted moves, which is a lower cost for moving during the nonpeak season. Most people move between May 15 and September 30–the peak season. If you move during a nonpeak season, be sure the cost is the only item that would change.

The next step is to decide how much, if any, of the packing you will do. Packing, unpacking, and the containers are not included in the actual

Household Check-Off List

There are so many things to remember before moving time... it seems like some of them are always forgotten until it's too late. Here's a list to help you remember these necessary details at the right time.

Transfer of Records

- ☐ School records
- ☐ Automobile and driver's license
- ☐ Bank-savings and loan
- ☐ Doctors and dentists
- ☐ Eyeglass prescription
- ☐ Pet immunization records
- ☐ Legal
- ☐ Church-fraternal organizations

Services to be Discontinued

- ☐ Telephone company (deposit refund?)
- ☐ Electric power company (refund?)
- ☐ Water department (refund?)
- ☐ Gas Company (refund?)
- ☐ Lay-away purchases
- ☐ Fuel oil company (measure remaining oil)
- ☐ Milkman
- ☐ Newspapers
- ☐ Laundry and dry cleaning service
- ☐ Cable TV
- ☐ Pest control
- ☐ Water softener
- ☐ Garbage collection
- ☐ Diaper service

Change of Address Cards

- ☐ Local post office branch
- ☐ Magazines
- ☐ Friends and relatives
- ☐ Insurance companies
- ☐ Creditors (charge accounts or credit cards)
- ☐ Lawyer

U-Haul International

4-30
Checklists can guide you through the steps you need to take when moving.

moving expense. However, the extra cost can be worth it. See 4-31. Packing takes time and it can be very hard work. Also, if an item you packed yourself is damaged in the move, it will be harder to file a claim with the moving company. It is a good idea to photograph expensive pieces to prove their condition and value.

When you are moving with children, special considerations need to be made. Moving may be traumatic for them. It is helpful to involve children in the move as much as possible. See 4-32. Tell them about the move as soon as possible. Involve children by letting them decide what to pack. Give them a floor plan of their new bedrooms, so they can have fun deciding where to put their furniture.

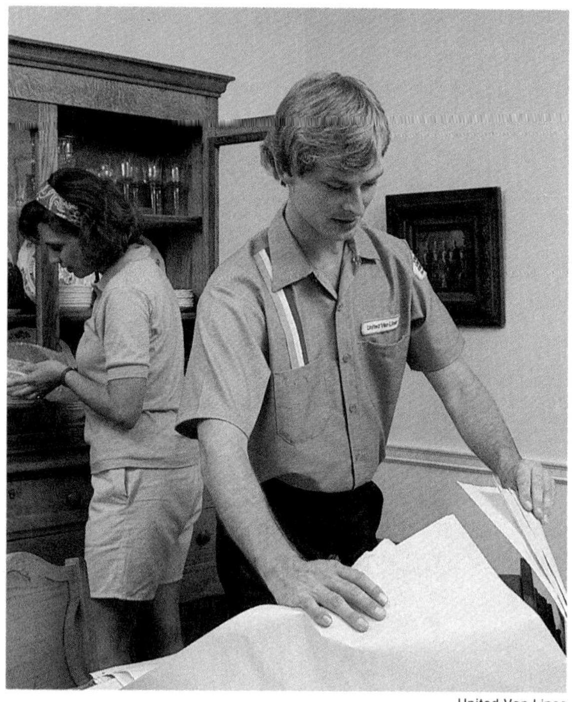

United Van Lines

4-31
Many people find it worth the expense to hire professionals to pack their household items.

Try to move when it is most convenient for all family members. For instance, children usually do not like to change schools, especially during the school year. When the children arrive at their new schools, make the change as easy as possible by having their records already there.

When the moving van arrives, be sure the dwelling is ready for occupancy. Clean or paint ahead of time, since this will be more difficult when your house is filled with moving cartons. Decide how you want your furniture arranged in each room and supervise the placement of it. Be sure that the items that have been taken apart are reassembled.

As your belongings are unloaded from the van, check for damaged or missing items. List any of these items on the driver's copy and your copy of the ***bill of lading,*** which is a receipt listing goods shipped.

If you file a claim for damaged or missing items, first list the lost items. Then make a list of damaged items and estimate the cost to repair them. Interstate movers are required by law to acknowledge and respond to your claim.

U-Haul International

4-32
Children adjust better to the move when they are involved.

Moving can be difficult. Therefore, it is important to weigh the advantages and disadvantages of the different ways to move. This will help you decide whether to move yourself or hire a moving company.

Summary

When choosing a place to live, you need to consider where it will be located and why you are choosing that location. You need to consider the region, neighborhood, site, and zone within the site. You also need to consider the restraints–natural and legal–of the locations you are thinking about.

There are many different types of housing. You will need to decide if you want to live in a multifamily house or single-family house. Multifamily houses include apartments, cooperatives, and condominiums. Single-family houses may be attached or freestanding. They can also be owner built, built by contractors or developers, or a type of manufactured housing. You can either rent or buy housing.

If an older person or someone with a disability is part of your living unit, you will need to consider his or her special needs when making housing decisions. If there are children, their needs must also be considered. You want to choose housing that promotes their development.

After you have chosen a place to live, you will need to move. The move may be a short move or across the country. When moving, you can choose to move yourself or you can hire a moving company. Both have advantages and disadvantages. After you have made your decision, there are certain steps you need to take to ensure a smooth move.

To Review

Write your responses on a separate sheet of paper.

1. List the five major decisions concerning the location of housing.
2. Give three reasons you might have for living in a certain region.
3. Regions are divided into communities and communities are divided into _____.
4. Neighborhoods in which all buildings are occupied by living units are called:
   a. Residential.
   b. Commercial.
   c. Industrial.
5. Explain the meaning of the following terms:
   a. MPS.
   b. FHA.
6. List two natural and two legal restraints that affect sites.
7. Name and describe the three zones within the site.
8. What are the differences among rentals, cooperative units, and condominium units?
9. A fixed house is one that:
   a. Shares a common wall with the dwellings on each side.
   b. Is not connected to another building.
   c. Is attached to a foundation that is anchored to the ground.
10. An architect _____ the dwelling and the contractor _____ it.
11. How does a tract house differ from a house that was custom-built from stock plans?
12. Describe three forms of manufactured houses.
13. Give three examples of special needs that need to be considered when choosing housing.
14. Describe the differences between the two methods of moving.

To Do

1. Choose a region other than your own where you would enjoy living. Study an atlas and encyclopedia to find out more about the region.
2. Make a list of the advantages of living in your own community.
3. Choose another community in which you would like to live. Write to its Chamber of Commerce to learn about the advantages of living there.
4. With a small group of classmates, prepare a brochure about your neighborhood.
5. At your public library, look up the zoning regulations and building codes of your community. Find out what control they have over housing.
6. Draw a dwelling on a site, showing the three zones of the site.
7. Look through the classified advertising section of a newspaper. Compare the information given for single-family houses with those given for multifamily dwellings. Which type is most often listed for sale? For rent?
8. In small groups, brainstorm lists of items to check when choosing a place to live.
9. Describe your ideal region, community, neighborhood, site, and house.
10. Visit a house that is for sale. List the features that need to be adapted for a person with a disability.
11. Research and write a report on one of the following topics:
    - Housing for older people.
    - Housing for people with disabilities.
    - Housing for children.
12. Pretend you are moving. Keep a diary for each day, describing the arrangements you make, the move itself, and evaluating the move.

CHAPTER 5

Acquiring Housing

Acorn Structures, Inc.

To Know

abstract of title
acquisition
adjustable rate mortgage
agreement of sale
appraiser
assign
bid
breach of contract
closed
closing costs
credit cards
conventional mortgage
cost
declaration of ownership
deed
earnest money
equity
eviction
FHA-insured mortgage
finance charge
foreclosure
gross income
inspector
installment buying

interest
lease
lessee
lessor
mortgage
net income
process
renegotiable rate mortgage
security deposit
sublet
title
VA-guaranteed mortgage

Objectives

After studying this chapter, you will be able to:

- Discuss the advantages and disadvantages of renting and buying houses.
- List several items to check before signing a lease.
- Explain the steps in buying a house.
- Define many legal and financial terms related to acquiring housing.
- Describe what to look for when buying condominium units or cooperative units.

At some time, you will have to decide how to spend money for housing. You will need to use rational decision making to choose between renting and purchasing a house. Your choice will depend on your life-style, your stage of the life cycle, and your other life situations.

Acquisition

Acquisition is the act of gaining something. Acquiring housing is divided into two parts: process and cost.

Process

Process is the method used to accomplish a task. In housing, process is the way you acquire housing. See 5-1. How did your living unit acquire the housing in which you live? Did you buy it, or do you rent? If you bought your housing, was it new or pre-owned? Did you have your house built, or was it built by a previous owner? Did you pay cash, or take out a mortgage on the property?

Additional processes are needed to maintain a household after the initial, or first, acquisition. You need to make arrangements to have the electricity and water turned on. You need to arrange to have your belongings moved to your house. You also need to repair or replace parts of the dwelling from time to time. It may mean something as simple as replacing a worn-out

The Process of Acquisition		
Decisions		Range of Available Choices
Possessing	Own	Buy Build Own to rent
	Rent	Privately owned Publicly owned Company owned
Financing	Cash	Currency Check
	Terms	Short term Long term
	Sources	Current income Savings Private loans Commercial loans Governmental loans
Operating		Furnish Maintain Repair
Replacing		Sell Trade Abandon
Adapting		Remodel Refinish Redecorate

5-1
When acquiring housing, you will want to consider all available choices.

washer in a leaky water faucet. It may also mean something as involved as adding an addition to the dwelling.

The way you pay for your housing is also a process. You can pay for items in several different ways:

- Full amount paid with cash, check, debit card, or automatic transfer of funds. (A debit card is like a check, except a debit card is used in place of a check.)
- Payment deferred by use of a credit card.
- Down payment made to secure a purchase, and the rest of the amount owed will be paid in regular installments of a lesser amount.

Cost

Cost is the amount of human and nonhuman resources used to achieve something. The money you spend for rent or mortgage payments, utilities, and home maintenance is part of your housing costs. The other resources you spend, such as time, energy, and skills, add to these housing costs.

For example, consider what is involved in replacing the plumbing in a house. First, you would have to pay for materials to replace the old pipes. Additional costs would be the time and energy you would spend removing the old plumbing and replacing it with the new plumbing. On the other hand, if you did not want to spend the time and energy to do it yourself, you could pay someone else money to use their resources to do the job.

Process as Related to Cost

Process and cost are closely related and should be considered together. For example, when you purchase an item, you pay for the cost of that item. When you pay in cash, you pay only that cost. However, when you pay by check, debit card, or automatic transfer of funds, you may have some banking costs. Some banks charge for checks and for providing checking, debit card, and automatic transfer of funds services.

Credit cards are also used to buy items. The cost of using them varies. Some credit cards charge an annual fee; others are free. If you pay only part of what you owe by the date listed on the bill, interest will be added to the rest of the amount you owe. ***Interest*** is the price paid for the use of the money. The credit card company is required by law to tell you exactly how much interest you will be charged. You can avoid paying interest by paying the entire amount of the bill by the due date.

To determine the cost of a credit card, ask the following questions:

- How much is the annual fee?
- What is the interest rate?
- Is interest charged starting at the time of purchase?
- Is the amount due paid in full?

Installment buying is the process of buying something by making a series of payments during a given length of time. It costs more to use than most other methods. This is because a person, company, or bank is *financing,* or providing credit, to you. They have paid your bill and are willing to wait for you to pay them back. Therefore, in addition to the original amount, you must pay extra for the privilege of using their money. This extra amount is called a ***finance charge.*** It includes the interest as well as any carrying charges. *Carrying charges* are the amounts of money, other than interest, that are added to the price of something when it is bought by the installment buying process. The finance charge is stated as an annual percentage rate of the amount borrowed.

You can pay back the money you borrow over a short or long period of time. The longer you take, the more interest you will pay. Most houses are purchased with *long-term financing.* You can take as long as 30 years to pay back the money you borrowed for a house. However, in the end, the interest may be more than the cost of the dwelling itself.

A Place to Rent

Over one-third of all people in the United States rent their housing. The majority of these are single people, young married couples, and older people. Many are people with low incomes.

Renters

Renters usually pay for their housing in monthly installments. When they first move into a building, the owner or building manager, usually requests a security deposit in addition to the first month's rent. The ***security deposit*** is a payment that insures the owner against financial loss caused by the renter. For example, the renter may fail to pay the rent or might damage the building. The amount of the security deposit commonly includes one month's rent and may include an additional amount.

Being a renter has a number of advantages. Renters are free to move as they desire. They do not need to worry about the value of property going up or down or about buying and selling. They have a clear idea of what housing will cost them. They have no hidden costs–like a new roof–that often come with ownership. Since they do not own the dwelling, they can save money that would be spent on improvements.

Any type of housing can be rented, but the most common are multifamily dwellings. Duplexes, triplexes, and apartment buildings are usually occupied by renters. Single-family houses can also be rented as well as condominiums and vacation houses.

As a renter, examine a rental unit closely before you move into it. It is helpful to use a checklist like the one in 5-2. Ask the owner of the unit questions, such as those in 5-3. Be sure that each question is answered and you are happy with the answers. You want your housing to bring you satisfaction, not frustration.

The Written Lease

Rental agreements can be on a month-to-month basis or for a specific length of time, such as one or two years. They can be either written or oral. The written lease, 5-4, is the preferred agreement between the renter and owner. A ***lease*** is a legal document spelling out the conditions under which the renter rents the property. It lists the rights and responsibilities of both the owner, or ***lessor,*** and the renter, or ***lessee.***

Read the written lease carefully. It should include the following:

- Address and specific apartment number.
- Date signed.
- Signatures of lessee(s) and lessor.
- Date of occupation and length of lease.
- Cost of rent–when and where it should be paid.
- Statement on lease renewal. Is it automatic? See 5-5.
- Allotment of specific responsibilities, such as shoveling snow, cutting the lawn, repairing, or painting.
- An entry clause allowing the lessor to enter the apartment for specific reasons with notice or in an emergency.
- A clause concerning who is responsible for water, electricity, gas, oil, or other bills.
- A statement concerning the security deposit: the amount, the conditions that must be met before it is returned, and when it will be returned.
- A clause on assigning and subletting. Check for any restrictions. (See "Assigning or Subletting a Lease.")
- A clause that states the final inspection of the premises will be made in the lessee's presence.
- A statement that the lease can be changed only upon written approval of both the lessor and lessee.

If the lessee does not like any of the provisions in the lease, he or she should try to have them removed from the lease. Similarly, if he or she desires additional provisions to be included in the lease, he or she should request to have them written down and added to the original lease. Such provisions might include necessary repairs, additional furniture, or the installation of appliances. A specific date should be included by which time all changes are to be made. Signatures of both parties should be obtained.

APARTMENT RENTERS' CHECKLIST

Laundry facilities

_____ How many washers and dryers are available?
(A good ratio is one washer and dryer for every ten apartments.)

_____ Are washers and dryers in good working order?

Building lobby

_____ Is the lobby clean and well lit?

_____ Is the main entrance locked so that only residents can enter?

_____ Is a security guard provided? If so, what hours?

Entrance, exit, and halls

_____ Are elevators provided? If so, are they in good working order?

_____ Are the stairs soundly constructed and well lit?

_____ Are fire exits provided?

_____ Is there a fire alarm or other warning system?

_____ Are halls clean, well lit, and soundly constructed?

Bathroom(s)

_____ Do all plumbing fixtures work? Are they clean?

_____ Does the hot water supply seem adequate?

_____ Do floors and walls around fixtures seem damp, rotted, or moldy?

Kitchen

_____ Is the sink working and clean? Does it have drain stoppers?

_____ Is there an exhaust fan above the range?

_____ Is the refrigerator working properly? Does it have a separate freezer compartment?

_____ If there is a dishwasher, does it work properly?

Air conditioning

_____ Is the building centrally air conditioned or are separate units present for each apartment?

_____ Does the air conditioning unit work properly?

Heating

_____ What type of heat is provided (gas, electric)?

_____ Does the heating system work properly?

_____ Is there a fireplace? If so, are there smoke stains or any other signs that it has not worked properly?

Wiring

_____ Are there enough electrical outlets? (There should be at least three to a room.)

_____ Do all switches and outlets work?

_____ Are there enough circuits in the fuse box or circuit breaker panel to handle all of your electrical equipment?

5-2
Check apartments carefully as you search for a place to rent.

Lighting

_____ Are there enough fixtures for adequate light? Are the fixtures in good working order?

_____ Does the apartment get a good amount of natural light from windows?

Windows

_____ Are any windows broken or difficult to open and close?

_____ Are windows arranged to provide good ventilation?

_____ Are screens provided?

_____ Are there drafts around the window frame?

_____ In high-rise buildings, does the landlord arrange for the outside of the windows to be cleaned? If so, how often?

Floors

_____ Are floors clean and free of gouges?

_____ Do floors have any water stains indicating previous leaks?

Ceilings

_____ Are ceilings clean and free of cracks and peeling?

_____ Are there any water stains indicating previous leaks?

Walls

_____ Are walls clean and free of cracks and peeling?

_____ Does the paint run or smear when rubbed with a damp cloth?

Soundproofing

_____ When you thump the walls, do they seem hollow or solid?

_____ Can you hear neighbors downstairs, upstairs, or on either side of you?

Telephone

_____ Are phone jacks already installed?

_____ Are phone jacks in convenient locations?

Television

_____ Is an outside antenna connection provided?

_____ Is a cable TV connection provided?

Storage space

_____ Is there adequate closet space?

_____ Are there enough kitchen and bathroom cabinets?

_____ Is additional storage space provided for tenants?

Outdoor play space

_____ Are outdoor facilities provided? If so, are the facilities well maintained?

5-2
Continued.

Questions for Lessors
Before you sign a lease, be sure to ask the lessor these questions:
• What is the rent per month? How and when is it to be paid? • Is a security deposit required? If so, how much is it? Under what conditions will it be returned? • Does the lease say that rent can be increased if real estate taxes or other expenses to the lessor are raised? • What expenses are there in addition to rent? (These may include utilities, storage space, air-conditioning, parking space, master TV antenna connections, use of recreational areas such as a pool or party house, installation of special appliances, and late payment of rent.) • How are deliveries of packages handled? • Is loud noise prohibited at certain hours?

5-3
Asking the lessor these questions will help you understand the conditions of your lease.

Leases vary a great deal. Some of them include restrictions about guests, pets, excessive noise, and the installment of extra locks. Be sure you are aware of any special restrictions in a lease before you sign it.

Sometimes the words in a lease are hard to understand. Assistance for lessees can often be obtained from a renter's association in the community or state. A member of the renter's association will be glad to explain the unfamiliar terms. Do not sign a lease until you understand each statement in it.

Assigning or Subletting a Lease

If you have signed a lease, but you wish to move out early, you have three options:

1. Continue paying the rent until the lease expires.
2. Assign the lease.
3. Sublet the lease.

To ***assign*** the lease, you transfer the entire unexpired portion of the lease to someone else. After the assignment is transacted, you can no longer be held responsible for the lease.

To ***sublet*** the lease, you transfer part interest in the property to someone else. For instance, you could turn over your apartment to another person for a period of time. Both you and the other person would be held responsible to the lessor for all terms of the lease.

Breach of Contract

Lessors and lessees are sometimes unable to fulfill promises. When this happens there is a ***breach of contract.*** This is a legal term for failure to meet all terms of a contract or agreement. If you cannot keep your agreement, you should try to work it out with your lessor. You should be aware that a lawsuit can be started against you for breach of contract. Lawsuits are costly and time-consuming.

The most common breach of contract on the part of the renter is failure to pay rent. For example, if you lose your job, you may not be able to pay the rent on schedule. You will need to make arrangements with your lessor, if possible.

A lessor may also be guilty of breach of contract. If there is failure to provide water or a means of heating your dwelling, the contract has been violated. Major repairs are usually the responsibility of the owner. If such repairs are needed, you should give written notice to your lessor. If the repairs are not made, you will have grounds for breach of contract.

Eviction

If a lessee fails to live up to his or her responsibilities, he or she can be evicted. ***Eviction*** is a legal procedure that forces a lessee to leave the property before the rental agreement expires. Lessors may begin a court action leading to eviction only after a lessee fails to live up to his or her responsibilities.

APARTMENT LEASE

UNFURNISHED

DATE OF LEASE	TERM OF LEASE		MONTHLY RENT	SECURITY DEPOSIT*
	BEGINNING	ENDING		

* *IF NONE, WRITE "NONE". Paragraph 2 of this Lease then INAPPLICABLE.*

LESSEE

NAME •

APT. NO. •

ADDRESS OF PREMISES •

LESSOR

NAME •

BUSINESS ADDRESS •

In consideration of the mutual covenants and agreements herein stated, Lessor hereby leases to Lessee and Lessee hereby leases from Lessor for a private dwelling the apartment designated above (the "Premises"), together with the appurtenances thereto, for the above Term.

ADDITIONAL COVENANTS AND AGREEMENTS *(if any)*

LEASE COVENANTS AND AGREEMENTS

RENT

1. Lessee shall pay Lessor or Lessor's agent as rent for the Premises the sum stated above, monthly in advance, until termination of this lease, at Lessor's address stated above or such other address as Lessor may designate in writing.

SECURITY DEPOSIT

2. Lessee has deposited with Lessor the Security Deposit stated above for the performance of all covenants and agreements of Lessee hereunder. Lessor may apply all or any portion thereof in payment of any amounts due Lessor from Lessee, and upon Lessor's demand Lessee shall in such case during the term of the lease promptly deposit with Lessor such additional amounts as may then be required to bring the Security Deposit up to the full amount stated above. Upon termination of the lease and full performance of all matters and payment of all amounts due by Lessee, so much of the Security Deposit as remains unapplied shall be returned to Lessee. This deposit does not bear interest unless and except as required by law. Where all or a portion of the Security Deposit is applied by Lessor as compensation for property damage, Lessor when and as required by law shall provide to Lessee an itemized statement of such damage and of the estimated or actual cost of repairing same.

CONDITION OF PREMISES; REDELIVERY TO LESSOR

3. Lessee has examined and knows the condition of Premises and has received the same in good order and repair except as herein otherwise specified, and no representations as to the condition or repair thereof have been made by Lessor or his agent prior to, or at the execution of this lease, that are not herein expressed or endorsed hereon; and upon the termination of this lease in any way, Lessee will immediately yield up Premises to Lessor in as good condition as when the same were entered upon by Lessee, ordinary wear and tear only excepted, and shall then return all keys to Lessor.

LIMITATION OF LIABILITY

4. Except as provided by Illinois statute, Lessor shall not be liable for any damage occasioned by failure to keep Premises in repair, and shall not be liable for any damage done or occasioned by or from plumbing, gas, water, steam or other pipes, or sewerage, or the bursting, leaking or running of any cistern, tank, wash-stand, water-closet or waste-pipe, in, above, upon or about said building or Premises, nor for damage occasioned by water, snow or ice being upon or coming through the roof, sky-light, trap-door or otherwise, nor for damages to Lessee or others claiming through Lessee for any loss or damage of or to property wherever located in or about said building or Premises, nor for any damage arising from acts or neglect of co-tenants or other occupants of the same building, or of any owners or occupants of adjacent or contiguous property.

5-4
Responsibilities of the lessor and the lessee are clearly stated in the lease.

USE; SUBLET; ASSIGNMENT

5. Lessee will not allow Premises to be used for any purpose that will increase the rate of insurance thereon, nor for any purpose other than that hereinbefore specified, nor to be occupied in whole or in part by any other persons, and will not sublet the same, nor any part thereof, nor assign this lease, without in each case the written consent of the Lessor first had, and will not permit anv transfer, by operation of law, of the interest in Premises acquired through this lease, and will not permit Premises to be used for any unlawful purpose, or purpose that will injure the reputation of the same or of the building of which they are part or disturb the tenants of such building or the neighborhood.

USE AND REPAIR

6. Lessee will take good care of the apartment demised and the fixtures therein, and will commit and suffer no waste therein; no changes or alterations of the Premises shall be made, nor partitions erected, nor walls papered, nor locks on doors installed or changed, without the consent in writing of Lessor; Lessee will make all repairs required to the walls, ceilings, paint, plastering, plumbing work, pipes and fixtures belonging to Premises, whenever damage or injury to the same shall have resulted from misuse or neglect; no furniture filled or to be filled wholly or partially with liquids shall be placed in the Premises without the consent in writing of Lessor; the Premises shall not be used as a "boarding" or "lodging" house, nor for a school, nor to give instructions in music, dancing or singing, and none of the rooms shall be offered for lease by placing notices on any door, window or wall of the building, nor by advertising the same directly or indirectly, in any newspaper or otherwise, nor shall any signs be exhibited on or at any windows or exterior portions of the Premises or of the building without the consent in writing of Lessor; there shall be no lounging, sitting upon, or unnecessary tarrying in or upon the front steps, the sidewalk, railing, stairways, halls, landing or other public places of the said building by Lessee, members of the family or other persons connected with the occupancy of Premises; no provisions, milk, ice, marketing, groceries, furniture, packages or merchandise shall be taken into the Premises through the front door of said building except where there is no rear or service entrance; cooking shall be done only in the kitchen and in no event on porches or other exterior appurtenances; Lessee, and those occupying under Lessee, shall not interfere with the heating apparatus, or with the lights, electricity, gas, water or other utilities of said building which are not within the apartment hereby demised, nor with the control of any of the public portions of said building; use of any master television antenna hookup shall be strictly in accordance with regulations of Lessor or Lessor's agent; Lessee and those occupying under Lessee shall comply with and conform to all reasonable rules and regulations that Lessor or Lessor's agent may make for the protection of the building or the general welfare and the comfort of the occupants thereof, and shall also comply with and conform to all applicable laws and governmental rules and regulations affecting the Premises and the use and occupancy thereof.

ACCESS

7. Lessee will allow Lessor free access to the Premises at all reasonable hours for the purpose of examining or exhibiting the same, or to make any needful repairs on the Premises which Lessor may deem fit to make; also Lessee will allow Lessor to have placed upon the Premises, at all times, notice of "For Sale" and "To Rent", and will not interfere with the same.

RIGHT TO RELET

8. If Lessee shall abandon or vacate the Premises, the same may be re-let by Lessor for such rent and upon such terms as Lessor may see fit; and if a sufficient sum shall not thus be realized, after paying the expenses of such reletting and collecting, to satisfy the rent hereby reserved, Lessee agrees to satisfy and pay all deficiency.

HOLDING OVER

9. If the Lessee retains possession of the Premises or any part thereof after the termination of the term by lapse of time or otherwise, then the Lessor may at Lessor's option within thirty days after the termination of the term serve written notice upon Lessee that such holding over constitutes either (a) renewal of this lease for one year, and from year to year thereafter, at double the rental specified under Section 1 for such period, or (b) creation of a month to month tenancy, upon the terms of this lease except at double the monthly rental specified under Section 1, or (c) creation of a tenancy at sufferance, at a rental of ____________ dollars per day for the time Lessee remains in possession. If no such written notice is served then a tenancy at sufferance with rental as stated at (c) shall have been created, and in such case if specific per diem rental shall not have been inserted herein at (c), such per diem rental shall be one-fifteenth of the monthly rental specified under Section 1 of this lease. Lessee shall also pay to Lessor all damages sustained by Lessor resulting from retention of possession by Lessee.

RESTRICTIONS ON USE

10. Lessee will not permit anything to be thrown out of the windows, or down the courts or light shafts in said building; nothing shall be hung from the outside of the windows or placed on the outside window sills of any window in the building; no parrot, dog or other animal shall be kept within or about said apartment; the front halls and stairways and the back porches shall not be used for the storage of carriages, furniture or other articles.

WATER AND HEAT

11. The provisions of subsection (a) only hereof shall be applicable and shall form a part of this lease unless this lease is made on an unheated basis and that fact is so indicated on the first page of this lease, in which case the provisions of subsection (b) only hereof shall be applicable and form a part of this lease.

(a) Lessor will supply hot and cold water to the Premises for the use of Lessee at all faucets and fixtures provided by Lessor therefor. Lessor will also supply heat, by means of the heating system and fixtures provided by Lessor, in reasonable amounts and at reasonable hours, when necessary, from October 1 to April 30, or otherwise as required by applicable municipal ordinance. Lessor shall not be liable or responsible to Lessee for failure to furnish water or heat when such failure shall result from causes beyond Lessor's control, nor during periods when the water and heating systems in the building or any portion thereof are under repair.

(b) Lessor will supply cold water to the Premises for the use of Lessee at all faucets and fixtures provided by Lessor therefor. Lessor shall not be liable or responsibie to Lessee for failure to furnish water when such failure shall result from causes beyond Lessor's control, nor during periods when the water system in the building or any portion thereof is under repair. All water heating and all heating of the Premises shall be at the sole expense of Lessee. Any equipment provided by Lessee therefor shall comply with applicable municipal ordinances.

STORE ROOM

12. Lessor shall not be liable for any loss or damage of or to any property placed in any store room or any storage place in the building, such store room or storage place being furnished gratuitously and not as part of the obligations of this lease.

5-4
Continued.

FORCIBLE DETAINER

13. If default be made in the payment above reserved or any part thereof, or in any of the covenants or agreements herein contained, to be kept by Lessee, it shall be lawful for Lessor or his legal representatives, at his or their election, to declare said term ended, to re-enter the Premises or any part thereof and to expel, remove or put out the Lessee or any other person or persons occupying the same, using such force as he may deem necessary in so doing, and again to repossess and enjoy the Premises as in his first estate; and in order to enforce a forfeiture of this lease for default in any of its conditions it shall not be necessary to make demand or to serve notice on Lessee and Lessee hereby expressly waives all right to any demand or notice from Lessor of his election to declare this lease at an end on declaring it so to be; but the fact of the non-performance of any of the covenants of this lease shall in itself, at the election of Lessor, without notice or demand constitute a forfeiture of said lease, and at any and all times, after such default, the Lessee shall be deemed guilty of a forcible detainer of the Premises.

CONFESSION OF JUDGMENT

14. Lessee hereby irrevocably constitutes any attorney of any court of record of this state to enter Lessee's appearance in such court, waive process and service thereof, and confess judgment from time to time, for any rent which may be due to Lessor or his assignees by the terms of this lease, with costs and reasonable attorney's fees, and to waive all errors and right of appeal from said judgment and to file a consent in writing that a proper writ of execution may be issued immediately.

RENT AFTER NOTICE OR SUIT

15. It is further agreed, by the parties hereto, that after the service of notice, or the commencement of a suit or after final judgment for possession of the Premises, Lessor may receive and collect any rent due, and the payment of said rent shall not waive or affect said notice, said suit, or said judgment.

PAYMENT OF COSTS

16. Lessee will pay and discharge all reasonable costs, attorney's fees and expenses that shall be made and incurred by Lessor in enforcing the covenants and agreements of this lease.

RIGHTS CUMULATIVE

17. The rights and remedies of Lessor under this lease are cumulative. The exercise or use of any one or more thereof shall not bar Lessor from exercise or use of any other right or remedy provided herein or otherwise provided by law, nor shall exercise nor use of any right or remedy by Lessor waive any other right or remedy.

FIRE AND CASUALTY

18. In case the Premises shall be rendered untenantable during the term of this lease by fire or other casualty, Lessor at his option may terminate the lease or repair the Premises within 60 days thereafter. If Lessor elects to repair, this lease shall remain in effect provided such repairs are completed within said time. If Lessor shall not have repaired the Premises within said time, then at the end of such time the term hereby created shall terminate. If this lease is terminated by reason of fire or casualty as herein specified, rent shall be apportioned and paid to the day of such fire or other casualty.

PLURALS; SUCCESSORS

19. The words "Lessor" and "Lessee" wherever herein occurring and used shall be construed to mean "Lessors" and "Lessees" in case more than one person constitutes either party to this lease; and all the covenants and agreements herein contained shall be binding upon, and inure to, their respective successors, heirs, executors, administrators and assigns and be exercised by his or their attorney or agent.

SEVERABILITY

20. If any clause, phrase, provision or portion of this lease or the application thereof to any person or circumstance shall be invalid or unenforceable under applicable law, such event shall not affect, impair or render invalid or unenforceable the remainder of this lease nor any other clause, phrase, provision or portion hereof, nor shall it affect the application of any clause, phrase, provision or portion hereof to other persons or circumstances.

WITNESS the hands and seals of the parties hereto, as of the Date of Lease stated above.

LESSEE:	LESSOR:
______________________ (seal)	______________________ (seal)
______________________ (seal)	______________________ (seal)

ASSIGNMENT BY LESSOR

On this ______________________, 19____, for value received, Lessor hereby transfers, assigns and sets over to ______________________ all right, title and interest in and to the above lease and the rent thereby reserved, except rent due and payable prior to ______________________, 19____.

______________________ (seal)

______________________ (seal)

GUARANTEE

On this ______________________, 19____, in consideration of Ten Dollars ($10.00) and other good and valuable consideration, the receipt and sufficiency of which is hereby acknowledged, the undersigned Guarantor hereby guarantees the payment of rent and performance by Lessee, Lessee's heirs, executors, administrators, successors or assigns of all covenants and agrements of the above lease.

______________________ (seal)

______________________ (seal)

5-4
Continued.

NOTICE TO TERMINATE TENANCY*

TO: Name ______________________

Address ______________________

City ____________ State ____________

You are hereby notified that I (we) shall be terminating my (our) tenancy of –

Apartment ____________ at ______________________ Street ______________________

State of ____________ on ____________ day of ____________, 19______.

Dated: ______________________, 19______.

Name ______________________

Address ______________________

City ____________ State ____________

* This form may be used by tenant as a 30 day notice to landlord to terminate month-to-month tenancy, or to give landlord 30 day notice prior to end of term created by rental agreement. It is also suggested that you retain a fully executed, and conformed copy of this notice, and on your copy, make a note of the name on whom same was served, and date and time of service.

Arizona Rental Residents Association

5-5
In some cases, if you do not give written notice that you will be moving when your lease expires, the lessor will automatically renew the lease. Once it is renewed, you are bound to the lease for another period of time.

The eviction process varies from state to state. However, nearly all states require that the lessee receives a warning before he or she can be evicted. The warning is a written legal notice.

A Place to Buy

A large number of people in the United States own their own houses. Instead of choosing to pay rent, they have chosen to stay in one place for a number of years and buy a house. House ownership has many advantages. It gives a real and emotional sense of freedom. For example, homeowners know they have a place to live and are not likely to be evicted. Also, they do not have to depend on the building owner or manager to make decisions about their housing.

There are also financial advantages to house ownership. It can be a hedge against inflation. This means houses tend to increase in value at a higher rate than the rate of inflation. People who pay rent must make higher payments for the same housing as inflation rises. Houses have increased in value on an average of 5 to 25 percent each year for 25 years. See 5-6.

As the value of your house increases, and you make payments on the principle of the mortgage, you build up equity. ***Equity*** is the money value of a house beyond what is owed on the house. Renters are not able to build equity in their houses. Homeowners can gain from equity if they sell or refinance their houses.

House ownership also gives a tax advantage. The federal government permits deductions for

If your home was built in:	and the original cost was:			
	$60,000	$80,000	$100,000	$120,000
	the approximate cost to rebuild in 1993 is:			
1970	$212,000	$282,700	$353,400	$424,000
1975	$141,300	$188,400	$235,500	$282,600
1980	$ 92,900	$123,900	$154,800	$185,800
1985	$ 70,500	$ 94,400	$117,500	$141,000
1990	$ 61,700	$ 82,300	$102,900	$123,400
These costs were developed using the 20-city national average index provided by E. H. Boeckh, Milwaukee, Wisconsin.				

Written permission was granted by the owner of the copyright, American Appraisal Associates., Inc., Milwaukee, Wisconsin, prior to its reproduction in its entirety in this book.

5-6
The dollar value of a house

the taxes you pay on your house and the interest paid on the mortgage. Some states allow these deductions, too.

The Right Price

Buying the right house is not a simple task. You want a house in which you are comfortable and happy. However, it must also be one that you can afford.

There are several ways to estimate your ability to pay housing costs. Three are discussed here. When you compare housing costs computed by each of these methods, you will be able to judge which one is best for you. To make figuring easy, suppose that your living unit has a $40,000 annual income.

Method one: Allow two-and-one-half times your ***gross income,*** or income before deductions, for the purchase price of a house. Using this method, you should be able to afford up to $100,000 for a place to live.

Method two: Divide your gross income by 60 and limit monthly housing costs to that amount. Using this method, you could spend up to $670 monthly for housing.

Method three: Keep monthly housing costs to approximately one-third of your monthly net income. ***Net income,*** or take-home pay, is the amount of money you receive after deductions such as social security and income tax have been taken from your paycheck. Because deductions vary from state to state and from job to job, this method can be used only when you know exactly what your take-home pay is. As a rule, method three allows you to spend more for monthly housing costs than method two. Both methods two and three can be applied to renters as well as to buyers.

Methods two and three mention "housing costs." These are more than just the regular, long-term installment payments. Housing costs also include property taxes; homeowners insurance payments; and the cost of utilities, such as water, gas, and electricity. Repairs and maintenance should also have a place in the monthly housing budget.

None of the methods described above is absolute. The amount you can afford depends on many other factors, such as the size of your savings account and if you have other debts. If you have a good job and expect your salary to grow, you may be able to spend more for housing. On the other hand, you may need to limit your housing costs if there are members in your living unit who are in poor health, or if your living unit is large, which means higher food, clothing, and education bills. Also, if your new house needs many repairs before you can live in it, you will have to set aside some of your money for this work.

To Build or to Buy?

Once you have decided how much you can afford to spend for a house, you will want to decide whether to build one or buy one that is already built.

Building a house. If you choose to build a house, you will need to buy the lot and then build the house. This involves four steps. They are done in the following order:

1. Choose a region, community, neighborhood, and site. Finding the right location may take weeks or months. (See Chapter 4, "Choosing a Place to Live.")
2. Find a house plan you like and that "fits" the site. The plan may be custom-designed by an architect or chosen from stock plans.
3. Select the contractor. Check the reputation and character of each contractor you are considering. Let each one look at your plans and list of the type and quality of materials being used for the house, 5-7.

When you have narrowed your choices down to a few contractors, you should ask each one for a ***bid,*** or what each one would charge to construct the house. The bid should include the cost for both materials and labor.

You also need to find out when work can be started and how long the job will take. Ask about the method and time of payments. Builders or contractors generally get paid by installments once the work is in progress.

4. Obtain enough money to pay for the house. If you don't have enough cash, you will have to borrow the money. When you apply for a loan, you must furnish the appraised value of the dwelling. This can be estimated using the information given in your plans. The first loan will be for construction of the house. After the house is finished, you can receive a long-term mortgage loan.

Buying a new house. If you want a new house, but do not want to build it, you can buy one that has just been built. See 5-8. This process requires much less time than buying a lot and having a house built on it.

If the house is built by a reputable builder, the workmanship will be guaranteed for a period of time, usually one to two years after completion. Some top builders guarantee their work for up to five years. Be sure to get the guarantee in writing for your protection.

Buying a new house has some unique advantages. One is that you can move in as soon as the deal is ***closed,*** or when all the legal and financial matters have been settled. Another advantage is that you can see the finished product

Pella Corporation

5-7
A contractor can help you choose the best materials for your house.

5-8
Some contractors build houses, such as this one, that are ready to sell.

before you buy. If you are a person who cannot visualize, or imagine, how a house will look by studying the plans, this will be important to you.

Buying a pre-owned house. Many house buyers choose houses that have been previously occupied. These houses have many advantages. The same number of rooms and amount of space in pre-owned houses will usually cost less than in new ones. Sometimes, you can see how the people who live there make use of the space. See 5-9. When you look at furnished rooms, you can get a better idea of their sizes. This can help you visualize how your furniture will fit into the same space. Another bonus is that taxes in established communities are not likely to increase as rapidly as those in new areas.

Also, some items that usually do not come with a new house may be included with a pre-owned one. Draperies and the hardware to hang them are sometimes left by the previous owner. The carpeting may also be left in the dwelling. The lot may have mature trees and shrubs. Fences, walls, and screens may have been added. These are costly in time, money, and effort if you add them yourself.

While you may find that some pre-owned houses are bargains, others are not. No house is perfect. You need to know the flaws before you buy. If you do not find out about the shortcomings until after you move in, it can be a shock. The shock becomes greater when you realize how much it will cost to fix them.

Before you sign a contract agreeing to buy a pre-owned house, you should check carefully for serious defects such as:

- The lack of a concrete foundation. This would indicate that the house will probably sag or shift, which will weaken the structure.
- Rotten or sagging roofs, walls, or supports. These are signs of poor care. They are also major construction defects and are costly to repair.
- Insect damage. The damage may need major repairs. It may also mean defects that are not visible to the inexperienced observer.

Schult Homes

5-9
A house may be easier to sell if shown with furnishings in place. This gives the potential buyers an idea how their furniture will look in it.

The following are less serious conditions that you may find. They can be repaired if you want to spend the time, money, and effort.

- The structure is good, but it needs paint.
- The plumbing is old and may need to be replaced soon.
- The walls, ceilings, or floors show slight damage.
- Windows are broken.
- The roof needs repair.
- Trash lying around the house.
- The yard looks shabby.

To learn about any shortcomings ahead of time, you may want to have the house inspected. An ***inspector*** will judge the construction and present condition of the house. You should also have the house appraised before you buy it. The ***appraiser*** will give you an expert estimate of the quality and value of the property.

TOM HENDRICKSON REAL ESTATE

121 N. Main Street
OPEN HOUSE
Saturday, May 22, 1993
&
Sunday, May 23, 1993, 1-4 PM
804 Lakeview
$139,500

Remodeled, updated, and delightful! 4 bedroom brick ranch with fireplace, 2 baths, utility room, 2 1/2 car garage and large deck off master bedroom. Great layout–quiet location. Plus as a bonus–160 feet lake frontage on South Lake. Get your fishing pole ready!
Directions: *Take Rt 50 to Western, Turn West at 3rd Street. North at Walnut, East at 6th Street, end of road. Signs are posted.*

5-10
Advertisements in local newspapers can help you find real estate firms.

Shopping for a Place to Buy

When you know what type of house you can afford and want, it is time to go shopping. One way to start is to contact a reliable real estate firm. Real estate firms are in the business of selling land and buildings. They often advertise properties in the real estate section of newspapers, 5-10. However, not all properties they have contracted to sell are advertised in the paper. They have additional listings in the real estate agent's catalog. See 5-11.

Real estate agents can give you information about the community and neighborhood you are considering. They can screen out places that would not appeal to you. Sometimes they can help you get financing.

Real estate agents charge a commission, or fee, for their services. The commission will range from 5 to 10 percent of the selling price. It is usually paid by the seller. However, the price of the house may be raised to cover this cost.

When shopping for a house, you should not totally rely on real estate agents. Tell people you know that you are looking for a place to buy. They may know about certain houses that you would like. They may even know of other people's plans to sell their houses in the near future.

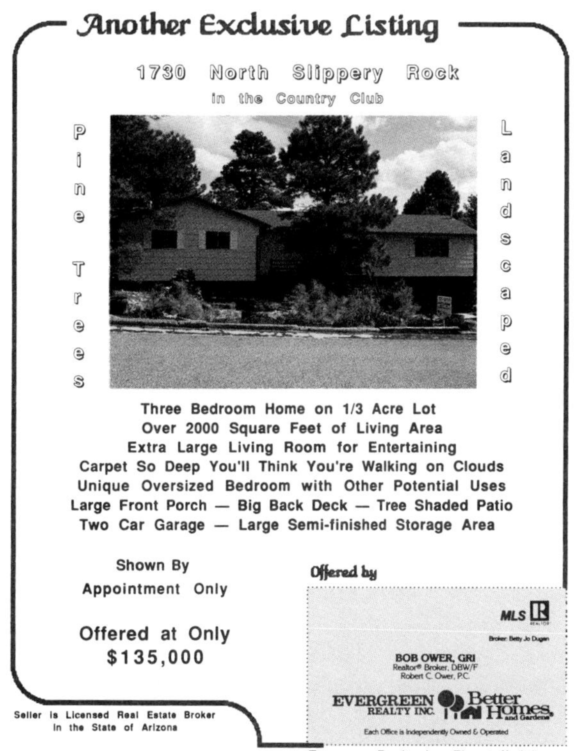

Evergreen Realty, Inc. Flagstaff, Arizona

5-11
In addition to the ads listed in newspapers, many property listings can be found in real estate agents catalogs.

You should also drive or walk through neighborhoods you like. You may find a model house on display. You may also find places with "for sale" signs in the front yards, 5-12.

Sometimes, you may buy directly from the owner and save the fees paid to the real estate agent. However, you need to have a great deal of time and knowledge to shop on your own. If you do not have a general knowledge about real estate deals, the mistakes you might make could be much more costly than real estate agent's fees.

As you look at houses and talk with people, keep a written record about each dwelling. Note the price and the location. Get the name and address of the owner. Write down the features of each house–the number of rooms, size of the rooms, size of the lot, condition of the structure, and any reactions you had when you saw it.

Steps in Buying a House

After you have found a house you want and have agreed to pay the price that is asked for it, you must settle many legal and financial matters. The first of these is agreement of sale.

Agreement of sale. When a buyer agrees to buy and a seller agrees to sell, they both sign a contract called an agreement of sale. The ***agreement of sale*** states all specific terms and conditions of the sale. This can also be called a contract of purchase, purchase agreement, or sales agreement. The agreement of sale is a legal document. Read all of the fine print, before signing it.

The agreement of sale should include a detailed description of the real estate and its legal location. The total purchase price, the amount of the down payment, and the delivery date of property should also be included. It should state that the sale will be complete only if the seller has clear title to the property.

Any specific terms and conditions of the sale should be spelled out in writing. For instance, an owner may agree to leave the draperies, carpeting, range, and refrigerator in the house. Each of these items should be listed in the agreement of sale. This way, the buyer knows exactly what he or she is buying. Other specific terms that should be explained are how the cost of property taxes will be divided at the end of the year and who bears the risk of loss to the property as a result of fire, wind, etc., while the deal is being completed.

Earnest money. ***Earnest money*** is a deposit the potential buyer pays to show that he or she is serious about buying the house. The money is held in trust until the closing of the deal. When the deal goes through, the earnest money is applied toward the payment of the total price. If the buyer does not qualify for, or cannot secure, a loan, the money is refunded. The buyer may lose the earnest money if he or she backs out of the agreement.

Abstract of title. Before a buyer buys a house, he or she must be sure the seller is the legal owner. An ***abstract of title,*** which is a copy of all public records concerning the property, is reviewed by a lawyer or title insurance company.

5-12
A real estate firm's sign advertises that a house is for sale.

The abstract reveals the true legal owner and any debts that are held on the property. This is important since the buyer becomes responsible for any such debts when he or she becomes the owner of the property. Often, the buyer purchases title insurance for protection against financial loss caused by errors in the abstract of title.

Survey. A survey is often done to assure the lender of the mortgage that a building is actually located on the land described in the legal description.

Securing a mortgage. A ***mortgage*** is a pledge of property that a borrower gives to a lender as security for the payment of a debt. The lender is usually a bank, savings and loan association, or insurance company. The seller may also be the lender.

For years, the standard home mortgage was a long-term, fixed-rate loan. This means that the mortgage was written for a long period of time, usually 20 to 30 years. During that time, the interest rate and monthly payments remained the same. The conventional, FHA-insured, and VA-guaranteed are three common fixed-rate mortgages.

A ***conventional mortgage*** is a two-party contract between a borrower and a lending firm. This type of mortgage is not insured by the government. Therefore, there is a greater risk in conventional mortgages than in other types of common fixed-rate mortgages.

FHA-insured mortgages are three-party contracts that involve the borrower, lending firm, and Federal Housing Administration (FHA). It is part of the U.S. Department of Housing and Urban Development (HUD). FHA does not make loans, but it insures the lender against the borrower's possible default.

Anyone can apply for an FHA-insured loan by going to an approved lending institution. The lending institution submits the application to the local FHA office.

When you compare FHA-insured loans to conventional ones, you will find that FHA-insured loans can often be secured with a smaller down payment. They have interest rates that are set by the government.

VA-guaranteed mortgages generally cost less than the other types of common, fixed-rate mortgages. They are three-party loans involving the borrower who is a veteran of the U.S. Armed Forces, lending firm, and Veterans Administration (VA).

Veterans may apply for a VA-guaranteed loan at a lending institution. Their applications will be submitted to a VA office. Eligibility requirements are set by Congress.

The VA does not require a down payment, but the lender may. The size of the down payment and the length of the repayment period are decided by the veteran and the lender.

Although conventional, FHA-insured, and VA-guaranteed mortgages are still popular, several alternative mortgages have come into existence. These alternatives keep lenders and borrowers from having to finance long-term mortgages at fixed interest rates. Lenders want greater flexibility, so they can keep up with changes in interest rates. Borrowers want affordable mortgages. Two alternative mortgage plans–the adjustable rate mortgage and renegotiable rate mortgage–are discussed below. Other creative house financing plans are presented in 5-13.

With an ***adjustable rate mortgage,*** the interest rate is adjusted up or down periodically according to a national interest rate index. Depending on interest rate changes, monthly payments may increase or decrease. However, some of these mortgages have rate caps. This means the interest rate will never exceed a certain rate regardless of the national interest rate index.

In a ***renegotiable rate mortgage,*** sometimes called a rollover mortgage, the interest rate and monthly payments are fixed for a stated length of time. When this length of time expires, interest rates are reviewed and may be changed according to the current rate of interest. If the new interest rate is below the original one, monthly payments will decrease. If the new interest rate is above the original one, monthly payments will increase.

House financing alternatives will vary from state to state and lender to lender. Research all the options to find the method of financing that is best for you.

Creative Home Financing	
Type	Description
Balloon Mortgage	Monthly payments based on a fixed interest rate, usually short term. Payments may cover interest only, with principal due in full at term end.
Shared Appreciation Mortgage	Below-market interest rate and lower monthly payments in exchange for a share of profits on a specified date or when property is sold.
Assumable Mortgage	Buyer takes over seller's original, below-market interest rate mortgage.
Land Contract	Seller retains original mortgage. No transfer of title until loan is fully paid. Equal monthly payments based on below-market interest rate with unpaid principal due at loan end.
Rent with Option	Renter pays "option fee" for right to purchase property at specified time and agreed-upon price. Rent may or may not be applied to sales price.

5-13
Many creative house financing plans are now available to meet the varying needs of house buyers or sellers.

Foreclosure. Suppose that you have secured a mortgage and have bought a house. It is the largest purchase you have ever made. You have agreed to make monthly payments for many years. What would happen if you lost your job or became ill and could not make your mortgage payments?

Legally, the lender could foreclose your mortgage. ***Foreclosure*** is a legal proceeding in which a lending firm takes possession of the mortgaged property of a debtor who fails to live up to the terms of the contract. To recover the money you borrowed, the lender could take your mortgaged property away from you and sell it.

You may be able to skip mortgage payments until your financial situation returns to normal. To find out if this is possible, make a personal visit to the lender. Let people there know you are concerned because you cannot make payments. Ask them for an extension of time. Know your financial situation and be prepared to answer these questions:

- Why did you miss your payments?
- From where are you currently getting income?
- When will you begin payments again?
- When can you pay the payments you missed?

Closing costs. Before a real estate sale is final, fees and charges for settling the legal and financial matters must be paid. They are called ***closing costs.*** These closing costs can amount to several hundred dollars. The buyers should ask for an estimate of the cost and be sure to have enough money to pay for them. They can be paid by cash or check.

Closing costs may include the following items:

- Recording the deed and mortgage.
- Escrow fees. (These are funds paid to an escrow agent to hold until a specified event occurs. After the event has occurred, the funds are released to designated people. In practice, this often means that when the homeowner makes mortgage payments, he or she pays an additional sum that is placed in a trust fund. This extra money is used to pay other expenses, such as taxes, insurance premiums, and special assessments.)
- Attorney's fee or fee to a title company.
- Abstract of title and title insurance.
- Appraisal.
- Survey charge.
- Points. (These are a type of interest paid to offset interest lost by the lender. One point equals one percent.)

The seller also has some closing costs. They may include the real estate commission and his or her share of the year's taxes, insurance, and any special assessments. The buyer and seller each pays the taxes, insurance, and special assessments for the portion of the year they owned the property. The seller's closing costs may actually be higher than those of the buyer, but the price of the house may be raised to cover them.

The title and deed. When the sale is closed, the title is passed to the new owner. The ***title*** is a document that gives proof of the rights of ownership and possession of particular property. The legal document by which the title is transferred from one person to another is called a ***deed.*** The deed describes the property being sold. It is signed and witnessed according to the laws of the state where the property is located.

Several types of deeds are used to transfer property. A *general warranty deed,* 5-14, transfers the title of the property to the buyer. It guarantees that the title is clear of any claims against it. If any mortgage, tax, or title claims are made against the property, the buyer may hold the

WARRANTY DEED
Statutory (ILLINOIS)
(Individual to Individual)

(The Above Space For Recorder's Use Only)

THE GRANTOR ____

of the ____ of ____ County of ____ State of ____
for and in consideration of ____ DOLLARS, in hand paid,

CONVEY __ and WARRANT __ to ____

of the ____ of ____ County of ____ State of ____
the following described Real Estate situated in the County of ____ in the State of Illinois, to wit:

hereby releasing and waiving all rights under and by virtue of the Homestead Exemption Laws of the State of Illinois.

DATED this ____ day of ____ 19__

PLEASE PRINT OR TYPE NAME(S) BELOW SIGNATURE(S)

____ (Seal) ____ (Seal)

____ (Seal) ____ (Seal)

State of Illinois, County of ____ ss. I, the undersigned, a Notary Public in and for said County, in the State aforesaid, DO HEREBY CERTIFY that ____

personally known to me to be the same person__ whose name ____ subscribed to the foregoing instrument, appeared before me this day in person, and acknowledged that __ h__ signed, sealed and delivered the said instrument as ____ free and voluntary act, for the uses and purposes therein set forth, including the release and waiver of the right of homestead.

IMPRESS SEAL HERE

Given under my hand and official seal, this ____ day of ____ 19__

Commission expires ____ 19__ ____ NOTARY PUBLIC

AFFIX "RIDERS" OR REVENUE STAMPS HERE

ADDRESS OF PROPERTY:

THE ABOVE ADDRESS IS FOR STATISTICAL PURPOSES ONLY AND IS NOT A PART OF THIS DEED.
SEND SUBSEQUENT TAX BILLS TO:
(Name)
(Address)

MAIL TO: (Name) (Address) (City, State and Zip)

OR RECORDER'S OFFICE BOX NO ____

5-14
A general warranty deed transfers the title of the property to the new owners and guarantees that the title is clear of any claims.

seller liable for them. This type of deed offers the greatest legal protection to the buyer.

A *special warranty deed* also transfers the title to the buyer. However, it guarantees that during the time the seller held the title to the property, the seller did nothing that would or will in the future impair the buyer's title.

A *quitclaim deed* transfers whatever interest the seller has in the property. By accepting such a deed, the buyer assumes all legal and financial risks for the property.

Insurance. A house is a big financial undertaking. Homeowners insurance or property insurance can help protect the homeowner's investment. Most mortgage holders require the house buyer to protect the house from loss through fire and other hazards. Several types of coverage are available, 5-15.

Refinancing. At some point after you have purchased your house, you may decide to refinance your mortgage. The main reasons people refinance are to lower monthly payments or to save money, because interest rates have dropped. Other reasons for refinancing include making house improvements and paying for expenses, such as college tuition.

You may need to lower monthly payments because you are having trouble meeting present payments. Using the equity in your house may allow you to get a loan with smaller payments that are spread over a longer period of time. Even though your payments are lower, refinancing for this reason probably won't save you money. Many times, it costs you more in the long run. In an emergency, however, refinancing can be an alternative to foreclosure.

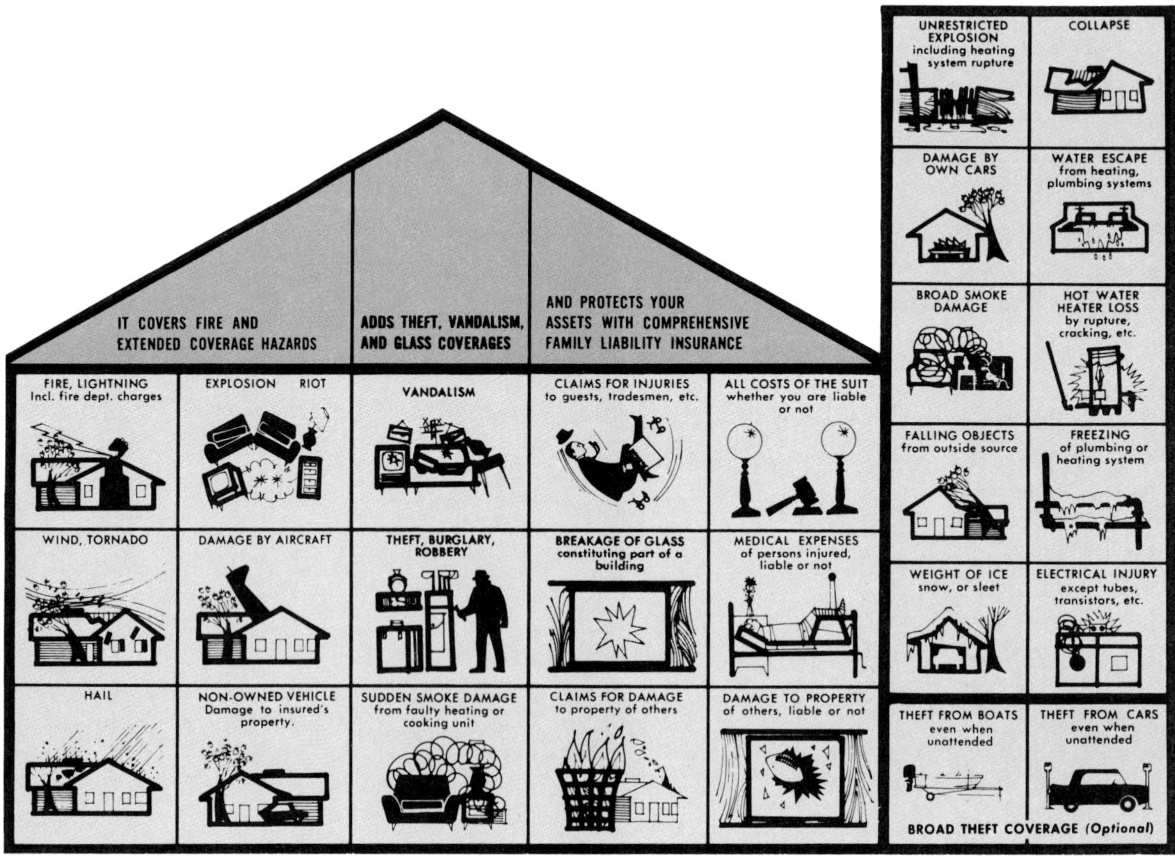

Cumis Insurance Society, Inc.

5-15
The basic coverage offered in this homeowners insurance policy is shown in the main part of the house. Additional types of coverage are shown in the "chimney".

You can refinance to save money if the going interest rate drops two or more percent below your rate. If you decide to refinance for this reason, shop for the best deal. Start with the institution carrying your present mortgage. By staying with them you may eliminate some costs, such as closing costs. Another institution would need to charge these fees.

Before making a decision about refinancing, get the answers to the following questions:

- Is there a prepayment penalty–will paying the old mortgage early cost more?
- Is a title search, appraisal, survey, or inspection required? (These will cost extra money.)
- Are there other costs?
- Who pays the recording and escrow fees?
- How much will your monthly payment change?
- How many months will it take for you to recover the cost of refinancing?
- Do you plan to live in the house long enough to make refinancing worthwhile?

Condominium Ownership

Buying a condominium unit is similar to buying any other house. You will need to choose a location you like and condominium unit you can afford. You will have to decide between a new and pre-owned unit. You will probably work with either a real estate agent or developer. You will sign an agreement of sale, make a down payment, secure a mortgage, pay closing costs, and sign a deed.

Condominium unit owners have the same financial advantages conventional homeowners have. They are investing in real estate and can take advantage of certain income tax deductions. They also build equity in their property.

Condominiums are usually less expensive to build than freestanding, single-family houses. However, because of the extras you buy, such as access to recreational facilities, the price may be high. These facilities may include a clubhouse, swimming pool, and tennis courts, 5-16. You will want to approach the purchase of a condominium unit carefully.

5-16
A tennis court may be part of the common use area when a condominium unit is the buyer's choice.

You should take some precautions if you plan to buy a condominium unit. First, be sure to read the ***declaration of ownership*** carefully. It contains the conditions and restrictions of the sale, ownership, and use of the property within a particular group of condominiums units. Check to see that you can sell your unit at any time and that you are liable for only the mortgage and taxes for your unit. Then, find out who has control of the management of the units. Finally, get a detailed breakdown of your monthly payments. Besides mortgage payments and taxes, you will have to pay utilities, insurance, and maintenance fees. Maintenance fees are used for the repair and maintenance of the common areas of the condominium. They vary widely and are usually subject to change. Check to see that the fee seems reasonable.

Cooperative Ownership

Buying a cooperative unit is different than buying a house. The first step–finding a unit–may be the most difficult one. Although the concept of cooperative dwellings is growing in popularity, relatively few exist today.

The legal and financial aspects of cooperative housing are unique. When a corporation buys an entire building and a lot to begin a cooperative housing project, it secures a mortgage on the property. When you move into a cooperative building, you cannot get a mortgage. This is because you are buying stock, not real estate. In many cases, you will need to pay the full price of the stock in cash. However, you will not pay closing costs, since you are dealing directly with the corporation.

The tax advantages of living in a cooperative unit are different than those for other types of house ownership. In a cooperative situation, the corporation owns the building. It pays real estate taxes and makes the mortgage payments. As a stockholder, you can deduct from your income tax a certain portion of what the corporation pays in real estate taxes and mortgage interest.

When you live in a cooperative dwelling, you will pay a monthly fee. This money is used for maintenance and taxes. It is also used to make the corporation's mortgage payments on the property. If some residents failed to pay this for any length of time, the corporation might be unable to make mortgage payments and would face the possibility of foreclosure. Because of this risk, check the financial stability of the corporation before you buy any stock.

Summary

When acquiring a house there are various processes and costs involved. You need to determine how much you will spend and how you will finance your house.

You may decide to rent your housing. Any type of dwelling can be rented, but the most common types are multifamily dwellings. Carefully inspect the dwelling you choose before you sign a lease. It is also important to know about assigning or subletting, breach of contract, and eviction.

If you decide to buy, it is important to know how much you can spend. There are several methods to help you determine this. Then you need to decide if you are going to have a house built, if you are going to buy a new house that is already built, or if you are going to buy a preowned house.

Once you have decided what type of house you want, you need to shop for one that is right for you. You may use a real estate agent or shop on your own. After you have found the house, you need to follow the correct steps for purchasing a house. This includes securing a mortgage and paying the closing costs. If you should need to refinance your house, you will need to go through many of the same steps.

Instead of buying a single-family dwelling, you may choose to buy a condominium unit or shares in a cooperative. When choosing a condominium unit, be sure to carefully read the declaration of ownership and understand what maintenance fees are required. When choosing a cooperative unit, be sure that you understand the unique legal and financial aspects of the corporation and make sure that it is stable.

To Review

Write your responses on a separate sheet of paper.

1. Acquisition is divided into _____ and _____.
2. Give examples of the following as related to housing:
   a. Initial acquisition.
   b. Maintenance cost.
   c. Replacement cost.
   d. Cost in money.
   e. Cost in time, energy, and skills.
3. List four advantages of renting a house.
4. Define the term written lease and name eight items it should include.
5. True or False. When you sublet your apartment, you are no longer responsible for it.
6. If a lessee fails to pay rent, the lessor could sue him or her for _____.
7. What are the three methods of estimating your ability to pay housing costs?
8. As the new owner of a house on which you have a mortgage, you want to figure your monthly housing costs. Which of the following items would you include?
   a. Income tax.
   b. Mortgage loan payments.
   c. House insurance payments.
   d. The heating bill.
   e. Car payments.
   f. Real estate taxes.
   g. Maintenance allowance.
9. An appraiser will tell you:
   a. What houses are available for sale.
   b. If your mortgage is accepted or rejected.
   c. How much a particular house is worth.
10. Define an agreement of sale and name five items it should include.
11. Why should the buyer of a house purchase title insurance?
12. Name three types of housing loans. Give one characteristic of each type named.
13. List two reasons for refinancing.
14. How are the terms title and deed related?
15. When you buy a condominium, you buy:
   a. Stock in a corporation.
   b. Your individual unit.
   c. Your individual unit and an undivided interest in all common areas.

To Do

1. Study the cost of buying a TV with cash, by check, with a credit card, or on an installment buying plan from the store. Which process costs the most in terms of money?
2. Visit an apartment building and ask the lessor for a copy of the lease used for those apartments. Does it include all that it should? Does it include any additional restrictions?
3. Have a class debate: Renting versus Buying.
4. Working in small groups, consider various incomes of living units. Figure out how much each one can afford to spend on housing.
5. Look through the classified ads in your local newspaper. Working with the figures obtained in the previous exercise, choose a house for each of those living units. Assume that some living units will rent and some will buy.
6. Discuss the advantages and disadvantages of buying each of the following types of housing:
   a. A pre-owned house.
   b. A new house that is already built.
   c. A new house that will be custom-built.
7. Find a classified ad offering a house for sale. Investigate the monthly cost of buying it using three different types of loans.
8. Ask the manager of a condominium complex for a copy of the declaration of ownership for the units. Examine it closely. Discuss the advantages and disadvantages of condominium unit ownership.

Chapter 6 The Evolution of Exteriors
Chapter 7 Understanding House Plans
Chapter 8 House Construction
Chapter 9 The Systems Within

FRONT

PART 3

From the Ground Up

SIDE

CHAPTER 6

The Evolution of Exteriors

To Know
balustrade
belvedere
bungalow
Cape Cod
contemporary
dormer
Dutch Colonial
earth-sheltered
Federal
French Manor
French Provincial
gable roof
gambrel roof
garrison
Georgian
Greek Revival
hillside ranch
hip roof
Mansard roof
modern
pediment
Pennsylvania Dutch Colonial
pent roof
portico
prairie style

raised ranch
ranch
saltbox
solar energy
Southern Colonial
Spanish
split-level
stucco
traditional
turret
Victorian

Objectives

After studying this chapter, you will be able to:

- Identify traditional, modern, and contemporary exterior house styles.
- Discuss the background of housing styles and the possibilities for future styles.

Housing in North America began with the Native Americans. They developed a wide variety of housing styles. When settlers arrived in North America, they brought styles from their homelands. Over time, these traditional styles have evolved into new types of housing.

Traditional Houses

The house styles described below are ***traditional*** styles. They are the good designs created in the past. They have survived the test of time and are still being used today. Each style has distinct characteristics that sets it apart from the other styles.

Native Americans

The many different styles of Native American housing have influenced housing. Early settlers sometimes copied the eight-sided mud and log hogans of the Navajo or the wood frame structures of the Seminole. The Pueblo in New Mexico still live in apartment-type adobe dwellings. See 6-1. The basic design used in these dwellings is copied in housing throughout the country, especially the Southwest. They are characterized by boxlike construction, flat roofs, and projecting roof beams.

Spanish

The ***Spanish*** style house came from the South and Southwest where the climate was warm and dry. It is still widely used there today. Its overall design is asymmetrical. Other characteristics are red tile roofs, enclosed patios, arch-shaped windows and doors, wrought iron exterior decor, and stucco walls. ***Stucco*** is a type of plaster applied to the exterior walls of a house. A Spanish style house is pictured in 6-2.

Scandinavian

The log cabin originated in Europe, and was brought to North America by Swedish and Finnish

David Muench

6-1
The Pueblo live in these adobe dwellings.

The Garlinghouse Company

6-2
This house includes many of the traits of the traditional Spanish style house.

immigrants. It was a popular style for those who traveled to the North American frontier. It is still used in wooded areas.

Typical log cabins are built of unfinished logs. They are small, one-story rectangular buildings with few windows and ***gable roofs,*** which are roofs that come to a point in the center and slope on both sides. See 6-3.

Dutch

Early Dutch settlers left their mark on architecture with what is known as the Dutch Colonial. See 6-4. The Dutch did not bring this style from their homeland, but instead created it after they had already settled in North America. The first

Fern Mountain Historic Homestead

6-3
The original log cabins looked very similar to this one.

H. Armstrong Roberts

6-4
The outstanding characteristic of the Dutch Colonial house is a gambrel roof that flares at the bottom.

Dutch Colonial houses were built in New York and Delaware. They were often built of fieldstone or brick, but sometimes wood was used. They had a ***gambrel roof*** with eaves that flared outward. Sometimes the flared portion extended out over an open porch. It became known as the "Dutch kick." Other characteristics of the Dutch Colonial are a central entrance; a chimney that is not centered; ***dormers,*** which are structures that project through a sloping roof and contain a window, in the second story; and windows with small panes.

German

Pennsylvania was where the first German-American homes were built. They are called ***Pennsylvania Dutch Colonial*** houses. They are characterized by gable roofs and thick, fieldstone walls. See 6-5. Some more elaborate houses were built. They have small roof ledges between the first and second floors called ***pent roofs.***

French

The French influenced American architecture in many ways. One example is the ***French manor.*** These symmetrical homes with wings on

Pennsylvania Dutch Convention & Visitors Bureau

6-5
Germans who settled in Pennsylvania built houses similar to this one.

each side and Mansard roofs on the main part of the house. See 6-6. A ***Mansard roof*** is a variation of the gambrel roof and was designed by a French architect named Mansard. When used on detached single family dwellings, the roof continues all around the house. Dormers often project from the steeply pitched part of the roof. When used on commercial buildings, the Mansard roof may be used only on one or two sides.

French influence is also seen in the house style called French Provincial. This style was introduced to New Orleans and became popular all over the country. A ***French Provincial*** house can be as tall as two-and-a-half stories. It has a delicate, dignified appearance and is usually symmetrical. The windows are a dominant part of the design. The tops of the windows break into the eave line. See 6-7.

Camerique

6-7
French Provincial houses are usually symmetrical with a formal appearance.

English/Colonial

The earliest homes in colonial America were simple, one-room buildings with a wooden or stone chimney at one end. As families grew larger, additions were built. The first addition to be made was a second room, often as large as the first. It was added next to the wall with the chimney. See 6-8. This is how the Cape Cod house design was created.

Pennsylvania Historical and Museum Commission

6-6
French manor houses are noted for their stately manner and Mansard roofs.

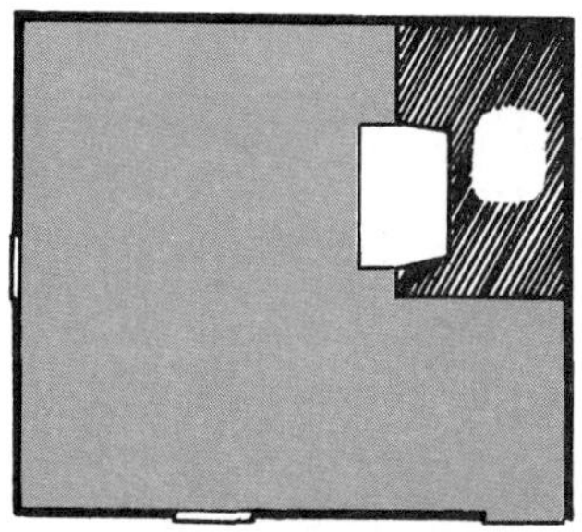

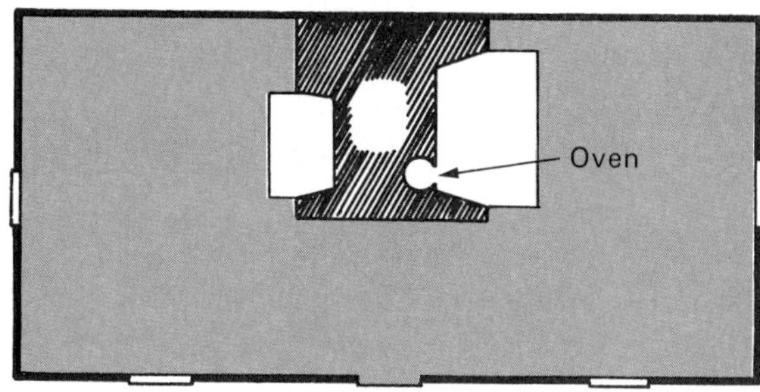

6-8
Colonists would make their houses larger by adding a room on the other side of the chimney.

Cape Cod. As shown in 6-9, the traditional ***Cape Cod*** is a small, symmetrical, one-and-one-half story house with a gable roof. It has a central entrance and a central chimney with several fireplaces. The eave line of the roof is just above the first-floor windows. The windows usually have shutters.

Oftentimes, the loft area of the Cape Cod is expanded and made into finished bedrooms. Openings are then cut in the roof for dormers that add light and air to the second story.

Saltbox. The ***saltbox*** house is a variation of the Cape Cod. See 6-10. It was created by adding a lean-to section to the back of the house. The name saltbox comes from the shape of the boxes salt was stored in during colonial times.

Saltbox houses are two or two-and-one-half stories high. They have steep gable roofs that extend down to the first floor in the rear. A large central chimney and large windows with small panes of glass are other typical characteristics.

Clois Kicklighter

6-9
The Cape Cod is a one-and-a half-story house with a gable roof and central entrance.

Western Wood Products Association

6-10
A saltbox house has narrow wood siding and windows without shutters.

Garrison. A later development was the ***garrison*** house, which is named after early garrisons, or forts. Like the old forts, they have an overhanging second story. See 6-11. The overhang allows extra space on the second floor without having to dig a larger foundation. It also has a supporting effect, so that the second story floor does not sag in the middle. This supporting effect is created when the second floor is supported by beams extending out from the first floor. The farther out the beams extend, the greater the support in the center.

The overhang is always on the front of the house and sometimes extends to the sides and rear. Carved drops or pendants below the overhang provide ornamentation. Other characteristics of the garrison house are a symmetrical design, a steep gable roof, and windows that have small panes of glass.

Later Developments

As colonial life prospered, better houses were built. The quality of building materials was better, and architects and architectural plans from Europe became available in North America.

Georgian. The ***Georgian*** style was adapted from English architecture. It is called Georgian because it was popular during the era when the Kings George I, II, and III ruled England.

Massachusetts Office of Travel & Tourism

6-11
This garrison style house, which was originally owned by Paul Revere, features an overhanging second story.

Georgian houses have simple exterior lines, dignified appearances, and are symmetrical. They have windows with small panes of glass and either gable or ***hip roofs,*** which are roofs with sloping ends and sloping sides. Hip roofs are sometimes topped by a flat area with a ***balustrade,*** or railing. This area is called a captain's walk or widow's walk. Georgian houses usually have a tall chimney at each end of the roof, and most have some ornamentation under the eaves. See 6-12.

As the style originally developed, it became more elaborate. More ornamentation was given to doors and windows. The style also changed according to the region where it was built. Wood was used in New England. Stone was used in the Mid-Atlantic region. In the South, brick was used, and a wing was added to each side of the main house.

Federal. Following the American Revolution, the Federal style was developed. See 6-13. The ***Federal*** style house has a boxlike shape. It is at least two stories high and is symmetrical. The roof is flat and is surrounded by a balustrade. Sometimes a small ***portico,*** which is an open space covered with a roof that is supported by columns, is added to the main entrance. Federal style houses also have ***pediments,*** which are architectural roof-like decorations that are usually found over the porticoes, windows, or doors. See 6-14. The pediments can be segmental or triangular.

Photograph by Thomas A. Heinz. Copyright 1993

6-12
Georgian houses have simple, dignified lines with ornamentation often found under the eaves.

Greek Revival. The next step in the evolution of exteriors was the ***Greek Revival.*** During this stage, the architecture of ancient Greece became popular. The main characteristic of the

6-13
This house can be identified as a Federal style house by the balustrade, portico, and pediments used.

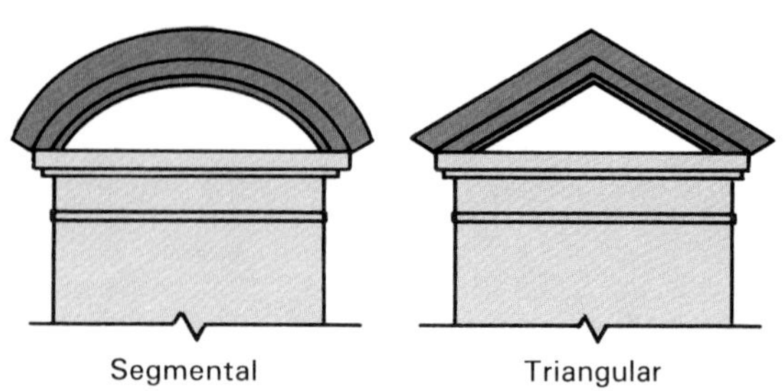

6-14
Pediments are used over doors and windows to add interest to a design.

Greek Revival style is a two-story portico. The portico is supported by Greek columns and has a large triangular pediment. See 6-15. Houses of this style are large and impressive. Some government buildings are designed in the Greek revival style.

Southern Colonial. An offshoot of the Greek Revival style is the ***Southern Colonial.*** The Southern Colonial is a large, two- or three-story frame house. See 6-16. The design is symmetrical. Two-story columns extend across the entire front, and they are covered by an extension of the roof. The roof style is hip or gable. Dormers, shutters, and a ***belvedere,*** which is a small room on the roof of a house used as a lookout, are often included.

Photograph by Thomas A. Heinz. Copyright 1993

6-15
A Greek Revival house is characterized by a two-story portico supported by Greek columns with a large triangular pediment.

Oak Alley Plantation, Louisiana Office of Tourism

6-16
The design of this Southern Colonial evolved from the Greek Revival style.

Victorian. Following the Civil War, the ***Victorian*** house style became popular. It is named after Queen Victoria of England. The main characteristic is an abundance of decorative trim. Other characteristics are high porches, steep gable roofs, tall windows, high ceilings, dark stairways, long halls, and a ***turret,*** or small tower. This style came to be associated with the "haunted" houses of horror movies.

As the style developed, owners tried to outdo one another in the amount of decorative trim on their houses. Quantity became more important than quality. Scrolls and other decorative trim made from wood appeared under eaves and around windows and doors. This came to be known as gingerbread. See 6-17.

Modern Houses

The housing designs that have been developed in the recent past, or within the twentieth century, are called ***modern*** house styles. These

Kindra Clineff, Massachusetts Office of Travel & Tourism

6-17
Excessive ornamentation called gingerbread is found on Victorian style houses.

styles are relatively new. They have been accepted by many people and will probably continue to be used in the future.

Bungalow

A **bungalow** is a one-story house with a low-pitched roof. It is usually made of wood or brick. The shingled roofs extend beyond the walls. Windows are set high, so furniture can be placed beneath them. A covered porch that is sometimes enclosed is common. See 6-18. The *California Bungalow* is similar in design but larger. Many bungalow houses are now called ranch houses.

Virginia Crossno

6-18
Bungalows typically have low-pitched roofs and covered porches.

Prairie Style

The ***prairie style*** house was designed by Frank Lloyd Wright, who is one of the most noted architects of modern times. He designed the prairie style house to accommodate changes that were taking place in family life.

The prairie house is unlike the traditional house. Instead of boxlike dividers, the spaces inside the house expand outdoors through porches, terraces, and windows. See 6-19. The houses are designed to blend well with their natural surroundings. They are built with wood, stone, and materials that are found in the natural environment.

Ranch

A ***ranch*** house is a one-story structure that often has a basement, 6-20. It has a low-pitched roof with a wide overhang. Large windows and sliding glass doors that open onto a patio are common. The building materials and the number of energy-saving features used vary according to the region where the house is located. For instance, in warm climates, light-colored materials, such as siding and paint, are used to reflect the heat.

Ranch houses that do not have stairs are easy to maintain and walk through. However, because they cover large areas, they are expensive to build. The large foundation and roof are costly. Another disadvantage is that they are less

Larry G. Morris

6-19
The many porches, terraces, and windows of this house designed by Frank Lloyd Wright are characteristic of the prairie style.

energy-efficient than other house styles because of their long, rambling structures.

The ranch style began in the West. The informal life-style, large plots of land, and generally warm climate made the ranch style ideal for this region. See 6-21. It has since become popular throughout the country.

There are many variations of the ranch style. One is the ***hillside ranch.*** As its name implies, the house is built on a hill. Part of the basement is exposed, 6-22. Depending on the layout of the lot, the exposed part may be anything from a living area to a garage.

Another variation is the ***raised ranch,*** or split entry. It is like a ranch, except the top part of the basement is above ground. See 6-23. This allows light to enter the basement through windows. The basement living area can be very pleasant if it is

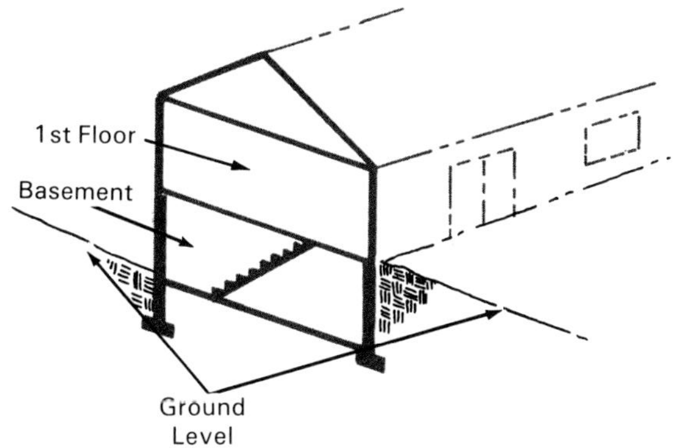

6-22
Part of the basement of a hillside ranch is above ground level.

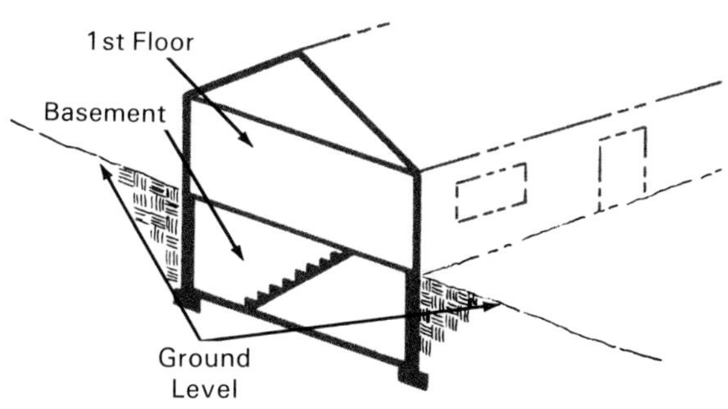

6-20
Some ranch houses have basements that are entirely underground.

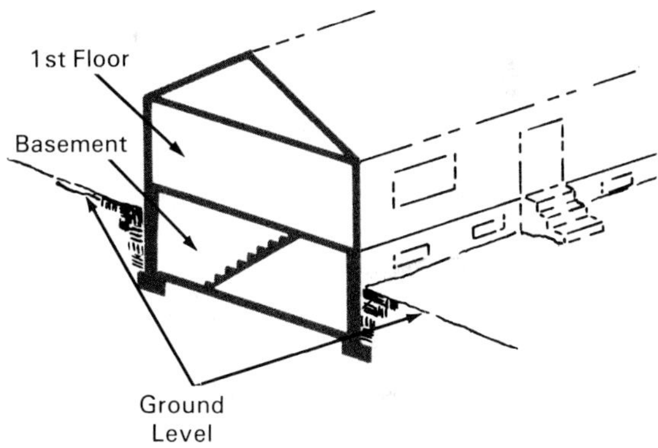

6-23
Since the top part of the basement of a raised ranch is above ground, the basement can be used as a living space.

6-21
Ranch houses are often found on farms and ranches where space is plentiful.

well-insulated and waterproof. A disadvantage is that stairs must be climbed to get anywhere in the house. This can be a problem for children, people with disabilities, and older people.

Split-level

A ***split-level*** house has either three or four levels. The levels can be arranged in many ways as shown in 6-24. The split-level was developed for sloping lots, although it is occasionally built on flat lots. See 6-25.

One advantage of a split-level house is that traffic into the social, quiet, and service areas can be separated easily. Also, there are few stairs to climb to get from one level to another. On the other hand, for a person to move from the living level to the bedroom level, he or she will have to climb stairs. This may be hard for some people with disabilities.

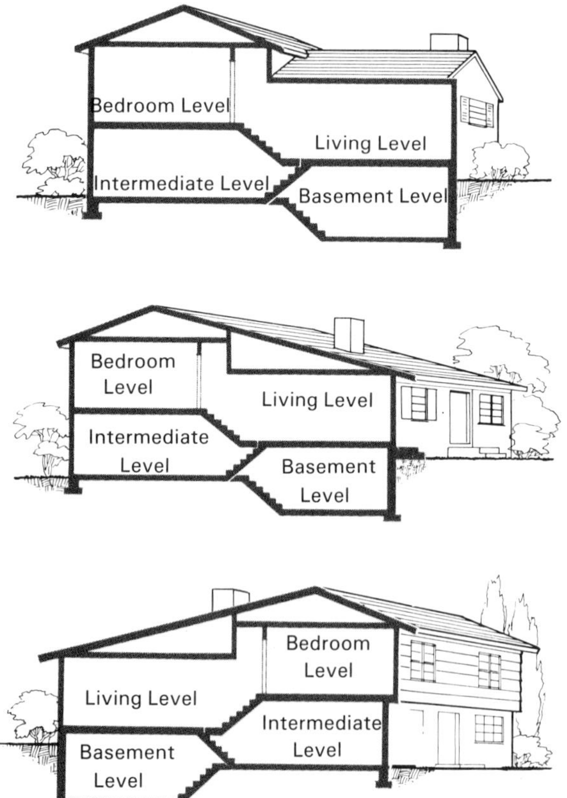

6-24
Changing the arrangement of levels in a split-level house also changes its outside appearance.

Contemporary Houses

Contemporary house styles are of the latest designs. The designs are surprising and often controversial. These houses look different and the architectural styles are not traditional.

Contemporary house designs cannot be described as easily as traditional or modern ones. This is because they vary so widely in shape, detail, and materials. However, there is one identifying trait of a contemporary design. That is uniqueness. Each contemporary house has an individual design, and the materials used may vary widely. For example, the exteriors of some contemporary homes are made of molded fiberglass or other plastic materials. Look at 6-26 to see a contemporary house design.

6-25
Split-level houses are designed to adapt to sloped sites.

California Redwood Association

6-26
This contemporary house uses a traditional building material–wood–but in an unusual way.

Roof styles used in contemporary houses can also vary widely. Study 6-27 to see the variety of roof styles available. While most of these styles are used in traditional houses, they can also be used in unique ways for contemporary housing. See 6-28.

Although contemporary houses do not fit easily into categories, there are two types that do. They are solar houses and earth-sheltered houses.

Solar Houses

Solar energy is energy derived from the sun. Today, many houses are being designed to use solar energy. They can use either active solar heating systems or passive solar heating systems. See 6-29.

Houses with active solar heating systems use special equipment, such as panels installed in the roof of the building, to capture the sun's

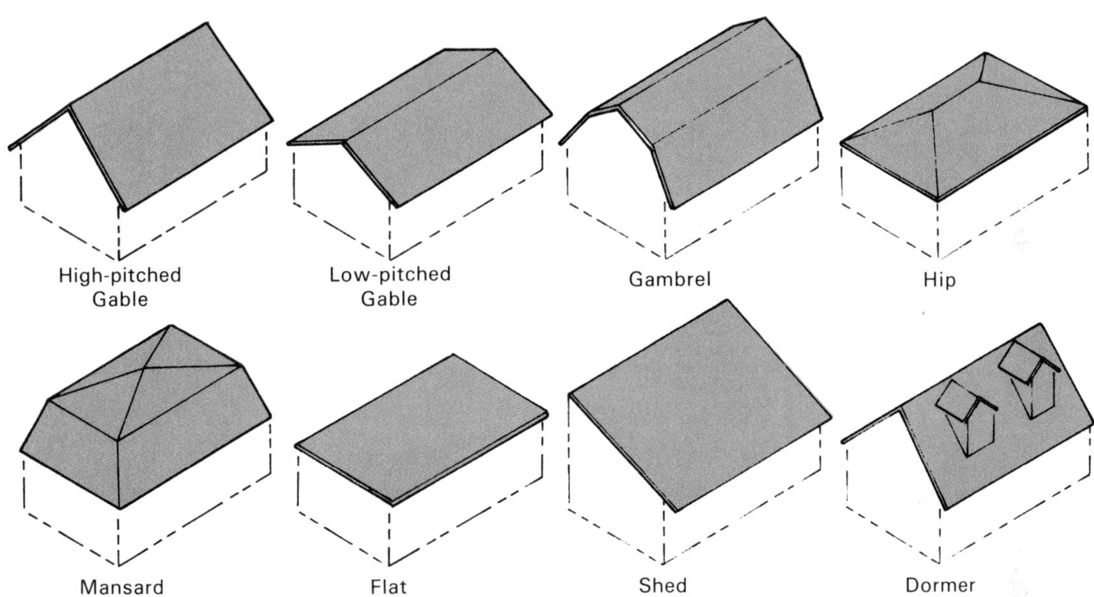

6-27
Roof styles have a great effect on the exterior design of buildings.

Photo courtesy of Lindal Cedar Homes, Inc. Seattle, Washington

6-28
The unusual use of the traditional gambrel roof makes this contemporary house stand out.

6-29
This house has both active and passive solar heating systems.

Concept 2000, Hermann J. Fraunhoffer

6-30
This earth-sheltered house is partially covered with soil. The soil helps insulate it from the desert heat.

energy and soak up the heat. Then fans and pumps move heated air or liquid from the panel to where the heat is needed or to a storage area.

Passive solar heating systems have no working parts. Instead, they include any design or construction material that makes maximum use of the sun for heating. A house with a passive solar system might include large areas of windows on the southern side of the house, cement pipe columns, or dark-colored walls that absorb heat from the sun and then gradually transfer the heat inside.

Earth-sheltered Houses

Another type of contemporary housing is ***earth-sheltered*** housing. Earth-sheltered houses are houses that are partially covered with soil. They are energy-efficient, since the soil is a natural insulation and helps protect the house from the elements and climate extremes, 6-30. Some earth-sheltered houses are designed to be partly underground. Others have soil placed against the side of the building. At other times the dwelling is built into a hill.

A number of earth-sheltered houses are powered in part by solar energy. They may be designed with active or passive solar heating systems or both.

Future Trends

What will housing be like in the years to come? That is something that only time can tell. However, today there are some housing trends that may help you visualize what will take place in the future.

According to the American Institute of Architects the following are current housing trends:

- Using less land.
- Finding multiple uses for inside space.
- Designing semidetached units for group living, with separate bedrooms and shared common spaces.
- Designing street layouts for economy and efficiency that mimic the 1940s grid plan.
- Renovating houses from the 1950s and 1960s as an alternate to new construction.
- Making housing more affordable.
- Receiving more input from home buyers.

Each of these trends can be incorporated with traditional, modern, or contemporary styles to create new styles of housing. This allows the evolution of exteriors to continue.

Summary

There is a wide variety of exterior housing styles in the United States. They have evolved from the housing styles of the Native Americans and those brought here by settlers from their homelands to housing that works with the environment to meet today's changing life-styles. Traditional styles include those from the Native Americans, Spanish, Scandinavians, Dutch, Germans, French, and English. During colonial times, other styles, which are unique to this country, began to evolve. They include the Cape Cod, saltbox, and garrison styles. Later, the Georgian, Federal, Greek Revival, Southern Colonial, and Victorian styles were developed. These are also considered traditional styles.

During the twentieth century, modern and contemporary housing was designed to fit and take advantage of the environment and changing life-styles. Modern houses include the bungalow; the prairie style, which was designed by Frank Lloyd Wright; the ranch and its variations; and different versions of the split-level. Contemporary housing designs are experimental in design and in the use of materials. Contemporary designs are hard to categorize. However, two that stand out are the solar house and earth-sheltered house.

What does the future hold for housing? That can only be seen in the years to come. However, looking at housing trends can help you predict the future.

To Review

Write your responses on a separate sheet of paper.

1. Red tile roofs, enclosed patios, and arch shaped windows and doors are characteristics of which style of housing?
   a. Native American.
   b. Spanish.
   c. Dutch Colonial.
   d. French Provincial.
2. The log cabin was brought to North America by _____ immigrants.
3. Which house style had its beginning as a one-room dwelling?
   a. Spanish.
   b. French Provincial.
   c. Cape Cod.
   d. Southern Colonial.
4. An overhanging second story is a characteristic of what house style?
5. Which housing style was named after an era when three similarly-named kings ruled England?
6. Describe a portico.
7. List four characteristics of a Victorian house.
8. Why did Frank Lloyd Wright design the prairie style house?
9. Name one advantage and one disadvantage of the ranch house.
10. What kind of lot is best suited to the split-level house style?
11. Draw sketches of a low-pitched gable roof and a high-pitched gable roof.
12. Which of the following words best describes contemporary housing designs?
    a. Steel.
    b. Rectangular.
    c. Expensive.
    d. Unique.
13. Two energy-efficient contemporary styles of houses are the _____ and the _____.

To Do

1. As a group activity, make a collage using sketches and magazine pictures of either traditional, modern, or contemporary house styles. Then divide into teams. Write stories about the life-styles of people who lived in the houses when the styles first evolved. Share your stories with the class.
2. Take pictures of different house styles in your community. Work together as a class to identify them.
3. Go to the library and research a house style. Then give an oral report on some of the factors that influenced the style.
4. Read real estate ads in the newspaper. Note the styles mentioned and how they are described.
5. Collect news items about contemporary architects and/or contemporary house designs.
6. Write a one-page report on Frank Lloyd Wright and how he influenced housing styles.
7. Observe a house being built. See how it fits the future housing trends mentioned in this chapter. Report your findings to the class.

C H A P T E R 7

Understanding House Plans

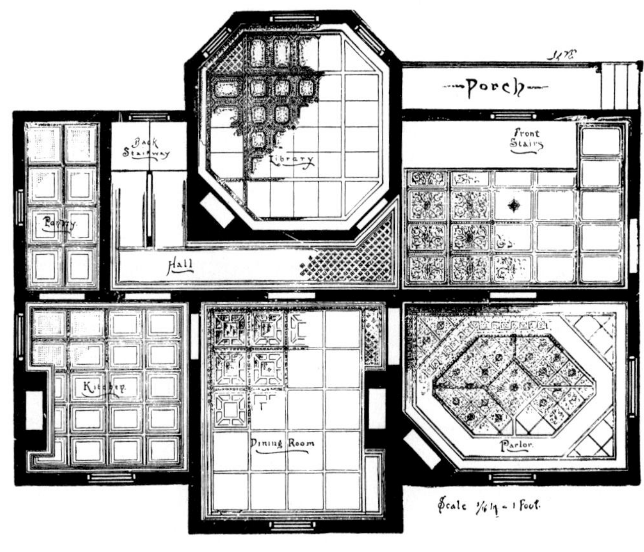

To Know
alcove
alphabet of lines
architectural drawings
built-in storage
common-use storage
detail view
elevation view
exterior elevations
floor plan
multipurpose room
plan view
print
quiet area
section view
social area
specifications
symbols
traffic patterns
work area
work triangle

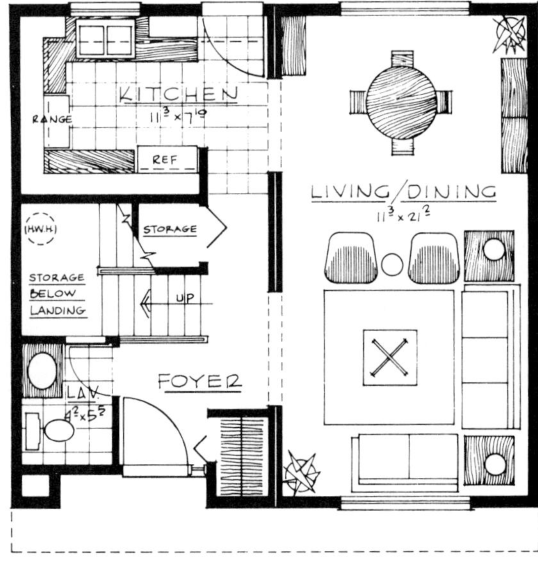

Objectives

After studying this chapter, you will be able to:

- Interpret architectural drawings.
- Organize space by grouping rooms according to function.
- Plan safe and convenient traffic patterns.
- Evaluate storage needs and space.
- List ways to modify housing for people with physical disabilities.

The design and construction of a house involves many people working together. These people include the owner, architect, designer, contractor, banker, and various tradespeople. These people and many others form the design and construction team. Members of the team communicate through house plans. If you are buying or building a house, it is important that you, as a member of the team, be able to interpret the house plans.

Architectural Drawings for a House

An important part of house plans is architectural drawings. ***Architectural drawings*** contain information about the size, shape, and location of all parts of the house. This universal language of the construction industry uses lines, symbols, views, and notes to convey ideas. To insure that architectural drawings are understood by everyone, standard rules of drafting regarding the types of lines, symbols, views, and where dimensions should be located are followed. These rules give meaning to each set of architectural drawings.

Architectural drawings are drawn in proportion to actual size. For instance, if a drawing is "half size," it is one-half as large as the actual object. When an architectural drawing is either smaller or larger than the actual object, it is drawn to *scale.* Drawings for a house are normally drawn at 1/4″ = 1′-0″ scale. One-fourth inch on the drawing equals 1 foot on the house. This scale can also be written as 1/4″ = 12″, 1″= 48″, or 1/48 size. The scale for each drawing is noted on the drawing.

Not all information about a house can be conveyed by architectural drawings. For example, it would be difficult to show texture or represent paint color on the drawings. However, wall texture and paint color are important parts of the finished house. Therefore, some information for the design and construction is prepared in written form called specifications or specs. The ***specifications*** tell the types and quality of materials to be used and give directions for their use, 7-1.

Prints of Architectural Drawings

Most architectural drawings in the past were made by drafters in architects' or contractors' offices using drafting machines and drafting instruments. Today, computer-aided drafting and design (CADD) drawings are often used.

When the drafter completes a set of architectural drawings, copies must be made for all members of the construction team. A ***print*** is a copy of a drawing. In the past, the term blueprint was used to refer to a reproduction of drawings.

Randy Rhoton

7-1
This specifications book contains written information about the methods and materials needed for the construction of the house shown in the prints.

It consisted of white lines on a dark blue background. The print was primarily blue, so it was called a blueprint. Today the drawings can be reproduced by the *diazo process,* which creates prints that have dark lines on a light background. Engineering copiers, which are similar to photocopy machines, are used to a large extent now. They reproduce black lines on a light background. Since the prints are no longer primarily blue, they are now referred to as prints.

Alphabet of lines. To understand the architectural drawings, you must first understand the lines used on the drawings. Seven different lines are commonly used on architectural drawings. These lines are called the ***alphabet of lines.*** They allow the drafter to communicate ideas clearly and accurately.

These lines vary in thickness or weight. They may be solid or a combination of dashes and breaks. The following examples are illustrated in 7-2:

- *Phantom lines* show alternate positions, repeated details, and paths of motion.
- *Visible lines* show the outline of the building and walls.
- *Hidden lines* show edges of surfaces that are not visible in a specific view of the house.

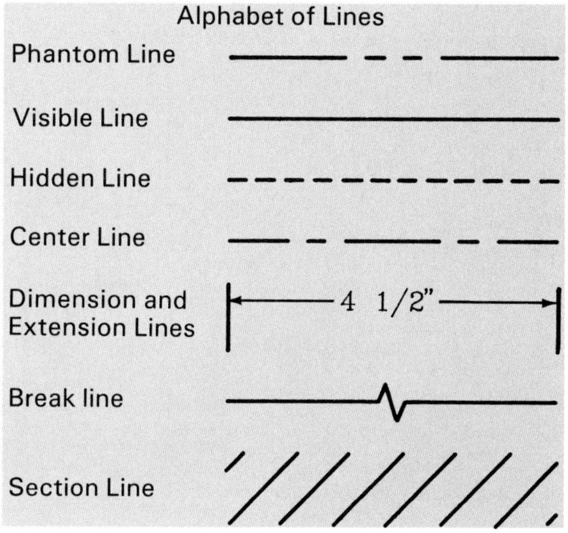

Alphabet of Lines

Phantom Line

Visible Line

Hidden Line

Center Line

Dimension and Extension Lines — 4 1/2"

Break line

Section Line

7-2
The alphabet of lines are basic lines that are used in all architectural drawings.

- *Center lines* show the center of an arc or circle.
- *Dimension and extension lines* show the extent and direction of measurements. Dimension lines show the size and location of the dimension. Extension lines show the termination points of a dimension.
- *Break lines* show the object continues on, but the complete view is not shown.
- *Section lines* show a feature that has been sectioned. These lines are often called crosshatch lines.

Symbols. Many features of a house cannot be drawn exactly as the finished product. Therefore, standard symbols are used on the drawings. ***Symbols*** represent plumbing and electrical fixtures, doors, windows, and other common objects in a house. Drafters use templates to trace symbols. CADD programs insert symbols or blocks to represent fixtures, doors, windows, etc. Notes on the drawings give additional explanation for symbols. In 7-3, you can see the more common symbols.

- *Door and window symbols* show the type of door or window and the direction each opens.
- *Mechanical symbols* indicate plumbing, heating, and air-conditioning fixtures used on a plan.
- *Electrical symbols* on a drawing include switches, receptacles, light fixtures, and appliances. Wiring is indicated by hidden lines drawn between switches, fixtures, and receptacles.

Views for Architectural Drawings

Architectural drawings of a house usually include different types of views. Among these are plan views, elevation views, and section and detail views. Imagine the house was enclosed in a large glass box. Each view is projected toward its viewing surface on the glass box, then brought into position as if unfolding the sides of the glass box.

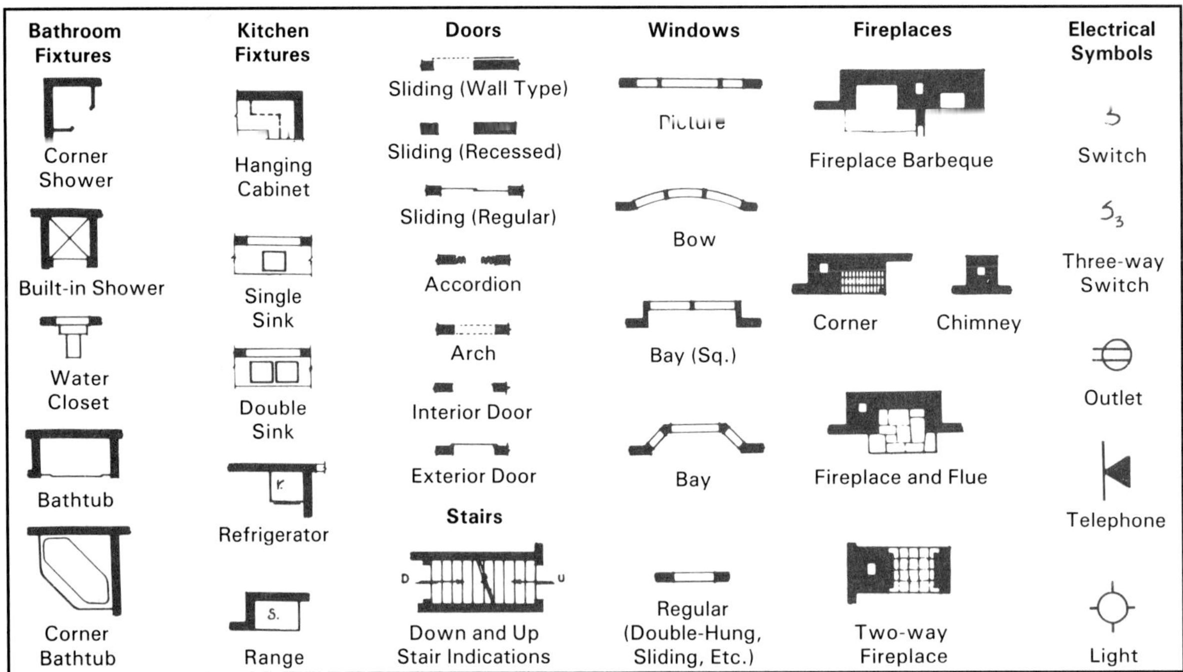

Master Plan Service, Inc.

7-3
These symbols are used on drawings to represent objects in the house.

Plan views. Views taken from the top of the imaginary glass box are called ***plan views.*** The site plan, floor plan, foundation plan, and roof plan are all plan views. The ***floor plan*** is the most important drawing on a set of house plans. It is a simplified drawing that shows the size and arrangement of rooms, hallways, doors, windows, and storage areas on one floor of a house. In 7-4 you can see the symbols used on the floor plans. Study them to learn how to read a floor plan.

Elevation views. Architectural drawings that show the outside views of the house are called ***exterior elevations.*** A set of drawings usually includes four elevations showing all four sides of the house. If the building is simple, there may be only the front elevation and one side elevation.

An ***elevation view*** shows the finished exterior appearance of a given side of the house. Height dimensions are usually shown on elevations. Elevation views help people visualize the completed house. By studying both the floor plan and the elevation views, you can envision the completed structure, 7-5.

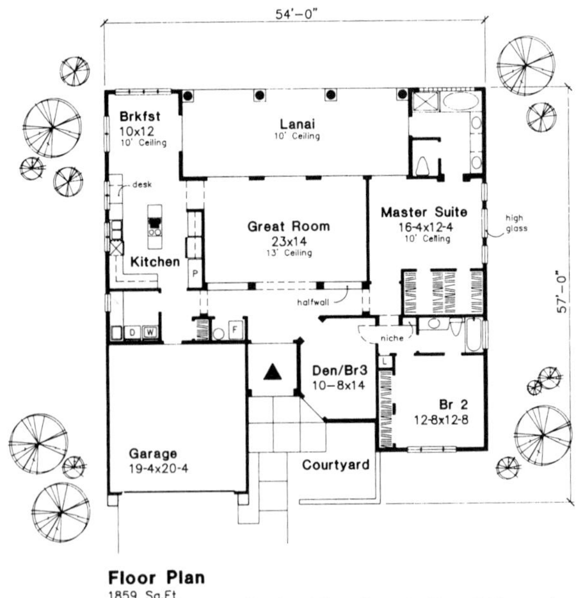

Bloodgood Sharp Buster Architects & Planners, Inc.

7-4
"Reading" an architectural drawing is a matter of picturing what the symbols mean.

Section views and detail views. In order to show how individual structural parts of the house fit together, section and detail views are used. For instance, the drafter may want to show the inside of the house. When a view is taken from an imaginary cut through a part, such as the walls, it is called a ***section view.*** This section view will provide information to the carpenter who will build the wall. See 7-6. The line labeled "B-B" in 7-5 shows where the section view was taken.

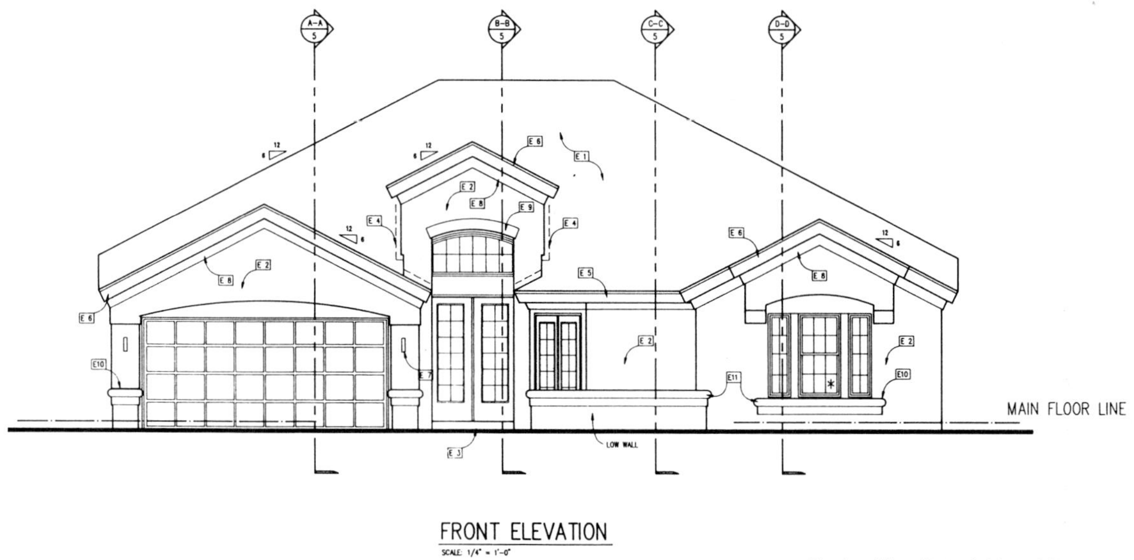

Bloodgood Sharp Buster Architects & Planners, Inc.

7-5
The main feature of this house is the great room in the center of the house.

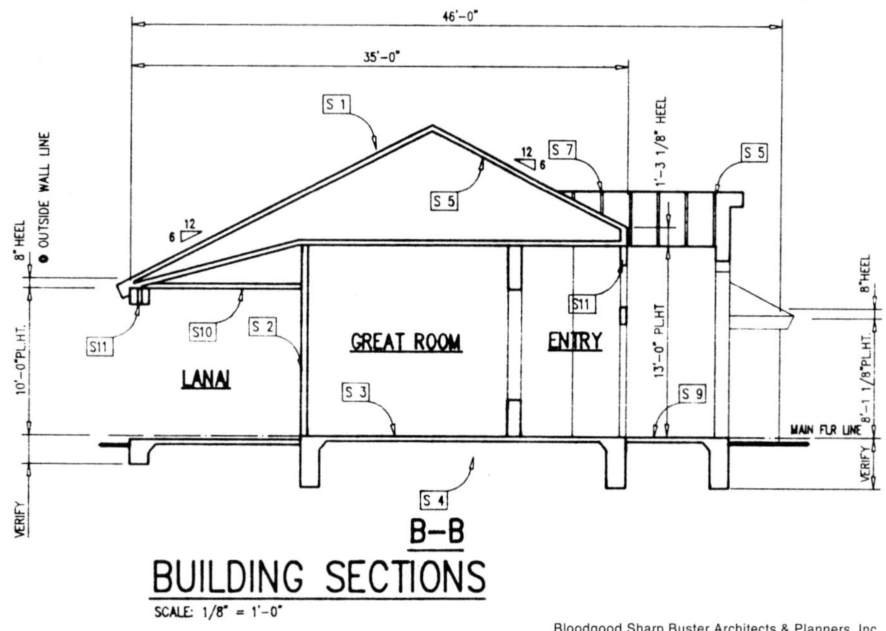

Bloodgood Sharp Buster Architects & Planners, Inc.

7-6
This section view shows that the ceiling height in the great room is different than the ceiling height in the lanai.

A ***detail view*** is usually an enlargement of some construction feature. The detail drawing often uses a larger scale than other drawings. It shows the details of a small part of the house. See 7-7 for a house and garage detail.

The Space Within

Once you understand the drawings for the house, you need to consider the space within.

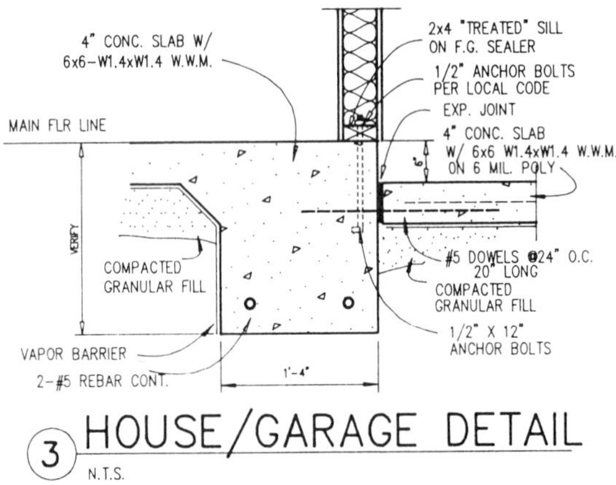

7-7
This detail view shows how the outside wall is fastened to the garage floor.

The way space is divided within the house is one of the most basic concerns in housing.

When planning how to use the space within a house, you need to consider the activities, habits, life-styles, and life situations of the living unit. Then you need to divide the interior space into areas according to the areas' intended uses. These space divisions should satisfy the needs and taste of the living unit.

Grouping by Function

As you look at floor plans, you will notice that certain rooms of a house are usually located next to one another. This is because these rooms are used for similar purposes, or *functions.* Grouping rooms together by function is an efficient way to organize space.

Most of the space within a house is divided into one of three areas. They are the quiet area, work area, and social area.

The quiet area. The ***quiet area*** in most houses consists of bedrooms and bathrooms, 7-8. These rooms provide space for sleeping, resting, grooming, and dressing. The quiet area of a house offers the best setting for rest and relaxation. It is usually a comfortable and private place.

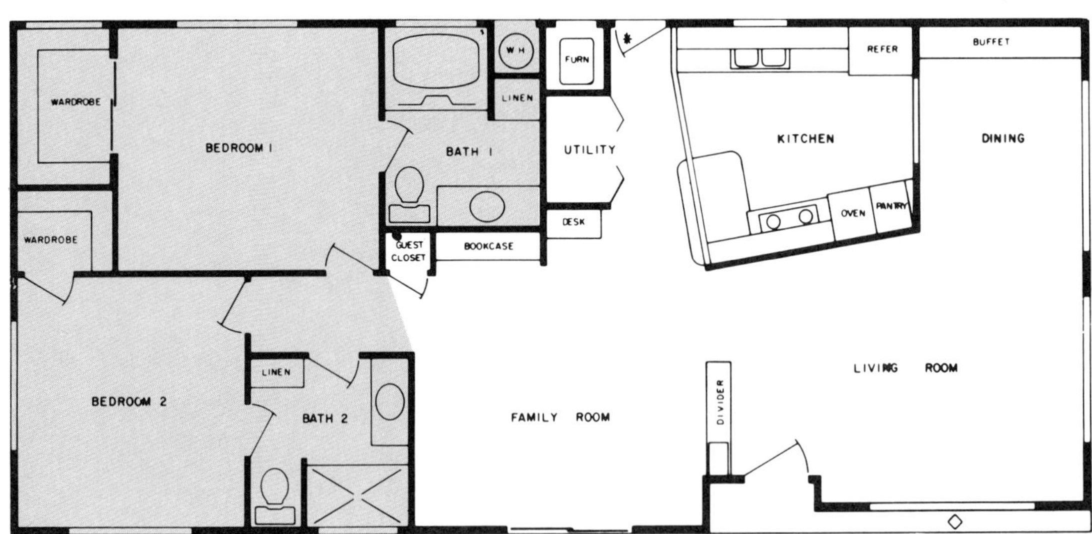

7-8
The shaded area of this floor plan represents the quiet area.

Since sleep and rest are basic needs, they should be one of the first needs to be considered when planning the use of space. In some homes, each person has a separate room. In other homes, this is not possible or desirable. The important goal is to insure the comfort of each person and put his or her spatial needs ahead of those of the group.

Dressing and grooming are other activities that take place in the quiet area. They require privacy and space for storing clothes and grooming supplies. Both bedrooms and bathrooms help fulfill these spatial needs.

Some bedrooms may provide space for other activities, such as reading, studying, watching TV, listening to music, and working on hobbies. When this is true, the rooms are called *multipurpose rooms.* They are used during waking as well as sleeping hours.

The work area. Some rooms in a home are set aside as the ***work area,*** 7-9. They include all parts of the house that are needed to maintain and service the other areas. Sometimes the work area overlaps with the service zone outside the house.

Rooms in the work area vary from house to house. The kitchen, laundry area, utility room, and garage are generally part of the work area. A workshop, home office, or sewing room may also be included.

In most homes, the kitchen is used more often than any other room in the work area. It has three activity centers. They are the food preparation and storage center, the cleanup center, and the cooking and serving center. The imaginary lines that connect these three centers form a ***work triangle.*** Anyone preparing a meal in a kitchen will walk along the lines of the triangle several times before the meal is ready. In a well-designed kitchen, the total length of all sides of the work triangle does not exceed 22 feet. Six basic kitchen designs are shown in 7-10.

The social area. Members of a living unit spend much of their time in the social area of the house. The ***social area,*** 7-11, provides space for daily living, entertaining, and recreation. It includes living rooms, family rooms, dining rooms, and entrances.

Living rooms provide space for family activities as well as for entertaining guests. If a dwelling has both a living room and a family room, the family room is often more casual. It is usually used for recreation and relaxation.

Some houses have separate dining rooms. They can be used for eating meals and entertaining guests. If a dining room is not used regularly, the cost of having a separate dining room may be too great. In that case, the living unit may prefer to eat in a room close to where the food is

7-9
The shaded kitchen and utility room represent the work area.

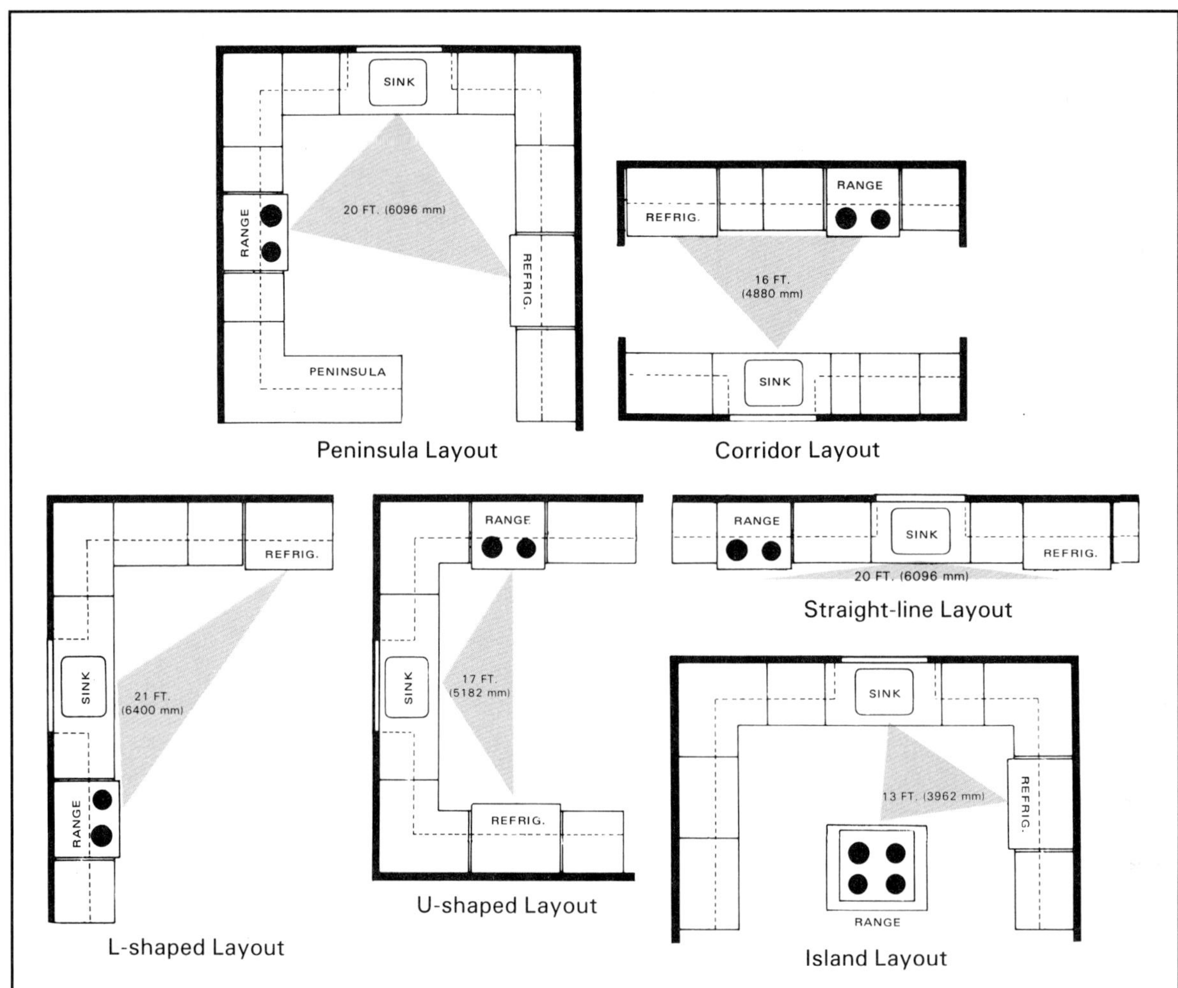

7-10
The distance around the work triangle in each of these kitchen designs is less than 22 feet.

prepared. This can be in the family room or living room. It can also be in the kitchen at a special counter or a separate table. If you enjoy being outdoors, you may want to use outside space for eating.

An entry or entrance is a place where guests are identified and greeted. It is here that outerwear is removed and placed in nearby coat closets. Entries also help direct the movement of people throughout the house. If a dwelling has more than one entrance, each may have a slightly different purpose. However, each is still part of the social area.

Separating areas and rooms. The quiet, work, and social areas can be separated in several ways. One way is to locate different areas on different ends or levels of the house. For instance, the quiet area may be upstairs, while the social and work areas are on the ground floor.

Hallways are another way to separate areas. Besides physically separating areas, hall space also acts as a buffer zone for noises. A hallway between the quiet area and social area makes it possible for some people to rest or sleep, while others are entertaining guests, dining, or watching TV. Hallways near work areas help reduce the amount of noise from appliances and tools that reaches the quiet and social areas.

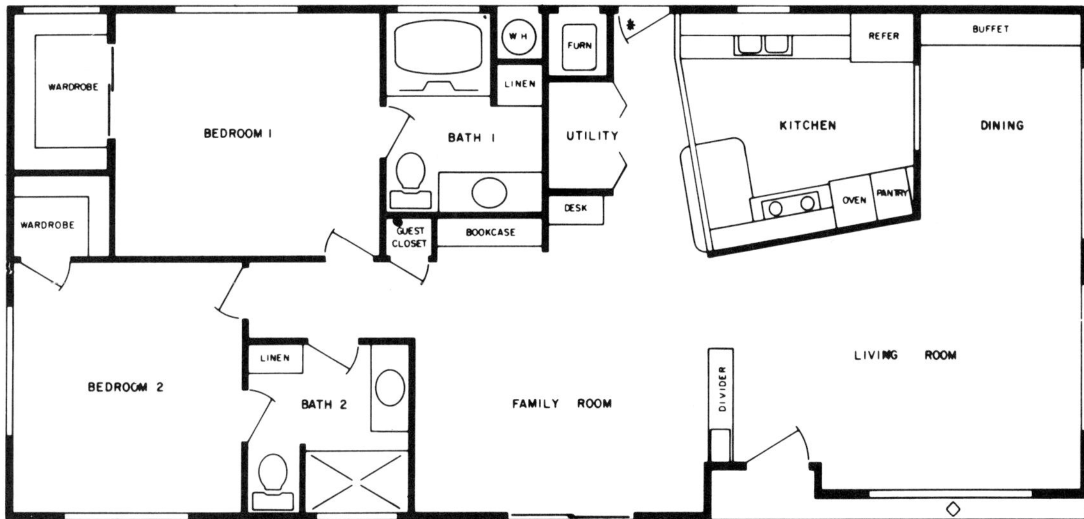

7-11

Hallways range from 36 inches to 42 inches wide. A 36 inch width is used for very short halls. A 40 inch width is the most common width used. A 42 inch width is used for very long halls or halls where wheelchairs are used regularly.

Individual rooms are usually separated by walls. However, some dwellings have large open areas that are divided into separate areas. ***Alcoves,*** which are small recessed sections of a room, and balconies are sometimes used. Screens, freestanding storage units, and careful arrangement of furniture can also be used to separate space according to function. Even when there are no walls dividing a room, you can see that the room is designed for different activities.

An advantage of open areas is that people in the home can be involved with more than one activity at a time. For instance, the kitchen may be open to the family room or living room. This allows the people preparing food or washing dishes to take part in other activities, such as watching TV.

Traffic Patterns

Have you ever been in a traffic jam as you were leaving a football game or concert? Often the police make plans to relieve the congestion by directing traffic and creating alternate routes.

Planning will also help prevent or reduce congestion in the traffic throughout a house. When space is organized well, people can move easily within a room, from room to room, or to the outside of the dwelling. The paths they follow are called ***traffic patterns.***

Traffic patterns need to provide enough space for people to move about freely. However, it is wasteful to use more space than is needed. As a rule, traffic patterns should be about 40 inches wide.

Traffic patterns should be designed so people can move throughout a house without disturbing other activities. For example, major traffic patterns should avoid the quiet area of a home, so it can remain quiet. Work areas are unsafe if people frequently walk through them. To avoid accidents, traffic patterns should lead to work areas, but not through them. Also, traffic patterns should not be located through social areas, since conversation, study, and TV viewing can be interrupted.

The easiest way to evaluate traffic patterns is to study floor plans. Look at the examples in 7-12. See if the following guidelines for safe and convenient traffic patterns have been followed. The traffic patterns

- Are convenient and direct.
- Provide adequate space, but do not waste space.

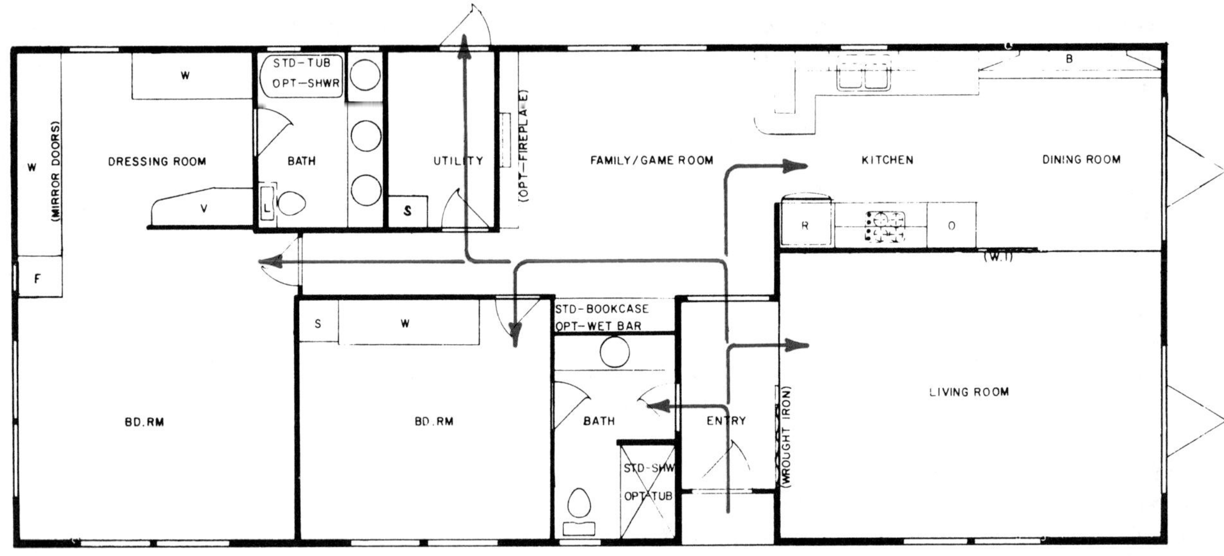

A

B

7-12
The main entry and the hall help direct traffic through house A. In house B, major traffic patterns go through the social area. Entertaining might be difficult in this house.

- Provide easy access from the entrances to other parts of the house.
- Separate traffic patterns to the work area from traffic patterns to the quiet and social areas.
- Avoid cutting through the middle of rooms.
- Do not interfere with a good furniture arrangement or interrupt activities within a room.
- Do not interfere with privacy in areas of the house where privacy is expected.
- Do not cut through kitchen work area or any other hazardous work area.

- Give the kitchen easy access to all areas of the home.
- Provide a direct access from the service entrance to a clean-up area.
- Provide access from service entrance to quiet area without going through social area.
- Provide direct access from utility area to outside service zone.

Space for doors. Outside doors and doors between rooms also help determine the flow of traffic. Other doors within a room may conceal storage. It is important that the space in front of these doors remain free. Blocked doors will stop traffic and cut off access to stored items.

Not only should the space immediately in front of doors be free, but there should be space for doors to swing and stand open. In 7-13, you can see the amount of space that is needed for different types of doors to swing open. People also need space to go through the doors or to get what they need from storage areas.

Survey the Storage Space

It is important to have plenty of storage space scattered throughout a house. When looking at house plans, look at what storage space is available. Make sure there is enough space to store all your belongings. Check to see if the storage space is located in convenient places. If you plan to use some rooms for more than one activity, make sure they have the storage space you need. For instance, you may plan to use the dining room as both a study area and a place to eat. Therefore, you will need space to store paper, pens, and reference books as well as dishes and table linens.

Looking at floor plans can help you evaluate the storage space of a home. A floor plan, such as the one in 7-14, shows the location of built-in storage units. ***Built-in storage*** cannot be sold, replaced, or moved like pieces of furniture. A section view would show the number of shelves and drawers in the storage unit. Floor plans also show how much floor space is available for additional storage, such as shelves and bookcases.

Planning for storage. If you plan to build a house or have one built for you, you will need to plan for storage. First, you need to determine the storage needs of each member of your living unit. Then you need to plan for ***common-use storage,*** which is storage used by all who live in a house. It includes the storage near the entrance where outerwear is kept and storage for food, tools, and other items that are shared.

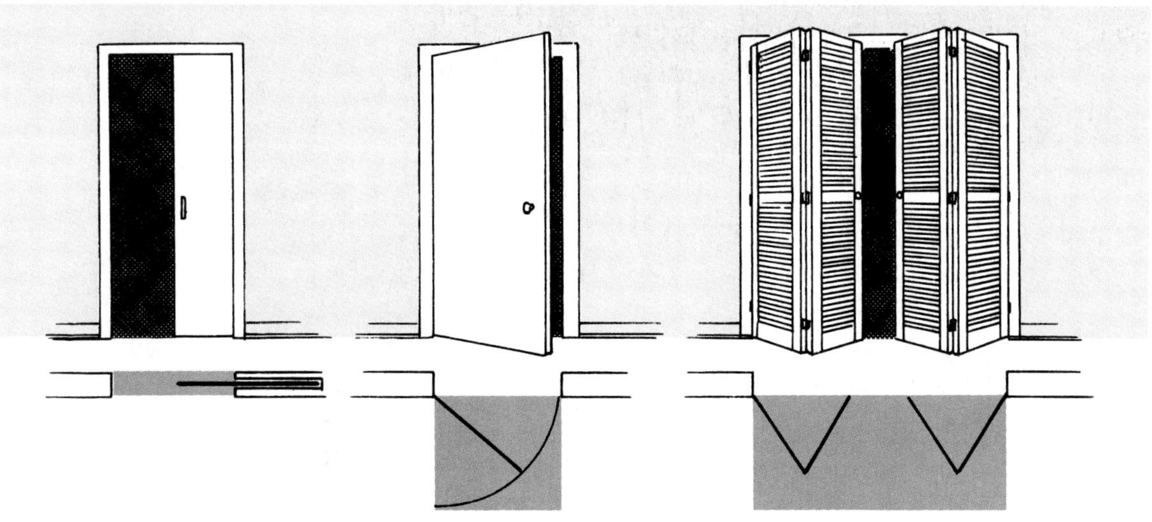

7-13
The colored areas show the amount of space that must be kept clear around each type of door.

7-14
This floor plan shows the location of closets, a pantry, and kitchen cabinets, which are all forms of built-in storage.

You can add to the amount of built-in storage available in a dwelling with storage units and storage furniture. Storage furniture includes desks, chests, and dressers. Another type is shown in 7-15.

Built-in storage, storage units, and storage furniture all have advantages. You cannot take built-in storage with you when you move, so you will not have the cost of moving it. Also, your home would increase in value if it includes built-in storage. Storage units, 7-16, can be moved easily, though some may need to be disassembled. Storage furniture can also be moved and taken with you.

Hold Everything

7-15
Armoires can be used in addition to built-in storage to hold household items.

Housing Modifications for People with Physical Disabilities

Housing should provide convenience, safety, and accessibility for all members of the living unit. This includes people with physical disabilities.

Hold Everything

7-16
These storage shelves can be easily disassembled and taken with you if you move.

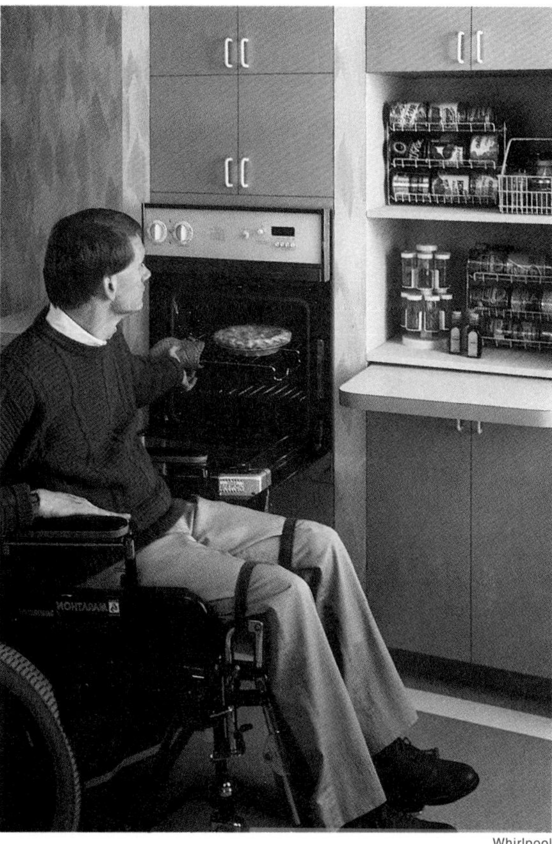

Whirlpool

7-17
Low overhead cabinets, C-shaped handles, and a wall oven make this kitchen more accessible for people with disabilities.

Houses for people with physical disabilities can be attractive and affordable. It is estimated that by spending only two percent above the base cost on a new house, it can be made barrier free. Also, the exterior and interior of existing houses can be modified at a reasonable cost to meet the needs of people with physical disabilities. The kitchen shown in 7-17 has been built for people with disabilities.

Exteriors. The exteriors of houses for people with physical disabilities should be as safe and accessible as possible. When building or choosing a house, keep the following points in mind:

- Lots should be flat for easy access.
- Entrance should face south, so ice and snow on sidewalks and the driveway will melt faster.
- Sidewalks, driveways, and garage floors should have nonskid surfaces, such as textured asphalt or concrete.
- Oil and debris should be kept off sidewalks, driveways, and garage floors.
- Driveways and garages should be wide enough to park cars and to move in and around wheelchairs.
- Garage door openers that light garages automatically should be used.
- Ramps with handrails should be installed for easy access to the house.
- Sidewalks, ramps, and entries need to be wide enough for wheelchairs to move easily. To allow for enough room on each side of a wheelchair, sidewalks should be four or five feet wide and entries should be three feet wide.
- Thresholds should be as level as possible to prevent stumbling.

- Automatic or push button-operated doors should be installed, since they are the easiest to use.
- Doors should be equipped with C or D shaped door levers or handles. They are easier to grasp and hold on to than conventional round knobs.
- Outdoor and entry areas should be well lit.

Interiors. The interiors of houses for people with physical disabilities should be even more barrier free than the exteriors. Since people spend most of their time inside, safety and accessibility are important. Keep the following points in mind when choosing a house:

- Stairs should have secure handrails that are thin enough to grip securely.
- Floors and stairs should be covered with wood or hard surface coverings for easy mobility. If carpet is used, it should have a low pile.
- Floor plans should allow for use of walker or wheelchairs.
- Open traffic lanes should lead directly to specific areas.
- Halls should be at least four feet wide to permit a wheelchair to turn into a room.
- Doors should be at least three feet wide. Doors that swing both directions or fold are easier to use.
- There should be room for wheelchairs to turn around inside a room.
- Storage space and equipment should be at a low level.
- Pull-out trays and drawers, 7-18, should be used. They are easier to use than cabinet shelves.
- Electric cooking appliances with easy access controls should be installed, since they are safe and convenient.
- Laundry equipment should be installed at convenient heights for the users.
- Electrical receptacles and switches should be placed at waist level.

Quaker Maid Cabinets

7-18
Pull-out storage is convenient for people with physical disabilities.

- Lavatories and toilets should be mounted on the wall for easy access.
- Showers or bathtubs should have doors for easy access.
- Faucet handles should be easy to grasp and use.
- A home elevator or stairway lift should be installed if the person's living quarters are on more than one level of the house.

If an existing house is not structurally suitable to be modified for a person with physical disabilities, a decision will need to be made. The person must decide if he or she can be satisfied living there anyway, or if he or she should look for another place to live. This is an important decision to make and should include all members of the living unit.

Summary

Architectural drawings contain information about the size, shape, and location of all parts of the house. They are drawn to scale, and prints are made. The drawings are often accompanied by specifications, which are written information about the drawings. To be able to understand architectural drawings, it helps to be familiar with the alphabet of lines and common symbols used on the drawings. Architectural drawings usually include different types of views. They include plan views, elevation views, and section and detail views.

After the drawings have been evaluated, the space within the house needs to be considered. Rooms in a house are usually grouped by function. The space is divided into three different areas–the quiet area, the work area, and the social area. These areas are separated by levels, hallways, walls, screens, freestanding storage units, and furniture arrangements.

Traffic patterns help prevent and reduce traffic congestion through the house. It is important to provide enough space for traffic and opening doors.

The space within should be organized to provide plenty of storage. Storage includes built-in storage, storage units, and storage furniture.

The exterior and interior space of a house sometimes needs to be modified to meet the needs of a member of the living unit who has physical disabilities. If a house is convenient, safe, and accessible for people with physical disabilities, it will meet the needs of anyone living in it.

To Review

Write your responses on a separate sheet of paper.

1. What does an architectural drawing contain?
2. If a drawing is drawn to 1″ = 1′-0″ scale, how can this scale also be written?
3. Which of the following would *not* be found in a print?
   a. Dimensions for the garage.
   b. Location of built-in storage.
   c. Location of furniture in a room.
   d. Room sizes and locations.
4. A(n) _____ _____ shows the arrangement of rooms, halls, and doors on one floor of a house.
5. Answer the following questions based on figure 7-4:
   a. How many windows are in the house?
   b. Where is the furnace located?
   c. The house has approximately how many square feet?
   d. The house has how many bathrooms?
   e. How many clothes closets are there?
6. The space in a house can be divided into three areas according to function. Name the three areas.
7. In a well-designed kitchen, what is the maximum length around a work triangle?
8. Explain two functions of hallways.
9. List five guidelines for good traffic patterns.
10. Name one advantage of built-in storage and one advantage of storage furniture.
11. Give two examples of how housing can be modified for people with physical disabilities.
12. Describe three features of a house interior that makes it barrier free.

To Do

1. Look at one of the floor plans shown in the chapter. Evaluate it as a house for your living unit by answering the following questions:
   a. Would all members of your living unit have enough space to satisfy their needs?
   b. Are the rooms grouped according to function?
   c. Are quiet areas away from public view and traffic?
   d. Which rooms could be used for more than one purpose?
   e. Are eating areas close to the kitchen?
   f. Is space provided for entertaining as well as day-to-day living?
   g. Are the entrances conveniently located?
   h. Are the traffic patterns safe and convenient?
   i. Is storage adequate and convenient?
   j. Is the house barrier free?
2. Using a number of floor plans, do each of the following:
   a. Shade the quiet areas, social areas, and work areas with different-colored pencils. Tell if they are divided as they should be. Justify your answer.
   b. Shade the traffic patterns. Check them with the guidelines listed in this chapter. Tell if they are safe and convenient.
   c. Tell which storage is for individual use and which is for common use.
   d. If living space has been modified for people with physical disabilities, indicate how it has been done.
3. Find or draw pictures to show one or more of the following:
   a. Ways to use a multipurpose room.
   b. Ways to modify housing for people with physical disabilities.
   c. Ways to increase storage space.

CHAPTER 8

House Construction

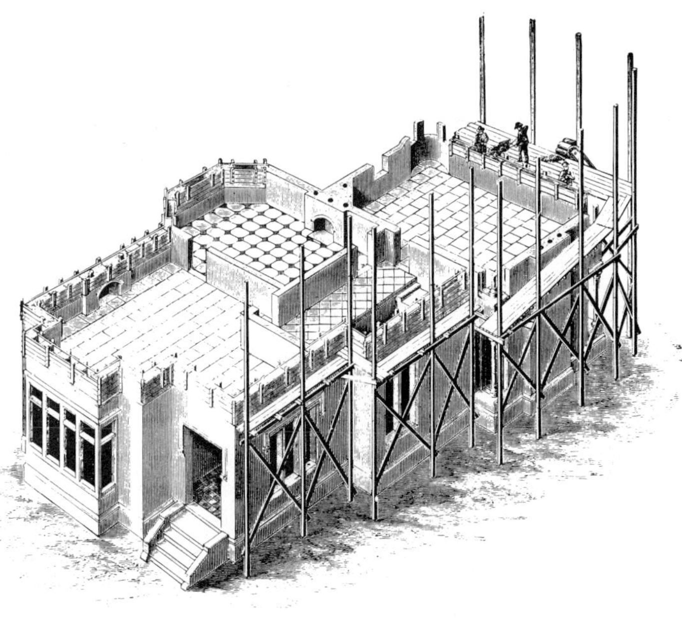

Lowden, Lowden and Co.

To Know
anchor bolt
bond
footing
foundation
foundation wall
frost line
girder
header
joist
rafter
ridge
siding
sill plate
shingle
stud
subflooring
truss rafter
veneer wall

Objectives

After studying this chapter, you will be able to:

- Describe how a house is constructed.
- List the parts of the foundation and frame of a house.
- List the advantages and disadvantages of different types of materials used for exterior construction.
- List basic types of windows used in houses.
- Distinguish between different types of doors.

When buying a pre-owned house or building a new house, it is helpful to understand how housing is constructed. You will be able to make good decisions and avoid poor investments. For example, in a pre-owned house, you will be able to detect structural damage or the need for major repairs, which are both expensive to correct. If you build a new house, you will know how it should be properly constructed.

Housing Begins with the Foundation and Frame

The foundation and frame are the basic structure of the house. Understanding how they are constructed is the first step in making an informed housing decision. When building a house, you will be able to observe the construction and make sure it is done correctly. When buying a pre-owned house, you may be able to inspect the foundation and frame for defects and needed repairs.

The Foundation

The ***foundation*** is the underlying base of the house. It is composed of the footing and the foundation walls. The very bottom of the foundation is called the ***footing,*** 8-1. Footings are usually made from concrete and are often reinforced with horizontal steel rods, called rebars, for added strength. The concrete and steel footing should be strong enough to support the rest of the foundation and the house. The footings need to be the correct width and thickness to support the weight of the foundation and house.

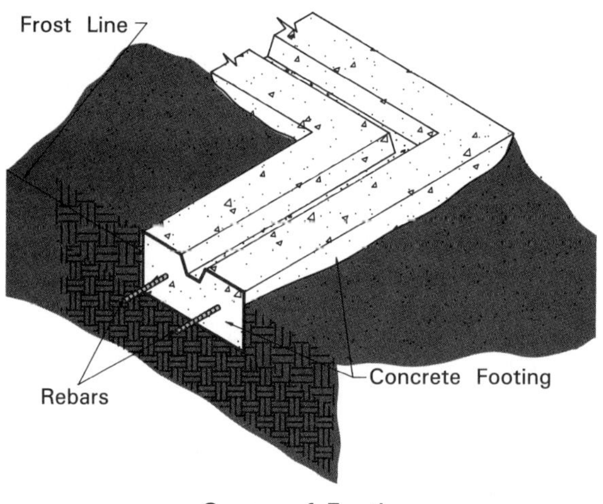

8-1
The footing is a wide concrete base that supports the foundation and the rest of the house.

Foundation walls support the load of the house between the footing and the floor. They form an enclosure for basements or crawl spaces. Foundation walls are commonly made from concrete or concrete block. Some may be constructed from pressure-treated timber. Thickness of the foundation wall varies from 6 to 10 inches. Wall thickness and requirements for reinforcements are normally controlled by local building codes.

Footings should be placed on undisturbed, compacted soil below the frost line. (The ***frost line*** is the depth to which frost penetrates soil in any climate.) If the footing is placed above the frost line, the soil under it could freeze and expand. This expansion causes the foundation to crack until the soil is compact again. It also causes cracks to appear in the foundation wall. In extreme cases, cracks will appear on inside walls. This cracking and settling will continue for years, and the cracks will continue to expand and lengthen.

Most foundations settle evenly as the house adjusts to the ground. The foundation and walls may show hairline cracks, which are cracks less than 1/8 inch wide. Cracks greater than 1/8 inch are considered excessive. The builder is required to surface patch these cracks.

Stress cracks differ from hairline cracks and are signs of possible structural problems. They are usually wider at one end than the other. Stress cracks can be caused when the footing has settled more at one point, and the foundation is beginning to be pulled apart from underneath. They can also indicate that one side of the house is settling more that the other.

How stress cracks are corrected depends on the extent of the damage and usually requires leveling the house and reinforcing the footing. This is a costly procedure. Unless the purchase price of the house is low enough to cover the cost of this problem, the prospective buyer should not purchase this type of house.

When looking at a pre-owned house, make sure that the foundation walls are straight and square at the corners. They should also be free from major stress cracks.

The Frame

The frame of the house consists of joists, studs, and rafters fastened together, so they work to support the house and its contents. See 8-2. When assembled and covered with sheet materials, they form floors, walls, and roof surfaces.

Lowden, Lowden and Co.

8-2
The framing members of the house provide the skeletal structure for the house.

Floor frame. After the foundation walls are completed, the floor frame is built. First, a sill sealer and sometimes a termite shield are placed on top of the walls. Then the first piece of lumber, which is called a ***sill plate,*** is bolted to the foundation wall with anchor bolts. ***Anchor bolts*** are set about six feet apart into the concrete of the foundation walls before the concrete hardens. If the foundation wall is made from concrete block, the top cores in the blocks are first filled with a sand and cement mixture called grout. Then the anchor bolts are embedded in the grout.

The floor frame is built on top of the sill plate or on top of wall frames when a second or third floor is desired. It consists of joists, girders, and subflooring. ***Joists*** are lightweight horizontal support members. Header joists and rim joists form the perimeter of the floor framing. The ends of the floor joists are nailed to the header joists at 16 inch intervals. They are supported by a girder, which is a horizontal piece of wood or steel. A ***girder*** is a large horizontal member in the floor that takes the end load of joists. It supports the load of the floor joists in the middle of wide rooms. The girder shown in 8-3 is built-up from three wooden planks nailed together. Subflooring covers the floor framing member. ***Subflooring*** is a covering of plywood sheets that is nailed directly to the floor joists.

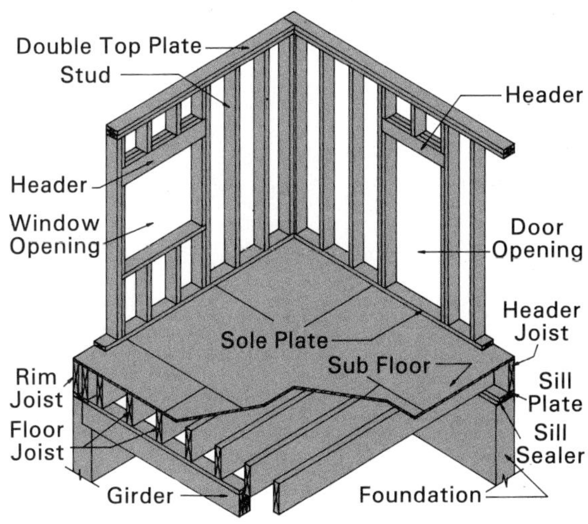

8-3
The floor and wall framing consists of joists, studs, girders, plates, headers, and subflooring.

The better the floor frame is constructed, the less likely it is to develop problems. Problems with floor frames are usually indicated by squeaky floors. Because normal vibrations over a period of time loosen the subflooring, many houses develop floor squeaks, especially in heavy traffic areas.

Wall frame. The wall frame is built on top of the floor frame. See 8-3. It is made from 2 inch by 4 inch or 2 inch by 6 inch vertical framing members called ***studs.*** Wall frames have a single *sole plate* on the bottom and a double *top plate* on top that support the ceiling joists and roof members. Exterior and interior walls are generally built flat on the subfloor and then raised and nailed into position on the floor frame.

Headers are small, built-up beams that carry the load of the structure over door and window openings. For a 6 inch-thick outside wall, headers are made from 2 inch by 10 inch lumber on edge with a piece of 1/2 inch plywood in between them to form a header that is 3-1/2 inches thick. See 8-3.

Wall frames are often plastered or covered with drywall. (See Chapter 14, "Creating Interior Backgrounds.") Cracks in these walls indicate that the wood in the frame has shrunk. Moisture from a leaky roof that causes the plaster to sag can be detected by sight or by hearing a dull sound when lightly tapping the wall.

Roof frame. The roof frame consists of a series of beams, called ***rafters,*** that support the roof. They extend from the exterior walls to the ridge. See 8-4. The ***ridge*** is the horizontal line at which the two slopes of the roof meet. It is the highest point of the roof frame.

In modern houses, most roof framing is done with truss rafters. A ***truss rafter*** is a group of members forming a rigid triangular framework for the roof. They are assembled at a factory and delivered to the job site. Then they are attached directly to the double top plate. Truss rafters usually span the distance between exterior walls.

As you evaluate the frame of the house, remember to look for stress cracks and hairline cracks. If you notice a sagging ceiling, it could indicate that the wrong size or type of lumber was used. Also, new houses have not settled yet and will not show problems. Pre-owned houses have had the chance to settle and probably will not deteriorate any further unless additions or remodeling takes place.

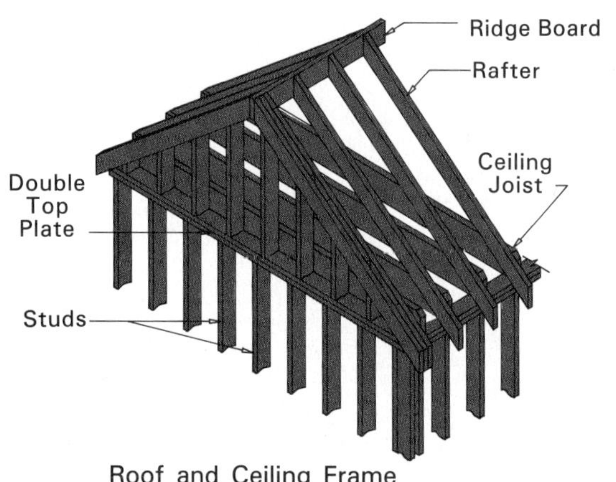

8-4
The roof and ceiling framing consists of plates, joists, rafters, and the ridge board.

Materials Used for Exterior Construction

After the foundation and frame are built, the exterior walls and the roof coverings are added. The materials used for exterior construction vary. The most common materials are wood, aluminum, vinyl, or acrylic-based. Masonry materials are also used. They include brick, block, stone, concrete, and stucco. The materials used depend upon the part of the country and the preference of the homeowners.

Wood Siding

Siding is the material forming the exposed surface of outside walls of a house. It is applied in strips, 8-5. Wood is the most common material used. It is suitable for a wide variety of exterior styles. It is also easy to cut and assemble. The ease of working with and fastening wood together with simple tools provides flexibility without extensive redesigning.

Wood siding is milled from cedar, redwood, pine, and cypress. One side is smooth and the

8-5
Wood siding is being applied to the side of this new house.

other is rough. Siding must be painted or stained and sealed to protect it against the elements.

Plywood siding is another type of wood siding. It can be applied horizontally or vertically. It covers large areas and saves installation time. Plywood siding must also be painted or stained and sealed unless a finish has been applied at the manufacturing mill.

Pressed wood siding is made from particleboard. Its surface is easy to paint but cannot be stained. It is less expensive than plywood siding. Special surface treatments, such as brushed, texture-embossed, and V-groove treatments, are available.

Manufactured Siding

Siding is also made from materials such as aluminum, vinyl, and fiberglass. Aluminum siding is durable and does not need to be repainted. It often has weather- and corrosion-resistant finishes. However, it does dent and may conduct electricity. Vinyl siding is also durable. It is less likely to dent and doesn't conduct electricity. However, it is brittle and more likely to crack or break. Fiberglass is used to make a siding that looks like wood shingles. This siding does not need finishes or to be painted.

When inspecting the exterior siding of a house, look for putty marks covered with paint. This may indicate that the siding was applied poorly or repaired. Also, a house that has siding covered up with putty and paint may have other problems that have been disguised.

Masonry Siding

Masonry products include brick, clay tile, concrete block, and stone. Sometimes, they are used to construct the entire exterior wall. Other times, a brick veneer wall is used to create the look of a masonry wall. A ***veneer wall*** is a nonsupporting wall tied to the wall frame that is covered with wallboard. See 8-6. (See Chapter 14, "Creating Interior Backgrounds.") Thin sheet metal ties are used to tie the veneer wall to the wallboard.

Masonry veneer walls are used in many areas of the country. Although masonry construction is often more expensive than wood construction, it is usually less expensive to maintain. Masonry houses usually last longer, too.

Masonry materials are available in a wide range of sizes, colors, and textures to produce different architectural effects. Other interesting effects can be created by the ***bond,*** or the way that masonry units are arranged together in a pattern. By varying the bonds and the depth and

Kate Shenberger Interiors, Flossmoor, Illinois

8-6
Brick is often used as an outside veneer on a wood frame to create a home with low maintenance and lasting beauty.

shape between units, additional depth dimensions and shadows can be added to the masonry wall.

When you examine a masonry house you need to look for cracks or bows in the walls. Hairline cracks in the joints are only normal expansion cracks. However, larger cracks can break bricks as they continue up or down the wall.

Roofing Materials

Common roofing materials include asphalt, fiberglass, vinyl, wood, tile, slate, concrete, and metal. These materials provide color and texture that make the exterior of the house more attractive. However, they must also provide a protective, watertight covering to keep out rain and snow. If the roof leaks, the structure of the house and its contents can be damaged.

Most houses have sloping roofs that are covered with shingles. ***Shingles*** are thin pieces of material for laying in overlapping rows on roofs. Asphalt shingles are the most common roofing material. They are inexpensive and easy to apply. Fiberglass and vinyl shingles are similar to asphalt shingles and come in a variety of textures and colors.

Wood shingles and *shakes,* a thicker shingle, are more expensive than asphalt shingles. They are treated with fire-retardant and decay-resistant chemicals. Shingles and shakes are popular because of their natural colors. They are most often used in parts of the country where cedar, redwood, and cypress trees grow.

In parts of the country with hot sun and little snowfall, tile, slate, and concrete roofing materials are often used. These materials are heavy and require proper roof design and structure to support the extra weight. See 8-7. These materials are very durable and will last the lifetime of the house.

Metal is also sometimes used as a roofing material. Aluminum and tin-plated steel are used in sheet form. Copper is used to accent small areas.

Most roofing materials are applied in the same manner. First, the roof frame is covered with sheathing, which is a sheet material such as plywood. Then the sheathing is covered with felt. This process will help keep out a limited amount of rain. Then, starting at the bottom of the roof, a starter strip of shingles is applied. The rest of the roof should be shingled in straight lines. The distance between the shingles should always be equal.

8-7
Roof tiles weigh about ten pounds each. This heavy load requires heavier rafters and other framing members to support the total weight of the roof.

When inspecting a roof, it is important to ask for reasons for every roof repair. You can tell if it has been patched instead of reroofed by looking for a change in the color of the shingles. Problems that required patching usually resurface at a later date.

Windows and Doors

When people first built dwellings, a window was an opening that provided ventilation. A door was an opening for entry and security. In the past, windows and doors did not fit houses well and allowed heat to escape from houses. They also provided very little insulation. Over time, many new types of windows and doors were developed. They were built to prevent air from escaping and to provide better insulation. Today a wide range of styles, shapes, and special options are available for both windows and doors.

Windows

Windows have many uses in a house. From the interior, they provide natural light, air circulation, and a view. They can also serve as a point of emphasis in a room or as a part of the background. On the exterior, their size, shape, and placement affect the appearance of the house.

Windows are made up of many parts. These parts include the frame, pane, sash, sill, and apron. See 8-8. Each sash may be divided into small sections by wooden dividers called *muntins* and *bars.* In the past, window frames were made from wood or aluminum. Today, as a result of strict local and national energy codes, new energy-efficient materials, such as vinyl and wood covered with aluminum or vinyl, are used.

There are three basic types of windows. They are *sliding* windows, *swinging* windows, and *fixed* windows. Other windows are a combination of these three. The type you choose for a house depends on the exterior style of the house, building codes, and personal preference. A traditional design, such as a Southern Colonial or French Provincial, looks best with a sliding window with muntins and bars. A contemporary house may feature large expanses of fixed windows.

Sliding windows. Sliding windows can operate either vertically or horizontally, 8-9. A *double-hung* window is a vertical sliding window. It provides an opening of about one-half the size of the window.

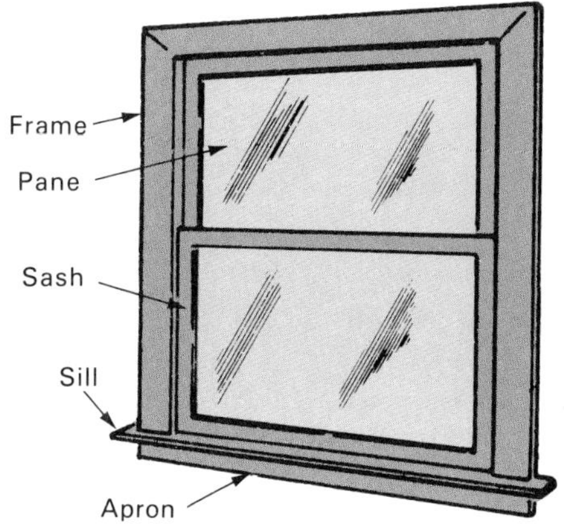

8-8
The five main parts of a window are the frame, sash, pane, sill, and apron.

Horizontal-sliding windows have two or three sashes. Two-sash windows have one sash that slides and the other that stays fixed. On a three-sash window, the center sash is fixed and the two outside sashes slide toward the center. Screens are mounted on the outside.

Swinging windows. There are four types of swinging windows. They are casement, awning, hopper, and jalousie windows, 8-10. *Casement* windows open and close with a crank and swing outward. Usually the entire window area can be opened for ventilation.

Awning windows swing outward at the bottom and are hinged at the top. This provides protection from rain. A similar window is the *hopper*

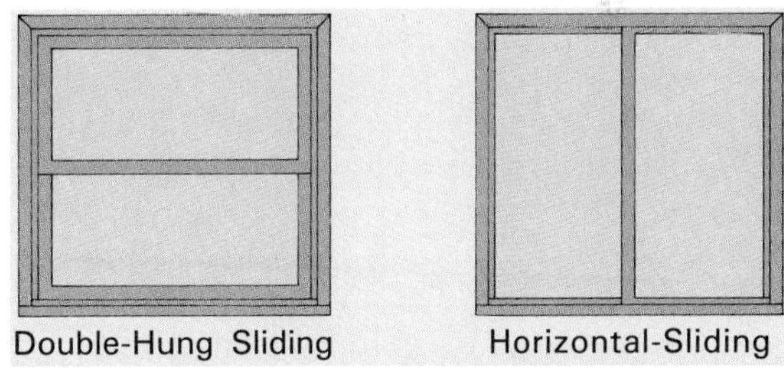

8-9
In double-hung windows, both sashes are operable. In two-sash horizontal-sliding windows, one sash is operable.

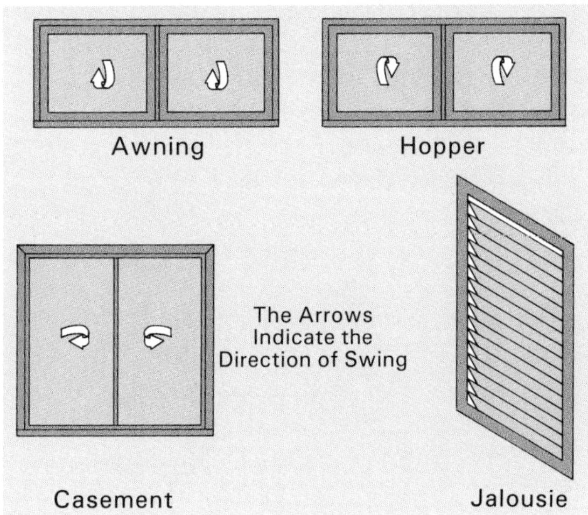

8-10
Awning, hopper, casement, and jalousie windows swing out to provide excellent ventilation.

window. It is hinged at the bottom, and the top of the sash swings inward.

Jalousie windows are a series of horizontal, adjustable glass slats fastened into a metal frame. They open and close with a crank and are used where ventilation is needed. Screens and storm windows are located on the interior.

Fixed windows. Fixed windows admit light and provide a view. However, they do not open. They come in many shapes and sizes including rectangular, 8-11, half-round, round, arched, and oval.

Combination windows. Fixed windows used in combination with other types of windows are called *combination windows.* For example, hopper windows are often used above a fixed window. A large fixed window can have a casement window on either side.

A *bay window* is a combination window that projects outward from the exterior wall of the house. It often has a large fixed window in the center and a double-hung window on either side.

Skylights and clerestory windows. Skylights and clerestory windows are used to let light into areas that get little or no natural light. They can also be used to add additional light to give a room an airy appearance. See 8-12. Skylights are normally located in the ceiling or roof. They can be a variety of shapes and sizes, depending on the design of the room. Clerestory windows are placed high on a wall. They can be standard windows or custom-made windows.

8-11
Fixed windows are used in areas where ventilation is not important.

Doors

Doors provide access, protection, safety, and privacy. They also provide a barrier against sound, extreme temperatures, and light. Exterior doors are made from wood or wood covered with metal or vinyl. Interior doors are made from wood, metal, or wood covered with vinyl.

Doors are often classified by their method of operation, 8-13. *Swinging doors* operate on

Velux-America, Inc.

8-12
The choice of windows plays an important part in the interior design of this house.

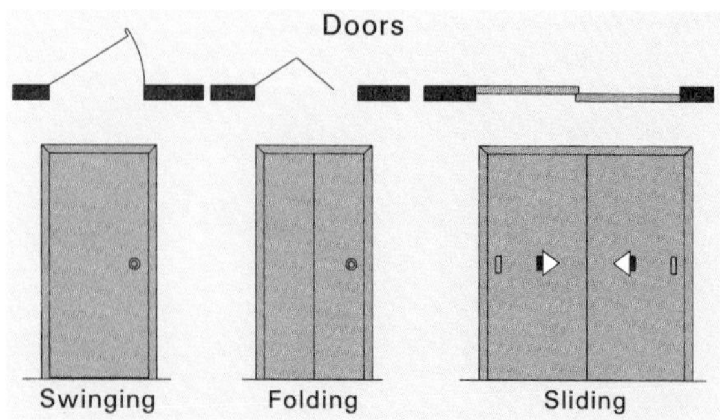

8-13
Doors operate in three different ways–by swinging, folding, or sliding.

hinges and usually swing open in one direction. Room needs to be left for the door to swing open and close. *Sliding doors* are set on a track and are opened or closed by gliding on the track. A *folding door* folds when open into a multisection stack.

Doors are also classified by their method of construction and assembly, 8-14.

Stile and rail doors. Stile and rail doors consist of stiles (solid vertical members), rails (solid horizontal members), and panels (space between stiles and rails). The panels may be decorative or glass. They may be raised or flat. Raised panels are cut from solid wood, and flat panels are usually cut from plywood. There is an unlimited number of panel combinations.

Flush doors. These doors are made by covering a framework core with wood or other material, such as metal or vinyl. There are two basic types of cores–solid and hollow. A *solid-core door* consists of tightly fitted blocks of wood covered with veneer. Sometimes particleboard is used as the core. These doors are heavy and are used mainly for exterior doors. A *hollow-core door* has a heavier outside frame combined with wood strips, stiff cardboard, or paper honeycomb as the core. This type of door is lightweight and is used mainly as an interior door.

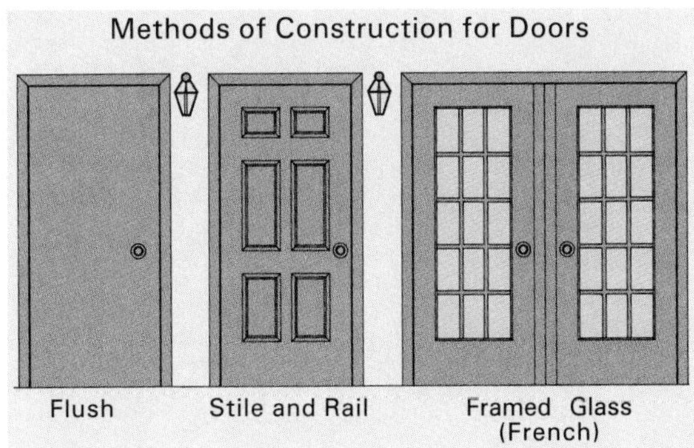

8-14
Doors can be constructed in many different ways including these three methods.

Framed-glass doors. These are stile and rail doors with glass panels. The glass may be single pane or insulating glass. *French doors* are framed-glass doors with the glass divided with muntins into small sections. French doors are usually installed in pairs. Sliding glass doors are another example of a framed-glass door. They often take the place of windows in small or medium-sized houses.

Summary

Understanding how houses are constructed helps house buyers make good decisions. The foundation and the frame are the basic structure of the house. The foundation supports the frame structure above it. It needs to be constructed correctly to prevent uneven settling. The frame consists of the floor frame, wall frame, and roof frame.

Once the foundation and frame are built, the exterior walls and the roof are added. A variety of materials are used. Those used for siding include wood, aluminum, vinyl, fiberglass, and masonry. Roofing materials include asphalt, fiberglass, vinyl, wood, tile, slate, concrete, and metal. It is important to closely inspect the exterior of the house.

Windows and doors complete the basic construction of the house. The three main types of windows are sliding, swinging, and fixed. Other windows are variations of these three types or combinations of them.

Doors are classified by their method of operation–swinging, sliding, or folding. They are also classified by the method of construction used to make them. These include stile and rail doors, flush doors, and framed-glass doors. There are also many variations of all these types.

To Review

Write your responses on a separate sheet of paper.

1. Why do footings need to be placed on undisturbed, compact soil below the frost line?
2. What structural problems might cause stress cracks?
3. List the three main parts of the frame that work together to support the house and its contents.
4. List three advantages of wood siding.
5. Compare the advantages and disadvantages of aluminum siding and vinyl siding.
6. List five types of roofing materials.
7. Match the names on the top with the types of windows below.

   _____ Jalousie.
   _____ Double-hung.
   _____ Awning.
   _____ Half-round.
   _____ Horizontal-sliding.
   _____ Casement.
   _____ Hopper.

   a. Fixed.
   b. Sliding.
   c. Swinging.
8. How is an interior door constructed differently from an exterior door?
9. What is the difference between a solid-core door and a hollow-core door?

To Do

1. Observe a house under construction. Then report what you saw to the class.
2. Make a sketch of the foundation and frame of a house and label each part.
3. Develop a house evaluation form that will help you inspect a structure for problems. Visit several houses that are for sale and evaluate them. Then, using the form, make a final evaluation as to which is the best house.
4. Research an exterior building material not discussed in the chapter and write a report on it.
5. Make a list of the sizes of the doors and windows in one room of your house. Take this list to a building supply company and obtain costs for replacing these windows and doors with energy-efficient units. Compare costs of various manufacturers.

CHAPTER 9

The Systems Within

The Kohler Company

To Know

ampere
central heat pump system
circuit
conductor
conduit
electric current
electricity
electric radiant heating system
fireplace insert
forced warm-air system
hydronic heating system
insulation
meter
overcurrent protection devices
R-value
service drop
service entrance panel
soil stack
trap
voltage
watt
weather stripping

Objectives

After studying this chapter, you will be able to:

- Describe the parts of the electrical system.
- Tell how natural gas and propane gas reach gas-burning appliances.
- Explain the functions of the two main parts of the plumbing system.
- List the different types of heating systems.
- Explain how a cooling system works.
- Identify ways to conserve energy in the house.

Almost every house has systems within it to make it more physically comfortable. These systems, usually called mechanical systems, control the interior temperature and provide electricity, gas, and water to the house.

Basic housing decisions regarding the systems within may include: Should I have gas or electric appliances? How can I make the house more energy-efficient? How much insulation do I really need? What type of windows are best for the climate? What new technology is being used in today's houses? These questions will be easier to answer after studying this chapter.

Electrical Systems

Almost all houses in the United States have electrical power. Electricity provides energy for lighting, the operation of appliances, 9-1, and the operation of most of the systems within the house.

Around your house, perhaps you've noticed words like "watts," "volts," or "amperes" on electrical appliances or even light bulbs. Understanding basic electricity will help you understand these terms and how the electrical system functions.

Electrical Terms

Electricity is the movement of electrons along a conductor. The ***conductor*** allows the flow of electricity and is usually a wire. The movement of electrons along a conductor is an ***electric current.*** This movement takes place at about the speed of light. The electrons follow a path from the source of the electricity to the device and back to the source. This is called a ***circuit.*** The circuit is made up of a delivery wire and a return wire.

Charlie Westerman/Zenith Electronics Corporation

9-1
Electricity allows this family to watch TV in a well-lit room.

The greater the number of electrons passing a given point in a circuit, the greater the current. The unit of current used to measure the amount of electricity passing through a conductor per unit of time is the ***ampere.*** A 100-watt light bulb requires a current of almost one ampere to make it work properly.

Voltage is a measure of the pressure used to push the electrical current along a conductor. This pressure is available in wiring circuits whether electricity is being used or not. The greater the voltage, the higher the current.

Electricity is delivered to your house by the electrical utility company at a voltage that will operate your lights, electrical appliances, and other electrical equipment. Lights and most small appliances require 120 volts. Larger appliances, such as the kitchen range, water heater, and furnace, may require 240 volts.

Electrical power is measured in ***watts.*** Watts are used by manufacturers and power companies to tell consumers how much electrical

power will be used when a device is being operated. For example, one watt of power is used when one ampere is used to light a 100-watt light bulb in a circuit with a force of one volt. This can be shown in the following equation:
Watts = Amperes x Volts.

Electrical Power Generation

Electrical power comes from a variety of sources. Power plants usually generate electrical current by converting the energy from falling water, atomic fission, or fossil fuels into electricity. Fossil fuels include coal, petroleum, and natural gas. These energy sources are often used to produce steam that turns turbines in generators to produce electricity.

Electricity is transmitted from the power plant at high voltages in wires held up by steel towers. When the electricity reaches the community, a transformer reduces the voltage and increases the current. The electricity is then distributed throughout a neighborhood in wires on poles or buried underground in a duct or conduit. A ***conduit*** is a metal or plastic pipe that surrounds and protects the wires.

Before the electricity reaches your house, another transformer lowers the voltage even further. A three-wire line from the transformer provides both 120 and 240 voltages for the house.

Electricity in the House

At the house, the electric company installs a service drop. A ***service drop*** is the connecting wires from the pole transformer to the point of entry to the house, 9-2. Wires can also be run underground to the house through a *service lateral.* In both instances, the three wires are run to the electric meter to the service entrance panel. The ***meter*** monitors electrical usage in the house. It is periodically read by a power company representative to determine how much power has been used.

The ***service entrance panel*** is a large metal box that receives power from the electric company's service drop or service lateral. It divides the power into individual circuits. These circuits are needed to provide electricity to each room or combination of rooms in the house. See 9-3. Each circuit is protected by either a *fuse* or *circuit breaker.* They are both ***overcurrent protection devices*** that stop the excessive flow of electrical current in the circuit if too much current is being drawn. If trouble develops on one circuit, only that circuit will be out of operation when the fuse blows or circuit breaker trips. Fuses were used mainly in older houses, and circuit breakers are used in newer houses.

Electricians install the wiring inside the house from the service entrance panel to all electrical appliances and devices requiring power.

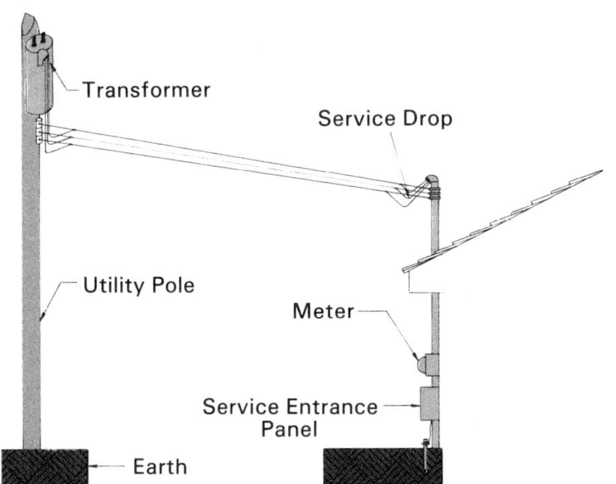

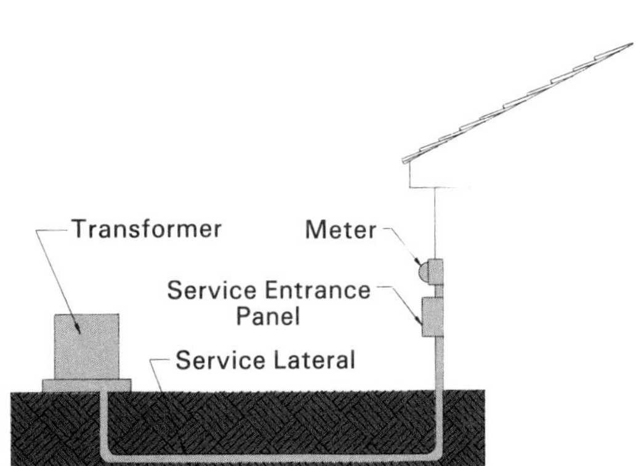

9-2
Electricity travels from the power plant to your house via conductors, which carry the electric current.

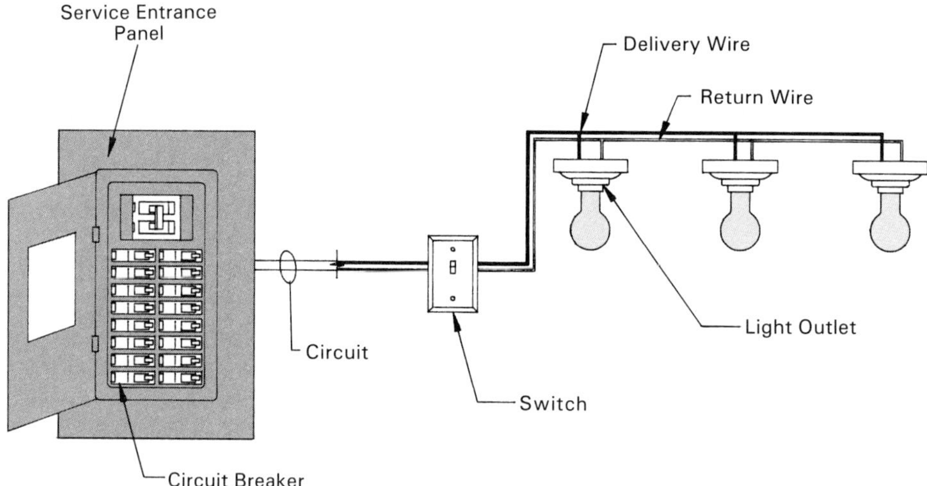

9-3
A circuit carries electricity from the service entrance panel to the electrical devices in your house.

They may include systems, such as telephone, doorbell, intercom, thermostat, fire detection, security, computers, and cable TV. (The installation of some systems may require workers with specialized electrical skills.) Wiring is installed while the wall framing is open and accessible. An electrical code authority is required to inspect the wiring installation while it is still visible.

Wiring requires advance planning of room use and possible furniture placement. No point along the floor line should be more than six feet from an outlet. Each room should have at least three outlets. Telephone jacks may be placed in each room. If cable TV is available, TV jacks may be installed in several rooms.

Gas As an Energy Source

Many houses use gas as an additional source of energy. It is a popular fuel for cooking, heating water, heating air in furnaces, and heating water in boilers. Gas fuels include natural gas, which is piped from a gas main to your house, and liquid propane gas, which is delivered in pressurized tanks to your house.

Natural Gas

Natural gas is taken from wells in the ground. From the gas fields, high-pressure pumps force the gas through large pipelines to communities, 9-4. Then the pressure is reduced, and the gas is distributed throughout the community in pipes called gas mains. To furnish gas to your house, the gas company taps the main and lays an underground pipe to your house. A gas meter is placed where the line enters your house. Like an electric meter, it records the amount of fuel used.

9-4
Natural gas is transported in large pipes to communities where it is distributed to houses through gas mains.

In the house, the plumber installs branch lines to all gas-burning appliances. Black pipe and fittings are used for the branch lines. A pipe thread compound, which prevents the leakage of natural gas, is used on all fittings. The system must be checked for leaks before it is used.

Liquid Propane Gas

Propane is a colorless, odorless gas. It is used as fuel by houses that normally do not have access to a natural gas line. Propane is produced at oil refineries from natural gas, crude oil, or oil refinery gases. Gas supply companies then deliver the liquid petroleum gas (LPG) in tanker trucks to each house as needed. It is required that LPG be stored in large, pressurized metal tanks on concrete pads in the yard. The tanks are then hooked up to the house.

LPG has about twice the heating value of natural gas per cubic foot. However, with the cost of delivery and storage requirements, it is normally more expensive than natural gas.

Plumbing Systems

The plumbing system in a house provides water to the house and removes water-borne waste from it. (The gas lines discussed above are also considered part of the plumbing system.) A water supply system supplies sufficient hot and cold water, so fixtures and appliances can function properly. A wastewater removal system removes the waste and used water and deposits them into a sewer line or private septic tank.

Water Supply System

Water is supplied, under pressure, to your house from a community water main or a private well or system. It enters the house through a pipe called the building main. Inside the house, the water may pass through a water softener, filter, or another treatment device. It then divides into cold and hot water mains. The hot water main starts at the water heater. Hot and cold water branch lines travel throughout the house to each fixture or appliance that has a water requirement.

Piping for the water supply system is located in the floor, walls, or ceiling of a house. Water lines are usually made of 3/4 inch diameter copper, plastic, or galvanized steel pipes. See 9-5. Local codes may restrict the use of certain types of pipe. The lines are usually under a pressure of 45 to 60 pounds per square inch (psi).

A shutoff valve is installed in the building main next to the water meter and on each branch line next to the fixture or appliance. Shutoff valves make it possible to repair separate parts of the system without shutting off the water for the entire house. A leak in the main water line requires that the valve at the meter be closed.

Wastewater Removal System

In the house, water-borne waste comes mainly from bathrooms, kitchens, and laundry areas. Since it tends to decompose quickly, the waste needs to be removed before it causes odors or becomes hazardous to your health.

Waste disposal pipes are completely separate from the water supply system. They are much larger than water supply lines and are not pressurized, 9-5. Instead, they rely on gravity to remove waste. The size of wastewater piping is

Lowden, Lowden and Co.

9-5
The small metal pipes are the cold and hot water lines. The large white pipes are the waste disposal pipe and soil stack.

determined by the number and type of plumbing fixtures that discharge into the line. Different types of piping, such as plastic, cast iron, copper, and brass alloy, are used. Local codes specify the types and size of pipes to use.

As the wastewater leaves the house, it is either transported to the community sewer lines or a private septic tank. Wastewater that goes through the community sewer lines ends up in treatment systems and is usually recycled. The recycled wastewater can be used for industrial and irrigation purposes.

A septic tank is used when access to community sewer lines is unavailable. In this case, the wastewater flows into the underground septic tank. Bacteria dissolve much of the waste that settles to the bottom of the tank. The liquid wastewater on top of the tank flows out into a system of perforated underground pipes called a *leach bed.* Here the wastewater is dispersed into the soil.

Gases from the wastewater removal system must also be removed. A ***soil stack*** is a vertical pipe that extends through the roof, so gases may vent outside. It also allows the water and waste to drain down. Each house has at least one soil stack for each toilet.

Each plumbing fixture has a ***trap,*** which is a device that catches and holds a quantity of water. This water forms a seal that prevents the sewage gases from coming back into the house. Traps are installed at each fixture unless the fixture has a built-in trap as in the case of a toilet.

Plumbing Fixtures

A plumbing fixture is a device that is connected to the plumbing system. Plumbing fixtures include kitchen sinks, lavatories, toilets, and bathtubs. Modern plumbing fixtures are made from a variety of materials. These materials include enameled cast iron, enameled steel, stainless steel, fiberglass, and plastics. These materials are chosen because they are durable, corrosion-resistant, nonabsorbent, and have a smooth, easy-to-clean surface.

A kitchen sink is a flat-bottomed plumbing fixture used for food preparation and cleaning dishes and other equipment used in food preparation. Sinks are available in a large variety of sizes and shapes. The most common is the double-compartment sink, which is installed on a cabinet countertop.

A lavatory is a plumbing fixture designed for washing hands and faces. It is commonly found in bathrooms. Lavatories come in a variety of colors, sizes, and shapes. They are available in wall-hung and vanity-top models.

A toilet is a water-flushed plumbing fixture designed to receive human wastes. Toilets are usually made of glass-like china. They are installed either directly on the floor or suspended from the wall.

A bathtub is a fixed tub designed to hold water for bathing. It comes in a variety of shapes. The most common is rectangular. Most tubs have shower heads installed above them.

Heating Systems

A house may be heated with one of four conventional heating systems. They are forced warm-air, hydronic, electric radiant, and central heat pump systems. Houses can also be heated by nonconventional heating systems, such as solar heat, fireplaces, and stoves.

Conventional Heating Systems

Electricity, gas, oil, or coal are used to fuel conventional heating systems. However, coal is rarely used in newly-built houses today. The choice of which energy source to use is based on availability and the cost of fuel and operation. Environmental concerns also influence the choice of fuels.

Forced warm-air system. In the ***forced warm-air system,*** the air is heated by a furnace and then delivered to the rooms through supply ducts. See 9-6. Gas, oil, or electricity is used to heat the air in the furnace. Then the blower moves the heated air through the supply ducts to the area being heated. Another set of ducts, called the cold air return, carries the cool air from each room back to the furnace. This movement of warm and cool air continues until the desired temperature is reached. A thermostat in the living area indicates and controls the desired temperature.

9-6
In a forced warm-air system, supply ducts are located under the floor and in the attic.

Forced warm-air systems are economical and easy to install. Heating ducts can also be used for cooling, and filters are often put in the system to control dust. The heating unit can be located in the house wherever it is convenient. However, the ducts require a large amount of space. Also, the rapid air movement is objectionable to some people and some systems are noisy.

Hydronic heating system. Circulating hot water systems are called ***hydronic heating systems.*** Water is heated in a boiler to a preset temperature, usually 180°F to 210°F. When the water reaches the proper temperature, it is pumped through pipes to radiators, 9-7. As the water cools, it returns to the boiler for reheating. Radiators are located throughout the living areas, usually along the outside walls to increase comfort and reduce cold air drafts.

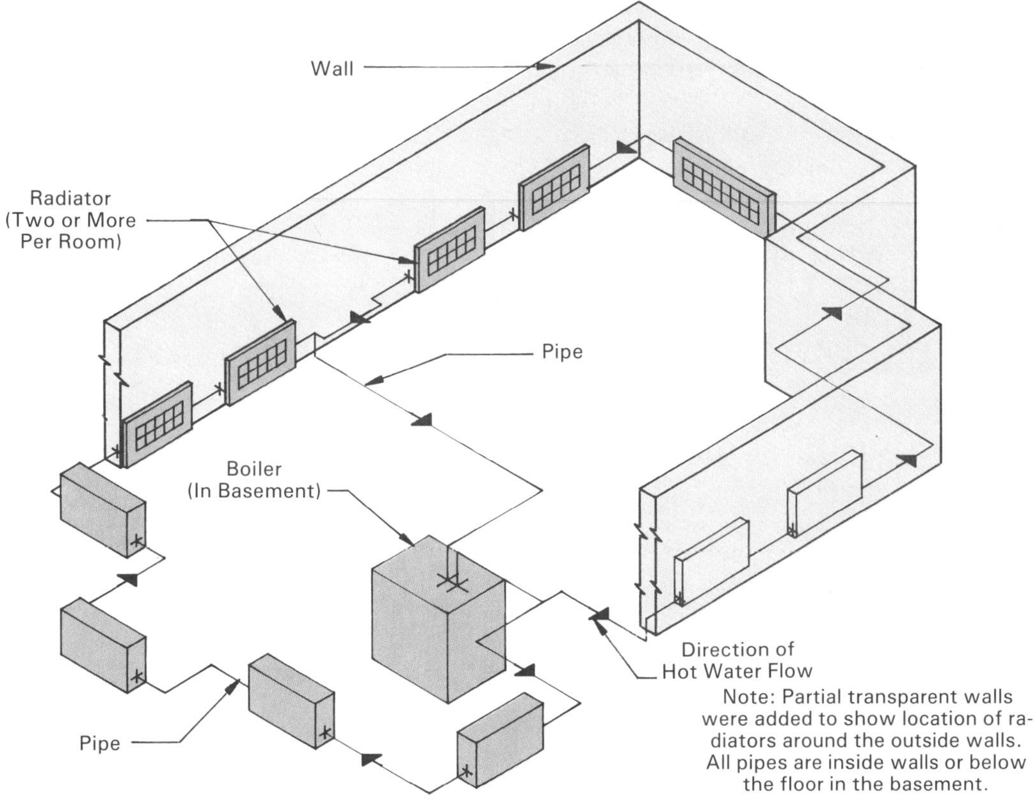

9-7
Hot water is pumped from the boiler to the radiators in individual rooms. Cool water is returned to the boiler for reheating.

Hot water may also be circulated through copper tubing embedded in a concrete floor or plaster ceiling. The tubing is laid in a coil or a grid configuration. The heat then radiates from the floor or ceiling into the room. This system is often used in mild climates. It may also be used as a back-up heating system.

Hydronic heating systems are a quiet, clean, and efficient type of heat that doesn't create drafts. However, a longer period of time is needed to bring the room temperature up to the desired level. Hydronic heating systems normally don't provide for cooling, air filtration, or humidification.

Electric radiant heating system. ***Electric radiant heating systems*** use resistance wiring to produce heat in the wire. The wire is placed in the ceiling, floor, or baseboards. The heat moves from the wiring through the air. This is because heat travels from hot objects to cooler objects. Individual thermostats control the temperature in each room.

This type of heating system allows complete freedom in furniture and drapery placement. No air is introduced, no radiators are used, and air movement from the system is almost nonexistent. Disadvantages of the electric radiant heating system include the high cost of electrical energy and the installation costs. This type of system should also be installed when the house is built.

Central heat pump system. A ***central heat pump system*** is an electric refrigeration unit used to either heat or cool the house. It removes heat from the outside air or ground in cold weather. In warm weather, it removes heat from the air in the house. The heat pump consists of liquid refrigerant, a compressor, and heat exchangers. A fan circulates the heated or cooled air through the house. See 9-8.

A central heat pump system is most efficient in moderate to mild winter climates above 20°F. It usually costs more than other heating systems. However, it does cost less than buying both a heating system and an air-conditioning unit.

Solar Heating Systems

Solar heating systems use energy from the sun to provide heating and oftentimes cooling and hot water for a house. Solar heating systems often have a back-up heating system, such as a wood or pellet stove, to compensate for long periods of cloudy weather. The two main types of solar heating systems are active and passive. Both systems consist of a collector and a storage area.

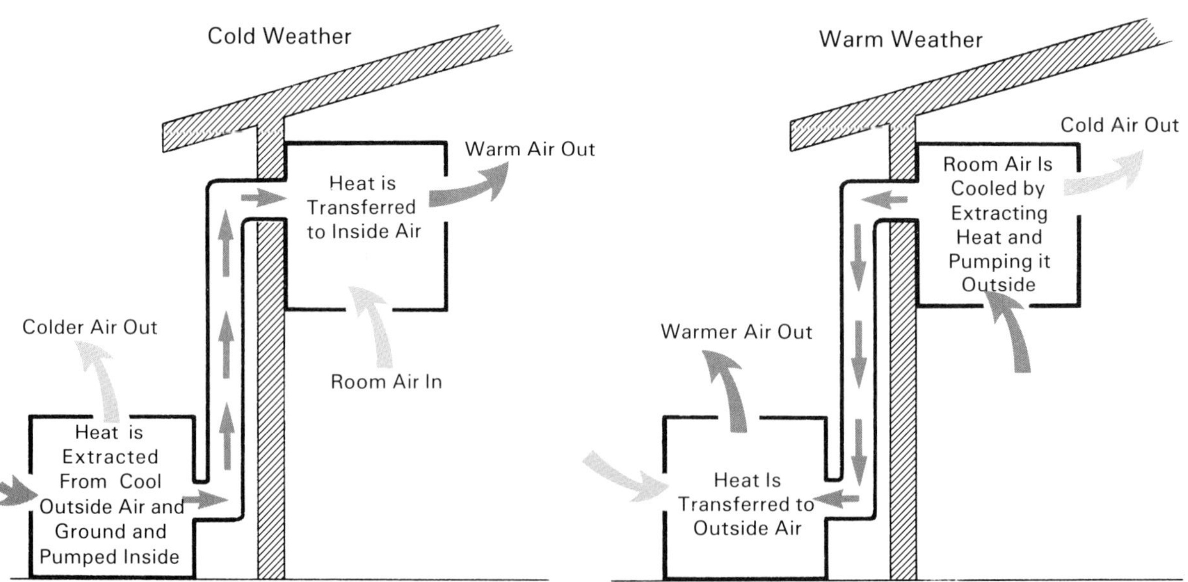

9-8
In cold weather, the heat pump absorbs heat from the air and ground outside and pumps it inside. In warm weather, the heat pump absorbs heat from the air inside the house and pumps it outside.

Active systems. Active systems have solar collector panels on the roof of the house. This type of system requires mechanical devices, such as pumps or fans, to move the heat from the collectors to a storage area or to the space requiring heat.

Passive systems. Passive systems have no solar panels. Instead, they rely on the construction materials to collect and store the sun's heat. Windows, doorways, greenhouses, or skylights act as solar collectors. Walls and floors made from masonry materials, such as concrete, concrete block, brick, stone, and adobe, absorb the heat and act as the storage areas. Water storage walls or tanks also store heat effectively.

Fireplaces and Stoves

Fireplaces and stoves are used as a heat source, as well as a focal point. They are different than the fireplaces and stoves used in the past. They are safer, cleaner, and more efficient. However, wood-burning fireplaces and stoves still require firewood that must be cut, split, and stacked. Moving wood from outside the house to the location of the fireplace or stove can leave debris on the floor. Also, after a long period of use, most stoves and fireplaces produce a light film of smoke in the room.

Fireplaces. Fireplaces need to be carefully designed and built to operate correctly and to prevent heat loss when not in use. Most fireplaces today are built with a single opening, or face, in the front. Some are also built with two or even three openings. Metal, freestanding fireplaces are often used in contemporary houses.

Traditional fireplaces are made from masonry, while newer ones are often made from metal. Metal fireplaces may be covered with brick or other materials, so they look like solid masonry. Many of these new units are wood burning. However, some use electricity or gas to give the appearance of a wood fire.

A fireplace consists of a hearth, firebox, damper, smoke shelf, chimney, and flue. See 9-9. The hearth is the flat area where the fire is built and the apron is in front of the fire area. The firebox is the combustion chamber. It is lined with firebrick, which is made from fire-resistant clay. A damper is a metal device that is used to close off the airflow when the fireplace is not in use. The smoke shelf is where the smoke collects before going up the chimney. It also prevents outside air currents from forcing smoke back into the room. The flue carries smoke up out of the house and creates a draft for the fire. The flue is lined with special tiles or metal liners that resist high temperatures. The chimney takes the smoke out of the house.

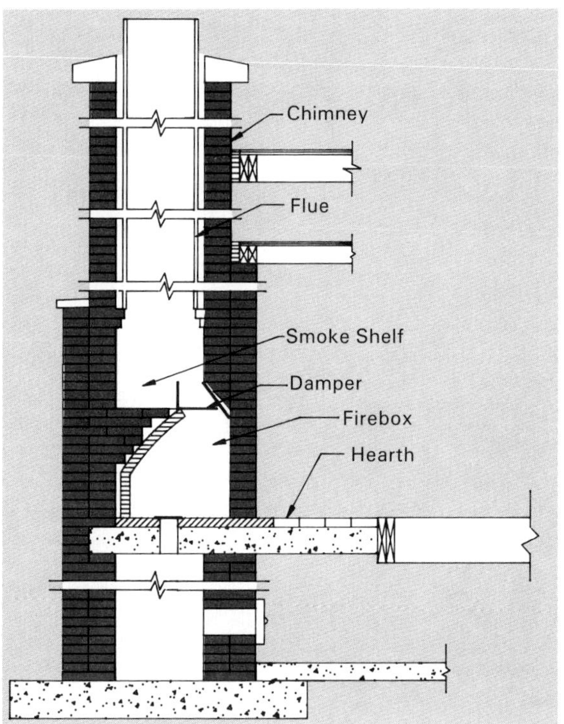

9-9
Each part of the fireplace plays an important role in the efficient burning of wood and removal of smoke.

A ***fireplace insert*** is a metal device that fits into an existing masonry fireplace (and some factory-built fireplaces) and attaches to the chimney liner. Fireplace inserts are used to transform a drafty fireplace into a more energy-efficient fireplace.

A fireplace insert draws air into the fireplace from the room. It circulates the air around a heat exchange and then blows the air back into the room. Heat detecting sensors on the insert automatically shut off the blower when the room reaches a set temperature. This results in energy costs savings, because fireplaces with inserts normally have an efficiency of about 70 percent. Fireplaces without inserts have an efficiency of 15 to 35 percent.

Stoves. Stoves usually produce more heat than fireplaces. They use coal or wood to generate heat. There are two main types of stoves. *Radiant stoves* produce heat that radiates through the room to cooler objects. The surfaces of these stoves are extremely hot. Flammable materials must be kept away from them.

In *circulating stoves,* the main fire area is separated from the outside of the stove by a compartment. Air circulates into and out of the compartment, taking heat into the room. Sometimes a fan helps the air move through the compartment. A thermostat is used to control the level of heat entering the room. These stoves are safer than radiant stoves, because they produce less smoke and exposed surfaces are not as hot.

Stoves have become more efficient and burn cleaner than in the past. This is because standards for stoves have been established by the Environmental Protection Agency (EPA). These standards require that stoves release a limited amount of smoke out of the chimney each hour. They must also produce more heat per unit of fuel. These two standards help to assure a cleaner and safer environment.

Another type of stove is the *pellet stove.* See 9-10. It is designed to burn waste wood or other organic materials. The waste materials are compressed into pellets resembling rabbit food. One ton of pellets generates about 17 million British thermal units (Btu) of heat. A wood-burning stove generates about 8 to 10 million Btu per cord of firewood. Usually, only a handful of pellets are burned at a time. This results in high combustion efficiency, which means less ash and no visible smoke. Instead of the conventional chimney, a vent is required.

9-10
A pellet stove is a highly-efficient and functional heating unit.

Cooling Systems

Cooling systems provide cool, clean, dehumidified air during hot, humid weather. Central air conditioners are the most common in houses. Room air conditioners are not cooling systems, but they are used for cooling rooms in houses.

The most common cooling system is the compressor-cycle system. It uses a compressed refrigerant to absorb heat and therefore, cool the air. The refrigerant absorbs heat as it passes through the evaporator coil and changes from a liquid to a gas. The gas passes through a compressor, where it is pressurized. The hot, pressurized gas passes through the condenser coil, where it gives up heat and changes back to a liquid. Moving through the liquid line, it passes through a metering device into the evaporator coil to begin the cycle again. See 9-11.

When the room air is cooled, moisture in the air condenses on the fins of the condenser and is drained away. This process dehumidifies the air and increases the comfort level. The cooler air is moved to various parts of the living space through a system of ducts. A blower is used to move the air through the ducts. These ducts may be the same as for the heating system.

In a central air-conditioning system, the compressor and the condenser unit are placed outside the building. In a room air conditioner, all components are contained in one unit. A part of this unit extends outside through a window, door, or wall opening.

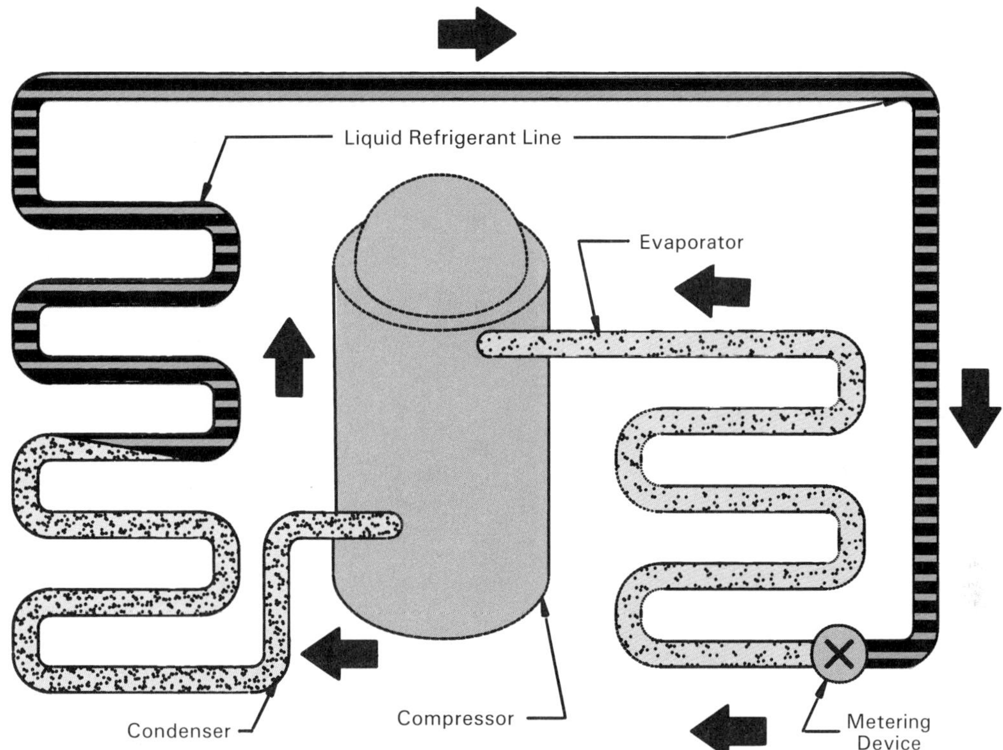

9-11
This diagram shows the path the refrigerant takes as it moves through the compressor-cycle system.

Conserving Energy

About one-fifth of all the energy used in this country is used in housing. Currently, legislation is pending that will enact strict measures to improve the energy-efficient construction of houses. The stated goal of the U.S. Department of Energy is to reduce energy consumption in houses by 50 percent. This applies to both new and existing houses. Building code authorities in cooperation with the National Association of Home Builders of the United States (NAHB) are promoting this new Model Energy Code.

Insulation and energy-efficient windows and doors can help conserve energy within the house. Computerized control systems for total energy management can also save energy.

Insulation

One of the best ways to conserve energy is by surrounding the living space with proper insulation during house construction. ***Insulation*** is material used to restrict the flow of heat from out of the house in the winter and into the house in the summer. It has millions of tiny air pockets that resist the flow of heat through the material. The resistance of a material to heat movement is called its ***R-value.*** The larger the R-value, the more resistance the material has to heat movement.

Insulation is made from a variety of materials that differ in efficiency, quality, and safety. These materials include fibrous glass, rock wool, cellulose, urethane, polystyrene, and urea formaldehyde. Insulation is available in blanket, board, and loose fill forms. Each has different uses and shapes and meets different requirements.

Blanket insulation comes in long rolls or *batts,* which are shorter rolls usually 4 to 8 feet long. Both rolls and batts come in 16 to 24 inch widths and in various thicknesses. The thicker the insulation, the shorter the roll. Blanket insulation is commonly used in attics, floors, walls, and around pipes and ducts. See 9-12.

Board insulation is made from rigid foamed plastics. It is available in sheets 1/2 inch to 4 inches thick. It is usually 2 feet by 4 feet or 4 feet by 8 feet in size. The R-value per inch of thickness is higher than for other forms of insulation. However, it also tends to be more expensive. Board insulation is used between concrete and earth, around foundation walls, and on one side of the footing. It is also used on the outside of studs as sheathing.

Loose fill is used in inaccessible spaces where other types of insulation are difficult to install. It may also be used in attics, inside frame walls, in cores of concrete block, and as filler between other types of insulation. It comes in bags and may be poured or blown into place.

As energy costs increase, adding additional insulation is usually justified to help increase lower energy consumption. In some areas of the country, heating costs determine how much insulation should be used; in others, air-conditioning costs are the major influence. In many areas, both heating and air-conditioning contribute to the recommendations shown in table 9-13. These figures reflect national, state, and local recommendations. To use this information, look on the map and find the zone in which you live. Then use the R-values shown for that zone as a guide for your insulation needs.

Lowden, Lowden and Co.

9-12
Blanket insulation is used here to insulate a wall.

Windows and Doors

Heat loss around windows and doors and through glass panes has always been an energy problem. Adding weather stripping to windows and doors helps prevent drafts and heat transfer. ***Weather stripping*** is a strip of material that covers the edges of a window or door to prevent moisture and air from entering the house. Another way to conserve energy is to add storm windows to single-panel glass windows. Dead air space between the storm windows and regular windows acts as an insulator.

It is possible to buy and install windows that have double or even triple the insulation value of single-panel windows. Other windows are available that contain two or three gas-filled insulating chambers that block almost all of the sun's ultraviolet rays. See 9-14. This means more daylight with less winter heat loss and less summer heat gain.

The need for energy efficiency is not limited to windows. Sliding patio doors feature the same double and triple panel system as windows. All types of doors can be weather-stripped. Wood doors can be covered with metal or other materials to prevent warping. Door construction and installation has evolved so that doors are now both attractive and energy efficient.

Energy Conservation through Computers

Personal computers, when used with certain software packages, can be used to manage the energy systems within a house. They can reduce energy use by 20 to 40 percent by monitoring anything within the house that can be controlled electronically. This includes appliances, mechanical products, electrical products, and communication products.

The computer can do a wide variety of tasks to conserve energy. It can control lighting, the interior climate, and maintenance systems. For example, it can:

- Turn lights on and off automatically as people enter and leave rooms.
- Roll shades up and down automatically to admit sun or block out cold.
- Adjust heating, ventilation, and air-conditioning systems to current outdoor weather conditions.
- Adjust the interior temperature according to activities going on in the house.
- Report maintenance and equipment problems automatically, so the total climate comfort and maximum use of equipment is maintained.
- Monitor climate control system for dirty filters, so the efficiency of this system can be maximized.

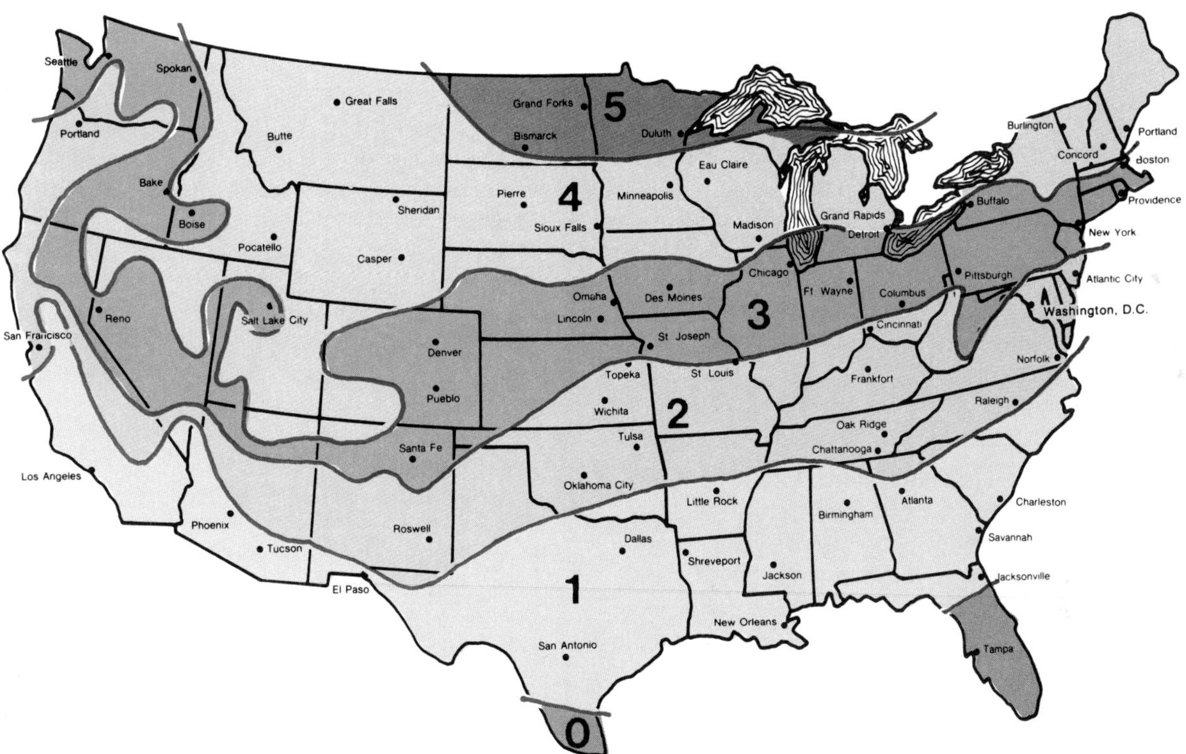

Recommended R-Values				R-Values Chart					
					Batts or Blankets		Loose Fill (Poured in)		
Heating Zone	Attic Floors	Exterior Walls	Ceilings Over Unheated Crawl Space or Basement		glass fiber	rock wool	glass fiber	rock wool	cellulosic fiber
1	R-26	R-Value of full wall	R-11	R-11	3½″-4″	3″	5″	4″	3″
2	R-26	insulation, which is	R-13	R-13	4″	4½″	6″	4½″	3½″
3	R-30	3½″ thick, will	R-19	R-19	6″-6½″	5¼″	8″-9″	6″-7″	5″
4	R-33	depend on material	R-22	R-22	6½″	6″	10″	7″-8″	6″
5	R-38	used. Range is R-11	R-22	R-26	8″	8½″	12″	9″	7″-7½″
		to R-13.		R-30	9½″-10½″	9″	13″-14″	10″-11″	8″
				R-33	11″	10″	15″	11″-12″	9″
				R-38	12″-13″	10½″	17″-18″	13″-14″	10″-11″

9-13
This map shows the five different heating zones in the continental United States.
The charts below show the recommended R-values for house insulation in each zone.

Hurd Millwork Company

9-14
These windows block almost all of the sun's ultraviolet rays, while adding character and beauty to the room.

A computer system can cut energy use, but it is expensive to buy and install. An inexpensive alternative to this system is to purchase a thermostat that can be programmed to control the heating and cooling system. See 9-15. Most can be programmed to adjust the temperature when you wake in the morning, leave for work, return home, and go to sleep at night. You can set the unit to change to four different temperatures each 24 hour period. A programmable thermostat is inexpensive and reduces energy use. Depending on energy use and cost, it should pay for itself in a short period of time.

Summary

The systems within a house provide electricity, gas, and water to the house to make it more physically comfortable. As you choose or evaluate systems for your house, you will have several options from which to choose.

Electricity provides energy for operating lights, appliances, and most of the systems within the house. Understanding the basic electrical terms–conductor, electric current, circuit, ampere, voltage, and watt–and how electricity works will help you use electricity wisely in your house.

Gas is another source of energy for the home. It can be in the form of natural gas, which reaches the house from a gas main. Liquid propane gas, which is delivered to the house in pressurized tanks, is another option.

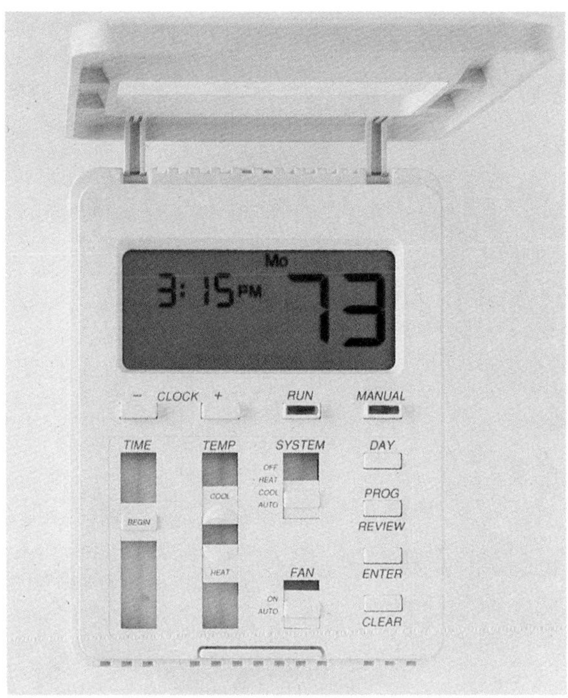

Lennox Industries, Inc.

9-15
A programmable thermostat is an inexpensive way to conserve energy in your house.

The plumbing system brings water to and through the house via the water supply system. Water-borne waste is removed from the house through the wastewater removal system.

The four types of conventional heating systems used to heat houses are the forced warm-air, hydronic, electric radiant, and central heat pump systems. Nonconventional heating systems include solar heat, fireplaces, and stoves. Central air conditioners and room air conditioners are used to provide cool, clean, dehumidified air during hot, humid weather.

When choosing systems for your house, look for ones that are designed to conserve energy. Other ways to conserve energy in your house are to use the proper insulation to keep the house warm in cold weather and cool in warm weather. Choosing energy-efficient windows and doors will also help. Computer systems can help you conserve energy in your home by controlling lighting and the interior climate and by maintaining the systems.

To Review

Write your responses on a separate sheet of paper.

1. Define electricity.
2. Which type of appliances require 240 volts of electricity?
3. Why are gas lines checked before they are used?
4. True or False. Hot and cold water supply lines rely on gravity to move the water.
5. True or False. The water supply system is separate from the wastewater system in the house.
6. List advantages and disadvantages of the four types of conventional heating systems.
7. Why might you choose a radiant heating system instead of a forced warm-air heating system?
8. Compare a fireplace, wood stove, and pellet stove and explain which you would choose for a new house.
9. What are the functions of the compressor and the condenser in a cooling system?
10. The type of insulation to use under a concrete floor would be _____.
11. How can a personal computer help conserve energy in a house?

To Do

1. Ask your parents to show you where the overcurrent protection devices are located in your house. Ask them to show you what to do when a fuse blows or a circuit breaker trips.
2. Locate the water shutoff valves for each fixture in your house.
3. Survey members of your class to see what type of heating and cooling systems they use in their houses.
4. Design a full page magazine advertisement that promotes energy conservation in the house.
5. Look through newspaper and magazine ads to find ads for windows and doors that are energy-efficient. Mount these on a bulletin board for others to look at.
6. Do library research to determine the cost of installing a computer system to manage energy systems in a house.

Wing Industries, Inc.

Chapter 10 The Elements of Design
Chapter 11 Using Color Effectively
Chapter 12 Using the Principles of Design
Chapter 13 Textiles in Today's Home
Chapter 14 Creating Interior Backgrounds
Chapter 15 Furniture Styles and Construction
Chapter 16 Arranging and Selecting Furniture
Chapter 17 The Finishing Touches
Chapter 18 Selecting Household Equipment

PART 4

The Inside Story

C H A P T E R 10

The Elements of Design

Andersen Windows, Inc.

To Know
abstract form
aesthetics
construction
curved line
design
diagonal line
form
free form
function
geometric form
high mass
horizontal line
low mass
mass
realistic form
space
tactile texture
texture
vertical line
visual imagery
visual texture

Objectives

After studying this chapter, you will be able to:

- List the three characteristics of design.
- Describe the different types of lines and explain what they do.
- Discuss the different types of form.
- Explain how space is used in design.
- Identify high mass and low mass.
- Describe tactile texture and visual texture.

Communication takes place in many ways. It can be verbal or nonverbal. Verbal forms of communication include expressing yourself by talking, writing a letter, or singing a song. Nonverbal communication includes using sign language, shaking hands, smiling, or giving a high five. In order for people to understand each other, they must understand the language. For example, the sender and the receiver must both know sign language or the meaning of high five.

Visual imagery is a type of nonverbal communication. It is the language of sight. When you see an item of clothing, piece of furniture, or an unusual object, you see a visual image. This image communicates a feeling to you. Look at 10-1 and 10-2. Each room's visual image communicates a certain personality or mood. This visual image is based on design. Understanding and creating good design is based on knowing design characteristics and the elements of design.

The word design has many meanings. To a fashion designer, it refers to the specific pattern in a fabric or a garment. A printer sees design as the way letters and pictures are arranged in a layout. Interior designers refer to the term ***design*** as the entire process used to develop a specific project. The project might be an object, a room, or a building. Design also refers to the product or result.

Design Characteristics

Design has three characteristics. They are function, construction, and aesthetics. They are used as guidelines in creating and evaluating any design.

The first characteristic is ***function,*** or how a design works. A design's function includes usefulness, convenience, and organization. Good design makes a product or room better or easier to use. It considers the needs of people using the

Lexington Homes

10-1
What feeling does this room communicate to you?

"Victoria and Albert Museum Collection" from Eisenhart Wallcoverings

10-2
How does the visual image of this room differ from the visual image of the room in 10-1?

product or room. Good functional design also accommodates people's ages, sizes, and physical abilities. Successful functional design provides easy access for all people and doesn't create any barriers.

The second characteristic is ***construction.*** Construction includes materials and structure. *Materials* are the different kinds of fabrics, woods, metals, plastics, or stones used to build a product or room. Appropriate materials need to be chosen to support the room's function. When selecting materials, consider design function, quality, initial cost, maintenance, and long-term costs, such as repair and replacement. Materials also need to meet industry standards, government codes, or regulations.

Structure refers to how the materials are assembled. Products need to be safe, durable, and well made. Like materials, structures must meet industry standards, government codes, or regulations.

The third characteristic of design is beauty, or ***aesthetics,*** which is a pleasing appearance or effect. Beauty is difficult to define, because each person has his or her own personal taste. However, good aesthetic design is pleasing to many people. It may communicate a message or stimulate an emotion, such as jolting or sedate, humorous or serious, or exciting or relaxing. See 10-3. Personalized design reflects the aesthetics a person wants to express in a room.

To create a successful design, function, construction, and aesthetics all need to be considered. For example, a room that is aesthetically pleasing but doesn't function well and is poorly constructed, is not good design.

Elements of Design

Successful designers use tools to create designs. These tools are called the elements of design. They include line, form, space, mass, and texture. Color is also an element of design. However, because it involves a lot of discussion, it will be covered in Chapter 11, "Using Color Effectively." You need all the elements of design to describe, plan, and evaluate your housing.

Line

A line is the most basic element of design. It is created when two dots are connected. Lines form the edges or outlines of objects and areas.

Velux-America, Inc.

10-3
This room's pleasing appearance communicates a feeling of relaxation.

They also show direction and cause the eyes to move from one point to another. For example, a line can cause you to look from objects on one end of a shelf to objects at the other end.

Types of lines. The two major types of lines are straight lines and curved lines. The different types of lines used create different emotional responses.

Straight lines can be horizontal, vertical, or diagonal. ***Horizontal lines*** are parallel to the ground. See 10-4. They often direct your eyes across. Horizontal lines communicate feelings of relaxation, calmness, and restfulness. For example, horizontal lines are associated with sunsets on the horizon. A sunset is a symbol that the day is ending, and it is time for rest. This is the same feeling you get when sleeping in a horizontal position.

Horizontal lines are found in many home furnishings. They can be seen in fireplace mantels, long sofas, or in fabrics or wallpaper used to decorate the room.

Vertical lines are perpendicular to the ground. They take your eyes up and down. This suggests height, strength, dignity, and stability.

In 10-5, notice how the columns visually communicate height. This is because the vertical lines direct your eyes upward. A feeling of strength is also communicated, since the columns support the pediment, which is an architectural roof-like decoration found over the door. Because the columns stand straight and tall, they communicate dignity. The vertical lines that rest on the ground show stability.

Vertical lines appear in many home furnishings. Look for vertical lines in window treatments, vertically-striped wallpaper, and decorative trims that carry your eyes upward. Grandfather clocks, highboys, armoires, tall mirrors, and most picture frames also have vertical lines.

Lines that angle between horizontal and vertical lines are called ***diagonal lines.*** They communicate different levels of activity, ranging from very little energy to chaos. See 10-6. The level depends upon the degree of the angle. For example, the symbol for a bolt of lighting has several sharp diagonal lines. This symbol communicates action, excitement, and a jolting feeling.

In home furnishings, diagonal lines create a feeling of transition from one level to another. They appear in roof lines, cathedral ceilings, staircases, lampshades, and various fabrics and paintings.

10-4
Horizontal lines can make a room feel more relaxing and informal.

Lexington Homes

10-5
These columns give the front of this house the feeling of height, strength, dignity, and stability.

Curved lines are the second major type of line. A ***curved line*** is a part of a circle. If you completely extend a curved line, it becomes a circle. The curved line may also be extended in a slightly different way to form an oval. Curved lines can also take a free form and range from slightly curved to very complex.

Interiors Classique, Nancy Folkers, ASID

10-6
The diagonal lines in the table and curtains create interest and movement.

Kohler Company

10-7
The curved lines found in the shapes of the jars are calm and organized. The curved lines in the pattern on the jars are flowing and active.

The different degrees of curves in lines communicate different ideas. Generally, curved lines seem softer than straight lines. A circle or oval reflects feelings of organization, eternity, and uniformity. Slightly-curved, free-form lines have a natural and flowing movement. They communicate softness, freedom, and openness. See 10-7.

Using lines in housing decisions. Applying different types of lines to specific decorating situations can result in different effects. For example, a space can appear larger, smaller, calmer, or busier just by using different types of lines. Repeating straight lines or curved lines can create a strong, intense statement. To create a more relaxed look, combine various types of lines.

Observe the use of various straight lines and curved lines in 10-8. The vertical lines in the drap-

Lexington Homes

10-8
Combining horizontal, vertical, diagonal, and curved lines can be very pleasing to the eyes.

ery draw your eyes upward. The horizontal lines in the fireplace mantle and brick wall make the room look wider. The diagonal lines in the lampshade create a gradual transition from the floor to the fireplace and ceiling. Meanwhile, the curved lines in the wall hanging, fireplace, and plants help soften all the straight lines shown.

Form

Form is the physical shape of objects. It outlines the edges of a three-dimensional object and contains volume and mass. Form also has height, width, and depth.

Types of form. There are four different types of form. They are realistic form, abstract form, geometric form, and free form.

When a form looks very much like the real thing, it has ***realistic form.*** Realistic form communicates a life-like, normal, and traditional feeling. For example, a chair has realistic form because of its specific form. It is easily recognized as a chair.

Abstract form rearranges or stylizes a recognizable object. The abstract item has traits that look like the real item, but altered. Abstract form communicates a contemporary, changing, creative, and artistic feeling.

Geometric form uses squares, rectangles, circles, and other geometric figures to create form. It communicates organization, order, planning, and a tailored look. Geometric forms are found in home furnishings, such as square tables, round lampshades, and various shapes of pillows. The room in 10-9 has many geometric forms.

Free form is random and flowing. It is found in nature–in plants, stones, and wood. It does not have any geometric design. Free form communicates a sense of freedom. Free form is different from realistic form in that it is not traditional.

Using form in housing decisions. There are three guidelines you can follow to help you use form in design. The first is that form follows function. In other words, the function of an object should be considered first. Then the form should

Kohler Company

10-9
Many different geometric forms, such as squares, rectangles, and triangles, are used in this kitchen.

be chosen. For instance, chairs for a family room should have a form that lets people sit comfortably and relax. If a chair had a seat that slanted to one side, or it had very short or very long legs, it would not be comfortable. Therefore, it would not be functional as a chair.

The second guideline is that using related forms is more agreeable than using several unrelated forms. When looking at similar forms, your eyes get comfortable looking at that specific form. For instance, in 10-10, square forms are dominant and are used throughout this room to give the room a crisp, organized look.

The third guideline is that a gradual change in form can direct the eyes smoothly. An abrupt change in form or too many different forms used together may be uncomfortable and cause confusion. When forms change, your eyes have to work harder to follow the different-shaped forms. However, sometimes the change in form can cause excitement.

Kohler Company

10-10
The related square forms used in this kitchen make looking at the room more comfortable.

Space

The term ***space*** refers to the area around a form, such as the area around a table. It also refers to the area inside a form, such as the area inside a room. When discussing space, two closely-related factors need to be considered. They are the size of the space and the arrangement of the space.

Size of the space. The size of interior space is often defined by its height, length, and width. The size affects who will use the space and how they will use it. For example, a bedroom that is 10 x 12 feet is probably too small for three teenagers who each need a bed, dresser, and desk at which to study. However, the same size bedroom is adequate for three smaller children who only need beds and one dresser for all three of them.

The size of a space can also communicate positive or negative feelings. For example, a large space can communicate feelings of openness, grandeur, or freedom. However, a large space, such as a sports arena, may make you feel small, lost, or overwhelmed. Also, a large living room, with a cathedral ceiling, 10-11, might create an open, drafty, or cold feeling, depending on how you look at it.

Lexington Homes

10-11
This cathedral ceiling creates an open and visually expanding space.

Small spaces can make you feel cozy, intimate, or comfortable. However, you might feel very big and uncomfortable in a small room. If more people and furnishings are added to this small room, it might feel very crowded.

Arrangement of the space. When using space in design, you first need to evaluate the space and decide what design effect you want to achieve. You can achieve different effects by arranging the space differently. For example, you can arrange space to make large spaces look smaller, and small spaces look larger.

To open and expand spaces, you can remove walls, expand window area, and use mirrors. To create the feeling of cozy quarters, the space can be divided into separate areas. This can be done by using area rugs, arranging furniture to create small areas, or even building a kitchen island. However, you need to be careful, because sometimes the area may be divided in a way that creates an unorganized and confused feeling.

Mass

Mass refers to the amount of pattern or objects in a space. It is also how crowded or empty a space appears. A space can have high mass or low mass.

High mass. *High mass* refers to a space that is visually crowded. A lot of pattern or lines are found in a high mass fabric design. A room with high mass has many items in it and may look crowded. High mass rooms may reflect a crowded feeling. See 10-12. Emotions communicated by high mass are full, packed, cluttered, formal, and heavy.

Low mass. *Low mass* refers to a space that is simple and sparse. It is the opposite of high mass. The least amount, or just the essential furnishings, are used in a low mass design. It communicates clean and airy feelings. The traditional design styles called Minimalism and Shaker reflect low mass, 10-13.

Using mass in housing decisions. Using a large amount of high mass or low mass can create a strong, heavy statement. Blending high and low mass can create variety in a room design. For example, placing a low mass design above a high mass design creates a very open feeling in the room. The two extremes may complement each other.

Texture

Texture refers to the way a surface feels or looks. There are two kinds of texture. They are called tactile texture and visual texture.

Tactile texture. *Tactile texture* is how the surface feels to the touch. You can see and feel tactile texture. For example, think of yourself standing next to a real stone wall. You can see the bumps on the stone with your eyes. You can feel the roughness of the stone with your hand. This stone wall has tactile texture.

"Victoria and Albert Museum Collection" from Eisenhart Wallcoverings

10-12
The use of high mass reflected in the patterned fabric and dark, heavy furniture gives this room a traditional feeling.

Photo by Paul Rocheleau, Shaker Hancock Village

10-13
The plain lines and lack of ornamentation give this Shaker room a sparse, airy feeling.

There are manyH tactile textures used in design. For instance, a surface might feel bumpy and rough, soft and smooth, grainy, porous, or hard. When selecting items for the home, you should consider the way they feel. For example, some upholstery fabrics may be too rough and uncomfortable to sit on.

Visual texture. ***Visual texture*** is texture that you see, but you cannot feel. It can be found in scenic wallpaper or fabric patterns as well as in pictures. For instance, in a photograph of a stone fireplace, you can visually see the texture. However, you cannot feel the roughness of the actual stone. You can only feel the smoothness of the photo.

Using texture in housing decisions. You can use specific textures to communicate different feelings in a room. For example, rough surfaces, such as concrete, create a more casual feeling. Smooth surfaces, such as glass, polished wood, or brass, may communicate an elegant feeling. Polished stone or marble can communicate both elegance and strength. Terms that are used to describe the roughness or smoothness of texture are nubby, crinkled, quilted, ribbed, uneven, and even. Rigid, crisp, harsh, flexible, and limp describe the hardness and softness of texture.

The use of textures can affect the visual size of a room. Heavy or rough textures absorb more light than smooth textures. They do not reflect light around the room, which makes the room look smaller. On the other hand, smooth surfaces make small rooms look larger. The light reflects off the smooth surface, creating the illusion of a larger space.

You can create variety by using both visual and tactile textures. When more than one texture is used in a room, the room looks more interesting. See 10-14. However, too many kinds of texture in one room may be confusing.

Carol G. Brown, ASID. Certified in the State of California

10-14
The wide range of textures used in this room give it a very interesting look.

Summary

Visual imagery is the language of sight. It communicates different feelings. Understanding visual imagery is based on knowing the design characteristics and the elements of design.

The three characteristics of design are function, construction, and aesthetics. They are used as guidelines in creating and evaluating design. The elements of design are color, line, form, space, mass, and texture. (Color is discussed in Chapter 11, "Using Color Effectively.") They are the tools used to create good design.

Using different types of straight and curved lines can create different emotions in a room. They can be used together in different combinations to create various effects.

The four types of form are realistic, abstract, geometric, and free form. Three guidelines can help you use form in design. They are (a) form follows function, (b) using related forms is more agreeable than using several unrelated forms, and (c) a gradual change in form can direct the eyes smoothly.

Space refers to the area inside and outside a form. When using space in design, you need to consider the size of the space and the arrangement of the space.

Mass can be high mass or low mass. High mass refers to a space that is visually crowded. Low mass refers to a space that is simple and sparse. You can use high mass or low mass to create a strong statement. You can also use both types together to create variety in a room.

Texture is the way a surface feels or looks. Tactile and visual texture can be used to communicate different feelings in a room, affect the visual size of a room, and create variety in a room.

To Review

Write your responses on a separate sheet of paper.

1. What is meant by the term visual imagery?
2. The three characteristics of design are _____, _____, and _____. Which characteristic of design is concerned with how a design works?
3. List the three types of straight lines and a feeling that each communicates.
4. Match the types of form on top with the descriptions on the bottom.
   _____ Realistic.
   _____ Abstract.
   _____ Geometric.
   _____ Free form.
   a. Life-like, normal, and traditional.
   b. Random and flowing.
   c. Organized, ordered, planned, and tailored.
   d. Rearranged or stylized.
5. List three guidelines for using form in design.
6. Why is using related forms more agreeable than using several unrelated forms?
7. What are three items that can be used to divide space to create smaller areas?
8. How are space and mass related to form?
9. A floral print fabric has _____ mass.
10. How are tactile texture and visual texture different?

To Do

1. Select pictures of three different rooms. Mount the pictures and describe how function, construction, and aesthetics are used in each of the rooms.
2. Look through old housing magazines and find pictures of rooms illustrating four of the following elements of design:
   a. The use of horizontal lines.
   b. The use of vertical lines.
   c. The use of diagonal lines.
   d. The use of curved lines.
   e. The use of form.
   f. The use of space.
   g. The use of low mass.
   h. The use of tactile texture.

   Mount the pictures on separate sheets of construction paper and label each with the element of design that is represented. Describe how the element of design is used in the picture.
3. Choose a word that describes a texture. Write the word in the middle of a large sheet of construction paper. Then, collect items, such as fabrics, woods, or stones, and pictures that represent the word. Using the items and pictures, make a collage on the sheet of construction paper.
4. Select a picture of a room and write a short report on how each element of design is used in the room.
5. Choose a room in your school and evaluate how each element of design is used in it. Then, on a sheet of paper, rate each element based on the following scale: 1 very poor, 3 average, and 5 very good. Share your evaluation with your classmates.

CHAPTER 11

Using Color Effectively

Ethan Allen, Inc.

To Know
analogous color harmony
color harmony
color wheel
complement
complementary color harmony
cool colors
double-complementary color harmony
hue
intensity
intermediate colors
monochromatic color harmony
neutral color harmony
pigment
primary colors
secondary colors
shade
split-complementary color harmony
tint
triad color harmony
value
warm colors

Objectives

After studying this chapter, you will be able to:

- Explain the meaning of different colors.
- Describe the relationships between colors on the color wheel.
- Give examples of color harmonies.
- Plan pleasing color harmonies.

In the previous chapter, you learned about the elements of design–line, form, space, mass, and texture. In this chapter, you will learn about another element of design–color. Color is probably the most important element of design. Deciding what color to use is usually the first decision made when decorating a room. It is one of the first things others notice about your housing. Color sets the mood in a room and leaves a lasting impression with most people.

Understanding Color

Color can help you create certain moods in your home. It can communicate excitement, calmness, or mystery. When you understand the meaning of color, you can use it to make your microenvironment attractive and satisfying.

Each color has certain psychological effects on people. For instance, red is associated with danger and power. It is bold, aggressive, exciting, and warm. It demands attention. Red can make you feel energetic. However, too much red in a room can be overpowering.

Orange is less aggressive than red. It is hopeful, cheerful, and warm. It can make a room feel energetic and friendly.

Yellow is friendly, happy, and warm. It is associated with sympathy, prosperity, and wisdom. Yellow rooms are light and airy.

Green is a natural color. It is cool, peaceful, and friendly. It is often associated with hope and envy. Green mixes well with other colors and looks especially good next to white.

Blue is cool, quiet, and reserved. It is associated with serenity and formality. Blue can be soothing and peaceful. See 11-1. However, too much blue in a room can be depressing.

Violet is a royal color. It is dignified, mysterious, and dramatic. It works well with most other colors.

Black is sophisticated. It is severe, dramatic, and mysterious. Small amounts of black help to give a room a crisp appearance.

White is fresh, youthful, peaceful, and pure. Like black, small amounts of white make rooms look cleaner and livelier.

People feel most comfortable when they are surrounded by colors that reflect their personalities. For instance, outgoing people might choose bright red or orange for the main color in a room. Shy people might feel awkward in a red room. Instead, they might prefer a room that is decorated with blue or green.

When making color decisions for your home, the preferences of each member of the living unit should be considered. No single color will satisfy everyone. However, the social area of the dwelling should be decorated to make all members feel as comfortable as possible. Individual preferences can be satisfied in the more private quiet and work areas.

Congoleum Corporation

11-1
The color blue creates a calm, soothing effect in this nursery.

The Color Wheel

The ***color wheel,*** 11-2, is the basis of all color relationships. It is made up of three rings. The center ring has three types of colors in it. They are primary colors, secondary colors, and intermediate colors. The ***primary colors*** are red, yellow, and blue. By mixing, lightening, and darkening the primary colors, all other colors can be made.

Mixing equal amounts of any two primary colors produces a ***secondary color.*** Orange, green, and violet are secondary colors. Orange is a mixture of red and yellow. Green is a mixture of yellow and blue. Violet is a mixture of blue and red. Look again at the color wheel in 11-2. Notice

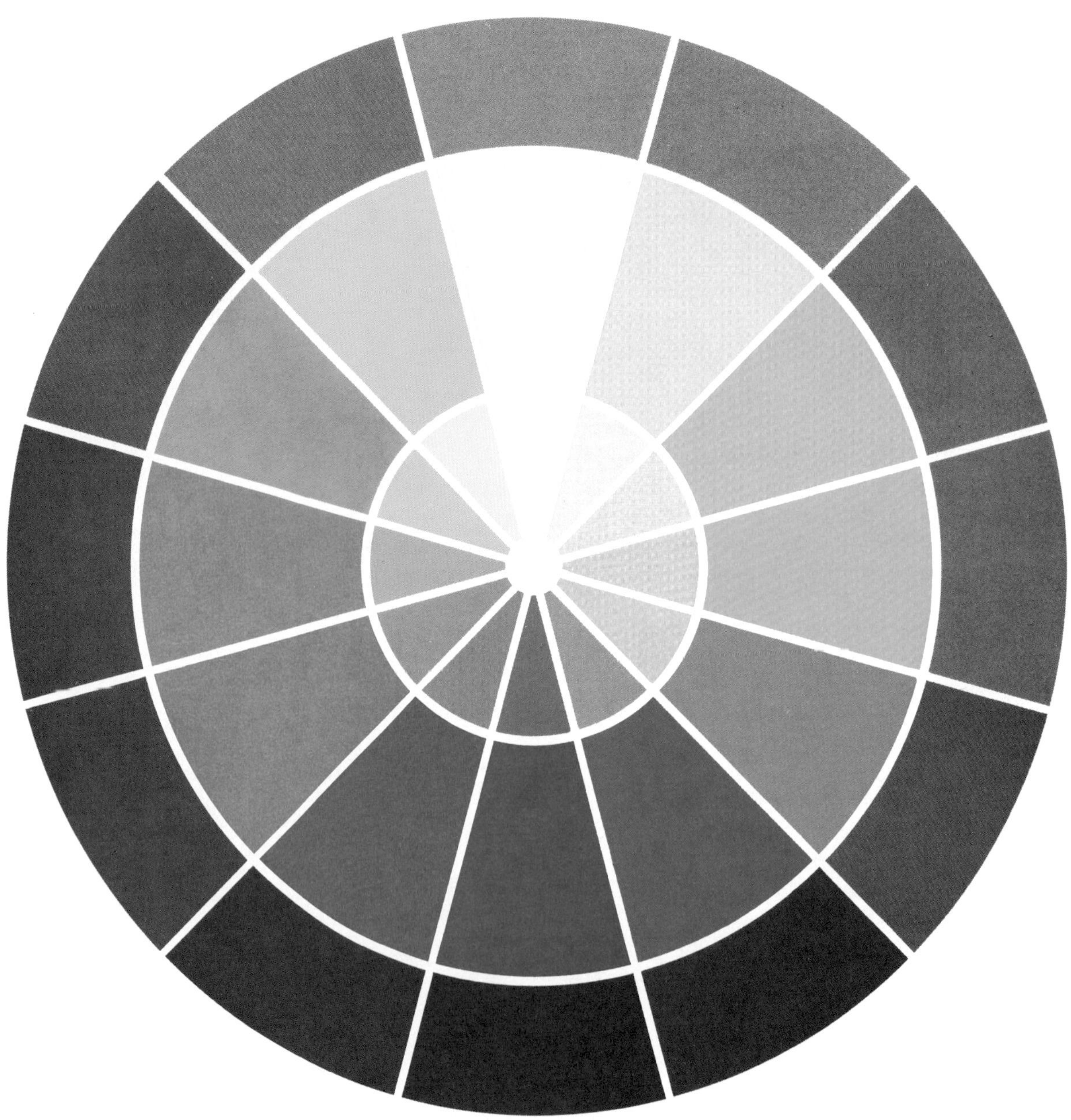

11-2
The arrangement of colors in a color wheel provides a basis for all color relationships.

that the location of each secondary color is halfway between the two primary colors used to make it.

The other colors in the center ring of the color wheel are ***intermediate colors.*** (They are sometimes called tertiary colors.) The intermediate colors are red-orange, yellow-orange, yellow-green, blue-green, blue-violet, and red-violet. They are named after the two colors used to make them. The primary color is always listed first.

Color Characteristics

Color has three characteristics. They are hue, value, and intensity.

Hue. A ***hue,*** or color name, is the one characteristic that makes a color unique. It is hue that makes blue different from red or yellow. If you make blue lighter, darker, brighter, or duller, you will not will not change the hue. It will still be blue.

Value. The ***value*** of a hue refers to its lightness or darkness. The normal value of a hue is shown on the center ring of the color wheel. The normal values of some hues are lighter than the normal values of others. For instance, yellow has the lightest normal value. As you move away from yellow on the color wheel, the normal values of hues become darker. Violet has the darkest normal value.

The value of a hue can be lightened by adding white to the hue. The result is called a ***tint.*** For instance, pink is a tint of red. It is made by adding white to red. For lighter tints, more white is added. Tints are shown on the inner ring of the color wheel.

The value of a hue can be made darker by adding black to a hue. The result is called a ***shade.*** Navy is a shade of blue. Burgundy is a shade of red. Shades are shown on the outer ring of the color wheel.

A *value scale* is pictured in 11-3. It shows the full range of values for the color blue from tints to shades.

Intensity. ***Intensity*** refers to the brightness or dullness of a hue. The normal intensity of hues are shown on the center ring of the color wheel. Most colors used in a home are low-intensity colors.

One way to lower the intensity of a color is to add some of its complement. The ***complement*** of a hue is the hue directly across from it on a color wheel. For instance, blue is the complement of orange. To lower the intensity of orange, add varying amounts of blue to it, 11-4.

Another way to lower the intensity of a color is to add some black or white to it. However, this method also changes the value of the hue.

Neutrals

Although neutrals are not really colors, they are usually classified as colors when discussing design. Black, white, and gray are neutrals. Black

11-3
Values for the color blue, ranging from tints to shades, are shown on this value scale.

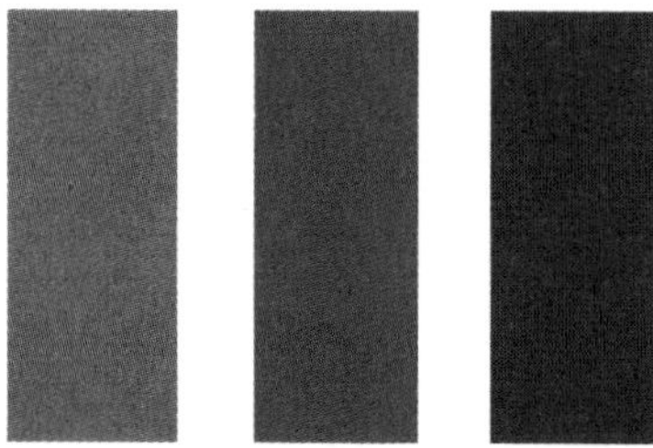

11-4
Adding blue to orange reduces the intensity of orange, making it a duller color.

when used as a ***pigment,*** or color used in paint or printed materials, is the combination of all colors. White when used as a pigment implies lack of color. Gray is a combination of black and white. Brown and its tints and shades are also considered neutrals. Brown is formed by combining equal amounts of complementary colors.

By adding a neutral color to a hue, the value of the hue is changed to either a tint or a shade. This makes the hue less intense. When any of these changes are made, the hue is neutralized. Neutralized hues blend better with other colors.

Warm and Cool Colors

Colors can be considered either warm or cool. All colors can be made to appear warmer or cooler than they are by changing the value. However, the normal value of the colors can be considered warm or cool.

Does your home have some rooms in which you always feel warm? If so, look at the colors used in those rooms. Do they appear on the left-hand side of the color wheel in 11-2? These colors–red, yellow, orange, and the colors near them–are called ***warm colors,*** since they remind people of fire and the sun.

Warm colors are called advancing colors. Warm-colored objects appear closer to you. Warm-colored walls look closer together. Therefore, a room that is painted red, yellow, or orange appears smaller than it really is.

Warm colors attract your attention. They can make you feel happy, energetic, and full of excitement. Many advertisements use warm colors to make you notice them. Restaurants use warm colors to increase your appetite. Locker rooms use them to generate excitement. They are used in homes to make members of the living unit feel lively and cheerful. Large amounts of warm colors, however, may make you feel nervous, especially if the colors are full-intensity colors.

On the opposite side of the color wheel are the cool colors. These include blue, green, violet, and the colors near them.

Cool colors are called receding colors. They make objects seem smaller and walls seem farther away than they really are. For example, a room painted light green seems larger than it is, 11-5.

Cool colors are quiet and restful. They are often used in hospitals to help keep patients calm and relaxed. They are also popular for bedrooms. However, if cool colors are overused, they may make people feel depressed.

Warm and cool colors are not different in temperature. They just create different moods that make people feel differently. For example, workers in an office complained that their lunchroom, which was painted light blue, was always cold. When the employer had the room painted orange, the workers quit complaining even though the temperature didn't change.

Color Harmonies

There are no right or wrong ways to use color. However, following one of the standard color harmonies is the surest and easiest way to achieve success with color. A ***color harmony*** is created when certain colors are used together in a pleasing manner.

Monochromatic Color Harmony

The ***monochromatic color harmony*** is the simplest color harmony. In it, a single hue is used. Variation is added by changing the value and intensity of the hue. For example, if you like green, you may use a dark green carpet, medium green upholstery, and light green walls. Accents of very intense green, white, and black can also add variety. Another type of a monochromatic color harmony is shown in 11-6.

Drexel-Heritage Furnishings, Inc.

11-5
The cool green color used in this room makes the room seem larger and more spacious.

Analogous Color Harmony

An ***analogous color harmony*** is made by combining related hues. These are hues that are next to each other on the color wheel. In an analogous color harmony, usually between three and five hues are used. Since they are related, they blend together well. One color seems to float into another. An example of an analogous color harmony is shown in 11-7.

An analogous color harmony will look best if you choose one color as the dominate color and use smaller amounts of the others to add interest and variety. You may also want to use a tiny amount of an unrelated color as an accent.

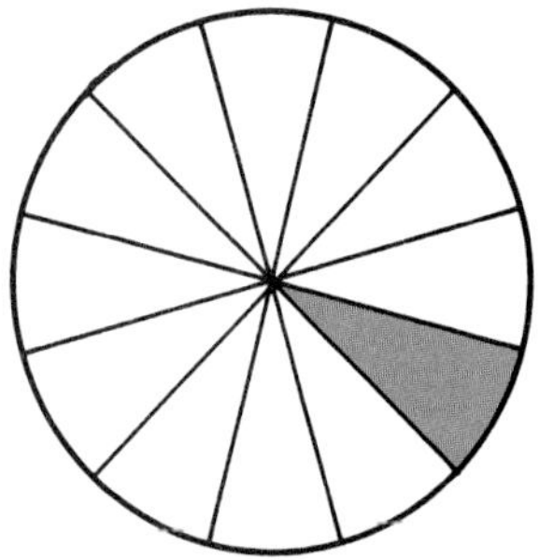

Spiegel

11-6
Blue is the basis for this monochromatic color harmony.

Complementary Color Harmony

A ***complementary color harmony*** is made by combining complementary colors. Complementary colors make each other look brighter and more intense. When blue is next to orange, the blue looks "more blue," and the orange looks "more orange." A complementary color harmony can make a room look bright and dramatic.

Although such a sharp contrast is fine for some rooms, most rooms look better if the contrast is lessened. This can be done by varying the values and intensities of the colors. See 11-8. Also, the colors can be used in varied amounts. The more one color is allowed to dominate the other, the less the contrast is noticed.

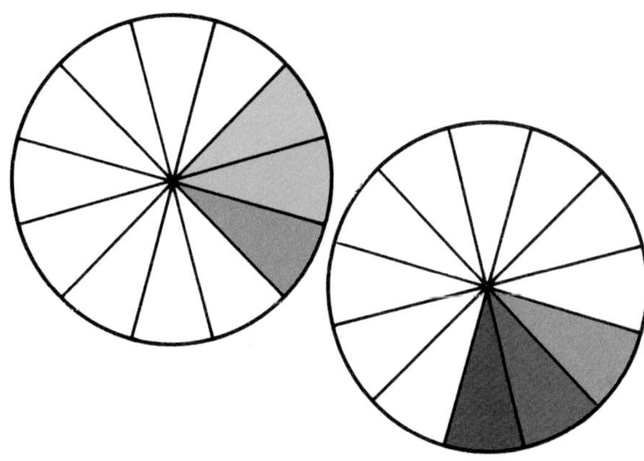

Crate & Barrel

11-7
An analogous color harmony using green, blue-green, blue, blue-violet, and violet gives this room a fresh appearance.

Split-complementary Color Harmony

A ***split-complementary color harmony*** is pictured in 11-9. One color is chosen. Then the two colors on each side of its complement are used with it.

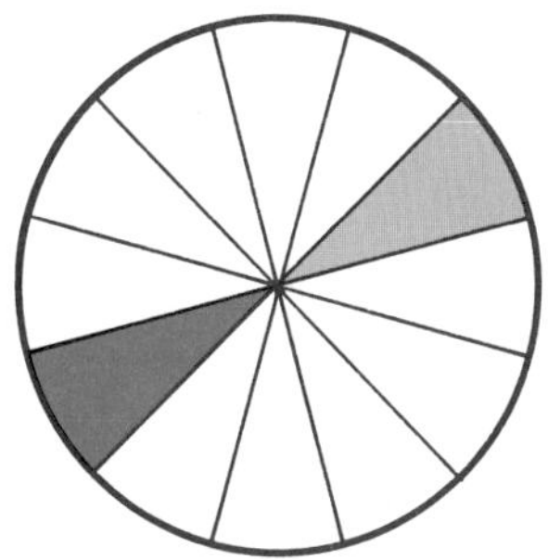

Kate Shenberger Interiors, Flossmoor, Illinois

11-8
Shades of green and tints of red are used to create this complementary color harmony.

Double-complementary Color Harmony

A ***double-complementary color harmony*** consists of two colors and their complements. The two colors are usually next to each other on the color wheel. They could also be colors on each side of complementary colors as in 11-10.

Triad Color Harmony

A ***triad color harmony*** uses three colors that are spaced evenly around the color wheel. The three primary colors form a triad color harmony, 11-11. The three secondary colors can also be used for this type of color harmony. Two other possible color combinations are yellow-orange, red-violet, and blue-green; or red-orange, blue-violet, and yellow-green.

Neutral Color Harmonies

Although black and white are not hues on the color wheel, they are the basis for ***neutral color harmonies.*** Combinations of black, white, and gray create neutral color harmonies. Brown, tan, and beige can also be used. Small amounts of other colors are sometimes added to neutral colors to give the room more interest. See 11-12.

Using Color Harmonies

Now that you have learned about color and the color harmonies, you can begin to use them in the home. The first step is to choose the right colors for your home and living unit. Then, you need to make sure you use them correctly.

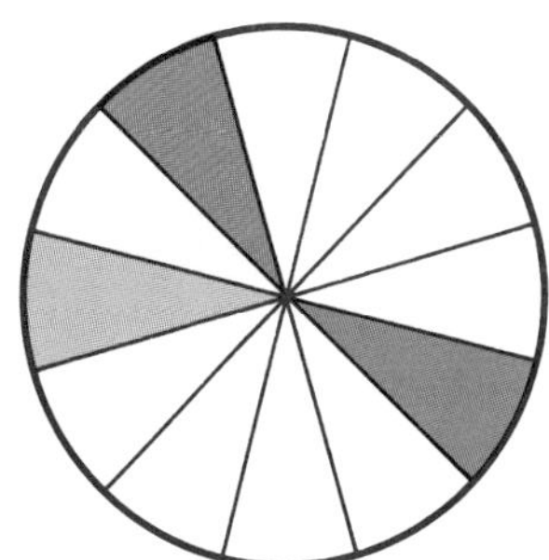

11-9
A split-complementary color harmony uses a main color and the colors on either side of its complement.

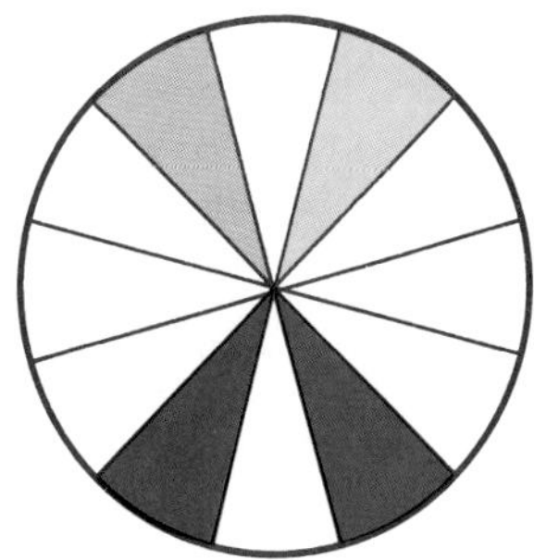

11-10
A double-complementary color harmony is made up of two sets of complementary color schemes.

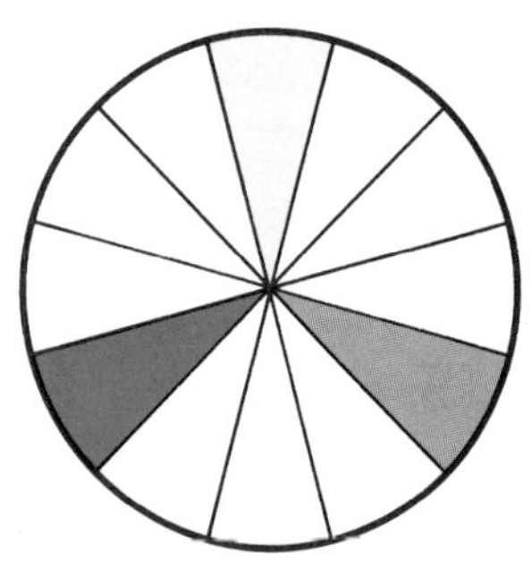

Tyke Corporation

11-11
Triad color harmonies are often used in childrens' bedrooms.

Choosing the Right Colors

The color harmonies you choose to use in your home depend on several factors. They include what mood or style you want to create, the life-style of the living unit, the items in the room, and the location of the room.

Moods and styles. You can create a variety of moods in a room through the use of color. For example, you might want a room to appear restful, or you may want it to seem exciting. Choosing cool colors that have similar values will create a restful mood in the room. Choosing warm colors with contrasting values will make the room feel exciting.

Spiegel

11-12
The green in the wall hangings is used as an accent in this neutral color harmony.

You can also choose colors that will create a certain style in a room. Different styles, such as southwestern and country, often suggest specific colors to use. You can use these colors in different color harmonies to achieve the style you want.

For example, in a southwestern-style room, you might choose a color harmony using the warm desert colors rust, orange, and beige. See 11-13. In a country-style room, you can choose low-intensity shades of reds, blues, oranges, and yellows.

Life-styles. Some people have active life-styles, while others lead quieter lives. The colors you choose depend on the life-styles of the members of the living unit. For instance, the main rooms in a house where a family with children lives requires a lot of care to keep clean. The family may want to choose dark colors for these rooms. This is because dark colors do not show dirt as easily as light colors. On the other hand, a couple without children may choose to use more light colors, since the upkeep of their house will be much easier.

Jessica Hall Associates. Certified in the State of California

11-13
A southwestern look is created in this room through the use of the colors orange, rust, brown, yellow, and black.

Spiegel

11-14
Primary and secondary colors are used in this child's room to give it a feeling of fun and excitement.

The colors you choose also depend upon the activities each room is used for. In a child's room, you should use normal intensity primary and secondary colors. See 11-14. In a bedroom where sleeping is the primary activity, you can decorate with the same hues but at lower-intensity levels.

Items in the room. Another way to choose color harmonies is to consider what items are going to be used in the room. For instance, you may have a favorite picture or a new couch that you intend to use in the room. To plan your color harmony around this item, you need to pull a color used in the picture or sofa fabric. This color becomes the base, or main, color. After choosing the base color, you can use the color harmonies to pick colors to go with it.

You also need to consider the type of lighting used in the room. Artificial light can make colors look warmer or cooler than they do in natural light. It can also change the value of a color. For instance, bright colors can look washed out in artificial light.

Most homes have both incandescent and fluorescent lighting. Incandescent lighting generally makes colors appear warmer. Fluorescent lighting makes colors appear warmer or cooler depending on the color of the tube or bulb. See 11-15. In general, most fluorescent lighting will make colors appear cooler than incandescent lighting will.

Location of the room. The direction the room faces is critical when choosing the base color and color harmony. If a bedroom is located on the north side of a house, the natural light of the northern exposure will make colors appear cooler. To make the room appear warmer, choose a color harmony that uses warm colors, such as yellow, yellow-orange, and orange. A southern exposure will make colors appear brighter and warmer. Therefore, cool colors should be chosen, 11-16, otherwise the room will appear too warm.

When considering location, you also need to think about the colors used in adjoining rooms. The colors you choose should blend with those used in those rooms. There shouldn't be any abrupt changes in color. If a dining room is located next to a living room, the same base color should be used in both rooms. You could use an

Color and Artificial Lighting					
Artificial Lighting	**Yellow**	**Orange**	**Red**	**Blue**	**Green**
Incandescent	warms	strengthens	enriches	dulls	darkens
Cool white fluorescent	slightly grays	strengthens	darkens, grays	cools	cools
Warm white fluorescent	intensifies, brightens	strengthens, brightens	brightens	darkens, grays	deepens
Deluxe cool white fluorescent	enriches, intensifies	close to true hue	warms	enriches	brightens
Deluxe warm white fluorescent	brightens	strengthens	enriches	darkens, enriches	enriches

11-15
Colors change when viewed under different types of artificial light.

American Fiber Manufacturers Association

11-16
Cool colors were chosen to decorate this sunny bedroom that has a southern exposure. These colors keep this room looking light and airy.

analogous color harmony with yellow as the base color in the living room. Then you could use a split-complementary color harmony with yellow as the base in the dining room. Since yellow is dominant in both rooms, it provides a smooth transition.

Using Color Correctly

As you work with color, there are several guidelines you should follow to help you use color well. They are as follows:

- Using contrasting colors draws attention. For example, a white sofa against a dark wall will draw more attention than a white sofa against a white wall. While you may want to guard against a totally neutralized room, you should remember that too many strong contrasts in a room can be confusing and tiring.
- Color harmonies look better when one color, the base color, dominates. When you use equal amounts of two or more colors in a room, your eyes become confused, and your color selection appears cluttered.
- When choosing colors for large areas, such as walls and floors, select low-intensity colors. If you use high-intensity colors in large amounts, they can become overpowering. Instead, high-intensity colors should be used in small amounts as accent colors in accessories or small pieces of furniture.
- Textured surfaces make colors appear dark. This is because the light strikes the surface at different angles, making the item appear

to have greater depth. Therefore, when you are trying to match fabrics, it is important to have samples of the fabrics you are matching. For example, if you are matching drapery fabric to a carpet make sure you have samples of the carpet with you.

- If a room is large, choose colors that will make it look smaller. These colors include shades, high-intensity colors, and warm hues, which have advancing qualities. Rooms decorated in these colors appear smaller. See 11-17.
- If a room is small, choose colors that will make the room appear larger. These colors include tints, low-intensity colors, and cool hues that have receding qualities. They make rooms appear larger.

Choosing the right colors, creating color harmonies, and following the color guidelines is important. This will let you make color work well for you and your living unit.

Summary

Color is one of the most important elements of design. It can communicate different moods. Each color has its own psychological effect on people.

The basis of all color relationships is the color wheel. Colors on the color wheel are primary, secondary, or intermediate colors. Color has three characteristics. They are hue, value, and intensity. Black, white, and gray are neutral colors. The cool colors are located on one side of the wheel, and the warm colors are located on the other side.

When colors are used together in a pleasing manner, color harmonies are created. Some color harmonies are: monochromatic, analogous, complementary, split-complementary, double-complementary, and triad.

When choosing a color harmony, you first need to choose the right colors for your home and living unit. Then, you need to follow certain guidelines to make sure you use the colors well.

Spiegel

11-17
The dark colors used in this large, open room make it look small and cozy.

To Review

Write your responses on a separate sheet of paper.

1. What moods are created by the colors red, green, and violet?
2. List the secondary colors and explain how each is made from primary colors.
3. Which color name is listed first in an intermediate color name?
4. Explain the difference between value and intensity of color.
5. Describe how to neutralize a hue.
6. _____ colors are related to red; _____ colors are related to blue.
7. Give an example of each of the following color harmonies:
   a. Monochromatic.
   b. Analogous.
   c. Complementary.
   d. Split-complementary.
   e. Double-complementary.
   f. Triad color.
8. True or False. Dark colors show more dirt than light colors.
9. _____-intensity colors should be used for large areas.

To Do

1. Look in magazines for five pictures of rooms that use color to create certain moods. Mount the pictures on pieces of paper. Write a caption under each picture explaining the mood of the room reflected by the color.
2. Using only red, blue, and yellow paints, mix colors to make a color wheel.
3. With paints, practice making a color less intense by adding varying amounts of its complement.
4. Place a piece of green paper next to a piece of red paper. Then place another piece of green paper next to a gray paper. Which green looks brighter? Discuss your observations with your classmates.
5. Find pictures in magazines to illustrate three of the six color harmonies discussed in this chapter. Share your findings with the class.
6. Make two small rooms without ceilings from cardboard. Cover the walls of one room with light, dull, cool colors. Cover the walls of the other room with dark, bright, warm colors. Which room looks larger?

CHAPTER 12

Using the Principles of Design

Jessica Hall Associates. Certified in the State of California

To Know

balance
emphasis
formal balance
golden mean
golden rectangle
golden section
gradation
harmony
informal balance
opposition
proportion
radiation
repetition
rhythm
scale
sensory design
transition
unity
visual weight

Objectives

After studying this chapter, you will be able to:

- Discuss how proportion and scale are related to objects.
- Give examples of formal and informal balance.
- Explain how emphasis creates a focal point.
- List the different types of rhythm.
- Describe the goals of design.
- Give examples of sensory design.

In the previous two chapters, you learned about the elements of design. When the elements of design are applied using the principles of design, you can achieve the goals of design. This chapter will tell you how to use this process to create well-designed rooms.

The Principles of Design

The principles of design are guidelines for working with the elements of design. When you understand the principles of design, you can use the elements of design successfully. The principles of design are proportion and scale, balance, emphasis, and rhythm.

Proportion and Scale

Proportion and scale are closely related though different. They both describe size, shape, and amount. They are both concerned with the relationships of objects and parts of objects.

Proportion. ***Proportion*** is the relationship of parts of the same object, or the relationship between different objects in the same group. For example, proportion is a consideration when choosing a shade for a lamp. The lamp base and the lampshade need to be in proportion to each other (parts of the same object). Proportion is also a consideration when choosing the surface on which to place the lamp. The lamp and table need to be in proportion to each other (different objects in the same group). The accessories that surround the lamp are also considered. The accessories must be in proper proportion to both the lamp and the table (different objects in the same group).

Proportion can also be described as the ratio of one part to another part or of one part to the whole. Ratios such as 2:3, 3:5, and 5:8 are more effective than ratios of 1:1 or 1:2. For instance, a rectangle has more pleasing proportions than a square. These ratios also apply to rooms, furniture, and accessories. See 12-1.

The Greeks were masters of the use of proportion. They developed guidelines that have been used for centuries. Three of these guidelines are the golden rectangle, the golden mean, and the golden section. Study 12-2 as you read about these guidelines.

The ***golden rectangle*** has sides in a ratio of 2:3. The short sides are two-thirds the length of the long sides. One example of the golden rectangle is the Parthenon in Athens, Greece. The golden rectangle can be found frequently in design. You can find many examples of the golden rectangle in houses and their furnishings.

The ***golden mean*** is the division of a line between one-half and one-third of its length. This unequal division is more pleasing to the eyes than an equal division or a division at less than one-third of the line's length. The golden mean is

Rea-Lynne Gilder

12-1
Good proportion is important in furnishing a room. The ratio of the dresser to the wall is 4:7.

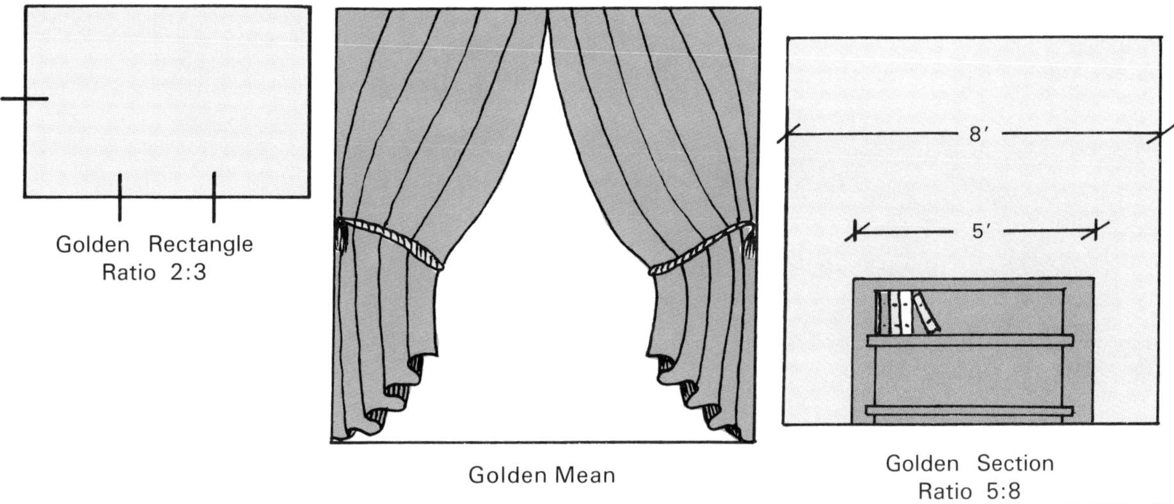

Rea-Lynne Gilder

12-2
The golden rectangle, golden mean, and golden section are all guidelines to help you achieve good proportion.

often applied when planning wall arrangements, tying draperies, and hanging pictures.

The ***golden section*** is the division of a line or form in such a way that the ratio of the smaller section to the larger section is equal to the ratio of the larger section to the whole. This relationship is based on the progression of the numbers 1, 2, 3, 5, 8, 13, 21, etc. Notice that each number is the sum of the two previous numbers.

When using the golden section to help you plan, you will find that the ratio of 2:3 is about the same ratio as 3:5 and other similar ratios. Using the concept of the golden section can help you develop more pleasing proportions in your designs.

Most people do not actually measure proportions. They can tell by looking at a rug on a floor if it is in the proper proportion. Likewise, they can tell if a bed or sofa fits the room it is in. People develop a sense of proportion that tells them if the proportions are right.

Scale. ***Scale*** refers to the relative size of an object in relation to other objects. For example, a chair is a small piece of furniture in comparison to a bed. A twin bed is small in comparison to a king-size bed. However, the twin bed is still larger than the chair.

When furnishings are scaled to the space they occupy, they are pleasing to the eyes. For example, large rooms require large-scale furnishings. A king-size bed is appropriate in a large bedroom. However, it might seem too large for a small room. Small rooms require small-scale furniture.

The furnishings within a room should be in scale with one another. For example, a large sofa requires a large coffee table. A small sofa would not go well with a large coffee table.

Furnishings also need to be in scale to the people using them. A large person will feel more comfortable in a chair of substantial size. Likewise, a child will feel more comfortable in a chair that is scaled to his or her size. See 12-3.

Another aspect of scale is visual weight. ***Visual weight*** is the perception that an object weighs more or less than it really does. For example, a wooden chair and an upholstered chair may have the exact same dimensions. However, the upholstered chair will look larger and heavier than the wooden chair. Thick lines, bold colors, coarse textures, and large patterns add to visual weight.

When decorating a small room, choose furniture that has light visual weight. This will prevent the furniture from making the room look crowded. Likewise, choose accessories that are in scale to the furniture. In a small room, it is wise to think small in regard to furniture and accessories.

Tyke Corporation

12-3
This child-size chair and table are scaled-down versions of adult-size tables and chairs.

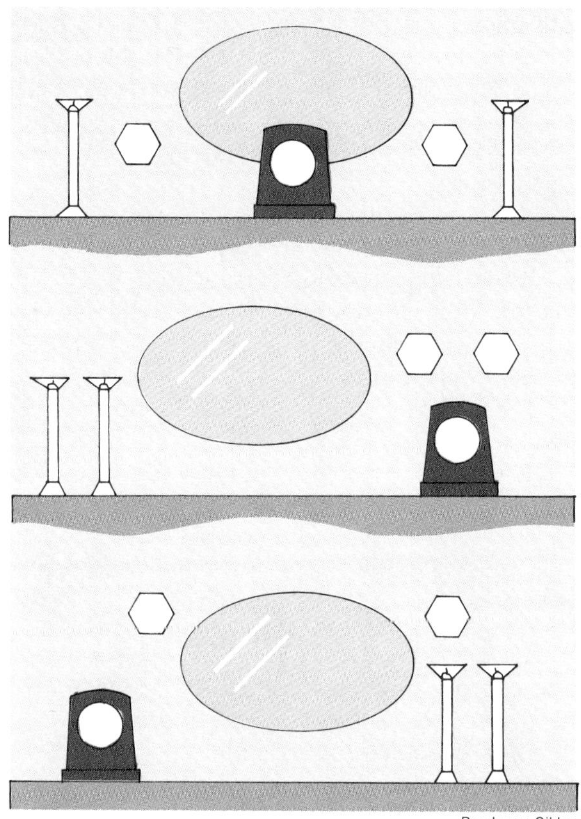

Rea-Lynne Gilder

12-4
The same objects can be arranged in many different ways and still create balance.

Balance

Balance implies equilibrium among parts of a design. It is a perception of the way arrangements are seen. When there is balance, there is a sense of equal weight on both sides of a center point. See 12-4. There is not a visual pull in one direction more than the other. Balance can be either formal or informal.

In ***formal balance,*** or symmetrical balance, identical objects are arranged on either side of a center point. Formal balance is often used in elegant and formal rooms. It is especially appropriate for traditional decorating styles. It can also be used in exterior design, 12-5. Formal balance is easy to achieve and makes people feel comfortable because of its orderliness.

In ***informal balance,*** also called asymmetrical balance, different, but equivalent, objects are arranged on either side of a center point. Although the sides are not alike, neither side overpowers the other. A feeling of equilibrium is created.

Informal balance can be achieved in various ways. In order to balance a heavy object and a

Lindal Cedar Homes, Inc. Seattle, Washington

12-5
The use of formal balance in the design of this house gives it a feeling of calm and orderliness.

light object, the heavier object must be placed closer to the center line than the light object. A single, large object can be balanced by several smaller ones, 12-6. If objects are the same size but of unequal distance from you, the object closest to you will appear larger.

A single, large object can also be balanced by an object that has visual weight. Color, texture, and form all create visual weight. Bold, warm colors will appear heavier than subdued, cool colors. Decorations added to an object give the object visual weight. See 12-7. Typically, large objects appear heavier than small objects.

Balance is a very important principle to follow when arranging furnishings. The furnishings on each half of a wall or opposite walls should balance with each other. The type of balance used helps determine the mood of a room. Formal balance creates an air of formality. Informal balance creates a casual atmosphere.

Marvin Windows & Doors

12-7
Although the two sides of the house are not identical, the vertical lines in the balconies on the right balance the horizontal rooflines on the left.

Emphasis

Emphasis creates a center of interest or focal point in a room. It is the feature that is seen first and repeatedly draws attention. Every well-designed room has a focal point. With one area of emphasis, the eyes are immediately drawn to that point when you enter a room. This gives a feeling of stability and unity to the room.

Marvin Windows & Doors

12-6
The large clock on the right balances the vase and small bottles on the left.

When planning a focal point, keep these guidelines in mind:

- The focal point should be worthy of the attention it will receive.
- The focal point should dominate the room, but not overpower the room or the design.
- No features should compete with the focal point. Otherwise, confusion will result.

Architectural features can provide a focal point for a room, or a focal point can be created. Common architectural focal points are picture windows and fireplaces. Created focal points include colorful rugs, striking works of art, mirrors, shelves of books or collections, and furniture groupings. Unusual objects or placement of objects can also serve as focal points. For example, a beautiful piece of antique furniture in a contemporary setting might be eye-catching. Special lighting cast upon an object can also create a focal point, 12-8.

The focal point gives order and direction to a room. Everything else in the setting should relate to it through color, texture, proportion, scale, and theme.

Carol G. Brown, ASID, Certified in the State of California

12-8
Lighting makes the art piece over the fireplace the focal point of this room.

The colors in a focal point are usually the first part to catch one's eyes. The color can be further emphasized if it is carried throughout the room in accessories, window treatments, and upholstery fabric. The texture of the focal point can be carried through the room in similar ways.

The size of the point of interest should be in proportion and scale to the room and furnishings. A massive focal point will be too large for a small room. However, a large room or a room with a cathedral ceiling demands a focal point that will not get lost because of the room size.

How a room will be used determines the theme of the room. The focal point should set the stage for the furnishings. For example, a living room will be used for socializing. If the fireplace is the focal point, comfortable seating that permits socializing should be grouped around the fireplace.

Rhythm

Rhythm smoothly leads the eyes from one area to another in a design. Rhythm results when an element of design forms an organized pattern. For example, a continuous line found in window and door frames produces rhythm. Rhythm can be achieved through repetition, gradation, radiation, opposition, and transition.

All types of rhythm are based on some repetition. Rhythm by ***repetition*** is created when an element of design–either color, line, form, or texture–is repeated, 12-9. Repetition is one of the easiest ways to achieve rhythm in a design. For instance, a dominant color can be repeated throughout a room. Lines that are repeated in shelves of a bookcase create rhythm. Repetition of form is found when rectangular end tables and a rectangular coffee table are used in the same setting. Texture may be repeated in fabrics used in draperies and upholstery.

Gradation is the type of rhythm created by a gradual increase or decrease of similar elements of design, 12-10. The eyes travel through

Andersen Windows, Inc.

12-9
The vertical lines in the windows, upholstery fabric, and fireplace create repetition in this room.

Rea-Lynne Gilder

12-10
These nesting tables are a good example of rhythm by gradation. The eyes move from the largest table to the smallest.

the levels of progression. For example, color value can change from dark to light or from light to dark. Lines can vary from thick to thin in a design. Objects that have the same form can increase or decrease in size. Textures can range from smooth to rough.

In rhythm by ***radiation,*** lines flow outward from a central point. A sunburst is an example of radiation. Radiation in home furnishings can usually be found in accessories. For example, a flower arrangement or a cushion may have radiating lines. See 12-11. A window that forms a half circle with a sunburst design is a good example of rhythm by radiation.

In rhythm by ***opposition,*** lines meet to form right angles. Rhythm by opposition is often found in the construction of a room as well as in the furnishings. It can be found in the corners of windowpanes, 12-12, picture frames, fireplaces, and the corners of tables and other furniture. It can also be created in simple ways as you decorate. For instance, a row of books may be held in place by three books lying on their sides. The three books form a right angle to the other books on the shelf.

Rhythm by ***transition*** is created when curved lines carry the eyes from one part of an object to another part. See 12-13. Transition leads the eyes in, through, and over a object until they have seen the whole object. Curved lines are found in architectural features and in furnishings. An arched window will lead your eyes from one side to the other. A drapery swag will draw your eyes from one part of the drapery to another.

Crate & Barrel

12-11
The lines in the backs and seats of these chairs show rhythm by radiation.

Marvin Windows & Doors

12-12
The corners of the many windowpanes used in this room create rhythm by opposition.

Armstrong World Industries, Inc.

12-13
Curved lines lead the eyes up the staircase to the second floor of this home.

Goals of Design

As you work with the elements and principles of design, you need to keep in mind the goals of design. The goals of design are function and appropriateness, harmony with unity and variety, and beauty. These goals help make sure that your design works together as a whole. The use, convenience, and satisfaction of members of the living unit should also be considered as you work to achieve the goals of design.

Function and Appropriateness

Function and appropriateness are closely related. If furnishings serve their various functions, they are considered appropriate. Rooms and furnishings within the rooms have functions that are determined by the people who live there. When furnishings provide service, comfort, and pleasure with minimum care, they are considered functional and appropriate.

There are three guidelines to follow when thinking about function and appropriateness in the home. First, furnishings should be appropriate for the function of the dwelling. For example, formal dining room furniture is not appropriate for a vacation cabin. Second, furnishings should also be appropriate for each room. For instance, a living room is not an appropriate place for a refrigerator.

Last, the form of furnishings should be appropriate for their function. Furnishings need to be designed to adapt to the structure of the human body. They also need to be designed and arranged to meet people's needs to stand, sit, move, and reach within a room.

Above all, your home should be appropriate and functional for all members of your living unit. It should fit the personalities, life-styles, needs, and wants of those who live there.

Harmony

Harmony is an agreement among the parts. It is created when the elements of design are effectively used according to the principles of design. One idea is used and carried throughout the design.

Harmony in design can be compared to the sounds coming from an orchestra in a concert. The instruments or "elements" are in tune, so the resulting sound is harmonious. The total effect is more important than any of the parts, 12-14.

Harmony results when there is unity among the elements. ***Unity*** occurs when all parts of a design are related by one design idea. When unity is present in a design, you see the room as a whole–not as separate pieces. Unity is achieved by repeating similar elements of design. For example, the furnishings and accessories in a room may all be square or rectangular. This ties the room together.

However, it would be monotonous for the room to have only square and rectangular furnishings and accessories. By adding a few circular or triangular accessories, variety can be created. Unity with some variety makes a design more interesting. See 12-15. Without variety, the limitations on the elements and principles of design can result in a boring, lifeless room.

While some variety is needed, too much variety can cause confusion. Variation is like seasoning in food. The right amount of a seasoning makes the food taste acceptable. Too little or too much may make it unacceptable. Therefore, the goal is unity with some variation.

American Fiber Manufacturers Association

12-14
When the elements and principles of design are used together effectively, a harmonious room, such as this one, results.

12-15
Using unity with variety in a design creates much more interest than simply using unity.

When working to achieve harmony, let only one type of each element of design dominate. For example, one color should dominate. This color can be the base color to your color harmony. Smaller amounts of a coordinating color can be used as an accent. This will assure harmony and unity with variety in the design. The overall appearance of a room will be pleasing. If several colors are used in equal amounts, the room will be a confusing combination of parts.

Beauty

In addition to being a characteristic of design, beauty is also a goal of design. Each person has a unique concept of beauty. However, the word beauty is generally used to describe well-designed and pleasing objects.

The elements and principles of design have been developed as a result of studying what most people see as being beautiful. If elements of design are arranged according to the principles of design, the result will appear beautiful to most people. The separate elements enhance one another and heighten the effect of beauty. Beauty gives a house, its furnishings, and its surroundings a distinction. Although beauty is not the only goal in planning and furnishing a home, it is what makes the visual appearance memorable.

Sensory Design

Good design responds to all sensory needs and serves people of all ages, sizes, and physical capabilities. Design that considers the senses enriches the total environment. ***Sensory design*** is the application of how to apply design in regard to the senses of sight, hearing, smell, and touch. It is used to make housing more accessible and functional for both people with disabilities and people without disabilities.

Most types of design can be seen by the majority of people. People can tell if they like a design by how it looks. However, in design, the other senses need to be considered too. The noise levels in a room can be controlled by using specific materials in construction and design. For instance, hard and smooth surfaces make sounds louder. Rough and soft surfaces absorb sound, which creates a quiet atmosphere. As you design a room, think about what kinds of sounds you want to hear in the room. Then think about the kinds of materials you need to include in your design to create this atmosphere.

The smell of a room can evoke feelings and emotions. Fresh flowers placed in a room may provide a sense of elegance. A lemon smell used in cleaners can create the sense of freshness. Pine reminds people of the outdoors. Candles, herbs, and spices used as accessories in design can be used to create certain atmospheres in a room. Some smells tend to be offensive and should be avoided. If odors, such as gas or smoke, are present in a room, they could indicate danger.

The sense of touch also affects your response to design. The texture of various materials used in design can communicate specific feelings. Marble is cold and hard, silk can be soft, and wood can be rough or smooth. Many people who are visually impaired use their sense of touch to direct them. For example, Braille used in elevators helps them identify specific floors.

The temperature of a room also affects design. People's skin is sensitive to temperature, which can affect their comfort level. Heating and cooling systems can be used to help control a room's comfortable temperature.

Summary

The elements of design are applied using the principles of design. The principles of design are proportion and scale, balance, emphasis, and rhythm.

Proportion and scale are both used to describe size, shape, and amount. They are also concerned with the relationships of objects and parts of objects. Guidelines for using proportion are the golden rectangle, the golden mean, and the golden section. Visual weight, an aspect of scale, is a perception that an object weighs more or less than it really does.

Balance can be formal or informal. It is a perception that both sides of an imaginary center line are equal. Informal balance can be attained through the arrangement of objects and the use of color, texture, and form.

Emphasis creates a focal point in a design. The focal point gives order and direction to a setting. Tips to keep in mind when planning a focal point include the fact that the focal point should be worthy of the attention it will receive. The focal point should dominate the room but not overpower it. Last, to prevent confusion, no other features should compete with the focal point.

Rhythm can be produced by repetition, gradation, radiation, opposition or transition. Repetition is when an element of design is repeated in a design. Gradation is created by a gradual increase or decrease of similar elements in a design. In radiation, lines flow outward from a central point. In rhythm by opposition, lines meet to form right angles. Rhythm by transition is created when curved lines carry the eyes from one part of an object to another.

The goals of design can be achieved when the elements and principles of design are used together well. The goals of design are function and appropriateness, harmony with unity and variety, and beauty. Function makes sure that furnishings meet their functions and are appropriate for their use. Harmony is when there is unity among the parts of a design. Variety is used to keep a harmonious design from becoming monotonous. What is beautiful to most people can be achieved when the elements of design are used according to the principles of design.

Sensory design incorporates the senses into design. The senses of sight, hearing, smell, and touch are all considered. When sensory design is used, housing becomes more accessible and functional for all people, regardless of age, size, or physical abilities.

To Review

Write your responses on a separate sheet of paper.

1. True or False. A sofa and coffee table in a 1:2 ratio is more pleasing than a sofa and coffee table in a 2:3 ratio.
2. Large-scale furnishings need ______-scale accessories.
3. Define formal balance and informal balance. Sketch an example of each.
4. How can emphasis be used to create a focal point? Give an example.
5. List the five kinds of rhythm.
6. How are function and appropriateness related?
7. What can be done to avoid monotony in a harmonious design?
8. What is the relationship between beauty and the elements and principles of design?
9. Give an example of how sensory design can benefit you.

To Do

1. Look in magazines to find pictures that illustrate each principle of design. Cut the pictures out, mount them on construction paper, and write the principle of design underneath the picture.
2. Look around your house and identify where the golden rectangle, golden mean, and golden section are used. If they are not used, make suggestions where they could be applied. Write a one-page paper on your observations.
3. Find a picture of a room with a definite focal point. Give an oral report explaining how the other features and objects in the room complement the focal point.
4. Visit a furnished model home. Identify how the goals of design are met in this house. Share your findings with the class.
5. Choose a room for a person who has special needs. It might be a bedroom for an older person, a playroom for a child who is visually impaired, or an office for a person who is hearing impaired. Give examples of how sensory design can enhance the room to make it more accessible to that person.

CHAPTER 13

Textiles in Today's Homes

Saxony Carpet Co.

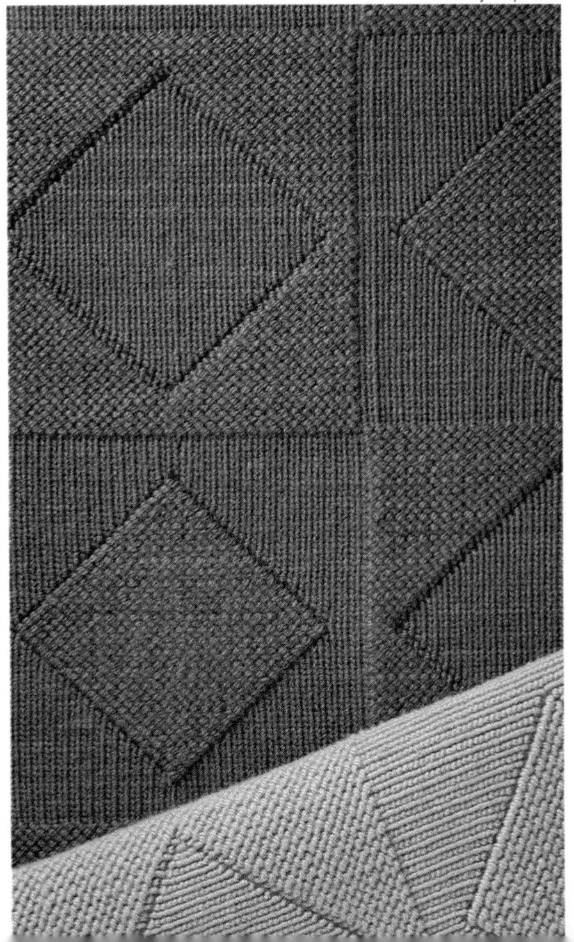

To Know
applied design
blend
bonded
cellulosic natural fiber
combination yarn
comforter
felting
fiber
finish
flammable
float
generic name
grain
knitting
manufactured fiber
nap
needlepunching
protein natural fiber
resiliency
structural design
tanned
textiles
trade name
tufted

wale
warp yarn
weaving
weft yarn
yarn

Objectives

After reading this chapter, you will be able to:

- Distinguish between natural fibers and manufactured fibers.
- List characteristics of various fibers.
- Describe the fabric construction processes.
- Identify appropriate textiles for various household uses.
- Explain the benefits of textile laws.

Textiles are any products made from fibers, including fabrics. You come in contact with a variety of textiles in your home every day. Your clothes are made from textiles and so are many other products. They include carpets, rugs, upholstery, curtains, tablecloths, towels, and sheets.

You need to choose textile products carefully when decorating and furnishing your house. It is important to understand the characteristics of the many fibers and fabrics used in textiles. You also need to know how to maintain and care for them.

Understanding Fibers, Yarns, and Fabrics

In order to understand how to use and care for textiles properly, you need to understand how they are made. Textiles begin as fibers. Then they are made into yarns, which are made into fabrics.

Fibers

Fibers are the raw materials from which fabric is made. They are long, thin, and hair-like. Fibers are obtained from either natural or manufactured sources.

Natural fibers. Natural fibers come from plant or animal sources. They are divided into cellulosic natural fibers or protein natural fibers.

Cellulosic natural fibers are made of the cellulose in plants. They are usually highly absorbent, launder well, and are seldom damaged by insects. However, they burn easily, can be stained by mildew, and prolonged exposure to sunlight can cause yellowing. The fibers are low in elasticity and may wrinkle easily. Specific traits and uses of some cellulosic natural fibers are listed in 13-1.

Cellulosic Natural Fibers			
Fiber	Source	Characteristics	Uses
Cotton	Cotton plant	Strong Dyes well Shrinks in hot water	Sheets Bedspreads Towels Upholstery Rugs Draperies
Linen	Flax plant	Strong Wears well	Tablecloths Kitchen towels Upholstery Draperies
Ramie	China grass	Dyes well High gloss or shine Shrinks	Table linens
Kapok	Kapok tree	Light Soft Not washable	Pillows and pad filling

13-1
Cellulosic natural fibers come from a variety of plant sources.

Protein natural fibers come from animal sources. They have good ***resiliency*** (ability to recover its original size and shape) and elasticity, and they burn slowly. However, they yellow in the sunlight and are weak. Care must be taken in cleaning them. They usually need to be dry-cleaned. Characteristics and uses of some natural protein fibers are listed in 13-2.

Manufactured fibers. ***Manufactured fibers*** are made from wood cellulose, oil products, and other chemicals. They are classified as cellulosic and noncellulosic fibers. Each fiber is given a ***generic name,*** which describes a group of fibers with similar chemical compositions. ***Trade names*** are used by companies to identify their own specific fibers.

Each manufactured fiber has its own characteristics. However, all manufactured fibers have some traits in common. For example, they generally launder well and are mothproof. They are also *nonallergenic,* which means you are not likely to develop an allergy to them. Some common manufactured fibers and their traits and uses are listed in 13-3.

Yarns

Fibers are spun or twisted into ***yarns,*** 13-4. Yarns are made from fiber *staples* (short fibers) and *filaments* (long, continuous fibers). A yarn may be made from a single type of fiber like wool or nylon. It can also be made from two or more different fibers, such as cotton and polyester. When two or more types of fibers are combined to make yarn, it is called a ***blend.*** Blends bring out the good qualities of the fibers and hide the bad. When two or more different yarns are combined, they create a ***combination yarn.***

Fabric Construction

Fabric traits are determined by the type, amount, and size of fibers and how they are used to make yarns. How fabrics are constructed is also important. There are many ways to construct fabrics. They include weaving, knitting, felting, tanning, or bonding.

Woven fabrics. Many fabrics used in the home are woven. See 13-5. ***Weaving*** is the interlacing of two sets of yarns at right angles to each other. The ***warp yarns*** run the lengthwise direction and form the lengthwise grain. ***Grain*** is the direction threads run in a woven fabric. Extra warp yarns form the *selvage,* which is the lengthwise woven edge of the fabric. The ***weft yarns*** are the filling yarns that run in the crosswise direction. They form the crosswise grain.

Protein Natural Fibers			
Fiber	Source	Characteristics	Uses
Silk	Silkworm cocoon	Strong Absorbent Dyes well Lustrous Water spots easily	Draperies Wall hangings Lampshades Upholstery
Wool	Hair of sheep	Absorbent Wrinkle resistant Not moth resistant Shrinks	Rugs Draperies Curtains Upholstery Blankets

13-2
Protein natural fibers are strong and absorbent.

Manufactured Fibers			
Generic Name; Some Trade Name(s)	Type	Characteristics	Uses
Acetate Celebrate Chromspun Estron	Cellulosic	Drapes well Does not shrink Dyes easily Weak Heat sensitive	Bedspreads Draperies Upholstery
Acrylic Acrilan Creslan Orlon	Noncellulosic	Warm Lightweight Resists wrinkles Low absorbency Heat sensitive	Blankets Carpets Draperies Rugs Upholstery
Glass Fiberglas Fiber Glass	Noncellulosic	Strong Resists sun fading Nonabsorbent	Curtains Draperies Insulation
Metallic Lame Lurex Chromoflex	Noncellulosic	Resists shrinking Durable Nonabsorbent	Draperies Rugs Tablecloths Upholstery
Modacrylic SEF	Noncellulosic	Warm Dyes easily Resists flames and wrinkling Weak Nonabsorbent Heat sensitive	Blankets Carpeting Curtains Draperies Rugs
Nylon Anso Cumaloft Zeftron	Noncellulosic	Strong Resistant to chemical damage and abrasions Does not stretch, shrink, or absorb water Creates static electricity	Carpets Curtains Draperies Rugs Slipcovers Tablecloths Upholstery
Olefin Alpha Essera Spectra	Noncellulosic	Lightweight Strong Resistant to abrasions Heat sensitive Nonabsorbent	Carpet backs Carpeting Slipcovers Upholstery
Polyester Dacron Fortrel Kodel	Noncellulosic	Strong Resistant to abrasions, creases, and shrinkage Holds its shape Low absorbency Heat sensitive	Bedding Carpeting Curtains Draperies Rugs Tablecloths Upholstery
Rayon Beau-Grip Zantrel	Cellulosic	Highly absorbent Soft Dyes easily Drapes well Weak Not resistant to mildew and sunlight	Bedding Draperies Slipcovers Tablecloths Upholstery

13-3
Each manufactured fiber has its own unique traits.

National Cotton Council of America

13-4
Cotton fibers are twisted and pulled into small strands to make fine yarns.

Carol G. Brown, ASID. Certified in the State of California

13-5
Many woven fabrics are used in this room. They can be found in the chair upholstery, window treatment, pillows, tablecloth, and napkins.

Woven fabrics are made from three basic weaves. They are the plain weave, twill weave, and satin weave. Each weave varies according to how the yarns are crossed or interlaced. All other weaves are variations on these three basic weaves. See 13-6.

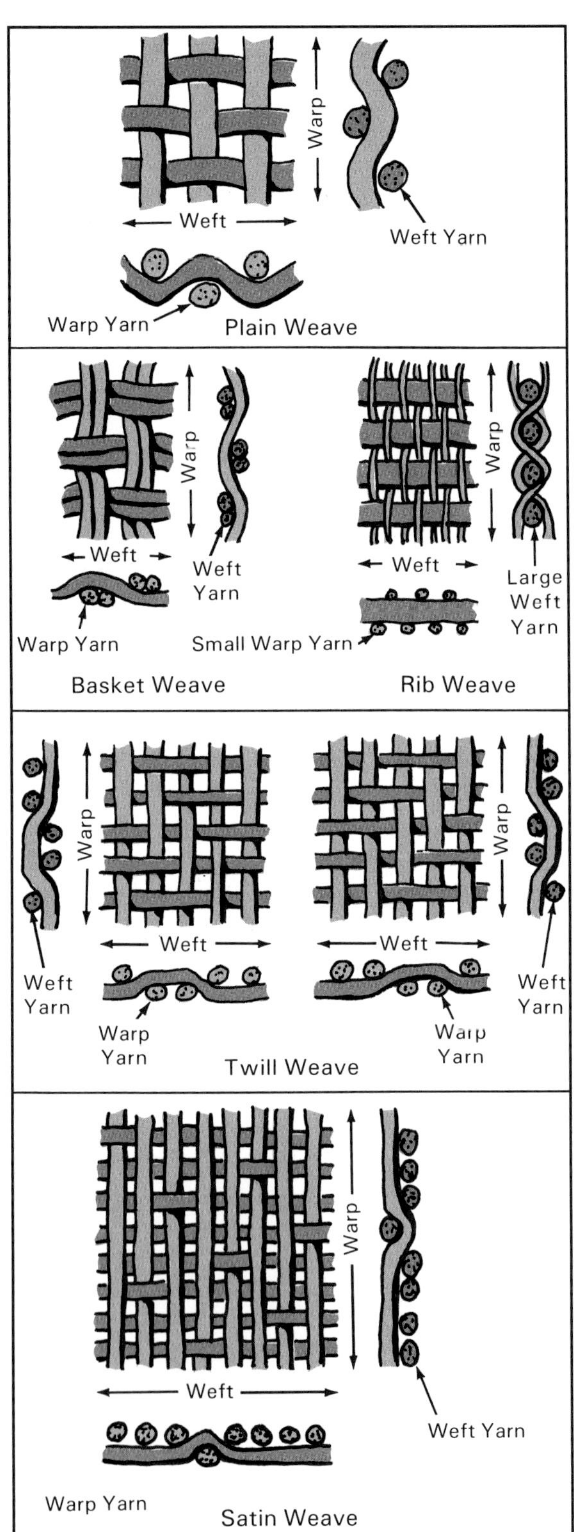

13-6
Each weave is constructed differently. This gives each type of fabric a different look and feel.

The *plain weave* is the simplest weave. The weft yarn goes over and under each warp yarn. A variation of the plain weave is the *basket weave.* Two or more weft yarns are interlaced with two or more warp yarns. The *rib weave* is another variation of the plain weave. Coarser weft yarns are combined with regular warp yarns to give a corded effect.

In the *twill weave,* the warp or weft yarn passes over two or more yarns. Each succeeding pass begins one yarn above or below the last one. The result is a ***wale,*** which is a diagonal rib or cord pattern.

A twill weave can be even or uneven. When the weft yarns go over and under the same number of warp yarns, an even twill weave is created. When the number of the weft yarns and the warp yarns are not the same, an uneven twill weave is created. Twill weave fabrics are stronger than plain weave fabrics. They also tend to show soil less quickly.

The *satin weave* has long ***floats,*** or portions of yarn, on the surface of the fabric. Either the warp yarns or weft yarns float over four or more opposite yarns, then go under one. Each successive float begins two yarns away from the beginning of the last one. The satin weave is smooth and slippery. It drapes well and is good for linings. However, it is less durable than the other basic weaves.

The *pile weave* is a variation of the plain and twill weaves. Pile fabrics have yarn loops or cut yarns that stand away from the base of the fabric. In 13-7, you can compare a plain weave, loop-pile weave, and a cut-pile weave. Examples of pile weave fabrics are velvet, velveteen, corduroy, terry cloth, and frieze.

Pile fabrics have a ***nap,*** which is a layer of fiber ends that stand up from the surface of the fabric. The nap appears different when you view it from varying directions. It is important that the nap runs in the same direction throughout a product. For example, if you make draperies that have two or more panels, the nap of the pile fabric needs to run the same direction on all of the panels.

Another weave used for home furnishings is the Jacquard weave. It is used for damask, tapestry, and brocade, 13-8. You will also find that

Plain Weave

Loop-Pile Weave

Cut-Pile Weave

Pile Weave

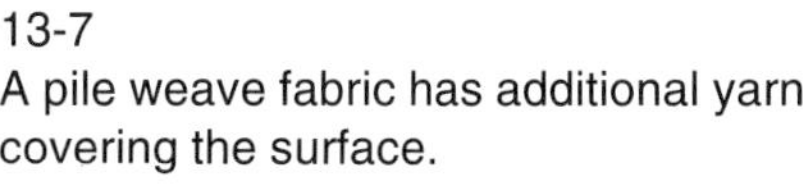

13-7
A pile weave fabric has additional yarn covering the surface.

Ethan Allen, Inc.

13-8
The Jacquard weave produces a decorative design on the fabric.

the leno weave, 13-9, is used for curtains and thermal blankets.

Knitted fabrics. ***Knitting*** is the looping of yarns together. The size of the loops and how close together they are varies, as well as the way the loops are joined. See 13-10. Depending on whether one or two needles are used, knits can be single or double knits.

Weft knits are either circular or flat. They produce single knits, double knits, jersey, rib knits, and Jacquard. Warp knits are flat. They are generally tighter, flatter, and less elastic than weft knits.

Knitted fabrics are mainly used in home fabrics as backing for other fabrics. This is because they lack the stability and body needed for many home textiles. However, they are increasingly being used for upholstery.

Other methods and types of fabrics. There are other fabrics used in the home that are not woven or knitted. They are constructed in a variety of ways.

Nonwoven fabrics are made by joining fibers together using heat, moisture, chemicals, friction, and pressure. During this process called ***felting,*** the masses of fibers interlock and hold together. Felt and fusible interfacing are examples of nonwoven fabrics. Nonwoven fabrics are generally not as strong as woven or knitted fabrics, and they do not have as much stretch.

Vinyl and other plastic materials are not made from fibers. Instead, they are thin, nonwoven sheets. These sheets can be finished to look like woven fabrics or leather. Vinyl is usually backed with a knit fabric to give it stability and strength.

Leather is sometimes classified as a nonwoven fabric. When it is ***tanned,*** or treated with a special acid called tannin, it is soft and resists stains, fading, and cracking. Since it is strong and durable, it is sometimes used in the home.

In ***bonded*** nonwoven fabrics, two layers of fabric are permanently joined together with an adhesive. Heat is used to set the bond. Often face fabric is bonded to a lining. Other times, the face fabric is bonded to synthetic foam.

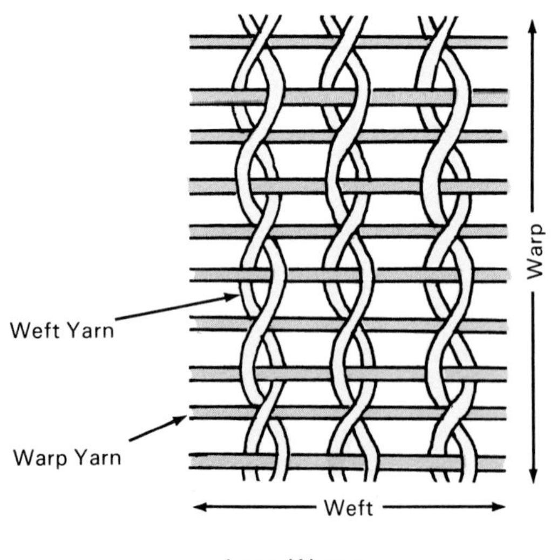

13-9
The leno weave is loosely-woven and has open spaces.

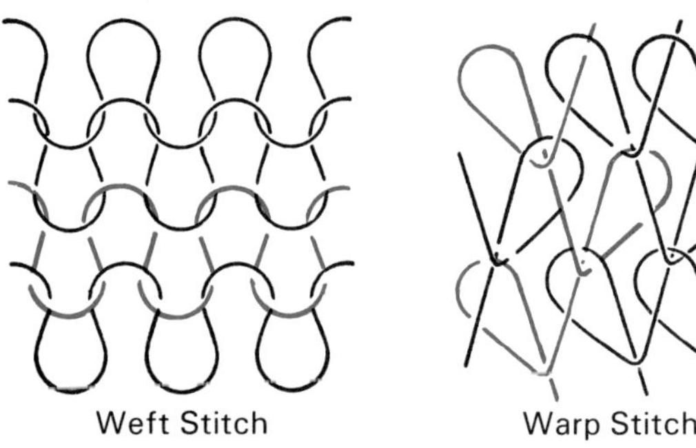

13-10
Knitted fabrics vary according to yarn size, yarn texture, and loop construction. The weft stitch allows more stretch than the warp stitch.

Fabric Modifications

Fabrics can be modified to improve their appearance, feel, performance, and durability. These changes can be made through design, dye, and finishes.

Design. Designs in fabrics may be structural or applied. ***Structural designs*** are made by varying the yarns as the fabric is either woven or knitted. The size, texture, and placement of the yarns all affect the final pattern. ***Applied designs*** are printed onto the surface of the fabric. They can be seen distinctly only on one side of the fabric.

Dye. Dyes are used to give color to fabric. There are three main methods of dyeing fabric. They are adding color to the fibers, adding color to the yarn, and adding color to the fabric.

When you add color to the fibers, it is called stock dyeing. It is done before the fibers are spun into yarn. The dying is uniform and long-lasting. Adding color to the yarn is one of the oldest methods. It is done before the yarns are made into fabric. This method is widely used and color absorption is good. The easiest and least expensive method is adding color to the fabric. It is called piece dyeing and usually a single color is used.

Finishes. The appearance, feel, and performance of fabrics can be improved by applying ***finishes.*** They are applied only to the fabric, not to the fiber or yarn. Manufacturers are able to produce many finishes for fabrics. See 13-11 for a description of common finishes and what they do.

Basic Textile Finishes
Antistatic: Prevents buildup of static electricity.
Bleaching: Whitens natural fabrics when they come from the mill.
Crease resistance: Prevents fabrics from wrinkling
Flame resistance: Prevents fabrics from burning easily.
Moth resistance: Discourages moths and carpet beetles from attacking wool fibers.
Napping: Produces a raised surface by pulling up fiber ends.
Permanent press: Prevents fabrics from wrinkling. Also known as **durable press.**
Preshrunk: Prevents fabrics from shrinking more than a small amount.
Sizing: Provides extra body and weight to fabric through a solution of starch.
Soil release: Makes stain removal easy.
Stain or soil resistance: Makes fibers less absorbent, so stains can be removed easier.
Waterproof: Prevents water from soaking into the fabric.
Water repellent: Resists water but does not make fabrics waterproof.

13-11
Finishes can be applied to fabrics to improve them in various ways.

Selecting Textiles for Home Use

The fabrics that are used in the home are referred to as household textiles. The textiles you choose will depend on where they will be used and for what purposes. You need to consider the appearance, durability, maintenance, and comfort of the fabric. You should also think about the ease of working with the fabric and the cost. Using what you have learned about fabric types and construction will help you make these decisions.

Appearance

Appearance is the visual effect. For instance, a fabric may appear soft or stiff. It may also appear bulky or sheer, light or dark, rough or smooth, bright or dull. Fabrics can make a room appear elegant or relaxed.

Durability

Durability is the ability to last. You want fabrics to last as long as possible to avoid replacement costs. Fabrics that receive heavy use need to stand up to wear. Tightly woven fabrics tend to last the longest.

Maintenance

Maintenance is the care needed to keep fabrics clean and looking their best. Proper cleaning techniques–dry cleaning or laundering–should be used. You need to follow instructions to ensure good results. You also need to consider the cost of maintaining fabrics. Textiles that can be laundered at home can help you avoid the costs of dry cleaning.

Comfort

You want fabric that makes you feel comfortable. Comfort is a psychological consideration and is different for each person. A fabric can give you visual comfort if you like its appearance. It can give you physical comfort if it feels good.

Ease of Use in Construction

If you are going to sew some of the textiles yourself, you need to consider the ease with which the fabric can be managed. Heavy, closely-woven fabrics are harder to handle than lightweight, loosely-woven fabrics. On the other hand, loosely woven-fabrics tend to catch on objects. Also, stitching is more difficult to see on dark fabric than light fabric.

Cost

You may be concerned about the cost. However, do not base your decision on the cost alone. You will want to buy the best fabric for its use. A good-quality fabric at a high price might be more economical in the long run than buying a low-quality fabric for a low price. You also need to keep in mind that besides the initial price, you have the costs of installation, maintenance, and replacement. Evaluate fabrics based on these important factors before you make the purchase.

Woven Carpet or Rug

Tufted Carpet or Rug

Needlepunched Carpet or Rug

13-12
The appearance and durability of carpet is affected by how it is constructed.

Textiles for Floor Treatments

Buying carpets and rugs for your house is a major purchase. There are many different construction methods, textures, fibers, and finishes from which to choose. In order to make a good decision, it is important to know what choices are available.

Construction methods. There are several methods used to construct carpets and rugs. Three are weaving, tufting, or needlepunching. See 13-12. Each of these methods combines the pile yarn, which is the part you walk on, with the backing material, which is the part that holds the yarn together.

Woven carpets and rugs are made on a loom. The pile yarns and the backing are interwoven. Axminster, velvet, and Wilton are the three main types of weaves used to make woven carpets and rugs. Only about two percent of today's carpeting is woven.

Tufted carpets and rugs are made when the yarn is looped into the backing material and secured with an adhesive to the backing and a second backing. Tufting is easy to do and is less expensive than weaving.

Needlepunching is the process of interlocking fibers by using felting needles. The process produces a flat carpet that resembles felt. It is mainly used for indoor/outdoor carpets and rugs.

Textures. Carpets and rugs come in a variety of textures. Different textures are created when the yarn is cut, left uncut, twisted, untwisted, or cut in different lengths. There are five different carpet textures. They are cut pile, level loop pile, multilevel loop pile, cut and loop pile, and shag pile. Level loop pile wears the best. Multilevel loop pile results when there is a combination of cut and looped yarns.

Texture can also be achieved by twisting the pile yarns. Other times, flecks of color are added and the appearance of texture results. The thickness of the yarn affects the texture, too. The thicker the yarn, the more plush the carpet. Density refers to the number of tufts or yarns per square inch. Carpets with a high density look better and are more durable.

Fiber content. Fiber content greatly affects the quality of rugs and carpets. Wool, nylon, acrylic, rayon, olefin, and cotton are the major fibers used for carpets and rugs. Each has unique traits that affect the carpeting.

Wool is an ideal fiber for carpets and rugs, because it is very resilient. It is also durable and soil and stain resistant. It is, however, expensive. Therefore, it is used only for luxury carpets and rugs.

Nylon is the most-used fiber for carpets and rugs today. It is very durable, resilient, and soil resistant. However, oily stains are difficult to remove. It is less costly than wool.

Acrylic looks like wool. It also has good resilience, durability, and soil-resistance like wool. However, oily stains are difficult to remove. It costs less than wool but more than nylon.

Rayon carpets and rugs are attractive, but not very practical. They are low in resilience, durability, and resistance to soil. They are, however, low in price. Therefore, they are used when quality is not an important factor. Scatter rugs and inexpensive room-size rugs are sometimes made of rayon.

Some kitchen, bathroom, and outdoor carpets are made of olefin. It is very durable and resistant to soil and stains. It is also fairly resilient. It ranges in price from medium to low.

Cotton rugs are attractive and durable, but low in resilience and soil resistance. Prices vary according to the type of cotton, but they are usually fairly low. Cotton is used mostly for washable scatter rugs.

Finishes. The application of finishes to carpet and rug yarns is mainly for functional reasons. For example, an antistatic finish reduces static buildup. A flame-resistant finish prevents the fabric from burning easily. Stain-resistant and soil release finishes make caring for rugs and carpets easier.

Textiles for Upholstered Furniture

Upholstered furniture is fully or partially covered with fabric, 13-13. When you choose upholstery fabric, you need to consider where and how the furniture will be used. For furniture that will receive hard wear, choose fabric that is durable, stain-resistant, and easy to clean. Wool, mohair, and manufactured fibers, such as nylon and acrylic, are very durable. They are often used in blends.

Masco Corporation/Scholz Design Architects

13-13
The chair in this room is partially upholstered, while the sofa is completely upholstered.

Knowing the fabric content will tell you how well the fabric will wear and how easy it will be to clean. These, along with other factors, are determined by the fibers used in producing the fabric and the finishes added to the fabrics.

Fabrics used for upholstery are chosen according to their use in formal and informal settings. Formal, or traditional, rooms have an elegant appearance. The fabrics most often used include plain or textured satins, damask, velvet or velveteen, brocade, faille, mohair, or matelassé. These fabrics can be made of silk or a blend of natural and manufactured fibers.

In informal, or casual, settings, the use of pattern is very important. The pattern can range from a very small print to a large scenic design. You can use a wide variety of fabrics, including chintz, polished cotton, gingham, sailcloth, burlap, denim, poplin, or corduroy.

Textiles Used in Window Treatments

As you choose fabrics for window treatments, which are draperies and curtains, there are many factors you will need to keep in mind. You need to consider the purpose and style of the room in which they are to be used. You need to consider the colors and patterns used throughout the room. You also need to consider their cost and care.

Purpose and Styles of Rooms

A window covering can regulate the natural light within a room. Sheer fabrics will filter the light. They will give you a feeling of privacy in the daytime. You will be able to see out, but others will not be able to see in the room. However, they do not provide privacy at night.

Opaque window treatments will not allow you to see out when window treatments are closed. They can shut out light and provide privacy both day and night. This is an important consideration when choosing fabrics for some rooms, such as bedrooms. Opaque fabrics are usually heavy and thick. Lighter weight fabrics may not give the privacy you desire.

As you choose window treatments, you need to consider the styles of the rooms in which they are used. If the room is informal or a work area, casual fabrics, such as denim or poplin, are good. In more formal settings, fabrics, such as damask and antique satin, should be used.

Colors and Patterns

The colors and patterns in window treatment fabrics should match or complement the furnishings in the room. You may choose a dominant color for your window treatments, 13-14. It could be a color that is in the upholstery or carpet. When choosing patterns, it is important to note that large patterns go well in large rooms. Also, small prints are better suited for small rooms.

Cost and Care

You can buy ready-made window treatments. You can also purchase fabric and have them made or make them yourself. However, it is important to keep in mind that the more fabric and

Carol G. Brown, ASID. Certified in the State of California

13-14
The peach color in the window treatments matches the upholstery and carpeting.

detail used in the window treatments, the more they will cost.

You should also consider the cost of caring for window treatments. Many types of fabrics are used for draperies. Most draperies and some curtains need to be dry-cleaned. This can be expensive. Others are made from fabrics that can be washed at home. However, if they are very large, they will need to be laundered professionally.

Textiles for Kitchen, Bath, and Bed

Textiles used in the kitchen, bathroom, and bedroom are called linens, although few are actually made of linen today. You need to consider the appearance, durability, and care of these linens as you do other textiles.

Kitchen

The main linens used in the kitchen or dining room are table coverings and towels.

Table coverings. Table coverings include tablecloths, place mats, and napkins. See 13-15. Silence cloths that go under the tablecloths to reduce noise are also considered a table covering.

Thinking about how the table coverings will be used will help you choose the best type. Is the table covering to be used everyday or for special occasions only? Is it to be used in a formal dining room or a breakfast nook? For instance, you may choose to use place mats for a less formal event or for everyday use.

Linen used to be the fabric of choice for table coverings. However, it requires ironing, and many people today are more interested in ease of care. Many table coverings are now available in fabrics that require little or no ironing and have soil-release finishes.

Towels. Kitchen towels include dishcloths, dish towels, and lint-free towels, which are used for drying glass. Kitchen towels are usually made of linen or cotton. Linen is good for lint-free towels because it does not have a nap, and it dries more quickly than cotton. All the towels you choose should absorb water quickly and easily, be durable, and be attractive, in that order. They should also be easy to launder.

Spiegel, Inc.

13-15
Tablecloths and napkins often coordinate with the tableware.

Towels are available in a variety of colors and patterns. Some have borders and woven-in designs. Any additional decoration, such as special borders or monograms, will increase the cost of towels. This, however, does not make them better-quality towels.

Bathroom

Household linens used in the bathroom include towels, bath mats, and shower curtains.

Towels. Bathroom towels come in several sizes. The extra large size is called a bath sheet. The large size is called a bath towel, the medium size is called a hand towel, and the small size is called a washcloth. Sometimes even smaller towels are available. They are called guest towels or fingertip towels. These towels often come in sets.

Many towels are made of cotton terry cloth because it is absorbent. Also, the loops absorb moisture well. Sometimes the cotton is blended with polyester. The polyester decreases drying time, adds strength, and reduces shrinkage. In both cases, the more closely woven the fabric is, the more durable and absorbent it is. Velour terry cloth is also used. It has a cut pile on one side of the towel, which gives it a velvet-like appearance.

Bath mats. Some bath mats are made of a similar, but heavier, material as towels. Others are tufted and have latex backing to keep them from slipping. Still others are made of yarn sewn onto a backing. You may see bath mats made from braided rags. Fibers used to make bath rugs include cotton, rayon, and various blends. They often come in colors that match or coordinate with bath towels.

Shower curtains. Shower curtains are used to prevent water from spraying outside of a shower. They are made from fabric that has been treated with a waterproof finish or from plastic. They come in a wide variety of colors and are often designed to coordinate with bath towels and bath mats, see 13-16.

J.P. Stevens & Company, Inc.

13-16
This shower curtain ties together the towel and wall treatment in this bathroom.

Bedroom

Linens used in the bedroom are called bedding. They include sheets, pillowcases, blankets, bedspreads, and comforters.

Bed linens. Bed linens include sheets and pillowcases. They usually come in matching sets. The sheets may be flat or fitted. A flat sheet can be used as either the top or bottom sheet. A fitted sheet is made to fit the shape of the mattress and is used only as the bottom sheet. Both sheets and pillowcases come in various sizes to fit the different-sized beds. These beds include cribs, twin beds, standard size beds, queen-sized beds, and king-sized beds. There are also sheets designed to fit waterbeds.

Sheets and pillowcases are usually made of cotton or a cotton/polyester blend. Cotton sheets are more absorbent, but polyester decreases wrinkling. Sometimes sheets are made from acetate or nylon. Cotton sheets are usually made from percale, muslin, or flannel. Percale is a high-quality, lightweight, plain-weave cotton product. Muslin is also a plain-weave cotton product that ranges from lightweight to heavyweight. Flannel has a napped surface that provides extra warmth.

When you purchase sheets and pillowcases, make sure you buy durable ones. The durability is determined to a great extent by the thread count. The higher the thread count, the more closely woven the fabric. Lower-count sheets are lower priced. Fine percale sheets may have a thread count of 180 to 200, while less expensive muslin sheets may have a count of only 112 to 140.

Last, you need to be concerned about the washability of sheets and pillowcases. Since they will be washed often, they need to be colorfast and durable.

Blankets, bedspreads, and comforters. These items come in weights suitable for different seasons of the year. In certain climates and air-conditioned homes, blankets are used year round. Light cotton or rayon blankets are ideal for summer. They are easy to launder and less expensive than heavy blankets. Wool, acrylic, or a combination are good for cold winter nights. Thermal blankets made using the leno weave are often a good choice. The open spaces in the weave form pockets that trap air and serve as insulation. Again, comfort, attractiveness, and durability are considerations in choosing blankets.

Bedspreads are usually purchased for their attractiveness. They come in a variety of fabrics. You can make a satisfying choice if you know your fabrics. While some bedspreads are washable, many need to be dry-cleaned.

In addition to your bedspread being attractive, it should be the correct size for the bed. It should also harmonize with the other furnishings in the room. Matching bedspread, window treatment, and sheet sets are available.

Filled bed coverings are called ***comforters.*** They are often used as bedspreads. They are chosen for their attractiveness and warmth. The covering makes a comforter attractive. See 13-17. Comforter coverings made from rayon, acetate, and silk can appear luxurious. Comforter covers made from sateen, polished cotton, and challis are not as luxurious appearing. However, they are still attractive and more durable.

The filling is what makes the comforter warm. The warmest comforters are filled with wool or down. Down is the soft, fine feathers from ducks or geese. It is both light and resilient. Since down is expensive, lower-quality feathers are sometimes used. Other fillings include polyester or cotton and kapok, which mat down in comforters.

Textile Laws

There are many laws in the United States that regulate textiles. They were passed to inform and protect the consumer from false labeling and advertising. Three major textile acts that apply to household textiles are discussed below.

The Textile Fiber Products Identification Act

This act says that fibers in a textile product are to be listed in order of predominance by weight. If the fibers are less than five percent of the fabric, they can be listed as "other fiber or fibers." Natural and manufactured fibers are listed by their generic names. Trade names can also be given. The information is to be attached to the product. However, certain items, such as already installed upholstery fabrics, mattress materials, and carpet backings are exempt.

Spiegel, Inc.

13-17
This comforter and the matching pillowcases and sheets makes this bed very attractive.

Wool Products Labeling Act

This act requires that all products made of wool include a label telling the kind and amount of wool used. Wool products are required to be identified as one of the following types:

- Wool: wool that has never been used before in fabrics.
- Recycled wool: wool from wool products that were never used or wool that has been used in other products.

Products made from wool must have labels identifying the percentage of each type of wool used. The name of the manufacturer is also required. Imported wool must be labeled with the name of the country where it was processed and manufactured.

The Flammable Fabrics Act

This act prohibits the sale of ***flammable*** fabrics, or fabrics that burn quickly. It includes fabrics found in textile products used in the home, such as carpets and rugs, mattresses, mattress pads, blankets, draperies, and upholstery. Many new flame-resistant finishes have been developed as a result of this act.

Summary

Natural fibers come from plant or animal sources. Manufactured fibers are made from wood cellulose, oil products, and other chemicals. Each fiber has its own traits. Fibers are made into yarns, which are then made into fabrics, or textiles.

You can make wise fabric choices by understanding fiber traits and the ways used to construct fabrics. Fabrics can be woven, knitted, felted, tanned, or bonded. Other factors to consider when choosing fabrics are the design, color, and finishes.

Some textiles are used for floor treatments, upholstery, and window treatments. Others are used in the kitchen, bathroom, and bedroom. The function and placement of the textiles are important. You need to consider how the fabrics will look with other furnishings in the room. Durability, maintenance, comfort, ease of use, and cost are other factors to consider.

Various textile laws inform and protect the consumer. Some laws require specific certain labeling information on textiles. Labels can help you wisely choose household textiles.

To Review

Write your responses on a separate sheet of paper.

1. Name two natural cellulosic fibers and two natural protein fibers.
2. List five manufactured fibers and give two characteristics of each.
3. What is the difference between natural fibers and manufactured fibers?
4. How do fibers and yarns differ?
5. Explain the difference between weaving and knitting.
6. How are bonded fabrics made?
7. List three factors that are included in the cost of fabric.
8. Describe the weaving and tufting processes used in carpet construction.
9. Name three fibers and give their uses in making carpets and rugs.
10. List three factors to consider when choosing upholstery fabrics.
11. _____ and _____ are types of window treatments using textiles.
12. True or False. Closely-woven fabrics are less opaque than loosely-woven fabrics.
13. What type of fabric are bathroom towels usually made of? Why?
14. Choose a textile act and explain how it protects consumers.

To Do

1. Collect a variety of household fabric samples and mount them on poster board. Underneath each sample, list the sample's fiber content and its household use.
2. Draw illustrations of the three basic weaves, labeling the warp yarns and weft yarns.
3. Using catalogs, find and list descriptions of the fabric, cost, and care required for fabrics suitable for one of the following:
   a. Upholstery.
   b. A window treatment.
   c. Bedroom linens.
4. Choose fabrics to decorate a kitchen, bathroom, or bedroom. Discuss what factors you need to consider when doing this. Explain why your choices are appropriate.
5. Choose five textile products from one room of your house. Read any labels found on them. Note on paper, the information required by law found on each. Share your findings with the class.

CHAPTER 14

Creating Interior Backgrounds

To Know
acoustical
floor coverings
flooring materials

Velux-America, Inc.

Objectives

After studying this chapter, you will be able to:

- Compare floor treatments.
- Describe several wall materials and wall treatments.
- Explain how ceiling treatments serve as interior backgrounds.
- Discuss how to plan satisfying interior backgrounds.

Floors, walls, and ceilings create interior backgrounds for furnishings and accessories in rooms. They also hide construction details and provide insulation. How they are treated helps determine the total look of the room and create a desired mood.

Floor Treatments

The floor treatment is usually the first background to be planned in a room. Floor treatments consist of flooring materials and floor coverings. There are many types of flooring materials and floor coverings from which to choose. However, before you choose a floor treatment, you should consider its appearance, comfort, durability, cost, and maintenance.

Flooring Materials

Flooring materials are materials that are used as the top surface of a floor. They do not include the subflooring, but they are structurally part of the floor and are fairly permanent. Commonly-used flooring materials include wood, ceramic tile, concrete, stone, brick, and terrazzo.

Wood. Wood is a popular flooring material. It looks good with all styles of furniture. It offers beauty and warmth to a room. Wood has some resilience. However, it is durable and resists dents.

The cost of wood flooring is moderate to high, depending on the type and quality of wood chosen. Hardwoods are typically more expensive than softwoods. Oak, hard maple, beech, birch, hickory, mahogany, cherry, and teak are common hardwoods used for floors. Oak is the most common because of its beauty, warmth, and durability. Hard maple is also common, because it is smooth, strong, and hard.

Southern yellow pine, Douglas fir, hemlock, and larch are common softwoods used for floors. Redwood, cedar, cypress, and eastern white pine are used where they are readily available.

Wood floors are applied in several ways. The most common method is to nail down thin strips of wood that are tongue and grooved to keep them close together. This is called strip flooring. Other methods include wood plank flooring and parquet flooring. Decorative patterns, such as alternate plank, 14-1, and parquetry, 14-2, can be created to add interest to a wood floor.

Wood finishes of plastic, wax, and oil make the task of maintaining wood floors easy. They protect the wood from moisture, stains, and wear.

Ceramic tile. Ceramic tile is available in a wide range of sizes, colors, and patterns. It is cool to the touch and hard and durable. Glazed ceramic tile is water and stain resistant, which

Bruce Hardwood Floors

14-1
This hardwood floor is a good example of alternate plank flooring.

makes it easy to maintain. Ceramic tile is expensive to install. It is most often used in bathrooms and entryways. However, it can be found throughout the house.

Quarry tile is the strongest of the ceramic tiles. It is available in a range of natural golds, reds, browns, grays, and blacks. See 14-3. The shapes and textures of quarry tile vary. Quarry tile is very strong and durable. It resists grease, chemicals, moisture, and changes in temperature. It can be glazed or unglazed. When needed, glazed quarry tile can be washed with warm water and soap. Unglazed tile may need to be waxed.

Bruce Hardwood Floors

14-2
Parquet floors are often assembled in factories for easier installation.

Lindal Cedar Homes, Inc. Seattle, Washington

14-3
This natural red and black quarry tile gives the room a pleasant rustic look.

Concrete. Concrete can have a smooth or textured surface. A smooth surface can be used as a finished floor. Color can be added to the concrete in powder form, or the concrete can be painted using a special paint. Concrete is uncomfortable to stand on for long periods of time. Because it is extremely sturdy and durable, it is often used for entryways, basements, patios, and garages. Indoor concrete floors need to be waxed for easy maintenance. Concrete floors are relatively inexpensive, because they do not require subflooring.

Stone. Stone floors are beautiful and durable, but costly. They can look either formal or informal. Stone comes in a variety of sizes and qualities. They may be used in their natural shapes or cut into geometric shapes. Colors are limited to natural grays and browns. Stone floors are fairly easy to maintain. A vinyl coating protects them from grease stains. Stone floors are used in areas of heavy traffic.

Brick. Brick floors are also beautiful, durable, and costly. They look best in informal settings. Bricks come in many sizes, colors, and textures. They can be used in a wide variety of patterns. The care of brick floors is similar to that of stone floors.

Terrazzo. Terrazzo is made of a mixture of cement and marble chips. It is often ground smooth and polished. For a more rustic appearance, gravel can be substituted for the marble, and the terrazzo can be left unpolished. Terrazzo comes in a limited range of colors, depending on the marble chips and gravel. Terrazzo floors are easy to maintain, because they are hard, durable, and very resistant to moisture. They are usually used in areas with heavy traffic, such as entryways and halls. Terrazzo, like stone and brick, is long lasting. However, it usually costs more than other flooring materials.

Floor Coverings

Floor coverings are placed on top of the structural floor. Although they are attached to the floor, they are not part of the structure. Floor coverings last several years and are expensive. However, they are not as expensive as flooring materials and can be changed more often. Floor coverings include soft floor coverings and resilient floor coverings.

Soft floor coverings. Carpets and rugs are types of floor coverings. They have many advantages. They serve as an insulation for cold floors and provide sound control and walking comfort. Soft floor coverings add color and texture to a room.

Soft floor coverings can cover the entire floor or portions of the floor. They are classified by how much floor they cover. Common soft floor coverings are wall-to-wall carpeting, room-size rugs, and area rugs.

Wall-to-wall carpeting covers an entire floor. It makes rooms appear large and luxurious. See 14-4. It can hide a poor floor. A disadvantage of wall-to-wall carpeting is that it usually cannot be moved without the help of a professional. Therefore, some parts of the carpeting show wear before other parts.

A *room-size rug* exposes a small border of floor. It can show off a beautiful wood floor while keeping the warmth and comfort of the soft floor covering. See 14-5. Maintenance, however, is a disadvantage. Separate cleaning processes are needed for the rug and the exposed part of the floor.

Area rugs vary in size, but they do not cover the entire floor. They are used to define areas of

Jessica Hall Associates. Certified in the State of California

14-5
A room-size rug combines the beauty of the original floor with the comfort of a rug.

Kate Shenberger Interiors, Flossmoor, Illinois

14-4
Wall-to-wall carpeting makes a room seem large, because the floor space is not divided into sections.

a room. See 14-6. Area rugs can add interest to a room and even serve as a focal point. They can be moved from one furniture grouping to another for a new look. They can be used in almost any room in any dwelling.

Padding is used under carpeting and rugs to lessen wear and increase resilience. It also adds luxury and warmth. Padding is made of hair, jute, sponge, or foam rubber.

Resilient floor coverings. Resilient floor coverings are nonabsorbent, durable, easy to maintain, and fairly inexpensive. They provide some walking comfort and noise control. Asphalt tile, vinyl, and cork tile are types of resilient floor coverings. They are available in a wide range of colors and patterns and can be used in any decorating scheme.

Asphalt tile is inexpensive. It is not affected by moisture and can be used in places where moisture is a problem, such as basement floors. Asphalt tile is durable, but it dents and stains easily.

Vinyl floor coverings, 14-7, are available in many colors, patterns, and textures. They are resistant to wear and stains, but abrasions can damage the surface. They are available in either tile or sheet form. Vinyl tile is the most costly kind of resilient tile, but it is the easiest to maintain. Little or no waxing is needed. Some sheet vinyl is made with a layer of vinyl foam behind it. The result is a floor with good walking comfort and good sound absorption.

Mannington Resilient Floors

14-7
This vinyl floor covering is beautiful and easy to keep clean.

Armstrong World Industries, Inc.

14-6
The use of the area rug on the right creates a conversational area and helps divide this open space into separate sections.

Cork tile has a beautiful, rich appearance. It is great for foot comfort and sound control, but it wears rapidly and dents easily. It is difficult to maintain and is damaged by grease stains. When covered with a coating of vinyl, it is water resistant, more durable, and easier to maintain than uncoated cork.

Walls

Walls make up the largest surface area of a room. They provide protection from the outdoors and reduce the amount of noise entering a room. They hide pipes, wiring, and insulation. They also divide space within a dwelling and provide privacy.

Wall Construction

How walls are constructed is an important factor to consider when planning backgrounds. It provides the basis for wall treatments.

A variety of materials can be used to construct interior walls. They include gypsum wallboard, plastic wallboard, paneling, plaster, and masonry. The materials used in wall construction will help determine what type of treatment will be used on it. Wall treatments will be discussed in the next section.

Gypsum wallboard. Gypsum wallboard, also known as drywall, is the most common material used for interior walls. It comes in 4 feet by 8 feet panels. Joints are taped, hidden by a fast-drying compound, and sanded. The smooth surface is covered by paint, wallpaper, or fabric.

Plastic wallboard. Plastic wallboard comes in both enamel and plastic laminate finishes, which makes it easy to maintain. It is used mostly in bathrooms and kitchens.

Paneling. Paneling is usually made of plywood. It is commonly available in 4 feet by 8 feet panels. Paneling can be applied directly to framing materials, but it is much more substantial if applied over gypsum board. Paneling comes in many different colors and textures. It is appropriate for any room. See 14-8.

Lindal Cedar Homes, Inc. Seattle, Washington

14-8
Paneling is used to give this contemporary room a feeling of warmth.

Plaster. Plaster is seldom used except in older homes and commercial buildings. Applying plaster requires special skills and facilities. Therefore, it costs more than most other types of walls. Plaster walls can be either smooth or rough. They are usually covered with paint.

Masonry. Masonry walls can serve as both the exterior and interior walls. *Cement blocks* can form both entire interior and exterior walls. They may be painted. Since they are large, they belong in large rooms decorated with large pieces of furniture, rough textures, and bold colors.

Brick or *stone* may form entire walls. However, they are both used mostly for decorative walls and fireplace walls, as in 14-9. They are beautiful and durable, and they require little or no upkeep. However, they are costly to install. Brick or stone is often found in informal settings, where it adds to a warm, cozy atmosphere.

Some of the materials used in wall construction can also serve as the wall treatment. For example, paneling, bricks, and stones do not need additional treatment. They can be used in their original state.

Masco Corporation/Scholz Design Architects

14-9
A brick wall is an attractive background for an informal room.

Wall Treatments

Walls may be treated in a variety of ways. Common wall treatments are paint, wallpaper, fabric, cork, ceramic tile, and plastic wallboard. These wall treatments vary from easy to difficult to apply. Some treatments are inexpensive while others are high in cost.

As you choose a wall treatment for a room, keep in mind that it should harmonize with the floor and ceiling. It should add to the general mood of the room. Most of all, it should reflect the personalities of the people who use the room.

Paint. Paint is the fastest and least expensive way to cover wall surfaces and to change the look of a room. See 14-10. Two types of paint commonly used for interior walls are water-based (latex) paint and oil-based paint. Water-based paint is easy to apply and dries quickly. Oil-based paint is thicker than water-based paint. It takes longer to dry and equipment is harder to clean.

Paints vary in the amount of gloss they have. *Enamel paints* have the most gloss. They give a protective and decorative finish to kitchen and bathroom walls, wood trim, windowsills, radiators, masonry, and heating pipes.

Spiegel

14-10
Paint has been used to give this room a cool, semiformal appearance.

Semigloss paints, sometimes called satin paints, have less gloss and are slightly less durable than enamel paints. They can be used in most of the same places as enamel paints.

Flat wall paints have no gloss. They give a soft finish to walls and ceilings. They should not be used for windowsills or kitchen or bathroom walls and woodwork. Flat paints are usually the least expensive.

When you choose paint, choose a color that is slightly lighter than the color you want. When color is applied to walls, it appears stronger and darker than the color on the can, because you see so much of it. Textured paints give walls a rough surface. They can be used to cover cracks or irregularities in walls and ceilings. Refer to the directions on the can label before applying paint.

When you have finished painting a room, paint one side of an index card. On the back of the card, write the brand name and color name of the paint. If you ever need to match it, you'll have the information you need. The painted index card can also be used to choose matching window treatments, floor treatments, or furniture.

Wallpaper. Wallpaper can copy almost any imaginable surface. It can look like brick, stone, wood, or leather. Murals of outdoor scenes can be created from wallpaper. Because of the variety of patterns available, wallpaper can be used to enhance any room.

Wallpaper is practical as well as beautiful. Some wallpapers are coated with thick layers of vinyl, which makes them durable and easy-to-clean. This type is often used in kitchens and bathrooms, because it resist stains and water. Other types of wallpaper can even be peeled off a wall and used again in another room.

Fabric. Fabric can be used to cover walls. It can be attached to the wall with glue, tape, or staples. Sometimes it is stretched over a frame and hung on the wall. Other times, it is stretched between two curtain rods–one at the ceiling and one at the floor. Fabric can add color, warmth, texture, and interest to a room. See 14-11. Closely-woven, medium-weight fabrics are the best choices for wall treatments. The fabric should resist fading, staining, mildewing, and shrinking.

Thomasville Furniture Industries, Inc.

14-11
The use of fabric on the walls and ceiling creates a very unique look and gives the room a cozy feeling.

Cork. Cork is a good wall treatment for rooms where sound insulation is needed. It adds warmth and textural interest to a room.

Ceramic tile. Ceramic tile comes in a wide variety of sizes, shapes, and patterns. See 14-12. The tiles are durable and easy to maintain. A wall treated with decorative ceramic tiles can be the point of emphasis in a room.

Mirrors and glass. Large mirrors, mirrored tiles, or mirrored strips can be used on all or part of a wall. Mirrors make rooms look larger, because the space is repeated in the reflection. If an entire wall is covered with mirrors, the room will look twice its actual size.

Large expanses of glass that are found in windows and glass doors also serve as a type of wall treatment. This is because they occupy wall space. Using glass extends the indoor space and brings the outdoors in. This creates the illusion of a larger space.

American Olean Tile Company

14-12
The ceramic tile used on the walls of this bathroom looks like wallpaper and is easy to clean.

The effect of mirrors and glass as wall treatments can be dramatic. However, they are expensive when compared to other wall treatments, such as paint and wallpaper.

As you can see, walls and wall treatments vary a great deal. Each one has its advantages and disadvantages. Choose the one that best meets your needs and wants and fits the mood of the room.

Ceiling Treatments

The ceiling of a room is the least-noticed background, but it performs many tasks. It holds and conceals insulating materials that help control the temperature in the house. It hides electrical wiring. Some ceilings also hide water lines and gas lines.

The height of the ceiling can help create certain moods. Average ceilings are 8 feet from the floor. Higher ceilings give a feeling of spaciousness and usually create a formal atmosphere. See 14-13. Lower ceilings make rooms seem smaller and usually create an informal mood.

Velux-America, Inc.

14-13
The high ceiling and use of skylights gives this room a spacious, formal appearance.

You can create the illusion of height by using vertical lines on the walls or by running the wall treatment up onto the ceiling a short distance. A ceiling will appear lower if you use horizontal lines on the walls or extend the ceiling treatment down a short distance onto the walls. Another way to make ceilings look lower is to use dark or patterned materials.

The three most common materials used for ceilings are plaster, acoustical plaster, and acoustical tile. ***Acoustical*** means to deaden or absorb sound.

Plaster, or wallboard finished to look like plaster, is appropriate for any room. Its surface can be either smooth or rough. It is usually covered with a flat paint. When painting a ceiling, you will need an extension handle for your paint roller. The extension handle permits you to paint without using a ladder as often, which is safer.

Acoustical plaster has a rough texture. It helps absorb sound and thus reduces the noise in a room. It is applied by spraying it onto the ceiling's surface. Acoustical plaster is difficult to paint and clean.

Acoustical tile, 14-14, is decorative and functional. It comes in many patterns and colors. It absorbs sound and is easy to clean.

When planning backgrounds for your home, keep the goals of design in mind. This will help you achieve pleasing results in any room throughout the dwelling.

Planning Your Background Treatments

The backgrounds in your decorating scheme set the stage for the furnishings you choose. Although they do not need to be costly, they do need to be planned carefully. This is especially true of floor and wall treatments.

Floor Treatments

Floor treatments receive more wear than other background treatments. They are also usually more expensive. Unless you plan to replace

Armstrong World Industries, Inc.

14-14
Vinyl-coated acoustical tile absorbs sound and is easy to clean.

a floor covering within a couple of years, choose one that is durable. Try to choose a color and style that is neutral enough to let you change your decorating scheme if you desire.

The floor treatment accents the entire room and helps tie the many parts of the room together. In many homes, a different floor treatment is chosen for each area. In other homes, a single treatment, such as carpeting, is used throughout the house. By using the same floor covering throughout the house, you can make the house seem larger and more unified. This can be important if your house is small.

Wall Treatments

Classic wall treatments are those that continue to be in style year after year. When you choose a classic wall treatment, you will save the cost of changing your wall treatment as styles change. Off-white is a classic wall treatment color. As a background, it lets you use a great variety of colors and designs in a room. It also helps make rooms appear more spacious. See 14-15.

Bold, bright wall treatments can be used to give a room a dramatic look. Painted graphic designs or murals and wallpaper with bold patterns make colorful focal points. Bold treatments tend to make rooms look smaller, so use them carefully. Be sure to choose wall treatments and furnishings that do not compete with each other.

Marvin Windows & Doors

14-15
This narrow room appears larger than it really is due to the use of off-white paint.

The most common wall treatment is paint. It is important to choose the right paint for the room. Washable paints should be used in rooms that receive a lot of use, such as kitchens and children's bedrooms. When painted surfaces can be cleaned, they do not need to be repainted as often. Enamel and semigloss paints are easier to clean than satin or flat paints.

Wallpaper is available in a wide variety of types and designs. Hanging wallpaper yourself can save you money. If you hang your own wallpaper, think about using prepasted wallpaper. It often costs a little more money, but it is easier to use. The time and effort saved makes prepasted wallpaper a better bargain for most people.

Summary

Floors, walls, and ceilings serve as backgrounds for the furnishings and accessories in a room. Floors may be treated with flooring materials or floor coverings. Flooring materials include wood–both hardwoods and softwoods–, ceramic tile, concrete, stone, brick, and terrazzo. Floor coverings consist of soft floor coverings and resilient floor coverings. Soft floor coverings include wall-to-wall carpeting, room-size rugs, and area rugs. Resilient floor coverings include asphalt tile, vinyl, and cork tile.

Wall construction provides the basis for wall treatments. Walls can be constructed from gypsum wallboard, plastic wallboard, paneling, plaster, and masonry. Other wall treatments–those applied to walls–include paint, wallpaper, fabric, cork, ceramic tile, and mirrors and glass.

The height and the treatment of ceilings are important factors. High ceilings give the feeling of formality and openness. Low ceilings create an informal, close feeling. The illusion of height can be created by using treatments that give the feeling of height. A ceiling can also appear lower if treated properly. Common ceiling materials are plaster, acoustical plaster, and acoustical tile.

Plan background treatments that will last for a long time and give the effect you desire. The colors and styles of your floor treatments, walls, and ceilings should be chosen to set the stage for furnishings and accessories.

To Review

Write your responses on a separate sheet of paper.

1. Why are interior backgrounds important?
2. What is the difference between flooring materials and floor coverings?
3. List three common flooring materials.
4. Name three types of materials used to construct walls.
5. Describe four wall treatments.
6. Explain how ceiling treatments can be used to make a ceiling appear lower than it actually is.
7. What is the benefit of using acoustical plaster or tile as a ceiling treatment in a room?
8. Why is it a good idea to use neutral backgrounds in a home?

To Do

1. Make two collages–one showing a variety of flooring materials and one showing a variety of floor coverings. Hang them up next to each other and compare.
2. Research a type of wall material or wall treatment. Find out how it is made and what the best ways to use it are. Then obtain a sample of the material or treatment. Report your findings in an oral report to the class.
3. Evaluate a room in your house in terms of its ceiling treatment. Think about how it could be treated differently to create a different mood. Write up your observations in a short report.
4. Make a miniature room from a box. Then, using samples from hardware and carpeting stores, create the interior backgrounds in the room.

C H A P T E R 1 5

Furniture Styles and Construction

Bernhardt Industries

To Know

antiques
bonded wood
box springs
butt joint
coil springs
collectibles
coniferous
corner blocks
deciduous
double dowel joint
dovetail joint
flat springs
foam mattress
innerspring mattress
mortise-and-tenon joint
pressed wood
reproductions
solid wood
tongue and groove joint
veneered wood
water bed
wood grain

Objectives

After studying this chapter, you will be able to:

- Describe various furniture styles.
- Identify ways to evaluate quality furniture construction.
- Tell how consumers are protected when buying furniture.

Once you have created the interior backgrounds for your home, you can start to furnish it. The first two steps in furnishing your home are choosing furniture styles and evaluating furniture construction. The next two steps–arranging and selecting furniture–will be discussed in Chapter 16, "Arranging and Selecting Furniture."

Choosing Furniture Styles

Choosing furniture styles is a matter of taste, or personal preference. The furniture you choose cannot be called "right" or "wrong" by anyone else. However, studying the various styles can give you a good idea of which styles you like. This will also help you use each style to its best advantage.

The style of furniture refers to design only. It does not refer to the cost or quality of construction. Any style, from Queen Anne to contemporary, can be made of good or poor materials using good or poor construction methods.

Traditional Furniture Styles

Traditional, or period, furniture styles were developed during different periods throughout history. Traditional styles from France, England, and the United States are discussed in this chapter. A general time reference for some traditional and nontraditional furniture styles is shown in 15-1.

Traditional styles from France. While *Louis XIII* was King of France, 1610-1643, furniture styles were grand and formal. Rich inlays, carvings, and classical motifs were typical.

Louis XIV, the Sun King, ruled France from 1643-1715. He built the Palace of Versailles. Its furnishings were extravagant. They had heavy ornamentation and gold overlays.

During the reign of *Louis XV,* 1715-1774, furniture styles had smaller proportions and became more delicate. Curved lines and soft colors were dominant.

Just before the French Revolution, 1774-1792, *Louis XVI* and Marie Antoinette ruled France. Simple, straight lines and classic motifs, such as fluted columns, were popular in furniture.

When Napoleon ruled France, 1804-1815, he dominated everything–even furniture styles. The dignified style called *Empire* became popular. The furniture was large and heavy. It was decorated with his initial and military symbols. Egyptian, Greek, and Roman motifs were also used.

During the seventeenth and eighteenth centuries, craftsworkers began copying styles that were popular in the court at Paris. The *French provincial* style was practical, functional, comfortable, and unpretentious. Local wood was used to copy this style and decoration was simplified. See 15-2.

During the 1800s and 1900s there was a revival of historical furniture styles. *Art Nouveau,* or new art, was a rebellion against this movement. The graceful lines of Art Nouveau furniture were based on flower forms.

Traditional styles from England. During the reigns of James I and Charles I, 1603-1649, *Jacobean* furniture became popular. Turning and fluting were used on oak furniture.

During the reign of *Queen Anne,* 1702-1714, there was an Oriental influence in furniture. Cabriole legs and carved fans and shells are characteristic of this graceful and comfortable style. See 15-3.

Several furniture styles became popular during the reigns of Kings George I, II, and III, 1714-1820. Sometimes these styles are called *Georgian.* Other times, they are labeled according to their designers–Thomas Chippendale, the Adam Brothers, George Hepplewhite, and Thomas Sheraton.

Thomas Chippendale was the first person to publish a book entirely about furniture designs, and his designs became popular around the world. Gothic and Chinese influences were a part of the Chippendale design. Splat-back chairs and curved top edges on the backs of chairs and sofas were typical. Early Chippendale furniture has

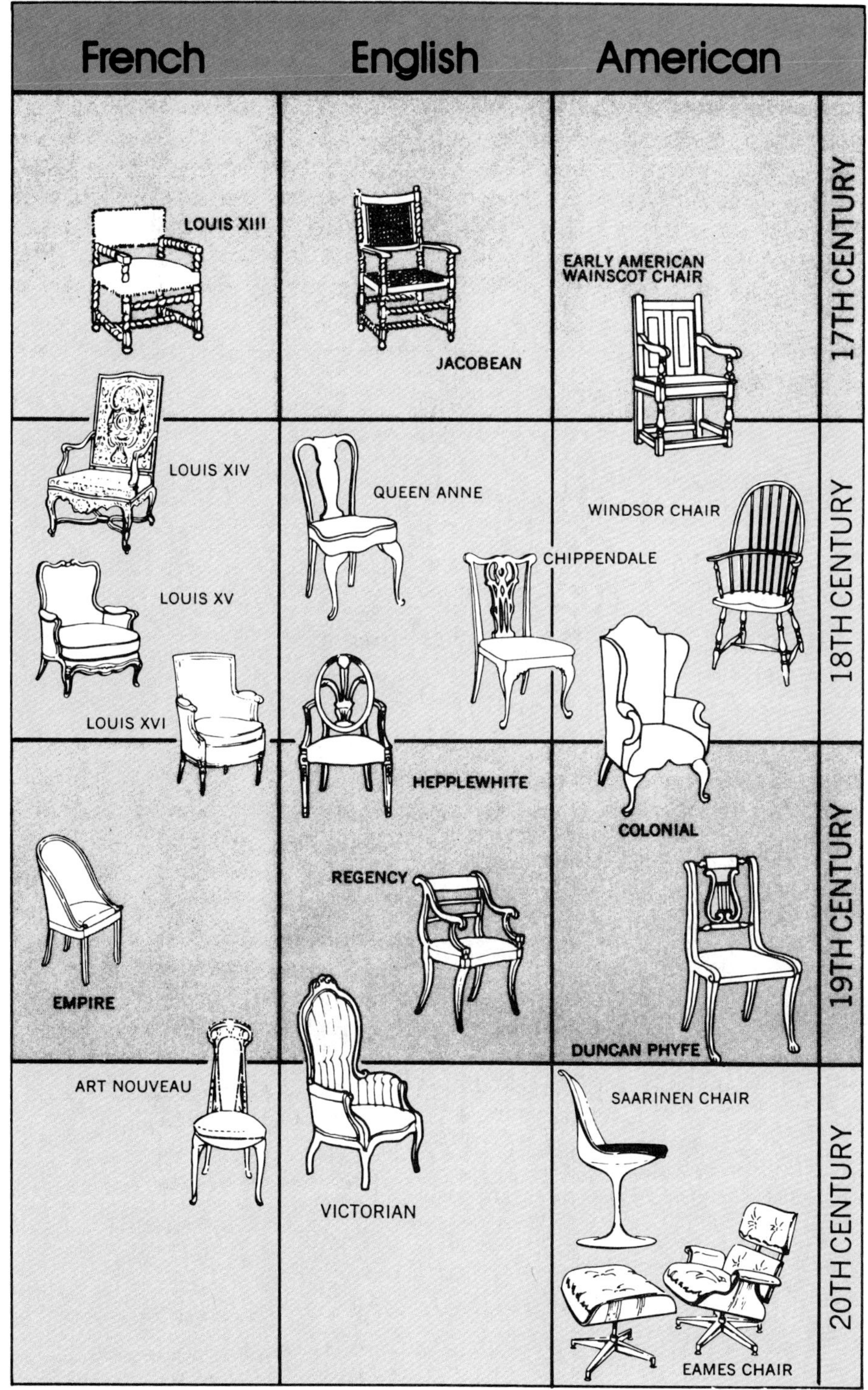

Ethan Allen, Inc.

15-1
New styles of furniture are continually being designed.

Thomasville Furniture Industries, Inc.

15-2
The French provincial style of furniture is frequently used today.

Drexel Heritage Furnishing, Inc.

15-3
This eighteenth century highboy is characteristic of the Queen Anne style of furniture because of its cabriole legs and carved fans.

"S-shaped" legs with claw and ball feet, 15-4. Later, due to Chinese influence, his furniture had straight legs.

Furniture designed by the *Adam Brothers,* Robert and James, was designed to complement their architectural designs. The furniture was classic and symmetrical. The pieces had simple outlines, rectangular shapes, and tapered, straight legs.

George Hepplewhite is most famous for his graceful chair designs. The backs of the chairs had shield, oval, and heart shapes, 15-5.

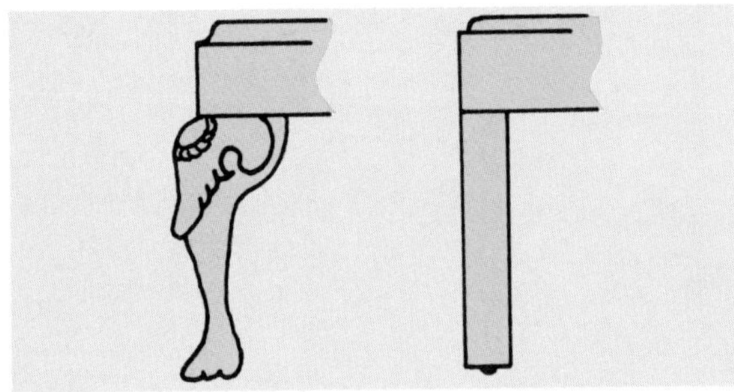

15-4
Curved legs with claw and ball feet were characteristic of early Chippendale designs. His later designs had straight legs.

Thomasville Furniture Industries, Inc.

15-5
This chair has a shield back, which is characteristic of Hepplewhite.

Thomas Sheraton designed furniture that had characteristic straight lines. He included motifs of urns, swags, and leaves. His furniture also included mechanical devices, such as disappearing drawers, folding tables, and secret compartments.

The *Regency* furniture style (1810-1837) is named after the Prince of Wales who reigned as Regent for nine years. The style reflects an interest in the ancient cultures of Greece, Rome, and Egypt. Bold, curved lines were dominant.

During the reign of Queen Victoria, 1837-1901, the *Victorian* furniture style became popular. Machines could make detailed pieces of furniture quickly and easily. This led to the excessive use of ornamentation that was typical of the style, 15-6. Other characteristics were massive proportions and dark colors.

Traditional American styles. The first settlers in North America built sturdy, practical furniture. This furniture was a simplified version of the Jacobean style, which was popular at that time in England.

The colonists used native woods, such as maple, pine, and oak. They began making furniture with less massive proportions. Ladder-back chairs and canopy beds were common. Windsor chairs also became popular, 15-7. These furnishings were generally called *Early American.*

Ethan Allen, Inc.

15-6
The American version of Victorian furniture is still found in homes today.

Rea-Lynne Gilder

15-7
The Windsor chair is typical of Early American furnishings.

Later, the *Colonial* style became popular. It was based on England's Georgian style. Graceful lines, "S-shaped" legs, and comfortable forms were typical.

After the American Revolution, England's influence declined in all areas, including furniture styles. The *Federal* style became popular in the United States. It combined classic influences with patriotic symbols, such as eagles and stars and stripes.

Duncan Phyfe was a major furniture designer of this period. He is noted for the lyre motif used for chair backs. Other characteristics of his designs are brass-tipped dog feet, curved legs, and rolled-top rails chair and sofa backs.

In the early 1800s, a religious group known as the Shakers, were recognized for their use of the circular saw in making furniture. *Shaker* furniture was very plain in design but often painted in bright colors. Shakers were best known for their side chairs and rockers, although they did make other furniture. See 15-8.

Photo by Paul Rocheleau, Hancock Shaker Village

15-8
These Shaker rocking chairs face a Shaker sewing stand that has a drawer on each side.

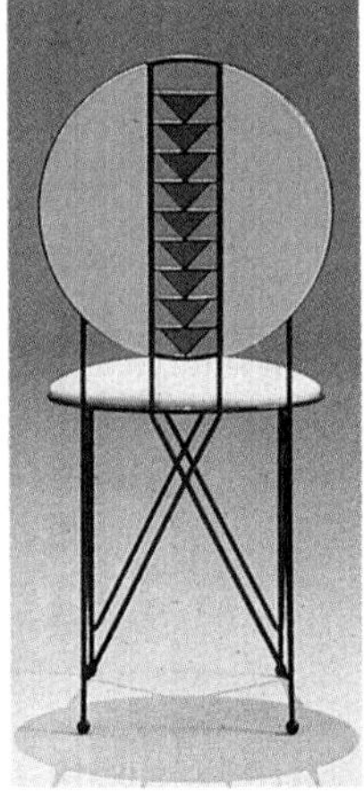

Courtesy of the Frank Lloyd Wright Foundation

15-9
Frank Lloyd Wright designed his modern furniture to correspond to his house designs.

Modern and Contemporary Furniture Styles

At the beginning of the twentieth century, designers reacted against the cluttered look of the Victorian era. They designed furniture with simple lines and forms. The furniture was designed for comfort and cost as well as the style. Two styles of twentieth century furniture are modern and contemporary.

Modern furniture. Modern furniture is comfortable, convenient, and durable. It is designed according to the guideline "form follows function." In other words, if the function of a chair is for sitting, it should be a comfortable place to sit. If the function of a table is to hold objects, it should be sturdy enough and large enough to hold them.

Unnecessary frills are avoided in modern pieces of furniture. This does not mean, however, that rooms must look boring. Colorful fabrics and accessories add beauty and variety to modern rooms. They enhance the simple lines of the furniture.

Frank Lloyd Wright designed modern furniture to go with the houses he designed. See 15-9. While the furniture designs varied according to the design of the house, they all used flat surfaces and geometric shapes.

Contemporary furniture. Contemporary furniture styles are the very latest designs. They take advantage of the newest materials and manufacturing methods. Plastics, metals, wood, and glass are used to create an endless range of visual effects. Pieces of contemporary furniture have simple lines and forms. Geometric shapes, such as circles, rectangles, triangles, cylinders, and cubes, are often used. See 15-10.

Spiegel, Inc.

15-10
Metal formed into geometric shapes was used to create the contemporary furniture for this home office.

Antiques, Collectibles, and Reproductions

While modern and contemporary furniture are the most current furniture styles, some people still prefer furniture styles from the past. Antiques, collectibles, and reproductions are all types of historical furniture that is available today.

Antiques. ***Antiques*** are furniture made over one hundred years ago in the style current at that time. As furniture styles become outdated, good-quality pieces have become hard to find. Some antiques can be found at a reasonable cost. However, the older the furniture and the better the quality of construction, the higher the cost. Fine antiques are those of good quality. The very finest antiques are museum quality as in 15-11. They can be very expensive.

Collectibles. ***Collectibles*** are highly-valued furnishings less than one hundred years old but no longer made. If kept long enough, they will become antiques.

Glencoe Plantation, Louisiana Office of Tourism

15-11
This fine antique bedroom set is on display in an historic plantation house.

Reproductions. ***Reproductions*** are copies of antique originals. Sometimes they are made to look worn. For example, false worm holes may be added to the finish. The reproductions may or may not be accurate imitations. Study 15-12 and see if you can determine if the style is authentic or if it is a reproduction.

Evaluating Furniture Construction

The furniture styles discussed above and many other furniture styles are constructed using wood, plastic, metal, wicker, or glass. The materials can be used alone or in combination with other materials. The ones you choose depend upon the desires of your living unit, the mood of the room, and the amount of money you can afford to spend. Being able to accurately evaluate furniture construction can help you choose the best-quality furniture for your money.

Wood

Wood used in furniture construction can be classified in many ways. Each of these classifications affects the quality of the furniture. When looking at furniture, be sure to consider each of these classifications to get the best-quality furniture for your money.

Grain. A ***wood grain,*** or pattern, is formed as a tree grows. See 15-13. The stump or base of a tree has a beautiful, irregular grain caused by the twisted and irregular growth of the tree's roots. Crotch wood has a special grain caused by branches growing out from the trunk of a tree. *Burls,* which are woody, flattened outgrowths on trees have a unique and highly-prized grain.

Lumber is cut to show off the grain. The way it is cut can affect the appearance of wood grain in your furniture. Quarter slicing, rotary cut, and flat slicing methods each give a different look to the same kind of wood.

Hardwood and softwood. Furniture can be made of all hardwood, all softwood, or a combi-

Spiegel, Inc.

15-12
Is the trunk in this room an original or a reproduction?

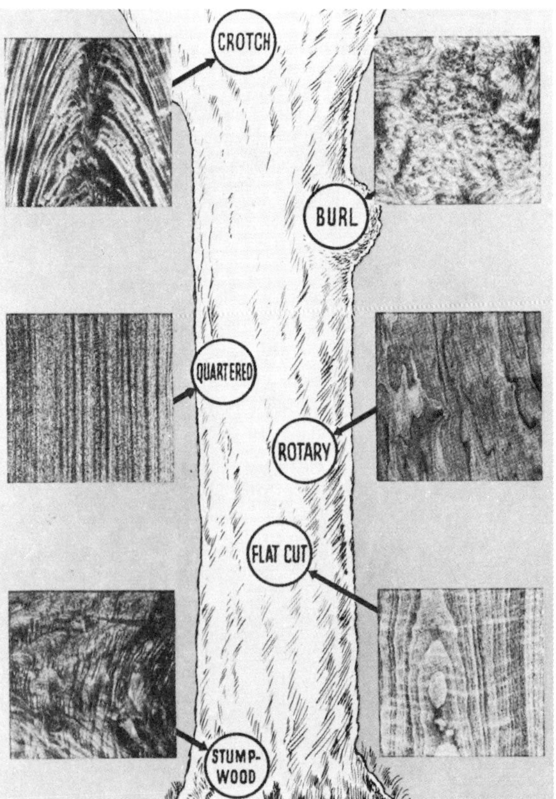

Fine Hardwoods–American Walnut Association

15-13
Wood grain varies according to the part of the tree from which the lumber comes and the way it is cut.

nation of the two. Hardwood comes from ***deciduous*** trees, or trees that lose their leaves. The most popular hardwoods used for quality furniture include walnut, mahogany, pecan, cherry, maple, and oak. Hardwood does not dent easily. It is usually stronger than softwood, and it costs more.

Softwood comes from ***coniferous*** trees, or trees that do not shed their leaves. Softwood does not have as beautiful a grain as hardwood, and it dents easily. Cedar, redwood, pine, fir, and spruce are the most common softwoods used for furniture. Some softwood is harder than some hardwood, so the names may be somewhat deceiving.

Solid wood and bonded wood. ***Solid wood*** means that all of the exposed parts of a piece of furniture are made of whole pieces of wood. Such furniture is usually expensive, especially if it is made of hardwood. The disadvantage of solid wood is that it has a tendency to warp, swell, and crack.

Bonded wood is wood that has been bonded by glue and pressure. Bonded woods include veneered wood and pressed wood.

Veneered wood, or plywood, is created by bonding three, five, or seven thin layers of wood to one another, to a solid wood core, or to a pressed wood core, 15-14. Fine woods are used for the outside layers. Less expensive woods are used for the inside layers or core.

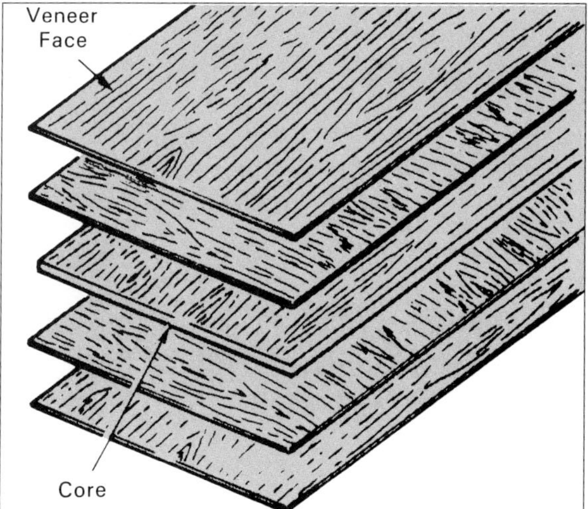

15-14
In plywood, the grains of alternate veneers run at right angles to one another. This adds strength to the plywood.

Since expensive woods are used only on the outside of veneered wood, veneering makes fine woods available at a moderate cost. Rare woods and beautiful grains can also be used. Veneering also permits the use of fragile woods, since the inside layers add strength. A disadvantage of veneered wood is that the adhesive may not stick, and the veneer may loosen and chip.

Most of the furniture made since 1900 is at least partly veneered. Today, veneered furniture is more common than solid wood furniture.

Pressed wood is made of shavings, veneer scraps, chips, and other small pieces of wood. These types of wood are less expensive than solid or veneered wood. Called particleboard, waferboard, or composite board, they are often used on parts of furniture that do not show. They may also be covered with a more expensive wood or with a plastic laminate, which is used on furnishings that need a tough, durable surface.

Wood joints. Wood pieces can be fastened together in many different ways, including wood joints. Common wood joints are pictured in 15-15. Glue is used on all joints to add strength.

A ***mortise-and-tenon joint*** is one of the strongest joints used for furniture. The glued tenon fits tightly into the mortise, or hole. No nails or screws are used. Mortise-and-tenon joints are commonly used to join legs or rails to tables, chairs, and headboards.

Double dowel joints are very common and very strong. Glued wooden dowels fit into drilled holes in both pieces of wood.

Dovetail joints are used to fasten corner joints. They can be found in drawers of good-quality furniture.

Tongue and groove joints are created when a tongue is cut on one board and matching groove is cut on the other. These joints are invisible if they are made skillfully. They are used where several boards are to be joined lengthwise, such as for tabletops.

Butt joints are the weakest of the joints. One board is simply glued or nailed flush to another board.

Corner blocks are small pieces of wood attached between corner boards. They support

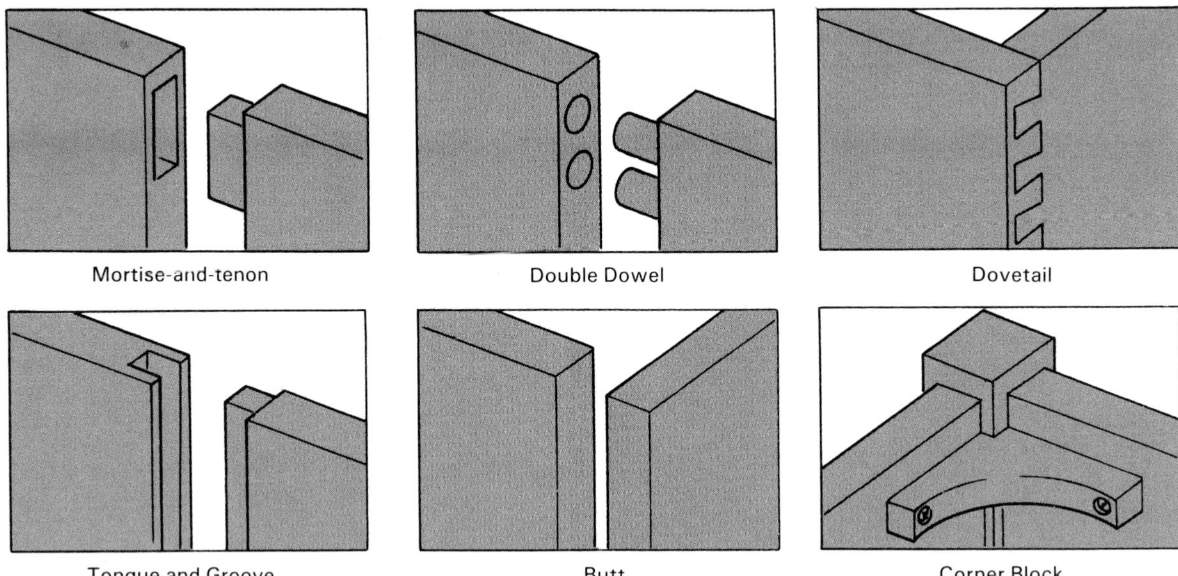

15-15
Joints are an important factor in determining the quality of pieces of furniture.

and reinforce the joint. They are used in the construction of chairs and tables. They keep one side from pulling away from the other.

Unfinished and finished wood furniture. Wood furniture may be left unfinished or given a finish for added protection or beauty.

In unfinished furniture, the wood is left as it was when the furniture was constructed. The surface of the wood has not been treated. You finish it yourself. The initial cost of unfinished furniture is low. Therefore, before you buy, be sure to consider the cost of finishing the furniture yourself. It will cost you money, time, and effort.

Finished furniture has been treated in some way to protect and improve the appearance of the wood surface. Some finishes include stains, sealers, waxes, and paints. Water-based stains and oil-based stains bring out the natural beauty of hardwoods and softwoods respectively. Sealers can be penetrating sealers or surface sealers. Plastic sealers resist moisture and are frequently used. Wax is used to preserve the wood and give it an attractive finish. Paint is sometimes used to hide a surface that is not attractive.

When you buy wood furniture, check the points listed in 15-16. You should also read the

Checklist When Shopping for Wood Furniture
___ Do doors shut tightly without sticking?
___ Have corner blocks been used for reinforcement?
___ Are dust panels provided between drawers?
___ Do drawers slide easily?
___ Are legs attached with mortise-and-tenon or dowel joints?
___ Do legs stand squarely upon the floor?
___ Have insides of drawers, backs of chests, and undersides of tables and chairs been sanded and finished?
___ Are surfaces smooth?
___ Are surfaces solid, veneered, or laminated?
___ Has a protective plastic coating been used on surfaces that will receive hard wear?
___ Will the furniture piece fulfill your use, style, color, and size requirements?
___ Is the furniture within your budget?

Sears Consumer Information Services

15-16
You may find this checklist useful when choosing wood furniture.

labels carefully. They will tell you what finishes have been applied, the purpose of the finishes, and the care they should receive. It is important to understand all the terms on the labels. For instance, "solid walnut" means that the exposed wood is the same wood throughout the thickness of the entire piece. "Genuine walnut" means that walnut was used as the face veneer; other woods were used as the core. "Walnut finish" means that the piece of furniture has been finished to look like walnut.

Plastic, Metal, Rattan and Wicker, and Glass Furniture

Plastic, metal, rattan and wicker, and glass are other materials used in furniture construction. They should also be evaluated for quality when buying furniture.

Plastic. Plastic furniture is usually less expensive than wood. It is lightweight, sturdy, easy to clean, and often brightly colored. Generally, it looks best in contemporary settings. See 15-17.

Plastic used for furniture should not imitate other materials, such as wood. Instead, the furniture design should take advantage of the special properties of plastic.

When you are choosing plastic furniture, ask yourself the following questions:

- Is the piece strong and durable?
- Are the edges smooth and the surfaces flawless?
- Are color and gloss uniform?
- Are the reinforcement parts hidden unless they are part of the design?

Metal. Metal is popular for both indoor and outdoor furniture. Wrought iron, steel, aluminum, and chrome are all used for different furnishings. Metal is often combined with other materials, such as wood, fabric, or glass. See 15-18.

When you are choosing metal furniture, ask yourself the following questions:

- Is the metal or metallic finish rustproof?
- Is the surface smooth?
- Are sharp edges coated or covered?

Rattan and wicker. Rattan furniture is made from the stringy, tough stems of different

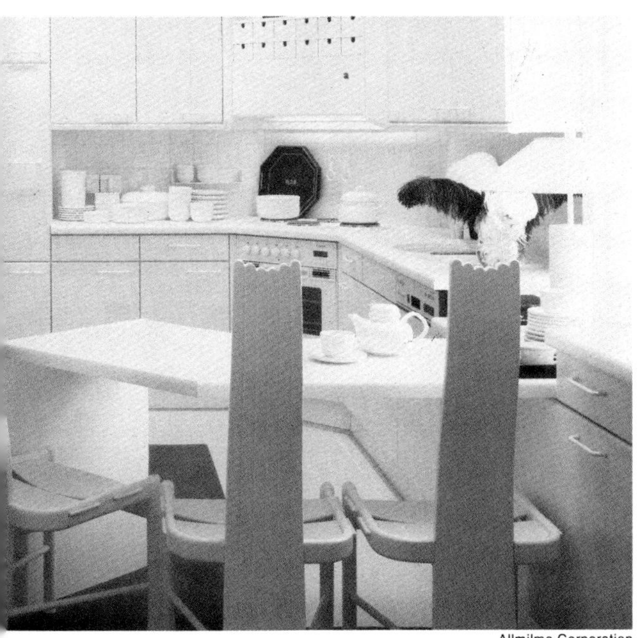

Allmilmo Corporation

15-17
Molded plastic gives this dining set a clean, contemporary look.

Armstrong World Industries, Inc.

15-18
Metal and glass are combined in this table.

kinds of palm trees. It bends easily and is strong. Wicker furniture is made by loosely weaving willow around a frame. Rattan, reed, and bamboo can be used in place of willow. Wicker bends easily, is lightweight, and durable. It is also water resistant and has a natural gloss. Although wicker was originally used for outdoor furniture, it is now also used indoors. See 15-19.

When you are choosing rattan or wicker furniture, ask yourself the following questions:

- Are the strands smooth and unbroken?
- Are the joints well wrapped and secure?
- Is the finish high quality?
- Are the legs even?

Glass. Glass is usually combined with metal or wood. It is popular for tabletops and cabinet doors.

When glass is a part of the furniture you are choosing, ask yourself the following questions:

- Is the glass tempered for safety and durability?
- Is the furniture designed to hold the glass firmly in place?
- Are glass surfaces free from bubbles, scratches, and other defects?

Upholstered Furniture

Chairs, sofas, and other pieces of padded furniture are called upholstered furniture. Most or all of the exposed surface of the furniture piece is covered with fabric. See 15-20. This outer covering hides the inner construction details. Because these details are hidden, choosing good-quality upholstered furniture can be difficult. The information below will help you evaluate upholstered furniture.

Upholstery fabrics. Fabric is an important part of upholstered furniture. It is also a clue to the overall quality of a piece. Good-quality furniture has durable, well-tailored upholstery fabric.

Upholstery fabrics are made primarily of blends or combination yarns. The yarns can be woven to create fabrics with different patterns and designs. Upholstery fabrics come in many

Thomasville Furniture Industries, Inc.

15-20
Upholstered furniture may be completely covered with fabric, or some wood may be exposed as in this sofa.

Georgia-Pacific Corporation

15-19
Wicker furniture looks good in informal indoor settings.

attractive colors and interesting textures. They can be heavy-, medium-, or lightweight. Lightweight fabrics do not wear as well as heavyweight fabrics.

When choosing upholstery fabrics, consider the following points:

- Woven fabrics with close, tight weaves are better quality than fabrics with open, loose weaves.
- Long floats, such as in the satin weave, tend to snag.
- Fabrics with equal number and size of warp and weft yarns are durable.
- Flame-resistant fabrics are safer than untreated ones.
- Stain-resistant finishes make woven fabrics easier to clean.
- Colorfast materials are preferred.
- Medium to dark colors, patterned materials, tweeds, and textured fabrics do not show soil easily.
- Labels on fabric samples give content and care information.

Upholstery tailoring. When evaluating upholstered furniture, you need to look at the tailoring details. A quick way to check is to evaluate a cushion cover. If the cover can be removed, check the seams, filling material, and see if it has an inside casing.

For a more thorough evaluation, check the entire piece of furniture. Use the following checklist:

- Is expert sewing evident?
- Are threads secure and trimmed?
- Is the fabric smooth, tight, and free from puckers?
- Does the fabric pattern, such as stripes and plaids, match?
- Are curved shapes and corners smooth?
- Are skirts lined and do they hang straight?
- Are buttons and trims securely fastened?
- Are staples and tacks concealed?

The more "yes" answers you have, the better tailored the upholstery is.

Frames, springs, and cushions. Upholstered furniture frames are made of wood or metal. As you evaluate the frames, keep in mind the points for choosing wood or metal furniture. You should choose a solid hardwood frame that is heavy and substantial. The joints should be secured with screws and corner blocks.

Springs are a part of the inner construction. The type and number of springs help determine the quality. There are two types of springs: coil and flat, 15-21. ***Coil springs*** are spiral-shaped springs without padding and covering. They are used in heavier furniture. You can "sink into" furniture with coil springs. Lightweight pieces of furniture with sleek lines usually have flat or zigzag springs. ***Flat springs*** are flat, S-shaped springs that may have metal support strips banded across them. They offer firm comfort at lower cost.

Cushions need to be the proper size. They should fit snugly into the furniture. They need to give body support. Cushions are often made of urethane foam or foam rubber. These materials are durable, lightweight, and resilient. They can be molded into any shape, and they come in many sizes and degrees of firmness.

Covered or pocketed coils are sometimes used in cushions. They are usually covered with a thin layer of foam rubber and a layer of fabric. Other cushions are filled with down and feathers. These are very comfortable, but not as durable as foam.

Loose fill can also be used as cushion filling. Shredded foam, kapok, and polyester fiberfill are all types of loose fill. They are less expensive than the shaped fillers. However, because loose

15-21
Coil springs are used in heavy furniture. Flat or zigzag springs are used when a minimum of bulk is desired.

fill takes the shape of the casing, it may not retain its original shape. Loose fill is used for styles that have soft pillow cushions.

The cutaway illustration in 15-22 shows the inner construction of an upholstered chair. You can see how different materials are combined to provide seating comfort.

When choosing upholstered furniture, comfort is a very important factor to consider. For example, a sofa that does not feel comfortable is a poor buy. Sit on it. Check the height and depth of the seat. Check the height of the back and arms. Be sure it fits your body's proportions. Other points to consider when shopping for upholstered furniture are listed in 15-23.

Beds

About one-third of your life is spent sleeping. Therefore, you should choose the best bed you can afford. A bed includes a mattress, frame, and springs. Headboards and footboards may or may not be added. Comfort is important when choosing a bed. Before you buy a bed, be sure to lie on it. That is the only way to see if it is comfortable for you.

Since you cannot see the inside construction of a mattress or box spring, you should choose a reliable brand. Many manufacturers have illustrations or miniature mattresses and box springs available for you to look at when you visit your bed dealer. Check them for support and durability.

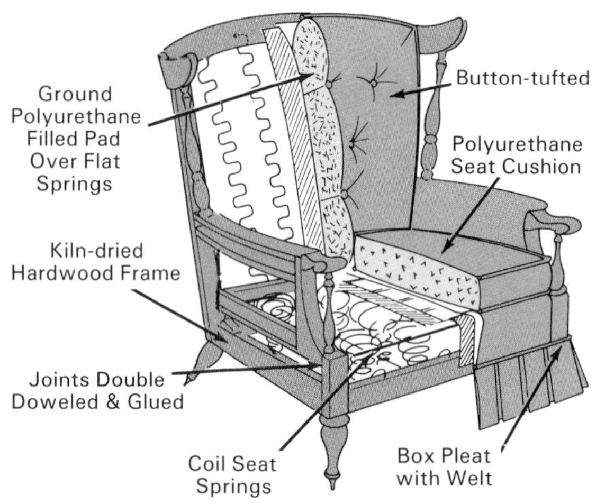

Monsanto Textiles Company

15-22
Much work goes in to the construction of an upholstered chair.

Checklist When Shopping for Upholstered Furniture

- ___ Are the legs and joints securely attached?
- ___ What kind of springs have been used?
- ___ Do you know the cushion materials and how they have been constructed?
- ___ Do the cushions have zipper closings?
- ___ Are the cushions reversible?
- ___ Does the outer covering have a well-tailored appearance?
- ___ Will the outer covering give good wearability for your purpose?
- ___ Does the outer covering have a stain-resistant finish?
- ___ Is it appropriate in style, design, and color for the room?
- ___ Is it within your preplanned budget?

Sears Consumer Information Services

15-23
Check these points before you buy pieces of upholstered furniture.

Mattresses. There are many types of mattresses available. The most popular type is the innerspring mattress. An ***innerspring mattress*** contains a series of springs covered with padding. The springs vary in number, size, placement, wire thickness (gauge), and whether or not they are individually pocketed. These are all factors that determine the firmness and comfort of the mattress. Manufacturers say that a regular size, good quality innerspring mattress should have the following features:

- At least 300 firmly-anchored, heavy coils.
- Good padding and insulation placed over and between coils.
- A tightly-woven cover with a border that doesn't sag, 15-24.

Foam mattresses are made of latex or polyurethane foam. The foam is cut or molded to shape and is usually covered with a tightly-woven

Sealy, Inc.

15-24
A good innerspring mattress will have several layers of padding and a tightly-woven cover.

cotton cloth. It may be of solid foam or molded foam, which is more pliable. Foam mattresses are lightweight and less expensive than innerspring mattresses.

Foam mattresses are often preferred by people with allergies. They vary in thickness, firmness, and quality. A good-quality mattress will be about 6 inches thick. It will have some holes or cores in it. The greater the number of cores, the softer the mattress will be.

A ***water bed*** is a bed with a mattress that is a plastic bag filled with water. It conforms exactly to body curves and provides good, firm support. Water beds consist of a heavy-duty plastic water bag, frame, and watertight liner, which goes between the mattress and frame to protect against leaks, and heating device used to warm the water. Water beds range from full motion to waveless.

When a standard-size water bed is filled, it weighs about 1,600 pounds. Buildings must have strong foundations to support them. Water beds are often prohibited in rented dwellings.

Air mattresses are easy to fill and empty. When empty, they require very little storage space. For these reasons they make good portable beds. They are primarily used for camping but are handy for overnight guests.

Springs. Most conventional beds have springs to support the mattress. Bed springs have three basic forms: box, coil, and flat. Many people prefer box springs even though they are the most expensive. ***Box springs*** consist of a series of coils attached to a base and covered with padding. The coils may vary in number, size, placement, and gauge. Coil springs are between box springs and flat springs in terms of quality and cost. Flat springs are the least expensive.

When buying an innerspring mattress and springs, they should be bought in a matching set. When they are purchased as a set, the coils in the mattress line up with the coils in the springs. This makes the bed more comfortable.

Frames. There are many types of bed frames. The most common type is a metal frame with springs and a mattress placed on top. Sometimes, springs, usually flat springs, are already built into the frame. An electric adjustable bed is like a metal frame bed, except the frame can be adjusted up and down according to the needs of the person sleeping in it. It is more expensive than a conventional metal frame.

Some bed frames, such as futons and sofa beds, can also be used for seating. A futon frame is a wooden bed frame that is low to the ground. A cotton mattress is placed on top of it to make a bed. Futons can be folded up to make a chair or sofa. A sofa bed is a sofa that can be made into a bed by pulling out a concealed mattress.

Consumer Protection

Buying furniture is a big investment. To help protect your investment, the government has agencies that protect consumers. The Federal Trade Commission (FTC) and the Consumer Product Safety Commission (CPSC) are two such agencies. As discussed in Chapter 13, "Textiles in Today's Homes," there are federal laws that protect you. The Flammable Fabrics Act prohibits the sale of highly flammable fabrics for apparel and home furnishings. The Textile Fiber

Products Identification Act requires that fibers be listed in their order of predominance by weight and the generic names of fibers appear on labels of all textile products, such as upholstery, carpets, and draperies.

There is also voluntary control of the quality of materials and construction methods used for furniture. Some fiber producers and fabric manufacturers set their own high levels of performance. Some furniture companies have also set high standards for themselves. These companies guarantee the durability and performance of their products after you buy them. Information about superior-quality materials and guarantees is given on the labels of furniture. It is your responsibility as a smart consumer to read the labels on anything you buy, so you will know what to expect from the product.

Summary

Furniture styles are always changing. The styles that have endured are known as traditional designs. They include styles from France, England, and the United States. Furniture styles designed during the twentieth century in opposition to traditional styles are known as modern and contemporary styles. Furniture that is over 100 years old are antiques. Those less than 100 years, yet no longer made, are collectibles. Reproductions are copies of antique originals.

Understanding furniture construction and the materials used can help you evaluate furniture. This will help you choose good-quality furniture. Furniture can be made of wood and wood veneers that are held together with joints. It can also be made of plastic, metal, rattan, wicker, and glass. Some furniture is upholstered. A knowledge of upholstery fabrics and construction details will help you make the right choices.

Your furniture investment is protected by government agencies and federal laws concerning consumer goods and textiles. Some manufacturers also set standards for their products.

To Review

Write your responses on a separate sheet of paper.

1. Name and describe three traditional styles of furniture.
2. Which of the following is NOT a traditional furniture style?
   a. Louis XV.
   b. Chippendale.
   c. Colonial.
   d. Frank Lloyd Wright.
3. The two furniture styles that were created in reaction to the traditional styles are _____ and _____.
4. What is the difference between an antique and a collectible?
5. True or False. Veneered wood is more expensive than solid wood.
6. List four joints used to fasten together wood furniture.
7. What is the difference between solid wood and genuine wood?
8. A type of furniture that can be used both indoors and outdoors is:
   a. Hardwood.
   b. Upholstered.
   c. Glass.
   d. Metal.
9. What is the difference between coil springs and flat springs in terms of comfort and cost?
10. Explain how manufacturers' high levels of performance help protect consumers.

To Do

1. Look through magazines for pictures of various furniture styles. Mount the pictures on pieces of paper and label them.
2. Choose and research a furniture style. Write a report about it and include illustrations.
3. Examine wood furniture in your home to find out how many different types of joints are used. Report your findings to the class.
4. Collect samples of fabric suitable for upholstery. Compare their characteristics.
5. Plan a study trip to a furniture store. Prepare a list of questions to ask your tour guide about furniture construction and furniture styles.
6. While doing the preceding activity, check the labels attached to three types of furniture. Make sure that all the consumer information is included.

C H A P T E R 16

Arranging and Selecting Furniture

To Know
close-out sale
comparison shopping
eclectic
loss leader sale
multipurpose furniture
prioritize
recycle
renew
restore
scale floor plan
seasonal sale
template
unassembled furniture

Ethan Allen, Inc.

Objectives

After studying this chapter, you will be able to:

- Describe how to use a scale floor plan to arrange furniture.
- List factors to consider when arranging furniture.
- Explain the steps to follow when selecting furniture.
- Compare places to shop for furniture.
- Give examples of ways to stretch your furniture dollars.

Now that you have learned about furniture styles and how to choose quality furniture, you can explore the second two steps of furnishing your home. These two steps are arranging and selecting furniture. As you select furniture, you may be tempted to choose items that will not fit into a good room design. Knowing how to properly arrange and select furniture will help you choose only the furniture you can really use. It will also help you get the most out of your home furniture budget.

Arranging Furniture

Before you select the furniture for a room, you need to plan how you will arrange it. This will let you know how much space is available in a room and how much furniture will fit in it. Using a scale floor plan and furniture templates are tools to help you plan the furniture arrangement.

Using Scale Floor Plans

A ***scale floor plan*** is a drawing that shows the size and shape of a room. A certain number of inches on the scale floor plan is equal to a certain number of feet in the room. You can use a scale floor plan from a print used to build your house, as described in Chapter 7. If a print is not available, you can make your own scale floor plan.

To create a scale floor plan, measure the length and width of each room. Then measure the features in the room, such as doors, windows, outlets, and air vents. Draw the dimensions of the room on graph paper using a scale of 1/4 inch equals 1 foot. Add the features, using the symbols from Figure 7-3 in Chapter 7, "Understanding House Plans."

After you have created your scale floor plan, you can create furniture templates. A ***template*** is a piece of paper cut in the shape of a piece of furniture to be used on a scale floor plan. The templates are drawn in the same scale as the floor plan.

To create furniture templates, measure the width and length of the furniture you want to place in the room. Draw each piece on graph paper using a 1/4 inch equals 1 foot scale. You may color the pieces of furniture the color you want the furniture to be and cut them out. Then, arrange the templates on the scale floor plan until you have found the best arrangement. See 16-1. Sometimes all the furniture may fit well. Other times it may not.

Factors to Consider When Arranging Furniture

There are some factors to consider that will help you find the best furniture arrangement for your room. These include how furniture is used, the space required for furniture, the features of the room, and the flow of traffic. You also need to consider the principles of design. See Chapter 12, "Using the Principles of Design."

Furniture and room use. How furniture is arranged depends upon how the furniture is used. Each piece of furniture in a room is selected for a specific use or uses. It will require a different amount of space than other pieces of furniture. For instance, a chest of drawers takes up floor space and wall space. Clearance space is also needed in front to open the drawers. See 16-2 for a list of furniture clearance space requirements.

Furniture arrangement also depends upon how the room is used. Before arranging furniture in a room, think about the activities that will take place in the room and the amount of space available. Then think about the areas within the room where the activities will take place. List the basic furnishings needed for each activity area and

Step 1. Draw the dimensions of the bedroom on graph paper showing windows and doors in their correct positions.

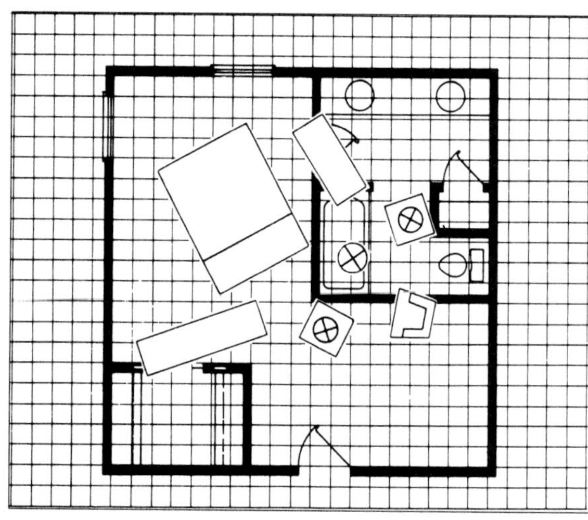

Step 2. Make furniture templates to be placed in the room, and cut them out.

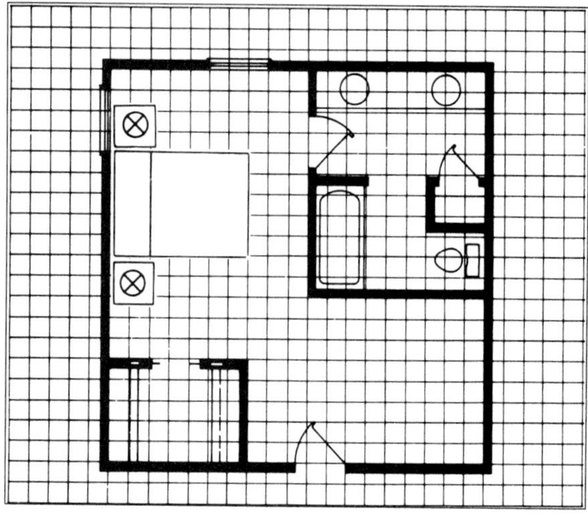

Step 3. Place the bed first.

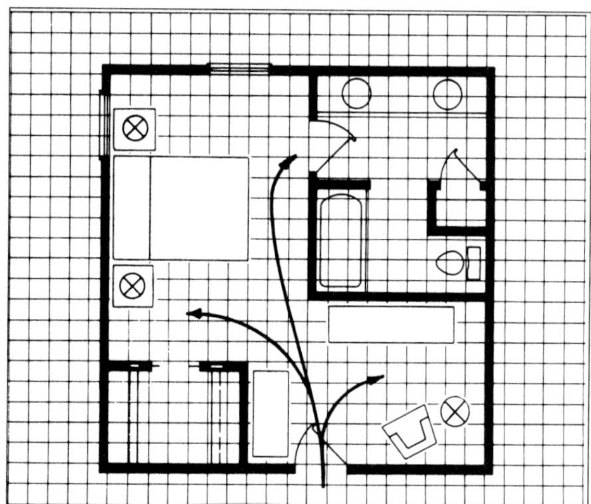

Step 4. Place the remaining furniture, keeping circulation paths clear.

16-1
Using a scale floor plan makes planning furniture arrangements easy.

determine the amount of space the furniture will occupy.

For instance, you might want to create a conversation area in the living room. See 16-3. A grouping of chairs, sofas, tables, and lamps should be no more than eight to ten feet across. To encourage conversation, the area should form part, if not all, of a circle. In the grouping, accessories, such as lamps, need to be conveniently arranged in relation to their use.

Room features. Plan furniture arrangements so they do not interfere with the features of the room, such as windows, doors, outlets, and air vents. Do not place furniture where it could get hit by a door. Do not place furniture in front of a window, making it difficult to open and close the

Space Recommendations for Furniture Arrangement	
Room	Clearance Space
Living Room	
Seating, such as chairs and sofas	18 - 30 inches
Between sofa and coffee table	15 inches
Dining Room	
Chairs–to get into and out of	24 - 36 inches
Occupied chairs	18 - 24 inches
Traffic around table	18 - 24 inches
Bedroom	
In front of dresser or chest of drawers	36 - 48 inches
Between twin beds	36 - 60 inches
Each side of bed–to make beds and get in and out of	18 - 24 inches

16-2
Suggested amounts of clearance space around furniture are given.

window. Try not to block electrical outlets or air vents.

Furniture arrangements also need to be planned around special architectural features. For example, you do not want to block a fireplace or built-in bookshelves with furniture.

Using a scale floor plan lets you see the placement of the features. If you have trouble visualizing how your furniture will be located in relation to the features, you can add walls to your plan and indicate the features. See 16-4. You will also indicate the placement of the furniture on the walls.

Traffic patterns. As you learned in Chapter 7, "Understanding House Plans," traffic patterns need to provide enough space for people to move about freely. Each piece of furniture should be placed so people can circulate easily throughout the room. Your furniture placement should not create an obstacle course or block traffic patterns between rooms.

Lindal Cedar Homes, Inc. Seattle, Washington

16-3
The furniture in this grouping is arranged to encourage conversation.

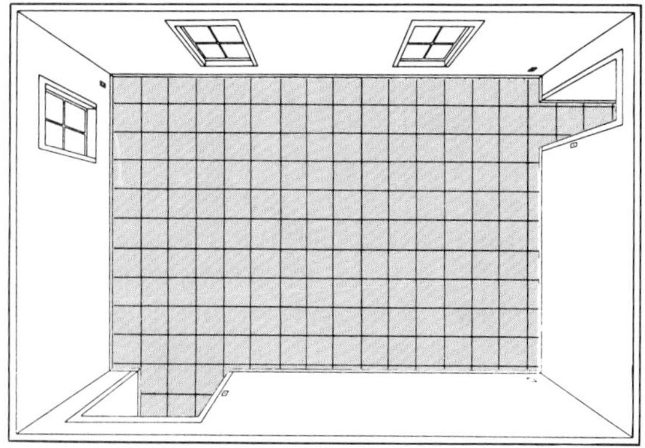

Drexel Furniture Company

16-4
A three-dimensional scale floor plan can be created by sketching doors and windows on walls drawn to scale. The walls can then be folded up, fastened at the corners, and placed on top of a scale floor plan.

Selecting Furniture

Selecting furniture is the next step in furnishing your home. This process involves many steps of its own.

Prioritizing Furniture Needs

Once you have determined how much furniture you can place in the rooms of your home, you need to prioritize your furniture needs. ***Prioritize*** means to rank goals in order of importance. This means deciding which pieces of furniture you need first and which can wait until later.

You should first buy the pieces you need the most, such as furniture for sleeping, eating, seating, and storage. Then you can buy accessories, which accent large pieces of furniture, and less-frequently used furniture.

You should also choose furniture that fits the life-style of your living unit. Furniture is of little value if it is not used. For example, if your living unit does not entertain with formal meals very often, having a formal dining room set is a waste of money and space.

Discuss furniture priorities with the other members of your living unit. Ask for input from all members of the living unit. This will let you make decisions that satisfy everyone. Listing everyone's ideas on paper will help prevent misunderstandings and make your decisions clear.

As you make your priority list, you should keep in mind that good design is always good design, even if it isn't the newest style. You should be familiar with decorating trends and be able to spot fads. They do not always last.

Deciding How Much You Can Afford

Once you have prioritized your furniture needs, you need to decide how much money you can spend. This will let you know how many items on your list you can afford. Each member of the living unit should have a say in the amount to be spent. Make a budget and be sure to follow it. Overspending is not likely to give you the same satisfaction as spending only what you can afford.

Smart shoppers buy the best merchandise for the best price. Sometimes, however, trade-offs are made. For example, if you spend more money for a kitchen table than you budgeted, you will need to cut back in other areas. You may have to wait longer than you wanted to purchase your next major piece of furniture. You may have to eliminate an item from your list.

Deciding Where to Shop

Furniture can be bought from many different types of stores. Generally, the more services a store provides, the higher the prices are. Therefore, you may want to do some ***comparison shopping,*** which is comparing the qualities, prices, and services provided for similar items in different stores before buying. See 16-5. You can save time and energy by checking prices using your telephone.

Retail stores. Retail stores, such as department stores and furniture stores, offer the most service to customers. For example, retail stores typically will deliver, unpack, and set up the merchandise in your home. However, the prices are usually higher to pay for these services. Some stores provide a decorating service. Decorating professionals will do a scale floor plan for you, visit your home, show you a wide selection of

Thomasville Furniture Industries, Inc.

16-5
By comparison shopping, a family was able to buy this love seat at the best price.

furniture, and take custom orders. Most custom-ordered furniture has to be ordered one to three months in advance.

Shop at retail stores with good reputations and buy furniture from manufacturers with good reputations. A good store will back up the merchandise it sells. A good manufacturer will replace defective products.

Furniture stores usually have a larger selection of furniture than department stores do. Both types of stores can order furniture they do not have in stock. Most custom-ordered furniture needs to be ordered one to three months in advance.

Discount houses. Discount houses often sell products at lower prices than retail stores. They also have less services than retail stores. You may have to wait for assistance or to receive your purchase. Delivery service for large items may not be available. If you have a problem with a product, you may not be able to get service from the store. If you are willing to give up these conveniences, discount houses may have bargains for you.

Warehouse showrooms. Generally, showrooms handle only a few brands of merchandise. They may also have off brands mixed in with the brand name merchandise. Since the furniture is already made, you will have less choice of fabrics. The advantages of shopping in warehouse showrooms are that they provide quick service and savings. You can take the item with you or have it delivered in a few days.

Catalogs. Catalogs let you shop by mail from anywhere. Catalogs carry store brand merchandise as well as name brand merchandise. Prices are usually lower, because the catalog house buys in large quantities. The main disadvantage of catalog shopping is that you cannot inspect the furniture for quality construction. You also cannot see the exact colors of the wood or upholstery. Shipping charges will add to the cost of the product.

Other places. Salvage stores, garage sales, auctions, and flea markets can provide great bargains if you have the time and shop carefully. Some items may need repairs or refinishing. You can decide whether the price is low enough to be worth the extra cost to refurbish the item.

Deciding When to Shop

When you shop is as important as where you shop. If you are in a hurry, tired, or shopping in crowded conditions, you may not make the best decisions. You may end up with purchases that you do not really want. Your choice of a time to shop will depend on your personal circumstances and desires.

Shopping at certain times can save you money. Stores sometimes have high-quality furniture on sale. Their sale prices can let you buy high-quality items at low prices. There are many different types of sales. Understanding each type can help you spend your money wisely.

Loss leader sales. ***Loss leader sales*** are held to get people to come into the store. The store management hopes that once you are in the store, you will buy other items that are not on sale. If you shop this kind of sale, buy only what you want and need at the price you want. For instance, you may find that a chair is on sale, but the matching sofa is not. If you want to buy only the chair, it may be a good bargain. However, if you want to buy a matching chair and sofa, you may be able to get a better deal somewhere else.

Seasonal sales. ***Seasonal sales*** are held so stores can get rid of stock to make room for new items. For instance, patio furniture is often on sale in August so that the store can make room for furniture for college dorm rooms. Many high-quality products are discounted during seasonal sales, 16-6.

Close-out sales. ***Close-out sales*** are held when a store is moving to another location or going out of business. It is better for the store to sell the merchandise at cost or at a loss than to move a large amount of goods. It is even more important to sell all the merchandise if the store is closing.

Damaged and discontinued item sales. Many stores mark down prices on items that are slightly damaged. Make sure you know where and how bad the damage is. A desk with a surface scratch may be a good bargain if the price is low. If the drawers don't slide easily, the desk may not be a bargain.

Discontinued item sales offer discontinued, high-quality goods at low prices. However, once the items are gone, you will not be able to purchase matching items. For example, you may find discontinued wallpaper on sale. If there is enough for you to wallpaper a complete area, it is a bargain.

As you shop at sales, keep in mind the expression, "Let the buyer beware." Sale items and less expensive items are priced that way for a reason. It's up to you, the buyer, to find out why and decide whether or not the lower price is worthwhile.

Information Sources

Before you make your final furniture selection, you should consult various sources for information on the furniture you are interested in buying. These sources will give you information on the quality and reliability of the furniture. They will also help you become familiar with what furniture is available.

Bargain Months		
January	February	March
Appliances, blankets, carpets and rugs, furniture, home furnishings, housewares, white goods.	Air conditioners, carpets and rugs, curtains and draperies, furniture, home furnishings, housewares, storm windows.	Laundry appliances, storm windows.
April	May	June
Gardening specials.	Blankets, carpets and rugs, linens, TV sets.	Building materials, fabrics, furniture, lumber, TV sets.
July	August	September
Air conditioners, appliances, carpets and rugs, fabrics, freezers and refrigerators, stereos, white goods.	Air conditioners, bedding, carpets and rugs, curtains and draperies, fans, gardening equipment, home furnishings, housewares, summer furniture, white goods.	Appliances, paint, TV sets.
October	November	December
China and silverware.	Blankets, housewares, home improvement supplies.	Blankets, housewares.

16-6
You can often find good bargains if you wait for seasonal sales.

Books and magazines. Home furnishing magazines and books can be found at the public library or can be purchased. Some books and articles tell how to refinish furniture. Some provide ideas on furniture selection and arrangement. Others give sources and costs for the merchandise featured. Money-saving ideas are often included.

Product ratings. *Consumer Reports* and *Consumer Bulletin* are publications that test and rate products. They give information about quality, price, and other factors, such as test results. The reports are available in their monthly magazines and annual buying guides. These publications can be found in the library, or you can subscribe to them.

Advertisements. Advertisements in newspapers and magazines and on the radio and TV often contain useful information. You can use advertisements to compare brand names, features, and prices.

Labels. Labels found on furniture may contain information about the materials used, coverings, fillings, country of manufacture, and origin of style. For example, if the product is made in the United States, the label will state "Danish Style" rather than "Danish." The label may indicate that the materials used are all new or partly made from used materials. Labels also include care information.

The Better Business Bureau. The Better Business Bureau (BBB) is a nonprofit organization sponsored by private businesses. It publishes pamphlets and booklets on products and services. Your local BBB can give you information about stores in the area. It also attempts to settle consumer complaints against local businesses.

Stretching Your Furniture Dollars

Stretching your furniture dollars can help you acquire more furniture for your money. There are many reasons you may need to do this. One is that when you move into your first home, your take-home pay may not be able to cover your many furniture needs. You may have to use rented or used furniture until you can afford to buy your own new furniture.

Another reason is that when the size of your living unit increases, your housing costs also increase. Therefore, finding ways to save money on furniture may be important as you move through the life cycle.

There are many ways to stretch your furniture dollars. They include shopping for bargains, using multipurpose furniture, unassembled furniture, reusing furniture, and creating an eclectic look.

Shopping for Bargains

As you read above, a good way to find furniture bargains is to buy furniture on sale. You need to keep in mind that no matter how much the item costs on sale, it is not a bargain unless you need it and can afford it. The item is also not a bargain if you would really rather have something else. A true bargain must improve the quality of your life.

You need to remember that what seems like a bargain may not be a bargain after all. While one item may cost less than a similar item, it may require more time or effort to acquire. For instance, carpeting at a store 50 miles away may cost 20 percent less than carpeting at a nearby store. This savings may be worth the long drive to some people, but not to others.

Although durable, simple furniture may not seem like a bargain, it really is. Complex furniture is often more expensive than simple furniture. Carving, latticework, turnings, and other extras add to the cost of furniture, 16-7. The appearance of furniture with simple lines and colors can be changed easily by changing accessories.

Using Multipurpose Furniture

Multipurpose furniture is furniture that can be used for more than one purpose. For example, a sofa bed can be used for sitting or sleeping. Flat-topped trunks and chests can be used as end tables and coffee tables, while also being used for storage.

Pennsylvania House

16-7
The detailed turning found in the legs of this table and chair set makes it more expensive than a set with simple, straight legs.

Unassembled Furniture

Unassembled furniture, which is furniture that does not come put together, may or may not be finished. It is often lower quality than most preassembled furniture. By assembling the furniture yourself, you save money. Since unassembled furniture usually takes up less room than assembled furniture, you can save money by hauling it yourself.

You can be creative and think of ways to assemble furniture from items not normally thought of as furniture. For example, you can use bricks and boards to assemble bookshelves. A round piece of board can be covered with a large circular cloth to produce a table. See 16-8.

Plastic or wooden cubes can be assembled in a wide variety of ways to create furniture. They can be used for shelves, tables, desks, and seats. See 16-9. Some cubes are divided to provide shelf space, or so drawers can be added. Plastic cubes come in many colors. Wooden ones can be painted to coordinate with your decorating scheme.

Spiegel

16-8
A round board mounted on any kind of a base can become a table.

Hold Everything

16-9
These cubes can be arranged in many different ways to create shelves and storage space.

Reusing Furniture

After you acquire new furniture, you can still reuse your old furniture. This will help you stretch your home furniture dollars even more. To reuse your furniture, you can recycle, restore, or renew it.

Recycling furniture. To ***recycle*** means to adapt to a new use. Recycling furniture means that you can use it for one purpose, and when you no longer need it for that purpose, you can use it for another purpose. For instance, outdoor furniture can be used in your first living room, dining room, or family room, 16-10. As your budget allows, you can replace the outdoor furniture with indoor furniture. The outdoor furniture can then be used to decorate your patio. Other outdoor furniture can be used indoors. For instance, patio benches can be used as coffee tables, end tables, or seating. Picnic tables and lawn chairs can also be used inside.

You can recycle furniture pieces in your own home or pass them on to someone else to use. You can also buy used furniture from other sources to recycle in your home. Garage sales, secondhand stores, and relatives are good sources of used furniture.

Brown Jordan

16-10
This wrought iron patio furniture is effectively used as indoor furniture.

Renovating furniture. Often furniture can be renovated, which includes restoring and renewing furniture. It usually costs less to renovate an old piece of furniture than to buy low-quality, new furniture. You can renovate furniture yourself, or you can hire a professional. If you choose to do it yourself, keep in mind that it takes time, patience, and work. It also takes money for supplies and equipment.

As you examine a piece of used furniture you are thinking about renovating, ask yourself the following questions:

- Is it well designed?
- Is it well constructed and worth repairing?
- Can it be used "as is"?
- Do I have the time, patience, and energy to do a good job?
- Do I have the necessary equipment and supplies to do the job?
- Do I have a suitable place to work?
- Will it blend with my other furnishings?

When you ***restore*** a piece of furniture, you are putting it back to its original state. There are steps to follow when you restore a piece of furniture. They are repairing, refinishing, and (possibly) reupholstering. For example, you may want to restore an antique chair. First, you would remove the paint and sand the wood down to the original state. Then you would make any necessary repairs, such as redoing the joints. After repairing the chair, apply a finish as close to the original as possible. Then do any reupholstering, if needed. This process takes a lot of time and skill. You must have an interest in restoring to make it worthwhile.

If a piece of furniture is still in good condition, but the upholstery fabric is worn or dated, you can ***renew*** it. The steps in this process are similar to those followed in restoration. However, in this case you are updating a piece of furniture, not restoring it to its original condition.

As an example, you might have a chair that is in good condition but the upholstery fabric is worn and soiled. To renew the chair, make any needed repairs to the frame. Then carefully remove the original upholstery fabric and use it as a pattern for the new upholstery, and reupholster the chair.

Creating the Eclectic Look

Another way to stretch your furniture dollars is to create the eclectic look in your home. ***Eclectic*** is a type of decor based on a mixture of furnishings from different periods and countries. See 16-11. You can choose to use this look as you are acquiring one style of furniture, or you can use it on a permanent basis.

Since a variety of styles are used in furnishing an eclectic room, care must be taken to avoid a busy appearance. Using the principles of design will help create a unified look. For example, the furnishings in an eclectic room should be in proportion to one another. They should be related in mood–formal or informal. The colors and textures should be carefully combined and balanced.

Summary

Using a scale floor plan aids in arranging furniture. It shows the dimensions and features of the room and allows you to move furniture templates around to find the best furniture arrangement. As you arrange furniture, you need to consider the following factors: furniture arrangement is dependent upon how the furniture and the room are used, furniture arrangements should be planned so they do not interfere with room features, and traffic patterns need to provide enough space for people to move about freely.

Selecting furniture involves many steps. First is prioritizing furniture needs. Then you need to decide how much you can afford, where to shop, and when to shop. Finally, you should consult information sources. All members of your living unit should have input in each step of the process.

Stretching your furniture dollars will allow you to acquire more furniture for your money. This can be done by shopping for bargains. You can also choose multipurpose furniture or furniture that needs to be finished or assembled. Reusing furniture can also save you money. You may do the work yourself or you can hire a professional. The eclectic look can be a solution to acquiring a certain furniture style over a period of time.

Ethan Allen, Inc.

16-11
This mixture of contemporary and traditional furnishings works well together to create an eclectic look.

To Review

Write your responses on a separate sheet of paper.

1. How does using a scale floor plan help you arrange furniture?
2. List three factors to consider when planning furniture arrangement.
3. Explain the importance of prioritizing your furniture needs.
4. Why do you need to decide ahead of time how much you can afford to spend on furniture?
5. Name three places to shop for furniture. Give one advantage and one disadvantage in shopping at each location.
6. Identify possible drawbacks for shopping at each of the following types of sales:
   a. Loss leader sale.
   b. Seasonal sale.
   c. Close-out sale.
   d. Damaged and discontinued item sales.
7. What are some sources of information for making purchases and how can they be used to select furniture?
8. Give examples of three ways to stretch your furniture dollars.
9. List two ways to reuse furniture.
10. Identify the steps in restoring furniture.
11. How can the eclectic look help you stretch your furniture dollars?

To Do

1. Draw a simple scale floor plan of your bedroom. Make templates of your furniture and use them to create different furniture arrangements on your scale floor plan. Allow for traffic patterns.
2. Compare prices on identical pieces of furniture, such as a sofa or dining room table. Go to two different stores and check the prices. If the prices are different, try to find out why. A salesperson may be able to help you. Share your findings with the class.
3. Look through the newspapers to find advertisements representing each type of sale discussed in this chapter. Cut out the advertisements, mount them on separate pieces of paper, and label them. Hang them in your classroom.
4. Look for a report on furniture in an issue of *Consumer Reports* or *Consumer Bulletin.* Read the article and report your findings to the class.
5. Look around your house for a piece of furniture that you think needs restoring or renewing. Research how to restore or renew that particular piece of furniture. Write a short report discussing your findings.

CHAPTER 17

The Finishing Touches

Spiegel

To Know
absorbed light
accent lighting
accessories
blinds
compact fluorescent bulb
curtains
diffused light
direct lighting
draperies
electronic lamp (E-lamp)
fluorescent light
footcandle
general lighting
incandescent light
indirect lighting
local lighting
nonstructural lighting
reflected light
shades
shutters
structural light fixtures
task lighting
tungsten-halogen light

Objectives

After studying this chapter, you will be able to:

- Describe types of window treatments.
- Explain the differences between incandescent and fluorescent lighting.
- Plan residential lighting for visual comfort, safety, and beauty.
- Distinguish between structural and nonstructural lighting.
- Give guidelines for using accessories.

Some of the final steps of furnishing a room are to select the right window treatments, provide good lighting, and choose accessories that show your personality. You will continue to use the elements and principles of design as you add the finishing touches.

Window Treatments

The style, size, and location of windows are all factors that need to be considered when choosing window treatments. Another very important factor is that windows let in natural light. Window treatments can help you control the amount of natural light that enters a room. Some window treatments let you block out all or part of the natural light. Others let in as much light as possible.

Window treatments include draperies, curtains, shades, shutters, and blinds. They have the ability to make a room look great. The right window treatments can help disguise design flaws that are costly to fix. For example, if windows are different sizes or unevenly spaced, window treatments can change the appearance within a room. Certain treatments can camouflage windows that are not in proportion to the rest of the room.

Some windows are left untreated. This often happens when privacy is not a concern, or the shape of the window makes it difficult to treat. In 17-1, the unusual-shaped windows are left uncovered. This gives the room a dramatic look and lets light enter the room freely.

Marvin Windows & Doors

17-1
These striking windows need no treatment.

Draperies and Curtains

Draperies and curtains are the most common window treatments. They are extremely versatile and can fit into any decor. The type of draperies or curtains you choose depends on the room's decor and the function of the windows.

Draperies. *Draperies* are pleated panels of heavy fabric that cover windows completely or are pulled to the side. They can be opaque or *translucent,* which means to permit the passage of light. They can be lined or unlined. Lining draperies protects them from the sun, adds body, and makes them hang better.

Draperies can be used alone or with other window treatments, such as curtains, shades, or blinds. In 17-2, pleated shades are used with draperies. The shades filter the light that enters the room and provide some privacy. When the draperies are closed, they block out almost all of the sunlight, provide complete privacy, and help insulate the room.

The different types of draperies are named for how they operate. *Draw draperies* open and close from the center or side with a pull stick or cord on one end of the curtain rod. *Stationary draperies* cannot be opened and closed. They

Kirsch

17-2
Draw draperies with coordinating pleated shades are an attractive part of this dining room.

Mannington Resilient Floors

17-3
A swag drapes across the top of a window.

are often positioned at the side of a window. *Swag draperies* hang in a curve across the top of a window, 17-3.

Curtains. ***Curtains*** are flat fabric panels that cover windows. Usually they have a pocket hem at the top, which is slipped onto a curtain rod and gathered to the desired fullness. The amount of light or privacy curtains provide depends on the fabric, 17-4. Curtains made of sheer fabric give a room a light, airy feeling. If more privacy is needed, heavier fabrics can be used. However, this may make the room appear darker.

Cafe curtains are horizontal panels hung in tiers to cover part of a window. The top of each panel is joined to rings that slip over a curtain rod. Cafe curtains cannot be opened by pulling a cord as draw draperies are. However, you can open cafe curtains by pushing them to the sides. This lets you control air, light, and privacy. When using cafe curtains, one tier can be used to cover only the bottom half of the window. More than one tier

Spiegel

17-4
The fabric in these curtains is opaque enough to shut out light and provide privacy as desired.

can be used to completely cover a window. By changing the width or the number of tiers, a variety of looks can be achieved with cafe curtains.

The length of draperies and curtains should fall at *sill length, apron length,* or *floor length.* If the bottom edge of a window treatment falls at any other place, it will look either too short or too long. To correctly measure the length of draperies and curtains, use the methods shown in 17-5.

Shades, Shutters, and Blinds

Shades block out unwanted light. This can be blocking out intense sunlight for a few hours in the afternoon or blocking out streetlight at night. Shades vary in appearance to go with almost any decor. *Roller shades,* 17-6, come in various colors. They also come in various degrees of opaqueness. Other shades can also be raised and lowered. *Roman shades,* 17-7, and *pleated shades* can be raised and lowered. They are available in many different colors and degrees of opaqueness. *Balloon shades* are yet another type. They received their name from the balloon shape they take when they are raised.

Windows that are used for ventilation cannot be covered, or air movement will be blocked. ***Shutters,*** movable hinged screens that cover part or all of a window, are appropriate for windows used for ventilation. See 17-8.

Blinds are window treatments made of slats that can be raised up and down or moved to the side. Horizontal blinds, often called *venetian blinds,* can be raised completely. *Miniblinds* are horizontal blinds with narrow slats. *Vertical blinds* move to one side to leave a window uncovered.

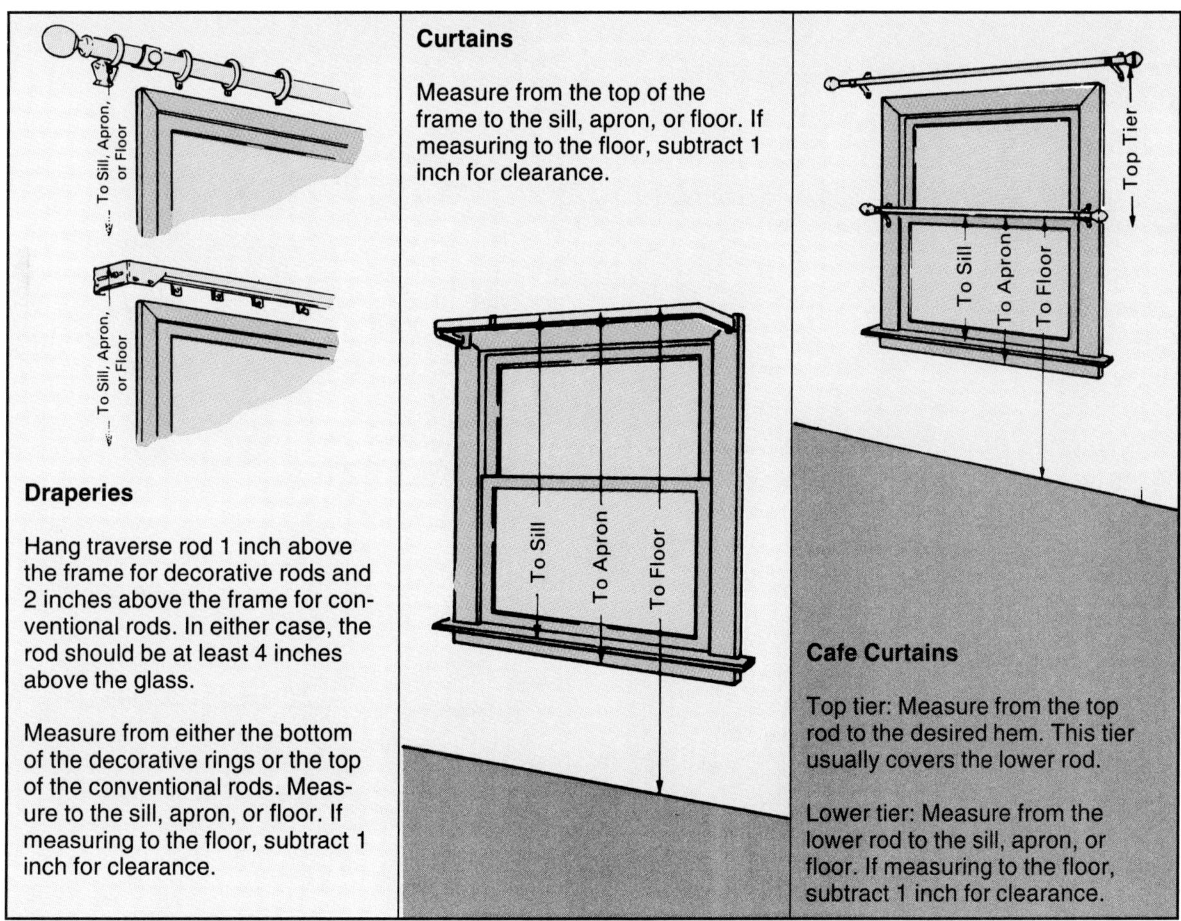

17-5
Different methods are used to measure for draperies, curtains, and cafe curtains.

Kirsch

17-6
This roller shade was designed to coordinate with the fabrics used in the room.

Armstrong World Industries, Inc.

17-7
As you raise Roman shades from the bottom, they form soft, accordion folds.

JCPenney Custom Decorating

17-8
These unique shutters are used to cover a sliding glass door.

The slats can be tilted to any degree to control the amounts of air and light that enter a room. Blinds are often made of wood, metal, plastic, or fabric. They can be custom-made to fit windows with unusual shape or placement. See 17-9.

Artificial Light

Natural light is not always available. Therefore, artificial light is also needed. The two main kinds of artificial light used in homes are incandescent light and fluorescent light.

Incandescent Light

Incandescent light is produced when an electric current passes through a fine tungsten filament inside a bulb. The filament is heated by the electricity until it glows and gives off light. See 17-10. Incandescent bulbs vary in shape and size. However, they all work the same way.

Incandescent light bulbs used in homes range from 15 to 300 watts. (See Chapter 9, "The

Velux-America, Inc.

17-9
Special miniblinds were installed between the panels of glass in these windows to control light.

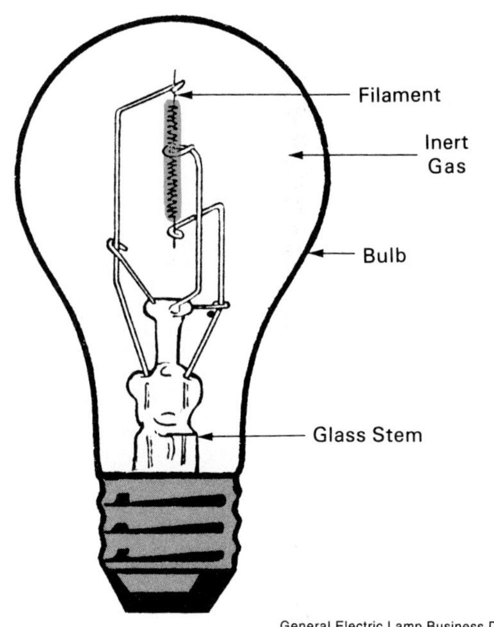

General Electric Lamp Business Division

17-10
Inside an incandescent light bulb, inert gas surrounds a filament. Electric current heats the filament and makes it glow.

Systems Within," for a discussion on watts.) When comparing two incandescent bulbs, the one with the higher wattage will give off more light. The chart in 17-11 lists the recommended wattage for some household activities.

Most incandescent bulbs used in homes have a *frost finish* that covers the entire inside surface of the bulb. The main purpose of the frost finish is to reduce glare, so the light appears smoother and shadows softer. The frost finish also makes the bulb last longer because it keeps the surface of the bulb fairly cool. Because of the coolness, a lampshade that accidentally touches this type of bulb is not likely to be scorched by it.

Selection Guide for Incandescent Bulbs	
Activity	Minumum Recommended Wattage*
Reading, writing, sewing	
Occasional periods	150
Prolonged periods	200 or 300
Grooming	
Bathroom mirror	
1 fixture each side of mirror	1–50 or 2–40s
1 cup-type fixture over mirror	100
1 fixture over mirror	150
Bathroom ceiling fixture	150
Vanity table lamps, in pairs (person seated)	100 each
Dresser lamps, in pairs (person standing)	150 each
Kitchen work	
Ceiling fixture (2 or more in a large area)	150 or 200
Fixture over sink	150
Fixture for eating area (separately from work space)	150
Shopwork	
Fixture for workbench (2 or more for long bench)	150
* white bulbs preferred	

U.S. Department of Agriculture

17-11
Your activities determine the quantity of light you need.

Bulbs without a frost finish produce a great deal of glare. They should be used only in fixtures that hide them completely from view.

Many kinds of special incandescent bulbs are available. One is the *three-way bulb.* Sets of filaments operate separately or together to give off different amounts of light, ranging from 30 to 250 watts.

Some bulbs have silver or aluminum coatings. These bulbs focus the light in certain directions. Other bulbs are coated with silicone rubber. This prevents the glass from shattering if the bulb breaks.

Another variation is colored bulbs. Colored bulbs can be used to create a mood in a room. Blue bulbs can make a room seem restful. Red bulbs create a feeling of excitement. Yellow-coated bulbs are used to keep insects away. They do not repel insects, but the yellow coating blocks the light rays that attract insects.

Tungsten-halogen lights. ***Tungsten-halogen lights*** are another form of incandescent lighting. In this type of bulb, a gas from the halogen family and tungsten molecules are combined to activate a filament. The special quartz bulb lights up instantly when the electric current is turned on.

Tungsten-halogen bulbs, 17-12, have many advantages over regular incandescent bulbs. They give off a better quality of light. The amount of light in an aging tungsten-halogen bulb does not decrease as much as in regular bulbs. Also, tungsten-halogen bulbs last up to three times as long as regular bulbs. However, the main disadvantage is that the tungsten-halogen bulbs are not as energy efficient as some other types. They are more energy efficient than other types of incandescent lights, but less energy efficient than fluorescent lights.

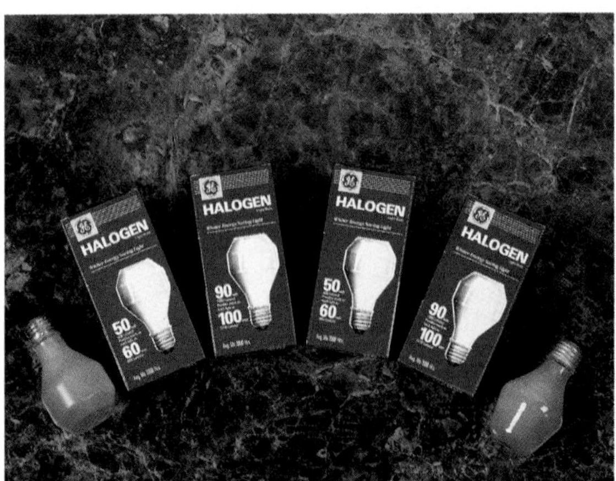

GE Lighting

17-12
Compared with standard incandescent bulbs of equal wattage, tungsten-halogen bulbs last longer and burn brighter.

The electronic 20-year lamp. The ***electronic lamp,*** or *E-lamp,* fits most sockets that use incandescent bulbs. It is expected to last up to 20,000 hours. If used four hours a day, those hours would equal 14 years. Incandescent bulbs, in comparison, are expected to last no more than 1,500 hours in the same amount of time.

Fluorescent Light

Fluorescent light is produced in a glass tube by releasing electricity through a mercury vapor to make invisible ultraviolet rays. These rays are converted into visible light rays by a coating of fluorescent material on the inside of the glass tube. There is a delay between when the electric current is released and light is produced.

Fluorescent light is more energy efficient than incandescent light. A fluorescent tube produces about four times as much light as an incandescent bulb with the same wattage. Fluorescent tubes are more expensive than incandescent bulbs, but they last longer and are less expensive to use. Fluorescent tubes can be expected to last up to 20,000 hours and use 40 watts or less of electricity.

Fluorescent tubes come in various shapes. Some are straight; others are circular. Fluorescent tubes are available in various sizes. Traditionally, the length of straight tubes or diameter of circular tubes determines the wattage. See 17-13.

The color of the light given off by fluorescent tubes can be varied by changing the coating of fluorescent material in the tube. Cool white light is very efficient, blends well with sunlight, and makes colors look good. Warm white is cost efficient, but it is not flattering to some colors. Cool white and warm white are most often used in kitchens and bathrooms. Deluxe cool white

Popular Sizes of Fluorescent Tubes		
	Wattage	**Length**
Straight Tubes	14	15 inches
	15	18 inches
	20	24 inches
	30	36 inches
	40	48 inches
	Wattage	**Outside Diameter of Circle**
Circular	22	8 1/4 inches
	32	12 inches
	40	16 inches

17-13
The wattage for fluorescent tubes depends on the length or diameter of the tubes.

closely imitates natural daylight. Full-spectrum fluorescent tubes now give both cool and warm colors.

Compact fluorescent bulbs. A new type of fluorescent light is the ***compact fluorescent bulb.*** Compact fluorescent bulbs are a little larger than regular incandescent bulbs and screw into regular light bulb sockets. See 17-14. They save energy and will operate about 9,000 hours, while using only 15 watts of electricity.

Compact fluorescent bulbs help the environment. The electricity saved by replacing an incandescent bulb with a compact fluorescent bulb will equal the energy generated by about 450 pounds of coal during the life of the bulb.

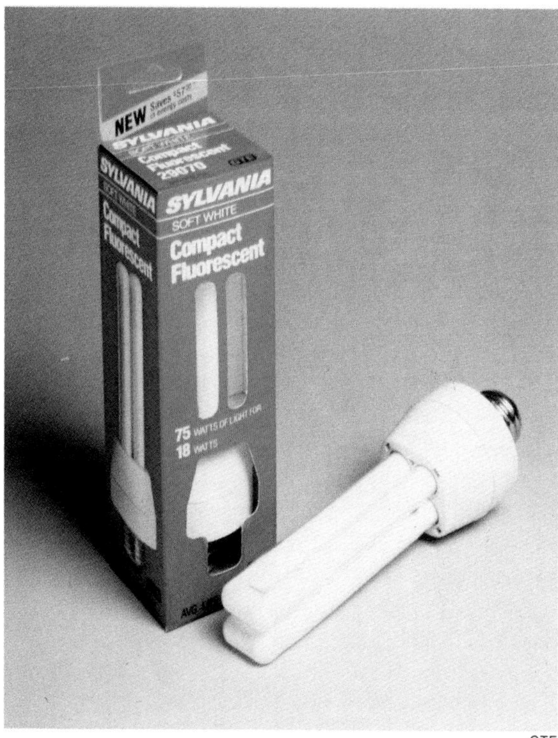

GTE

17-14
Although compact fluorescent bulbs look different than regular incandescent light bulbs, they can be used in the same outlets.

Let Light Work for You

You can use light to achieve several different effects in your home. To do this, you first need to understand the various properties of light. Light can be reflected or absorbed. It can shine directly on a certain spot or lighten a whole room.

Reflected Light

Light, color, and texture are closely related. Without light, there is no color. In turn, colors reflect and absorb various amounts of light. Surfaces with rough textures look dark because tiny shadows form where the light does not reach. Together, light, color, and texture greatly affect the appearance of rooms.

Reflected light is the light that bounces off surfaces. It seems to come from these surfaces as well as from its source. Light is reflected by light colors and smooth, shiny surfaces. Light is also reflected by background treatments in the home. Study 17-15 to learn how much light can be reflected by background areas.

Absorbed Light

Absorbed light is light that is drawn in by a surface. Rough textures and dark colors absorb most of the available light rays. If light is absorbed, it cannot be reflected.

In your home, use rough textures and dark colors in large areas. This will make the areas appear smaller, since the light is being absorbed.

Background	Minimum	Maximum
Ceilings		
Pale Color Tints	60%	90%
Walls		
Natural Wood	5%	50%
Light Colors	70%	80%
Medium Colors	35%	60%
Dark Colors	5%	25%
Floors		
Carpeting, Tiles, Woods	15%	35%

17-15
This chart gives minimum and maximum amounts of light that can be reflected by background areas.

Summitville Tiles, Inc.

17-16
Direct lighting is used here to make preparing and cooking easier and safer.

Diffused Light

Diffused light is light that is scattered over a large area. It has no glare, which is the most troublesome aspect of lighting. Instead, it creates a soft appearance. The devices used to diffuse light are called diffusers. Diffusers spread the light evenly. An example of a diffuser is the frosted or white finish on incandescent and fluorescent bulbs. Other diffusers are more apparent, such as the covers for light fixtures. These diffusers are usually made of frosted or translucent glass.

Lighting for Visual Comfort

To create visual comfort in your home, you need two basic types of lighting: general and local. The type and amount needed vary from room to room.

General lighting. ***General lighting*** provides a uniform level of light throughout a room. General lighting can be achieved through both direct and indirect lighting. ***Direct lighting*** shines directly toward an object, 17-16. It provides the most light possible to a specific area. If used alone, direct lighting creates a sharp contrast between light and dark, which can cause eye fatigue. Therefore, if direct lighting is needed for a task, use other lighting in the room.

General lighting can also be achieved through indirect lighting. ***Indirect lighting*** is directed toward a surface, such as a ceiling or wall, that reflects the light into the room. See 17-17. Indirect lighting may provide soft light for a large area. However, it does not provide enough light for detailed work.

General lighting should light up a room, so you can see objects clearly and move about safely. The amount of general lighting needed depends on the shape, size, and use of the room.

Local lighting. General lighting does not always supply enough light for visual comfort. In these cases, it can be supplemented by local lighting. ***Local lighting*** is lighting used in specific areas requiring more light. Having the right amount of local lighting will prevent eyestrain. When it is used to help you see well enough to do a certain task, such as writing letters, carving wood, or sewing, it is called ***task lighting.***

Randall Whitehead/Lighting Designer: Randall Whitehead, Light Source

17-17
Indirect lighting is reflected by the ceiling and wall around this plant.

The amount of local lighting you need depends on the activity. The finer the detail or the faster the action taking place, the more light you need. For instance, playing table tennis requires more light than shooting pool.

Local lighting in one part of a room can serve as general lighting for another part. For instance, if you are reading in one corner of a family room, the lamp that you use for local lighting adds to the general lighting of the entire room.

To get the right amount of good quality light, combine general and local lighting. Together, they give adequate light without sharp contrast.

Measuring light. The amount of light needed or used can be measured with the use of a light meter. The unit of measure is the footcandle. A ***footcandle*** is the amount of light a standard candle gives at a distance of one foot. Amounts of light needed for various activities are listed in 17-18.

As an example, if you plan to read for quite awhile, you need about 70 footcandles of light over the reading area. A lamp in the correct position with a 200 watt bulb can give this amount of light. See 17-19.

Lighting for the Home	
Seeing Task	**Amount of Light (in footcandles)**
Dining	15
Grooming	50
Ironing	50
Kitchen Duties	
Food preparation and cleaning that involves difficult seeing tasks	150
Serving and other noncritical tasks	50
Laundry Tasks	
Preparation, sorting, hand wash	50
Washer and dryer areas	30
Reading and Writing	
Handwriting, reproductions, poor copies	70
Books, magazines, and newspapers	30
Sewing	
Dark fabrics	200
Medium fabrics	100
Light fabrics	50
Occasional, high contrast	30
Studying	70
Playing Table Games	30

U.S. Department of Agriculture

17-18
Use this chart to determine the approximate amount of light needed for certain activities.

Lighting for Safety

Lighting for safety is very important. It can help prevent accidents and fires. Accidents can occur in the dark and where there is not enough light. To guard against accidents, plan lighting where it will work best for you. If you can answer yes to the following questions, you will know your lighting is planned for safety. If you answer no, you will need to do some planning.

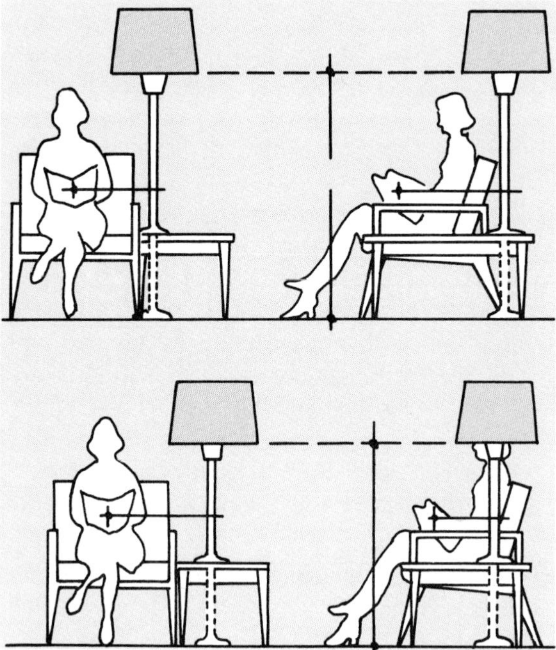
Agricultural Research Service

17-19
Lampshades above eye level should be farther behind you but closer to your side than lampshades at eye level.

17-20
The Underwriters Laboratories seal on a lamp assures you that the lamp was made according to safety guidelines.

Can you:

- Light your way as you go from room to room?
- Switch lights on or off from each doorway?
- Turn on stairway lighting as you go up or down the stairs?
- Light entrances as you enter?
- Control garage or carport lighting from the house?
- Control outside lighting from inside the house?

Another aspect of lighting for safety concerns safe wiring. If wiring is unsafe, it can start fires in the home. To assure safety, the wiring used for lighting should meet standards set by various groups. For example, the National Electrical Code is a standard with which all wiring should comply. There are often local requirements as well.

When you purchase electrical lighting fixtures, buy only those with an Underwriters Laboratories (UL) seal attached. See 17-20. It tells you that the light was manufactured according to safety standards. However, it does not assure you that the parts will continue to be safe. You need to use lights safely and watch for possible dangers. If instructions for the use and care of the lights are available, read them and follow them.

Electrical circuits should not be overloaded. Do not plug too many lights into one socket. The excess load could blow a fuse or trip a circuit breaker, and you would be without electric power in all or part of your home. Even worse, a fire could start.

Lighting for Beauty

While all light can be decorative, some lighting is used for beauty alone. Soft light can create a quiet, restful mood. Sharp light can be used to highlight the focal point in a room. When lighting is used in this way, it is called ***accent lighting.***

Decorative lighting can also be used outside the home, 17-21. Huge yard lights are often used in rural settings, while smaller ones are used in urban areas. Lights near entrances are also common. Patios can be lighted for night use. In such areas, the light should be attractive. Harsh and glaring light should be avoided. With the right choices, you can have pleasant, glowing light.

Structural and Nonstructural Lighting

Lighting affects the appearance of a room. So does the means by which the light is delivered. The two ways of delivering light are through structural and nonstructural lighting.

Photography: Ken Rice/Lighting Design: Jan Moyer Design

17-21
Exterior lighting gives this home a dramatic appearance.

Structural Lighting

When a light fixture is permanently built in a home, it is called a ***structural light fixture.*** It is either included in the original plans or added during a remodeling project.

When you choose structural light fixtures, they should be in harmony with other aspects of the room's design. When choosing fixtures, consider the following points:

- Diffused light gives more visual comfort than exposed bulbs, which can produce glare.
- Fixtures that can change position can be used in more than one way. Some fixtures may be raised or lowered. Others swing or swivel for a variety of effects.
- Fixtures that provide for changing the quantity of light, such as three-way bulbs or dimmer switches, have more uses.

There are many types of structural lighting fixtures. Some are pictured in 17-22. *Valance lighting fixtures* are mounted over windows. Fluorescent light is directed upward and downward, giving both direct and indirect lighting. Valance lighting restores the daytime lighting balance to a room.

Bracket lighting fixtures are just like valance lighting fixtures, except that they are used on walls or over work areas. Fluorescent light is directed both upward and downward. Bracket lighting can be used for general or accent lighting.

Cornice lighting fixtures are mounted to the wall near the ceiling. Fluorescent light shines downward, giving direct light only. Cornice lighting can be used on almost any wall for a variety of effects.

Cove lighting fixtures are also mounted near the ceiling. Fluorescent light is directed upward, giving indirect light only. Cove lighting is good general lighting, but it must be supplemented with local lighting. It also gives a room a feeling of height.

Recessed downlights are small, circular lights installed in the ceiling. When several are used together, they supply good general lighting. A few of them can be used for accent lighting. The typical "scalloped" pattern of light and shadow gives a dramatic look.

Surface-mounted downlights are similar to recessed downlights. However, the housing can or cylinder is in plain view below the ceiling.

Wall washers are also installed in the ceiling. They have a contoured inner reflector that directs nearly uniform light on walls from ceiling to floor. It gives walls a smooth look.

Soffit lighting fixtures consist of an enclosed box attached to the ceiling. Soffit lighting is used where a large amount of local light is needed.

Luminous ceilings are made of panels that cover recessed lights. They make a room feel spacious.

Track lighting consists of several light fixtures mounted on a metal strip. The fixtures can be arranged in varying positions to shine in different directions and create different effects.

Nonstructural Lighting

Nonstructural lighting is lighting that is not a structural part of the house. These lights can be moved, changed, and replaced more easily than any other form of lighting.

General Electric Lighting Institute

Cove Lighting

Capri Lighting, Thomas Industries

Track Lighting

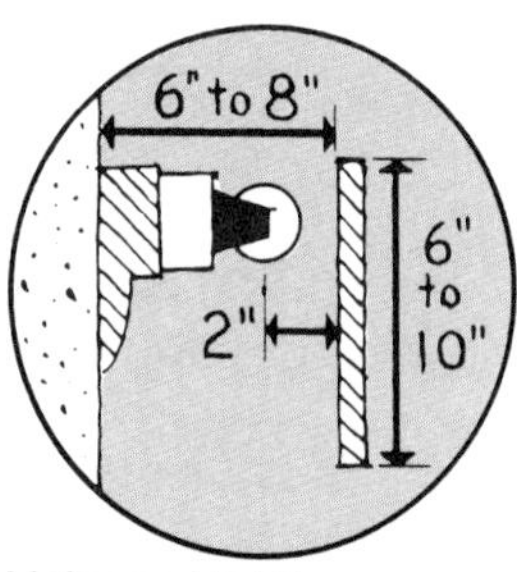

Valance Lighting

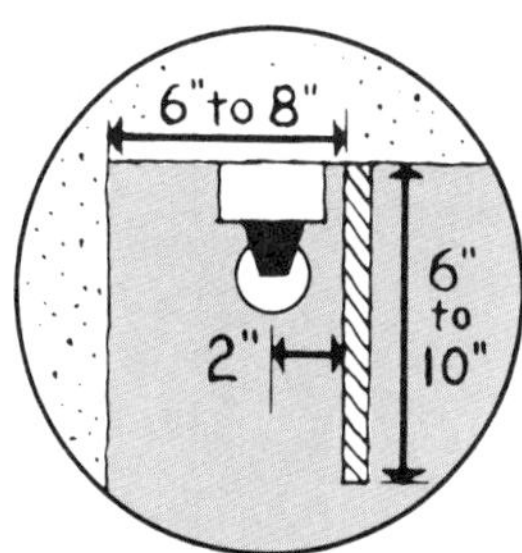

Cornice Lighting

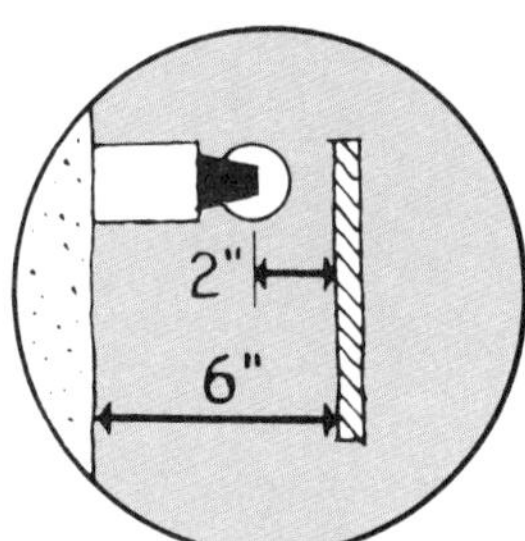

Bracket Lighting

Kate Shenberger Interiors, Flossmoor, Illinois

Recessed Downlights

17-22
Structural lighting can create special effects in a room. It must be planned while the dwelling is being built or remodeled.

Lamps are the most common type of nonstructural lighting. They can be used for decorative purposes and to provide good lighting and safety. When choosing lamps, keep the following points in mind:

- A sturdy or heavy base prevents tipping.
- A diffusing bowl prevents glare.
- A harp makes it possible to change the height of the lampshade. (A *harp* is a metal hoop or arch that supports a lampshade.)
- The colors and textures of lamps and lampshades should harmonize.
- Light-colored, translucent lampshades give off the most light.
- Lamps that can be adjusted are the most practical. Some can be raised and lowered, such as swag lamps. Some have swinging arms, and some use three-way bulbs.

Structural and nonstructural lighting can be combined in many different ways. See 17-23. The goal is always to achieve good lighting throughout the dwelling.

Choosing Accessories

Accessories are items smaller than furnishings that accent the design of a room. They can be used for decorative purposes or for functional purposes. Some accessories serve both purposes. *Decorative accessories* add beauty to a room. Some examples of decorative accessories are plants, flowers, pictures, wall hangings, and figurines. *Functional accessories* accent the room, while also serving another purpose. They include pillows, quilts, lamps, mirrors, and clocks. Functional and decorative accessories are often used together. An example of an accessory that is both decorative and functional is a lamp shade of a special design.

The accessories in your home reflect the personalities of the living unit, 17-24. They can show a preference for items such as clocks, antiques, or Oriental objects. Some items may have sentimental value. Others may be parts of collections.

Keep in mind that accessories should not be used just to fill up space. Each accessory should

Marvin Windows & Doors

17-23
Cove lighting and lamps provide artificial light for this room. A large window area provides natural light during the day.

Ethan Allen, Inc.

17-24
What do you think this bedroom says about the personality of the person who sleeps here?

Accessories	
Decisions	**Range of Available Choices**
Location	In room In relation to other objects
Form Type Style	 Functional or decorative Traditional Modern Contemporary Eclectic
Acquisition Process and cost	 Initial Maintenance Replacing Financing

17-25
As you decorate with accessories, it is important to think about location, form, and acquisition.

be chosen for a purpose. It should also blend in with the style and period of the room. While an accessory may be useful, beautiful, or meaningful to you, it may not fit into the scheme of the room. At that point, you should ask yourself if it really belongs.

Accessories placed near one another should have something in common. It may be color, style, or purpose. This shared element will help tie the furnishings in the room together. Other decisions concerning accessories are outlined in 17-25.

Summary

The finishing touches of furnishing a room are window treatments, lighting, and accessories. The style, size, and location of windows influence how they are treated. The amount of natural light you want to let in is also a factor. There are a variety of window treatments available. They include draperies, curtains, shades, shutters, and blinds and are made from a variety of materials.

Artificial lighting is used to supplement natural light. You can choose between the two main types of artificial lighting–incandescent or fluorescent lighting. Each type has its advantages and disadvantages. The E-lamp and compact fluorescent bulb are new, energy-efficient types of artificial lighting.

Light can be used to achieve different effects. Light can be reflected, absorbed, and diffused. It can be used to create visual comfort through general and local lighting. As you work with light, you need to consider using it for safety and beauty.

Some lighting comes from structural fixtures, which are a part of the house. Other lighting comes from nonstructural items, which are not a part of the house. The types you choose will depend on the type of lighting that you need or desire.

Accessories are part of the decorative scheme. They can be decorative or functional, or a combination. They reflect your personality. They need to fit with one another and the other furnishings.

To Review

Write your responses on a separate sheet of paper.

1. How do draperies and curtains differ?
2. Why are shutters and blinds appropriate for windows that are used for ventilation?
3. How do incandescent lights and fluorescent lights differ in terms of purchasing cost and operating cost?
4. List two energy-efficient types of light bulbs.
5. List three ways light can work for you in your home. Give an example of each.
6. Why do you need general lighting and local lighting?
7. List five structural light fixtures.
8. Explain the difference between functional and decorative accessories.
9. Why should accessories placed near one another have something in common?

To Do

1. Find and mount pictures of each of the five types of window treatments on a bulletin board.
2. Compare light from several different sources: a frosted bulb, colored bulbs, a cool white fluorescent tube, and a warm white fluorescent tube. Place lights near one another. Compare each light with sunlight. Turn on all lights and observe the different colors of light. Shine all lights on a white surface and note the differences. Then shine them all on a colored surface and note the differences.
3. Change four incandescent light bulbs in your house to compact fluorescent bulbs. Then evaluate your electric bill over several months to see if you notice a savings.
4. Research your local electrical wiring requirements. Find out who is responsible for inspection.
5. Look for the Underwriters Laboratories seal of approval on lamps and electrical appliances in your classroom and home.
6. Walk through your home and note all the different types of structural lighting used. Make a list of the different types you find and give reasons you think they were chosen.
7. Make a bulletin board entitled, "Types of Structural Lighting." For each type of structural lighting discussed in this chapter, include the following:
   a. Picture or drawing of the fixture as it is used within a room.
   b. Description of the type of lighting provided by the fixture.
   c. Suggestions for locations where the fixture would be most suitable.
8. List the accessories used in your bedroom. List which ones are functional, which are decorative, and which are a combination of the two.

CHAPTER 18

Selecting Household Equipment

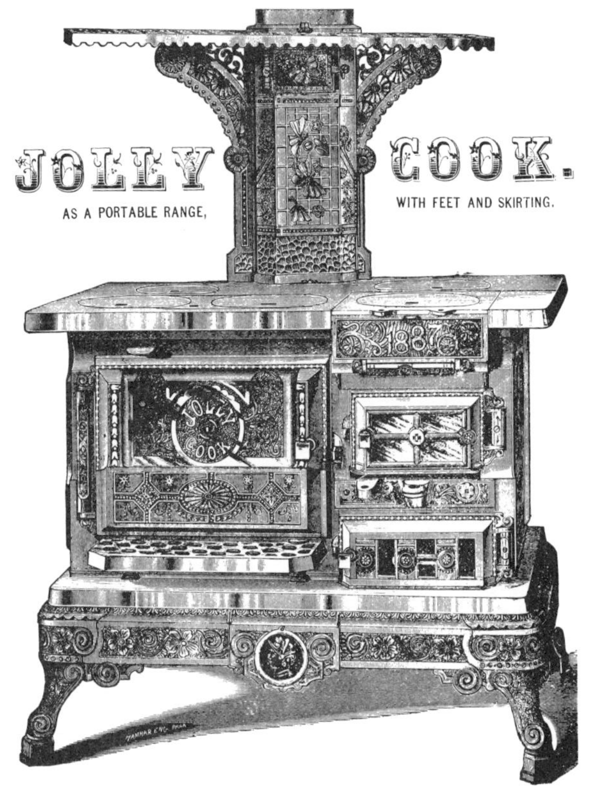

Magic Chef

To Know
appliance
continuous cleaning oven
convection oven
dehumidifier
EnergyGuide label
full warranty
hardware
humidifier
induction cooktop
limited warranty
microwave oven
self-cleaning oven
software
warranty

Objectives

After studying this chapter, you will be able to:

- Discuss factors to consider when selecting household appliances.
- Describe styles and features of various kitchen, laundry, and climate control appliances.
- Choose household appliances to fit your needs.

Making a home attractive is only part of the inside story. To meet needs and personal values, a home must also be functional. Appliances greatly increase the usefulness of various areas in the home.

Appliances are household devices powered by gas or electricity. Appliances play a major role in the kitchen and laundry room. They are also used in other areas throughout the home. Appliances help people meet their basic needs. Choosing appliances carefully can help create a home environment that is safe and healthy as well as efficient.

Appliance Considerations

Most major appliances can be expected to last 10 years or more. When buying appliances, therefore, you must consider your future needs as well as your present needs. Will your living unit be expanding or compacting in the next decade? Will you be moving at some point? If you move, will you want to take your appliances with you?

Major appliances account for a large part of a housing budget. This is especially true when you completely equip a home, 18-1. If you rent a home that has appliances in it, part of your rent goes toward the cost of the appliances. Because appliances are so costly, you need to consider their purchase carefully. Cost, features, size, safety, and quality are among the factors you should consider.

Cost

When considering a major appliance purchase, you must ask yourself if the appliance fits your budget. The cost of appliances can vary greatly from brand to brand and from model to model. Larger appliances with many features will cost more than smaller, more basic models. Prices also vary from one retailer to another. Therefore, smart consumers shop around and compare prices.

The purchase price of an appliance is only part of its true cost. When shopping, you should inquire about delivery and installation charges. If you pay for an appliance on an installment plan, you will also pay a finance charge.

Frigidaire Company

18-1
A fully-equipped kitchen is a convenient, but costly, part of housing.

Energy costs are another part of the expense of major appliances. When shopping, look for ***EnergyGuide labels,*** which state the average yearly energy cost of operating an appliance. These labels are required on refrigerators, refrigerator-freezers, freezers, dishwashers, clothes washers, water heaters, room air conditioners, and furnaces. They enable you to compare average cost estimates for similar appliances, 18-2. This helps you determine which appliance would be the most energy efficient and least costly to operate.

Features

Appliances are available with a wide range of features. Careful planning will help you choose the features that best meet your needs. Ask yourself some questions when shopping. Do I like the color of the appliance? Will it look good with the other furnishings in the room? Is the appliance easy to use? Does it perform all the tasks I want it to do? Does it have extra features I do not need? (Extras will add to the price.)

When deciding what features you need on an appliance, you must consider the people who will be using it. Does anyone in your household have special needs that must be met? For instance, a person who uses a wheelchair does not have the same range of reach as other people. An appliance feature needed by this person might be front-mounted controls. Electronic touch pads might be a feature needed by someone who has trouble turning knobs.

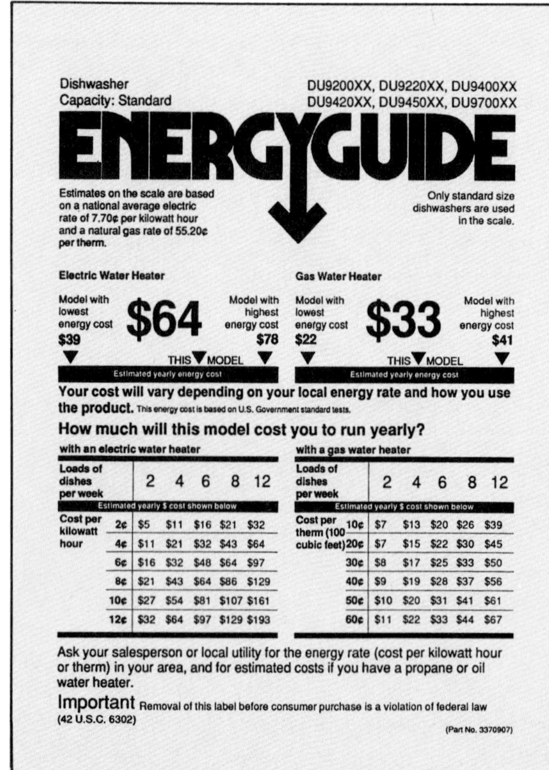
Dishwasher
Capacity: Standard

DU9200XX, DU9220XX, DU9400XX
DU9420XX, DU9450XX, DU9700XX

ENERGYGUIDE

Estimates on the scale are based on a national average electric rate of 7.70¢ per kilowatt hour and a natural gas rate of 55.20¢ per therm.

Only standard size dishwashers are used in the scale.

Electric Water Heater

Model with lowest energy cost $39 — $64 THIS MODEL — Model with highest energy cost $78

Estimated yearly energy cost

Gas Water Heater

Model with lowest energy cost $22 — $33 THIS MODEL — Model with highest energy cost $41

Estimated yearly energy cost

Your cost will vary depending on your local energy rate and how you use the product. This energy cost is based on U.S. Government standard tests.

How much will this model cost you to run yearly?

with an electric water heater

Loads of dishes per week		2	4	6	8	12
		Estimated yearly $ cost shown below				
Cost per kilowatt hour	2¢	$5	$11	$16	$21	$32
	4¢	$11	$21	$32	$43	$64
	6¢	$16	$32	$48	$64	$97
	8¢	$21	$43	$64	$86	$129
	10¢	$27	$54	$81	$107	$161
	12¢	$32	$64	$97	$129	$193

with a gas water heater

Loads of dishes per week		2	4	6	8	12
		Estimated yearly $ cost shown below				
Cost per therm (100 cubic feet)	10¢	$7	$13	$20	$26	$39
	20¢	$7	$15	$22	$30	$45
	30¢	$8	$17	$25	$33	$50
	40¢	$9	$19	$28	$37	$56
	50¢	$10	$20	$31	$41	$61
	60¢	$11	$22	$33	$44	$67

Ask your salesperson or local utility for the energy rate (cost per kilowatt hour or therm) in your area, and for estimated costs if you have a propane or oil water heater.

Important Removal of this label before consumer purchase is a violation of federal law (42 U.S.C. 6302)

(Part No. 3370907)

18-2
EnergyGuide labels allow consumers to compare the average yearly energy costs of similar major appliances.

Size

Size is another consideration when purchasing a major appliance. How large should the appliance be to meet the needs of your household? How many people will be using the appliance now and in the future? Will the appliance fit the space where it is to be placed? Can it be brought up stairways and through doors to reach the place where it will be used?

Safety

When purchasing major appliances, you also must evaluate whether they meet safety standards. Electrical appliances should have the Underwriters Laboratories (UL) seal. If the symbol is on the body of the appliance, all parts of the appliance meet the UL standards. Look for the blue star emblem of the American Gas Association (AGA) on gas appliances. This certification symbol indicates that an appliance meets standards of safety, performance, and durability. See 18-3.

Make sure you have the proper electrical or gas connections to hook up appliances and use them safely. Major 120-volt electrical appliances should have a three-prong plug. The third (round) prong grounds the appliance. If a grounded appliance has damaged wiring, electric current will flow to the ground rather than through your body. The grounding prong, therefore, prevents electrical shock and should not be removed.

18-3
The UL seal and the AGA blue star emblem indicate that appliances have met safety standards.

Quality

The quality of an appliance is a key purchase consideration. Appliances that require frequent repairs are costly and troublesome to operate. You want appliances that will work dependably for many years.

Asking a few questions might help you evaluate quality. Is the appliance well constructed? Is it from a reputable manufacturer? Is the instruction book thorough and easy to understand? Is after-sale service offered?

Assessing quality also involves reading the warranty. A ***warranty*** is a manufacturer's written promise that a product will perform as it is intended. A warranty may be full or limited. Under a ***full warranty,*** you may have the item repaired or replaced free of charge (at the warrantor's option). You cannot be asked to do anything unreasonable to have it repaired or replaced. Under a ***limited warranty,*** you can be charged for repairs. You may have to ship the item back to the warrantor or take other steps to get repairs.

When reading a warranty, be sure to find out what is covered–the entire product, or only certain parts? Are labor fees included? Also, find out how long the warranty lasts.

Consumer Satisfaction

Your satisfaction with your appliances will depend largely on the choices you make as a consumer. However, your satisfaction will also be affected by appliance manufacturers and retailers.

As a consumer, you have a responsibility to be informed about the appliances you buy. You need to know the various options that are available. These should be matched to the needs and desires of the people in your household. You need to determine the amount of money you can afford to spend on an appliance. You will want to ask about warranties and service. You need to read and understand use and care information before operating an appliance. Fulfilling these responsibilities will help improve your satisfaction with your appliances.

Manufacturers have a goal of keeping consumers happy with the appliances they buy. If people are not satisfied with a manufacturer's products, the manufacturer will soon be out of business. To assure your satisfaction, manufacturers strive to make safe, dependable, and economical appliances. They generally conform to performance standards set by the Association of Home Appliance Manufacturers (AHAM). Manufacturers provide a variety of models to meet your needs. They give warranties and instructions for the use of their appliances. Some manufacturers also provide educational programs about the use of their products.

The success of retail appliance businesses also relies on customer satisfaction. To meet your needs, retailers provide a selection of models. They have trained salespeople to explain the features of the models in which you are interested. Most retailers will deliver and install appliances. They often offer maintenance service, too. Retailers act as go-betweens for you and the manufacturer. They see that the conditions of warranties are met.

Choosing Kitchen Appliances

Kitchen appliances are used for all facets of food storage and preparation, and for cleanup, 18-4. The purchase considerations discussed above relate to all of these appliances. Some specific information will help you make educated consumer choices when choosing particular appliances.

Refrigerators

Refrigerators are a necessity for keeping foods fresh. Perhaps that is why at least one refrigerator can be found in nearly every home in the United States.

Styles. Refrigerators are available in a few basic styles. A *one-door refrigerator* does not have a freezer. Instead, it has a frozen food storage compartment. This compartment is colder than the rest of the refrigerator, but its use is limited. It is not designed to freeze foods. It provides only short-term storage for commercially frozen foods, and it keeps ice cubes.

A variation of the one-door refrigerator is the *compact* refrigerator. It is suitable for rooms in college residence halls or small apartments. It can be purchased or rented at a fairly low price. Compact models may be capable of freezing ice cubes, but they are not suitable for storing frozen foods.

Most refrigerators made today are *two-door refrigerator-freezers.* These models have a separate freezer section that is capable of freezing foods. The temperature in the freezer section remains at about 0°F. The freezer section may be above, below, or at the side of the refrigerator. See 18-5.

Features. Refrigerators and refrigerator-freezers are sold in different colors to fit many decors. Other special features of refrigerators include compartments for meat, produce, and dairy products with separate temperature controls. Adjustable shelves allow you to easily store large items. Reversible doors give you better access to counter space, so you can add or remove food quickly and easily. Message centers and ice and water dispensers are also features that many people find convenient.

Magic Chef Company

18-4
The tasks of storing foods, cooking meals, and washing dishes are all made easier with the help of appliances.

KitchenAid

18-5
The freezer section of a refrigerator-freezer may be mounted on the bottom of the appliance. This reduces the need to bend when getting items out of the refrigerator compartment.

The type of defrosting a refrigerator requires is a feature you will want to consider. One-door models often require *manual defrosting.* This means that frost accumulates inside the refrigerator, reducing the efficiency of the appliance. When the frost becomes 1/4 inch thick, the appliance must be turned off so the frost can melt. The refrigerator compartment should be dried before turning the appliance on again.

Refrigerator-freezers may have partial automatic defrosting or full automatic defrosting. *Partial automatic defrosting* models do not accumulate frost in the refrigerator compartment. However, the freezer compartment must be defrosted manually. In *full automatic defrosting* models, frost does not accumulate in either the refrigerator or the freezer. These frostless models are convenient, but they cost more. They also use more electricity.

Along with features, you need to consider space requirements. Space inside a refrigerator is measured in cubic feet. A basic guideline is that every adult needs about four cubic feet of refrigerator space and about two cubic feet of freezer space. These amounts are for people who shop once a week for food. If you shop more often, you will need less storage space.

When shopping for a refrigerator, you should consider how much storage space you need. A range of sizes is available to meet the needs of various households. Think about whether or not you need a separate freezer section. Another consideration is the amount of kitchen space you have for a refrigerator. Measure the height, width, and depth of the space you have. Take the measurements with you when you shop. A checklist for refrigerators is shown in 18-6.

Checklist for Refrigerators
___ Does the refrigerator require defrosting?
___ Are interior and door shelves adjustable for more flexible use of space?
___ Is space available for heavy and tall bottles?
___ Is interior well lighted?
___ Does the refrigerator have a porcelain interior–best for durability and resistance to scratches, rust, and stains?
___ Are shelves made of strong, noncorroding, rust-resistant materials?
___ Are all interior parts easily removable and/or accessible for cleaning?
___ Are door shelf retaining bars strong and securely attached?
___ Does the meat pan have adequate ventilation and does it maintain proper cooling temperature?
___ Is crisper space adequate?
___ Is crisper tray designed to keep moisture in?
___ Is the freezer section easy to reach, use, clean, and organize?
___ Do the exterior doors have magnetic gaskets on all edges?
___ Is refrigerator easy to move for cleaning?
___ Does refrigerator have switch to turn off door heater when not needed to prevent condensation?
___ Is refrigerator's energy consumption figure available?

Sears Consumer Information Services

18-6
Consider these points before choosing a refrigerator.

Freezers

If a refrigerator-freezer does not provide enough storage space for frozen foods, you may want to buy a separate freezer. It can help you save money if you use it to store food purchased at low prices.

The size freezer you need depends on how many people will be using it. A basic guideline allows about six cubic feet for each person.

Styles. The two styles of freezers are chest and upright. Large, bulky packages are easier to store in a chest model, 18-7. Chest freezers use less electricity because less cold air escapes when the door is opened. One disadvantage of chest freezers is that they require more floor space. Another is that food must be lifted when it is removed.

Food is easier to see and remove in an upright freezer. Only a small amount of floor space is needed, but upright freezers cost more to operate.

You can choose a freezer with either a *manual* defrost or a *frostless* system. Frostless models are convenient, but their purchase and operation costs are higher.

A checklist for freezers is shown in 18-8.

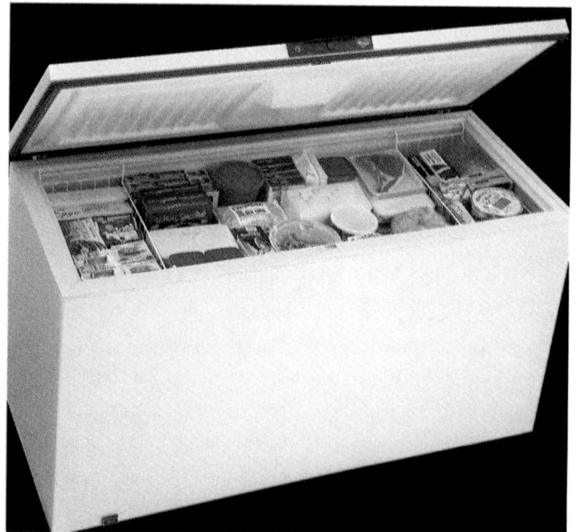

Whirlpool Appliances

18-7
Chest freezers provide energy-efficient storage space for frozen foods.

Checklist for Freezers

- ___ Will model fit your floor space and weight limitations?
- ___ Will the type of opening be convenient in its location?
- ___ Are shelves and/or baskets adjustable?
- ___ Are all sections readily accessible?
- ___ Is the interior well lighted?
- ___ Does it have a safety signal light to let you know that power is on?
- ___ Is the freezer frostless? If not, does it have a fast-defrost system?
- ___ Does it have easy-to-read and accessible controls?
- ___ Does it have magnetic gaskets to seal cold air in more completely?
- ___ Does it have a power-saver switch to allow for lower use of energy when activated?

Sears Consumer Information Services

18-8
Consider these points before choosing a food freezer.

Ranges

Many changes have been made in ranges. These changes have been due to advances in technology and growing concern about energy conservation. You will have many factors to consider before choosing a range.

Your first decision concerns fuel. Your choice of either electricity or gas depends on the availability and cost of each, as well as your personal preference.

Electric ranges. Electric ranges come with several styles of cooking surfaces. The *conventional coil* range has wires encased in coils. The electric current flows from the coils to cookware by conduction and radiation.

Some electric ranges feature a smooth *glass-ceramic* cook top, which makes the range easy to clean. This surface may hide conventional coils or *halogen cartridges,* which give instant infrared heat. The heat travels mainly by conduction.

A range with *solid elements* has disks covering the elements that are sealed to the cooktop. The heated disks conduct heat to the cookware.

Induction cooktops use a magnetic field to generate heat in the bottom of cooking utensils. Cookware must be made of a ferrous metal, such as cast iron or steel. These materials offer resistance to the passage of electrical current, which is what generates the heat. Heat from the cookware is then transferred to the food. No heat is created in the range surface. Cleanup is easy because spills do not burn and the induction coils are located under a glass-ceramic surface.

Gas ranges. The heat in gas ranges is produced by the combustion process between gas and oxygen in the air. The heat is controlled by regulating the flow of gas through a valve. More gas means higher flames and hotter temperatures.

Gas ranges are available with two types of burners–conventional and sealed. *Conventional* burners are open, whereas the *sealed* burners are located under a one-piece surface that makes cleaning easier.

Styles. Ranges come in many styles and sizes. Your choice depends on the capacity you need and the space you have. *Freestanding* models are very common. They offer many options in sizes, colors, and features. They may have an oven below the cooking surface, at eye level, or both. They may stand alone or be located between counters for a built-in look. See 18-9.

Slide-in (or drop-in) models fit snugly between two base cabinets. Chrome strips are often used to cover the side edges and provide a built-in look. The oven is below the cooking surface.

Built-in models separate the cooking surface from the oven. This allows flexible kitchen arrangements. The surface units are installed in a countertop. The oven is installed in a wall or specially-made cabinet.

Features. Both gas and electric ranges are available in split-level styles with a microwave oven on top. Some electric ranges have a single oven that works as both a conventional and a microwave oven.

Mannington Resilient Floors

18-9
Freestanding ranges can look like built-in models when they are placed between cabinets.

Hoods are a useful range feature. They are used over the cooking surface to help vent heat and odors from the kitchen. Hoods can be vented to the outside or the attic. Some models are not vented but use a special filter to collect odors and grease. An alternative to a hood is a *downdraft ventilation* system. Fumes are pulled down by a fan located below the cooktop.

Many consumers find a self-cleaning oven to be a desirable range feature. ***Self-cleaning ovens*** can be set at extremely high temperatures to "burn" soil away. Only a little ash remains to be wiped clean. Because such high temperatures are reached during cleaning, these ovens have extra insulation. This helps to save energy during normal baking periods. The self-cleaning feature adds to the price of the range. However, the cost of operating the cleaning cycle is less than the cost of chemical oven cleaners.

Another option in cleaning features is a continuous cleaning oven. ***Continuous cleaning ovens*** have a special coating on the oven walls. Food spatters on the walls are oxidized over a period of time during the normal baking process.

Models with this feature cost less than those with self-cleaning ovens. However, most people find them less effective. Also, continuous cleaning ovens do not have extra insulation.

Other range features to consider include clocks, timers, and programmed cooking cycles. Some ranges have thermostatically controlled surface units or oven rotisseries. Others have modular surface units that can be replaced with grills, griddles, or cutting boards. See 18-10. Study the checklist for ranges in 18-11.

Convection Ovens

Convection ovens bake foods in a stream of heated air. Because heated air is forced directly onto foods and is constantly in motion, foods cook faster at lower temperatures. Convection ovens require about two-thirds the time and half the energy of conventional cooking. The diagram in 18-12 shows how a convection oven works.

Jenn-Air

18-10
The modular surface units in this cooktop have been replaced with a grill.

Checklist for Ranges

- ___ Is range suitable for cooking needs and kitchen space?
- ___ Is cooktop height convenient and comfortable for user?
- ___ Are cooktop burners or units an adequate size for pans to be used?
- ___ Is oven capacity adequate to meet regular cooking needs?
- ___ Are controls placed for convenient and safe use?
- ___ Are control settings and numbers easily read?
- ___ Is range designed to simplify cleaning? (Smooth, wipeable background; removable burners or units; removable liners or self-clean feature; absence of grooves, crevices.)
- ___ Does range offer features that are important to family needs and use?
- ___ Does gas range have pilot-free electronic ignition?

Sears Consumer Information Services

18-11
Consider these points before choosing a range.

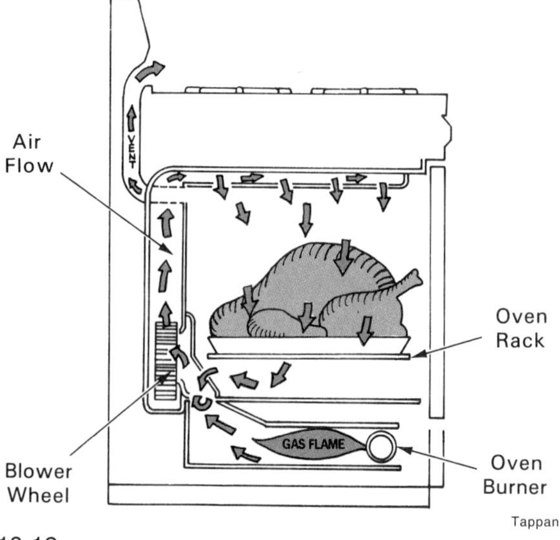

Tappan

18-12
In a convection oven, heated air is recirculated inside the oven.

Convection ovens are being used more and more in home kitchens. Although they are available by themselves, they are usually found in combination with conventional or microwave ovens. The combination models allow you to use two different cooking methods.

Microwave Ovens

Microwave ovens cook food with high frequency energy waves called *microwaves.* These appliances can cook, defrost, and reheat foods in a fraction of the time required for conventional ovens. Microwave cooking can also save up to 75 percent of the energy used by conventional ovens.

As food absorbs microwaves, the molecules within the food vibrate against one another. The friction that is produced creates the heat that cooks the food.

The time required to cook foods depends on the type of food being cooked and the power level used. Most microwaves have at least four or five power levels. Low power levels are needed for cooking delicate foods, such as eggs, cheese, meats, and sauces. High power levels can be used for most other foods.

Oven-proof glass, paper, and plastic can be used as cooking containers because microwaves pass through them. Metal containers should not be used since they reflect microwaves.

Styles. Several styles of microwave ovens are available. Countertop models are the most popular and offer the greatest choices of features. They can be placed on a countertop, table, or cart.

Microwave ovens with exhaust hoods are made to be attached to the wall and cabinet above a range. These models are similar to countertop models. However, they may have less capacity, less cooking power, or fewer feature options. See 18-13.

Upper microwave ovens of two-oven ranges are available with gas and electric ranges. These ovens are also similar to countertop models but may have fewer options.

Combination ovens combine the microwave oven with a conventional or convection oven. Combination ovens are available in range and countertop models.

Whirlpool Appliances

18-13
Exhaust hood microwave ovens are specially designed to withstand heat and gases created by cooking.

Mounted ovens go on the wall or under a cabinet. Some of these ovens have a smaller capacity. They may have less power, which means slightly longer cooking times.

Features. Various features are available on microwave ovens. These include automatic programming, automatic settings, browning elements, temperature probes, and turntables.

A microwave oven with *automatic programming* automatically shifts power levels at preset times. This feature allows you to program the oven to do several operations in sequence. For instance, you might set the oven to defrost a food product, cook it, and then keep it warm.

Automatic settings determine cooking times and correct power levels for you. You just set the controls for the type and amount of food, and the oven does the rest.

Browning elements are electric heating coils on the ceiling of the oven. They give added top browning and crispness to food following microwave cooking.

A *temperature probe* (sometimes called a food sensor) helps you control cooking. It automatically turns off the oven or switches to a warm setting when food reaches a preset temperature.

Temperature probes are helpful when cooking roasts, casseroles, soups, and stews.

Study the checklist for microwave ovens that is given in 18-14.

Dishwashers

Your household size and the time you have determine your need for a dishwasher. This appliance can save you time and energy.

Another advantage of a dishwasher is that it can get your dishes cleaner than you can by hand. It uses hotter water and stronger detergents. It can also dry dishes, so they don't have to be wiped with towels that may carry germs.

Most dishwashers are *built-in* styles, as shown in 18-15. Other models are *portable.* They are on casters, so they can be moved easily from storage to the sink.

Features. Dishwashers often feature a variety of cycles to meet various needs. For instance, some models have special cycles for scrubbing pans or sterilizing baby bottles. An adjustable upper rack is a feature that makes it possible to wash large or odd-sized items. Many models offer energy-saving features, such as a cool drying cycle. This can save up to one-third the electricity used in a normal drying cycle.

Study the checklist in 18-16 before choosing a dishwasher.

KitchenAid

18-15
This built-in dishwasher is attractive and convenient.

Checklist for Microwave Ovens
___ Is microwave oven cavity large enough for your needs?
___ Does it have the kind of power settings you need?
___ Is there a signal that tells when microwave oven finishes cooking and shuts off?
___ Does the timer have enough minutes to allow you the flexibility you need?
___ Are the controls solid state or mechanical?
___ Does a cookbook come with the microwave oven?

Sears Consumer Information Services

18-14
Consider these points before choosing a microwave oven.

Checklist for Dishwashers
___ Are the tub and door lining materials made of porcelain enamel?
___ Does the wash system have two levels? (A single system takes a great deal of care in loading.)
___ Will it hold at least 10 place settings? Pots and pans?
___ Does it offer more than one cycle, such as rinse/hold or prerinse cycle?
___ Is an automatic wetting agent dispenser provided?
___ Is the dishwasher insulated to eliminate excessive noise and heat?
___ Does it have forced air drying? A no-heat drying cycle?
___ Does it have an energy saver where the heating element is partially or completely off during some cycles?

Sears Consumer Information Services

18-16
Consider these points before choosing a dishwasher.

Trash Compactors

Trash compactors compress household trash to about one-fourth of its original volume. The trash is put into heavy-duty paper bags that are lined with plastic.

Compactors are available as freestanding and built-in models. They will handle almost any kind of trash, such as bottles, tin cans, plastic cartons, and food scraps. They will not handle highly-flammable materials and aerosol cans. These should be discarded separately. You may also want to separate paper, plastic, glass, and metal that can be recycled.

Food Waste Disposers

The smell and mess of food scraps are easily eliminated by a food waste disposer. This appliance fits below a sink. It catches and grinds all types of food scraps. It is connected to the city sewer or drained into a septic tank.

Both batch-feed and continuous-feed models are available. In *batch-feed* models, the food is placed in the grinding chamber. Then cold water is turned on and the lid is put in place. When the food has been ground, the water is turned off and the lid is removed. In *continuous-feed* models, food is added to the disposer as it is running.

Choosing Laundry Appliances

Doing laundry is a routine household task. Having an automatic washer and dryer in your home is highly convenient. You can do laundry whenever you want without the hassle of taking it to a laundromat.

Automatic Washers

Size is one of the most important variables in automatic washers. If your home is small, a compact machine may be best for you, 18-17. Some are permanently installed, and others are portable. Some have only the basics: washing, rinsing, and spin-drying. Other compact washers have the features of full-size machines.

Maytag

18-17
This compact washer/dryer combination would be a wise choice for people with limited space.

To suit a variety of fabrics, many washers have several different cycles, such as normal, permanent press, and delicate. All cycles have the same basic steps: fill, wash, rinse, and spin. They vary in the length of time, speed of agitation, water temperature, and number of rinses.

Features. Features on automatic washers include dispensers that release detergent, bleach, and fabric softener into the wash water at the right time. Some washers have water-saving features. These include an adjustable water level setting that lets you choose the water level according to the load size. Another feature saves water by retaining the wash water so it can be reused. (The rinse water is always fresh.)

Use the checklist in 18-18 when buying an automatic washer.

Dryers

Automatic clothes dryers are often bought at the same time as washers. They are usually available as a matching set. The dryer you choose should be large enough to dry a full load from your washer.

Checklist for Automatic Washers
___ Will the washer fit your space limitations?
___ Does the washer have a self-cleaning lint filter?
___ Is a water level selector provided?
___ Is a water temperature selector provided?
___ Is more than one cycle available including a presoak cycle? A permanent-press cycle? A knit cycle? A delicate cycle?
___ Does it have an off-balance switch that stops machine and signals when load is unbalanced?
___ Are bleach, fabric softener, and detergent dispensers offered?
___ Is an optional second rinse selector provided?
___ Has porcelain enamel been used for the tub and lid?
___ If a portable compact model, does it have an agitator and single tub for wash, rinse, and spin cycles?
___ If a portable compact model, does it connect to sink faucet for automatic filling?

Sears Consumer Information Services

18-18
Consider these points before buying an automatic washer.

Dryers can be operated by either gas or electricity. Compare installation and operating costs as well as purchase prices before you buy.

Features. Basic dryer models have a preset temperature that is safe for most fabrics. The drying time is the only variable. More expensive machines have both time and temperature settings. You can set the temperature at high, medium, or low. A permanent press feature prevents wrinkles from forming by tumbling clothes without heat at the end of the drying time. An air only option, which has no heat, may be featured to fluff items.

Deluxe dryer models have a moisture-sensing system. The dryer shuts off when clothes reach a selected degree of dryness. Another feature of deluxe models guards against wrinkles. It tumbles dried clothes without heat for a few seconds every few minutes until you unload the dryer.

Look at the checklist for dryers in 18-19.

Choosing Climate Control Appliances

Appliances can help control the climate in your home. They can maintain humidity levels and temperatures that increase the comfort of the environment in which you live.

Dehumidifiers and Humidifiers

The humidity level of the air in your home will determine your need for a dehumidifier or a humidifier. A ***dehumidifier*** is a small appliance that draws moisture out of the air. Excess humidity can cause mildew, musty odors, rust, and other problems. A dehumidifier is generally not needed if you have an air conditioner because the air conditioner also draws out moisture.

A ***humidifier*** performs the opposite function of a dehumidifier. It puts moisture into the air. Dry

Checklist for Dryers
___ Is lint trap conveniently placed for ease in removing, cleaning, and replacing?
___ Is there an automatic pilot light or electronic ignition on gas dryer?
___ Is control panel lighted? Interior lighted?
___ Is there a finish signal–buzzer or bell at end of drying period?
___ Is there a safety button to start dryer?
___ Does dryer offer one heat setting meant for use on most fabrics?
___ Does it have an automatic sensor to prevent overdrying?
___ Does it offer a wrinkle-guard feature? An air-only, no-heat setting?
___ Does it have a touch-up cycle to remove creases in dry clothes?

Sears Consumer Information Services

18-19
Consider these points before choosing a dryer.

air is a problem in some climates, especially during winter months when homes are heated. Static electricity build up is only one result of air that is too dry.

Dehumidifiers and humidifiers can be built-in or portable. Your best bet if you are purchasing a unit is to follow the recommendations of the manufacturer. A type and size will be recommended for your situation.

Room Air Conditioners

A room air conditioner is a small appliance used for cooling a small area. The air conditioner should be the proper size for the area to be cooled. It must also be the proper size for the space in which it will be installed, 18-20. *Portable* room air conditioners are designed to be placed in window openings. *Built-in* units are designed to be installed through another type of opening.

When you shop for an air conditioner, have the information you need with you. What is the size and the shape of the area to be cooled? How many people normally use the space at the same time? How much glass and insulation are in the area?

Whirlpool Appliances

18-20
Room air conditioners come in different sizes to cool various sizes of rooms.

Your retailer will help you choose the right air conditioner. Check the British thermal unit (Btu) rating. That is the measure of the efficiency of the air-conditioning unit. Look at the controls. Are they easy to reach and use? Can you change the level of cooling to meet your needs? Check the louvers for air direction. Turn on the unit to observe the noise level.

Choosing Other Appliances

Many other appliances, both essential and optional, are available for home use. Water heaters, vacuum cleaners, personal computers, and a variety of portable appliances are among those that you might consider buying.

Water Heaters

Hot water in a home is needed for bathing, laundry, and a variety of cooking and cleaning tasks. Water heaters are operated by either gas or electric heat. The type of water heater you choose will depend on the heating system in your home.

If you are in the market for a water heater, you will need to consider the size you need. This will depend on the amount of hot water you use. The more people living in your home, the more hot water you are likely to use. Also consider whether you have other appliances that require hot water, namely a dishwasher and an automatic washer.

Heating water greatly adds to home energy costs. Therefore, it is wise to make sure your water heater is properly insulated. An insulating jacket can be wrapped around the water heater to provide added insulation. You may also wish to insulate hot water pipes to reduce heat loss. Set the thermostat no higher than 140°F. If possible, install the water heater near the kitchen and laundry areas. These steps will help save energy, too.

Vacuum Cleaners

A vacuum cleaner can be a useful appliance for removing loose dirt from rugs and carpets. It can also be used to clean hard surface flooring, draperies, and upholstery. Attachments allow vacuum cleaners to perform still other cleaning tasks.

Your choice of a vacuum cleaner will depend on what you want it to do for you. There are many types available. These include canisters, uprights, minicanisters, hand-held vacuums, and wet/dry vacuums, 18-21. Some people choose to own more than one type to meet their specific needs.

Canisters. Canister cleaners are easy to handle and do an adequate job of house cleaning. They are effective on bare floors, stairs, and upholstery. Canister cleaners, as well as other types, may feature a power attachment that increases carpet cleaning capability with rotating beaters and brushes.

Uprights. Upright cleaners are the choice of three-fourths of those purchasing vacuum cleaners. They are made primarily to clean carpets. Most are adjustable for low, medium, and high carpet depths. Some adjust automatically, others are set manually. Nearly all uprights have attachments for other house cleaning tasks.

Central vacuum systems. A central vacuum system is a built-in system. The heavy machinery stays in one place. A flexible, lightweight hose is carried from room to room and inserted into conveniently located outlets, 18-22. The system can also have a power attachment and special cleaning attachments. The air is filtered to the outside of the home rather than through a dirt-filled bag. Some have a special foam filter for better filtering efficiency.

The best cleaning device is probably a system that uses *aerodynamics* (air in motion) and *hydrodynamics* (water in motion). Such a

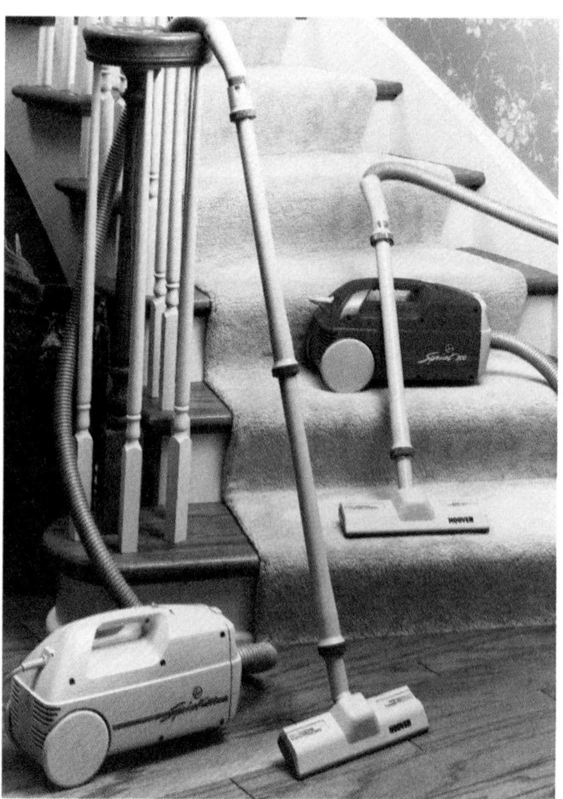

Hoover Company

18-21
A light-weight minicanister vacuum cleaner can easily be carried throughout a home.

Electrolux Corporation

18-22
This central vacuum system is ducted to the outside. The hose connects to special outlets in each room.

vacuum cleaner draws air through a compartment containing water. The air is "washed" before it returns to the room. This is the type that will remove lead particles. See 18-23.

Personal Computers

A versatile appliance that many people are choosing to purchase for their homes is the personal computer (PC). PCs can be used to tutor students, entertain children, and organize entrepreneurs. They can process information, store records, control thermostats and alarm systems, activate appliances, send and receive communication, and play games.

When considering the purchase of a home computer, you must first decide what you want it to do for you. ***Software*** is a program of instructions that tells a computer what to do. Software most often comes on disks or tapes. Programs are available to do everything from establishing household budgets to analyzing the nutritional value of meals. You should look at the software programs designed for the tasks you want to perform. Then find out what type of computer system and how much computer memory you need to operate them.

Hardware refers to the components in a computer system. These components include *input devices,* such as keyboards and scanners. These devices are used to enter data into a computer. A *central processing unit (CPU)* is another hardware component. It follows built-in instructions and those on software programs. The CPU generally includes a disk or tape drive, which reads the information on software programs and stores information on tapes or disks. An *output device,* such as a video display terminal or a printer, allows a computer user to view data.

When buying a computer, consider all the people who might use it and all the different ways it might be used. Find out if the computer's memory capacity can be expanded to meet future needs. Inquire about classes to help you learn to use the computer. Ask whether telephone support service is available if you have questions about how to operate the computer. Carefully investigating your purchase will help you get the most use and value out of this appliance. See 18-24.

Portable Appliances

Portable appliances are those that can be moved easily from one area to another. They include everything from toasters to electric blankets to hair dryers.

Rexair

18-23
This vacuum cleaner uses aerodynamics and hydrodynamics to keep dust in the appliance.

Ralph Wilson Plastics Co. (Wilsonart)

18-24
A personal computer can be a valuable addition to a home appliance inventory.

In today's society, many major appliances tend to be viewed as basic necessities. Operating a home without a refrigerator or water heater, for instance, would require a big adjustment in your life-style. Portable appliances, however, are more optional. They should be chosen to meet the specific needs of household members.

Portable appliances tend to be less costly than major appliances. However, the procedure for choosing them is much like choosing major appliances. The first step is always to determine your needs and your resources. Then do some comparison shopping. Compare construction details, warranties, and prices. Decide which of the latest features you want and can afford. Look for recognized brands. Be sure appliances carry the UL seal as an indication that safety standards have been met. Read use and care information to help you select appliances that are easy to operate, clean, and maintain. Following these guidelines will help you feel confident that you have made wise appliance choices. See 18-25.

Summary

Choosing household equipment, including both major and portable appliances, is a part of your housing decisions. If you want satisfactory performance from appliances, you must choose products that meet your needs. You should consider cost, features, size, safety, and quality when making appliance purchases.

Kitchen appliances include refrigerators, freezers, ranges, convection and microwave ovens, dishwashers, trash compactors, and food waste disposers. These appliances are all available in a range of styles and with a variety of features. Careful consideration will help you select those appliances that best meet your needs.

Other appliances, including those used for laundry and climate control, must also be chosen with your needs in mind. Although they are a big investment, these appliances can improve the convenience, efficiency, health, and safety of your household.

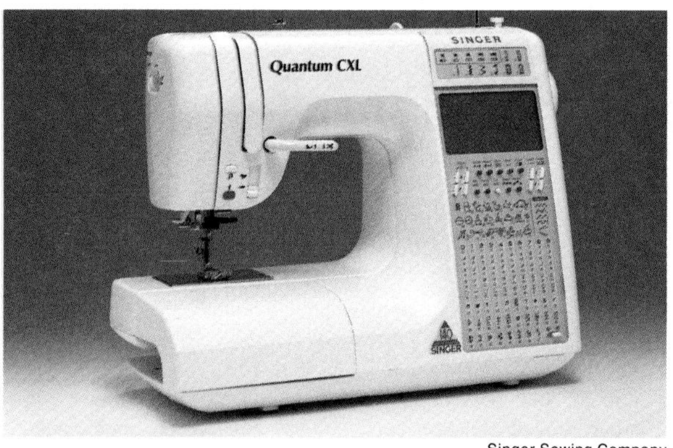

Singer Sewing Company

West Bend Company

Technic Tool Corporation

18-25
Portable appliances are available for a wide range of personal care, cooking, and home maintenance tasks.

To Review

Write your responses on a separate sheet of paper.

1. Name the two symbols that indicate that safety standards have been met on electrical and gas appliances.
2. Explain the difference between a full warranty and a limited warranty.
3. Which style of freezer is most energy efficient?
4. Of what kind of material must cookware used on an induction cooktop be made? Why?
5. Why does a convection oven cook foods faster and at lower temperatures than conventional ovens?
6. How is heat produced in a microwave oven?
7. True or False. A dishwasher can get dishes cleaner than dishes washed by hand.
8. Describe two water-saving features that are available on some automatic washers.
9. Tell the difference between a dehumidifier and a humidifier.
10. Why is insulation on a water heater important?
11. How does air filtering on a central vacuum system differ from that on most canister and upright vacuum cleaners?
12. List three questions you might ask before purchasing a personal computer.

To Do

1. Compare prices, energy costs, performance features, size, safety features, and quality of two similar major appliances. Use the checklists given in this chapter to help you evaluate the two products. Share the findings of your comparison with your classmates.
2. Find a use and care manual for a major appliance. List the kinds of information that it gives.
3. Find and read two magazine or newspaper articles on appliances. Report your findings to the class.
4. Design a brochure that tells about a portable appliance.

Massachusetts Office of Travel & Tourism

Chapter 19 The Outdoor Living Space
Chapter 20 Keeping Your Home Safe and Secure
Chapter 21 Maintaining Your Home

PART 5

A Safe and Attractive Environment

CHAPTER 19

The Outdoor Living Space

California Redwood Association

To Know

annuals
biennials
conservation
enclosure elements
ground cover
landscape
landscape zones
man-made landscape elements
natural landscape elements
perennials
soil conservation
sun-room
water conservation
xeriscape

Objectives

After studying this chapter, you will be able to:

- Identify the goals of landscaping.
- List natural and man-made landscape elements.
- Determine zones in a landscape site.
- Select furnishings for outdoor living.
- List conservation measures for landscaping.
- Design an outdoor living space.

You are surrounded by the beauty of nature. When making housing decisions, you should find ways to enhance and enjoy this beauty. People spend much of their time indoors–in schools, offices, and homes. The ***landscape*** is the outdoor living space. A beautifully landscaped area, or even a small balcony in city housing, can draw people outdoors. Everyone can find ways to enjoy the beauty of nature.

Nature is "stirred up" when a site is prepared for construction. The construction process often changes the layout of the land. If you leave the landscape alone after construction, it may never bring you pleasure. On the other hand, if you work in partnership with nature, you can have an outdoor living space that is psychologically rewarding. Note how the landscaping shown in 19-1 enhances the appearance of the home. Your outdoor living space should permit the positive development of each member of your living unit. The right landscape will help this happen.

A

B

Melka Landscaping, Orland Park, IL

19-1
After construction is complete, the proper landscaping can make the site much more attractive. A–Site has been graded and is ready for landscaping. B–Finished landscape.

Planning the Landscape

The basic goal of landscaping is to create pleasing outdoor spaces for various activities. The landscape should be private, comfortable, attractive, safe, and convenient. If you are like most people, you will also want the area to be easy to maintain. Any or all of these qualities can be achieved in a well-planned landscape.

Identify Your Goals

You will have more successful results if you identify your landscaping goals. Your goals may include some of the following:

- Privacy–attained by enclosures that set the space apart from the public.
- Comfort–allows you to relax in an inviting space and perhaps read a book.
- Beauty–draws attention away from areas that you do not want others to view and highlights attractive areas.
- Recreation–may include a children's play area or a place for family games.
- Entertainment–provides for the use of the outdoors for a party, barbecue, or family wedding.
- Safety–achieved by installing adequate lighting. Paths and walks can be constructed to safely lead to various areas in the landscape.
- Creativity–evident in the ways that you express yourself in the landscape.
- Ease of maintenance–lets you benefit from labor-saving ideas, such as raised planters, watering systems, and ground covers that do not need to be mowed.

The right environment can be created only if the needs and values of your living unit are considered in the planning process. Take time to identify your goals before you start your plan. As you formulate your goals, ask yourself these questions:

- What is the life-style of your living unit? Are there children and pets to consider?
- If you are concentrating on one area of the site, how will it affect other areas? Will the addition of a patio, deck, or swimming pool reduce the lawn area to less than you like?
- Do you understand the use of the materials that are available?
- What activities are likely to take place in the area?
- How much space do you want to maintain?
- How much time, money, and effort are you willing to spend?
- What energy-saving measures can you take? Are there possibilities for other conservation measures?

You should answer these and other questions before designing your outdoor living space.

Landscape Elements

Before you begin planning a landscape, you should recognize the various landscape elements. There are two basic types of landscape elements: natural elements and man-made elements.

Natural Landscape Elements

Natural landscape elements are those that are found in the natural environment. The terrain and soil are natural elements that are already on the site. Other natural elements include trees, shrubs, flowers, ground covers, boulders, stones, wood, bark, water, sun, and wind. Some natural elements, such as rocky soil, cannot be changed. Other elements can be altered to a certain degree. For instance, trees and shrubs can be planted, and large rocks can be moved.

Topography. The topography, or contour of the land, is basic to the landscape. Level land is the easiest and the least expensive to landscape. The ideal topography is a gentle, rolling terrain with natural drainage.

Soil. Good soil encourages plant growth and provides plants with the right nutrients. It has a proper balance of sand, silt, and clay. The soil must drain well, yet hold enough water to sustain plant life.

Trees and shrubs. Trees and shrubs range in size from small to large. Trees can provide shade, as well as shelter from wind. As mentioned in Chapter 15, *coniferous* trees and shrubs remain green year round. *Deciduous* trees and shrubs, on the other hand, lose foliage in the fall. New leaves are produced in the spring, 19-2.

Flowers. Flowers add fragrance and color to the landscape. They are divided into three types: annuals, biennials, and perennials. ***Annuals*** and ***biennials*** last one and two years respectively. Most of these flowers are planted yearly. ***Perennials,*** on the other hand, come up for several years without replanting. Some perennials never need replanting. Many gardeners prefer perennials because they require less work than annuals or biennials. Most flowers grow from seeds or bulbs. If you desire, however, you can plant seedlings. Seedlings are young plants that were started from seeds. You can start the seedlings yourself or purchase them from a nursery. With the right choices, you can have flowers blooming at all times during the growing season.

Ground covers. There are a variety of ***ground covers*** used in landscaping. Ground covers include grasses and various types of low-growing plants. *Grass* is the most common ground cover. Many types of grasses are available for lawns. Some are more appropriate for use in warm climates, while others thrive in cool climates. The growth cycle of grasses varies with the climate. Some grow well in the shade. Others need full sun. Some grasses can stand heavy traffic, while others will tolerate very little.

Other ground covers include *low-growing plants* that can be used in places where grass is not desired or cannot be maintained. Ground covers can be purchased in the form of vines, woody plants, or herb-like plants. They are perennials; some are coniferous and others are deciduous. Ground covers are commonly used when low maintenance is desired. They are also used in places that are difficult to maintain. Most ground covers are not suitable for high traffic areas. Compare the ground covers in 19-3.

Boulders and stones. Boulders and stones are available in various sizes and are commonly used for landscaping. Boulders with unusual forms, textures, or colors will add interest to any landscape.

Water, sun, and wind. Water, sun, and wind will always be a part of the outdoors. They

19-2
Many deciduous trees and shrubs flower in the spring as they get their new leaves.

19-3
Note the types of ground cover used in this landscape.

are considered natural landscape elements. Water is a basic need of any plant life. Yet, high water levels can cause swampy yards, wet basements, and poor plant growth. Orientation to the sun and wind affect the use of outdoor living areas. At times, you need protection from these elements. At other times, you want to take advantage of them.

Man-made Landscape Elements

Man-made landscape elements are those elements not found in the natural environment. They are, however, a common sight in most landscapes. These elements include hard surfaces, such as walks, driveways, and steps, and various structures, such as walls, fences, patios, and decks. Numerous other items, such as lighting and outdoor furnishings, are landscape elements.

Hard surfaces. When hard surfaces are needed, they can be created with *brick* or *concrete.* See 19-4. Concrete can be made into brick-like blocks, stepping stones, and slabs. You can purchase these items ready to use, or you can make your own by placing the concrete into forms. *Asphalt paving* produces a hard surface and is relatively inexpensive to apply. In some cases, *soil* is of the right composition to create a hard surface. Flagstone, which is a flat stone found in certain areas of the country, can be set in concrete or placed on a bed of sand. It can be used in its natural form to create a walk, 19-5.

Enclosure elements. Walls and fences are ***enclosure elements.*** This means they enclose a space. They can be used to keep children or pets in. They can also be used to keep unwanted visitors out. Enclosure elements can be constructed of a variety of materials–wood, brick, stone, concrete, plastic, metal, or a combination of these. *Freestanding walls* are often found on property lines. They give privacy and serve as a boundary, 19-6. *Retaining walls* have soil against one side as shown in 19-7. They are used for terracing and can serve as boundaries for yards and planting beds.

A *fence* is usually less expensive than a wall and is easy to construct. There are many types and heights from which to choose, 19-8. Most fences do not provide as much privacy as walls.

Unlike a row of hedges or trees, enclosure elements do not need time to grow. Both walls and fences can be used immediately after construction or installation.

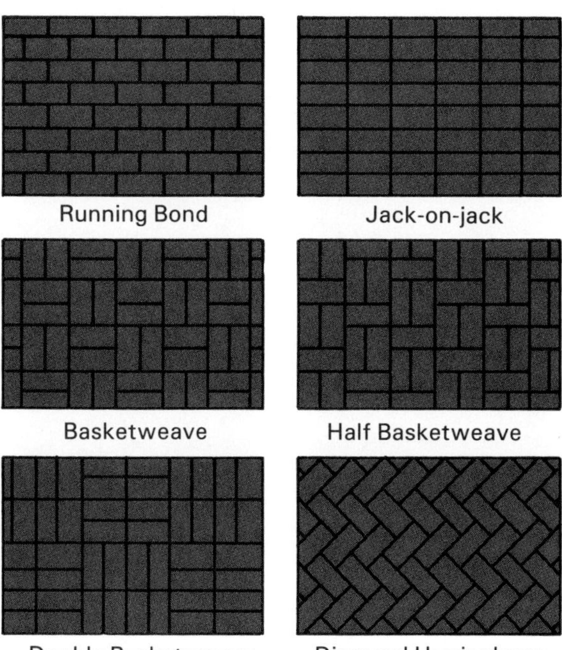

19-4
Bricks can be placed to form a variety of designs.

19-5
This attractive walk is constructed of flagstone.

Georgia-Pacific Corporation

19-6
A freestanding wall can provide privacy and beauty.

Versa-Lok Retaining Wall Systems

19-7
Retaining walls are used to hold soil in place.

There are many types of structures used in landscaping. You may build them or buy them ready to put in place. Courtyards, patios, decks, and terraces can enhance and extend your outdoor living space, 19-9. Other structures you might consider include fountains, barbecue pits, gazebos, playhouses, and storage structures. You may also want to add plant containers to your landscape.

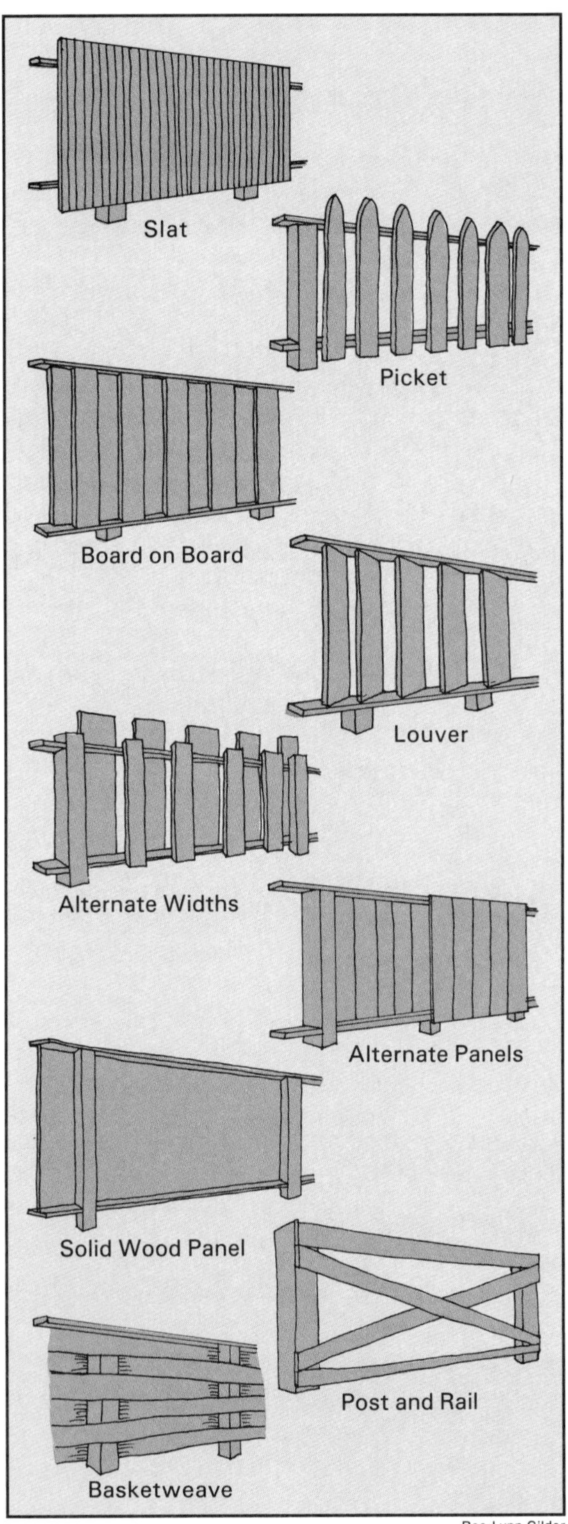

Rea-Lynn Gilder

19-8
Fences are available in a variety of designs. Nine popular styles are shown.

Lindal Cedar Homes, Inc., Seattle, WA

19-9
This house has a series of areas that enhance outdoor living.

California Redwood Association

19-10
The raised portions of this deck can be used as benches.

A variety of materials are available to build structures, including wood, brick, block, concrete, and flagstone. All of these materials are appropriate, and some are easy to use.

Outdoor furniture. Outdoor furniture is another man-made landscape element. The furniture is usually constructed of metal, wood, fiberglass, plastic, or glass. It can be made of a single material or a combination of materials. A variety of furniture styles are available to meet any need. Sometimes enclosure elements and other structures serve as furniture. See 19-10.

Artificial lighting. Another important element of the landscape is artificial lighting. Outdoor lighting should be functional, providing for safety and security. Lighting allows nighttime work or leisure activities. It can also add beauty to an outdoor setting.

Floodlights, spotlights, and underlighting can be used to accent a landscape site. *Automatic timers* are available for security lighting. These timers are designed to turn lighting on and off at predetermined times. *Photoelectric cells* are commonly used to turn lights on at dusk and off at dawn. *Motion detectors* activate lights when there is movement within a given area. Some lights are designed to conserve energy. Many manufacturers produce low-voltage outdoor lighting kits that operate on 12 or 24 volts. Other lights use solar energy. These lights store energy directly from the sun.

As you can see, some natural landscape elements are predetermined by the location of your property. Other natural elements, as well as all of the man-made elements, can be chosen by members of your living unit. Recognizing these elements can help you design an outdoor living space that meets your needs and goals.

Designing the Outdoor Living Spaces

Designing a landscape is similar to designing the interior of a home. Think of the areas you are landscaping as outdoor rooms. Just as the inside of the house is divided according to certain activities, the grounds are divided into three ***landscape zones***–the public zone, the private zone, and the service zone. The public zone is the part of the site that can be seen from the street. The service zone includes sidewalks, driveways, and storage areas for tools, trash cans, lawn equipment, etc. The private zone is for recreation and relaxation and is generally separated from the public zone. These zones were discussed more thoroughly in Chapter 4. Only you can decide how much landscaping you want for each zone. The landscape plan should include backgrounds and accents. Be sure to allow for activities and traffic. You can be innovative in your use of the landscape elements as you plan any area of the outdoor living space.

As you plan the "rooms" in your landscape, review the elements and principles of design. Recall the ways to use color effectively. You can apply what you have learned to the form, line, color, and texture of the landscape elements you choose. The landscaped space should have unity and balance. Landscape elements should be in proportion to one another and to the structures they surround.

Landscape Backgrounds

Floors, walls, and ceilings serve as the backgrounds in your landscape. The topography and the soil are the floor. Hard surfaces and ground covers are the floor coverings.

You may not have good soil on the site. If not, with knowledge and effort, you can improve it. Soil can be improved by the use of compost and mulch. These are organic materials, such as straw, peat moss, bark, and leaves. Compost is a decomposed or rotted natural material; mulch is not. Compost is worked into the soil, while mulch is used to cover the surface. Both compost and mulch are important to soil building. They increase the penetration of water and air, help the soil hold water, and control soil temperatures. If you plan to include grass or any other plants in your landscape, the condition of the soil is important.

Grass makes up one of the most appealing parts of the landscape. It creates a pleasing floor covering for the landscape site and can provide recreational areas for the members of your living unit. It also prevents soil erosion and supplies oxygen to the air. When grass is mowed, the clippings produce organic matter for the soil. Grass is commonly used to unify or connect the other parts of the landscape, 19-11.

Melka Landscaping, Orland Park, IL

19-11
This lawn ties various elements of the landscape together.

Plantings other than grass may be used as ground cover in areas where there is no traffic. They typically do not need as much care as grass. A variety of plants can be used as ground cover. Local conditions may limit your choices, since some plants will grow only in very good soil. Some ground covers require full sunlight and a warm climate.

Loose aggregate, such as sand, gravel, cinders, and bark or wood chips, is suitable for sections of the site that are difficult to water or have poor soil. It is used when low maintenance is desired or water is scarce. Sometimes loose aggregate is used as a mulch in planting areas.

Sections of the floor of the landscape will be paved or covered with other hard materials. These surfaces include driveways, sidewalks, and other areas. Hard surfaces on your lot should be sloped away from your house to provide proper water drainage. You do not want water standing or freezing on your driveway and sidewalks.

Walks are one of the easiest landscape elements to construct. They can be made of any durable material and are often used as borders. Walks divide the landscape site into separate areas and act as guideways to these areas. You should choose an attractive pattern in which to lay the walk, 19-12. If the level of the ground varies, you can include steps in the route. Most walks are permanent. However, changes are sometimes necessary when plant life matures and becomes larger. If you anticipate changing the route at some point in the future, steppingstones should be used to form the walk. They are easier to move than most other materials used for walk construction.

The walls of the landscape are created by trees, shrubs, walls, and fences. Walls can act as a screen, giving visual privacy. They also curb noise and serve as a windbreak. See 19-13. You must decide which areas to enclose with walls. If you have a good view in one direction, you may want to take advantage of it by leaving it open.

Suitable shrubs or evergreens can be planted close together to form a wall. If you want a dense grouping, combine trees with shrubs. Plant short shrubs among the tall trees. You could also plant two rows of trees, staggering the plantings to make a continuous barrier.

Melka Landscaping, Orland Park, IL

19-12
A walk does not have to be placed in a straight line. This walk was designed to complement the landscape.

19-13
This fence provides privacy and protects the house from the wind.

Walls were originally built to keep enemies away. Today, they serve different functions. They may be used to separate one property from another, provide privacy, and block wind. Many walls are decorative, using such materials as wood, stone, or concrete.

Fences are often used for the same purposes as walls. Some are solid; others can be seen through. Fences that can be seen through are often covered with vines for more privacy.

Gates are part of the landscape's wall. They can add an interesting touch to the enclosure, 19-14. Gates must blend with the walls of the landscape.

The sky, with its clouds and color, is the ultimate ceiling of your landscape. Tall trees may frame the sky to create part of the ceiling. The spreading branches of some trees give a canopy effect. The trees may be located for the shade they produce. If needed, shade can also be provided by an overhead structure. Ceilings can be constructed of canvas, bamboo, fiberglass, louvers, or lath. See 19-15.

Accents

Accents in your landscape are the finishing touches. They are the colorful flower beds, the boulders and stones, and the special features you choose. Some accents become background elements for smaller accents. For example, a boulder may serve as a background for a cluster of flowers as shown in 19-16. You should include a variety of accents in your landscape plan.

19-14
A wrought iron gate can be attractive and functional.

California Redwood Association

19-15
This redwood ceiling is designed to provide shade.

Jackson & Perkins, Medford, OR

19-16
The boulders in this flower bed serve as both an accent and a background.

Flowers are not a permanent landscape element. They die in dormant seasons, so they are considered an accent. When in bloom, they are spectacular in their color and show. There are many forms, heights, and colors of flowers from which to choose.

Flower plantings should be simple. Too many types or colors in a single bed will produce a disorganized appearance. Some flowers need full sunlight. Others do well in the shade or partial sunlight. Find out which flowers will do best in your landscaping project.

Planting beds are good choices for flowers. These beds are the spaces that are reserved for plants. Raised beds or planters are effective. They are ideal for older people or people who use wheelchairs. Portable planters can be moved from one outside area to another, then moved inside during the cold season.

Choices of materials for planters include wood, plastic, glass, metal, concrete, and glazed ceramics. You can also use recycled materials, such as cans, jars, baskets, tubs, tires, and boxes, to construct planters. Look for planters that are durable and decorative.

Boulders and stones are often chosen as accent pieces. They can look as if they belong where they are placed as in 19-17. They can also serve as borders along paths and flower beds. Look again at 19-14. Place boulders and stones to show off their interesting features. Rock gardens are popular in landscaping.

Sculptures, murals, and mosaics can enhance your landscape design. The selection of these accents is very personal. In expressing your tastes, consider form, color, and texture. Usually a landscape will appear cluttered if you use too many of these accents. Most accents should be placed at eye level. Sculpture fits well against a background of foliage. You may, however, want to combine it with some type of structure.

Other Landscape Features

Throughout your landscape, you can use many different features. You can have fun planning them and may even enjoy building some of them.

You might want a gazebo in your landscape. A gazebo is a raised platform that has four, six, or eight open sides. You can enjoy the landscape as you relax in a gazebo. It can double as a playhouse. Some gazebos have a regular roof. Others have lattice or vine-covered roofs. You can adapt a gazebo to fit your desires.

19-17
Boulders and stones are attractive additions to this landscape.

A water fountain is another popular landscape feature. Water projects can be very enjoyable. The sound and sight of running water has a soothing effect. Sounds can be produced by having water fall from a high level to a lower one. Jets, bubbles, and sprays can also make soothing water sounds.

Water in motion has a special attraction. A small, inexpensive circulating pump may be installed to move the water. If you use water as a landscape element, it should be recycled. It can be used again in the landscape or used to water plant life.

You may want to attract birds to your property. You can do this by including a pool or pond in your landscape. The pool can be small or large. Small pools work best if they are near a group of plantings. See 19-18.

Birds will also be attracted to your yard if you put out feeders and birdhouses. Plan for the birds. Be sure there are good places for nests in your landscape.

Furnishing Your Outdoor Living Space

Outdoor furnishings can be used to extend your living space. They invite you outside. The furnishings can help make the landscape site enjoyable and functional for the entire living unit.

19-18
Water in a landscape is an appealing feature. Note that this pond is surrounded by various plantings.

Outdoor furnishings generally include tables, chairs, accessories, and cooking equipment. Furnishings that are durable and weather resistant are best for outdoor use. They should be of quality construction. Choose furnishings that resist the deterioration caused by heat, sun, and water. The furnishings should also resist soilage. See 19-19 for a description of materials commonly used in outdoor furniture. Many of these materials are also used for other outdoor accessories.

If you plan to move the outdoor furniture frequently, it should not be too heavy. You may want to store the furniture during the winter or use it in another location. Some furniture is appropriate for both indoor and outdoor use. If you want furniture for dual-purpose use, keep this in mind when making your selection. See 19-20.

Materials For Outdoor Furniture
Metals • Aluminum: lightweight and rustproof; sometimes has a finish to prevent corrosion. • Wrought iron: heavy and not very portable, rusts without the proper finish. • Molded cast iron: heavier than wrought iron, brittle, rusts, cracks, and breaks easily. • Steel: strong, durable, and weather resistant.
Woods • Cedar, cypress, and redwood: needs a protective coating to prevent deterioration. • Rattan, wicker, and bamboo: cannot be finished to withstand continuous outdoor conditions. Works well for sun-room furnishings.
Plastics • Urethane: durable, requires minimal maintenance; used for molded items. • Polyester and acrylic: used for furniture tops. • Fiberglass: lightweight, strong, durable, and weather resistant; can be designed to fit body contour; comes in colors.
Glass • Glass: common for tabletops; a high quality is needed.

19-19
Outdoor furniture is made from a variety of materials.

Carpeting is sometimes a part of the furnishings. It is best if outdoor carpeting is made of 100 percent synthetic fiber. Olefin, acrylic, and nylon are suitable fibers for outdoor use. The best outdoor carpeting is of needlepunched or tufted construction. The needlepunch process produces a felt-like carpeting. Tufting produces loops. The loops may or may not be cut. Either type of carpeting needs to be glued or taped down to a hard surface. For more information on carpet construction, see Chapter 13.

Additional furnishings include decorative and functional accessories. Accessories add the finishing touches to the furnished area. Common examples of decorative accessories include wind chimes, sculpture, driftwood, and urns. Examples of functional accessories include pillows and pads, cooking equipment, and waste containers.

Pillows and pads can be made of woven or knitted synthetic fibers. They must be filled with weather-resistant filler. This type of material can usually withstand moisture. Nevertheless, the pillows and pads should be protected from standing water.

Your outdoor living space may not seem complete unless you add cooking equipment. You may choose a portable unit or a stationary unit. A portable unit should be located so it does not interfere with the landscape. Position it in an area that is protected from strong winds and hot sun. You will not want the smoke from the unit to be a bother. Portable equipment can be stored when not in use.

If you choose stationary cooking equipment, place it in a convenient spot. However, do not allow it to detract from its surroundings. A well-planned unit can add pleasure to the landscape.

Cooking equipment can be fueled by charcoal, natural gas, or propane. Equipment fueled by propane or natural gas is generally more convenient than equipment fueled by charcoal.

Accessories often set the mood for the landscape area. There is no end to the choices you have when you select accessories.

Coordinate the style and color of your outdoor furnishings and accessories. Consider what is needed and determine where and how it will be used. When selecting furnishings and accessories, consider the following: comfort, convenience, durability, portability, storability, quality, design, and maintenance.

When selecting furnishings, use what you have learned about organizing space and traffic patterns. The principles apply to outdoor living spaces as well as indoor spaces.

Grosfillex

19-20
This plastic outdoor furniture can be moved easily.

Lighting the Outdoor Living Space

Lighting can create a type of magic in the landscape. It can extend the use of the outdoor living space. The lighted area invites you outside at night. Lights also enhance the view from inside the house. See 19-21.

Appropriate lighting is important for each area of your property. Outside lighting should illuminate the sidewalks and driveways. It should provide a clear view to and from your house. At the same time, lighting should discourage intruders. Lighting at entryways can help you see who is approaching.

Floodlights can be used for large areas, while spotlights are good for lighting specific features. You can highlight a garden sculpture or flowing water with a spotlight. Underlighting is especially appropriate for small areas. Underlighting is the practice of directing the light upward from the ground level into plants or other landscape features. If you desire, you can choose colored lights. Any of the lighting may be colored. Colored lights can add an interesting aspect to your landscape design.

If possible, light fixtures should be situated so they are hidden from view. Ground-level lights can be placed behind plants or structures. Higher fixtures can be installed under eaves or on rooftops.

Landscaping for Conservation

Conservation is the process of protecting or saving something. Your landscaping decisions can help to conserve soil, water, and energy.

Efforts at conservation should begin when a house is being built. Disturbances to the soil occur during construction. If ground covers are planted at this time, erosion of the topsoil can be prevented. In steep areas, terraces can be built to prevent erosion. Builders should be encouraged to employ these and other conservation measures.

Once construction is complete, permanent conservation efforts can begin. Even if you have been in your home for some time, you can make a significant contribution to conservation. The life-style of the living unit is probably the most important factor in conservation. If you are environmentally conscious, you will want to conserve natural resources. If you value economy, you can conserve to save money.

Homeowners want their outdoor space to be comfortable and attractive. They can accomplish this and still conserve natural resources through landscaping.

Lindal Cedar Homes, Inc., Seattle, WA

19-21
Well-planned outdoor lighting can help extend the use of outdoor living spaces.

Water and Soil Conservation

Awareness is the first step in ***water conservation.*** If you live in an arid part of the country, you realize how important it is to conserve water. The six-year drought that started in the late 1980s brought the need for water conservation to the attention of people in California. People throughout the United States must be aware of the need to conserve water.

After awareness, the next step is to plan a water-efficient landscape design. ***Xeriscape*** is the term used to describe landscapes that are designed to conserve water. Xeriscaping involves grouping plants according to the amount of water they need. Then the plants are encouraged to develop deep roots by watering less often and deeper. Water retention is promoted by using mulches and increasing the number of trees and the amount of grass.

Plan to use the most water in areas that receive the most use. These areas will include the lawn, play areas, and gardens. If you can use runoff water from roofs and gutters, you can reduce water costs.

Patios and similar areas need water only for accent plants. Areas near the property boundary may require little or no watering. If you use native plants, you should have low water use. Native plants are better adapted to the climate and usually need less watering than other plants, 19-22.

Watering, if needed, should supply plants with enough moisture to live. Too much water can lead to plant disease. Excess water also prevents plants from developing properly. It is better to water less often and water deeply. Deep watering can help roots grow deeper and plants become more drought resistant.

The most effective watering method is trickle or drip irrigation. In this technique, water is delivered to the base of the plants, reducing evaporation and runoff. In some trickle irrigation systems, narrow tubing is routed under the ground and surfaces at the delivery site. In other systems, water is delivered to the plants through a porous hose. The most common watering method involves the use of sprinklers. Sprinklers spray plants with a mist of water. Portable sprinklers can be moved to various positions in the landscape. Built-in sprinkler systems have several stationary sprinkler heads, which are located throughout the landscape. Built-in systems are generally more convenient than portable sprinklers because they do not have to be moved. A considerable amount of water is lost to evaporation when using sprinklers. If sprinklers are not controlled, there may be excessive water runoff. See 19-23.

19-22
The native plants in this landscape require very little water.

Melka Landscaping, Orland Park, IL

19-23
The sprinklers in this built-in system are controlled to conserve water.

Irrigating at night saves water. However, some plants are susceptible to certain diseases if they are watered at night. Know the characteristics of your plants. Irrigating when there is no wind will help reduce evaporation. A system controlled by a timer will also help save water. If possible, recycle water. You can use water from a pond to water grass or plants. Can you think of other ways to recycle water?

Soil conservation includes improving, as well as taking care of, the soil. Analyzing the soil is a very important part of soil conservation. Soil samples can be sent away to be tested or an on-site survey can be made. The results of these tests can be used to determine what should be done to improve the soil. Sometimes natural materials or chemicals can be added to improve the soil.

Soil can be improved by mixing organic matter with the native soil. The organic matter creates air space in the soil. It also retains moisture so less watering is needed. Improved soil increases the chances for good plant growth. When planning a landscape, water and soil conservation should be taken into account.

Energy Conservation

Homeowners are becoming increasingly aware of the possibility of energy conservation through landscaping. With the proper use of landscape elements, the climate in and around a home can be modified. Heat gains in the summer and heat losses in the winter can be reduced. In areas where air-conditioning is used, cooling costs can be reduced by up to 75 percent. This is achieved by providing plenty of summer shade. In regions where air-conditioning is not used, the home interior can be made more comfortable. Properly placed vegetation and man-made landscape elements can block prevailing winds. Windbreaks can save enough energy to lower heating bills by 10 to 15 percent.

Trees with high branches and many leaves provide summer cooling by blocking the sunlight. Tall trees provide less shade than those that are wide spread. Since deciduous trees lose their leaves in the winter, they will provide summer cooling and still allow you to benefit from the warmth of the winter sun. Deciduous trees are a good choice for placement on the south and east sides of buildings. Coniferous trees are good as windbreaks on the north and west sides of buildings. The types of trees that do best vary from region to region.

Shrubs and vines provide good shade for the walls of a house. Most walls retain heat in the summer sun. Shrubs and vines act as insulation to reduce the heat reaching the walls. Coniferous shrubs and vines will also help prevent heat loss in the winter. If you have enclosures that you want to collect heat from the winter sun, use deciduous plantings.

Overhangs and roof extensions offer shade. They can be planned to shut out summer sun and take in winter sun.

A ***sun-room,*** or garden room, is another structure that can alter the climate. A sun-room is a structure that traps heat. The trapped heat is a source of energy to heat water or air. Like plants, a sun-room can be used to help conserve energy. The room may be a part of a house or entirely separate, 19-24.

Lindal Cedar Homes, Inc., Seattle, WA

19-24
This sun-room is connected to the house. Note that a tile floor is used to absorb the heat from the sun.

To ensure that a sun-room conserves energy, it must be correctly positioned. For instance, it must be positioned at the correct angle to the sun and located in areas that are not shaded by trees or shrubs.

The conservation of natural resources for future generations should be everyone's concern. You can do your part, too. There is plenty of information available to help you make decisions about conservation. Before you decide which measures you are going to include in your landscape, find out all you can. Since the role of landscaping varies from region to region and from season to season, you need specific information. Information about conservation measures is available from landscape dealers or county extension offices. Libraries are excellent sources of information. You might want to look for publications by the United States Department of Agriculture (USDA). There are probably a number of landscape specialists in your community. Most large communities have at least one garden club. The members of these clubs will generally be willing to help you with your landscaping questions.

Complete Scaled Plans

After you have listed the needs, interests, and desires of your living unit and considered the climate, topography, and soil of the landscape site, analyze the orientation to the sun. Note the sunny and shady areas. Determine the best natural resources on the site. What is attractive and what is unattractive about your outside environment?

After you have compiled all the information you need, you are ready to complete your plan on paper. It is a good idea to begin your plan for the outdoor space with a map of the entire property. Use graph paper and draw the plan to scale. If possible, one-fourth inch should equal one foot. North should be at the top of the drawing. The map should include the following information:

- Property boundaries.
- Location of the residence, showing windows and doors.
- Location of other structures.
- Orientation to the sun and wind.
- Location of the driveway and sidewalks.
- Position of both underground and above-the-ground utilities.
- Location of existing plant life, rocks, and other features.

Develop the Landscape Design

After creating a scaled map of the property, 19-25, you are ready to design your landscape. Do not be afraid to experiment. You may want to make several separate designs. Use tracing paper for overlays on your map. This is the best way to add features and to experiment with your design. Clearly mark spaces for specific uses. Laying the

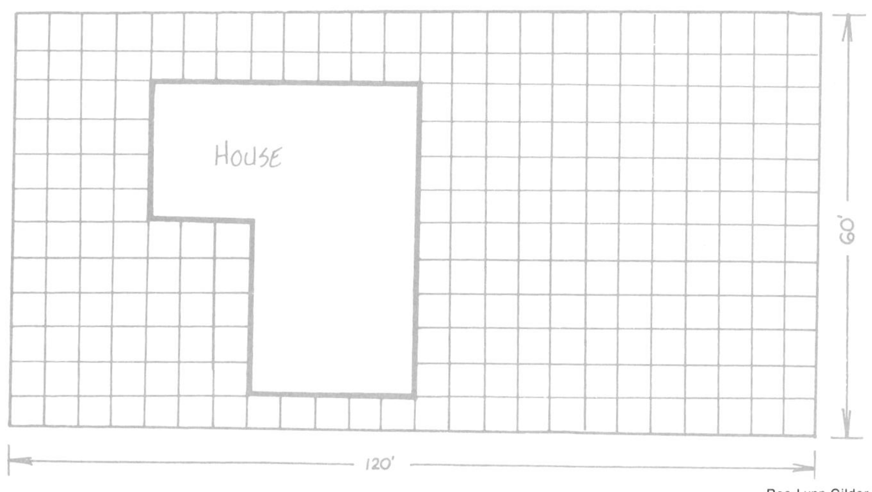

Rea-Lynn Gilder

19-25
Landscape plans should be drawn on graph paper.

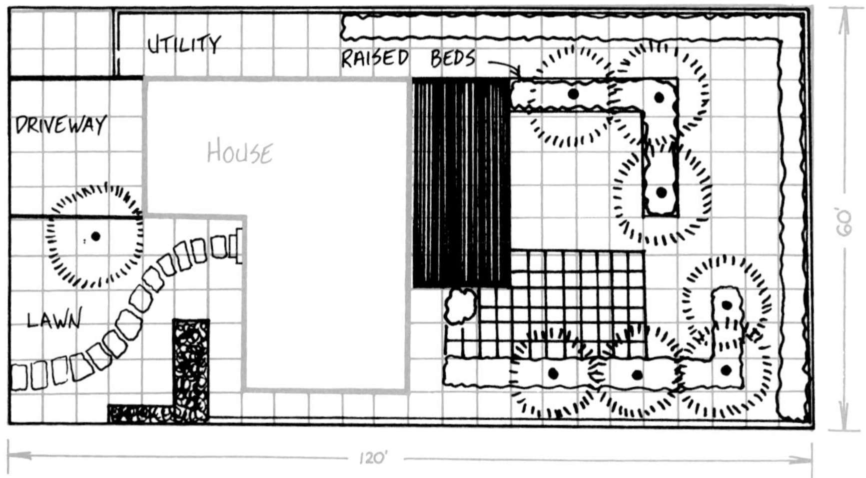

Landscape design A.

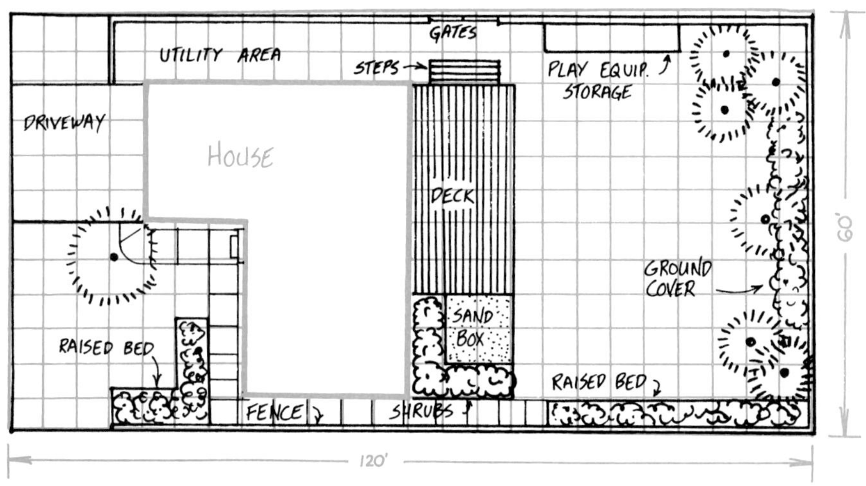

Landscape design B.

Rea-Lynn Gilder

19-26
Two alternate landscape designs are shown for the homesite in 19-25.

various tracing paper overlays on the map lets you choose the design you like best, 19-26. You may want to combine two or more overlays when designing your landscape. Complete the drawing by arranging the outdoor furnishings. Remember to allow for traffic and convenience when planning furnishing arrangements.

Once you have decided on a landscape plan, it is time to roll up your sleeves and go to work. You and the other members of your living unit may enjoy working together to create your outdoor living environment. You may choose to hire a landscape firm to carry out your plans. Many nursery owners are trained in landscape design. They are knowledgeable about plants and can help you with the planning. If you desire, you can hire specialists to help you care for your outdoor living area, 19-27.

Summary

When you plan the outdoor living area of your home, you need to identify your goals. Your goals will depend on the life-style, needs, and desires of your living unit.

The Service Master Company

19-27
This lawn-care specialist is applying fertilizer to a grass-covered area.

You will use several elements in landscaping. Recognizing the types of elements and their uses will help you make your plans. There are many natural landscape elements, including soil, rocks, trees, flowers, water, sun, and wind. Man-made landscape elements include hard surfaces, enclosures, structures, and outdoor furniture. You must determine which natural elements are suitable for the site being landscaped. You will choose the man-made elements that fit your situation.

Planning a landscape is much like planning the rooms inside your house. Just as a house is divided into several areas, the landscape site is divided into three zones–the private zone, the public zone, and the service zone. Each zone will be treated differently in your plan. As you plan your landscape "rooms," you will have floors, walls, and ceilings to consider. You will furnish the "rooms" and put accents in them. Lighting should be included in your plans so that you can use the outdoor living area at night.

You must understand the topography and the condition of the soil. This will help you to practice soil and water conservation. You should also plan the landscape to conserve energy.

Detailed plans of your outdoor "rooms" and zones will be needed for you to receive the satisfaction you want. The plans should be drawn to scale.

You can use various resources to help you make your decisions. After your plans are complete, you must decide who will do the work.

To Review

Write your responses on a separate sheet of paper.

1. What is the basic goal of landscaping?
2. What are natural landscape elements? Name three examples.
3. Which of these is not a ground cover?
   a. Deciduous shrub.
   b. Grass.
   c. Loose aggregate.
   d. Low vines.
4. List five man-made landscape elements.
5. When landscaping a zone, think of it as a _____.
6. Give three functions for the "walls" in a landscape design.
7. Name three accents used in landscaping.
8. List five factors to consider when selecting outdoor furniture.
9. List three reasons for including lighting in any landscape plan.
10. Explain the term xeriscaping.
11. For energy conservation, _____ trees should be located on the south side of a building.
12. Name five items to include on a site map.

To Do

1. Draw to scale a map of the site on which your house sits. Draw the arrangement of the dwelling. Divide it into zones. Show how you would design the outdoor living space.
2. Take a walk through your neighborhood. Do one or more of the following:
   a. List the natural and man-made landscape elements.
   b. Count the enclosure structures you find.
   c. Notice the different methods of watering.
   d. Look for low-maintenance landscapes.
   e. Look for deciduous and coniferous trees. Note their locations.
   f. List the types of ground covers.
3. Survey the members of your living unit. List the activities they would like to include in the planning of your landscape.
4. Watch newspapers and magazines for gardening news. Report landscaping ideas that are suitable for your area.
5. Look through seed catalogs. Find five annuals and five perennials for sale. Indicate how they can be purchased (seeds, bulbs, plants).
6. Look at outdoor furnishings. Make a list of the items you would choose. Give reasons for each choice.
7. Make a plan for outdoor living for someone who lives in an apartment.

CHAPTER 20

Keeping Your Home Safe and Secure

GE Plastics

To Know
alarm system
combustible
deadbolt locks
decibels
electrical shock
escape plan
GFCI
hand limitations
hearing impaired
mobility impairment
physical disabilities
precautions
radon
smoke detector
toxic
ventilation
visually impaired

Objectives

After studying this chapter, you will be able to:

- List the types and causes of the most frequent home accidents.
- Describe ways to keep the air in your home clean.
- Explain how to make your home safe and secure.
- Describe changes that can make the home safe and secure for those with special needs.

You face a variety of risks as you go about your daily life. Some of these risks cannot be avoided without restricting your activities. Other risks may be avoided by using common sense and taking preventive measures. The housing decisions you make can reduce the risk of accidents in your home. You can also make decisions that will help you feel more secure in your home.

A Safe Home

You probably think of home as a safe place. Surprisingly, it is *not*–more injuries take place at home than anywhere else. Home accidents are a major cause of death and serious injury. Each year, they hurt more people than traffic and work accidents combined. What about your home? Is it really safe?

Preventing Accidents

You should not wait until an accident happens to take some preventive measures. Survey your home for danger spots. Guard the members of your living unit against accidents that can have painful or even fatal results. Be sure that they know and follow safety rules.

Preventing falls. Falls are the most common type of home accidents. People of all ages suffer from falls, but the vast majority of those who suffer serious injury are older people. Children often experience falls because they are curious.

Taking a few simple ***precautions*** (preventive actions) can help avoid many falls. Wet floors can cause people to slip and fall. Wipe up water or other spilled liquids immediately. Loose rugs also can cause falls. Choose rugs with a nonskid backing. Remove tripping hazards by picking up any toys, shoes, or other items left on floors or stairs.

The bathroom can be especially dangerous, because wet surfaces cause many falls. Soap left in the bathtub creates a slippery, hazardous surface. You can reduce the danger of falling in the bathroom by using suction-type nonslip mats or safety strips in the shower and bathtub, 20-1. Firmly attached grab bars also can help prevent falls.

The most dangerous room in the home, according to the National Safety Council, is the bedroom. Many falls take place in the bedroom; so do fires. One reason for the high rate of bedroom accidents is that people move around while half-asleep. Placing lamps next to each bed (or on both sides of a double bed) will help prevent falls caused by stumbling in the dark.

Stairways should have light switches at both the top and bottom, and a sturdy, secure handrail. When climbing or descending stairs, always keep one hand free to use the rail. Keeping stairs clutter-free will help prevent falls.

Falls also occur on the outside of the home, often as a result of slipping on wet leaves, snow, or ice. Promptly removing snow and ice from sidewalks will help prevent falls. Toys, garden tools, and other possible tripping hazards should be removed from walks.

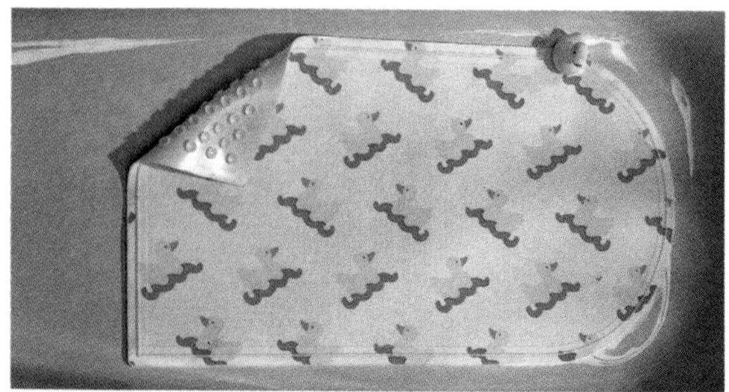

Lillian Vernon Corporation

20-1
Using a nonslip mat or self-adhesive safety strips in the bathtub or shower can help prevent injury from a fall.

When you use a ladder or stepladder, make sure it is securely in place before climbing. Whenever possible, a second person should support the ladder. After using a ladder, store it properly so that children will not be tempted to climb.

Preventing burns. Burns are another major type of injury resulting from home accidents. Children under four years of age and elderly people are most likely to be victims.

Scalding water can cause serious burns. Lowering the temperature of your home's hot water supply to 120°F can prevent scalding burns. Hot cooking utensils can cause burns. Turn pan handles away from the edge of the range when cooking to avoid spills. Open steam-filled pans on the side away from your body. To move hot utensils, use pot holders or oven mitts. Be sure the mitt or pot holder is not damp–the heat from the cooking utensil could cause steam burns. Be careful of other household heat sources, such as toasters, hair dryers, and the iron you use to press your clothes.

Preventing electrical shock. Electricity in our homes is convenient and makes possible a high standard of living. However, the home's electrical system must be properly designed, installed, and maintained to prevent it from being a safety hazard. An ***electrical shock***, electric current passing through your body, can be fatal.

Most electrical shocks result from the misuse of household appliances. Since water conducts electricity, electrical appliances must not be used near water or with wet hands. Dry your hands before using, connecting, or disconnecting electrical equipment. Do not stand on a damp floor while connecting or disconnecting an appliance's power cord. When disconnecting a power cord, grip the plug, not the cord. Pulling on the cord can weaken wires and eventually could result in a shock or a fire.

Use heavy-duty extension cords, whenever possible. An extension cord should never be lighter than the appliance cord that is plugged into it. To avoid damage to electrical cords, do not tie knots in them or run them under rugs. Damaged or frayed cords and defective plugs must be replaced promptly. Do not plug too many lamps or appliances into one outlet. Overloading circuits can cause electrical fires.

The National Electric Code requires safety grounding of all outlets. In kitchens, bathrooms, laundry rooms, and other locations near water, a special type of electrical outlet must be installed. The outlet includes a safety device called a ***Ground Fault Circuit Interrupter (GFCI)*** to help prevent shocks. Outlets on the exterior of your home should have weatherproof covers or caps. Circuit breakers and fuses are safety devices. They interrupt electrical power if too much current flows. Always replace a fuse with one of the same rating. Using a fuse with higher rating could let wires overheat and cause a fire.

Preventing poisonings. Another major cause of home injuries and fatalities is poisoning. Most such accidents are caused by swallowing common household products. Laundry and cleaning aids, medicines, and cosmetics can be ***toxic*** (poisonous). So can garden chemicals, materials used in the workshop, and many items found in the garage. The leaves or other parts of some house plants are poisonous if eaten. The list of dangerous items is long. You can probably think of others.

To help prevent poisoning, always keep products in their original containers. Read and understand the product labels. Follow the directions for use. Then properly dispose of the container and any leftover product. Use the safety checklist for hazardous materials in 20-2. You may wish to use nontoxic alternatives for chemical products that are considered harmful. See 20-3.

Keeping Children Safe in Your Home

Children are often the victims of home accidents. When they are present, extra precautions must be taken. To prevent falls, you should install gates, bars, railings, and other types of protection. Keep children away from open windows, porches, and stairways. To help prevent falls in the dark, you can install night-lights.

Keep electrical appliances and cords where children cannot get to them. Install safety covers on unused outlets to prevent possible electrical shocks. Guard against fire–keep matches and lighters out of the reach of children. It is especially important to involve children in fire drills, so they will know what to do in case of a fire.

Hazardous Materials Safety Checklist	Yes	No
Do you always read the label before using hazardous material and follow directions?	☐	☐
Do you store hazardous material in their original labeled containers?	☐	☐
Do you keep hazardous materials out of the reach of children, pets, and irresponsible people?	☐	☐
Do you avoid smoking while using hazardous materials when directions so indicate?	☐	☐
Do you avoid inhaling hazardous materials and wear protective clothing and masks when directed to do so?	☐	☐
Do you avoid spilling hazardous materials on your skin and wash immediately when they are spilled accidently?	☐	☐
Do you wash hands thoroughly after handling hazardous materials and before eating or smoking?	☐	☐
Do you cover food and water containers of pets when using hazardous materials such as pesticides which might contaminate them?	☐	☐
Do you always dispose of empty hazardous material containers so they pose no hazards to humans, animals, wildlife, or valuable plants?	☐	☐
Do you wash contaminated clothing before reuse when this is directed?	☐	☐
Do you always observe label directions to keep the residues of hazardous materials, such as pesticides applied to plants, within the limits permitted by law?	☐	☐
Do you store your hazardous materials in locked cabinets and in a well ventilated storage facility?	☐	☐

20-2
How much do you know about proper methods for handling household products and other chemicals that may be hazardous if not correctly used?

Children can learn to read labels that indicate poison. However, many dangerous products are not clearly labeled as poison. For example, how many laundry and cleaning products carry a warning label like the one shown in 20-4? Where are these products stored in your home? Too often, they are kept under the kitchen sink, where children can reach them easily. Store dangerous products in a safe place. Install safety latches or locks on cabinet doors.

A home swimming pool can be fun and healthy for your family. However, it can be a source of danger, especially to children. For children under five years of age, drowning is the second leading cause of accidental deaths around the home. If you have a pool, observe the following safety precautions:

- Young children must be supervised at all times.
- The pool must be completely surrounded by a fence or wall.
- Install gates that are self-closing and self-latching. The latch must be located out of reach of young children.
- Keep a phone and emergency numbers handy.
- Learn cardiopulmonary resuscitation (CPR), a lifesaving method you can use in an emergency.

Keeping the Air Clean

Clean air in the home is more of a concern now than it has been in the past. To save energy used for heating and cooling, houses have become more airtight. Such airtight houses, however, have increased the problem of inside air pollution.

Few people realize that the air inside the average home may be badly polluted. In some homes, the situation is critical. Inside pollution comes from many sources. Fuels burned for heating and cooking emit polluting chemicals. Some insulating materials give off vapors that are pollutants. Tobacco smoke, dust, pets, household cleaning and beauty products, all add pollutants to the air in the home. Even stagnant water left in containers like vaporizers and humidifiers pollutes the air.

Safe Alternatives for Chemical Products

Most of the household products you use can be substituted by simply using vinegar, baking soda, borax, ammonia, and soap. You can use different combinations of these products for your different household needs. The following is an all-purpose cleaner you can make yourself using non-toxic ingredients:

1 gallon hot water
2/3 cup of baking soda
1/4 cup ammonia
1/4 cup vinegar

Doubling the ingredients (excluding water) will make the solution even stronger for tough cleaning jobs.

Disinfectants ***Hazardous Ingredients:*** diethylene or methylene glycol, sodium hypochlorite, phenols ***Alternative:*** Mix 1/2 cup borax in 1 gallon water.	**Ammonia-Based Cleaners** ***Hazardous Ingredients:*** ammonia, ethanol ***Alternative:*** Use a vinegar, salt, and water mix for surfaces; baking soda and water for the bathroom.
Drain Cleaners ***Hazardous Ingredients:*** sodium or potassium hydroxide, sodium hypochlorite, hydrochloric acid, petroleum distillates ***Alternative:*** Plunger; flush with boiling water, 1/4 cup baking soda, and 2 oz. vinegar.	**Enamel or Oil-Based Paints** ***Hazardous Ingredients:*** pigments, ethylene, aliphatic hydrocarbons, mineral spirits ***Alternative:*** Latex or water-based paints.
Floor and Furniture Polish ***Hazardous Ingredients:*** diethylene glycol, petroleum distiates, nitrobenzene ***Alternative:*** Mix 1 part lemon juice with 2 parts olive or vegetable oil.	**House Plant Insecticide** ***Hazardous Ingredients:*** methoprene, malathion, tetramethrin, carbaryl ***Alternative:*** Mixture of bar soap and water or old dishwater; spray on leaves, then rinse.
Bleach Cleaners ***Hazardous Ingredients:*** sodium or potassium hydroxide, hydrogen peroxide, sodium or calcium hypochlorite ***Alternative:*** For laundry, use 1/2 cup white vinegar or baking soda or borax.	**Roach and Ant Killers** ***Hazardous Ingredients:*** organophosphates, carbamates, pyrethrins ***Alternative:*** Roaches–traps or baking soda and powdered sugar mix. Ants–chili powder to hinder entry.

Abrasive Cleaners or Powders

Hazardous Ingredients: trisodium phosphate, ammonia, ethanol

Alternative: Rub area with 1/2 lemon dipped in borax, rinse, and dry.

20-3
By recognizing and understanding the dangers of using hazardous products, you can choose to use less-harmful substitutes. The alternatives listed here are considered safe for you and the environment.

Perhaps the most dangerous of all indoor pollutants is ***radon,*** a natural radioactive gas. Radon is found in high concentrations in soils and rocks containing uranium and some other minerals. It is also found in soils with certain types of industrial wastes. Radon is believed to be a cause of lung cancer. Your risk of developing lung cancer from radon depends on the concentration and the length of time you are exposed to the gas.

20-4
This "Mr. Yuk" label was developed to help warn children about dangerous products.

You cannot see, smell, or taste radon. Many states, as well as the federal government, are working to identify high-risk areas and provide information on dealing with the problem. The federal government recommends that you measure the level of radon in your home. See 20-5. A radon test is the only way you will know whether or not it is there.

Except in the case of radon, no single source creates a great pollution problem. The problem arises when all the sources are combined and locked in an airtight house. The air can become so polluted it affects health. People may develop allergies, become very ill, or feel tired and listless.

Proper ***ventilation,*** or air circulation, reduces pollution levels. The living spaces of the house need to be ventilated to allow an exchange of fresh and stale air. Ventilation must also be provided for the attic and any basement or crawl space under the floor. If your house did not have vents built in, they can be installed. Exhaust fans can be added to increase ventilation. If ventilation is planned, air will be exchanged at a good rate. See 20-6 for steps in diagnosing a too-tight house.

Air pollution can be reduced by eliminating or controlling the source of the pollutants. For example, you can use fewer chemicals in your house. Learn the effects of the chemicals you have around. Eliminate or reduce the use of those that are the most polluting. Some types of pollutants, such as asbestos, can be sealed or enclosed to prevent fibers or vapors from being released and polluting the air.

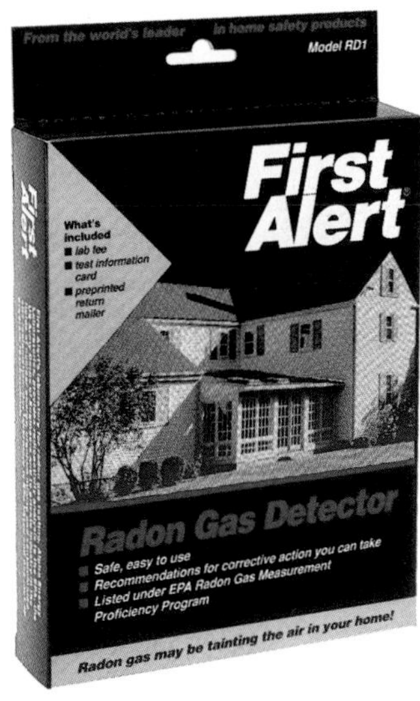

First Alert®

20-5
A number of companies make test kits for radon gas. The detector is exposed to household air for a period of time, then sent to a laboratory for analysis.

Providing proper ventilation and eliminating the sources of pollutants are effective solutions. Another solution you may want to consider is the use of an air purifier. However, such devices are not effective with some pollutants, such as radon.

House cleaning methods also affect the pollution level. For instance, using a feather duster merely moves dust around. The dust remains in the air until it settles on another surface. The best cleaning device is probably a vacuum cleaner that "washes" dust out of the air it draws in by passing the air through a compartment containing water. (See 18-23 in Chapter 18.) A central vacuum system also helps clean the air, because air is filtered and exhausted to the outside.

You probably will combine the various methods to eliminate or control air pollution in your home. The Environmental Protection Agency (EPA) is concerned about air quality. You can request more information from them.

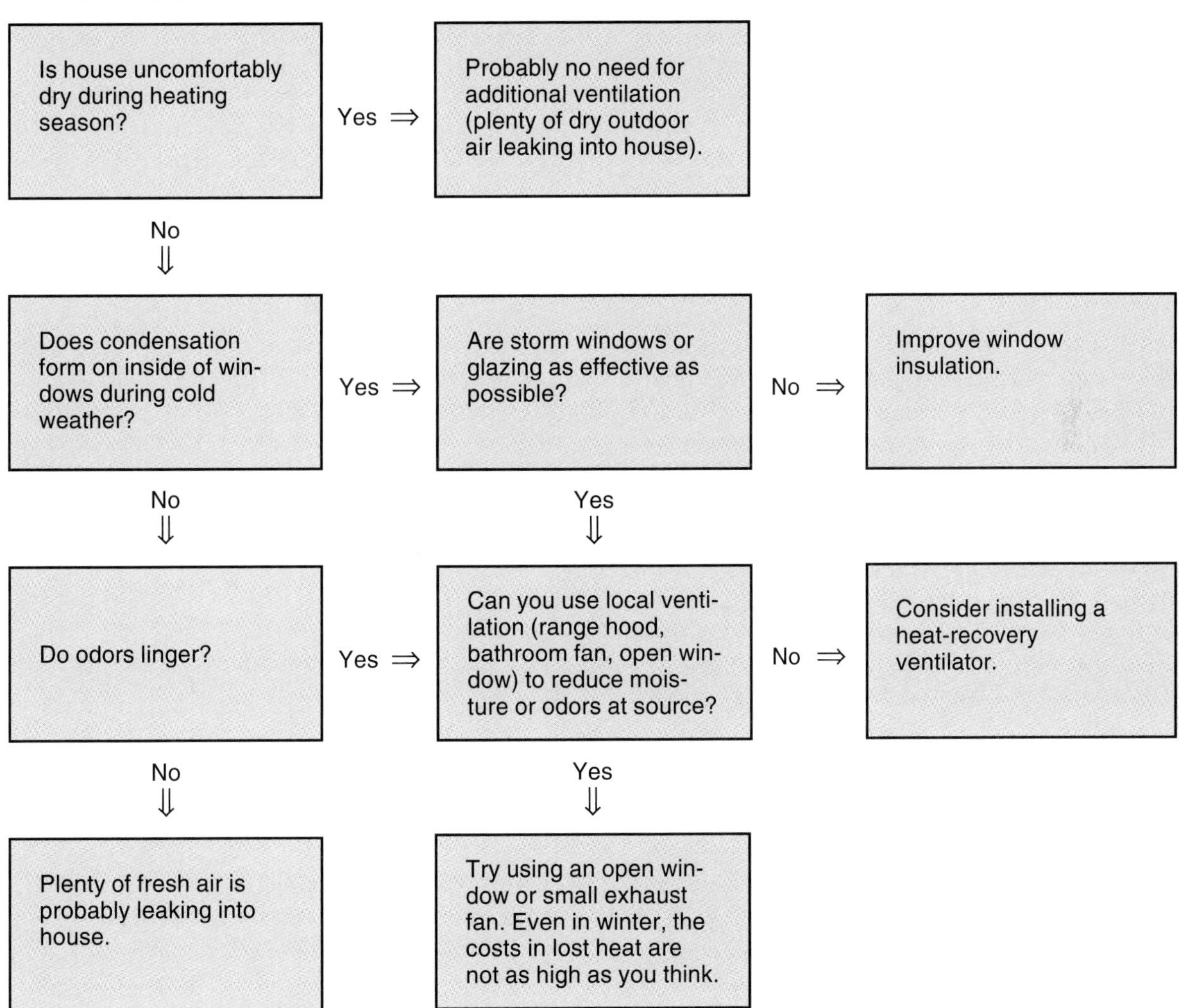

Copyright 1985 by Consumers Union of United States, Inc., Mt. Vernon, NY. Reproduced by permission from Consumer Reports, October, 1985.

20-6
If you spot problems with ventilation in your house, you can correct them with a few simple steps.

Controlling Noise Pollution

Noise is unwanted sound. It may be the most widespread nuisance in the nation. According to government studies, it is the leading cause of neighborhood dissatisfaction. Medical research indicates that noise is a cause of physical and psychological stress. Noise interferes with conversation. It hampers concentration and slows down work efficiency. Noise can cause accidents and interfere with sleep. Researchers are even trying to learn more about the possible harmful effects of noise on unborn babies.

Sound is measured in units called ***decibels***, abbreviated as dB. The quietest sound that can be heard is rated at 0 dB. Normal conversation is about 60 dB. The loudness of a sound, and how long you are exposed to it, determines its effect on you. Continued exposure to loud noise can cause permanent hearing loss.

Reducing noise pollution. Listen to your house. Evaluate the noises you hear. Do they interfere with conversation? Are there sounds that threaten the invasion of privacy? Are there small sounds that are distracting?

Sound levels of some typical household appliances are given in 20-7. Compare them to the level of normal conversation. The EPA has set noise standards for home products. If you listen before you buy, you can choose products that will contribute as little as possible to noise pollution of your home.

Solving some noise problems may be a simple matter. Solving others may take more effort. Inside your home, you can install sound-absorbing materials, such as acoustical ceiling panels. Carpets and draperies also help absorb sound. Pleasant sounds, such as music, can muffle unwanted sounds. You can close off rooms that are noisy.

Noise from outside the house may be controlled by insulating exterior walls. Storm windows or multiple-pane glass can keep out some of the noise. Landscaping techniques, such as building berms (earth mounds), erecting walls, and planting shrubs can help reduce noise, as well.

Household Noisemakers	
Appliance	**Sound Level in Decibels**
Floor fan	38 to 70
Refrigerator	40
Washing machine	47 to 78
Dishwasher	54 to 85
Clothes dryer	55
Hair dryer	59 to 80
Vacuum cleaner	62 to 85
Sewing machine	64 to 74
Food disposal	67 to 93
Electric shaver	75
Electric lawn edger	81
Home shop tools	85
Gasoline-powered mower	87 to 92
Gasoline-powered riding mower	90 to 95
Chain saw	100
Stereo	up to 120

20-7
These appliance sound levels are for someone who is close to or operating the device. Normal conversation level is about 60 dB.

A Secure Home

Your home should provide security (protection) from physical harm. It should be a place where you can feel safe and protected from the unknown.

If you live in a well-built dwelling, located in a neighborhood that is basically free from crime, you are likely to feel secure. However, to more fully satisfy your need for security, you should include some protective devices in your home.

Security from Fire

Home fires are one of the most serious types of accidents, and often claim small children and the elderly as victims. Fires not only can cause bodily injury or death, they can also be responsible for costly damage to property. The leading causes of fire include:

- Placing ***combustible*** (burnable) materials too close to a source of fire.
- Falling asleep while smoking.
- Starting fires with flammable materials.
- Operating defective electrical or heating equipment.

Fire department officials stress that fire prevention is a matter of common sense. By following a few simple rules, you can help to prevent a fire in your home:

- Store flammable liquids properly. Use only approved containers.
- Keep matches in a safe place, where children cannot reach them. Dispose of lighted matches and cigarettes in a safe manner.
- Do not overload electrical wires.
- Dispose of rubbish regularly.
- Have your heating system inspected yearly.
- In wood-burning stoves and fireplaces, burn only seasoned (dry) wood. Do not use green wood, which can cause creosote build-up that may result in a fire.
- Choose upholstered furniture that is constructed to make it more resistant to smoldering cigarettes. Such furniture carries a gold-colored hangtag from the Upholstered Furniture Action Council (UFAC), 20-8.

UFAC

20-8
This label on upholstered furniture certifies that it is constructed to make it more resistant to smoldering cigarettes.

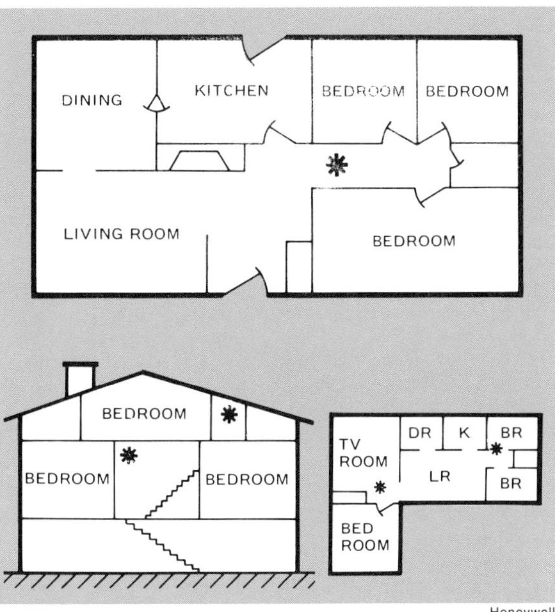

Honeywell

20-9
Smoke detectors should be placed on each floor of a dwelling, especially near bedrooms. They can be mounted on the ceiling or a wall.

Although some fire deaths result from burns or injuries caused by panic, deadly smoke and gases released by the fire claim most fire victims. Some simple precautions can help you escape injury by smoke and gases. For example, by sleeping with your bedroom door closed, you can greatly delay the spread of smoke and flames, if a fire should occur.

Smoke detectors. An inexpensive ***smoke detector*** will give a loud warning signal if a fire starts. The detectors are easy to install, and one should be placed on each floor of a building. The diagrams in 20-9 suggest good locations for smoke detectors.

There are two basic types of smoke detectors: ionization and photoelectric. The ionization type responds more rapidly to fires where flames are present. The photoelectric detector is quicker to detect a smoldering, slow-burning fire. Both types are effective at providing an early warning of fire, however. Most detectors are battery operated, but some are available that operate on the house's electrical current. It is important to choose smoke detectors that are approved by the Underwriters Laboratories, Inc.

If a smoke detector is battery operated, a fresh battery should be installed once a year. Most smoke detectors emit a sharp beep or have a flashing light to indicate that the battery needs replacing. It is a good idea to check smoke detectors for proper operation every 30 days. Most units have a test button that can be pressed for this purpose.

Fire extinguishers. Fire extinguishers are classified according to the type of burning material on which they should be used. The Class A extinguisher is for fires involving paper, wood, fabric, and other "ordinary combustibles." Class B extinguishers are used for burning liquids (such as a fire in a deep fryer), and Class C extinguishers are best for use on electrical fires. The three classes are described in 20-10. In practice, many extinguishers available today can be used on fires of any type. They are marked "ABC." Fire extinguishers should be located where they are easy to find and use, 20-11.

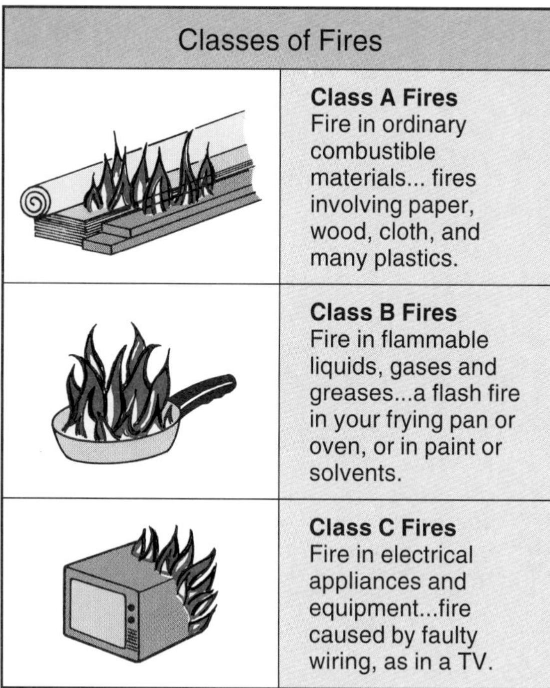

Classes of Fires	
	Class A Fires Fire in ordinary combustible materials... fires involving paper, wood, cloth, and many plastics.
	Class B Fires Fire in flammable liquids, gases and greases...a flash fire in your frying pan or oven, or in paint or solvents.
	Class C Fires Fire in electrical appliances and equipment...fire caused by faulty wiring, as in a TV.

20-10
Fire extinguishers are labeled for use on one, two, or all three classes of fire.

Plan for fire emergencies. The members of your living unit should have a plan of action, or ***escape plan***, in case a fire occurs. Draw a scale floor plan of your home. On it, mark a main escape route and an alternate route from each room. Remember that children and older people will need special assistance in escaping from a fire. Make sure that all members of your living unit know the way an alarm will be sounded. For example, a loud whistle or a bell might be used to awaken and alert everyone in the home.

Everyone must understand that speed in leaving the burning building is essential. There is no time to waste getting dressed or collecting possessions. Be sure each person knows how to make the *door test*: If the knob or panels of the closed door are warm, *do not* open the door. Use an alternate escape route. If the doorknob or panels are not warm, open the door slowly. If no smoke or hot air greets you, it is probably safe to use that exit.

Part of your plan should be to decide on a place to meet once everyone is outside. After everyone is safely outside, go to the nearest telephone and call the fire department. In many ar-

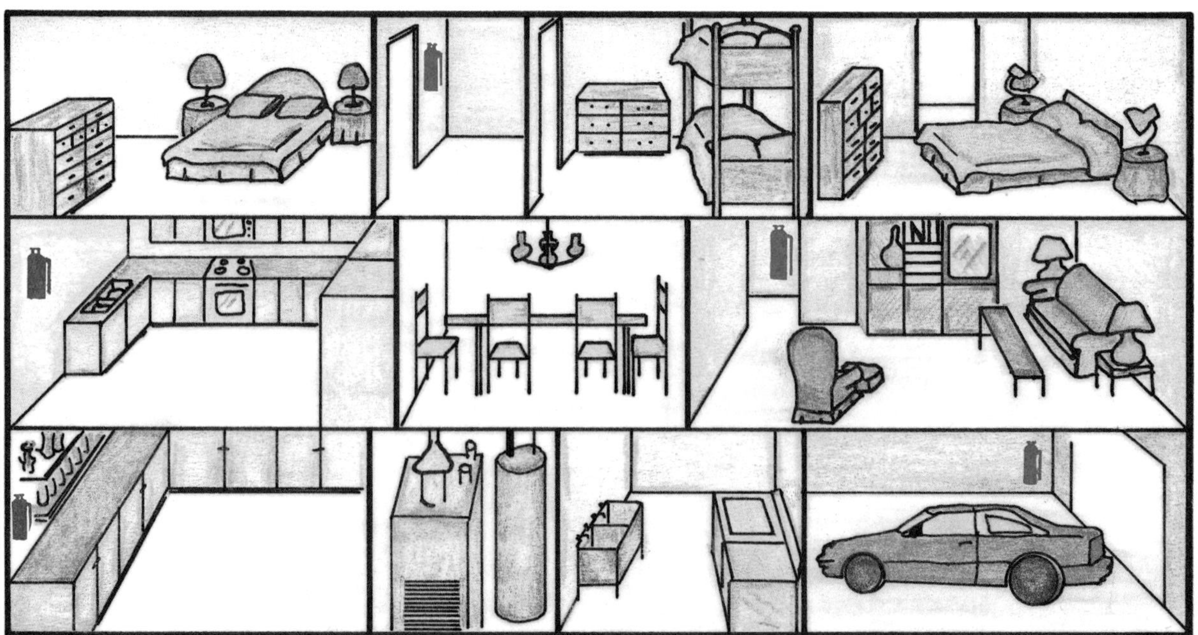
General Services Administration

20-11
Fire extinguishers should be located in the garage, kitchen, basement, and at an easily reached spot on each floor. If possible, they should be near exits and not more than 75 feet from any point on that floor.

eas, dialing 911 will connect you to an emergency services dispatcher. Some areas will have a local emergency number, instead. Give your name and address and describe the situation.

Once everyone knows the emergency plan, hold a practice drill. Repeat the drills periodically. Be sure to practice the use of alternate routes, as well as main escape routes.

Security from Home Intruders

In the United States, a private residence is burglarized about every 15 seconds. You can take some measures to keep this from happening to your home. Many security measures are merely common sense. For instance, do not publicize your absence when you are away from home. Most burglaries are committed during the day, while people are away at work or shopping. Take steps to make your home look lived-in, even when you are gone. The following will give a home that lived-in look:

- Leaving a vehicle in the driveway.
- Keeping newspapers off the porch.
- Returning emptied trash cans from the curb.
- Taking mail out of the box.
- Using a variable timer to turn lights on and off.
- Keeping yard mowed or snow removed from walks.
- Opening drapes during the day and closing them at night.
- Turning on a radio or TV.
- Keeping a dog that barks at strange noises.

Do not let strangers into your home. You should have some way of knowing who is at the door without opening it. A peephole or a chain lock permits you to see who is there. Monitoring devices are available that permit you to see and hear the person at your door before that person sees you. See 20-12. If a stranger asks to use your telephone, offer to make the call for him or her. Other security precautions include the use of outside lighting at every entrance to your home and installing secure locks on all doors and windows. You can also install an alarm system.

If a child is home alone, there are additional rules to be observed. The child should know how to use the phone and have important numbers available. When answering the phone, no details should be given. For example, the caller should not be told the child is home alone, or what time someone is expected back.

Make the exterior of your home as visible as possible. Install a system to light exterior doors and the yard. Use automatic timers, so that lights are on from dusk to dawn, 20-13. An alternate

Nutone

20-12
This video door-answering system lets you hear and see a caller at your door.

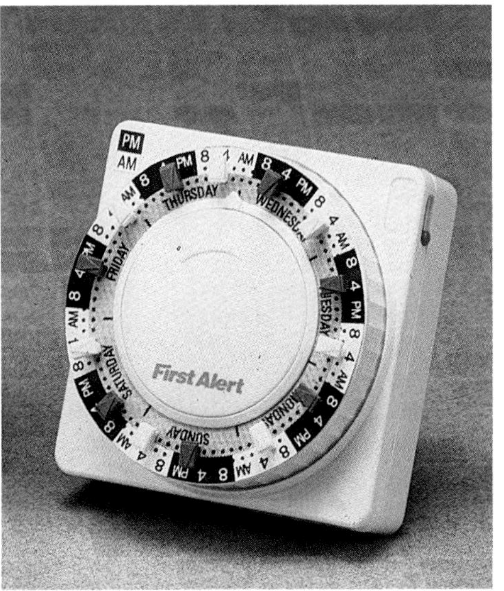

First Alert®

20-13
A timer can be used to turn lights on at dusk and shut them off at dawn.

method is the use of motion-detecting lights that will go on when someone comes near the house. Trim all shrubs so that doors and windows can be seen clearly from the street. If shrubs are growing under windows, make sure that they are thorny or that they cannot be used as a hiding place or shield for an intruder.

Locks and other security devices. To make doors as secure as possible, install ***deadbolt locks***, 20-14. Use the type that requires a key to unlock from the inside, as well as the outside. This type is called a double cylinder lock. When you move to a new residence, change lock cylinders (they are less expensive than complete locks.) This will prevent entry by anyone who previously had a key to the door.

Keep all windows and exterior doors locked. If there is a door between the garage and the house, keep it locked as well. Never leave keys in the locks. Also, do not hide keys near the house. Intruders can usually find them easily. Install extra locks or take other measures to make sliding doors and windows secure. See 20-15.

Install strong exterior doors that are made of metal or have solid wood cores. (Many doors are so weak that they can be broken down with a strong kick.) Hang the doors so that the hinge pins are on the inside. If the pins are on the outside, a burglar can remove them and open the door. If you have a glass pane door, a good extra security measure is to install a panel of rigid transparent plastic, such as acrylic, inside the glass.

Another deterrent to burglary is to mark your valuables with an identification number. Your driver's license number is one that can be traced in any state. Marking valuables can deter a thief, since they would be harder to dispose of than unmarked items. If they are stolen, however, the identification number makes them easier to trace and identify. Keep valuable items, such as jewelry and savings bonds, safely locked away. You may wish to store them in a home safe, a private security vault, or a safe deposit box at your bank.

Alarm systems. Electronic ***alarm systems*** are being installed in many homes. A typical system has window and door sensors. The sensors will set off an alarm if someone forces open a door or window. Some systems also have sensors that are triggered by vibrations, body heat, or noise. Some systems also include smoke de-

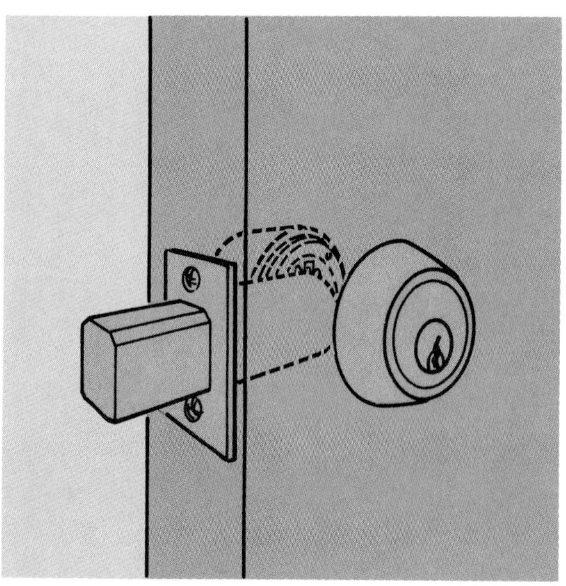

20-14
Deadbolt locks help make entrances more secure. The type that requires a key to open from either side is best.

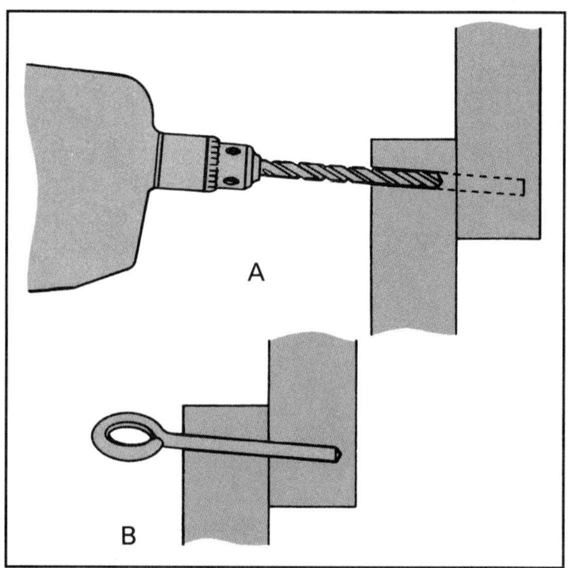

20-15
To make windows and sliding doors more secure, drill through both frames where they overlap (A). Then place a pin in the hole (B).

tectors, or even waterflow alarms to signal a plumbing problem. Many alarm systems will signal a burglary attempt with flashing lights, a siren, an alarm bell, or a combination of these. Some systems are connected to a monitoring station. If you are away, someone will know when the alarm goes off. The fire department or police will be notified. You can expect to pay a monthly fee for the monitoring service in addition to the installation charge.

Often the presence of an alarm system will ward off intruders. A barking dog may serve the same purpose. Some dogs are also trained to protect their owners. People who live on the same street may form a Neighborhood Watch program. People in such a program report any suspicious activities on their street to police. Some people prefer to live in a place that has security guards in stations or gatehouses.

Your personal needs and beliefs will affect the way you choose to keep your home secure. For instance, some people feel safe with a security guard nearby. Having a guard may make other people feel as if they are giving up some of their freedom. No matter what your situation, you will probably want to take some security measures. Choose those that make you feel as comfortable and safe as you can within your home.

Whether you own or rent, you can take measures to prevent home accidents and safeguard your home against intruders. You also want to make your home safe and secure for a special person who may be a member of your living unit.

Equipping a Home for People with Disabilities

Sometimes, ***physical disabilities*** (limitations) may make it necessary for a person to move from his or her home. However, if the present home can be modified, the move often may be postponed, or made unnecessary. A home now can be equipped to meet the needs of people with physical disabilities. This includes people with visual and hearing impairments.

Some appliance companies have designed kitchens to meet the needs of people with disabilities. With careful selection of features, appliances from regular stock can be used in these kitchens. For example, the range needs to have front controls, as shown in 20-16.

A person who is ***visually impaired*** may have any degree of vision loss. For most people, changes in vision begin after the age of 50. These changes often become more severe after age 65. One in 20 people over the age of 85 is legally blind.

People who are visually impaired live most comfortably and safely in familiar surroundings. You can take these measures to adapt living areas to the needs of a visually impaired person:

- Prominently mark changes in floor levels.
- Place furniture away from traffic lanes.
- Increase the amount of lighting and make sure it is evenly distributed.
- Use highly visible colors, such as yellow-oranges and reds.

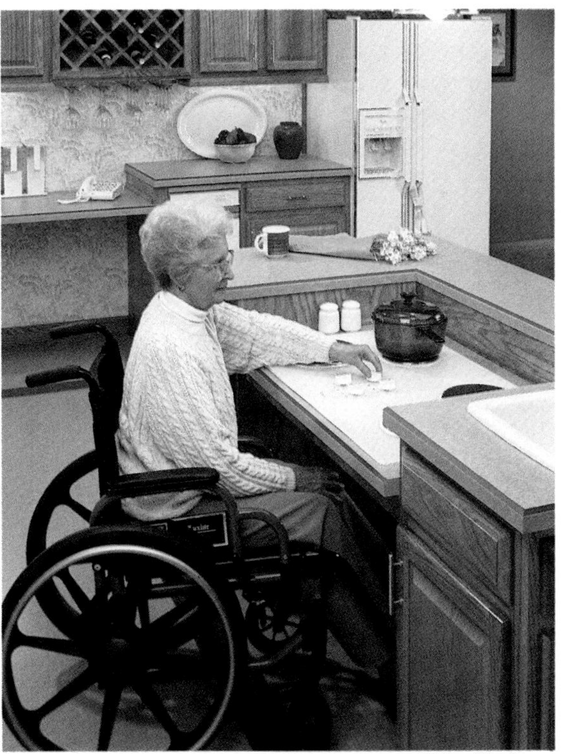

Whirlpool Appliances

20-16
Front controls on a gas or electric range make operation more convenient for people with physical disabilities.

- Avoid using similar colors together. Instead, use contrasting colors to separate items.
- Keep a consistent light level in bedrooms and halls. Use night-lights.
- Where appropriate, use Braille in cookbooks and on controls, 20-17.

The checklist in 20-18 will help you analyze how well the home is adapted for the needs of visually impaired persons.

The most common disability among older people is hearing loss. Hearing ability declines gradually, so a ***hearing-impaired*** person may have any degree of hearing loss. Hearing-impaired persons need communication systems that correspond to their level of deafness. Amplifying devices on doorbells and phones may be sufficient. People who are totally hearing impaired will need visual signals, 20-19.

Hand limitations result from arthritis and other conditions limiting movement and gripping ability. This calls for large lever-type controls on doors and faucets. Special faucets are also available with proximity sensors or electric eyes to turn them on and off, 20-20. Appliance knobs may need to be larger and thus easier to grasp and turn. Light switches that can be pressed are easier to use than those that must be moved up and down. On outside doors, keyless push-button locks are good.

Whirlpool Appliances

20-17
A Braille cookbook and Braille controls on the microwave help this visually impaired person to be more independent.

Checklist for Meeting Needs of Visually Impaired

__ Are raised number or letters used on entrance doors (especially in apartment dwellings)?
Note: These numbers should be at side of door near handle, 5 feet above floor.

__ Have all hanging objects under 6 feet, 2 inches (depending on height of the blind person) been eliminated?

__ Is there a minimum of low tables, stools, or other obstructions near major trafficways?

__ Are sliding doors used on closets and elsewhere to eliminate walking into an edge of a partially open door?

__ Are handles treated with knurling (or a special adhesive) on doors that lead directly to steps or other potentially dangerous areas?

__ Are all pushbutton controls identifiable by touch (such as *off* and *on* switches for lights)?

__ Are all control dials marked or shaped so fingers can feel location of dial and be able to interpret setting? (In some cases, click stops may be substituted).
  __ range
  __ oven
  __ mixer faucets

__ Is storage adequate, so that items can be stored separately (or like items on like) upon adjustable shelves–not piled high?

__ Are faucets in lavatories always arranged do the hot water faucet is on the left and the cold water faucet on the right of the user of the sink?

20-18
This checklist will help you see how well living spaces are adapted to the needs of those with visual impairment.

A person who has ***mobility impairment*** finds it difficult to walk from one place to another. Living spaces that are all on one level will eliminate the need for stair climbing. If stairs are unavoidable, they must be easy to use. They must have handrails and a nonskid surface. Risers and treads need to be lower and wider. See 20-21.

Some mobility-impaired persons can use a walker, 20-22; others require a wheelchair. Accessibility requirements change drastically when

Nutone

20-19
A visual signal, such as a lamp flashing on and off, can be used to signal the ringing of a telephone or doorbell to a deaf person.

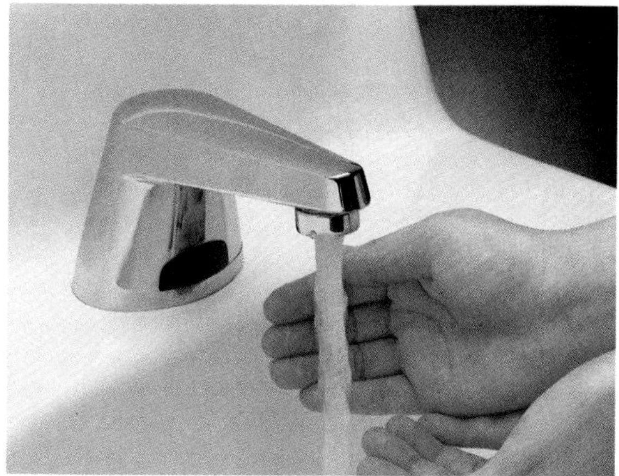

Kohler Co.

20-20
A proximity sensor turns the water on when a hand is placed under the faucet, and shuts off water flow when the hand is removed.

Azrock Industries, Inc., San Antonio, TX

20-21
Stairs in a building where a mobility impaired person lives should have short risers and a wide tread. They should be surfaces with a nonskid material.

Whirlpool Appliances

20-22
Certain changes must be made in a house or apartment to permit greater independence for persons who use walkers or wheelchairs.

the needs of a person using a walker or wheelchair must be taken into account.

The checklists in 20-23 will help you determine if your home is accessible and adaptable for persons with mobility impairment that requires use of a walker or wheelchair.

Often, even rented housing can be adapted for people with disabilities. Before you modify a rental unit, of course, check with the building owner. In one instance, a nurse studied an apartment to determine what changes would be needed for a person with multiple sclerosis. With only a few minor changes in the living space, the physically impaired person was able to live independently. The changes were:

- Moving the telephone, door latch, and heat controls so they could be reached from a wheelchair.
- Installing a built-up toilet seat.

Checklist for Home Adaptability

A home is considered adaptable if it has all or most of the following key structural features. These will allow reasonable entry and circulation without extensive modification:

- ☐ Located on relatively flat or level site with paved walkways from parking (covered is preferred) and sidewalk areas to level entry.
- ☐ A ground-level entrance or a one- or two-step entrance clear of any major obstructions, i.e. trees, building corners, etc., that would accept a ramp with a slope no greater than 1″ height per 12″ in length.
- ☐ No steps or abrupt level changes on main floor.
- ☐ Wider-than-standard doorways (32″ or more clear width).
- ☐ 1/2″ high maximum thresholds at doorways.
- ☐ Wide hallways at least 42″, preferably 48″-60″.
- ☐ At least one bathroom with a 32″ clear door opening.
- ☐ Clear 5′×5′ floor space in bathroom.
- ☐ A kitchen large enough for easy wheelchair mobility (U or L shaped or open plan preferred).

A

Checklist for Accessibility

This list will provide you with a measure of existing accessibility features. Not all of these features are necessary to meet the needs of a given individual with a disability. This checklist is intended to let people interested in accessibility features know if a given home warrants consideration.

- ☐ One-story building.
- ☐ Multi-level house with main level accessible entrance, bathroom, and bedroom.
- ☐ Level entryway, or ramp with entry level landing for easy door opening.
- ☐ Wide doorways (32″-36″ clear width).
- ☐ Wide hallways (42″-60″).
- ☐ Low-pile carpeting with thin padding.
- ☐ Chair-height (48″-54″) doorbell/mailbox.
- ☐ Chair-height electrical controls/outlets (excluding the kitchen, generally controls are 6″ lower and outlets are 6″ higher than standard).
- ☐ Chair-height push-button telephones/jacks.
- ☐ Accessible, easily operated window controls.

B

Easter Seal Society/Century 21

20-23
These checklists provide a method of measuring home adaptability (A) and accessibility (B) for people with physical disabilities.

- Installing grab bars on the bathtub, and putting a straight chair in the tub.
- Lubricating the windows, so they would be easy to open.
- Lowering a clothes rack.
- Trading the range for one with front controls.

Sometimes new products are introduced that are designed specifically to solve a problem for physically impaired persons. For example, a new type of bathtub is now available with a door in its side wall, 20-24. This allows easy entry for a person who might find it difficult or impossible to step over the rim of a traditional tub.

Ideally, a home should provide a quiet, peaceful, healthy environment for those who live and visit there. How would you rate your home?

Summary

A safe home provides freedom from accidents and offers security. Home accidents can happen to people of all ages. Special precautions should be taken to assure safety for older people, children, and people with disabilities.

Preventive measures can eliminate many falls and other accidents. They also can lessen the possibility of injury as a result of fire, burns, and electrical shock. Special considerations need to be taken when there are children in the home.

A healthy home environment will be free of air and noise pollution. You want to know about pollutants and how to reduce them or control their sources. Proper ventilation and wise use of cleaning methods and materials are steps toward having a healthy home. Noise inside a home can be controlled in various ways.

Your home can be made more secure by using protection and warning devices. You can reduce the possibility of injury or death from fire by installing smoke detectors and fire extinguishers. An emergency plan is important in case of the need to evacuate. Good locks and an alarm system will help make your home more secure. Marking valuables may deter theft, or make stolen items easier to recover.

Your home can be equipped so that people with disabilities are safe and secure. The equipment depends on the type of disability. Rental units as well as homes that are owned can be modified to meet the needs of people with disabilities.

Kohler Co.

20-24
The door on the side of this tub swings open for ease of entry by a physically impaired person. A special seal inflates to prevent leaks when the tub begins to fill with water.

To Review

Write your responses on a separate sheet of paper.

1. List three types of home accidents. Give two possible causes for each one. For each cause, describe a precaution that could have prevented the accident.
2. The victims of home accidents are most often the _____ and _____.
3. Name three health problems that may result from inside air pollution.
4. Compare the terms noise and sound. The unit of measure for sound is the _____.
5. List three products commonly found in the home that are considered hazardous.
6. Every home needs _____ and _____ to prevent injury from fire.
7. List five ways to make your home appear occupied when you are not there.
8. Give two guidelines that a child who is home alone should follow.
9. _____ locks should be used on exterior doors.
10. What is a monitoring device?
11. A good identifying number to use when marking your valuables is _____.
12. List three ways to make a home safe for people with disabilities.
13. List five conditions to check for accessibility in a home.

To Do

1. Find a newspaper article describing a home accident. Explain how the accident could have been prevented.
2. Find out how to use a fire extinguisher.
3. Write a report on radon, emphasizing how it affects housing choices.
4. Find and read two or three magazine or newspaper articles on inside air pollution. Report your findings to the class.
5. Design a brochure that gives guidelines for safety in the home.
6. Make a floor plan that shows the routes for fire escape from your house or apartment.
7. Make a safety checklist for your home.

CHAPTER 21

Maintaining Your Home

To Know

American Society of Interior Designers (ASID)
box nail
circuit breaker
finish nail
fuse
interior designer
redecorating
remodeling
short circuit

White Home Products

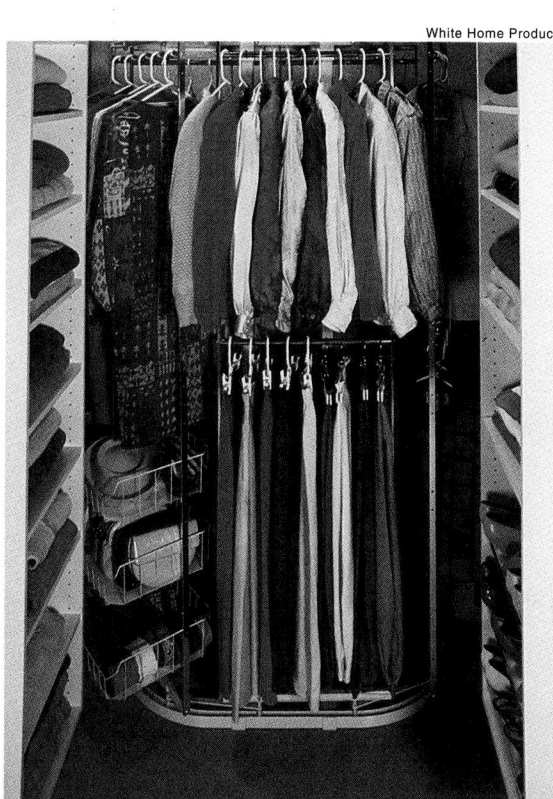

Objectives

After studying this chapter, you will be able to:

- Choose cleaning tools and products to keep your home clean.
- Make a schedule for house cleaning and yard maintenance.
- List basic tools for making home repairs.
- Make simple home repairs, including plumbing and electrical.
- Understand estimated life of house parts and appliances and need for replacement.
- List ways to improve storage and organize space.
- Choose redecorating methods.
- Understand advantages of remodeling.
- List resources for home care, maintenance, and improvements.

Maintaining a home involves keeping it clean and safe. It also involves making sure that equipment, electrical and plumbing systems, and other parts of the home are in proper working order. Maintenance is needed to keep the home environment secure and comfortable. You will use the decision-making process to choose how and to what level you maintain your home.

Keeping the Home Clean

Every house is different, and everyone has different standards of cleanliness. One person wants every part of a room spotless with each object in its place. Another person may not mind some clutter. When people share a home, they should come to an agreement on acceptable cleaning standards. The standards should be realistic. Everyone should be able to work together to meet the standards.

A certain minimum of standards is needed for the health and safety of family members. Garbage must be contained and removed from the dwelling regularly. If garbage is left for a long period of time, it can attract rats, roaches, and other insects. In addition, any items that cause odors should be removed or properly stored. This helps to keep the air fresh.

It is important to decide how much time you can devote to cleaning. Your decision affects your choices in home furnishings. For instance, if you don't want to spend much time cleaning, you would choose a floor covering that does not show soil readily. Also, you would not choose furniture and accessories that require much care. These would include items that tarnish and those made of fine woods.

Cleaning is easier if there is little clutter. Any room in your home can gather clutter. It can be taken care of in a number of ways. You can recycle many items such as newspapers and cans. Items that are obviously junk should be discarded. If you are like most people, you will keep some "treasures" even though they produce clutter.

Cleaning Tools

Cleaning chores are easier if you have the right equipment, or cleaning tools. There are two main types of cleaning tools. The first type is used to remove loose dust and dirt. These tools include the following:

- A broom and dustpan for sweeping hard floors and steps.
- A dust mop for picking up dust on hard floors.
- A vacuum cleaner with attachments for carpets, hard floors, woodwork, furniture, upholstery, and curtains.
- Cloths for dusting and polishing.

The second type of cleaning tool includes those tools used to remove soil that is stuck to surfaces. These include the following:

- A pail to hold cleaning solutions.
- A wet mop for cleaning floors.
- Sponges for washing walls, woodwork, and appliances.
- A toilet bowl brush.
- A stepladder or stool for reaching high places.

See 21-1 for a variety of cleaning tools.

Rubbermaid, Inc.

21-1
Tools and supplies for cleaning generally have a specific purpose.

Cleaning Products

Cleaning products include the chemicals that aid you in your cleaning tasks. The basic cleaning products you should always have on hand are:

- A glass cleaner that can be used for bathroom fixtures, counters, and kitchen appliances, as well as glass.
- A grease-cutting liquid.
- A mild abrasive powder.

Some cleaning agents and waxes and polishes are listed in 21-2. Most chemicals come in dry and liquid forms. Before you purchase any cleaning product, check your supplies. Look for those that can be used for more than one purpose. There are many multipurpose cleaning products. You may already have what you need.

You also must be aware of dangers associated with many cleaning products. Check labels to see if the products are toxic. Many cleaning compounds are poisonous or flammable. In addition, always read labels on cleaning products to make sure they will not damage the surface you are cleaning. Follow directions carefully. Finally, do not mix different cleaning products. Some products produce toxic gases when mixed with other cleaning compounds.

To help make cleaning easier, keep all cleaning items in an organized area. See 21-3. Always store cleaning products out of the reach of children or in locked cabinets. Keep cleaning products away from heat sources.

Cleaning Schedule

Some people have a high energy level. They may like to get their work done early in the day. Other people like to "sleep in" and work better at night. Some people like housework, others do not. Whatever your energy level or your work pattern,

Cleaning Products	
Cleaning Agents (Used to remove soil from surfaces.)	
Agent	**Method of Action**
Water	Dissolves and flushes away dirt.
Alkalies soaps washing sodas some general purpose cleaners	Break down surface tension of water, allowing water to penetrate and pick up dirt better.
Synthetic detergents	Relieve surface tension more than soaps to clean and cut grease better. Unlike soaps, detergents do not react with minerals to form scum deposits.
Acids ammonia vinegar lemon juice	Cut grease; act as a mild bleach.
Fat solvents	Dissolve soil held by grease.
Fat absorbents fuller's earth talcum bentonite cornmeal	Dry materials are sprinkled over oily soil. Agents absorb the oils; oils are brushed away with the absorbent.
Abrasives silver polish scouring powder steel wool soap pads	Rub dirt away with a scraping or polishing action. Used dry or with water depending on type.
Waxes and Polishes (Used to protect and add shine to surfaces.)	
Agent	**Method of Action**
Solvent-base cleaning waxes liquid wax paste wax	Used on hard floors. Loosen soil. Remove old coats of wax. Form new coating of wax.
Water-base cleaning waxes emulsion wax solution wax	Used on hard floors other than wood or cork. Lift out soil. Form new coating of wax. Do not remove old coats of wax; must use remover to strip floor occasionally.
Furniture polishes aerosol spray creamy liquid paste polishes	Lift out soil. Remove old coats of wax. Form new coating of wax.
Multipurpose cleaner waxes	Used on counter tops, tile, appliances, paneling, furniture, cabinets. Lift out soil. Remove old coats of wax. Form new coating of wax.

21-2
Using the proper cleaning agent for the job is important.

Quaker Maid

21-3
Storing cleaning supplies neatly in one place helps make cleaning easier.

setting up an agenda of cleaning tasks allows you to better use your cleaning time. A list of common tasks is shown in 21-4.

Your cleaning schedule may vary from day to day or week to week. It depends on the use of your facilities. The more often facilities are used, the greater the cleaning need. Less use usually means less cleaning. The larger the living unit, the greater the cleaning task.

When making a cleaning schedule, include the name of the person responsible for each task. Divide the tasks among household members.

Weekly cleaning tasks are easier if each family member helps with daily maintenance. For example, each person can be responsible for cleaning the bathtub or shower after bathing. An immediate wipe down should leave it clean. Supply a sponge, brush, squeegee, or towel. You may need to use a glass cleaner. Keep everything needed for the task in the bathroom.

Checklist for Cleaning

Daily Cleaning Tasks

___ Make bed.
___ Straighten up bedroom, bathroom, living, and eating areas.
___ Wash dishes.
___ Wipe kitchen counters and cooking surface; clean sink.
___ Sweep kitchen floor.
___ Empty wastebaskets, ashtrays, and other garbage containers.

Weekly Cleaning Tasks

___ Change bed linens.
___ Do laundry and mending.
___ Wash kitchen garbage pail or change liner.
___ Wash kitchen floor.
___ Clean bathroom sink, tub, and toilet.
___ Wash bathroom floor.
___ Dust accessories.
___ Dust and polish furniture.
___ Vacuum lampshades.
___ Vacuum carpet.
___ Shake out small rugs.

Monthly Cleaning Tasks

___ Vacuum and turn mattress.
___ Wash mattress pad.
___ Remove old wax and rewax hard floors.
___ Vacuum drapes, wipe blinds.
___ Vacuum upholstered furniture.
___ Wash windows and mirrors.
___ Clean and wax furniture.
___ Clean kitchen shelves.
___ Clean refrigerator (defrost if needed).
___ Clean range, including oven.
___ Wash bathroom walls.

Bi-yearly Cleaning Tasks

___ Clean closets.
___ Dry-clean or wash bedding.
___ Clean drapes thoroughly.
___ Wash seldom-used glasses and dinnerware.
___ Clean silverware.
___ Replace shelf paper.
___ Wash all walls.
___ Clean woodwork.

21-4
A checklist for your cleaning will help keep you on schedule.

Outdoor and Lawn Care

After you have spent time, money, and energy in making the outdoor living space attractive and inviting, you need to maintain it. You should make a maintenance schedule for that part of your environment. Some special tools will be needed to maintain the outdoor living space.

Tools for Outdoor Tasks

If you have a lawn, a lawn mower is probably the most expensive and most used outdoor tool. Most lawn mowers are powered by gasoline or electricity. The mower shown in 21-5 not only cuts grass, but shreds it for mulch. Since landfills are filling up, people are being encouraged to use clippings as mulch on grass or other plants. Many communities charge extra to accept yard waste. Some areas will not accept it at all.

Lawn trimmers and weed cutters are also powered tools. They are used for cutting down unwanted plants. Outdoor hand tools include pruning and lopping shears, shovels, rakes, and hoes.

Many yard tasks involve the use of tools that cut through plants or soil. This is true of all of the tools mentioned thus far. The more frequently you sharpen these tools, the easier they are to use. In addition, sharp tools are safer and less likely to damage plants. You may want to sharpen your tools yourself, or you can have them sharpened professionally.

Troy-Bilt

21-5
This mower not only cuts the grass, it shreds it for mulch.

Yard Maintenance

Yard maintenance should be scheduled according to the season. The specific outdoor tasks will vary depending upon where you live. In the fall, plant life may need to be winterized to withstand the cold winter months. Watering is continued, but fertilizing is stopped. Mulch is applied around the bases of trees, shrubs, and bushes. The mulch insulates the roots and helps to retain moisture. Sensitive plants, such as roses and some shrubs, may need to be wrapped for more protection from the cold.

Some bulbs, such as gladiolus, need to be dug after the leaves have dried. These bulbs can be replanted in the spring. Other bulbs, which bloom in the spring, need to be planted in the fall. Bulbs that bloom in the spring generally are not dug and replanted. Perennials need the dead foliage removed after the first killing frost.

While the winter chill is still in the air, it is time to prune and trim most trees and shrubs. Your trees and shrubs will last many years with proper care. The care is generally easy. Long-handled lopping shears are the best tool for pruning and trimming.

At the first sign of sprouting in the spring, the roses and other plants should be uncovered. As soon as the ground is thawed, it is time to begin watering and fertilizing. This is also time to plant or replant summer-blooming bulbs and flower seeds. You can divide and set out perennials at this time.

When watering your plants and lawn, it is better to water thoroughly and less often than to underwater often. Thorough watering encourages deeper root growth. The soil should remain moist between eight and 12 inches under the ground. Keeping a mulch around plants will inhibit weed growth as well as retain the moisture in the ground. If plants begin to wilt, it is usually an indication that watering is needed. Watering once every three to six days is considered plenty. However, the age of the plants, the soil characteristics, and the weather are all factors in determining your watering schedule.

A lawn requires regular care from spring to late summer. Like other plants, lawns need regular watering and inspection for pests and diseases. A green carpet of lawn is very inviting.

Weeds compete for space, moisture, and nutrients in the lawn. They are also unsightly. Weeds can be eliminated by hand weeding or by chemical methods. Any products that are used in yard care should be carefully used. Like household cleaning products, yard care products may be poisonous. Use and store them according to directions.

Mowing the grass is a critical part of lawn care. If you mow the grass in a diagonal direction, you will prevent a striped look. Change directions each time you mow. Mowing the lawn too closely will prevent the development of a healthy root system. A general rule is to cut only the top third of the grass, 21-6.

Your mowing schedule is related to the rate your grass grows. It will vary from 5 to 14 days, depending on whether the season is wet or dry.

Making Home Repairs

Keeping a home safe and comfortable requires regular care and maintenance. Homeowner maintenance includes the inspection and repairs needed to keep the home safe and to prolong the life of the house. You can often do the repairs yourself with the right tools and some basic knowledge of the item needing repair.

In cases where your knowledge is limited, you may want to hire a professional to do the work. Electrical or gas repairs can be dangerous. Utility companies normally have professional service people handle home repairs. Even the best do-it-yourself person needs to call on a skilled professional from time to time.

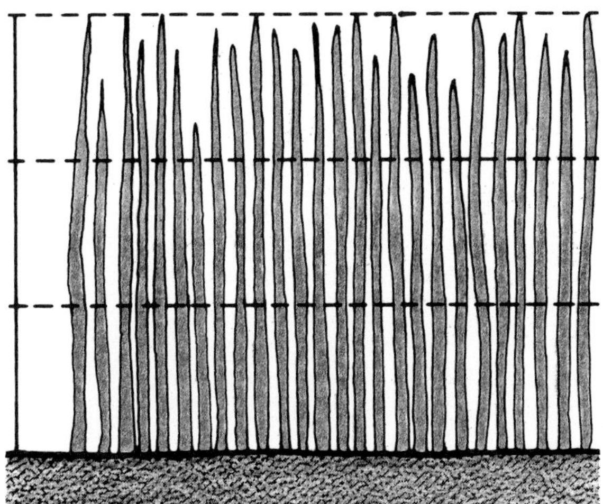

21-6
Grass grows green on top and turns brown near the base. You should cut only the top third of the blades.

The Basic Tools

Tools can be expensive. You should buy quality tools because they last longer. Consider shopping around or buying from discount stores. You can build your supply of tools by buying only what you need. To get the right tool for your job, ask for advice where you shop. The following are the basic tools you will need. Some of these tools are shown in 21-7.

Hammer. A general purpose 16 ounce model with a curved claw is used for driving and pulling nails and other tasks. The curved claw provides leverage when pulling nails. The medium-weight head performs finish work as well as rough work.

Screwdrivers. A screwdriver is used for driving and removing screws. You need a *straight blade screwdriver* and a *Phillips tip screwdriver.* Both come in various sizes. The blade of a screwdriver should fit the slot in the screw.

Adjustable wrench. A wrench is used to tighten and loosen nuts and bolts. This tool is adjustable, so it will fit nuts of different sizes. If a nut is hard to turn, apply a few drops of a lubricant. Let it soak from two hours to overnight. If the wrench slips off the nut, turn the wrench over.

Plumbing plunger. The plunger (force cup) is called the plumber's friend because it will often clear a blocked drain. There are two types. A molded plunger is used for curved surfaces, such as the toilet bowl. The flat plunger is for surfaces like sinks, showers, and tubs.

Side-cutting pliers. These are sometimes called linesman's pliers by electricians. They are used for cutting wire and removing insulation from wire. Take care to not cut into the wire when removing the insulation.

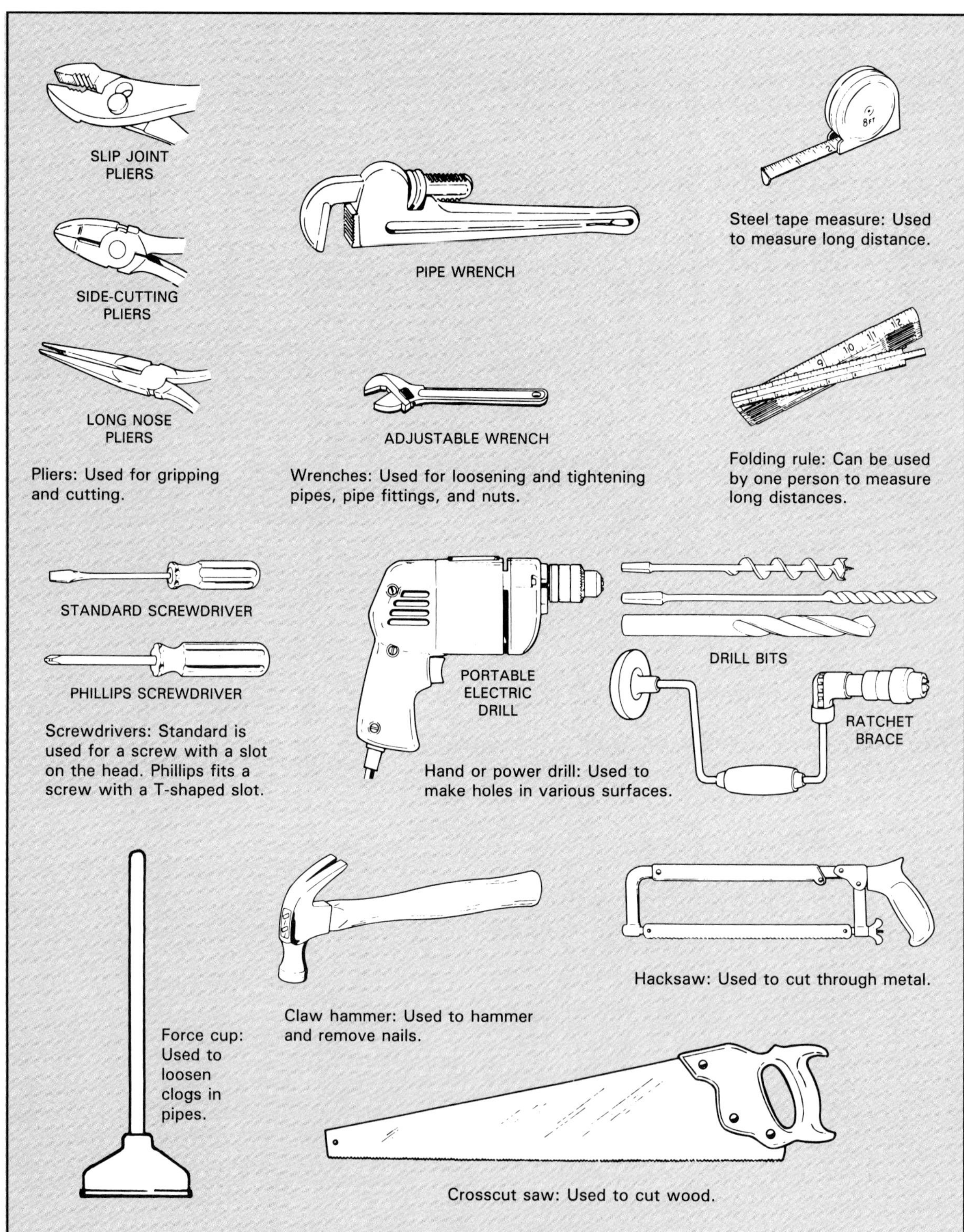

21-7
These basic tools will help you handle many household maintenance tasks.

Long-nose pliers. These pliers are appropriate for bending wire and positioning small components into close and difficult work areas. This tool is not a substitute for a wrench to tighten small nuts.

Tape measure. Choose a retractable tape measure that is at least 16 feet long and three-fourths inch wide. There is a wide range of measuring tapes on the market. A common choice has a thumb lock to keep the tape from retracting when in use.

Channel-lock pliers. Sometimes called slip-joint pliers, this is a handy tool for tightening nuts and bolts. This basic plumbing tool is also used for holding pipe.

Pipe wrench. The pipe wrench is a holding tool for assembling fittings on pipe. Teeth are set at an angle in one direction. The teeth are designed to grip a rounded fitting firmly and produce a ratchet effect. This effect makes the wrench grip in only one direction.

Hacksaw. The hacksaw is a general purpose tool for cutting metal. The hacksaw can cut pipe from one side, cutting as it is pushed forward.

Crosscut saw. This saw, used to cut across the grain of the wood, can also be used as a general purpose saw for sheeting materials such as plywood. Of the many types available, a ten-point crosscut, one that has 10 points per inch of saw blade, works well for most purposes.

Electric drill. An electric drill is a light-duty tool for drilling holes. It can also be used as a nut/screwdriver and a light-weight buffer or grinder. The size of a drill is determined by the drill chuck. The chuck is the clamping device that holds the drill bit. Common sizes are one-fourth inch and three-eighths inch. For versatility, you need a three-eighths inch chuck, variable speed, and a reversible motor.

You need a variety of drill bits for your electric drill. Straight-shank drill bits will drill holes in metal and wood. They are sized by diameter in one of three systems: fractional, decimal, and letters. Fractional drills are common for home repairs.

Closet auger. When there is blockage in the toilet caused by cloth or some other item that should be retrieved, the closet auger is a useful tool. In some cases blockage is caused by a comb, pencil, or some other object that cannot be retrieved. Then you can usually force the object through the piping by using the closet auger and plumbing plunger alternately.

Electric tester. Electrical circuits can be tested safely with an electrical tester (neon tester). Most hardware stores sell this item. It is inexpensive. The tester is designed to light up in the presence of 110 volts and 220 volts. To use, firmly press each lead against the terminals. If the circuit is "hot", the light will go on.

Flashlight. This tool rounds out the tools needed for basic home repairs. A two-cell unit is sufficient. An industrial rated flashlight will prove most durable.

Toolbox. Metal or plastic toolboxes are affordable and come in a variety of sizes and shapes. The main purpose of a toolbox is to keep your tools in the same location for use when repairs are necessary.

Plumbing Repairs

Plumbing problems can occur in any home at any time. Some problems come on suddenly, such as when an item is accidentally dropped into a toilet. Other problems develop over time. Drains become sluggish or faucets and pipes begin to leak. Certain problems can result in water damage to parts of the home, adding to the repair costs. If you can handle minor plumbing repairs yourself, you can save the expense and inconvenience of hiring a plumber. One of the most common problems is a clogged drain. Pipes tend to clog when foreign matter finds its way into waste lines.

Clogged drains. The most common cause of a clogged drain is foreign matter, such as grease and hair, in the drainage system. Stoppages in the drainage system rarely occur in straight, horizontal, or vertical runs of piping. They usually occur where two pipes are joined together with a fitting, creating a change of direction. Stoppages may also occur in the trap, 21-8. A *trap* is a fitting or device that provides a liquid seal to prevent sewer gases from coming back into the home.

If a drain is *partially* clogged, one method of cleaning it is to use a chemical drain cleaner. Drain cleaners come in liquid or crystal form. Liquid drain cleaners are heavier than water and settle into the trap to dissolve grease, food, soap, and hair. Crystal cleaners in granular form begin the chemical cleaning process when they come in contact with the water in the trap.

Use these chemicals with caution. These chemicals are poison. They are also caustic, which means they will burn your skin. Wear protective gloves and keep you face away from the drain opening. Carefully read the directions on each container. Use acid drain cleaners to dissolve soap and hair. Alkalis cut grease. Do not mix chemical cleaners as they may form a toxic gas.

If a drain is completely clogged, chemical cleaners may not work. The tool to use in this case is a flat plumbing plunger, as shown in 21-9.

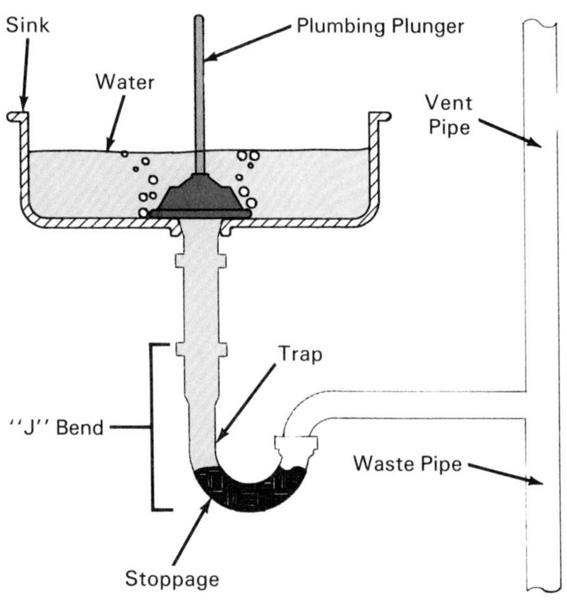

21-8
Since there is a curve in the trap, stoppage is likely to occur here.

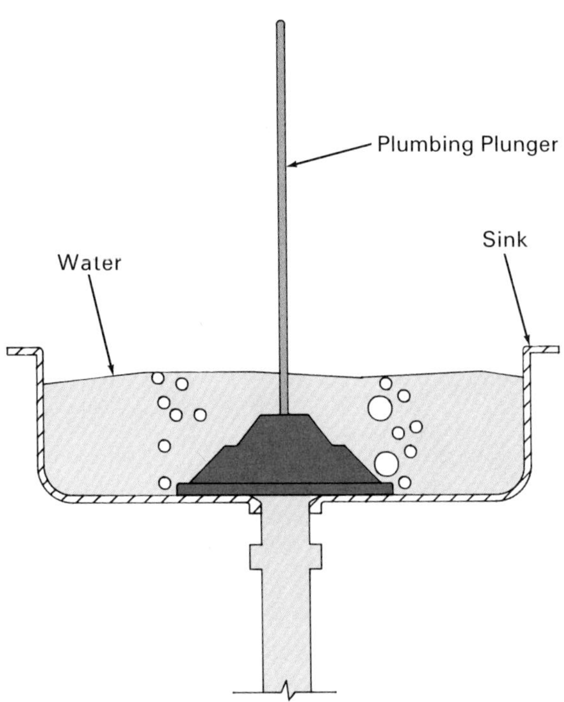

21-9
A plunger is pumped up and down to form a suction and a surge in the drain.

First remove the basket strainer in the sink waste outlet. If it is a double compartment sink, plug the other waste outlet with a rag to prevent loss of pressure in the drain. Place the flat force cup of the plunger directly over the drain opening. Two inches of standing water will provide the necessary seal for the force cup to take hold. Grip the plunger handle firmly with both hands and push down with a slow, even pressure. Pull up quickly and repeat the process several times. This will unstop most sink drains.

If the stoppage still exists, try a flexible spring cable. Place a container under the trap. Loosen two nuts on the trap and remove the "J" bend. Use a small auger with a one-fourth inch spring cable. Feed the cable slowly into the drain pipe. Rotate the cable as you feed it. Turn the handle until the obstruction is broken up. See 21-10. When finished, remove the cable, replace the "J" bend, and tighten the nuts. Flush the drain with hot water and check for leaks.

When a toilet is clogged, try to determine the cause of the stoppage. If the substance will not cause additional blockage when forced into the

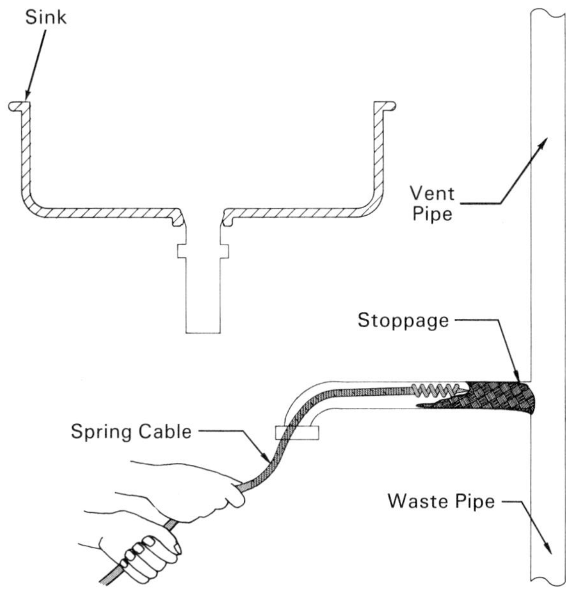

21-10
The auger, which has a flexible spring cable, may need to be placed near the blockage to remove it.

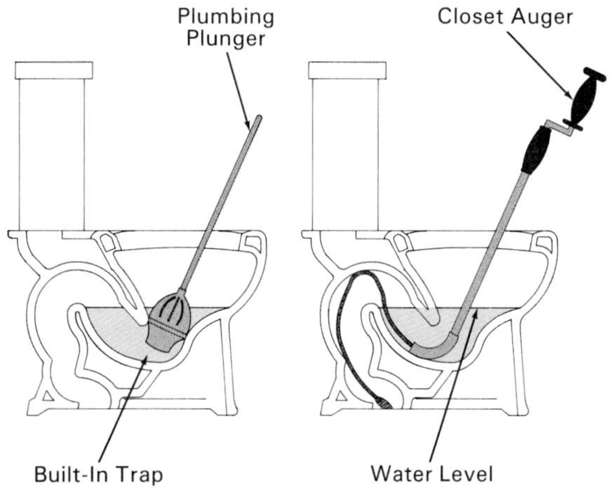

21-11
Both the plumbing plunger and the auger may be needed for toilet blockage.

drainage system, use the molded plunger. If material, such as a diaper, caused the stoppage, use the closet auger. Since an auger has a flexible spring cable, it can make sharp turns in a drain.

For certain items you may need to use the plunger and auger in alternating sequence. Compare the two methods in 21-11. Should these methods fail, the only solution is to remove the toilet and retrieve the object from the underside. If the toilet is removed, the rubber or wax ring that serves as a seal must be replaced.

Installing Nails and Screws

Nails and screws are fastening devices. Each has special uses in household repairs. Nails can be driven easily, but may be difficult to remove. Screws can be removed easily.

Nails come in two basic shapes. ***Finish nails*** have a very small head. You can drive them below the surface by using a tool called a nail set or with another nail. Holes can be filled with wood filler or putty. Use finish nails when appearance is important. Putting up paneling or building shelves are two examples. ***Box nails*** have large, flat heads. Use them for rough work when appearance is less important.

To drive nails, use one hand to hold the nail in place and the other to start the nail into the surface. Drive the nail holding the hammer by the handle. When the nail is secure, drive the nail until the head is seated on the surface, leaving no mark on the surface.

If you are placing nails or screws in walls, location on the wall is important. To secure heavy objects, place fasteners where a stud is behind the wall surface. Studs are the upright boards in the framing of the wall. This allows the fastener to be driven into the wood of the stud for additional support. See 21-12. You can find studs by tapping on the walls lightly. You will hear a hollow sound between studs. When you tap a stud, the sound will be lighter and more solid. You can also purchase inexpensive stud-sensing devises at any hardware store. After you find one stud, you can find others by measuring 16 inch intervals to the left or right.

To install a wood screw, drill a pilot hole. Use the proper type of screwdriver (Phillips or straight) for the screw. Try to match the size of the screwdriver to the head of the screw. Undersizing the screwdriver makes the task more difficult and can damage the screw head.

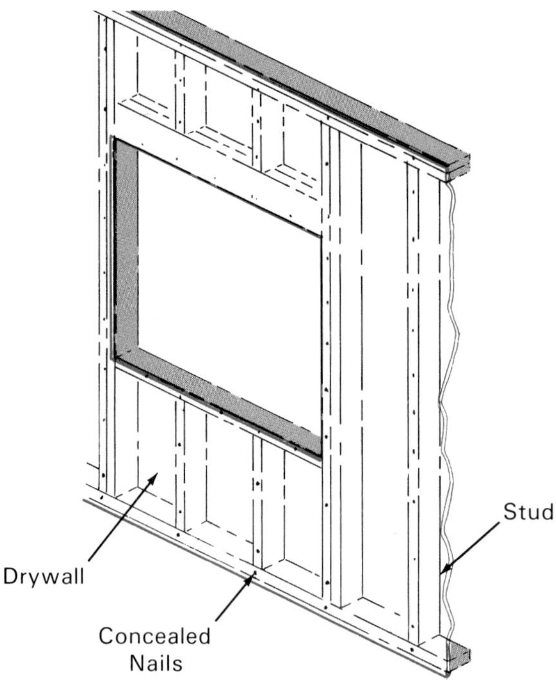

21-12
Studs are placed 16 inches apart behind walls. Find a stud before hanging anything heavy on the wall.

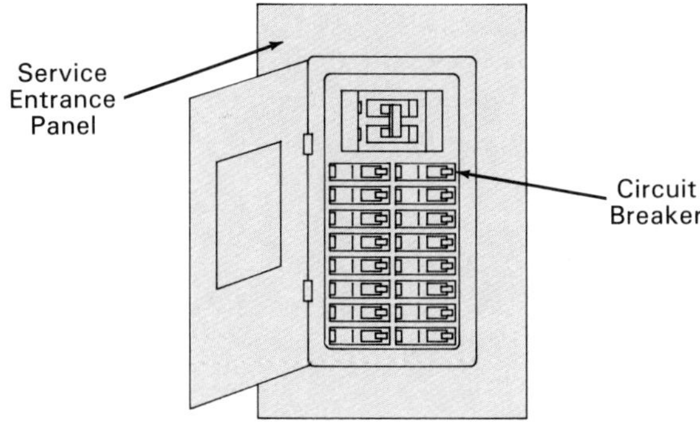

21-13
The service entrance panel monitors the electrical system for the house.

Electrical Repairs

When electricity enters a house, the wires are connected into the service entrance panel. Service entrance panels contain either circuit breakers or fuses. Circuit breaker entrance panels are more common than panels with fuses, 21-13. If any circuit in your house is overloaded with appliances or other electric items, the fuses or circuit breakers cut off the power. This prevents damage to wiring and possible electrical fires.

A ***short circuit*** is probably the most common cause of electrical problems. It is an undesirable current path that allows the electrical current to bypass the load of the circuit. Sometimes the short occurs between two wires due to faulty insulation. It can also occur between a wire and a grounded object, such as a metal frame on an appliance. If an arc occurred with the short, a black carbon deposit will show where the short occurred. A short must be repaired before a breaker is reset or a fuse is replaced.

Circuit breakers. A ***circuit breaker*** is a switch that automatically interrupts an electrical current under an abnormal condition. The switch on each breaker switches to the "off" position when a problem occurs. This disconnects the power.

Usually a circuit breaker goes off when the circuit is overloaded. This happens when too many electrical appliances are used at one time. Disconnect some appliances before restoring electricity to the circuit. To restore the electricity, move the handle of the circuit to the "reset" position, then to the "on" position. The "reset" position is usually on the opposite side of the "on" position.

Fuses. A ***fuse*** is the simplest device for opening an electric circuit when an overload occurs. You must replace the fuse to restore power. There are two types of fuses–plugs and cartridges. Plug fuses screw into the entrance panel like light bulbs. A plug fuse has a clear window with a metal strip across it. The metal strip is called a fuse link. When current level exceeds the rating of the fuse, the link melts and a gap is formed. The result is a broken circuit with no flow of current.

To replace a plug fuse, remove the main fuse or turn off the connection switch. This will disconnect all power, so a flashlight may be needed. Locate the blown fuse. The window of a blown fuse is black or the fuse link is broken.

Cartridge fuses are held in place by spring clips. These fuses often show no sign of being blown. If the power is off, follow the same steps as in replacing a plug fuse. Always replace the blown fuse with a new one of the exact size. To avoid electrical shock, stand on a dry surface and be sure your hands are dry.

Wall switches. All types of electrical switches can wear out as they get older. Do not attempt to replace a wall switch unless you know how to do so. Electric shocks can occur.

To replace a wall switch, 21-14, turn off the power at the service entrance. Remove the screws and the cover plate to the wall switch. Carefully pull the switch and wires out from the box. To check if the power is off, use a voltage tester. Place one of the voltage tester leads against each screw on the switch. The tester should show a voltage level of zero.

With the power off, loosen the two screws and remove the two black wires. If there are more than the usual two black wires, make a sketch of the way the wires are attached to the switch. Reattach the wires to the new switch. Hook up the new switch securely. Place the new switch in the switch box and attach with screws. Replace the cover plate. Turn on the power and test the switch.

Power cord plugs. For the safety of members of the living unit, replace damaged or worn electric plugs before using them. When replacing a plug on a flat two-wire cord, use a snap-down plug.

To attach the snap-down plug, lift the top clamp. Slit the cord apart to one-fourth inch from the end of the cord. Push the cord into the plug, and tightly close the clamp. Test the cord to see that it works. Hold the plug after use to make sure it is not overheating.

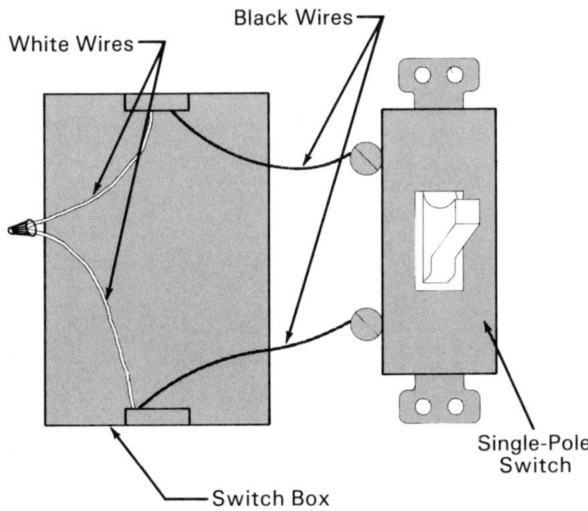

21-14
Take extra precaution when repairing electrical switches. Be sure the electricity is off.

Making Replacements

Home maintenance includes more than making repairs. It includes replacing the parts of your house that are worn out or obsolete. It includes replacing appliances that are no longer worth repairing.

All parts of your house can be expected to function for a certain number of years before they need to be replaced. Research has determined about how many years you can expect major household parts and appliances to function. This is referred to as life expectancy. If you know the life expectancy of the various parts of your house and your appliances, you can plan for replacements. Study 21-15 to see when various items may need to be replaced and how much these might cost.

Meeting Storage Needs

If your home is small, you need to make the most of your space. Having organized storage helps you make more room in your living spaces. It also makes finding stored items easier.

Organize for Storage

You can reorganize closets in many ways using a variety of storage devices, 21-16. These can make it easier to use your storage space.

Adding shelf space above the hanging rod in a closet is helpful. In most closets there is only one shelf and it is about half the width of the closet. To triple your shelf space, get two more boards and cut to the size of the existing shelf. Fit one in place just in front of the one already there. You may need to extend the frame or base on which it rests. The other shelf can be placed between the first shelf and the ceiling. You will need to put a base in place for it. The shelves need not be nailed in place. If you move, the boards can go with you.

Space under a stairway or at the end of a hall or room can often be converted to storage. You

When Your House Will Fall Apart

Listed below are the estimated life expectancies for all major household parts and appliances, and the cost of replacing them.

Household Item	Life Expectancy	Replacement Cost
Chimney & Liner	100 years	$4,500-$12,000
Siding	40 years	$8,000-$20,000
Toilet	35 years	$300+
Septic System	30 years	$3,000-$12,000
Bathtub/Tile	25 years	$1,500+
Asphalt Shingle Roof	25 years	$1.15-$3.50 per sq.ft.
Vinyl Kitchen Floor	25 years	$3-$12 per sq.ft.
Plumbing	20-60 years	$1,500-$4,000
Oven/Range	20 years	$800-$1,200
Hot-air Furnace	18 years	$1,000-$2,000
Bathroom Basin	16 years	$200-$350
Asphalt Driveway	15 years	$2-$3 per sq.ft.
Wood Deck	15 years	$10-$15 per sq.ft.
Refrigerator	14 years	$600-$1,000
Washer and Dryer	13 years	$650-$800
Dishwasher	12 years	$600-$1000
Faucets	12 years	$150+
Central Air-conditioning	11 years	$800-$2,000
Garbage Disposal	10 years	$150-$400
Garage-door Opener	10 years	$300-$450
Water Heater	10 years	$350-$800
Exterior Paint	5 years	$1,000-$2,500
Sump Pump	5 years	$150-$250
Carpet	Indefinite	$25-$60 per sq.ft.

Kiplinger's Personal Finance Magazine, copyright Nov., 1991. The Kiplinger Washington Editors, Inc.

21-15
The various parts of a house and the appliances within all have a certain life expectancy. This information will help you plan replacements.

can buy ready-to-use shelves or other storage items for this space, 21-17. They can be purchased in components, so you can adapt them to the space that exists. You can also build your own storage units.

Often utility rooms and garages have poorly-organized storage space. Shelves can make storage in these areas more efficient. Some

Closet Works

21-16
Storage areas can be organized in many ways to meet your needs.

types of shelves can be attached to the ceiling joists (wood boards that support the ceiling) as shown in 21-18.

Shelves can also be placed in window nooks and over radiators. Shelf arrangements on bare walls provide open storage for displays.

White Home Products

21-17
Ready-made storage pieces like these can turn unused space into an efficient storage area.

The Hirsh Co.

21-18
Shelves, such as this, add storage space to garages and work areas.

Racks can be attached to doors or walls. They can hold magazines, books, or supplies.

Cardboard storage boxes come in many sizes and styles. Many have drawers or doors. Some fit under beds; others will fit in small spaces throughout the house. They can also be used to organize closet storage. Boxes can be painted, papered, or covered with fabric to match room decor.

Hooks and poles can be used for some types of storage. They are popular for hanging coats. They can be used in bathrooms to hang towels and bathroom supplies. (The supplies can be placed in buckets or plastic bags with handles.)

Space Savers

Many furniture pieces are designed to help save space. A sofa bed and a daybed are two such pieces. They double as sofas and beds, 21-19. This saves room if you don't have space for both.

You can replace your regular bed frame with a platform that has drawers. This provides storage and sleeping space in the same area. You can also use stacking beds in a children's room to save space.

Masco Corporation/Scholz Design Architects

21-19
To save space, daybeds can double as couches.

Stacking chairs and folding chairs are other types of space-saving furniture. Padded chests used for seating and storage also save space.

A drop-leaf table takes up little space when the leaves are down. It can easily be expanded when extra space is needed. You can build a hinged table surface or desk that is attached to the wall. It can have legs that fold out or a hinged support that swings out from the wall. The table lies flat against the wall when it is not being used. Other household furniture and equipment can be mounted to the wall to save space.

In the kitchen, lost space can be regained by using small appliances that are installed on the wall or hung under kitchen cabinets. Many smaller appliances are available to be used where space is at a premium.

Well-organized storage helps make living easier. It keeps your living spaces from becoming too cluttered. Having enough storage helps you make the most of your housing.

Redecorating

Some time after you have decorated for the first time, you will probably want to change your decorating scheme. This is called ***redecorating.*** Parts of your home may look out of fashion. Some furnishings may be worn. You may just be tired of a room and ready for a change. As your life situation changes, so will your needs and values. In turn, you may redecorate part or all of your home to meet your needs and values.

Redecorating is different from decorating because you already have a base from which to start. If you decorated wisely the first time, there should be several items that you will want to keep when you redecorate. Old and new items do not need to match. They only need to agree.

Use the same steps in planning to redecorate that you used to decorate. Planning is important if you are to find new items that blend with the old. Determine what you want to keep and what you want to replace. Evaluate why you want to get rid of items. You may find that some can be kept with a few changes. For instance, your sofa may be sturdy, but you may not like its color or pattern. Reupholstering may satisfy your decorating needs at a lower cost than replacing the sofa. This is especially true if you can do the work yourself.

You may decide to keep more of what you have after you explore the possibilities of making them look good. Look at 21-20 to see how you can have bathroom fixtures renewed. Sometimes what you already have can be redone to meet your needs.

You may redecorate in a single stage, or you can redecorate in a series of stages spread over time. Time and money limits may cause you to take this approach. After you decide what you want to change, you can divide your project into stages. For instance, to redecorate the living room, you may replace the carpet as one stage.

Perma Ceram Enterprises, Inc.

21-20
These "before" and "after" pictures show how a bathtub can be refinished by a professional.

Changing the curtains may be another stage. Replacing some of the furniture and accessories could be another stage. Your priorities and budget will help you determine the order of the stages.

Remodeling

Remodeling is usually more expensive than redecorating. This is because it involves changes to the structure, such as adding a wall or a room. There are times when remodeling is more of a bargain than moving or trying to live in your home the way it is.

Remodeling may improve what is already there, like redoing the kitchen or basement, 21-21. Usable space such as a family room or a garage may be added. You may enclose a porch or build a patio. Some kinds of remodeling increase the market value of your home. Other remodeling gives you more satisfaction, but does not increase the value of the home.

The cost of remodeling is measured in many ways. You need to ask yourself if the cost of remodeling is a better value than moving or keeping your living space the same. Will remodeling increase the quality of life in your home? Will the process cause too many inconveniences for the members of your living unit? Adding a room is not likely to be as inconvenient as remodeling the kitchen or bathroom. Will you remodel, then realize that you need to move anyway?

You also need to decide whether to use professionals or do the work yourself. You can save about half the money by remodeling yourself. However, the work could take you twice as long or longer. If your project is not too complex and you know what you are doing, remodeling yourself may be worthwhile. If tasks like rewiring and adding plumbing are involved, you may be better off hiring a professional. You may do some tasks yourself and hire people for others, or you may have a remodeling service do the whole job.

Getting Your Money's Worth

Do your homework before you start a remodeling project. This will help you avoid making changes that cost you more than they are worth. Start by researching information about remodeling products, trends in design, and financing. Get estimates on how much your remodeling project

Georgia-Pacific Corp.

21-21
This family has increased its living space by remodeling the basement.

will cost. If you need a home improvement loan, shop to find the best rate. Consider whether you will regain the costs of remodeling when you sell your house. See 21-22.

If you decide to use a contractor to do your remodeling, select carefully. Find out answers to these questions:

- Is the contractor licensed? By whom?
- How long has the contractor been in business?
- How have other clients felt about the contractor's work? (Ask the contractor for references or find names of clients at the local building department.)
- Will the contractor show you a similar completed project?
- Does the contractor have insurance coverage for all workers?
- Will the contractor give you lien waivers to show that supplies and subcontractors used for the project have been paid? (A lien waiver prevents you from being held liable if your contractor does not pay for items used to remodel your house.)

Do not pay for the entire remodeling project until all of the work is finished the way you want it. The best arrangement is to pay 25 percent of the total fee before work starts. Pay the rest after the project is finished and you have inspected all the work. Contractors are more likely to complete a project the way you want it if they are waiting to be paid.

As you make your remodeling plan, keep your neighborhood in mind. Keep your improvements in line with nearby houses. Try not to raise the value of your home more than 20 percent over the value of neighboring homes. If you do, you may not be able to get the full value when you sell your house.

Consider adding features that conserve energy when you remodel. Such features are bargains because they lower your monthly energy

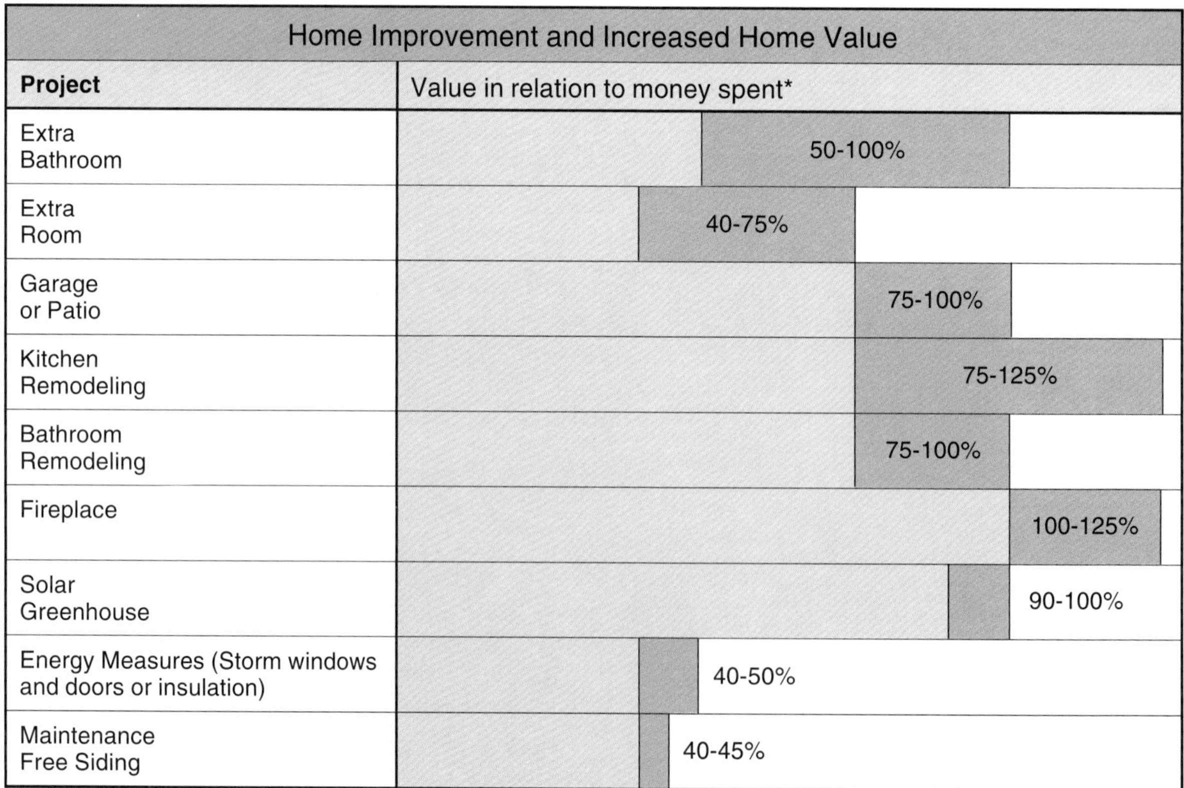

Home Improvement and Increased Home Value	
Project	Value in relation to money spent*
Extra Bathroom	50-100%
Extra Room	40-75%
Garage or Patio	75-100%
Kitchen Remodeling	75-125%
Bathroom Remodeling	75-100%
Fireplace	100-125%
Solar Greenhouse	90-100%
Energy Measures (Storm windows and doors or insulation)	40-50%
Maintenance Free Siding	40-45%

*This means you can regain this much of your costs if you sell your house. There will be some loss in value as the house becomes older.

21-22
Remodeling improves your home. It can also increase your home's value.

bills. They also increase the resale value of your home. You may remove a drafty window and replace it with a wall or with an insulating window. Insulating windows provide a view, and they insulate better than standard windows, 21-23. You may add insulation to your walls or replace old doors with insulating doors as you remodel. You may also replace older appliances with other models that use less energy.

Resources for Home Care, Maintenance, and Improvements

There are resources for you to use if you need help in maintaining your home. Resource people can offer advice, or they can do the work for you. You might seek both advice and help with the work.

Help with Home Care and Maintenance

If you don't have the help you need in your family, or their time is limited, you can hire people to clean for you. House cleaning services have employees that work by the hour, by the day, or by the job. You contract with the service rather than with the employee. You can also hire people who do not work for a cleaning service. They set their own rates.

The cost of house cleaning services varies according to the size and location of your house. Your cost can be decreased if you provide the cleaning products and tools.

If you hire a cleaning service, it is important that you ask what services will be provided. You may have to find someone else or pay more for certain cleaning tasks. For instance, window-washing is not usually considered part of a weekly cleaning service.

You can also hire someone to help with outside maintenance. You may have someone mow your lawn and trim the trees and shrubs. You can employ the services of commercial landscaping companies or those who do yard maintenance on a regular basis. They can do complete maintenance, or you can schedule what part you want them to do.

Marvin Windows & Doors

21-23
Remodeling improves your home. It can also increase your home's value.

Help with Decorating Decisions

There are professional services to help you decorate or redecorate. An ***interior designer*** can plan your decorating, make purchases for you, and see that the work is done correctly. A designer will save you time and help you avoid costly mistakes. A designer also has contacts that you cannot make on your own, such as sources for the furnishings you want.

Interior designers are paid for their knowledge and services. Members of the ***American Society of Interior Designers (ASID)*** are required to have a high level of preparation and training. You may want to ask about professional training and membership before using a designer's services.

Only you can decide how much help you want from a designer and how much you want to do on your own. Most designers expect to do the bulk of the planning and let the client do some of the purchasing. Determine your needs, and then identify the work you want the designer to do.

You can also use the services of a decorator who is employed by a furniture store. No charges are made for this service, but you are expected to purchase some furniture from the store.

Knowing what you want will help you communicate your desires to a professional. You will be the one living with the decisions, so make your wishes known.

Remodeling Services

Some contractors specialize in remodeling projects. If you do not want to do the work yourself, you may engage a contractor to remodel. As discussed earlier, use a licensed contractor and one who will guarantee the work. If you choose to do it yourself, you can save money. Be sure you have the necessary time and skills for the remodeling jobs.

Other Resources

You can learn more about how to maintain your home yourself. A neighbor or a longtime gardener may be a good resource for you. Courses are offered at community colleges and technical schools on home maintenance. You can learn about the use of tools and other aspects of home maintenance. You can buy books and magazines or go to the local library. Newspapers often feature articles pertaining to home maintenance. Clip the articles, and start your own resource file.

Summary

The first step in maintaining your home is to keep it clean. The proper tools and cleaning products are important. Tools and cleaning products need proper care and storage.

You can involve other members of your living unit in the maintenance tasks. A cleaning schedule helps you get the tasks done. You will need the schedule that is right for you.

Yard maintenance also requires some tools and products. Outdoor maintenance can be scheduled by the seasons. Much of the maintenance needs to be done in the fall and the spring. Other tasks are done on a regular basis during the growing season.

The right tools can speed up home repairs. Basic tools and a knowledge of their use can help you in making simple plumbing and electrical repairs. Safety factors are important as you make repairs. Not only repairs, but also replacements are a part of home maintenance.

Meeting storage needs and organizing storage space can simplify home maintenance. Some ideas for storage are easy to do and cost very little. Many of them tell you how to save space.

Redecorating and remodeling have their place in home maintenance. Both are more likely to be satisfactory if a plan is made and followed. There are a number of helpful resources for redecorating and remodeling, as well as for other home maintenance. You can do the work yourself or employ the assistance of people outside your home.

To Review

Write your responses on a separate sheet of paper.

1. True or False. Brooms and vacuum cleaners are the best tools for removing soil that is stuck to surfaces.
2. The three basic cleaning products are _____, _____, and _____.
3. What is the advantage of a cleaning schedule?
4. When mowing the grass, it is important to mow it at a certain length because _____.
5. True or False. Watering and fertilizing are parts of yard maintenance.
6. List five home repairs that you are likely to need.
7. Name five basic tools needed for home repairs and give their uses.
8. Name two methods of cleaning a clogged drain.
9. Describe the difference between finish nails and box nails.
10. What is an electrical short circuit?
11. Name five places where you can add shelves to increase storage space.
12. True or False. To redecorate, you must change all of the backgrounds, furnishings, and accessories in a room.
13. True or False. Remodeling is usually more expensive and complex than redecorating.
14. Give three guidelines to follow when remodeling.
15. List three resources to help you in maintaining your home.

To Do

1. Set up a cleaning agenda for your home. Use the checklist in 21-4 as a guideline. Then list the cleaning tools and supplies needed to perform the tasks on your agenda.
2. As a class, visit a hardware store. Have the manager describe some of the tools and supplies. Have the manager demonstrate how to use some basic tools.
3. Demonstrate to the class a simple home repair.
4. Make a model of a well-organized storage closet.
5. Compare prices on a piece of storage furniture. Go to different stores or find different models in the same store. Try to find out why similar pieces have different prices. A salesperson may be able to help you. Share your findings with the class.
6. Divide into groups of three to five students and make a redecorating plan for a living room. Include a budget, a rough sketch, samples of colors and dimensions needed, and prices from nearby stores.
7. Make a list of guidelines to follow when you are planning to redecorate.
8. Make a list of remodeling projects that you think are good do-it-yourself projects. Make a list of those you would want to turn over to a professional.

GE Plastics

Chapter 22 Housing for Tomorrow
Chapter 23 Careers in Housing

PART 6

Progress in Housing

CHAPTER 22

Housing for Tomorrow

THE PHONOGRAPH.

GE Plastics

To Know
biosphere
ecology
geothermal energy
hazardous wastes
hydroelectric power
integrated waste management
nuclear energy
photovoltaic array
pollution
recycling
solid waste
visual pollution

Objectives

After studying this chapter, you will be able to:

- Explain the impact of technology on housing.
- Identify ways to provide and conserve energy.
- Summarize the importance of a healthy environment.
- Describe ways to provide for a healthy environment.
- Describe new solutions in housing.

How can people have better housing for tomorrow? No one knows just what the future holds. However, by learning from the past and watching for new developments, people can make tomorrow's housing better.

Recent Developments in Housing

As the needs of people have changed, so has their housing. Housing designs and construction are influenced by many factors. One factor having a great influence on developments in housing is new technology. Some people living today can remember when houses did not have electricity, indoor plumbing, refrigerators, or air conditioners. These are all related to advances in technology. New technology systems are continually being developed for use in homes today. New construction materials and methods of construction are being developed, as well.

SMART HOUSES

Many of these new technologies are showcased in specially built SMART HOUSES located throughout the country. (SMART HOUSE is a for-profit partnership that gives member manufacturers license to its technology.)

SMART HOUSES feature a simple and easy-to-use home automation system based on computer technology. The main control system operates and controls many sub-systems. These sub-systems include security, lighting, entertainment, appliances, heating, and cooling. Telephones, handheld remotes, control panels, programmable wall switches, and sensors control the system.

The SMART HOUSE system begins with the *service center.* Electricity, telephone service, and cable television are brought in from the outside through the service center, 22-1.

A *system controller* is the main component in the SMART HOUSE system. It has two main functions. First, it is a network manager, routing the electronic signals that control the sub-systems. To do the routing, the system controller must keep track of everything that is connected to the system. The controller functions from the database it has of the house. Second, the system controller has some logic. It can manage different software to direct simple functions. For example, appliance manufacturers can install microprocessors in their appliances that are compatible with the SMART HOUSE system. These appliances can then be programmed for specific functions via the system controller. Such a program might operate a dishwasher at night when the utility rate is lowest.

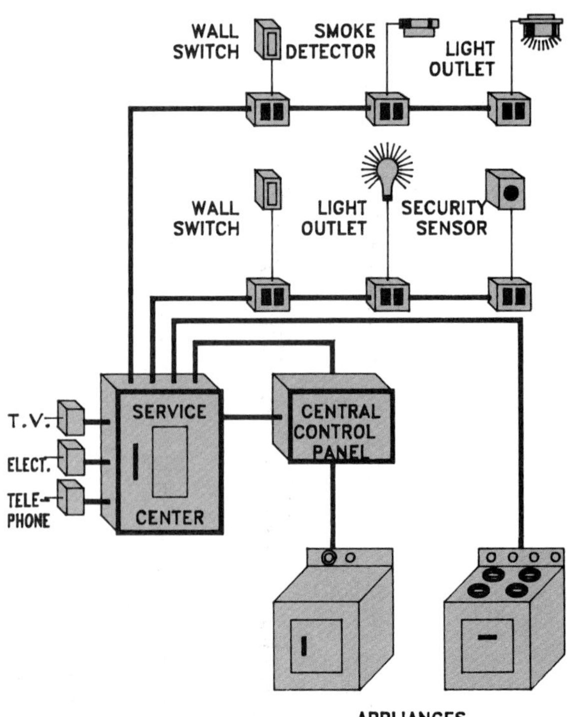

22-1
Typical circuits for a "smart house" are shown in this illustration.

The system controller operates continually, monitoring the various sub-systems. It will check all of the windows several times a second. It can tell if one has been forced open. Each room, as well as the outside area, is checked for security. The computer will take indoor and outdoor temperatures and constantly compare them. Indoor heating or cooling is then adjusted as needed. The computer will check each room to see if anyone has entered, and turn lights on or off as needed. The system can monitor energy consumption, detect gas leaks, and even call the fire department in case of fire. These are typical activities of the computerized system controller in the SMART HOUSE.

A "smart" house, one that uses a computer management system, looks like any other house from the outside. See 22-2. "Smart" house technology is being installed in many new houses today. It is believed that by the year 2000 most new houses will have computer management systems of some type.

The Living Environments Concept House

General Electric, in partnership with more than 50 other companies, has designed a model house known as the *Living Environments concept house*. The 3,000 square foot house is a showcase of building design, construction materials, and assembly systems that will influence future home construction, 22-3.

The goal of the project was to design attractive, functional, and affordable housing. The use of *standardized modular components* was one of the keys to achieving this goal. These components include a roof component, a modular wall system, a modular floor system, and a foundation system. The heating, ventilation, and air conditioning form another component or system, 22-4. Many of these components would be constructed on factory assembly lines. Roof, wall, floor, and foundation panels would be produced in factories. The panels would arrive at the building site

SMART HOUSE, L.P. 400 Prince George's Blvd., Upper Marlboro, Maryland

22-2
Passing by, you cannot tell this SMART HOUSE from any other house.

GE Plastics

22-3
The Living Environments concept house is shown here in a back view.

already cut to size, with doors and windows installed. The final assembly of the house at the site would then proceed quickly.

The reliance on the use of components and systems in housing is expected to increase in the future. In addition, new materials are being developed and old materials are being put to new uses. Advances in technology can also make materials last longer. For example, pine shingles can now be treated to have a projected life span of up to 50 years. Other types of roofing materials, such as asphalt, have a life expectancy of 25 to 30 years.

GE Plastics

22-4
This component houses the functions of five home comfort appliances.

Housing Concerns

You can see that technology is bringing about many changes in housing. Many of these changes are the result of the concerns of people. For example, there is a concern regarding the affordability of housing. This has resulted in the development of new products to bring down spiralling housing costs. Many of the technologies described above will make future housing more affordable.

There are also concerns regarding energy usage. Many natural fuels are being depleted. Can alternate fuel sources be developed? Can recycling strategies be put in place to keep from depleting natural resources?

Another concern is for the health of the environment. What needs to be done to preserve a healthy environment for people today and all future generations?

Alternative Energy Sources

Fuel provides heat, and people need heat to live. Like all forms of energy, fuel begins as solar energy, or energy derived from the sun. Nature converts solar energy to raw materials such as oil and coal. The conversions take millions of years to complete. The raw materials are then refined and used as fuel for electricity. The chart in 22-5 shows that coal continues to be our nation's main source of energy.

The supplies of such common sources of fuel as oil and coal are being depleted. These sources of energy are *nonrenewable.* Researchers are working to find new sources that will supply enough fuel for the future. They are looking toward *renewable* sources of energy–those that replenish themselves regularly. These include the sun, wind, water, and geothermal energy.

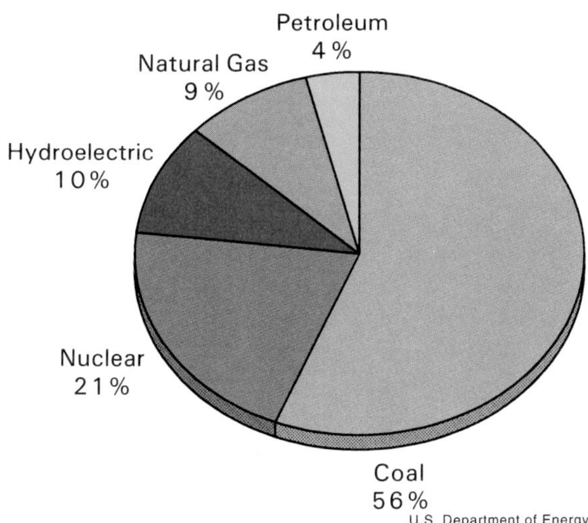

22-5
The U.S. continues to rely heavily on coal to fuel the generation of electricity for industrial use.

Nuclear energy and hydroelectric power are providing more and more of our energy needs. Other new energy sources are being evaluated to determine their ability to produce electricity. They include solar, geothermal (heat from underground), wind, and solid wastes.

Nuclear Energy. In 1951, nuclear energy was discovered. Its discovery marked the beginning of the "atomic age." This was a monumental breakthrough for scientists and energy experts worldwide.

Nuclear energy is produced in a nuclear reactor by the fissioning of Uranium-235. Heat is released when the nucleus of an atom "fissions" or splits into two pieces. A large amount of energy can be produced with only a small amount of fuel. One nuclear pellet the size of a small marshmallow contains the equivalent amount of energy as 1,780 pounds of coal or 149 gallons of oil.

More than 110 nuclear energy plants provide nearly as much electricity as oil, natural gas, and hydroelectric power combined, 22-6. Only coal produces more electricity than nuclear energy. In some states, nuclear energy is the leading source of electrical power. Over 400 nuclear plants are also operating in 27 foreign countries. These plants supply almost 20 percent of the world's electricity. In many countries, the percentage is higher.

Nuclear energy will continue to play a major role in providing electric power. Its benefits have been proven over the past four decades. Nuclear energy does not pollute the air with gases or dust. However, there are concerns about the effects of nuclear energy on the environment. Though nuclear plants produce only a small amount of radioactive waste, the waste remains radioactive for many years. This waste must be carefully disposed of to protect people from potential hazards. People also fear incidents at nuclear plants that might cause radioactive materials to be released.

Hydroelectric power. Another important source of energy is ***hydroelectric power***. This is electrical power that is generated by water in dams and rivers. Water as a source of energy is not new. Water power was first converted into electricity using waterwheels in the late 1800s.

Arizona Public Service

22-6
The Palo Verde Nuclear Plant in the Arizona desert is the largest in the world.

Today's hydroelectric plants use turbines to drive electric generators. A *turbine* is a series of blades placed around a shaft. The turbine is powered by flowing water. The turbine's speed is determined by the swiftness of the water. The higher the speed of the turbine, the greater the generation of electricity. See 22-7 for an example of a hydroelectric system.

Most of the hydroelectric generating systems are located on major rivers. They are usually placed at dams, but small plants can be placed at any point along a river.

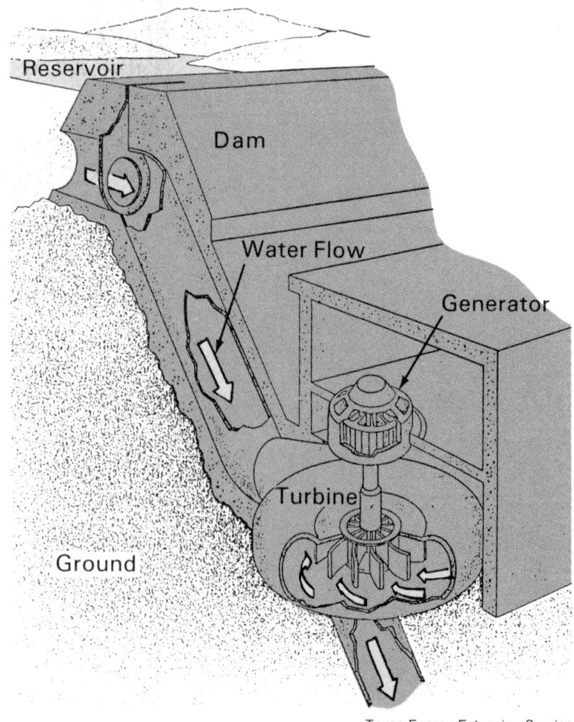

Texas Energy Extension Service

22-7
This illustration shows how water flowing from a reservoir powers a hydroelectric generator.

Solar energy. Many houses are being built that use solar energy. See 22-8. Solar energy could supply a majority of the energy needed to heat and cool buildings throughout the United States, 22-9. Solar heating systems are expensive to install. However, utility bills are greatly reduced when solar energy is used. In the long run, solar heating systems usually cost less than conventional systems. The two types of solar heating systems–active and passive–were described in Chapter 6, "The Evolution of Exteriors" and Chapter 9, "The Systems Within."

In an active solar system, a ***photovoltaic array*** converts sunlight into electricity. This solar cell array can power a computer system that regulates energy usage in the house, conserving electricity stored in the solar system's batteries. The downside of photovoltaics is that they can generate electricity only when the sun shines.

22-8
This house has windows placed to take advantage of passive solar heating.

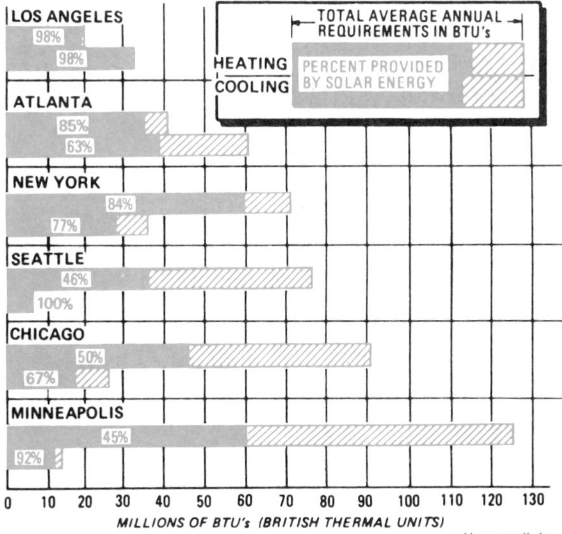

Honeywell, Inc.

22-9
This chart shows the amount of heating and cooling that could be done with solar energy in some major cities in the United States.

Though the system's batteries can store enough energy to power a house for several days, persistent overcast weather can deplete the electricity supply. Deluxe systems can match the reliability of power supplied by utility companies, but the price tag is much larger. As the cost of solar electric systems declines, more environmentally conscious homeowners will likely invest in this technology.

Some solar energy heating systems are designed to supply more energy than is needed. The excess is sold to a utility company or stored in their lines until needed by the producer. It can also be stored in a bank of batteries. Two electric meters are needed. One is to measure power that comes into a dwelling, the other is to measure power that goes out. See 22-10.

Geothermal energy. ***Geothermal energy*** comes from steam, hot water, or very hot rock stored deep beneath the surface of the earth. In certain locations, it is present near the surface. In others it can be reached by drilling extremely deep holes through lava (a type of volcanic rock). Reykjavik, Iceland, is the first city in the world to become almost entirely heated by geothermal

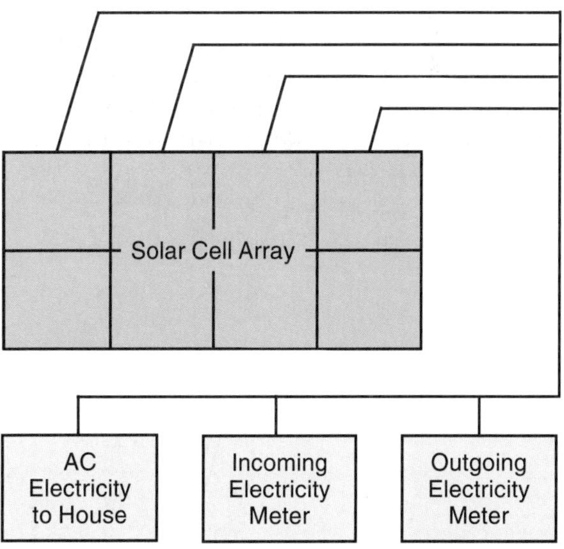

22-10
In a photovoltaic system, silicon chips are joined by electrical wires to form solar cell arrays. The arrays collect solar energy. The amount of energy depends on the season, the time of day, and the cloud cover.

energy. Approximately half a million people in California, Mexico's Baja, and the Mexicali Valley have their fuel needs met with geothermal energy. Other geothermal projects are being developed in the United States.

Geothermal energy has advantages and disadvantages. One advantage is that it has been shown to be less expensive than other fuels. It also is a source of heat that does not emit harmful pollutants into the environment. A third advantage is that geothermal energy is considered a renewable resource. However, some geothermal waters contain chemicals that require responsible disposal. A second disadvantage is that geothermal energy can be used only near the sites where it is produced. Hot water cannot be transported over long distances.

Wind as energy. The use of wind as energy dates back some 2,000 years. At that time, windmills were used to pump water and grind grain. Wind is experiencing a new popularity as an energy source. Although a wind energy system is relatively high in cost, wind is a clean and inexhaustible energy source. A minimum average annual wind speed of ten miles per hour is necessary to run a wind generator. If the average is above 12 miles per hour, an excellent wind system can be developed.

Some regions of the United States have strong, shifting winds that can be used for power. Wind turbine generators grouped together to form wind farms can convert air motion to electrical current. The current that is produced is fed into utility lines or storage systems. The systems keep the power flowing even when the air is still, 22-11.

Bergey Windpower Company/Excel 10kW Wind Turbine

22-11
A wind generator is connected to a utility system to supply electricity to customers.

Conserving Energy

Between 1974 and 1985, when oil prices began a rapid rise, laws were enacted to encourage conservation of energy. There were acts to encourage research on making solar energy more useful. Tax credits were given for adding energy-saving features to houses. Many people took advantage of these laws and added such energy-saving features to their houses. Though the tax laws have changed, they raised the awareness of the general public to the need for energy conservation. This awareness and concern continues today.

When buying a house, the prospective homeowner should consider energy efficiency. Energy-efficient features not only save money, but they also help make the house more comfortable. The checklist in 22-12 can help you choose an energy-efficient house. Also see Appendix B.

A Healthy Environment

Ecology is the relationship between all living things and their surroundings. People harm the environment each time they put undesirable items into their surroundings. ***Pollution*** is all the harmful changes in the environment caused by human activities. Look at 22-13 to see the many types of pollution that can harm your surroundings.

Humans have made many demands on the environment. They cannot continue "taking with-

Checklist for Buying an Energy-Efficient House

Look for and evaluate these features for home energy efficiency.

Orientation and Landscaping

___ Orientation of long side of house (N, S, E, or W)
___ Windows facing east (Note number and compute area in square feet.)
___ Windows facing west (Note number and compute area in square feet.)
___ Shade from landscape features on east or west sides
___ Unobstructed southern exposure or shaded by deciduous trees

Thermal Resistance

___ Attic insulation (Note the type of insulation and its thickness.)
___ Wall insulation
___ Under-floor insulation, especially in homes with crawl spaces, cold basements, and garages
___ Insulated ducts
___ Insulated hot water pipes
___ Insulated hot water heater
___ Double or triple-glazed (paned) windows
___ Solid-core wood or metal door
___ Storm doors

Lighting and Windows

___ Fluorescent lighting is used in work areas
___ Windows or skylights over work areas
___ Windows should not make up more than 10 percent of the total wall area (Measure the total window area and calculate its percentage of the total wall area.)

Appliances

___ Kitchen arrangement locates refrigerator away from stove and dishwasher and away from direct sunlight

Ventilation

___ Ceiling fans
___ Wholehouse fan
___ Window/door placement appropriate for cross-ventilation
___ Attic vents near the roof ridge
___ Attic vents beneath the eave

Air Infiltration

___ Weatherstripping around doors
___ Weatherstripping around windows
___ Weatherstripping around attic entry door
___ Caulking around door frames
___ Caulking around window frames
___ Caulking around penetrations for pipes, wires, etc.
___ Tightly fitted windows

Texas Energy Extension Service

22-12
Use this checklist to compare houses for energy efficiency.

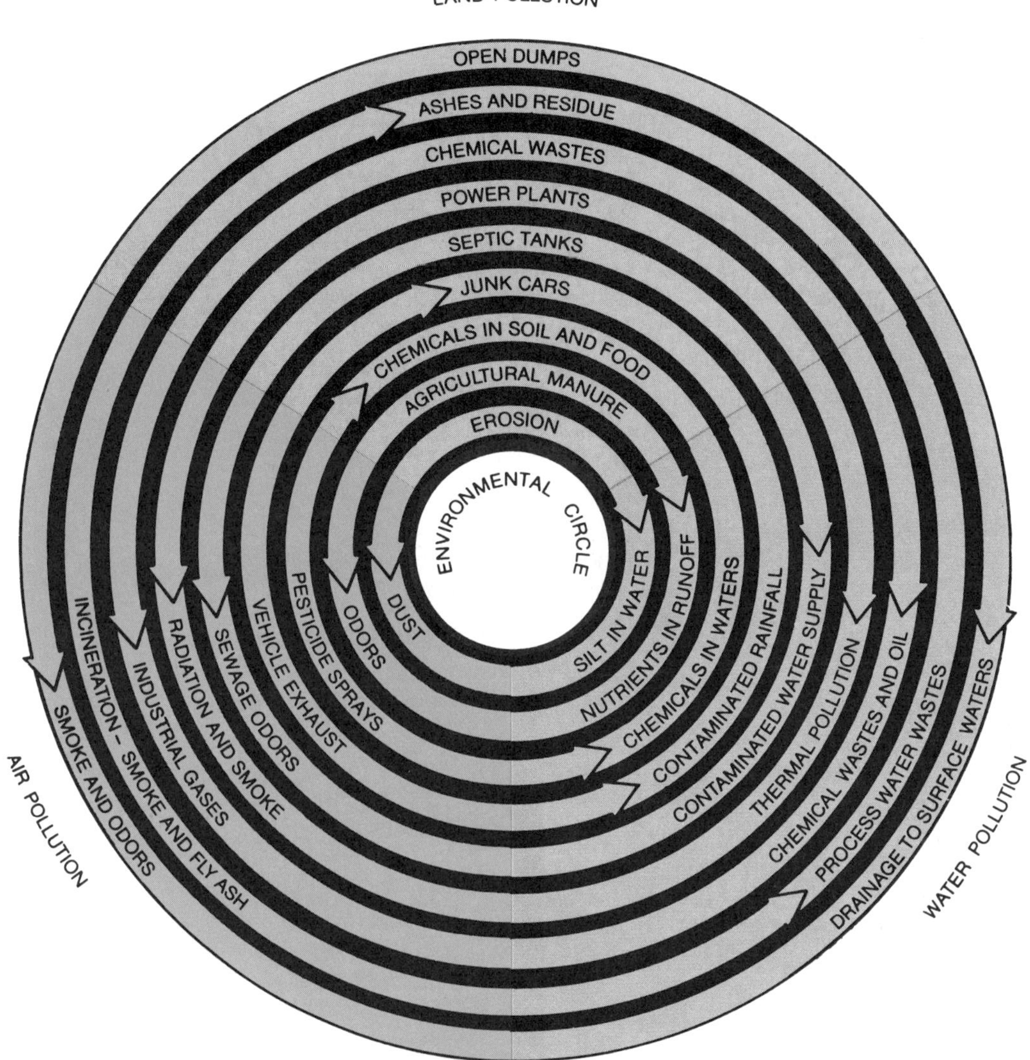

22-13
This environmental circle shows many kinds of pollution. Notice that each kind can affect land, air, and water.

out giving." If the environment is to continue to satisfy so many human needs, people must care for it. A solution must be found for the increasing amounts of garbage.

A healthy environment also helps people be healthy. There is increasing concern about the pollutants in the environment. Water and air pollution affect your health. Other forms of pollution also affect how you feel.

Solid waste. Every year people throw away tons of solid waste materials. ***Solid waste*** is any discarded material that isn't a liquid or a gas. Much of the waste comes from our homes in the form of garbage. The total output of garbage is called the *solid waste stream.* Most solid waste is either dumped into sanitary landfills or incinerated. Both of these methods have drawbacks.

Nearly 73 percent of solid waste is landfilled, but solid waste experts project that more than half of the landfills will be filled by 1995. Suitable sites are difficult to find because of the toxic substances that seep from landfills into groundwater stores despite safeguards.

With landfills becoming filled, incinerators are used more often. Over 14 percent of solid waste is incinerated. Incinerators don't pollute the groundwater, and they can generate energy. The downside is that incinerators can pollute the air, and they produce a highly toxic ash. For every ten tons of waste burned in an incinerator, one ton of ash is produced.

Some wastes are particularly harmful. ***Hazardous wastes*** are poisonous waste materials that damage the environment and cause illness. The Environmental Protection Agency's (EPA) definition of hazardous wastes includes all corrosive, ignitable, reactive, or toxic substances. Modern industry produces many toxic substances that are hazardous to the environment. However, the average household also contains a variety of hazardous materials that require special disposal methods. Among the most common chemical hazards in the home are aerosols, batteries, bleach, disinfectants, drain cleaners, insect sprays, medicines, and metal polishes. Certain lawn and home workshop products are also hazardous. Special ways of disposing of these toxic wastes are required.

Water pollution. Half of all Americans use groundwater for drinking water. Groundwater can become contaminated. This contamination occurs when hazardous chemical wastes, pesticides, or other agricultural chemicals seep down through the soil into underground water supplies.

Few people know where their drinking water comes from. Many people believe that all toxins have been removed from drinking water before it reaches their homes. Generally, water is properly treated at municipal treatment plants or in private septic systems. However, most plants are not set up to treat hazardous wastes. In septic systems, most hazardous waste is untreated. Since 1977, federal law has required water suppliers to periodically sample and test the water supplied to homes. If tests show that national water standards are being violated, the supplier must correct the situation. Homes with private wells should have the water tested periodically.

Even if the water that enters your home is pure, your house can contribute to its pollution. Many homes built prior to 1988 contain plumbing systems that use lead-based solder in pipe connections. Older homes may even have lead pipes. In such systems, lead can enter drinking water as a corrosion byproduct. Some galvanized and plastic pipes may give off harmful chemicals to the water supply.

Modern technology can make a water supply safe. However, you will want to check to be sure you are not drinking polluted water. Samples of the water in your home can easily be tested.

Other types of pollution. Air and noise pollutants exist outdoors as well as indoors. Safety and health issues related to air and noise pollution were discussed in Chapter 20. ***Visual pollution*** is the harm done to the appearance of the environment as a result of human activities. Signboards, debris in yards and along roadsides, and the destruction of natural surroundings are examples of visual pollution.

Researchers continue to learn more about the effects of the various pollutants on people. All pollutants are harmful in one way or another. People should welcome research and technology that helps them have a healthy environment. A healthy environment will help make tomorrow's housing better.

Solving Housing Concerns

An approach is now being used that addresses some of these housing concerns–the need for energy and the desire for a clean environment. The concept is called ***integrated waste management.*** It is based on a hierarchy of preferred waste handling options developed by the EPA. See 22-14. The EPA is encouraging every community to use this approach when considering ways to dispose of its garbage.

Beginning with the most preferred option, the hierarchy is:

- Source reduction. This means reducing the amount and toxicity of waste by altering the design, manufacturing process, sale, or use of products or packaging.
- Recycling and reuse.
- Incineration with resource recovery. This involves using the energy released in the incineration process.
- Incineration without energy recovery.
- Landfills.

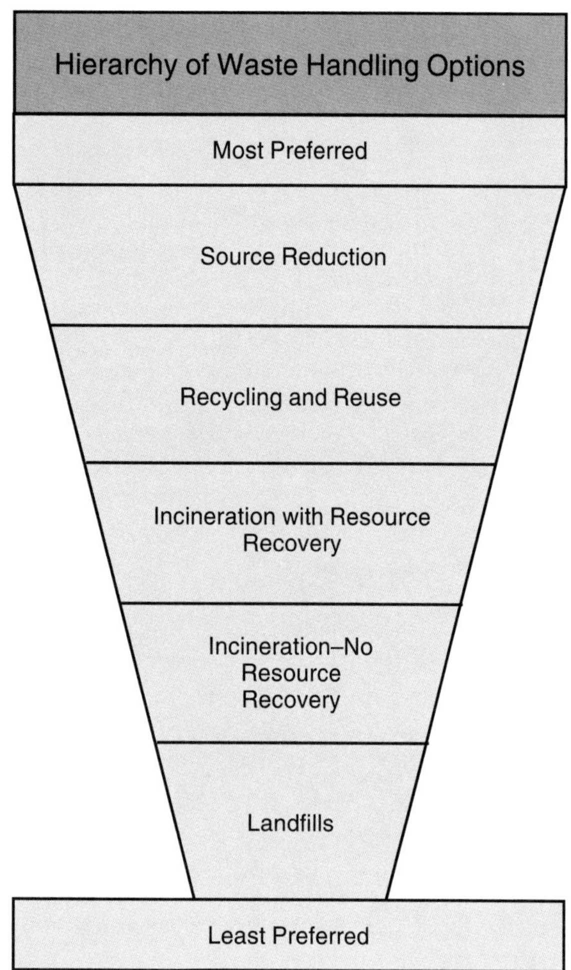

22-14
This illustration shows the most and least preferred options for handling waste.

As you can see, this hierarchy strongly supports efforts to reduce the growing volume of waste as the best approach to waste management. Though industry is playing the major role in source reduction by reducing the amount of packaging, you can also play an important role. Think about some of the ways your buying decisions can help the environment. Buy only those items that are the least environmentally harmful to produce. Also buy those that are safe to use and less of a burden to dispose of. Consider the amount and kind of packaging used on each item you buy. Some packaging is necessary, but much of it adds to the solid waste problem. Finally, deciding *not* to buy something you don't really need has the greatest environmental impact of all.

The second level in the hierarchy is to recycle and reuse. ***Recycling*** means reprocessing resources to be used again. The EPA estimates that Americans recycle only 13 percent of their solid waste. The EPA's goal is to increase that amount to 40 percent by the year 1996. Many communities have recycling programs. If they don't, they will soon. You play a very important role in recycling.

Newspapers, aluminum cans, glass, and plastic can all be recycled. Newspapers are made into many other products, such as newsprint, molded fiber packaging, home insulation, cereal boxes, and roofing felt. Aluminum is recycled into new beverage containers, storm doors, and gutters. Recycled glass is crushed, melted, and made into glass containers. Some recycled glass is crushed and used for asphalt pavement mixes or permeable media in foundation drains.

When plastic products become solid waste, they take hundreds of years to decompose. Thus, plastic recycling is becoming more and more important. A type of plastic used in soda bottles called PET (polyethylene terephthalate) is being recycled successfully. It is being used as a fiber in carpeting. A similar type of plastic is being recycled into a wood-like material. This material is being used to make outdoor items, such as bird feeders, benches, fences, and decks.

Many people believe that the United States can recycle on a large scale. Many recycled materials can be used to build new homes. If recycled materials become more widely available, the cost will be even less. Recycling saves energy, natural resources, and landfill space.

The third level on the hierarchy is incineration with resource recovery–waste to energy. Waste-to-energy processes are still in the developing stages. Most involve incineration of solid waste and recovery of methane gas from landfills. The energy created from the incineration of garbage is used to provide heat and electrical power for homes and businesses. At least 40 states have programs for converting garbage to energy. The recovery and use of methane gas from landfills is more costly and more difficult to transport to the user.

New Solutions in Housing

The growing and shifting population, the changes in life-styles, and the longer life span dictate attention to new housing solutions. The designs of the future will reflect these and other life-style changes.

Housing should be designed and constructed for the people who are to use it. Needs and values of people should be considered. Housing must allow for the changes taking place in the lives of people. It should also take advantage of new technologies. At the same time, care must be taken to protect the environment.

Planned Communities

Planned communities are one answer to today's housing problems. Instead of just "happening" one building at a time, these communities are designed to meet present and future needs. Careful consideration is given to the use of resources and to the needs and values of humans.

Planned communities are described as "one-stop living." They are made as self-sufficient as possible. Businesses, shops, recreation, and schools are included in the planning. Homes in these communities are an escape from the suburbs and high traffic enroute to work.

An example of a planned community is Columbia, Maryland. This is one of several communities planned by architect James W. Rouse. It is located on 15,000 acres of land between Baltimore and Washington, D.C. About 3,200 acres are set aside for parks, lakes, and a golf course.

The city of Columbia is really a group of seven villages. They are built around an urban downtown. In this arrangement, the villages are called *satellite communities.*

The total number of residents in Columbia can reach 110,000. It is planned as an integrated community for people from different backgrounds. The homes are in a wide range of prices and styles. Some can be purchased, and others can be rented.

Included in the planning of Columbia were specialists from many fields: architects, sociologists, educators, religious leaders, and doctors. They tried to answer the question, "What should be included in a well-planned community?" The factors they considered are listed in 22-15.

Factors to be Considered When Designing a Planned Community

- The desired life-styles of the occupants.
- The occupants must be able to afford the housing.
- The neighborhood must be arranged so people have easy access to schools, religious buildings, stores, and health facilities.
- Recreational facilities should be provided for all age groups from the very young to the very old.
- A community should be broken up into neighborhoods by the use of green belts, parks, and playgrounds.
- A public transportation system should be provided to move people where they need to go without great expense.
- There should be opportunity for employment for all who need work.
- Educational opportunities should be available for all at the level they need.
- There should be health facilities that provide care (both to prevent and remedy poor health) at a cost people can afford.
- There should be a communication system, so that people will know about one another and community activities.

22-15
These factors were considered when the planned community of Columbia, Maryland, was being designed.

A community association is needed to govern a planned community. A well-run association can raise the quality of life, as well as property values. The number of such associations is expected to double during the 1990s.

Experimental planned communities. Arcosanti, designed by Paolo Soleri, is another example of a planned community that is experimental in nature. Paolo Soleri was a student of Frank Lloyd Wright. His first dwellings are found near Taliesin West, the Frank Lloyd Wright School of Architecture. Soleri has designed cities for as few as 3,000 and as many as 170,000 people.

Soleri's idea is to build his structures from the least expensive durable materials that are close at hand. His structures are of concrete made with sand and gravel taken from a nearby riverbed. In 22-16, you can see one of the megastructures being built. His designs are modular. The large structures are repetitions of a basic module that are stacked 30 high. Unlike modular complexes of other designers, Soleri's modules are irregular or angular shapes rather than rectangular.

Millennium City is another concept of a planned community. An Austrian, Hermann J. Fraunhoffer, is the designer. In this city of the future, buildings are in the shape of disks or rings, 22-17. Each ring provides housing for about 100,000 people. The rings reach a diameter of one mile and are 400 feet high. They contain housing units ranging in size from 300 to 2,200 square feet. Durable building materials such as glass, steel, and concrete are used. The structures are expected to last 500 years.

A mass transit system (a monorail), bicycle paths, and walkways provide easy access to all areas of the city. Since each structure is in the form of a circle, everything is close together. A person can get to any place within the circle in a minimum amount of time. People of any age can travel anywhere in the city easily. Parking space for personal vehicles is provided. However, vehicles are needed only for transportation outside of the city.

Each ring is designed to include shops, schools, and churches. These and other community services occupy the bottom levels of the rings. Inside the rings are open areas. They include features such as lakes, zoos, and golf courses.

One of the concepts used in Fraunhoffer's design is that of *cluster housing*. Clustering provides the best use of space. It creates high density housing, but the land that is saved can be used for gardens and parks. These "green spots" make high density housing more satisfying.

New Living Spaces

Many of today's housing problems relate to space. About 75 percent of the people in the United States are living on less than 10 percent

Arcosanti: Paolo Soleri

22-16
Modular structures make it possible for the entire city of Arcosanti to be built on only seven acres of land.

Concept 2000, Hermann J. Fraunhoffer

22-17
Perhaps cities of the future will resemble Millennium City.

of the land, yet space for housing is difficult to find. It is also expensive. In just 40 years the cost of land has risen dramatically. It has risen from about 10 to 25 percent of the purchase price of a home. In some areas, the cost will be as much as 50 percent. To solve this problem, some new sources of living space are being explored.

Biosphere refers to living beings and their environment. Biosphere 1 is Earth. *Biospere 2* is a community under glass in Oracle, Arizona. The goals of Biosphere 2 are to test life support systems for future space colonies and to help scientists understand global processes. They also want to generate new methods of food production and waste management. In 1991, eight volunteers entered the airtight, watertight building for a two-year stay. Their environment includes a desert, ocean, tropical rain forest, marsh, and one-half acre farm. See 22-18.

Some people think living space could be extended downward. Caves, cellars, and basements all have their place in the story of housing. Earth-sheltered housing has been used. (See Chapter 6, "Evolution of Exteriors.") The idea of building whole communities underground has not yet been proven successful.

Paolo Soleri's first home in Scottsdale, Arizona, was an "earth house." You can walk on the roof without realizing that there is a dwelling underneath. Only when you approach the entrance are you aware of the underground dwelling.

Living space may be found on and in bodies of water. The SS United States, once the world's fastest ocean liner, has been converted into a seagoing condominium. However, the prices of its 282 housing units are very high.

Less costly seagoing living quarters are available. Some are on ocean sites, and others are on smaller bodies of water. Most of them are houseboats. However, the same idea may be used in the future to lessen the shortage of space for housing.

Some of these housing predictions may not come true. Some may just be science fiction. It will be interesting to see which directions housing of the future will take. What do you expect to happen during your lifetime?

C. Allan Morgan/Space Biosphere Ventures

22-18
Sections of Biosphere 2, called biomes, produce food for the people and animals. Pictured is an intensive agriculture biome.

Gill Kenny/Space Biosphere Ventures

Biosphere 2 covers 3 1/4 acres of land. It is the largest and most complex ecosystem ever built.

Summary

Of the recent developments in housing, the greatest impact has been that of new technology. The SMART HOUSE is an example of housing that is based on new advances in technology. New materials continue to be developed for housing, as shown in the Living Environments concept house.

Producing and conserving energy are present-day concerns related to housing. Energy can be produced from a variety of sources. All forms of energy begin as energy from the sun. Nature converts them to raw materials that can be refined for fuel. Nuclear energy is one of the most recent forms of energy that has been harnessed. Energy can also be conserved in various ways. Use of renewable sources of energy and materials are conservation measures.

Each individual, as well as researchers, desire a healthy environment. The environment needs to be free of pollutants. Land, water, and air pollution are major concerns.

Citizens of the United States create more garbage than any other industrialized nation. This amounts to nearly a ton per person annually. The garbage in most communities is simply burned or buried. In places where garbage is recycled, it is sorted. The combustible materials are used as fuel for operating power plants or for heating. Metal cans, plastic, and glass are sent back to industries to be reused. Scientists are trying to find more ways of recycling garbage.

Trends in housing offer new solutions to the concerns of people regarding their housing. Planned communities are one solution, as well as a look to new living spaces. Planned communities now exist on the land. In the future, they may exist below the ground or out in space.

To Review

Write your responses on a separate sheet of paper.

1. Give a brief description of a "smart house".
2. The goal of the Living Environments concept house was to design _____, _____, and _____ housing.
3. List the five major sources of energy in the U.S. today.
4. Give one advantage and one disadvantage of nuclear energy.
5. Compare hydroelectric energy and geothermal energy.
6. How is wind used as an energy source?
7. List five features to look for when buying an energy-efficient house.
8. _____ is the relationship between all living things and their surroundings.
9. List the five waste handling options from the most preferred to the least preferred.
10. Name four waste products that can be recycled and give an example of a recycled product made from each one.
11. Describe a planned community and name two examples.

To Do

1. Find magazine articles that describe ways in which technology influences housing. Report your findings to the class.
2. Check with a home builder to find out how he or she uses new technology in building houses.
3. Survey your class or school to find which types of fuel or energy are used in the homes of students and teachers.
4. Work with other members of your class to determine ways you can conserve energy.
5. Check the buildings in your community to see how many have solar heating systems.
6. Collect articles from the local newspaper related to pollution that affects your environment. Report to the class.
7. Find out which waste products can be recycled in your community. Make a list of products made from recycled materials.
8. As a small group activity, make a list of questions to ask people about their housing. Include some questions about the types of housing they expect in the future.
9. Bring news items and magazine articles about housing of the future to class.
10. Find out more about the people who are concerned about housing of tomorrow. You may choose from this list or find others:
    a. Rouse, James.
    b. Fraunhoffer, Hermann.
    c. Soleri, Paolo.
11. Write a "science fiction" story about housing of tomorrow.

CHAPTER 23

Careers in Housing

Arcosanti, Paolo Soleri

To Know
apprentice
career cluster
career ladder
career lattice
cooperative education
dual-career families
entrepreneurs
high-tech
job descriptions
leadership
multiple roles

Objectives

After studying this chapter, you will be able to:

- Describe several careers that are related to the field of housing.
- Explain which job skills and personal qualifications are required for housing careers.
- Describe the relationship between careers and personal and family life.

The number of living units in the United States is growing. About two million new housing units are needed each year to house them. There are many career opportunities available in providing housing for these people. Perhaps one of these careers will be of interest to you.

Who Provides Housing?

The efforts of people from many career areas are combined to provide housing that satisfies people of all life-styles, 23-1. People who work in the building industry are perhaps the first ones who come to mind when thinking about who provides housing. They are an important part of housing, but they do not provide all that is needed in a good housing environment. People who work for health agencies and other community improvement groups contribute to housing environments. Fire fighters and police officers help you feel secure. Garbage and refuse collectors help keep your environment clean, safe, and beautiful. People who work for the telephone company make it possible for you to contact plumbers, carpenters, family members, and friends. All of these people are not in "housing" industries, but they make housing environments more satisfying.

Career Clusters

Since careers related to housing are so varied, they do not all fit in one category. Instead they are grouped into several smaller categories. Jobs or careers that are closely related make up a ***career cluster***. In 23-2, you can see how the career cluster related to housing design and interior design can be broken down into individual careers according to the jobs that need to be done. Sometimes a career cluster is called a *career web*. Look at 23-3 to see why this name is appropriate.

One cluster of careers in the building industry is with the Manufactured Housing Institute. They represent about 25,000 firms and businesses in the United States and Canada. They identify five *subclusters* within their career cluster. These are listed in 23-4. Each subcluster can be divided into individual jobs. The jobs offered in the subcluster of mobile home parks are listed and described in 23-5.

23-1
Many people from different career groups were involved in building, selling, and furnishing this house.

Career Cluster	Subclusters	Jobs
Housing design, interior decoration	Design and decoration	House designing and planning Interior decorating Counseling on house design and decoration
	Furnishings selectivity	Selecting paint and finishes Selecting furniture styles, draperies, and slipcovers Selecting and combining home accessories Selecting household equipment
	Refurbishing and refurnishing	Upholstering Refinishing furniture Repairing furniture
	Product testing	Serviceability testing of furnishings Comparative testing of household equipment Counseling on home furnishing and equipment Demonstrating home furnishings and equipment

U.S. Office of Education

23-2
The career cluster related to housing design and interior decoration offers several distinct types of jobs.

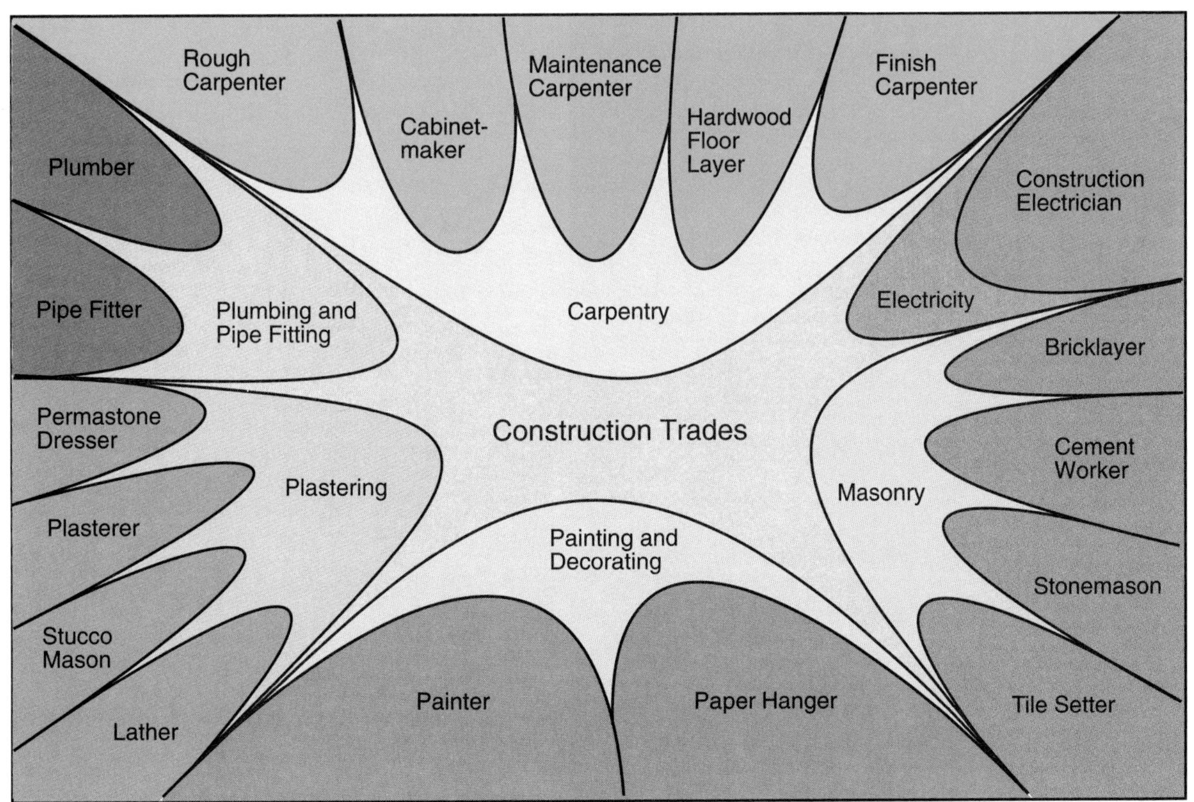

23-3
A career web for construction trades shows related areas of work and kinds of workers needed.

Career Cluster	Subclusters
Manufactured housing	Manufacturers–more than 900 manufacturing plants in USA and Canada
	Mobile home trade associations (national and state)–more than 60 associations in USA and Canada
	Manufactured house suppliers–more than 1000 major suppliers in USA and Canada
	Manufactured house dealerships–more than 10,000 dealers in USA and Canada
	Mobile home parks–more than 13,000 rated parks in USA and Canada

23-4
The career cluster related to the manufactured housing industry has five subclusters and many job opportunities.

Positions in the Subcluster of Mobile Home Parks	
Job Title	What Person Does
Developer	Obtains satisfactory zoning. Leases or buys land in order to build a mobile home park. Hires land planners, architects, and engineers to design a park. Installs water and utility connections. Builds streets, foundations, service, and recreational buildings. Prepares site for each home.
Park manager	Supervises all functions of park operation. Maintains services and contact with home owners. Collects rent. Plans activity program for residents in a "service" or retirement park.
Social director	(Sometimes position is combined with that of park manager.) Plans activity program for park residents.
Office administration	
clerk/typist	Does clerical work, typing, and filing.
secretary	Takes dictation, does typing, filing, and perhaps purchasing of supplies.
accountant	Controls all accounting systems and procedures including payroll, accounts receivable, accounts payable, insurance. Prepares tax report and financial statements.
Maintenance manager/ groundskeeper	Keeps lawns and grounds clean. Maintains service buildings such as community pool, laundromat, and office. Assists home owners in certain home repairs.
Advertising and public relations manager	Found in large parks only. In most instances, the job is probably conbined with the park manager's. Determines advertising program and media to use in cooperation with manager's recommendations. Maintains good public relations with community and park residents.

Manufactured Housing Institute

23-5
Many skills and personal qualities are needed to run a mobile home park.

Look at 23-6, 23-7, and 23-8. These illustrations show career clusters in other areas related to housing.

Career Information

Many kinds of careers are a part of the housing industry. Special skills and training are needed to carry out the assigned tasks of each one. When you think about possible future careers, you need to know what qualifications are needed for the different kinds of jobs. You also need to know what the job is like and what would be expected of you if you had the job.

Usually school counselors can provide you with job descriptions and a list of qualifications that are needed for the jobs. Sometimes this information can be obtained from a vocational teacher. Libraries are another source of career information. They have many publications dealing with careers. Two such publications are the *Dictionary of Occupational Titles, Volumes I* and *II* (Washington, D.C., U.S. Department of Labor) and the *Occupational Outlook Handbook* (U.S. Department of Labor, Bureau of Labor Statistics). Most libraries have many additional sources of career information. They may have sets of job guides or career briefs that tell about specific jobs. These may include such information as:

- Definition of the job title.
- List of duties.
- Personal qualifications needed.
- Education and training needed.
- How and where to receive the education and training needed.
- Future outlook on employment.
- Earnings.
- Opportunities for advancement.
- How and where to find a job.
- Related careers.

Ask your librarian for help in finding the career information you need.

Job Descriptions

The biggest questions when considering careers are "What is available?" and "What is that job like?" ***Job descriptions*** provide the answers to those questions. The following job descriptions are related to housing.

Architects

An architect's job is to design buildings that satisfy people. Such buildings must be safe, attractive, and useful. There is more to the job than design. Architects must be sure that the proper materials are used and that the builder follows the plans.

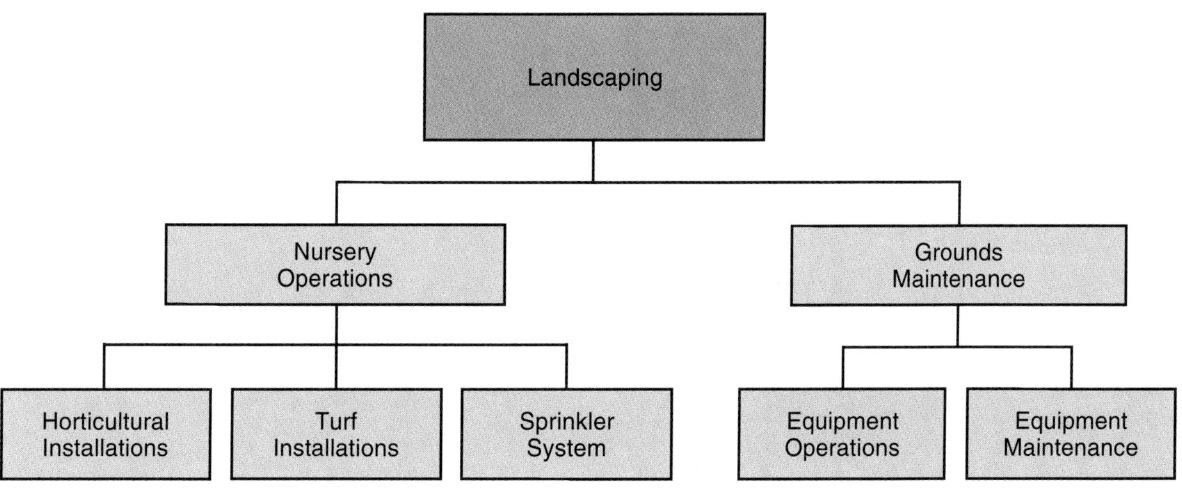

23-6
All jobs in this career cluster are related to landscaping.

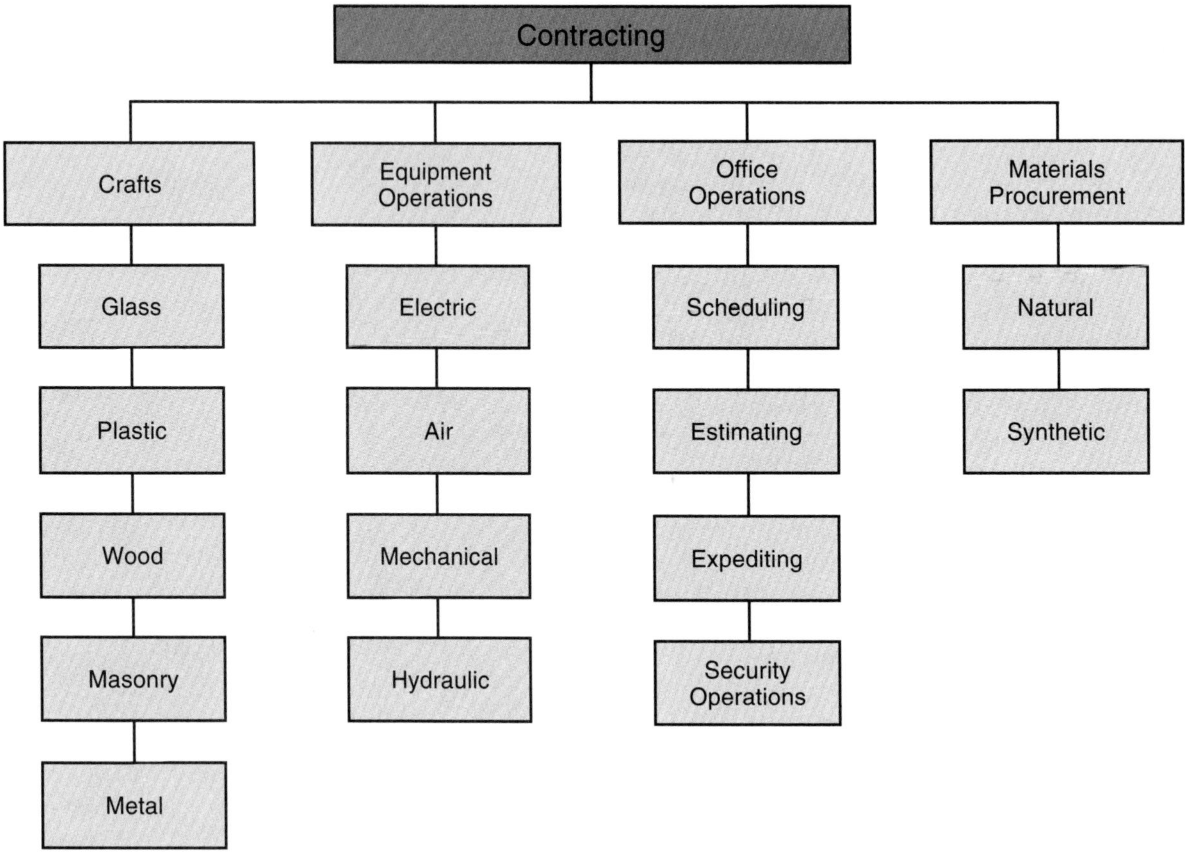

Contracting
Crafts
Glass
Plastic
Wood
Masonry
Metal
Equipment Operations
Electric
Air
Mechanical
Hydraulic
Office Operations
Scheduling
Estimating
Expediting
Security Operations
Materials Procurement
Natural
Synthetic

23-7
The career cluster of contracting has a wide variety of job opportunities.

Distribution
Packaging
Packaging Development
Packaging Manufacturing
Marketing
Retailing
Wholesaling
Distributing
Advertising
Product Promotion
Transportation
Air
Truck
Rail
Pipeline
Vessel
Warehousing
Packing
Storing/Inventory

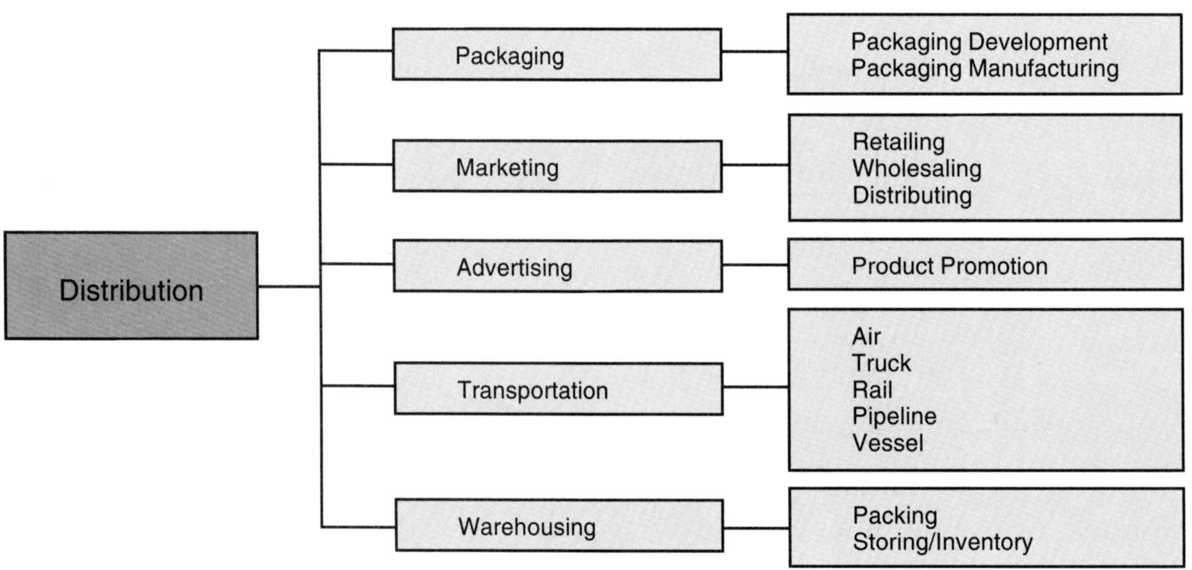

23-8
The distribution of manufactured products for housing offers many types of positions.

Architects tend to be paid well, but they must take much care to be sure that their work is accurate. Architects also have a long training period. Five years are required to earn a bachelor's degree. Then a two-day examination must be taken to receive a license. Becoming established often takes many years of hard work and experience.

Landscape Architects

Landscape architects work with organizations, committees, governments, private firms, and individuals to beautify the land surrounding structures. Their work entails planning the placement of trees, shrubs, walkways, parking lots, and open areas around buildings. They usually study four or five years in college. Required courses include surveying, sketching, horticulture, landscape construction, botany, science, and mathematics. About half the states require licensing.

Drafters

From an architect's sketches and instructions, a drafter prepares the detailed working drawings used by the builder. See 23-9. These drawings tell what materials to use, give exact dimensions, and what and how much work is to be done by the contractor or builder.

Standard Oil of California

23-9
Drafters make precise, detailed drawings to specify the kind of work that will need to be done as a building is constructed.

Drafters must be able to produce neat, accurate drawings using compasses, dividers, and other drafting equipment. A knowledge of construction is needed as are patience, good eyesight, and a steady hand. More and more drafting is being done with computers using CADD programs. In order to do computer drawings, a drafter must have knowledge of and experience with computers, 23-10.

Drafters may specialize in certain aspects of the job. One such specialist is the architectural illustrator. He or she prepares the presentations and renderings that are used in brochures or shown to clients who want to know how the finished structure will look.

Modelmakers

To help clients visualize large projects, an architect may have a scale model of the project built. See 23-11. A modelmaker will be hired to do this. Most modelmakers are self-employed. Necessary skills include being able to read and interpret prints, to use scales, and to visualize drawings in three dimensions. Modelmakers must do precision work, while shaping materials in miniature.

Surveyors

Using various tools, the surveyor locates corners and boundaries of tracts of land. Instrument findings are used to draw a map of the surveyed area.

Assisting the surveyor are other workers. *Instrument workers* adjust and operate the surveying instruments. *Chain workers* measure distances between survey points. *Rod workers* use a level rod and range pole to help measure distance and angles. Surveying involves outdoor work with much walking while carrying heavy instruments. Knowledge of mathematics is essential.

Engineers

Engineers are educated in programs leading to bachelor of science degrees. Engineers whose work is related to housing take courses in mathematics, print reading, drafting, computer science, physics, humanities, and English. Four or five years might be spent in preparation, depending on the school.

In many cases, the architect may assume the tasks of determining the ability of the building

Andersen Windows, Inc.

23-10
Much drafting is done by computers today.

23-11
Modelmakers build three-dimensional models from an architect's drawings.

to withstand stresses. As structures become larger and more complex, the *structural engineer* is asked to advise the architect on design for safety and strength. This person estimates the weight the building must carry, the pressure of air movement against the sides and roof, pressures against the foundation, and extraordinary pressures from earth tremors. Many structural engineers are self-employed. Others are employed by large engineering or architectural firms.

Mechanical engineers are concerned with the design of equipment for plumbing, heating, ventilating, and air-conditioning. They plan the way this equipment will be used in buildings and oversee its installment.

Civil engineers are responsible for preparing the site. They level the land, design drainage and sewer systems, and lay out streets, driveways, and sidewalks. Another part of their work is to study the soil of the site. They must know how much weight it will support without settling. Many civil engineers work for federal, state, and local governments. Others are employed by housing developers.

Electrical engineers plan the electrical services needed for the operation of household appliances, such as ranges, washers, dryers, air conditioners, and furnaces. Their calculations are included in the working drawings supplied to the builder.

Construction Careers

A variety of skilled people work on building an average dwelling. These people include estimators, masons, carpenters, plumbers, plasterers, electricians, drywallers, roofers, and flooring specialists. Training is obtained on the job, in vocational schools, or in apprenticeship programs. Many are employed by builders and contractors. Others have their own businesses.

Estimators study the working drawings and determine how much the building will cost in materials, labor, and overhead. In large construction projects, this person may be an expert in the engineering field. In such cases, he or she is called a *construction cost engineer* or a *cost analysis engineer.* Estimators must know about materials, methods, and costs of construction. Some estimators have a background in construction work. Others enter the field after training programs beyond high school.

Masons and *cement workers* set up forms for footings, foundation walls, patios, and floors. They place concrete and use various hand and power tools to smooth and finish it. They must know the materials. They also must be familiar with cement additives that speed or retard the setting of concrete.

Bricklayers and *stonemasons* build walls, partitions, fireplaces, and other structures, 23-12. They use brick, block, and stone as well as other natural or manufactured materials. They work with hand tools for the most part. Reading working drawings and making careful measurements are among the important skills they must master. Bricklayers must also be able to construct various bonds (patterns). They must be able to use accepted construction methods for safety and reinforcement and to work rapidly and neatly.

Carpenters put up the wooden framework in buildings, 23-13. They install windows, doors, cabinets, stairs, and paneling. They also lay hardwood floors, asphalt, and other types of rigid

Lowden, Lowden & Co.

23-12
Bricklayers use bricks and stones to form the exteriors of many houses.

23-13
These carpenters are putting up the framework for a house.

Lowden, Lowden & Co.

23-14
This electrician is wiring a circuit breaker panel in a large, multifamily structure.

flooring materials. Rough carpenters build only the framework or set up the concrete forms. Finish carpenters install millwork, cabinets, stairs, etc. Some carpenters learn their work on the job. Others prepare through special vocational programs.

Electricians are people who install wiring in new constructions and make repairs on older wiring systems. The electrician must know how to read the electrical diagrams in the builder's working drawing. In addition, a knowledge of electrical codes and electrical loads is essential. See 23-14.

Floorcovering installers put down or replace resilient tile, vinyl flooring, and carpeting. Their work may include removing an old covering and sanding and cleaning the surface to be covered. They must be able to read architectural drawings and measure, mark, and cut accurately.

Painters apply paints, varnishes, and other finishes to decorate and protect surfaces. Painting involves surface preparation by scraping, burning with a torch, sanding, washing, priming, and sealing. Then a new painted surface is applied with brushes, rollers, pads, and sprayers.

Paperhangers attach wallpaper or cloth to walls and ceilings. Sometimes they must first remove old wallpaper by soaking or steaming it, and sometimes minor patching of plaster is done. Then they prepare the wall surface by cleaning it and applying sizing. The sizing makes the surface less porous. Workers measure, cut, and hang materials, applying paste as needed.

Roofers apply shingles and other protective materials to make roofs weatherproof. They may also apply waterproofing to walls and other parts of the building. Roofers use a variety of materials including wood or asphalt shingles, hot tar and gravel, slate, tile, aluminum, copper, or steel.

Plumbers and *pipe fitters* install pipe systems that carry water, steam, air, or other liquids and gases. They also install plumbing fixtures, appliances, and heating, or refrigeration units. They will install piping between walls and under floors during early stages of construction. Then they will return during final construction stages to attach fixtures and install appliances.

Plasterers and *drywall installers* finish the framed walls with plaster or with smooth sheets of plaster-like material. Their methods differ, but their results are much alike. Plasterers apply wet, cement-like material to the wall in successive coats using trowels and other hand tools to smooth it.

Installing drywall is a task that is done in two steps. Installers attach large sheets of drywall to the walls and ceilings of rooms and nail or glue them in place. Finishers then apply mastics and perforated tape to conceal joints and nail heads after the drywall is attached, 23-15.

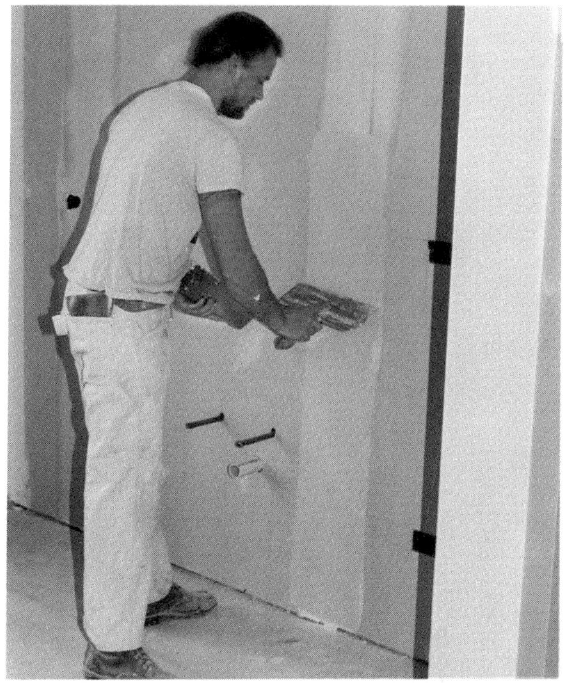

Lowden, Lowden & Co.

23-15
This drywall finisher is concealing nail heads and joints in walls and ceilings.

Construction Machinery Operators

Handling dirt or heavy construction units would be difficult, if not impossible, without heavy machines to lift and carry them. These machines are controlled by skilled workers who are often called *operating engineers.* They are at the controls of cranes, bulldozers, backhoes, forklifts, pavers, and trucks, 23-16. Good eyesight and coordination are required. Unless carefully controlled, such equipment could endanger the lives of other construction workers.

Concept 2000. Hermann J. Fraunhoffer

23-16
A crane operator must work carefully to avoid damage to this building module or injury to other workers.

Real Estate Agents

Careers in real estate include many kinds of tasks such as renting and managing property for clients, making appraisals on property, developing new building projects, and arranging loans for home buyers.

The most common career in the field of real estate is the *real estate agent*, 23-17. Real estate agents help people buy, sell, rent, and lease property. Real estate agents must be familiar with their communities, real estate laws, banking laws, and building codes. A license is required by all states and is issued only after successful completion of a written test. Most real estate agents have a college background although it is not a requirement. Needed personality traits include a pleasant disposition, honesty, neatness, tact, enthusiasm, and maturity. A good memory for names, faces, and facts is helpful.

Interior Designers

Interior designers plan and supervise the design and arrangement of building interiors and furnishings. They work from prints to make floor

Century 21

23-17
Real estate agents must know many facts about the housing they show to clients.

American Society of Interior Designers

23-18
Interior designers plan fabric, carpet, and window treatments for their clients. They also prepare room floor plans prior to furniture selection and placement.

plans to scale and to prepare elevation drawings. Their drawings help clients visualize how the rooms will look.

Interior designers must have knowledge of basic housing principles. They should also have a creative, artistic flair. Designers must be good at evaluating clients' needs and tastes and designing rooms that fulfill the clients' wishes.

Interior designers work for either individual clients or for firms that sell furnishings, or for planning and designing services. They select and estimate costs of furniture, floor, and wall coverings and accessories, 23-18. When plans are approved, the designer may arrange the purchase of furnishings and hire and supervise various workers.

Three or four years of training in a professional school are required. Courses include principles of design, history of art, freehand and mechanical drawing, painting, furniture design, and textiles. A knowledge of antiques, art pieces, and furnishings is also needed.

Salespeople and Consultants

Retailers of building materials, appliances, and home furnishings hire people with a background in housing and furnishings. Their job is to demonstrate and sell their employer's products.

Some firms hire consultants who will help customers select the right furnishings, equipment, or materials. They also advise customers on installation and use of the products. Such personnel need to understand design, materials, and methods.

Secretaries and Computer Operators

No business could operate efficiently without the assistance of office workers, 23-19. The smaller the firm is, the more the worker's duties vary.

Work might include typing, filing, filling out reports, taking dictation, handling visitors and phone calls, scheduling appointments, bookkeeping, and operating duplicating equipment and printers. Many secretaries function as special assistants to architects, engineers, builders, and contractors.

Computers have become important in the housing industry. They are used in every career cluster and at all levels, 23-20. Because of this, computer operators are needed to assist many

Sally Riggs

23-19
Office workers are called upon to do a variety of jobs.

Sally Riggs

23-20
Today's office workers often use computers to help them with their tasks.

people in the housing industry, such as architects, engineers, interior designers, and real estate agents.

Occupations with Utility Companies

Utility companies that supply electricity, gas, and telephone services offer job opportunities related to housing. Gas and electric companies, for example, employ consultants who advise consumers on appliances. This requires not only knowledge of the product but sales ability as well. Department stores and large chain stores often have a public relations department in which people prepare materials on proper selection, use, and care of furnishings and appliances.

Service people are hired by private firms or utility companies to repair and adjust appliances. Telephone companies employ phone *installers* and *line workers* to install equipment and lines and to keep them in repair.

Positions with Government

Government positions related to housing occur at federal, state, and local levels. Some of the positions are concerned with legislation. They influence the passing, monitoring, and enforcing of laws concerning housing. People in government positions often deal with building codes, housing standards, and zoning.

Other government workers help with finances or money matters related to housing. They deal with appraisals, mortgages, and interest rates. Some workers help secure affordable housing for low- to middle-income living units. Other government employees study housing trends and engage in research related to housing.

High-Tech Careers

Many future positions related to housing involve emerging technologies. These are new technologies that are not widely used today, but may become common in the future. These technologies are called high technology or ***high-tech.***

New communication systems are being developed that are considered high-tech today, but will become common tomorrow. For example, there are communication systems that respond to voice-activated instructions. Computer technology using microprocessors (miniature circuits) has opened the door to many of these new technologies.

Career opportunities in which computers are utilized will continue to grow in number. *Programmers* develop the programs or software (set of instructions) that tell computers what they are to do. *Computer systems analysts* plan methods of computerizing business and scientific tasks. *Computer operators* set controls, load the equipment, and monitor computer operations. *Computer service technicians* are called upon to repair computer systems when they break down.

The list of job descriptions becomes even longer when you consider the many other areas related to housing. Is there a position that appeals to you? Do you know the qualifications? Can you become qualified?

Career Levels

You can see that career opportunities related to housing are many and varied. They do not all carry the same amount of responsibility nor do they require the same qualifications. Career opportunities can be divided into three career levels:

1. The professional level.
2. The mid level.
3. The entry level.

Professional-Level Positions

Some of the people who help provide housing work on a *professional level.* Generally, a college degree is required for these jobs. Special training and experience may be needed in addition to a degree.

Those in professional careers related to housing influence the quality of life for themselves and others. They make decisions that affect the lives of individuals, families, and whole communities.

Architects, engineers, and interior designers are a few of the people with professional-level positions. Land use planners are also professionals. They work in both urban and rural areas. Wherever they are, they consider the needs and priorities of people using land. They also consider those who are affected by the way land is used. Will a certain use of the land pollute the environment? If so, what effect will the pollution have on those using the land or what is built on the land? How will those living nearby be affected? Will it make a difference to those who pass by? How will it affect future generations? These and other questions will be considered as decisions are made by land use planners.

Mid-Level Positions

Professionals are key people because they make decisions that affect the work of others. They do need others to support them in their choices. The people who help carry out decisions that have been made are called *supportive personnel.*

People in *mid-level positions* are often supportive of professionals. Their work sometimes involves supervising people in positions that carry less responsibility, 23-21.

For example, housing construction supervisors oversee the work of others. They usually do not do the wiring, plumbing, or roofing. However, they need to know how to do these tasks to determine if others are doing their jobs correctly.

Andersen Windows, Inc.

23-21
People who check for accuracy are in mid-level positions.

The mid level of career opportunities is very broad, and it has many sublevels. Thus, many people who work under a supervisor are also in mid-level positions. Others include carpenters and lighting specialists. The fact that they are supervised does not make their work any less important.

Those in mid-level positions are expected to have schooling beyond high school. It may be through a special class or by service as an ***apprentice***. An apprentice is one who is going through an organized program of job training that is coupled with vocational classes.

Entry-Level Positions

People in *entry-level positions* are supportive of those in both professional and mid-level positions. The qualifications for entry-level positions are not high. You can enter a career area and be successful with less preparation than at the other levels. You are likely to learn much of what you need to know on the job, 23-22. There is often opportunity to move up if you do your job well.

Some of the entry-level positions related to housing include helpers. They might help a mover, upholsterer, or carpenter. There are entry-level jobs in every career area.

A few entry-level positions still do not require a high school education. However, you are more likely to be sure of securing a position if you finish high school. Some courses related to housing careers are identified in 23-23.

Does your school have a program in ***cooperative education***? (Cooperative education programs offer opportunities to work part-time and attend classes part-time.) You may be able to secure a job through this kind of program. It will probably be an entry-level position. You will receive training on the job. You will also receive help from a vocational teacher in your school.

Entrepreneurial Careers

Many careers in housing allow you the opportunity to start and run your own business. People who do this are called ***entrepreneurs***. Entrepreneurial opportunities in housing include starting a cleaning, redecorating, or remodeling service. Entrepreneurs might also create and sell their own home decorations, 23-24. You may consider becoming an independent realtor or architect.

Andersen Windows, Inc.

23-22
Entry-level workers are often trained on the job to do specific tasks.

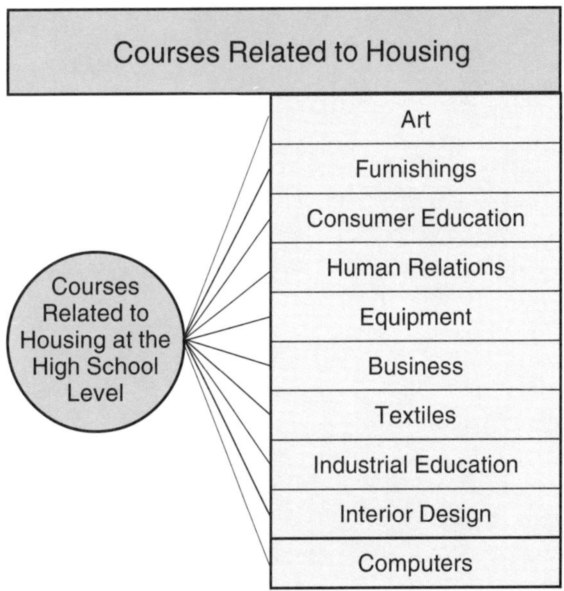

23-23
How many of these courses are offered in your school? Are there others related to housing?

Texas Dept. of Transportation

23-24
This entrepreneur uses her creative skills to produce home accessories.

Knowledge and skill in your career area is important to success as an entrepreneur. However, many other skills and qualities are important for successful entrepreneurs. You must be willing to take risks and be financially prepared to handle slow times in your business. You need to be self-motivated to work, because you will not have a supervisor telling you what to do. You will also need to understand the legal and financial aspects of running a business. You may even need to handle advertising or supervise your own employees.

Entrepreneurship is a good way to have a successful career that you control. However, success is not guaranteed. People who want to become entrepreneurs need to be prepared for the risks and responsibilities of running their own businesses.

Career Ladders

When the jobs in a career cluster are "stacked" according to the qualifications they require, they form a ***career ladder*** or a ***career lattice.***

A career ladder shows the steps from entry-level jobs to mid-level or professional-level ones. You can climb a career ladder by gaining more knowledge and experience. Study the career ladder shown in 23-25.

A career lattice shows that you can move in more than one direction as you change jobs within a career cluster. See 23-26. You can move either up or across the lattice. You may even be

Ladder for Home Furnishings Service

High School	Adult	Post-secondary	College or University
Window display aide Decorator's aide Drapery or slipcover aide Home lighting aide Home furnishings maintenance aide	Decorator's assistant Home lighting and appliance assistant Home furnishings maintenance specialist Window display assistant	Color consultant Drapery and upholstery estimator Appliance and consumer consultant Window display designer	Merchandising specialist Interior designer

23-25
There may be more than one position on each step of a career ladder. Education can help you climb a career ladder.

Career Lattice for Housing Design and Interior Decoration			
Professional	• Environmental Designer • Interior Designer • Home Economist • Home Service Director • Home Service Advisor • Textile Researcher		
	Service positions: Care and renovation	Advisory and design positions	Production positions: Construction
Supervisory	• Home furnishings laboratory technician	• Home furnishings advisor • Color coordinator • Drapery advisor • Home lighting advisor • Florist • Scenic arts supervisor • Scenery designer • Window display designer • Household equipment advisor	• Home furnishings sewing specialist • Drapery room supervisor • Textile technician • Laboratory tester • Household products technician
Mid level	• Home furnishings maintenance specialist • Rug cleaner • Upholstery cleaner • Floor care specialist • Maintenance specialist	• Decorator's assistant • Drapery and slipcover aide • Home lighting assistant • Accessories assistant • Floral assistant • Decorative arts craftsperson	• Drapery and slipcover constructionist • Sewing specialist
Entry level	• Home furnishings maintenance aide • Assistant upholstery cleaner • Assistant rug cleaner	• Home furnishings aide • Drapery and slipcover aide • Appliance and equipment aide • Home lighting aide • Floral aide	• Drapery and slipcover constructionist aide

23-26
The career lattice shows horizontal and vertical changes you can make within a career cluster.

able to move at an angle–both up and across at the same time.

The terms *open entry* and *open exit* are sometimes used to describe moving on a career lattice. They mean that you can enter at any level for which you are qualified and move across to any other position for which you are qualified.

Qualities for Success

Did you notice the magic word that determines your place on a career ladder or lattice? It is the word *qualified.* You become qualified by learning job skills.

Job Skills

Any job you do requires some skills. If you are *competent* on a job, you can perform each skill well.

Suppose you own a lawn mower and take a job mowing lawns. Some of the job skills you will need to perform include the following:

- Moving large objects out of the way.
- Adjusting the mower to the desired height.
- Refueling the mower engine.
- Starting the mower engine.
- Mowing the grass evenly.

- Shutting off the mower engine.
- Catching or raking the grass clippings.
- Trimming and edging grass.
- Disposing of trash.

You can learn job skills by working with someone else on the job. This is especially true of entry-level jobs. Other places to learn job skills are in school and training programs.

Leadership Skills

Leadership skills are needed at times in all careers. ***Leadership*** can be defined as the ability to guide and motivate others to complete tasks or achieve goals. It involves communicating well with others, accepting responsibility, and making decisions with confidence.

Leadership roles are often part of mid-level and professional-level positions in the housing industry. People in these positions may be expected to supervise work crews or secretarial staff. However, people in entry-level positions often take on informal leadership roles by setting examples and motivating fellow workers to do good jobs. Entry-level workers who show leadership ability have better chances of being promoted.

Leadership qualities may seem to come naturally to some people. However, you or anyone can improve leadership skills with practice. Becoming involved in a school club or organization can help. Taking a role as an officer or committee chair will give you even more practice. A part-time job can be another good place to gain leadership skills.

Personal Qualifications

It is important to have an interest in your job. Sometimes a special interest helps to make you qualified for a position. If you like art and have a special talent for it, you may qualify for a job that requires artistic abilities.

Many housing careers require artistic ability. Architects, landscape architects, furniture designers, and textile designers work with art.

Your personal preferences, or what you like, help to determine your qualifications. Do you like to work alone or with someone else? Examine the career clusters in this chapter and find positions in which you would probably work alone much of the time. Then find ones in which you would work with others. Which ones appeal to you more?

Do you enjoy being outdoors, or would you rather stay inside? What kind of life-style appeals to you? Do you like to sleep late in the morning? Can you work best during the day or during the night? Will your career choice let you spend as much time away from work as you would like? Are you work-oriented? Do you want your career to be the focal point of your life? Are you willing to work evenings and weekends?

Working Conditions

When you are looking for a job, you will want to know about the working conditions. Then you will know what to expect. Some of the conditions that you should find out about include the following:

- Physical surroundings. Where will you be working? Is the place clean and safe?
- Work schedule. What are your working hours and days?
- Pay scale. How much will you be paid? Does everyone doing the job you are doing get the same pay? On what is the pay increase based?
- Advancement. Is there opportunity for advancement? How soon and how often can you expect to move up the ladder? Are there special expectations of you before you advance?
- Fringe benefits. Are there insurance benefits? How much sick leave is granted during the year? Does it accumulate? Is there personal or emergency leave? Are training programs provided? Is there a credit union?
- Dues and fees. Will you be expected to join a union or other organization? If so, what are the costs? Will it require some of your time?

You may also want to find out about public transportation to and from work. If you drive, where will you park your car? Are there eating facilities nearby? Are rest breaks provided? The conditions under which you work have a great effect on the amount of enjoyment you receive from your job.

Careers and Life-style

Your success in a career will affect your satisfaction with your personal and family life. Likewise, your roles and responsibilities related to home life will affect your career. Balancing career and home life is important in any life-style.

The career you choose affects your life-style in many ways. It affects your income. For instance, most architects earn more money than drafters. Your income determines how much you can spend on housing, clothing, food, and luxury items. If you choose to be a drafter, you may need to live in a smaller, less elaborate home than an architect can afford. You may not be able to spend as much money on restaurant dining, entertainment, and other luxury items.

Your career choice may also affect where you live. If you choose a career in construction, you may need to live in a suburban or urban community where much new building is taking place. If you become an interior designer, you may not be limited to urban settings. You may have an easier time than a construction worker finding work in smaller towns and more established communities.

Your friendships are affected by your career choice, too. You are likely to become friends with some of your work associates. You may meet other friends through people you know from work.

Your leisure time is affected by the hours and vacation policies of your job. If you choose to be a carpenter, you may need to work frequently on weekends. Vacations during the warm, summer months may be out of the question. If you become an office worker, your hours may be more regular. You would not have to work weekends often. If you start your own architectural firm, you may need to put in many hours to keep your business running. You may not have as much leisure time as an architect who is employed by a firm.

Career Satisfaction and Life-Style

How you feel about your career affects your attitudes toward your personal and family life. If you are content in your work, you tend to be more relaxed and pleased with your personal life and relationships. If you feel stress and dissatisfaction because of your work, this may create personal and family problems.

Satisfaction in your career helps your personal and family life. If you enjoy your work, you are less likely to bring home problems and frustrations at the end of the day. You will be able to focus on home satisfactions or responsibilities.

Job success helps you feel good about yourself. This success might include mastering a new job skill or having one of your ideas accepted by your manager. You may feel successful after completing a project to a client's satisfaction. Being given a promotion or raise is another form of job success. Job success may give you more confidence and help you feel more contented at home, 23-27.

Some situations at work can cause stress or job dissatisfaction. Working twelve-hour days or taking on extra responsibilities during the regular work day can lead to stress. Doing work that you don't like can cause stress and dissatisfaction. Not getting along with employers or fellow employees may also cause these problems.

When work becomes unpleasant, your personal and family life can be affected. Your concern about work may interfere with other personal and family relationships. You may be too tired or busy to devote enough time to family and friends. Some people even allow stress from work to interfere with their personal health.

You may need to make adjustments if work-related stress becomes too great. For instance, you may need to cut back on overtime, so you can spend more time with your family. You may need to resolve conflicts with fellow employees,

Sally Riggs

23-27
This woman's success as an engineer influences her attitude toward her personal and family life.

so you can relax more when you are away from work. If you cannot work out a solution where you work, you may need to find a new job that is more satisfying or less stressful.

Balancing Work and Family

Belonging to a family involves many roles and responsibilities. Family roles might include spouse, parent, and homemaker. These roles involve many reponsibilities. Spouses need to work together to have satisfying, loving relationships. Parents need to provide safe, loving environments for their children. Being a homemaker involves keeping home life orderly by managing cleaning, nutrition, and child care tasks.

Career roles help to meet some family responsibilities by providing the money to meet family needs. However, careers involve other roles and responsibilities that may sometimes conflict with family roles. People with ***multiple roles***, such as parent, homemaker, and engineer, must balance their responsibilities to fully meet family needs.

Sometimes, you may need to make career decisions based on family responsibilities. For instance, you may be offered the chance to open a remodeling business with a partner. You must consider the needs of family members as well as your own. Will the demands of a partnership interfere with the time you can spend with your family? Will you be able to meet family financial needs if the business does not go well right away? Can you take on the responsibility of managing a business and still devote mental energy to family members when they need you? These questions and many more will affect your final choice.

In many families, both parents are employed. These families are called ***dual-career families***. When both parents work outside the home, meeting family needs can be challenging. Single parents who work have similar challenges in meeting family needs. Parents face many decisions about how child care and homemaking needs will be met.

Unless one or both parents work from the home, parents need to provide substitute care for their children. They must choose a child care service that best fits their needs and the needs of their children. Some employers offer benefits related to child care, such as on-site care or vouchers to help pay for child care. Employers may also offer days off with pay to be used when children are sick. Such benefits help lessen the strain on parents who work.

Parents who work may also need to adjust their homemaking practices. Both parents and the children may all need to contribute to caring for the home. Families may decide that they cannot spend as much time on homemaking as they would like. They may contract a cleaning service, buy more convenience foods, or let some less important home care tasks go.

Dual-career families often need to make special efforts to keep communication open. Since family members may be away from home often, they must make the most of their time together. Families do not always need to plan special activities for family time. This can cause extra pressure when family members may already be tired from work. However, parents and children need to know that they can talk with one another and share their feelings.

Some parents feel strain and guilt from trying to balance the responsibilities of work and home life. For instance, a parent may not be able to attend a school function because of work. This may cause feelings of guilt for the parent. It may even cause the child to feel resentment. Such feelings can cause problems at work due to lack of concentration.

Families need to make adjustments to keep responsibilities in balance. Sometimes this may involve supporting one another, so family members do not need to feel guilty or resentful about work responsibilities. Single parents may look to close friends and relatives for extra support. At other times, parents may adjust work responsibilities so they can spend more time with the family. These adjustments might include working less overtime, changing to a part-time job, or working from the home.

Summary

All people need some kind of housing, and many people work together to create housing. Careers are related to the designing, construction, and use of housing. The careers can be arranged in clusters according to the housing category to which they belong. Job descriptions help in understanding the types of jobs that are available.

Many people are involved in the design of a building. They include architects, drafters, and model makers. A number of people, including surveyors and different types of engineers, work on the building plans. Then many workers in construction, such as masons, bricklayers, electricians, and plumbers, are busy erecting the building. After the building is complete, painters, carpet layers, and interior designers are at work.

There are many other careers related to the housing industry. People who work in real estate, retail businesses, and offices contribute to the housing industry. People in government positions and those employed by utility companies are working for better housing. Those in high-tech positions are involved with new technologies.

Jobs can be divided into career levels. The higher the level, the greater the need for training and the higher the pay scale. There are those who work at the professional level. Others are at mid-level or entry-level positions. As you advance, you move up the career ladder.

Opportunity for advancement is determined, in part, by the levels of jobs or positions within a career cluster. Advancement is also determined by the qualities a worker possesses. Your job skills and leadership ability are important. The ability to balance your career responsibilities and your other roles will influence your career satisfaction. Working conditions also influence career satisfaction.

To Review

Write your responses on a separate sheet of paper.

1. True or false. People who work in the building industry provide all that is needed for a good housing environment.
2. Define a career cluster.
3. List three sources of career information.
4. Name four career areas related to housing.
5. Write a job description for a position in a career related to housing.
6. Name one position in each of the career levels:
   a. Professional level.
   b. Mid level.
   c. Entry level.
7. People who help carry out decisions that have been made by higher authorities are called _____ _____.
8. Define the term apprentice.
9. What is the difference between a career ladder and a career lattice?
10. _____ _____ are the abilities you need to perform well on a job; _____ _____ include interests, natural talents, and personal preferences.
11. List five facts you should know about working conditions before you decide to take a job.
12. List three ways in which career choices affect life-styles.
13. True or false. Employer benefits can help reduce strain on dual-career and single parents.

To Do

1. Find descriptions of several jobs related to housing and arrange them into career clusters. Use current editions of *Dictionary of Occupational Titles* and *Occupational Outlook Handbook* to find job descriptions.
2. Examine telephone directories to identify businesses that are related to housing.
3. Look through the classified advertising section of your newspaper. Find ads that are seeking employees in positions that help provide housing.
4. Make a collage using advertisements, pictures, and news articles about careers related to housing.
5. Choose a career related to housing that interests you. Research it further, and report to your class on it.
6. Draw a career ladder in the area of your interest. Begin with an entry-level position and progress to a professional-level position.
7. List the courses in your school that help prepare students for housing careers.
8. Ask your school counselor to give you an aptitude test. Determine which types of housing careers offer the best chances for you to succeed.
9. Write a feature article for your school or local newspaper telling about a career related to housing.
10. Write, call, or visit a local firm that employs people in housing careers. Find out employer expectations and working conditions.
11. Have a class discussion about attitudes in the "world of work." Determine which attitudes lead to success on the job and which do not.
12. Visit a local employment service to find out what careers related to housing are available in your area and across the nation.
13. Interview people who have jobs related to housing. Find out what they like and dislike about their jobs. Ask them to share situations in which satisfaction or dissatisfaction on the job has affected their personal and family life.
14. As a class, discuss ways in which dual-career families can meet their parenting and home care needs.
15. Read all you can about the SMART HOUSE and list the high-tech careers associated with it.

APPENDIX A

Housing Legislation

Few items affect housing as much as government policy. The what, where, and how of buildings are legislated. Even cost is affected by government controls. Some major developments at the federal level are listed below.

1901–The Tenement House Act was passed to improve conditions in tenement houses. It applied to those already constructed and set standards for building new ones.

1918–U.S. Housing Corporation was established to provide housing for war workers.

1932–President Hoover's Conference on Home Building and Home Ownership discussed the decline in building and shrinking mortgage credit.

1932–As a result of the Conference, the Federal Home Loan Bank Act of 1932 was passed. This act established 12 district Federal Home Loan Banks as the framework of a reserve credit organization for home financing institutions. It failed in its purpose to provide an adequate volume of funds for mortgage credit.

1933–Home Owners' Loan Act of 1933 set up a corporation to refinance the mortgages of distressed home owners. It financed over one million mortgages in three years, investing three and a half billion dollars in the process. It was considered quite successful.

1934–The Housing Act of 1934 created the Federal Housing Administration (FHA), an agency that still exists today. It also set up the Federal Savings and Loan Insurance Corporation to protect deposits. FHA revolutionized home financing methods by making possible lower interest rates and longer amortized mortgage periods. Improvements in housing standards were also brought about by setting up minimum physical property standards as a basis for FHA participation.

1937–The Housing Act of 1937 started the public housing program with the objective of providing decent, sanitary housing for low-income families. The Act set the principle of basing rental payments on the individual family's ability to pay. It provided for annual subsidy contracts whereby the federal government pays the difference between costs of managing the project, including debt amortization, and the rental revenues received.

1940–Lanham Act provided for federal financing of war housing. Two million dwelling units were built under this Act during the war.

1942–The National Housing Agency created by executive order was the first attempt to coordinate all federal housing programs.

1946–Veteran's Emergency Housing Act was passed. It established the VA program for mortgage insurance.

1947–The Housing and Home Finance Agency was created by the President's Reorganization Plan No. 3. The Federal Housing Administration, the Public Housing Administration, and the Home Loan Bank were all brought under the supervision of the Housing Administrator.

1949–Many cities and states were attempting to deal with the slum problem, and different renewal-type efforts were made. They usually fell short of their goals for lack of money. As a result, the desire for federal assistance was made known to Congress from the major cities all over the nation. From this experience came the Housing Act of 1949 with its now well-known title of a "decent home and suitable living environment for every American family." To support this effort, the Act permitted, for the first time, that land areas cleared with federal aid could be sold or leased to private developers for residential development. It gave recognition to the fact that private financial resources must be attracted to the housing field if the broad objective of the Act was to be realized. The 1949 Act became the symbol of the joint effort between public and private interests to clean and redevelop certain areas and decently house the population.

1953–President Eisenhower established a special committee on government housing policies and programs. This committee's efforts were reflected in the 1954 Housing Act. The objective was to create a total program against housing blight. Their conclusion was that federal assistance should be available only to communities willing to undertake a long-range program of slum prevention through sound general planning and enforcement of housing and building codes. This became the basis for the Workable Program.

1954–The Housing Act of 1954 incorporated the many recommendations of the President's Committee. Besides the Workable Program, it established the Urban Planning Assistance Program, sometimes called the 701 Program. It added a great stimulus to public acceptance of the comprehensive plan and the planning process. The Act also established the concept of rehabilitation by recognizing the desirability of retaining and improving essentially sound structures in an urban renewal area. It recognized, for the first time, the need for nonresidential urban renewal projects to attack blight in business and industrial areas. This Housing Act also instituted the demonstration grant program, whereby the federal government would participate in some research-oriented projects. The 1954 Housing Act was an extremely significant piece of legislation in the housing and urban renewal field because it oriented the program toward the comprehensive goal of urban revitalization, rather than the single goal of good housing.

1956–The Housing Act of 1956 established relocation payments for families and businesses; aid for housing for older people; and the General Neighborhood Renewal Program. The GNRP was an urban renewal plan for areas too large for a single project.

1959–The Housing Act of 1959 further extended the urban renewal program and created the Community Renewal Program (CRP). This grew out of the need for a comprehensive, long-range programming of a city's renewal activities, both public and private, closely tied to capital financing and land economics. The Act also established special credits for college and university urban renewal projects.

1961–The Housing Act of 1961 shifted more of the financial burden from local communities to the federal government. In cities with less than 50,000 population, the federal government would pay three quarters of the net project costs. This reduction of local financial obligations to a point where the locality put up just one dollar out of every four made the program almost irresistible for any city that was willing to fight the problems of blight. The Act also established the Open-Space Program and the Mass Transportation Program. It greatly liberalized various programs of the Federal Housing Administration.

1964–The Housing Act of 1964 authorized code enforcement urban renewal projects intended to attack the beginnings of blight in basically sound areas. To reinforce this technique, special low-interest loans for residential rehabilitation were also authorized. The Act also liberalized relocation procedures and aid.

1965–The Housing and Urban Development Act of 1965 provided for the formation of a cabinet-level Department of Housing and Urban Development (HUD). The Act authorized a variety of new approaches to urban improvement, including grants for neighborhood facilities, demolition grants, grants for public works and facilities, grants for urban beautification, grants to low-income home owners for rehabilitation, and municipal grants for open spaces. It set new public housing policies such as rent supplements, leased private housing, and purchase of existing units. The code enforcement "renewal project" of the 1964 Act, having proved unworkable, was revised as an "aid program."

1966–The Demonstration Cities and Metropolitan Development Act of 1966 authorized the Model Cities Program to rebuild or restore extensive blighted areas. The act stated that physical and social development programs should be coordinated, using local private and governmental resources. The original emphasis on renewal of housing was reasserted in the Act. It required the provision of a substantial number of low and moderate-cost standard housing units in the development of an urban renewal area. This rule did not apply when redevelopment was for predominantly nonresidential uses. As incentives for the Model Cities Program and for coordinated metropolitan planning, supplemental federal funds were authorized. Other significant features of the Act included "new town" development through

FHA financing; a new FHA sales housing program for low-income families; grants for surveys of structures and sites to determine historical value; a liberalized noncash policy permitting up to 25 percent of the cost of a public building; and authorization of air rights projects for industrial development.

1968–The Housing and Urban Development Act of 1968 was considered to be the most important piece of housing legislation since the 1949 Act. It added two new programs to house low and moderate income families whose incomes were above the level of public housing. Under the Home Ownership for Lower Income Families Program, the government helped to pay the cost of the home mortgage and the mortgage interest of the housing project sponsor. This permitted the sponsor to charge lower rents.

Other significant features were:

- Provisions that relaxed mortgage insurance in urban neighborhoods.
- A special FHA risk fund for mortgages in declining urban areas.
- Credit assistance to enable low income families to become eligible for mortgage insurance.
- Assistance to private developers of new towns.
- Creation of a new approach to renewal, known as the "Neighborhood Development Program," which provided more flexibility in planning and permitted staged development on a one-year basis.
- An increase in rehabilitation grants from $1500 to $3000.
- Authorization to close out a renewal project when only small parcels of land remain.
- Aid in alleviating harmful conditions in blighted areas where renewal action was programmed, but immediate action was needed before renewal could be started.

1970–The Housing and Urban Development Act of 1970 extended and amended laws relating to housing and urban development. The Act authorized the establishment of a national urban growth policy to encourage and support orderly growth of populated areas. It gave emphasis to new community and inner city development, encouraging the coordinated effort of state and local governments. Some specific features of the Act include provisions for parks, especially in low-income areas; preservation and restoration of historic and architectural sites; and curbing urban sprawl and spread of urban blight.

1970–The Federal Equal Housing Opportunity Council was established by the Office of Fair Housing and Equal Opportunity. Representatives of 50 federal departments and agencies participated. They coordinated efforts to assure all persons, regardless of race, creed, sex, or national origin, equal and unhindered access to the housing of their choice.

1970–The Clean Air Act was passed to control smoke pollution and provide a healthy treatment of solid wastes.

1974–The Housing and Community Development Act provided funds that went directly to the general local government. These funds were in the form of "community development block grants" (CDBG). They were provided to begin or continue urban renewal or neighborhood development programs. Benefits were directed mainly toward low and moderate income families. They were assisted in securing decent, safe, and sanitary housing.

1974–The Emergency Housing Act of 1974 authorized HUD to buy up $7.75 billion in mortgage loans at below-market interest rates so lenders could offer mortgages at subsidized interest rates. The Act was extended in 1975.

1974–The Real Estate Settlement Procedures Act was designed to give consumers more information about costs related to buying or selling a home.

1974–The Solar Energy Research, Development, and Demonstration Act had two main goals. One was to pursue a vigorous program of research and resource assessment of solar energy as a major source of energy for the nation. The second goal was to provide for the development and demonstration of practical ways of using solar energy on a commercial basis.

1975–The Energy Policy and Conservation Act mandated appliance labeling. The Department of Energy and the Federal Trade Commission jointly oversee the implementation of this act.

1975–The Emergency Homeowner's Relief

Act of 1975 authorized temporary assistance to help defray mortgage payments on homes owned by persons who were temporarily unemployed or underemployed as the result of adverse economic conditions. The Act made it possible for unemployed persons to retain possession of their homes. It was passed because the nation was judged to be in a severe recession, reducing employment opportunities.

1975–The National Housing Act was amended to increase the maximum loan amounts for the purchase of mobile homes.

1976–The Housing Authorization Act of 1976 amended and extended many laws relating to the fields of housing and commercial development.

1976–The Energy Conservation and Production Act required states and localities to adopt Building Energy Performance Standards. Many new energy-saving ideas were encouraged.

1976–An extension of the National Housing Act included $850 million for subsidized housing. Of that amount, $85 million was to be used for the construction of new public housing. The bill also provided a major increase in funding for a housing program for the elderly.

1977–The Housing and Community Development Act made it easier for people to buy and improve their dwellings. It revised many loan regulations, which had become outdated because of inflation. It increased the ceiling for home loans made by federal savings and loan associations. It provided a new system whereby savings and loan associations would have more money available for larger loans. It increased the limit on FHA Title I home improvement loans. It also increased mortgage loan limits for purchases of manufactured houses.

1977–Housing weatherization programs were initiated by the Department of Energy, Community Service Act, and Farmers Home Administration. (Weatherization means the addition of insulation, weather stripping, insulating glass windows, etc., to conserve energy.)

1978–The National Energy Conservation Policy Act was passed to confront serious energy problems. The act established the following provisions related to housing:

- Utility companies to provide energy conservation information and services to residential customers and promote the financing of energy conservation improvements.
- Energy conservation grants and loans for low to moderate income families, rural families, the elderly, and the handicapped.
- Income tax credits (through 1984) for homeowners, including weatherization items as well as systems using renewable resources (solar, geothermal, and wind).
- Energy efficiency standards for major home appliances.
- Increased regulation of rates for electricity and gas and lower rates during periods of low usage.

1978–The Housing and Community Development Act amended and extended provisions for community projects, especially for those with special needs.

1979–The Housing and Community Development Act was revised to extend programs and appropriate funds to carry out the initial purpose of the Act.

1979–Congress authorized the Office of Technology Assessment to make a detailed study of the potential for conserving energy in homes. The study reviewed existing and promising technologies and reasons for using or not using them.

1979–Energy Assistance Program provided money for low income families to help pay winter home heating bills.

1979, 1980 and 1982–The Housing and Community Development Act for each of these years was revised to extend programs and appropriate funds to carry out the act's initial purposes.

1980–The Household Moving Bill was passed to allow movers to offer binding estimates of what a move would cost. This increased movers' freedom to raise or lower prices. It also established standards for informal dispute settlements. Panels were set up by movers to resolve conflicts.

1980-1986–Programs were authorized by the Housing and Community Development Act of 1980. These programs were continued under appropriation measures and temporary extension bills each year. In 1985, the extensions provided emergency food and shelter for the homeless.

Housing assistance was also provided for older people.

1981–The Reagan administration agreed to increase subsidies to builders of low-income housing. The increase was granted in an attempt to revive construction, which had been virtually halted by high financing.

1982–President Reagan presented the following measures to help people buy homes:

- Easing of regulations on mortgage revenue bonds, making lower-cost mortgage money available to some home buyers.
- Action to increase the money available for home buyers.
- Revision of Federal Housing Administration rules to permit more first-time home buyers to qualify for loans.
- Reduction of the processing time for FHA loan applications.
- Relaxation of government restrictions that limited real estate firms' participation in related businesses such as providing title insurance.

1983–An antiforeclosure aid bill worth $760 million was passed to provide federal loans to homeowners facing foreclosure or falling far behind on mortgage payments because of the recession. Loans were made available to homeowners who had suffered "substantial loss" of income "through no fault of their own" and who were delinquent for at least 90 days or who had notice of intent to foreclose.

1985–The energy crises laws and policies of the 1970s were dismantled. Tax credits for energy saving measures in housing no longer existed.

1986–Programs to clean up hazardous wastes were expanded. The EPA was mandated to study problems, set standards, decide methods, and establish timetables for cleanup.

1987–Congress authorized funds for the Community Development Block Grants. A permanent extension was made to insure home mortgage loans.

1987–A requirement was made to inspect and remove lead-based paint in federally assisted housing.

1987–The Federal Omnibus Act included reforms in residents' rights and care standards in nursing homes.

1987–The McKinney Homeless Assistance Act was enacted to protect and improve the lives and safety of the homeless. Special emphasis was on older people, people with disabilities, and families with children. Grants became available for shelters. Subsidies were provided for low-income renters. Child care programs became available in public housing. The Act was amended in 1988 and 1990 to provide transitional housing and permanent housing with supportive services, such as education for homeless children.

1988–The Fair Housing Act gave HUD the authority to penalize those practicing discrimination in housing. Rentals, as well as home sales, were included. Discrimination could not be against any of the following:

- People with disabilities, physical or mental.
- Any race, color, or religion.
- Any national origin.
- Any familial status.
- Occupants with children under 18 years.

The Act also provided architectural accessibility and adaptable design requirements in new multifamily housing.

1988–The Indian Housing Act legally separated the federal government's efforts for Native Americans from other housing programs.

1988–Money from the Community Development Block Grant and the Farmers Home Administration could be used to improve housing conditions along the Mexican border.

1988–A program was begun to determine radon levels in housing and to remove radon. Also, there was to be screening for lead in drinking water, and efforts to reduce lead poisoning.

1990–The Cranston-Gonzalez National Affordable Housing Act was passed to help families purchase homes. The supply of affordable housing was to be increased, especially for older people, the homeless, and people with disabilities. Financial assistance was to be provided for certain first-time home buyers. Rental assistance was available for low-income families.

1991–The Cranston-Gonzalez Act was amended to include veterans and residents of Indian Reservations.

Energy-saving Tips

Americans use more energy per person than any other people in the world. We have only six percent of the world's population, but we use about one-third of all the energy consumed on this globe.

Where does all this energy go? Industry takes about 36 percent. Commerce uses about 11 percent for enterprises including stores, offices, schools, and hospitals. Transportation accounts for about 27 percent, and residences take about 26 percent.

Where does residential energy go? The largest amount, 46 percent, is used to heat and cool homes. An additional 15 percent goes for heating water, and another 15 percent for refrigerators and freezers. The remaining 24 percent goes into lighting, cooking, and running other household appliances.

Americans can cut energy use and living costs by making homes energy efficient, even if they have to spend some money to do it. The money spent now will be returned through lower utility bills month after month.

Protect Your Home from Outside Heat and Cold

Millions of single-family homes in the United States are not adequately protected from outside weather, according to U.S. Department of Energy estimates. (Utility companies will do an energy check of your home for a small fee.) Here are some tips to make sure yours is not one of them:

Insulation

- Find out if your home needs insulation. Your needs will depend on the climate in which you live and the amount of insulation, if any, you already have.
- Find out about R-values before you buy your insulation material. Then buy the thickness of insulation that will give you the R-value you need. R-values or numbers are insulation efficiency ratings. The "R" stands for resistance to winter heat loss or summer heat gain. The higher the R-number, the more effective the insulating capability. The numbers should appear on packages of all insulation materials.
- Insulate or increase the amount of insulation in your attic floor or top floor ceiling to the recommended R-values for your climate. Check the insulating qualities (R-values) of the floor coverings, draperies, etc.
- Don't insulate over eave vents or on top of recessed lighting fixtures or other heat-producing equipment on the attic floor.
- Consider insulating exterior walls. This is an expensive measure that requires the service of a contractor, but it may be worth the cost if you live in a very hot or very cold climate.
- Insulate floors over unheated spaces, such as crawl spaces and garages.

Windows and Doors

- Test your windows and doors for air-tightness. Move a lighted candle around the frames and sashes of your windows. If the flame dances around, you need caulking and/or weather-stripping. Try slipping a quarter under your door. If it goes through easily, you need weather-stripping.
- Install storm windows and doors. Combination screen and storm windows and doors (triple-track glass combination) are the most

convenient and energy efficient, because they can be opened easily when there is no need to run heating or cooling equipment. Alternatives range from single-pane storm windows to clear plastic film that can be taped tightly to the inside of the window frames.

Heating and Cooling

To prevent wasting energy, follow these tips during both heating and cooling seasons:

- Close off unoccupied rooms and close their heat or air-conditioning vents. (This does not apply if you have a heat pump system. Leave it alone; closing vents could harm a heat pump.)
- Use kitchen, bath, and other ventilating fans sparingly.
- Keep your fireplace damper closed unless you have a fire going.
- Install ceiling fans that have a reverse switch, so the air can be circulated whether you are heating or cooling your home.
- Clean or replace filters on furnaces and air conditioners as recommended by the manufacturer (usually at least once per month).
- Open and close drapes and shutters according to the time of the day and year to allow or prevent heat transfer.

Heating Energy Savers

If you use electric furnace heating, consider a heat pump system. The heat pump uses thermal energy from outside air for both heating and cooling.

- If you plan to buy a new gas heating system, ask your gas utility or public service commission about the savings potential of electronic ignition. Ask also about possibilities for retrofitting the system you may already own.
- Consider the advantages of a clock thermostat for your heating system. The clock thermostat will turn the heat down for you automatically at a set hour before you go to sleep and turn it up again before you wake.
- Consider buying a properly-sized gas furnace that incorporates an automatic stack damper or an induced draft fan. These devices reduce the loss of heat when the furnace is turned off.
- Lower your thermostat to 65°F during the day and 60°F at night (unless your physician advises you otherwise).
- Keep windows near your thermostat tightly closed. Otherwise, it will keep your furnace working after the rest of the room has reached a comfortable temperature.
- Install an insert in your fireplace. Some models allow you to retain the beauty of your fireplace yet are energy efficient.
- Have your oil furnace serviced at least once a year.
- Check the duct work for air leaks about once a year if you have a forced-air heating system. To do this, feel around the duct joints for escaping air when the fan is on. Relatively small leaks can be repaired simply by covering holes or cracks with duct tape. More stubborn problems may require caulking as well as taping.
- If you have oil heat, have someone check to see if the firing rate is correct.
- Don't let cold air seep into your home through the attic access door. Check the door to make sure it is well insulated and weather-stripped.
- Dust or vacuum radiator surfaces often. Dust and grime impede the flow of heat. If the radiators need painting, use flat paint, preferably black. It radiates heat better than glossy.
- Keep draperies and shades open in sunny windows; close them at night.
- For comfort in cooler indoor temperatures, use the best insulation of all–warm clothing.

Cooling Energy Savers

- If you need central air-conditioning, select a unit with the lowest suitable capacity and highest efficiency. A larger unit than you need not only costs more to run, but probably won't remove enough moisture from the air.

- Make sure the ducts in your air-conditioning system are properly insulated, especially those that pass through the attic or other uncooled spaces.
- If you don't need central air-conditioning, consider using individual units in rooms that need cooling from time to time.
- Install a whole-house ventilating fan in your attic or in an upstairs window to cool the house, even if you have central air-conditioning. It will pay to use the fan rather than air-conditioning when the outside temperature is below 82°F. When windows in the house are open, the fan pulls cool air through the house and exhausts warm air through the attic.
- Set your thermostat at 78°F. This is a reasonably comfortable and energy-efficient indoor temperature.
- Don't set your thermostat at a colder setting than normal when you turn your air conditioner on. It will not cool faster.
- Set the fan speed on high except in very humid weather. When it's humid, set the fan speed at low. You'll get less cooling, but more moisture will be removed from the air.
- Turn off your window air conditioners when you leave a room for several hours.
- Consider using a fan with your window air conditioner to spread the cooled air farther without greatly increasing your power use. However, be sure the air conditioner is strong enough to help cool the additional space.
- Don't place lamps or TV sets near your air-conditioning thermostat. Heat from these appliances is sensed by the thermostat and could cause the air conditioner to run longer than necessary.
- Keep out daytime sun with outdoor awnings or indoor draperies or shades.
- Open the windows instead of using your air conditioner or electric fan on cooler days and during cooler hours.
- If you don't use air-conditioning, be sure to keep windows and outside doors closed during the hottest hours of the day.
- Do your cooking and use other heat-generating appliances in the early morning and late evening hours when possible.
- Use vents and exhaust fans to pull heat and moisture from the attic, kitchen, and laundry directly to the outside.

Hot Water Energy Savers

Heating water accounts for about 15 percent of all the energy used in homes. Don't waste it.

- Repair leaky faucets promptly.
- Do as much household cleaning as possible with cold water.
- Insulate your hot water storage tank and piping.
- Buy a water heater with thick insulation on the shell. While the initial cost may be more, the savings in energy costs will more than repay you.
- Add insulation around the water heater you now have if it is inadequately insulated. Be sure not to block off needed air vents. That would create a safety hazard.
- Check the temperature on your water heater. Most water heaters are set for 140°F or higher, but you may not need water that hot unless you have a dishwasher. A setting of 120°F can provide adequate hot water for most families.

Energy Savers in the Kitchen, Laundry Room, and Bathroom

- Install an aerator in your kitchen sink faucet. By reducing the amount of water in the flow, you use less hot water and save energy.
- If you need to purchase a gas oven or range, look for one with an automatic (electronic) ignition system instead of pilot lights. If you have a gas range, make sure the pilot light is

burning efficiently with a blue flame. A yellowish flame indicates an adjustment is needed.

- Never boil water in an open pan. Water will come to a boil faster and use less energy in a kettle or covered pan.
- Keep range-top burners and reflectors clean. They will reflect the heat better, and you will save energy.
- Match the size of pan to the heating element. More heat will get to the pan; less will be lost to surrounding air.
- If you cook with electricity, get in the habit of turning off the burners before the end of the allotted cooking time. The heating element will stay hot long enough to finish the cooking without using more electricity.
- When using the oven, cook more than one food at a time.
- Watch the clock or use a timer. Don't continually open the oven door to check food. Every time you open the door, heat escapes and more energy is used.
- Use small electric pans or ovens for small meals rather than the kitchen range or oven. They use less energy.
- Use pressure cookers and microwave or convection ovens if you have them. They can save energy by reducing cooking time.
- When cooking with a gas range-top burner, use moderate flame settings to save gas.
- When you have a choice, use the range-top or a countertop oven rather than the oven.
- When buying a dishwasher, look for a model with air-power and/or overnight dry settings. These features automatically turn off the dishwasher after the rinse cycle.
- If your dishwasher doesn't have an automatic air-dry switch, turn off the control knob after the final rinse. Prop the door open a little and let the dishes air dry.
- Be sure your dishwasher is full, but not overloaded, when you turn it on.
- Wash clothes in warm or cold water and rinse them in cold water. Use hot water only if absolutely necessary.
- Fill clothes washers and dryers, unless they have small-load attachments or variable water levels.
- Do not run the dryer longer than necessary to dry clothes.
- Separate drying loads into heavy and lightweight items. Since the lighter ones take less drying time, the dryer does not have to be on as long for these loads.
- Dry your clothes in consecutive loads. Once the dryer is warm, it cuts down on initial energy consumption.
- Save energy needed for ironing by hanging clothes in the bathroom while you're bathing or showering. The steam often removes the wrinkles for you.
- Take showers rather than baths, but limit your showering time and check the water flow if you want to save energy.
- Consider installing a flow restricter in the pipe at the shower head. These inexpensive, easy-to-install devices restrict the flow of water.

Appliance Energy Savers

About 20 percent of the energy that people use goes into running electrical home appliances, so appliance use and selection can make a considerable difference in home utility costs.

- Don't leave your appliances running when they're not in use.
- Keep appliances in good working order so they will last longer, work more efficiently, and use less energy.
- When buying appliances, read labels carefully. Compare energy use information and operating costs of similar models by the same and different manufacturers. Look for yellow and black "EnergyGuide" labels on the following major appliances: refrigerators, refrigerator-freezers, freezers, dish-

washers, water heaters, clothes washers, air conditioners, and furnaces.

- Before buying new appliances with special features, find out how much energy they use compared with other models that may be less convenient. A frost-free refrigerator, for example, uses more energy than one you have to defrost manually.
- Use appliances wisely. Use the one that takes the least amount of energy for the job. For example, toasting bread in an oven uses three times more energy than using a toaster.

Lighting Energy Savers

Most Americans overlight their homes, so lowering lighting levels is an easy conservation measure. About 15 percent of the electricity we use in our homes goes into lighting.

- Turn off lights in any room not being used.
- Light-zone your home and save electricity. Concentrate lighting in reading and working areas and where it's needed for safety, such as stairwells. Reduce lighting in other areas, but avoid very sharp contrasts.
- To reduce overall lighting in nonworking spaces, remove one bulb out of three in multiple light fixtures and replace it with a burned-out bulb for safety. Replace other bulbs throughout the house with bulbs of the next lower wattage.
- Consider installing solid state dimmers or hi-low switches when replacing light switches. They make it easy to reduce lighting intensity in a room and thus save energy.
- Use one large bulb instead of several small ones in areas where bright light is needed.
- Use compact fluorescent lights whenever you can. They give out more lumens per watt. These new lights can fit into many incandescent lamp sockets and provide the same quality of light.
- Turn three-way bulbs down to the lowest lighting level when watching TV. You'll reduce the glare and save energy.
- Use fluorescent lights whenever you can. They give out more lumens per watt.
- Keep all lamps and lighting fixtures clean. Dirt absorbs light.
- Use outdoor lights only when and where they are needed. A photocell unit or timer will turn them on and off automatically.

Yard and Workshop Energy Savers

- Do not allow gasoline-powered yard equipment to idle for long periods.
- Use hand tools, hand lawn mowers, pruners, and clippers whenever possible.
- Maintain electrical tools in top operating condition. They should be clean and properly lubricated.
- Keep cutting edges sharp. A sharp bit or saw cuts more quickly and therefore uses less power.
- Buy power tools with the lowest horsepower adequate for the work you do.
- Remember to turn off shop lights, soldering irons, glue pots, and all bench heating devices right after use.

U.S. Department of Energy

GLOSSARY

A

absorbed light: light that is drawn in by a surface and cannot be reflected. (17)

abstract form: the physical shape of an object that rearranges or stylizes a recognizable object. (10)

abstract of title: a copy of all public records concerning a property. (5)

accent lighting: sharp lighting that is used for decorative purposes, especially to focus on the point of emphasis in a room. (17)

accessories: items smaller than furnishings that accent the design of a room. They may be either decorative (as pictures and figurines) or functional (as ashtrays and lamps). (17)

acoustical: a common material used for ceilings that deadens or absorbs sound. (14)

acquisition: the act of getting something. (5)

adjustable rate mortgage: a payment contract in which the interest rate is adjusted up or down periodically according to a national interest rate index. (5)

adobe: building material made of sun-dried earth and straw. (1)

aesthetics: a pleasing appearance or effect. (10)

agrarian: people who earn their living from the land. (2)

agreement of sale: a contract that states all specific terms and conditions of a sale. Also called a contract of purchase, purchase agreement, or sales agreement. (5)

alarm system: sensors set off an alarm if someone forces open a door or window. (20)

alcove: a small recessed section of a room. (7)

alphabet of lines: lines used on an architectural drawing that allow the drafter to communicate ideas clearly and accurately. (7)

American Society of Interior Designers (ASID): a professional organization that requires members to have a high level of preparation and training in interior design. (21)

ampere: the unit of current used to measure the amount of electricity passing through a conductor per unit of time. (9)

analogous color harmony: a color harmony made by combining related hues–those next to each other on the color wheel. (11)

anchor bolts: bolts set about six feet apart into the concrete of the foundation walls. (8)

annuals: flowers that must be replanted every year. (19)

antiques: furniture made over one hundred years ago in the style popular at that time. (15)

appliances: household devices powered by gas or electricity to help people meet their basic needs. (18)

applied design: patterns that are printed onto the surface of a piece of fabric. (13)

appraiser: an expert who estimates the quality and value of a property. (5)

apprentice: one who is enrolled in an organized program of job training that is coupled with vocational classes. (23)

architect: a person who designs buildings and supervises their construction. (4)

architectural drawings: a house plan containing information about the size, shape, and location of all parts of the house. (7)

assign: to transfer the entire unexpired portion of a lease to someone else and relinquish responsibility. (5)

attached houses: housing designed for one living unit, but sharing a common wall with the houses on each side. (4)

B

balance: a perception of the way arrangements are seen. It is the equilibrium among parts of a design. (12)

balustrade: a railing found on the flat area of hip roofs. (6)

batts: shorter rolls of blanket insulation. They are usually 4 to 8 feet long. (9)

beauty: the quality or qualities that give pleasure to the senses. (1)

belvedere: a small room on the roof of a house used as a lookout. (6)

bid: a charge for construction that includes the cost of materials and labor. (5)

biennials: flowers that must be replanted every other year. (19)

bill of lading: a receipt listing the goods shipped in a moving van. (4)

biosphere: the relationship of living beings and their environment. (22)

blend: yarn that is made up of two or more types of fibers. (13)

blended family: parents and children from a previous marriage living together in the same family. (1)

blinds: window treatments made of slats that can be raised up and down or moved to the side to control the amounts of air and light that enter a room. (17)

bond: the way that masonry units are arranged together in a pattern. (8)

bonded: two layers of fabric that are permanently joined together with an adhesive. (13)

bonded wood: wood that has been bonded by glue and pressure. (15)

box nails: nails with large, flat heads. (21)

box springs: a series of coils attached to a base and covered with padding. (15)

breach of contract: a legal term for failure to meet all terms of a contract or agreement. (5)

building codes: established minimum standards for materials and construction methods. (2)

built-in storage: shelves and drawers built into a storage room. (7)

bungalow: a one-story house with a low-pitched roof. (6)

butt joint: a board that is glued or nailed flush to another board. (15)

Note: Numbers in parentheses refer to the chapter in which each term is defined.

C

cafe curtains: horizontal panels that are hung in tiers to cover part of a window. The top of each panel is joined to rings that slip over a curtain rod. (17)

Cape Cod: a style of housing that is small, symmetrical, and one-and-one-half stories with a gable roof. (6)

career cluster: a group of several careers that are closely related. (23)

career ladder: a progression of related careers, each one requiring more qualifications than the previous one. (23)

career lattice: a chart showing related career opportunities organized in such a way that by moving up the chart, the careers require more qualifications, and by moving across the chart, the careers are in a slightly different subject area. (23)

carrying charges: amounts of money, other than interest, that are added to the price of an item when it is bought by the installment method. (5)

cellulosic natural fiber: fiber made of the cellulose in plants. It is usually highly absorbent, launders well, and is seldom damaged by insects. (13)

census: an official count of the population taken by the government. (2)

central heat pump system: an electric refrigeration unit used to either heat or cool a house. (9)

central-satellite decision: a group of decisions consisting of a major decision that is surrounded by related, but independent, decisions. (3)

chain decision: a sequence of decisions in which one decision triggers others. (3)

circuit: the path electrons follow from the source of the electricity to the device and back to the source. (9)

circuit breaker: a switch that automatically interrupts an electrical current under an abnormal condition. (21)

climate: prevailing weather conditions of a region as determined by the temperature and meteorological changes over a period of years. (2)

closed: when the legal and financial matters of moving into a new home have been settled. (5)

close-out sale: a sale held when a store is moving to another location or going out of business. (16)

closing costs: the fees for settling the legal and financial matters of buying and selling property. (5)

coil springs: spiral-shaped springs without padding and covering that are used in heavier furniture. (15)

collectibles: highly-valued furnishings that are less than one hundred years old but no longer made. (15)

color harmony: certain colors are used together in a pleasing manner. (11)

color wheel: a particular circular arrangement of primary, secondary, and intermediate colors; the basis of all color relationships. (11)

combination yarn: a continuous strand of yarn made up of two or more different yarns. (13)

combustible: the quality of being burnable. (20)

comforter: a filled bed covering that is often used as a bedspread. (13)

common-use storage: storage used by all who live in a house. It includes the storage near the entrance where outerwear is kept and storage for food, tools, and other items that are shared. (7)

community: a particular area that is smaller than a region, but larger than a neighborhood. Examples include a large city, small village, or rural area. (4)

compact fluorescent bulb: a light bulb that uses only 15 watts of electricity and operates for 9,000 hours. (17)

comparison shopping: comparing the qualities, prices, and services provided for similar items in different stores before buying. (16)

complement: a hue that is directly across from another hue on a color wheel. (11)

complementary color harmony: a color harmony made by combining complementary colors–those opposite one another on the color wheel. (11)

computer-aided drafting and design (CADD): software and hardware used to create designs using a computer. (2)

condominium: a type of ownership where the buyer owns individual living space and has an undivided interest in the common areas and facilities of the multiunit building. (4)

conductor: allows the flow of electricity; usually a wire. (9)

conduit: a metal or plastic pipe that surrounds and protects wires. (9)

coniferous: trees that do not lose their leaves. (15)

con-ops: a blend of condominium and cooperative units. In con-ops, the buyers own their individual living spaces as in a condominium ownership; however, the common areas and facilities are owned cooperatively. (4)

conservation: the process of protecting or saving something from loss or waste. (19)

contemporary: a housing style in which the designs are surprising and often controver-sial. (6)

continuous-cleaning ovens: an oven with a special coating on the walls to keep it clean. Food is oxidized over a period of time during the normal baking process. (18)

contractor: a person who contracts or agrees to supply certain materials or to do certain work for a stipulated fee, especially one who contracts to build buildings. (4)

convection oven: a stream of heated air that is forced directly onto foods and cooks food faster at lower temperatures. (18)

conventional mortgage: a two-party contract between a borrower and a lending firm. This type of mortgage is not insured by the government. Therefore, a greater risk is involved. (5)

cool colors: blue, green, violet, and the colors near them in a color wheel. Also called receding colors. (11)

cooperative: a type of ownership where people buy shares of stock in a nonprofit corporation. These shares entitle them to occupy a unit in the cooperative building. (4)

cooperative education: schooling that includes working part-time and attending classes part-time. (23)

corner blocks: small pieces of wood attached between corner boards that support and reinforce the joint. (15)

cost: the amount of human and nonhuman resources used to achieve something. (5)

creativity: the ability to create. (1)

credit cards: cards used instead of cash to buy goods and services. Only part of what is owed needs to be paid by the date listed on the bill, and interest is added to the remaining amount. (5)

culture: beliefs, social customs, and traits of a group of people. (2)

curtains: flat fabric panels that cover windows. They have a pocket hem at the top, which slips onto a curtain rod. (17)

curved line: a line that is a part of a circle or an oval. (10)

custom-designed and custom-built: the most individualistic type of house that is designed and built by an architect and a contractor. (4)

D

deadbolt locks: a lock that requires turning a knob or a key to unlock the door from the inside, as well as the outside. (20)

decibels: unit of measure for the volume of sound. (20)

deciduous: trees that lose their leaves. (15)

declaration of ownership: a legal document containing the conditions and restrictions of the sale, ownership, and use of the property. (5)

deed: the legal document by which the title is transferred from one person to another. It describes the property being sold. (5)

dehumidifier: a small appliance that removes excess moisture from the air. (18)

density: the number of people in a given area. (2)

design: the entire process used to develop a specific project. It also refers to the product or result. (10)

detail view: an enlargement of a construction feature. (7)

developers: people who develop plots of land into subdivisions, neighborhoods, apartment complexes, and shopping centers. (4)

diagonal line: a line that angles between a horizontal and a vertical line. (10)

diffused light: light scattered over a large area. It has no glare and creates a soft appearance. (17)

direct lighting: lighting that shines directly towards an object. It provides the most light possible to a specific area and very little is reflected from other surfaces. (17)

disabilities: the impairing or limiting of a person's abilities. (2)

dormer: a window set in a structure that projects through a sloping roof. (6)

double-complementary color harmony: a color harmony consisting of two colors and their complements. (11)

double dowel joint: glued wooden dowels that fit into drilled holes in two pieces of wood. (15)

dovetail joint: fastened corner joints in which tightly fitting teeth are carved on both pieces of wood. (15)

down payment: a payment that is made to secure a purchase. (5)

draperies: pleated panels of fabric that cover windows completely or are pulled to the side. (17)

dual-career families: families in which both parents are employed. (23)

dual-income family: when both the husband and wife are employed outside the home. (2)

Dutch Colonial: houses built of fieldstone or brick, but sometimes wood. They feature gambrel roofs, central entrances, off-center chimneys, and dormer windows. (6)

dysfunctional: when the behavioral environment produces a negative effect on members of the living unit. (2)

E

earnest money: a deposit the potential buyer pays to show that he or she is serious about buying the house. The money is held in trust until the closing of the transaction. (5)

earth-sheltered: houses that are partially covered with soil. (6)

eclectic: a type of decor based on a mixture of furnishings from different periods and countries. (16)

ecology: the study of the relationship between living organisms and their surroundings. (22)

electric current: the movement of electrons along a conductor. (9)

electronic radiant heating system: a heating system in which resistance wiring is used to produce heat in the wire, which is placed in the ceiling, floor, or baseboards. (9)

electrical shock: an electric current that passes through one's body. (20)

electricity: the movement of electrons along a conductor. (9)

electronic lamp (E-lamp): a lamp that lasts up to 20,000 hours and fits most sockets that use incandescent bulbs. (17)

elevation view: the finished exterior appearance of a given side of the house. (7)

emphasis: a center of interest or focal point in a room. (12)

enclosure elements: barriers that confine a space. (19)

EnergyGuide label: a label that states the average yearly energy cost of operating an appliance. (18)

entrepreneur: a person who starts and runs his or her own business. (23)

environment: the conditions, objects, places, and people that surround a living organism. (2)

equity: the money value of a house beyond what is owed on the house. (5)

escape plan: a plan of action in case a fire occurs. (20)

esteem: having the respect, admiration, and high regard of others. (1)

eviction: a legal procedure that forces a lessee to leave the property before the rental agreement expires. (5)

extended family: a living unit consisting of several generations of a family. (1)

F

family life cycle: a series of stages through which a family passes during its lifetime. (1)

Federal: a style of housing that has a box-like shape. It is at least two stories high and is symmetrical with a flat roof. (6)

felting: the process of using heat, moisture, chemicals, friction, and pressure to interlock and hold fibers. (13)

FHA-insured mortgage: a three-party contract that involves the borrower, lending firm, and Federal Housing Administration (FHA). (5)

fiber: the raw material from which fabric is made. (13)

finance charge: a fee paid for the privilege of using credit. It includes interest and carrying charges. (5)

financing: a form of credit in which the borrower and lender agree to a payment plan. This includes an interest fee and a transfer of ownership should the borrower become delinquent in payment. (5)

finish: a substance that is applied to fabric to improve its appearance, feel, or performance. (13)

finish nails: a nail with a very small head that can be driven below the surface. (21)

fireplace insert: a metal device that fits into an existing masonry fireplace and attaches to the chimney liner. It is used to transform a drafty fireplace into a more energy-efficient fireplace. (9)

flammable: fabrics that burn quickly.(13)

flat springs: flat, S-shaped springs that may have metal support strips banded across them. (15)

float: portions of yarn that lie on the surface of the fabric. (13)

floor coverings: flooring materials, such as carpets and rugs, that are placed on top of the structural floor. (14)

flooring materials: materials that are used as the top surface of a floor, such as wood, ceramic tile, and brick. (14)

floor plan: a simplified drawing that shows the size and arrangement of rooms, hallways, doors, windows, and storage areas on a floor of a house. (7)

fluorescent light: light produced as electricity activates mercury vapor within a sealed tube to create invisible ultraviolet rays. These rays are converted into visible light rays by a fluorescent material that coats the inside of the glass tube. (17)

foam mattress: latex or polyurethane foam that is cut or molded to shape and is covered with a tightly-woven cotton cloth. (15)

footcandle: a unit of measure for illumination. It is the amount of light a standard candle gives at a distance of one foot. (17)

footing: the bottom of the foundation, which supports the rest of the foundation and the house. (8)

forced warm-air system: a heating system in which the air is heated by a furnace and then delivered to the rooms through supply ducts. (9)

foreclosure: a legal proceeding in which a lending firm takes possession of the mortgaged property of a debtor who fails to live up to the terms of the contract. (5)

form: the physical shape of objects. It outlines the edges of a three-dimensional object and contains volume and mass. (10)

formal balance: the arrangement of identical objects on either side of a center point. Also called symmetrical balance. (12)

foundation: the underlying base of the house, which is composed of the footing and the foundation walls. (8)

foundation wall: the walls supporting the load of the house between the footing and the floor. (8)

free form: a shape that is random and flowing and communicates a feeling of freedom. It is found in nature. (10)

freestanding houses: single-family houses that stand alone and are not connected to another unit. (4)

French Manor: a symmetrical house with wings on each side and a Mansard roof on the main part of the house. (6)

French Provincial: a style of housing that has a delicate, dignified appearance and is usually symmetrical. The windows are a dominant part of the design, and the tops of the windows break into the eave line. (6)

frost line: the depth to which frost penetrates soil in any climate. (8)

full warranty: a written agreement which allows a consumer to have a broken appliance repaired or replaced free of charge (at the warrantor's option). (18)

function: purpose of the designed room; the way in which a design works. This includes usefulness, convenience, and organization.
(7, 10)

fuse: device used to open an electric circuit when an overload occurs. (21)

G

gable roof: a roof that comes to a point in the center and slopes on both sides. (6)

gambrel roof: a two-pitched roof with the lower slope steeper than the upper slope. (6)

garrison: a style of housing in which an overhang allows extra space on the second floor. (6)

general lighting: lighting that provides a soft, even level of light throughout a room or area. (17)

general warranty deed: transfers the title of a property to the buyer. It guarantees that the title is clear of any claims against it. (5)

generic name: a name given to describe a group of fibers with similar chemical compositions. (13)

geometric form: the physical shape of an object that uses squares, rectangles, circles, and other geometric figures to create form. (10)

Georgian: a style of housing that has simple exterior lines, a dignified appearance, and is symmetrical. Georgian houses have windows with small panes of glass and either gable or hip roofs. (6)

geothermal energy: energy coming from the heat of the earth's interior. (22)

girder: a large horizontal member in the floor that takes the end load of joists. (8)

golden mean: the division of a line between one-half and one-third of its length, which creates a more pleasing look to the eye than an equal division. (12)

golden rectangle: a rectangle having sides in a ratio of 2:3. The short sides are two-thirds the length of the long sides. (12)

golden section: the division of a line or form in such a way that the ratio of the smaller section to the larger section is equal to the ratio of the larger section to the whole. (12)

gradation: the type of rhythm created by a gradual increase or decrease of similar elements of design. (12)

graduated-care facilities: a life care community for older people in which the residents move from their own apartments to a nursing home unit as needed. (4)

grain: the direction that threads run in a woven fabric. (13)

Greek Revival: architecture imitating ancient Greece, where the main characteristic is a two-story portico. The portico is supported by columns and has a large triangular pediment. (6)

Gross Domestic Product (GDP): the value of all goods and services produced within a country during a given time period, regardless of who owns the production facilities. (2)

gross income: income before deductions. (5)

ground cover: low-growing plants that cover the ground in place of sod. (19)

Ground Fault Circuit Interrupter (GFCI): safety device used in outlets to help prevent shocks. (20)

H

habitual behavior: actions that are done as routine without thought. (3)
hand limitations: conditions that limit hand movement and gripping ability. (20)
hardware: the components in a computer system. (18)
harmony: agreement among parts. It is created when the elements of design are effectively used according to the principles of design. (12)
hazardous wastes: poisonous waste materials that damage the environment and cause illness. (22)
header: small, built-up beams that carry the load of the structure over door and window openings. (8)
hearing-impaired: degree of hearing loss. (20)
high mass: a space that is visually crowded. (10)
high-tech: a high level of technology. (23)
hillside ranch: a type of ranch style house that is built on a hill. The basement is often partially exposed. (6)
hip roof: roofs with sloping ends and sloping sides. They also are sometimes topped by a flat area with a balustrade railing. (6)
hogan: buildings made of logs and mud. (2)
home: any place a person lives. (4)
horizontal line: a line that is parallel to the ground. (10)
house: any building that serves as living quarters for one or more families. (4)
housing: any dwelling that provides shelter. (1)
housing market: the transfer of dwellings from the producers to the consumers. (2)
hue: the name of the color. It is the one characteristic that makes a color unique. (11)
human ecology: the study of people and their environment. (1)
human resources: resources that are available from people, such as abilities, knowledge, attitudes, energy, and health. (3)
humidifier: a small appliance that adds the desired amount of moisture into the air. (18)
hydroelectric energy: electrical power that is generated by water in dams and rivers. (22)
hydronic heating system: a circulating hot water system in which water is heated in a boiler to a preset temperature and then pumped through pipes to radiators. (9)

I

incandescent light: the light produced when an electric current heats a tungsten filament inside a bulb so that it glows and gives off light. (17)
indirect lighting: lighting that is directed mainly towards a ceiling or wall. It is reflected from these surfaces to produce soft, general lighting for a room. (17)
individual life cycle: a series of stages through which a person passes during his or her lifetime. (1)
induction cooktops: a range that cooks food by using a magnetic field to generate heat in the bottom of cooking utensils. (18)
informal balance: the arrangement of different, but equivalent, objects on either side of a center point. Also called asymmetrical balance. (12)
innerspring mattress: a series of springs covered with padding. (15)
inspector: a person who judges the construction and present condition of a house. (5)
installment buying: the process of buying something by making a series of payments during a given length of time. (5)
insulation: material used to restrict the flow of heat from out of the house in winter and into the house in the summer. (9)
integrated waste management: a waste handling concept that conserves energy and cleans the environment. (22)
intensity: the brightness or dullness of a hue. (11)
interest: the price paid for the use of borrowed money. It is usually stated as an annual percentage rate of the amount borrowed. (5)
interior designer: a person who plans the decorating of an interior, makes the purchases, and sees that the work is done correctly. (21)
intermediate colors: colors made by mixing equal amounts of a primary color and a secondary color. Also called tertiary colors. (11)

J

job descriptions: a brief explanation of what a particular job is like: what duties it involves, what qualifications are needed, and what opportunities it offers. (23)
joist: lightweight horizontal support members. (8)

K

kit house: housing shipped to the site in unassembled parts or as a finished shell from the factory. (4)
knitting: the process of looping yarns together. (13)

L

landscape: outdoor living space. (19)
landscape zones: the ground around a building that is divided into three areas–the public zone, the private zone, and the service zone. (19)
landscaping: altering the topography and adding decorative plantings to change the appearance of a site. (4)
lavatory: a plumbing fixture designed for washing hands and faces. (9)
leadership: the ability to guide and motivate others to complete tasks or achieve goals. (23)
lease: a legal document spelling out the conditions under which the renter rents the property. It lists the rights and responsibilities of both the owner and the renter. (5)
lessee: the person who has signed a lease and pays rent. (5)
lessor: the person who owns the property to be rented. (5)
life cycle: a series of stages through which an individual or family passes during a lifetime. (1)
life situations: circumstances that affect people and the way they live. (1)
life-style: a living pattern or way of life. (1)
limited warranty: a written agreement that only obligates a warrantor to do certain kinds of repairs at no charge to the

consumer or to replace the product under certain conditions. (18)

living unit: people who share the same living quarters. (1)

local lighting: lighting that is used in specific areas that require more light. (17)

loss leader sale: a type of sale in which a store greatly reduces the prices on a few items hoping that customers will also buy items that are not on sale. (16).

low mass: a space that is simple and sparse. (10)

M

maintenance fees: payment that is used for the repair and maintenance of the common areas of a condominium. (5)

man-made landscape elements: landscape components that are not found in nature. (19)

Mansard roof: a variation of the gambrel roof designed by a French architect named Mansard. The roof continues all around the house and dormers often project from the steeply pitched part of the roof. (6)

manufactured fiber: fiber made from wood cellulose, oil products, and other chemicals. (13)

manufactured housing: housing built in factories and then moved to a site and assembled. (4)

mass: the amount of pattern or objects in a space. It is also how crowded or empty a space appears. (10)

meter: a gauge that monitors electrical usage in the house. (9)

microenvironment: a small and distinct part of the total environment in which a person lives. (1)

microwave oven: an oven that cooks food with high frequency energy waves called microwaves. (18)

minimum property standards (MPS): standards set by the Federal Housing Administration (FHA) that regulate the size of lots. (4)

mobile home: a factory-built, single-family dwelling that can be moved by attached wheels. (4)

mobility impairment: conditions that make it difficult for a person to walk from one place to another. (20)

modern: housing styles developed in the twentieth century. (6)

monochromatic color harmony: the simplest color harmony. It is based on tints and shades of a single hue. (11)

mortgage: a pledge of property that a borrower gives to a lender as security for the payment of a debt. (5)

mortise-and-tenon joint: one of the strongest joints used for furniture. The glued tenon fits tightly into the mortise, or hole. (15)

motor home: an automotive vehicle equipped as a house. (4)

multifamily house: a structure that provides housing for more than one living unit. (4)

multiple roles: filling more than one position, such as parent, homemaker, and engineer, with each position having different responsibilities. (23)

multipurpose furniture: furniture that can be used for more than one purpose. (16)

multipurpose room: a room used for many types of activities, such as reading, studying, watching TV, listening to music, and working on hobbies. (7)

N

nap: a layer of fiber ends that stand up from the surface of the fabric. (13)

natural landscape elements: landscape components found in the natural environment, such as terrain and soil. (19)

needlepunching: the process of interlocking fibers by using felting needles to produce a flat carpet that resembles felt. (13)

needs: the basic items that people must have in order to live. (1)

neighborhood: a section of a community consisting of a group of houses and people. (4)

net income: the amount of money left after deductions. (5)

neutral color harmony: a color harmony using combinations of black, white, and gray. Brown, tan, and beige can also be used. (11)

new town: an urban development consisting of a small to medium-sized city with a broad range of housing and planned industrial, commercial, and recreational facilities. (2)

nonhuman resources: resources that are not directly supplied by people. Examples include money, property, and community resources. (3)

nonstructural lighting: lights that are not permanently built into a home. They can be moved, changed, and replaced easily. (17)

nuclear energy: the heat released when Uranium-235 is fissioned (split) in a nuclear reactor. (22)

nuclear family: a living unit consisting of parents and their children; also, a childless married couple. (1)

O

one-person living unit: housing occupied by single people. (1)

opposition: lines meeting to form right angles. (12)

overcurrent protection devices: a fuse or circuit breaker that stops the excessive flow of electrical current in the circuit if too much current is being drawn. (9)

owner-built houses: housing constructed by the living unit. Although a contractor may be hired to put up the shell of the house, the living unit does the interior work. (4)

P

pediment: an architectural roof-like decoration that can be segmental or triangular and is usually found over porticoes, windows, or doors. (6)

Pennsylvania Dutch Colonial: a style of housing characterized by gable roofs and thick, fieldstone walls. (6)

pent roof: small roof ledges between the first and second floors. (5)

perennials: flowers that bloom for several years without replanting. (19)

photovoltaic array: solar cell array that converts sunlight into electricity. (22)

physical disabilities: limitations of the human body, such as visual or hearing impairments. (20)

physical needs: basic survival essentials, including shelter, food, water, and rest. (1)

physical neighborhood: the actual dwellings, buildings, and land that make up a neighborhood. (4)

pigment: color. (11)
planned neighborhood: determining the size and layout of individual lots before building begins. (4)
plan views: views from the top of an imaginary glass box. (7)
pollution: all the harmful changes in the environment that are caused by human activities. (22)
portico: an open space covered with a roof that is supported by columns and added to the main entrance. (6)
prairie style: a style of housing using wood, stone, and materials found in the natural environment. This style was designed by Frank Lloyd Wright. (6)
precautions: preventive actions that can help avoid accidents. (20)
pressed wood: a board made of shavings, veneer scraps, chips, and other small pieces of wood pressed together. Often used on unseen parts of furniture. (15)
primary colors: the colors of red, yellow, and blue. All other colors are made from these colors. (11)
print: a copy of an architectural drawing. (7)
prioritize: ranking in order of importance. (16)
privacy: need to be completely alone. (1)
private zone: the part of a site hidden from public view. It provides space for recreation and relaxation. (4)
process: the method used to accomplish a task. (5)
proportion: the relationship of parts of the same object, or the relationship between different objects in the same group. (12)
protein natural fiber: silk and wool; fibers made from animal sources. (13)
psychological needs: needs related to the mind, and feelings that must be met in order to live a satisfying life. (1)
public zone: the part of a site that can be seen from the street or road. It is usually in front of the house. (4)

Q

quality of life: the degree of satisfaction obtained from life. (1)
quiet area: space in a house provided for sleeping, resting, grooming, and dressing. (7)
quitclaim deed: a legal document that transfers whatever interest the seller has in the property. By accepting such a deed, the buyer assumes all legal and financial risks for the property. (5)

R

radiation: lines flowing outward from a central point. (12)
radon: a natural radioactive gas found in the earth. (20)
rafter: a series of beams that support the roof. (8)
raised ranch: a type of house similar to a ranch, but the top part of the basement is above ground. (6)
ranch: a style of housing characterized by a one-story structure that often has a basement. It also features a low-pitched roof with a wide overhang. (6)
rational decision: a decision based on reasoning. (3)
realistic form: the physical shape of an object that communicates a life-like, normal, and traditional feeling. (10)
recycle: adapting to a new use. (16)
recycling: the reprocessing of resources to be used again. (22)
redecorating: a change of decorating scheme. (21)
reflected light: light that bounces off a surface. (17)
region: a specific part of the world, country, or state. (4)
remodeling: changing a structure, such as adding a wall or a room. (21)
renegotiable rate mortgage: a payment contract in which the interest rate and monthly payments are fixed for a stated length of time. When this length of time expires, interest rates are reviewed and may be changed according to the current rate of interest. Also called a rollover mortgage. (5)
repetition: repeating an element of design. It is one of the easiest ways to achieve rhythm in a design. (12)
reproductions: copies of antique originals. (15)
resiliency: ability to recover original size and shape. (13)
resources: objects, qualities, or people that can be used to reach a goal. (2)
restore: changing a piece of furniture back to its original state. (16)
reverse mortgage: a payment plan designed for older people. A mortgage company converts the money tied up in a house into income, until the people no longer live in the house. At that time, the mortgage company assumes ownership of the dwelling. (4)
rhythm: a sense of movement that smoothly leads the eyes from one area to another in a design. The result of an organized pattern. (12)
ridge: the horizontal line where the two slopes of the roof meet. It is the highest point of the roof frame. (8)
row houses: a continuous group of dwellings connected by common side walls. (2)
R-value: the resistance of a material to heat movement. (9)

S

saltbox: a style of housing that is a variation of the Cape Cod. It was created by adding a lean-to section to the back of the house. (6)
scale: the size of an object on an architectural drawing, proportioned according to the determined drawing size. The relative size of an object in relation to other objects. (7, 12)
scale floor plan: a drawing that shows the size and shape of a room. (16)
seasonal sale: a sale held at the end of a selling season to get rid of stock so that a store can make room for new items. (16)
secondary colors: the colors of orange, green, and violet. These colors are made by mixing equal amounts of two primary colors. (11)
section view: a view taken from an imaginary cut through a part of the building, such as the walls. (7)
security deposit: a payment that insures the owner against financial loss caused by the renter. (5)
self-actualization: when a person develops to his or her full potential as a person. (1)
self-cleaning oven: an oven that can be set at extremely high temperatures to burn soil away. (18)
self-esteem: an awareness and appreciation of a person's own worth. (1)
self-expression: showing a person's true personality and taste. (1)
sensory design: the application of how to apply design in regard to the senses of sight, hearing, smell, and touch. (12)

service drop: the connecting wires from the pole transformer to the point of entry to the house. (9)

service entrance panel: a large metal box that receives power from the electric company's service drop or service lateral. It divides the power into individual circuits. (9)

service zone: the part of the site that is used for necessary activities. It includes sidewalks, driveways, and storage areas for such items as trash, tools, lawn equipment, and cars. (4)

shade: a value of a hue that is darker than the hue's normal value. (11)

shades: screens that block out unwanted light. (17)

shingle: a thin piece of material for laying in overlapping rows on roofs. (8)

short circuit: an undesirable current path that allows the electric current to bypass the load of the circuit. (21)

shutters: movable hinged screens that cover part or all of a window. (17)

siding: the material covering the exposed surface of outside walls of a house. (8)

sill plate: a piece of lumber bolted to the foundation wall with anchor bolts. (8)

single-family house: housing designed for one family or living unit. (4)

single-parent family: a family with only a mother or a father. (1)

site: the piece of land on which a dwelling is built. (4)

smoke detector: a small appliance that gives a loud warning signal if a fire starts. (20)

social area: an area providing space for daily living, entertaining, and recreation. (7)

software: a program of instructions that tells a computer what to do. (18)

soil conservation: the act of improving and taking care of the soil. (19)

soil stack: a vertical pipe that extends through the roof, so gases may vent outside. (9)

solar energy: energy derived from the sun. (6)

solid waste: any discarded material that is not a liquid or a gas. (22)

solid wood: furniture in which all exposed parts are made of whole pieces of wood. (15)

Southern Colonial: a style of housing that features a large, two- or three-story frame with a symmetrical design. (6)

space: the area around a form and inside a form. (10)

Spanish: a housing style that emanated from the South and Southwest. Its overall design is asymmetrical; other characteristics are red tile roofs, enclosed patios, arch-shaped windows and doors, wrought iron exterior decor, and stucco walls. (6)

special warranty deed: transfers the title to the buyer. It guarantees that during the time the seller held the title to the property, the seller did nothing that would or will in the future impair the buyer's title. (5)

specifications: information for design and construction that is prepared in written form and communicates the types and quality of materials to be used and give directions for their use. (7)

split-complementary color harmony: a color harmony created by choosing one color and then adding the two colors on each side of its complement. (11)

split-level: a type of house that has either three or four levels. It was developed for sloping lots. (6)

spur-of-the-moment decision: a decision that is made quickly, with little thought of the possible consequences. (3)

structural design: the pattern created by varying the yarns of woven or knitted fabric. (13)

structural light fixtures: fixtures that are permanently built in a home. (17)

stucco: a type of plaster applied to the exterior walls of a house. (6)

stud: vertical 2 inch by 4 inch or 2 inch by 6 inch framing members. (8)

subdivision: a smaller version of the new town concept. (2)

subflooring: a covering of plywood sheets that is nailed directly to the floor joists. (8)

sublet: to transfer part of the unexpired portion of a lease to someone else and maintain responsibility. (5)

substandard: houses that are not up to the standards that are best for people. (2)

Sunbelt: the southern and southwestern states of the United States. (2)

sun-room: a structure that traps heat. The trapped heat is a source of energy to heat water or air. (19)

symbols: icons used on architectural drawings to represent plumbing and electrical fixtures, doors, windows, and other common objects in a house. (7)

T

tactile texture: how the surface feels to the touch. (10)

tanned: leather treated with tannin, a special acid, that makes it soft and resistant to stains, fading, and cracking. (13)

task lighting: light that is used to help one see well enough to do a certain task, such as writing letters, carving wood, or sewing. (17)

tax exemption: not having to pay taxes on a designated portion of income. (2)

technology: a scientific discovery achieved through research and development. (2)

template: paper cut in the shape of a piece of furniture to be used on a scale floor plan. (16)

textiles: any products made from fibers, including fabrics. (13)

texture: the way a surface feels or looks. (10)

tint: a value of a hue that is lighter than the hue's normal value. (11)

title: a document that gives proof of the rights of ownership and possession of a particular property. (5)

tongue and groove joint: a joint created by matching a tongue cut on one board to a groove on another. (15)

topography: the physical features of the land, such as hills and rivers; the art of representing such features on maps and charts. (2)

toxic: poisonous. (20)

tract houses: groups of similarly-designed houses built on a tract of land. (2)

trade name: names used by companies to identify their own specific fibers. (13)

traditional: a style or design created in the past that has survived the test of time and is still being used today. (6)

traffic patterns: the paths followed from room to room, or to the outside of the dwelling. (7)
transition: carrying the eyes from one part of an object to another part. (12)
trap: a plumbing device that catches and holds a quantity of water. (9)
triad color harmony: a color harmony using three colors that are spaced evenly around the color wheel. (11)
truss rafter: a group of members forming a rigid triangular framework for the roof. (8)
tufted: yarn looped into backing material and secured with an adhesive to the backing and a second backing. (13)
tungsten-halogen light: the light produced when a gas from the halogen family and tungsten molecules are combined to activate a filament. (17)
turret: a small tower that is characteristic of Victorian style houses. (6)

U

unassembled furniture: furniture that does not come put together and may or may not be finished. (16)
unity: repeating similar elements of design to relate all parts of a design by one idea. (12)

V

VA-guaranteed mortgage: is a three-party loan involving the borrower (veteran), lending firm, and Veterans Administration (VA). (5)
value: the lightness or darkness of a hue. (11)
values: strong beliefs or ideas about what is important. (1)
veneered wood: wood made by bonding several thin layers of wood together at right angles to each other. Fine wood is often used for the top layer. (15)
veneer wall: a nonsupporting wall tied to the wall frame that is covered with wallboard. (8)
ventilation: the circulation of air. Proper ventilation helps reduce pollution levels. (20)
vertical line: a line that is perpendicular to the ground. (10)
Victorian: a style of housing named after Queen Victoria of England. The main characteristic is an abundance of decorative trim. (6)
visual imagery: a type of nonverbal communication. It is the language of sight and communicates a certain personality or mood. (10)
visually impaired: a degree of vision loss. (20)
visual pollution: the destruction of the appearance of the environment as a result of human activities. (22)
visual texture: the texture that is seen, but cannot be felt. (10)
visual weight: the perception that an object weighs more or less than it really does. (12)
voltage: a measure of the pressure used to push the electrical current along a conductor. (9)

W

wale: the diagonal rib or cord pattern of yarn. (13)
warm colors: red, yellow, orange, and the colors near them on a color wheel. They remind people of fire and the sun. Also called advancing colors. (11)
warp yarn: lengthwise strand that forms the lengthwise grain. (13)
warranty: a written guarantee of a product's performance and of the maker's responsibilities concerning defective parts. (18)
water conservation: the act of saving water from waste. (19)
watt: a unit of measure for electrical power. (9)
weather stripping: a strip of material that covers the edges of a window or door to prevent moisture and air from entering the house. (9)
weaving: two sets of yarns that are interlocked at right angles to each other. (13)
weft yarn: crosswise filling yarns that form the crosswise grain. (13)
wood grain: the natural decorative characteristics of wood. The pattern depends to a great extent on how the wood is cut from the log. (15)
work area: parts of the house that are needed to maintain and service the other areas. (7)
work triangle: the imaginary lines connecting the food preparation and storage center, the cleanup center, and the cooking and serving center of a kitchen. (7)

X

xeriscape: landscapes that are designed to conserve water. (19)

Y

yarn: a continuous strand made from fibers. (13)

Z

zoning regulations: controlled land use in certain areas. These regulations state that only specific activities can take place in a certain area. (2)

INDEX

A
Absorbed light, 259
  definition, 259
Accent lighting, definition, 262
Accents, 296, 297
Accessibility, chart, 322
Accessories, 265, 266
  chart, 266
  definition, 265
Accidents, preventing, 308, 309
Adjustable wrench, 331
Advertisements, 247
Agents, real estate, 375
Air, 310-312
Air conditioners, 281
Alarm system, 318, 319
  definition, 318
American Society of Interior Designers, definition, 343
Annuals, definition, 290
Appliance considerations, 269-271
  cost, 269, 270
  features, 270
  quality, 271
  safety, 270
  size, 270
Appliances, 269-284
  climate control, 280, 281
  definition, 269
  kitchen, 272-279
  laundry, 279, 280
  portable, 283, 284
Apprentice, definition, 379
Architects, 369, 371
  landscape, 371
Arrangement and selection of furniture, budgeting money, 247-250
Artificial light, 256-259
  fluorescent light, 258, 259
  incandescent light, 256-258
Artificial lighting, 293
Automatic washers, 279
  chart, 280
  features, 279
Abstract form, definition, 166
Abstract of title, 96, 97
  definition, 96
Acceptance and love, 13
Acoustical, definition, 220
Acquiring housing, 81-103
  acquisition, 82, 83
  buying a place, 91-101
  condominium ownership, 101, 102
  cooperative ownership, 102
  renting, 83-91
Acquisition, 82, 83
  cost, 83
  definition, 82
  process, 82, 83
  process and cost, 83
  process chart, 82
Active systems, 153
Adjustable rate mortgage, 97
Adobe, definition, 11
Aesthetics, definition, 163
Affordable housing, 34
Agrarian, definition, 29
Agreement of sale, 96
  definition, 96
Alcove, definition, 127
Alphabet of lines, 121
  definition, 121
Ampere, definition, 146
Analogous color harmony, 177
  definition, 177
Anchor bolts, definition, 137
Antiques, 229
  definition, 229
Antiques, collectibles, and reproductions, 229, 230
  antiques, 229
  reproductions, 230
  collectibles, 229
Appearance, 203
Applied design, definition, 202
Appraiser, definition, 95
Appropriateness and function, 192
Architect, definition, 71
Architectural drawings, definition, 120
Architectural drawings for a house, 120-124
  prints, 120, 121
  views, 121-124
Area,124-127
  quiet, 124, 125
  separating, 126, 127
  social, 125, 126
  work, 125
Arrangement, factor of furniture, 241-243
Arrangement and selection of furniture, 241-251
Arrangement of space, 168
Assign, definition, 87
Assigning and subletting a lease, 87
Attached houses, 70, 71
  definition, 70

B
Background treatments, 220, 221
  floor treatments, 220, 221
  wall treatments, 221
Backgrounds, 212-222, 294-296
  interior, 212-222
  landscape, 294-296
Balance, 188
  definition, 188
Balustrade, definition, 110
Bargain shopping, 247
Basic life-style, 22
Bath, bed, and kitchen, textiles for, 207-209
Bath mats, 208
Bathroom, 207, 208
  bath mats, 208
  shower curtains, 208
  towels, 207, 208
Beauty, 13, 14, 193
  definition, 13
Bed, kitchen, and bath, textiles for, 207-209
Bed linens, 208
Bedroom, 208, 209
  bed linens, 208
  blankets, bedspreads, and comforters, 208, 209
Beds, 236, 237
  frames, 237
  mattresses, 236, 237
  springs, 237
Bedspreads, 208, 209
  comforters, and blankets, 208, 209
  definition, 209
Behavioral environment, 37
Belvedere, definition, 111
Better Business Bureau, 247
Bid, definition, 93
Biennials, definition, 290
Bill of lading, definition, 78
Blankets, bedspreads, and comforters, 208, 209
Blend, definition, 198
Blended family, definition, 17
Blinds, definition, 255
Biosphere, definition, 361
Bond, definition, 139
Bonded, definition, 202
Bonded wood, definition, 231
Boulders and stones, 290
Box nail, definition, 335
Box springs, definition, 237
Breach of contract, 87
  definition, 87
Brick, 214
Budget for furniture, 244
Budgeting money, 247-250
  bargain shopping, 247
  eclectic decor, 250
  multipurpose furniture, 247
  reusing furniture, 249
  unassembled furniture, 248
Building codes, definition, 42
Building or buying a house, 92-95
  building, 92, 93
  buying a new house, 93, 94
  buying a pre-owned house, 94, 95
Built-in storage, definition, 129
Bungalow, 112
  definition, 112

Burns, 309
Butt joint, definition, 231
Buying a house, 91-101
  building or buying, 92, 95
  chart, 92
  price, 92
  shopping for a house to buy, 95, 96
  steps to, 96-101
  new house, 93, 94
  pre-owned house, 94, 95
Buying or building a house, 92-95

C

Canisters, 282
Cape Cod, 108
  definition, 108
Care, decisions according to, 48
Care and cost, 206, 207
Care and maintenance, home, 343
Career clusters, 366-369
  career information, 369
  definition, 366
Career information, 369
Career ladders, 380, 381
  definition, 380
Career lattice, definition, 380
Career levels, 378-381
  career ladders, 380, 381
  entrepreneurial careers, 379, 380
  entry-level positions, 379
  mid-level positions, 378, 379
  professional-level positions, 378
Career satisfaction and life-style, 383, 384
Careers and life-style, 383, 384
  work and family, 384
  career satisfaction and life-style, 383, 384
Careers in housing, 365-386
  career clusters, 366-369
  career levels, 378-381
  careers and life-style, 383, 384
  housing providers, 366
  job descriptions, 369-378
  qualities for success, 381, 382
Catalogs, 245
Ceiling treatments, 219, 220
Cellulosic natural fibers, chart, 197
  definition, 197
Census, definition, 30
Central heat pump system, 152
  definition, 152
Central-satellite decision, 48, 49
  definition, 48
Central vacuum systems, 282, 283
Ceramic tile, 213, 214, 219
Chain decision, 49, 50
  definition, 49
Changes in housing, 30
Changing roles of society, 34
Channel-lock pliers, 333
Chemical products, chart, 311
Child safety, 309, 310
Children, housing needs, 75, 76
Circuit, definition, 146
Circuit breakers, 336
  definition, 336
Cleaners, vacuum, 281, 282
Cleaning, 326-329
  chart, 329
  cleaning products, 327
  cleaning schedule, 327-329
  cleaning tools, 326
Clerestory windows, 142
Climate, definition, 36
Climate control appliances, 280, 281
  dehumidifiers and humidifiers, 280, 281
  room air conditioners, 281
Clogged drains, 333-335
Closed, definition, 93
Close-out sales, 246
  definition, 246
Closet auger, 333
Closing costs, 98, 99
  definition, 98
Clusters, career, 366-369
Coil springs, definition, 235
Close-out sales, 246
  definition, 246
Collectibles, 229
  definition, 229
  reproductions, and antiques, 229, 230
Color, 172-184, 206
  artificial lighting chart, 182
  color harmonies, 176-179
  color harmonies usage, 179-183
  color wheel, 174-176
  patterns, 206
  understanding color, 173
Color characteristics, 175
  hue, 175
  intensity, 175
  value, 175
Color harmonies, 176-179
  analogous color harmony, 177
  complementary color harmony, 178
  double-complementary color harmony, 179
  monochromatic color harmony, 176
  neutral color harmonies, 179
  split-complementary color harmony, 178
  triad color harmony, 179
Color harmonies usage, 179-183
  life-styles, 180, 181
  moods and styles, 180
  room items, 181
  room location, 181, 182
Color harmony, definition, 176
Color wheel, 174-176
  color characteristics, 175
  definition, 174
  neutrals, 175, 176
  warm and cool colors, 176
Combination windows, 142
Combination yarn, definition, 198
Combustible, definition, 314
Comfort, 203
Comforters, blankets, and bedspreads, 208, 209
  definition, 209
Common-use storage, definition, 129
Community, 58, 59
  chart, 59
  definition, 58
  planned, 359, 360
Community life-style, 22, 23
Community resources, 52
Compact fluorescent bulbs, 259
  definition, 259
Compactors, trash, 279
Companies, utility, 377
Comparison shopping, definition, 244
Complement, definition, 175
Complementary color harmony, 178
Computer-aided drafting and design (CADD), definition, 41
Computer operators and secretaries, 376, 377
Computers, 156-158
  personal, 283
Concrete, 214
Condominium, definition, 70
Condominium ownership, 101, 102
Condominium units, 70
Conductor, definition, 146
Conduit, definition, 147
Coniferous, definition, 231
Con-ops, definition, 70
Conservation, 155-158, 300-303, 354
  definition, 300
  energy, 354
  landscaping for, 300-303
  water and soil, 301, 302
Constructed environment, 37
Construction, 135-144, 163, 198-202, 204, 230-237
  definition, 163
  fabric, 198-202
  furniture, 230-237
  house, 135-144
  materials for exterior, 138, 139
Construction and styles of furniture, 223-239
Construction careers, 373-375
Construction machinery operators, 375
Construction methods, 204
Consultants and salespeople, 376
Consumer protection, 237, 238
Consumer satisfaction, 271
Contemporary, definition, 114
Contemporary and modern furniture styles, 228
Contemporary furniture, 228
Contemporary houses, 114-116
  earth-sheltered houses, 116
  solar houses, 115, 116
Continuous cleaning oven, definition, 275
Contract, breach of, 87
Contractor, definition, 71
Convection ovens, 276, 277
  definition, 276
Conventional heating system, 140-152
  central heat pump system, 152
  electric radiant heating system, 152
  forced warm-air system, 150, 151
  hydronic heating system, 151, 152
Conventional mortgage, definition, 97

Cool and warm colors, 176
Cool colors, definition, 176
Cooling systems, 154
Cooperative education, definition, 379
Cooperative, definition, 69
Cooperative ownership, 102
Cooperative units, 69, 70
Cork, 219
Corner blocks, definition, 231
Cost, 83, 204, 269, 270
  definition, 83
Cost analysis, 341-343
Cost and care, 206, 207
Cost and process, 83
Creativity, 14
  definition, 14
Credit cards, definition, 83
Crosscut saw, 333
Cultural influences on housing, 32, 33
Culture, definition, 32
Curtains, 254, 255
  definition, 254
Curved line, definition, 165
Cushions, frames and springs, 235, 236
Custom-designed and custom-built, definition, 71

D

Damaged and discounted item sale, 246
Deadbolt locks, definition, 318
Decibels, definition, 313
Deciduous, definition, 231
Decision-making procedure, 53, 54
  alternative solutions, 53, 54
  choosing and acting on an alternative solution, 54
  problem identification, 53
Decision-making process, 52-54
  chart, 53
  procedure, 53, 54
  skills, 47-55
  steps in decision-making, 53
  resources for housing decisions, 50-52
  type of decisions 48-50
Decisions, interrelated, 48-50
Decisions according to thought and care, 48
Declaration of ownership, definition, 102
Decorating, 343, 344
Deed, definition, 99
Dehumidifier, definition, 280
Dehumidifiers and humidifiers, 280, 281
Density, definition, 29
Design, 161-171, 185-195, 202
  definition, 162
  elements of, 161-171
  goals of, 192, 193
  principles of, 185-195
  sensory, 193, 194
  characteristics, 162, 163
Designers, interior, 375, 376
Designing outdoor living space, 293-300
  accents, 296, 297
  furnishings, 298, 299
  landscape backgrounds, 294-296
  landscape features, 297, 298
  lighting, 300
Detail and section views, 123, 124
Detail view, definition, 124
Developers, definition, 59, 60
Developments, housing, 348-350
Diffused light, 260
  definition, 260
Diagonal lines, definition, 164
Direct lighting, definition, 260
Disabilities, definition, 34
Disabled, 74, 75, 130-132, 319-323
  housing design modifications for the, 130-132
  housing needs, 74, 75
Discounted and damaged item sales, 246
Discount houses, 245
Dishwashers, 278
  chart, 278
  features, 278
Disposers, food waste, 279
Door space, 129
Doors, 142, 143
  flush doors, 143
  framed-glass doors, 143
  stile and rail doors, 143
Doors and windows, 140-143, 156
Dormers, definition, 107
Double dowel joint, definition, 231
Double-complementary color harmony, 179
  definition, 179
Dovetail joint, definition, 231
Drafters, 371, 372
Draperies, 253, 254
  definition, 253
Draperies and curtains, 253-255
  curtains, 254, 255
  draperies, 253, 254
Drawings, architectural, 120-124
Dryers, 279, 280
  chart, 280
  features, 280
Dual-career families, definition, 384
Dual-income family, definition, 34
Durability, 203
Dutch, 107
Dutch Colonial, definition, 107
Dwelling, chart, 73
Dye, 203
Dysfunctional, definition, 37

E

Early shelter, 27-29
  housing of colonists, 27-29
  housing of Native Americans, 27
Earnest money, 96
  definition, 96
Earth-sheltered, definition, 116
Earth-sheltered houses, 116
Eclectic, definition, 250
Eclectic decor, 250
Ecology, 24, 354
  definition, 354
  human, 24
Economic influences on housing, 38, 39
  effects of housing on the economy, 38
  effects of the economy on housing, 38, 39
Economy, 16, 17, 38
  effects of housing on, 38
Elderly, 72-74
Electric current, definition, 146
Electric drill, 333
Electric heating system, 152
  definition, 152
Electric ranges, 274, 275
Electrical tester, 333
Electrical power generation, 147
Electrical repairs, 336, 337
  circuit breakers, 336
  fuses, 336
  power cord plugs, 337
  wall switches, 337
Electrical shock, 309
  definition, 309
Electrical systems, 146-148
  electrical power generation, 147
  electrical terms, 146, 147
  electricity in the house, 147, 148
Electrical terms, 146, 147
Electricity, definition, 146
Electricity in the house, 147, 148
Electronic lamp, definition, 258
Elements, 289-293
  landscape, 289-293
  man-made landscape, 291-293
  natural landscape, 289-291
Elements of design, 161-171
  design characteristics, 162, 163
  form, 166, 167
  line, 163, 164
  space, 167, 168
Elements of style, 168, 169
  mass, 168
  texture, 168, 169
Elevation view, 122
  definition, 122
Emphasis, 189, 190
  definition, 189
Enclosure elements, 291-293
  definition, 291
Energy, gas, 148, 149
Energy conservation, 155-158, 302, 354
  computers, 156-158
  insulation, 155, 156
  windows and doors, 156
Energy sources, 351-354
  geothermal energy, 353, 354
  hydroelectric power, 351, 352
  nuclear energy, 351
  solar energy, 352, 353
  wind, 354
Energy-efficient home, chart, 355
EnergyGuide label, definition, 270
Engineers, 372, 373
English/Colonial, 108, 109
  Cape Cod, 108
  garrison, 109
  saltbox, 109
Entrepreneurial careers, 379, 380
Entrepreneurs, definition, 379

Entry-level positions, 379
Environment, 36, 37
behavioral, 37
constructed, 37
definition, 36
healthy, 354-357
interactions between the different environments, 37, 38
natural, 36, 37
Environmental influences on housing, 36-38
behavioral environment, 37
constructed environment, 37
interaction of the environments, 37, 38
natural environment, 36, 37
Equipment, household, 268-285
Equity, definition, 91
Escape plan, definition, 316
Esteem, 13
Esteemed, definition, 13
Eviction, 87-91
definition, 87
Experimental planned communities, 359, 360
Extended family, definition, 17
Exterior elevations, definition, 122
Exteriors, 105-118, 131, 132, 138-140
construction materials, 138-140
contemporary houses, 114-116
housing trends, 116
modern houses, 111-114
traditional houses, 106-114

F

Fabric, 218
Fabric construction, 198-202
knitted fabrics, 202
method and types of fabrics, 202
woven fabrics, 198-202
Fabric modifications, 202, 203
design, 202
dye, 203
finishes, 203
Fabrics, fibers, and yarns, 197-203
Factors of furniture arrangement, 241-243
furniture and room use, 241, 242
room features, 242, 243
traffic patterns, 243
Falls, 308, 309
Family and work, 384
Family life cycle, chart, 19
Family unit, 16
Features, 270
Federal, 110
definition, 110
Felting, definition, 202
FHA-insured mortgages, definition, 97
Fiber content, 204, 205
Fibers, 197, 198
definition, 197
manufactured fibers, 198
natural fibers, 197, 198
Fibers, yarns, and fabrics, 197-203
fabric construction, 198-202
fabric modifications, 202, 203
fibers, 197, 198
yarns, 198
Finance charge, definition, 83
Finish nail, definition, 335
Finished and unfinished wood furniture, 232, 233
Finishes, 203, 205
chart, 203
definition, 203
Finishing touches, 252-267
accessories, 265, 266
artificial light, 256-259
lighting, 259-262
structural and nonstructural lighting, 262-265
window treatments, 253-256
Fire, 314-317
fire emergencies, 316, 317
fire extinguishers, 315
smoke detectors, 315
emergencies, 316, 317
extinguishers, 315
Fireplace insert, definition, 153
Fireplaces, 153, 154
Fireplaces and stoves, 153, 154
fireplaces, 153, 154
stoves, 154
Fixed windows, 142
Fixtures, plumbing, 150
Flammable, definition, 210
Flammable Fabrics Act, 210
Flashlight, 333
Flat springs, definition, 235
Floats, definition, 201
Floor coverings, 215, 216
definition, 215
resilient floor coverings, 216
soft floor coverings, 215, 216
Floor frame, 137, 138
Floor plan, definition, 122
Floor treatments, 213-216, 220, 221
floor coverings, 215, 216
flooring materials, 213, 214
textiles for, 204, 205
Flooring materials, 213, 214
brick, 214
ceramic tile, 213, 214
concrete, 214
definition, 213
stone, 214
terrazzo, 214
wood, 213
Flowers, 290
Fluorescent light, 258, 259
chart, 259
compact fluorescent bulbs, 259
definition, 258
Flush doors, 143
Foam mattress, definition, 236
Food waste disposers, 279
Food and water, 12
Footcandle, definition, 261
Footing, definition, 136
Forced warm-air system, 150, 151
definition, 150
Foreclosure, 98
definition, 98
Form, 166, 167
definition, 166
form and housing decisions, 166, 167
types of form, 166
Form and housing decisions, 166, 167
Formal balance, definition, 188
Foundation, 136, 137
Foundation and frame, 136-138
foundation, 136, 137
frame, 137, 138
Foundation walls, definition, 136
Frame, 137, 138
floor frame, 137, 138
roof frame, 138
wall frame, 138
Frame and foundation, 136-138
Framed-glass doors, 143
Frames, 237
Frames, springs, and cushions, 235, 236
Free form, definition, 166
Freestanding houses, 71, 72
definition, 71
Freezers, 273, 274
chart, 274
styles, 274
French Manor, definition, 107, 108
French Provincial, definition, 108
Frost line, definition, 136
Full warranty, definition, 271
Function, definition, 162
Function and appropriateness, 192
Funding for housing, 42, 43
housing for people in need, 42, 43
Furnishings, 298, 299
Furniture, 234-236, 244-246
budget for, 244
multipurpose, 247
reusing, 249
stores to buy, 244, 245
time to buy, 245, 246
unassembled, 248
upholstered, 234-236
Furniture and room use, 241, 242
Furniture arrangement, 241-243
chart, 243
factors of furniture arrangement, 241-243
scale floor plans, 241
Furniture arrangement and selection, 240-251
furniture arrangement, 241-243
furniture selection, 244-247
Furniture construction, 230-237
beds, 236, 237
plastic, metal, rattan and wicker, and glass furniture, 233, 234
upholstered furniture, 234-236
wood, 230-233
Furniture needs, 244
Furniture selection, 244-247
budget for furniture, 244
furniture needs, 244
information sources, 246, 247
stores to buy furniture, 244, 245
time to buy furniture, 245, 246
Furniture styles, 224-230

antiques, collectibles, and reproductions, 229, 230
modern and contemporary furniture styles, 228
traditional furniture styles, 224-227
Furniture styles and construction, 223-239
consumer protection, 237, 238
furniture construction, 230-237
furniture styles, 224-230
Fuses, 336
definition, 336

G

Gable roofs, definition, 107
Gambrel roof, definition, 107
Garrison, 109
definition, 109
Gas as an energy source, 148, 149
liquid propane gas, 149
natural gas, 148, 149
Generic name, definition, 198
Geometric form, definition, 166
Georgian, 109, 110
definition, 109
Geothermal energy, 353, 354
definition, 353
German, 107
Girder, definition, 137
Glass, 234
Glass, wicker and rattan, plastic, and metal furniture, 233, 234
Glass and mirrors, 219
Goals of design, 192, 193
beauty, 193
function and appropriateness, 192
harmony, 192, 193
Golden mean, definition, 186
Golden rectangle, definition, 186
Golden section, definition, 187
Government, 377
Governmental influences on housing, 41-43
environmental protection, 43
funding for housing, 42, 43
legislation, 41, 42
Gradation, definition, 190
Graduated-care facilities, definition, 74
Grain, 230
definition, 198
Greek Revival, 110, 111
definition, 110
Gross Domestic Product (GDP), definition, 39
Gross income, definition, 92
Ground covers, 290
definition, 290
Ground Fault Circuit Interrupter (GFCI), definition, 309
Gypsum wallboard, 217

H

Habitual behavior, definition, 48
Hacksaw, 333
Hammer, 331
Hand limitations, definition, 320
Hard surfaces, 291
Hardware, definition, 283
Hardwood and softwood, 230, 231
Harmonies, color, 176-179
Harmony, 192, 193
definition, 192
Hazardous materials, chart, 210
Hazardous wastes, definition, 357
Headers, definition, 138
Heating systems, 150-154
conventional heating systems, 150-152
fireplaces and stoves, 153, 154
solar heating systems, 152, 153
High mass, 168
definition, 168
High technology, 40, 41
definition, 377
careers, 377, 378
Hillside ranch, definition, 113
Hip roofs, definition, 110
Historical influences on housing, 27-32
early shelter, 27-29
housing during the 1700s and 1800s, 29, 30
housing in the 1900s, 30-32
Hogans, definition, 32
Home, 69, 196-211
definition, 69
textiles for home use, 203, 204
textiles in today's, 196-211
Home adaptability, chart, 322
Home care, maintenance, and improvements, resources for, 343, 344
Home care and maintenance help, 343
Home improvement, 325-345
cleaning, 326-329
home repairs, 331-337
outdoor and lawn care, 330, 331
redecorating, 340, 341
remodeling, 341-343
resources for home care, maintenance, and improvements, 343, 344
storage, 337-340
Home repairs, 331-337
electrical repairs, 336, 337
nails and screws, 335
plumbing repairs, 333-335
replacements, 337
tools, 331, 333
Home safety and security, 307-325
disabled, 319-323
safety, 308-314
security, 314-319
Horizontal lines, definition, 164
House, 69, 91-101, 147, 148
buying, 91-101
definition, 69
electricity in the, 147, 148
House construction, 135-144
foundation and frame, 136-138
materials for exterior construction, 138-140
windows and doors, 140-143
House plans, 119-134
architectural drawings for a house, 120-124
interior space, 124-132
Household, 33
composition, 33
size, 33
Household appliances,
appliance considerations, 269-271
canisters, 282
central vacuum systems, 282, 283
personal computers, 283
portable appliances, 283, 284
uprights, 282
vacuum cleaners, 281, 282
water heaters, 281
Household equipment, 268-285
climate control appliances, 280, 281
consumer satisfaction, 271
kitchen appliances, 272-279
laundry appliances, 279, 280
Household items, chart, 338
Houses, 69-72, 106-144, 348, 349, 359-361
attached, 70, 71
contemporary, 114-116
earth-sheltered, 116
freestanding, 71, 72
modern, 111-114
multifamily, 69, 70
"smart," 348, 349
solar, 115, 116
solutions in, 359-361
traditional, 106-111
Housing, 10, 26-45, 69-72
cultural influences, 32, 33
decisions, 72
definition, 10
economic influences, 38, 39
effects of economy on, 38, 39
governmental funding for housing, 42, 43
governmental influences, 41-43
historical influences on, 27-32
influences on, 26-45
multifamily houses, 69, 70
single-family houses, 70-72
societal influences, 33-36
solutions to shortages, 31
technological influences, 39-41
urban, 29, 30
Housing and human needs, 9-25
housing and meeting needs, 10-14
housing and the quality of life, 24
housing needs, 17-20
life-styles and housing decisions, 20-24
people and housing, 10
values and housing choices, 15-17
Housing and meeting needs, 10-15
human needs, 11, 12
needs, 13-15
physical needs, 10
psychological needs, 12, 13
Housing and needs, 72-76
children, 75, 76
elderly, 72-74
people with disabilities, 74, 75
Housing and people, 10

Housing and the quality of life, 24
human ecology, 24
personal quality of life, 24
quality of life for society, 24
Housing choices and values, 15-17
Housing concerns, 350-358
energy conservation, 354
energy sources, 351-354
healthy environment, 354-357
solutions, 357, 358
Housing decisions, 20-24, 50-52, 166-169
resources for, 50-52
form, 166, 167
life-styles, 20-24
lines, 165, 166
mass, 168
texture, 169
Housing design modifications for the disabled, 130-132
exteriors, 131, 132
interiors, 132
Housing developments, 348-350
living environments concept house, 349, 350
smart houses, 348, 349
Housing during the 1700s and 1800s, 29, 30
changes in housing, 30
urban housing, 29, 30
Housing for tomorrow, 347-364
housing concerns, 350-358
housing developments, 348-350
solutions in housing, 359-361
Housing in the 1900s, 30-32
solutions to housing shortages, 31
steps to improve housing, 31, 32
Housing market, definition, 39
Housing needs, 17-20
life cycles and housing needs, 18-20
living units, 17, 18
Housing of colonists, 27-29
Housing of Native Americans, 27
Housing shortage solutions, 31
Housing standards, 41, 42
Housing, steps to improve housing, 31, 32
Housing styles, 109-111
Federal, 110
Georgian, 109, 110
Greek Revival, 110, 111
Southern Colonial, 111
Victorian, 111
Housing trends, 116
Hue, 175
definition, 175
Human ecology, 24
definition, 24
Human needs, 11, 12
food and water, 12
Human needs and housing, 9-25
Human resources, 50, 51
definition, 50
Humidifier, definition, 280
Humidifiers and dehumidifiers, 280, 281
Hydroelectric power, 351, 352
definition, 351
Hydronic heating system, 151, 152
definition, 151

I

Incandescent light, 256-258
chart, 257
definition, 256
electronic 20-year lamp, 258
tungsten-halogen lights, 258
Indirect lighting, definition, 260
Individual life cycle, 18
Individualistic life-style, 21
Induction cooktops, definition, 275
Industrialization, 40
Influences on housing, 26-45
cultural, 32, 33
economic, 38, 39
environmental, 36-28
governmental, 41-43
historical, 27-32
societal, 33-36
technological, 39-41
Influential life-style, 23, 24
Informal balance, definition, 188
Information, career, 369
Information sources, 246, 247
advertisements, 247
Better Business Bureau, 247
books and magazines, 247
labels, 247
product ratings, 247
Innerspring mattress, definition, 236
Inspector, definition, 95
Installment buying, definition, 83
Insulation, 155, 156
definition, 155
Insurance, 100
Integrated waste management, definition, 357
Intensity, 175
definition, 175
Interactions of the environments, 37, 38
Interest, definition, 83
Interior backgrounds, 212-222
background treatments, 220, 221
ceiling treatments, 219, 220
floor treatments, 213-216
walls, 216-219
Interior designer, 343, 375, 376
definition, 343
Interior space, 124-132
housing design modifications for the disabled, 130-132
spaces, purposes, 124-127
storage space, 129, 130
traffic patterns, 127-129
Interior systems, 145-159
cooling systems, 154
electrical systems, 146-148
energy conservation, 155-158
gas as an energy source, 148, 149
heating systems, 150-154
plumbing systems, 149, 150
Interiors, 132
Intermediate colors, definition, 175
Interrelated decisions, 48-50
central-satellite decisions, 48, 49
chain decisions, 49, 50
Intruders, 317-319
alarm system, 318, 319
locks and security devices, 318

J

Job descriptions, 369-378
architects, 369, 371
construction careers, 373-375
construction machinery operators, 375
definition, 369
drafters, 371, 372
engineers, 372, 373
government, 377
high-tech careers, 377, 378
interior designers, 375, 376
landscape architects, 371
modelmakers, 372
real estate agent, 375
salespeople and consultants, 376
secretaries and computer operators, 376, 377
surveyors, 372
utility companies, 377
Job skills, 381, 382
Joists, definition, 137

K

Kit houses, definition, 72
Kitchen, 207
table coverings, 207
towels, 207
Kitchen appliances, 272-279
convection ovens, 276, 277
dishwashers, 278
food waste disposers, 279
freezers, 274
microwave ovens, 277, 278
ranges, 274-276
refrigerators, 272, 273
trash compactors, 279
Kitchen, bath, and bed, textiles for, 207-209
Knitted fabrics, 202
Knitting, definition, 202

L

Labels, 247
Ladders, career, 380, 381
Landscape, definition, 288
Landscape architects, 371
Landscape backgrounds, 294-296
Landscape design, developed, 303, 304
Landscape elements, 289-293
manufactured landscape elements, 291-293
natural landscape elements, 289-291
Landscape features, 297, 298
Landscape plans, 289
goals, 289
Landscape zones, definition, 294
Landscaping for conservation, 300-303
energy conservation, 302
water and soil conservation, 301, 302

Landscaping, definition, 64
Laundry appliances, 279, 280
automatic washers, 279
dryers, 279, 280
Lawn and outdoor care, 330, 331
Laws, textile, 209, 210
Lease, 84-87
assigning, 87
definition, 84
subletting, 87
written, 84-87
Leadership, definition, 382
Leadership skills, 382
Legal restraints, 66
Legislation, 41, 42
housing standards, 41, 42
Leisure time, 34, 35
Lessee, definition, 84
Lessor, 84, 87
chart, 87
definition, 84
Levels, career, 378-381
Life, housing and the quality of, 24
Life, personal quality of, 24
Life, quality of life for society, 24
Life cycle, definition, 18
Life cycles, 18, 19
chart, 18
family life cycle, 18, 19
individual life cycle, 18
Life situations, definition, 17
Life-style, definition, 20
Life-styles, 180, 181, 383, 384
career satisfaction, 383, 384
careers, 383, 384
Life-styles and housing decisions, 20-24
basic life-style, 22
community life-style, 22, 23
individualistic life-style, 21
influential life-style, 23, 24
supportive life-style, 22
Light, 256-259
absorbed, 259
artificial, 256-259
diffused, 260
fluorescent, 258, 259
incandescent, 256-258
reflected, 259
Light measurement, 261
Lighting, 259-262, 300
absorbed light, 259
beauty, 262
chart, 260
chart, 261
diffused light, 260
lighting for beauty, 262
reflected light, 259
safety lighting, 261, 262
structural, 263
structural and nonstructural, 262, 265
visual lighting, 260, 261
Limited warranty, definition, 271
Line, 163, 164
types of line, 164, 165
Lines and housing decisions, 165, 166
Liquid propane gas, 149
Living unit, definition, 17
Living units, 17, 18
Local lighting, 260
Locks and security devices, 318
Long-nose pliers, 333
Location, 57-68
community, 58
neighborhood, 59-62
region, 57, 58
room, 181, 182
site, 62-66
zones within the site, 66-68
Loss leader sales, 245, 246
definition, 245
Love and acceptance, 13
Low mass, 168
definition, 168

M

Magazines and books, 247
Maintenance, 203, 325-345
Maintenance and care, home, 343
Manufactured landscape elements, 291-293
artificial lighting, 293
definition, 291
hard surfaces, 291
outdoor furniture, 293
enclosure elements, 291-293
Mansard roof, definition, 108
Manufactured fibers, 198, 199
chart, 199
definition, 198
Manufactured housing, definition, 71
Manufactured siding, 139
Maslow's chart of human needs, 11
Masonry, 217
Masonry siding, 139, 140
Mass, 168
definition, 168
high mass, 168
low mass, 168
mass and housing decisions, 168
Mass and housing decisions, 168
Materials,140, 213, 214
flooring, 213, 214
roofing, 140
Materials for exterior construction, 138-140
manufactured siding, 139
masonry siding, 139, 140
roofing materials, 140
wood siding , 138, 139
Mattresses, 236, 237
Metal, 233
Metal, rattan and wicker, glass, and plastic furniture, 233, 234
Meter, definition, 147
Microenvironment, definition, 10
Microwave ovens, 277, 278
chart, 278
definition, 277
features, 277, 278
styles, 277
Mid-level positions, 378, 379
Minimum property standards (MPS), definition, 66
Mirrors and glass, 219
Mobile homes, definition, 72
Mobile society, 35, 36
Mobility impairment, definition, 321
Modelmakers, 371, 372
Modern, definition, 111
Modern and contemporary furniture styles, 228
contemporary furniture, 228
modern furniture, 228
Modern furniture, 228
Modern houses, 111-114
bungalow, 112
prairie style, 112
ranch, 112-114
split-level, 114
Modifications, fabric, 202, 203
Money, 51, 52, 247-250
budgeting, 247-250
Monochromatic color harmony, 176
definition, 176
Moods and styles, 180
Mortgage, definition, 97
Mortise-and-tenon joint, definition, 231
Motor homes, definition, 72
Moving, 76-79
chart, 76
moving company, 77-79
yourself, 77
Multifamily houses, 69, 70
condominium units, 70
cooperative units, 69, 70
definition, 69
rentals, 69
Multiple roles, definition, 384
Multipurpose furniture, 247
definition, 247
Multipurpose rooms, definition, 125

N

Nails and screws, 335
Nap, definition, 201
Native American, 106
Natural environment, 36, 37
Natural fibers, 197, 198
Natural gas, 148, 149
Natural landscape elements, 289-291
boulders and stones, 290
definition, 289
flowers, 290
ground covers, 290
soil, 289
topography, 289
trees and shrubs, 290
water, sun, and wind, 290, 291
Natural restraints, 62-66
Needlepunching, definition, 204
Needs, 10-14, 72-76, 244
beauty, 13, 14
creativity, 14
definition, 10
furniture, 244
housing, 72-76
human, 11, 12
meeting through housing, 10-14
physical, 10

self-expression, 14
Needs relationship to values, 15
Neighborhood, 59-62
definition, 59
physical, 59
social neighborhood, 62
zoning and other regulations, 59-62
Net income, definition, 92
Neutral color harmonies, 179
definition, 179
Neutrals, 175, 176
New town, definition, 31
Noise pollution, 313, 314
reducing noise pollution, 314
Nonhuman resources, 51, 52
community resources, 52
definition, 51
money, 51, 52
property, 52
Nonstructural and structural lighting, 262-265
definition, 263
Nuclear energy, 351
definition, 351
Nuclear family, definition, 17

O

Older population, 33
One-person living unit, definition, 17
Operators, 375-377
computer and secretaries, 376, 377
construction machinery, 375
Opposition, definition, 191
Organization, 337-339
Outdoor and lawn care, 330, 331
tools for outdoor tasks, 330
yard maintenance, 330, 331
Outdoor furniture, 293
Outdoor living space, 287-306
designing outdoor living space, 293-300
landscaping for conservation, 300-303
scaled plans, 303, 304
Ovens, 276-278
convection, 276, 277
microwave, 277, 278
Overcurrent protection devices, definition, 147
Owner-built houses, definition, 71

P

Paint, 218
Paneling, 217
Passive systems, 153
Patterns, traffic, 127-129
Patterns and colors, 206
Pediments, definition, 110
Pennsylvania Dutch Colonial, 107
Pent roofs, definition, 107
People and housing, 10
People with disabilities, 34
Perennials, definition, 290
Personal quality of life, 24
Personal computers, 283
Personal qualifications, 382
Photovoltaic array, chart, 353
Photovoltaic array, definition, 352
Physical disabilities, definition, 319
Physical needs, 10
definition, 10
shelter, 10
Physical neighborhood, 59
definition, 59
Pigment, definition, 176
Pipe wrench, 333
Places to live, 56-80
housing, 69-72
housing and special needs, 72-76
location, 57-68
moving, 76-79
Plan views, 122
definition, 122
Planned communities, 359, 360
chart, 359
experimental planned communities, 359, 360
Planned neighborhood, definition, 61
Planning for storage, 129, 130
Plans, 119-134, 303, 304
house, 119-134
scaled, 303, 304
scale floor, 241
Plaster, 217
Plastic, 233
Plastic, metal, rattan and wicker, and glass furniture, 233, 234
glass, 234
metal, 233
plastic, 233
rattan and wicker, 233, 234
Plastic wallboard, 217
Plumbing fixtures, 150
Plumbing plunger, 331
Plumbing repairs, 333-335
clogged drains, 333-335
Plumbing systems, 149, 150
plumbing fixtures, 150
wastewater removal system, 149, 150
water supply system, 149
Poisonings, 309
Pollution, definition, 354
Portable appliances, 283, 284
Portico, definition, 110
Positions, 378, 379
entry-level, 379
mid-level, 378, 379
professional-level, 378
Power, electrical 147
Prairie style, 112
definition, 112
Precautions, definition, 308
Pressed wood, definition, 231
Preventing accidents, 308, 309
burns, 309
electrical shock, 309
falls, 308, 309
poisonings, 309
Price of buying a house, 92
method one, 92
method three, 92
method two, 92
Primary colors, definition, 174
Principles of design, 185-195
balance, 188, 189
emphasis, 189, 190
goals of design, 192, 193
proportion and scale, 186-188
rhythm, 190, 191
sensory design, 193, 194
Print, 120
Prints, 120, 121
alphabet of lines, 121
symbols, 121
Prioritize, definition, 244
Privacy, 15, 16
Private zone, 66
Process, 82, 83
definition, 82
Process and cost, 83
Process of buying a house, 96-101
abstract of title, 96, 97
agreement of sale, 96
closing costs, 98, 99
earnest money, 96
foreclosure, 98
insurance, 100
refinancing, 100, 101
securing a mortgage, 97
survey, 97
title and deed, 99, 100
Product ratings, 247
Products, cleaning, 327
Professional-level positions, 378
Property, 52
Proportion, 186, 187
definition, 186
Proportion and scale, 186-188
proportion, 186, 187
scale, 187
Protection, consumer, 237, 238
Protein natural fibers, definition, 198
Providers, housing, 366
Psychological, love and acceptance, 13
Psychological needs, 12, 13
definition, 12
esteem, 13
security, 13
self-actualization, 13
Public zone, 66

Q

Qualifications, personal, 382
Qualities for success, 381, 382
job skills, 381, 382
leadership skills, 382
personal qualifications, 382
working conditions, 382
Quality of life, 24
definition, 24
society, 24
Quiet area, 124, 125
definition, 124

R

Radiation, definition, 191
Rafters, definition,138
Rail and stile doors, 143
Raised ranch, definition, 113
Ranch, 112-114

definition, 112
Ranges, 274-276
chart, 276
electric ranges, 274, 274
features, 275
gas ranges, 275
styles, 275
Rational decision, definition, 48
Rattan and wicker, 233, 234
Real estate agents, 375
Realistic form, definition, 166
Recycle, definition, 249
Recycling, definition, 358
Recycling furniture, 249
Redecorating, 340, 341
definition, 340
Reducing noise pollution, 314
Reflected light, 259
definition, 259
Refrigerators, 272, 273
chart, 273
styles, 272
features, 272, 273
Region, 57, 58
chart, 58
definition, 57
Remodeling, 341-343
cost analysis, 341-343
definition, 341
Remodeling services, 344
Renegotiable rate mortgage, 97
Renew, definition, 249
Renovating furniture, 249
Rentals, 69
Renters, 84
Renting, 83-91
assigning and subletting a lease, 87
breach of contract, 87
eviction, 87-91
renters, 84
written lease, 84-87
Repairs, 331-337
electrical, 336, 337
home, 331-337
plumbing, 333-335
Repetition, definition, 190
Replacements, 337
Reproductions, 229, 230
antiques, and collectibles, 229, 230
definition, 230
Resiliency, definition, 198
Resilient floor coverings, 216
Resources, 38, 50, 51
definition, 38
human, 50, 51
nonhuman, 51, 52
Resources for home care, maintenance, and improvements, 343, 344
decorating, 343, 344
home care and maintenance, 343
remodeling services, 344
Resources for housing decisions, 50-52
human resources, 50, 51
nonhuman resources, 51, 52
Restore, definition, 249
Retail stores, 244, 245
Reusing furniture, 249
recycling furniture, 249
renovating furniture, 249
Reverse mortgage, definition, 74
Rhythm, 190, 191
definition, 190
Ridge, definition, 138
Roof frame, 138
Roofing materials, 140
Room air conditioners, 281
Room and furniture use, 241, 242
Room features, 242, 243
Room location, 181, 182
Rooms, purpose and style, 206
Row houses, definition, 29
R-value, definition, 155

S

Safety, 270, 308-314
air, 310-312
child safety, 309, 310
noise pollution, 313, 314
preventing accidents, 308, 309
Safety and security, home, 307-325
Safety lighting, 261, 262
Salespeople and consultants, 376
Saltbox, 109
definition, 109
Scale, 186-188
definition, 187
proportion, 186-188
Scale floor plans, 241
definition, 214
Scaled plans, 303, 304
developed landscape design, 303, 304
Scandinavian, 106, 107
Screwdrivers, 331
Screws and nails, 335
Seasonal sales, 246
definition, 246
Secondary color, definition, 174
Secretaries and computer operators, 376, 377
Section and detail views, 123, 124
Section view, definition, 123
Securing a mortgage, 97
Security, 13, 314-319
fire, 314-317
intruders, 317-319
Security and safety, home, 307-325
Security deposit, definition, 84
Security devices and locks, 318
Selection and arrangement of furniture, 240-251
Self-actualization, 13
definition, 13
Self-cleaning oven, definition, 275
Self-esteem, definition, 13
Self-expression, 14
definition, 14
Sensory design, 193, 194
definition, 194
Separating areas and room, 126, 127
Service drop, definition, 147
Service entrance panel, definition, 147
Service zone, 66
Services, remodeling, 344
Shade, definition, 175
Shades, definition, 255
Shades, shutters, and blinds, 255, 256
chart, 255
Shelter, 10, 27-29
early, 27-29
Shingles, definition, 140
Shopping, 95, 96, 247
bargain, 247
for a house to buy, 95, 96
Short circuit, definition, 336
Shower curtains, 208
Shrubs and trees, 290
Shutters, blinds, and shades, 255, 256
Shutters, definition, 255
Side-cutting pliers, 331
Siding, 138-140
definition, 138
manufactured, 139
masonry, 139, 140
wood, 138, 139
Single-family houses, 70-72
definition, 70
attached houses, 70, 71
freestanding houses, 71, 72
Single-parent families, definition, 17
Site, 62-66
chart, 63
definition, 62
legal restraints, 66
natural restraints, 62-66
Size, 167, 168, 270
of space, 167, 168
Skills, 47-55, 381, 382
decision-making, 47-55
job, 381, 382
leadership, 382
Skylights and clerestory windows, 142
Sliding windows, 141
"Smart" houses, 348, 349
Smoke detectors, 315
definition, 315
Social area, 125, 126
definition, 125
Social neighborhood, 62
Societal influences on housing, 33-36
affordable housing, 34
changing roles, 34
household composition, 33
household size, 33
leisure time, 34, 35
mobile society, 35, 36
older population, 33
people with disabilities, 34
Soft floor coverings, 215, 216
Software, definition, 283
Softwood and hardwood, 230, 231
Soil, 289
Soil and water conservation, 301, 302
Soil conservation, definition, 302
Soil stack, definition, 150
Solar energy, 115, 352, 353
definition, 115
Solar heating systems, 152, 153
active systems, 153
passive systems 153

Solar houses, 115, 116
Solid waste, 356, 357
  definition, 356
Solid wood, definition, 231
Solid wood and bonded wood, 231
Solutions, housing concerns, 357, 358
Solutions in housing, 359-361
  living spaces, 360, 361
  planned communities, 359, 360
Southern Colonial, 111
  definition, 11
Space, 15, 124-132, 167, 168, 287-306
  arrangement of, 168
  definition, 167
  designing outdoor living, 293-300
  interior, 124-132
  outdoor living, 287-306
  size of space, 167
  storage space, 129, 130
Spaces' purposes, 124-127
  quiet area, 124, 125
  separating areas and rooms, 126, 127
  social area, 125, 126
  work area, 125
Spanish, 106
  definition, 106
Specifications, definition, 120
Split-complementary color harmony, 178
  definition, 178
Split-level, 114
  definition, 114
Springs, 237
Springs, cushions, and frames, 235, 236
Spur-of-the-moment decision, definition, 48
Stile and rail doors, 143
Still plate, definition, 137
Stone, 214
Stones and boulders, 290
Storage, 337-340
  organization, 337-339
  space savers, 339, 340
Storage space, 129, 130
  planning for storage, 129, 130
Stores to buy furniture, 244, 245
  catalogs, 245
  discount houses, 245
  other places, 245
  retail stores, 244, 245
  warehouse showrooms, 245
Stoves and fireplaces, 153, 154
Structural and nonstructural lighting, 262-265
  nonstructural lighting, 263-265
  structural lighting, 263
Structural design, definition, 202
Structural light fixture, definition, 263
Structural lighting, 263
Stucco, definition, 106
Studs, definition, 138
Styles, 109-111, 224-230
  furniture, 224-230
  housing 109-111
  modern and contemporary furniture, 228
  traditional furniture, 224-227
Styles and moods, 180
Subdivision, definition, 32
Subflooring, definition, 137
Sublet, definition, 87
Subletting and assigning a lease, 87
Substandard, definition, 30
Success, qualities for, 381, 382
Sunbelt, definition, 36
Sun-room, definition, 302
Supportive life-style, 22
Survey, 97
Surveyors, 372
Swinging windows, 141, 142
Symbols, 121
  definition, 121
Systems, 150-154
  conventional heating, 145-159
  cooling, 154
  electrical, 146-148
  heating, 150-154
  interior, 145-159
  plumbing, 149, 150
  solar heating, 152, 153
  wastewater removal, 149, 150
  water supply, 149

T

Table coverings, 207
Tactile texture, 168, 169
  definition, 168
Tanned, definition, 202
Tape measure, 333
Task lighting, definition, 260
Tax exemption, definition, 39
Technological influences on housing, 39-41
  early technology, 39
  high technology, 40, 41
  industrialization, 40
Technology, 39
  definition, 39
  early, 39
Template, definition, 241
Terms, electrical, 146, 147
Terrazzo, 214
Textile Fiber Products Identification Act, 209
Textile laws, 209, 210
  Flammable Fabrics Act, 210
  Textile Fiber Products Identification Act, 209
  Wool Products Labeling Act, 210
Textiles, definition, 197
Textiles for floor treatments, 204, 205
  construction methods, 204
  fiber content, 204, 205
  finishes, 205
  textures, 204
Textiles for home use, 203, 204
  appearance, 203
  comfort, 203
  construction, 204
  cost, 204
  durability, 203
  maintenance, 203
Textiles for kitchen, bath, and bed, 207-209
  bathroom, 207, 208
  bedroom, 208, 209
  kitchen, 207
Textiles for upholstered furniture, 205
Textiles in today's homes, 196-211
  fibers, yarns and fabrics, 197-203
  floor treatments, 204, 205
  home use, 203, 204
  kitchen, bath, and bed, 207-209
  textile laws, 209, 210
  upholstered furniture, 205
  window treatments, 206, 207
Textiles used in window treatments, 206, 207
  color and patterns, 206
  cost and care, 206, 207
  purpose and styles of rooms, 206
Texture, 168, 169, 204
  definition, 168
  tactile texture, 168, 169
  texture and housing decisions, 169
  visual texture, 169
Texture and housing decisions, 169
Thought, decisions according to, 48
Time to buy furniture, 245, 246
  chart, 246
  close-out sales, 246
  damaged and discounted item sales, 246
  loss leader sales, 245, 246
  seasonal sales, 246
Tint, definition, 175
Title, definition, 99
Title and deed, 99, 100
Tongue and groove joint, definition, 231
Tool, screwdriver, 331
Toolbox, 333
Tools, 330-333
  adjustable wrench, 331
  channel-lock pliers, 333
  cleaning, 326
  closet auger, 333
  crosscut saw, 333
  electric drill, 333
  electric tester, 333
  flashlight, 333
  hacksaw, 333
  hammer, 331
  long-nose pliers, 333
  outdoor tasks, 330
  pipe wrench, 333
  plumbing plunger, 331
  side-cutting pliers, 331
  tape measure, 333
  toolbox, 333
Topography, 36, 289
  definition, 36
Touches, finishing, 252-267
Towels, 207, 208
Toxic, definition, 309
Tract houses, definition, 31
Trade name, definition, 198
Traditional, definition, 106
Traditional American styles, 227
Traditional furniture styles, 224-227

American, 227
English, 224-227
French, 224
Traditional houses, 106-114
Dutch, 107
English/Colonial, 108, 109
French, 107, 108
German, 107
housing styles, 109-111
Native Americans, 106
Scandinavian, 106, 107
Spanish, 106
Traffic patterns, 127-129
definition, 127
door space, 129
Transition, definition, 191
Trap, definition, 150
Trash compactors, 279
Treatments, 213-216, 219- 221, 253-256
background, 220, 221
ceiling, 219, 220
floor, 213-216, 220, 221
wall, 221
windows, 253-256
Trees and shrubs, 290
Triad color harmony, 179
definition, 179
Truss rafter, definition, 138
Tufted, definition, 204
Tungsten-halogen lights, 258
definition, 258
Turret, definition, 111

U

Unassembled furniture, 248
definition, 248
Unfinished and finished wood furniture, 232, 233
Unity, definition, 192
Upholstered furniture, 234-236
chart, 236
frames, springs, and cushions, 235, 236
textiles for, 205
upholstery fabrics, 234, 235
upholstery tailoring, 235
Upholstery, 234, 235
fabrics, 234, 235
tailoring, 235
Uprights, 282
Urban housing, 29,30
Utility companies, 377

V

Vacuum cleaners, 281, 282
VA-guaranteed mortgages, definition, 97
Value, 175
definition, 175
Values, definition, 15
Values and housing choices, 15-17
economy, 16, 17
family unit, 16
privacy, 15, 16
relationship between values and needs, 15
space, 15
Values, relationship to needs, 15
Veneer wall, definition, 139
Veneered wood, definition, 231
Ventilation, definition, 312
Vertical lines, definition, 164
Victorian, 11
definition
Views, 121-124
elevation views, 122
plan views, 122
section and detail views, 123, 124
Visual imagery, definition, 162
Visual lighting, 260, 261
general lighting, 260
light measurement, 261
local lighting, 260, 261
Visual pollution, definition, 357
Visual texture, 169
definition, 169
Visual weight, definition, 187
Visually impaired, definition, 319
Voltage, definition, 146

W

Wale, definition, 201
Wall construction, 216, 217
gypsum wallboard, 217
masonry, 217
paneling, 217
plaster, 217
plastic wallboard, 217
Wall frame, 138
Wall switches, 337
Wall treatments, 218, 219, 221
ceramic tile, 219
cork, 219
fabric, 218
mirrors and glass, 219
paint, 218
wallpaper, 218
Wallpaper, 218
Walls, 216-219
wall construction, 216, 217
wall treatments, 218, 219
Warehouse showrooms, 245
Warm and cool colors, 176
Warm colors, definition, 176
Warp yarns, definition, 198
Warranty, definition, 271
Washers, automatic, 279
Wastewater removal system, 149, 150
Water and food, 12
Water and soil conservation, 301, 302
Water bed, definition, 237
Water conservation, definition, 301
Water heaters, 281
Water pollution, 357
Watts, definition, 146
Weather stripping, definition, 156
Weaving, definition, 198
Weft yarns, definition, 198
Wicker and rattan, 233, 234
Wind, 290, 291, 354
Window treatments, 253-256
draperies and curtains, 253-255
shades, shutters, and blinds, 255, 256
textiles used in, 206, 207
Windows, 141, 142
combination windows, 142
fixed windows, 142
skylights and clerestory windows, 142
sliding windows, 141
swinging windows, 141, 142
Windows and doors, 140-143, 156
doors, 142, 143
windows, 141, 142
Wood, 213, 230-233
grain, 230
hardwood and softwood, 230, 231
solid wood and bonded wood, 231
unfinished and finished wood furniture, 232, 233
wood joints, 231, 232
Wood grain, definition, 230
Wood joints, 231, 232
Wood siding, 138, 139
Wool Products Labeling Act, 210
Work and family, 384
Work area, 125
definition, 125
Work triangle, definition, 125
Working conditions, 382
Woven fabrics, 198-202

X

Xeriscape, definition, 301

Y

Yard maintenance, 330, 331
Yarns, 198
definition, 198

Z

Zones, 66-68
Zoning regulations, 59-62
chart, 59-62
definition, 42
other regulations, 59-62